Sandra Lumpkin

PENGUIN CLASSICS DELUXE EDITION

THE TIBETAN BOOK OF THE DEAD

The translation of *The Tibetan Book of the Dead* was carried out with the support of His Holiness the Dalai Lama and with the commentarial guidance of revered contemporary Tibetan masters including the late Head of the Nyingma School of Tibetan Buddhism HH Dilgo Khyentse Rinpoche, Zenkar Rinpoche and Garje Khamtrul Rinpoche.

GYURME DORJE (PhD) is a leading scholar of the Nyingma tradition of Tibetan Buddhism. His seven major publications include works on Tibetan lexicography, medicine, divination and pilgrimage guides to Tibet and Bhutan, as well as the translations of HH Dudjom Rinpoche's *The Nyingma School of Tibetan Buddhism*. His forthcoming titles include *The Guhyagarbha Tantra: Dispelling the Darkness of the Ten Directions*.

GRAHAM COLEMAN is President of the Orient Foundation (UK), a major Tibetan cultural conservancy organization. Writer/director of the acclaimed feature documentary *Tibet: A Buddhist Trilogy* and editor of the *Handbook of Tibetan Culture*, he has been editing Tibetan Buddhist poetry and prose texts in cooperation with various distinguished translators since the mid-1970s.

THUPTEN JINPA (PhD) is the senior translator to His Holiness the Dalai Lama and President of the Institute of Tibetan Classics. His works include the translation of twelve books by the Dalai Lama, including the *New York Times* bestseller *Ethics for the New Millennium* and the forthcoming *The Universe in a Single Atom*, the Dalai Lama's perspective on the meeting of Buddhism and modern science.

Padmasambhava (Guru Rinpoche)

THE TIBETAN BOOK OF THE DEAD

First Complete Translation

[*English Title*]

THE GREAT LIBERATION BY HEARING IN THE INTERMEDIATE STATES

[*Tibetan Title*]

Composed by
Padmasambhava

Revealed by
Terton Karma Lingpa

Translated by
Gyurme Dorje

Edited by
Graham Coleman with Thupten Jinpa

Introductory Commentary by
His Holiness The Dalai Lama

PENGUIN BOOKS

PENGUIN BOOKS
Published by the Penguin Group
Penguin Group (USA) Inc., 375 Hudson Street,
New York, New York 10014, U.S.A.
Penguin Group (Canada), 90 Eglinton Avenue East, Suite 700, Toronto, Ontario,
Canada M4P 2Y3 (a division of Pearson Penguin Canada Inc.)
Penguin Books Ltd, 80 Strand, London WC2R 0RL, England
Penguin Ireland, 25 St Stephen's Green, Dublin 2,
Ireland (a division of Penguin Books Ltd)
Penguin Group (Australia), 250 Camberwell Road, Camberwell, Victoria 3124,
Australia (a division of Pearson Australia Group Pty Ltd)
Penguin Books India Pvt Ltd, 11 Community Centre,
Panchsheel Park, New Delhi – 110 017, India
Penguin Group (NZ), 67 Apollo Drive, Mairangi Bay, Auckland 1310, New Zealand
(a division of Pearson New Zealand Ltd)
Penguin Books (South Africa) (Pty) Ltd, 24 Sturdee Avenue,
Rosebank, Johannesburg 2196, South Africa

Penguin Books Ltd, Registered Offices:
80 Strand, London WC2R 0RL, England

First published in Great Britain by Penguin Books Ltd 2005
First published in the United States of America by Viking Penguin,
a member of Penguin Group (USA) Inc. 2006
Published in Penguin Books (UK) 2006
Published in Penguin Books (USA) 2007

7 9 10 8

Thangkas painted by the late Shawu Tsering of Repkong and photographed by Jill Morley Smith are from the private collection of Gyurme Dorje.

ISBN 0-670-85886-2 (hc.)
ISBN 978-0-14-310494-0 (pbk.)
CIP data available

Printed in the United States of America

May all sentient beings,
children of buddha nature,
realise
the ultimate nature of mind:
insight and compassion,
in blissful union.

Contents

List of Illustrations x

Acknowledgements xi

Acknowledgements for the Illustrations xiv

Introductory Commentary by His Holiness the XIVth Dalai Lama xv

Editor's Introduction xxxi

A Brief Literary History of the *Tibetan Book of the Dead* by Gyurme Dorje xxxviii

THE TIBETAN BOOK OF THE DEAD 1

Appendix One: *Peaceful and Wrathful Deities* and the *Tibetan Book of the Dead* 381

Appendix Two: Symbolism of the Maṇḍala of the Peaceful and Wrathful Deities 387

Notes 403

Bibliography 436

Glossary of Key Terms 443

Thematic Index by Chapter 529

List of Illustrations

Guru Padmasambhava iv
Karma Lingpa xlvi
The Mantra Circle of the Peaceful and Wrathful Deities 346

Colour Plates

1. The assembly of the Forty-two Peaceful Deities
2. Samantabhadra with Samantabhadrī, and the Peaceful Deities of the Buddha Family
3. Peaceful Deities of the Vajra Family
4. Peaceful Deities of the Ratna Family
5. Peaceful Deities of the Padma Family
6. Peaceful Deities of the Karma Family
7. The Six Sages
8. The Eight Gatekeepers
9. The Assembly of the Fifty-eight Wrathful Deities
10. Mahottara Heruka with Krodheśvarī
11. Wrathful Deities of the Buddha Family
12. Wrathful Deities of the Vajra Family
13. Wrathful Deities of the Ratna Family
14. Wrathful Deities of the Padma Family
15. Wrathful Deities of the Karma Family
16. The Eight Mātaraḥ and the Eight Piśācī

Acknowledgements

Our project began in 1988 when HH the Dalai Lama kindly offered to request HH Dilgo Khyentse Rinpoche, the late head of the Nyingma school, to give an oral commentary to me on key sections of the *Tibetan Book of the Dead*. The Dalai Lama knew that various translations had been made of 'The Great Liberation by Hearing', our Chapter 11, but that so far no one had translated the entire *Tibetan Book of the Dead*. HH Dilgo Khyentse graciously agreed to the Dalai Lama's request and over a period of four weeks gave the empowerments and an incisive and illuminating oral commentary to the core elements of the text, which was eloquently translated each day by Sogyal Rinpoche.

While in Kathmandu, receiving the oral commentary from HH Dilgo Khyentse Rinpoche, I had the good fortune to meet Dr Gyurme Dorje, who had previously translated Longchen Rabjampa's commentary to the *Guhygarbha Tantra*, the root text on which the *Tibetan Book of the Dead* is based. During our first meeting, Gyurme agreed to make a new annotated translation of the entire *Tibetan Book of the Dead*, a task he undertook with exceptional care and dedication over the years that followed. While Gyurme was working on the translation he was also employed at the School of Oriental and African Studies in London as a research fellow, translating into English the *Greater Tibetan–Chinese Dictionary* (*Bod-rgya tshig-mdzod chen-mo*). During this time, Gyurme worked closely with the highly regarded Nyingma master Zenkar Rinpoche, who is one of the foremost contemporary lineage holders of the *Tibetan Book of the Dead*. Zenkar Rinpoche kindly advised Gyurme throughout the translation of our text and also gave an extensive oral commentary to us on Chapter 4, 'The Introduction to Awareness'.

At various stages of the project, the Dalai Lama answered my questions about difficult points, and he also dictated to me the lucid and succinct Introductory Commentary. At the Dalai Lama's request, Khamtrul Rinpoche, an adviser to the Dalai Lama on Nyingma studies, also gave a beautiful oral commentary to key sections of Chapter 8 and dictated the introduction to Chapter 11.

Throughout the editing process I had the happy good fortune of working with Geshe Thupten Jinpa, senior translator to the Dalai Lama, whom I had first met in 1977 and who has been a close friend since he came to England to study philosophy at Cambridge in 1989. Jinpa translated the Dalai Lama's Introductory Commentary and reviewed every line and word of all fourteen chapters of the edited translation with me twice, in the course of which he made countless important and inspiring suggestions. Everyone who knows Jinpa's work is aware of his special talent and skill both as a translator and writer and these have played an invaluable role in this project. Finally, the individual introductions to each of the chapters, except Chapter 11, were written by Dasho Sangay Dorji, a Bhutanese scholar, who comes from a family whose paternal line has been lineage holders of the *Tibetan Book of the Dead* for several generations and who throughout his childhood accompanied his father every time he was called to a household to carry out these practices.

Needless to say it has been a wonderful privilege for us to work with all those who helped to make this project possible. Our insights and skills as writers would not even register on the most sensitive of detectors compared to those of the composers of the original cycle of teachings or the lineage holders who gave the commentarial explanation that guided us. Throughout this endeavour therefore we have tried to substitute hard work and attention to detail for our lack of ability and to let the original magnificence of the text shine through the clouds of our shortcomings as much as we were able.

My work on this project would not have been possible without the life-long friendship of the Orient Foundation's chairman David Lascelles. It is difficult to thank him enough for all that he has made possible, beginning with our work together on the making of our films *Tibet: A Buddhist Trilogy*, in the 1970s, and ever since. Two other special friends, Elinore Detiger and Elsie Walker made it possible for this project to be initiated, and their kindness and confidence, together with that of Michael Baldwin, will never be forgotten. My sincere appreciation goes also to Johnnie and Buff Chace, Lucinda Ziesing, Faith Bieler, Lavinia Currier, Cynthia Jurs, Catherine Cochran, Margot Wilkie, Basil Panzer, Bokara Patterson and Lindsay Masters for their important contributions in the early stages of this work.

At Gyurme Dorje's request, Gene Smith of the Tibetan Buddhist Resource Center in New York generously made available a digital version of the three-volume manuscript from the library of the late *Kyabje* Dudjom Rinpoche, on which our translation is largely based. HH Dilgo Khyentse Rinpoche had previously provided copies of the text reprinted under his supervision in Delhi. Other versions of the text which we consulted, including the Varanasi reprint and other versions of Bhutanese and Chinese origin, are all from Gyurme Dorje's private collection. Some source materials were also kindly provided by Zenkar Rinpoche, Tulku Jigme Khyentse, Dr Burkhard Quessel of the British Library, and Dr Fernand Meyer of CNRS in Paris. Gyurme Dorje also especially acknowledges the kindness and profound advice of all of his teachers within the Nyingma tradition, including the previous Kangyur, Dudjom and Dilgo Khyentse Rinpoches, as well as Tulku Pema Wangyal and Zenkar Rinpoche, and he thanks his wife Xiaohong for all her encouragement and sustenance during the final years of this project.

I am very grateful to Gillon Aitken, my agent, for introducing this project to Penguin, our publishers, and to Simon Winder, our editor at Penguin, for his patience and unfailing enthusiasm during the long genesis of this work. Our thanks go also to Dr Martin Boord and Andrew Bell for their proofreading of the text and to Robert Chilton for compiling the thematic index.

GRAHAM COLEMAN
Bath, England

Acknowledgements for the Illustrations

The colour illustrations that appear in our text have never previously been published. The two painted scrolls depicting the Hundred Peaceful and Wrathful Deities in Repkong style, which were commissioned by Gyurme Dorje in 2002, are from the studio of the late master artist Shawu Tsering of Sengeshong Yagotsang in Amdo.

The line drawings of Guru Padmasambhava (p. iv) and Karma Lingpa (p. xlvi) are the work of Robert Beer. The circular chart of mantras (*btags-grol*) (p. 346) is reproduced from Fremantle and Trungpa, *The Tibetan Book of the Dead* (Shambhala Classics, 2000), p. 32.

Introductory Commentary

by His Holiness the XIVth Dalai Lama

The question of whether or not there exists a continuity of consciousness after death has been an important aspect of philosophical reflection and debate from ancient Indian times to the present. When considering these matters from a Buddhist point of view, however, we have to bear in mind that the understanding of the nature of continuity of consciousness and the understanding of the nature of the 'I' or 'self' are closely interlinked. Therefore, let us first look at what it is that can be said to constitute a person.

According to Buddhist classical literature, a person can be seen as possessing five interrelated aggregates, technically known as the five psycho-physical aggregates.[1] These are the aggregate of consciousness, the aggregate of form (which includes our physical body and senses), the aggregate of feeling, the aggregate of discrimination, and the aggregate of motivational tendencies. That is to say, there is our body, the physical world and our five senses, and there are the various processes of mental activity, our motivational tendencies, our labelling of and discrimination between objects, our feelings, and the underlying awareness or consciousness.

Among the ancient schools of thought, which accepted the notion of continuity of consciousness, there were several non-Buddhist philosophical schools which regarded the entity, the 'I' or 'self', which migrated from existence to existence as being unitary and permanent. They also suggested that this 'self' was autonomous in its relationship to the psycho-physical components that constitute a person. In other words they believed or posited that there is an essence or 'soul' of the person, which exists independently from the body and the mind of the person.

1. See the glossary for a description of the five psycho-physical aggregates and other Buddhist terms used in the commentary. *Ed.*

However, Buddhist philosophy does not accept the existence of such an independent, autonomous entity. In the Buddhist view, the self or the person is understood in terms of a dynamic interdependent relationship of both mental and physical attributes, that is to say the psycho-physical components which constitute a person. In other words our sense of self can, upon examination, be seen as a complex flow of mental and physical events, clustered in clearly identifiable patterns, including our physical features, instincts, emotions, and attitudes, etc., continuing through time. Further, according to Prāsaṅgika-Madhyamaka philosophy, which has become the prevailing philosophical view of Tibetan Buddhism today, this sense of self is simply a mental construct, a mere label given to this cluster of dependently arising mental and physical events in dependence on their continuity.

Now, when we look at this interdependence of mental and physical constituents from the perspective of Highest Yoga Tantra,[2] there are two concepts of a person. One is the temporary person or self, that is as we exist at the moment, and this is labelled on the basis of our coarse or gross physical body and conditioned mind, and, at the same time, there is a subtle person or self which is designated in dependence on the subtle body and subtle mind. This subtle body and subtle mind are seen as a single entity that has two facets. The aspect which has the quality of awareness, which can reflect and has the power of cognition, is the subtle mind. Simultaneously, there is its energy, the force that activates the mind towards its object – this is the subtle body or subtle wind. These two inextricably conjoined qualities are regarded, in Highest Yoga Tantra, as the ultimate nature of a person and are identified as buddha nature, the essential or actual nature of mind.

Now, before we look more closely at the nature of the subtle body and mind, let us look at how the gross body and mind are thought to originate. The notion of dependent origination lies at the very heart of Buddhist philosophy. The principle of dependent origination asserts that nothing exists in its own right independent of other factors. Things and events come into being only in dependence on the aggregation of multiple causes and conditions. The process through which the external world and the sentient beings

2. The perspective of the *Tibetan Book of the Dead* is that of Highest Yoga Tantra. *Ed.*

within it revolve in a cycle of existence propelled by karmic propensities and their interaction with misapprehension, attraction and aversion and conditions is described in terms of twelve interdependent links. Each cycle of the process begins with a misapprehension of the nature of actual reality. This fundamental ignorance acts as a condition for the arising of the propensities created by our past actions, mental, verbal and physical, which condition our dualising consciousness. Our dualising consciousness, in turn, conditions the qualities and mode of interaction of our psycho-physical aggregates, which condition our sensory fields, which generate contact, which generates sensations, and then in turn attachment, grasping, and maturation towards rebirth. At this point there is an interaction with the genetic constituents of the parents and subsequent interaction with the environment, and then finally we have birth, ageing and death. This cycle can be viewed as both illustrating the underlying processes of life, death and rebirth and as an illustration of the processes to be transformed on the path to liberation from suffering in cyclic existence.

The notion that there is a connection between this life and the events of both our previous existence and our future existence, follows from the Buddhist understanding of the natural law of cause and effect. For example, although we can speak of yesterday's weather and today's weather as distinct, today's weather is inextricably linked with the weather patterns of yesterday. Even at the bodily level, in the case of our physical health for example, we know that events in the past affect the present and those of the present the future. Similarly, in the realm of consciousness the Buddhist view is that there is also this same causal continuum between the events of the past, present and future.

The Buddhist understanding of the continuity of personal experience, including our memories, can also be considered here. The Buddhist view is that the continuity of personal experience is primarily founded on the capacity for retention, which can be further developed during one's meditative practice in this life. However, generally speaking, it is thought that if a person dies after a prolonged period of illness that has led to a prolonged degeneration of both physical and mental capacities, there will be a greater chance of many of the personal characteristics, including memories etc., being lost. On the other hand, in the case of someone who dies a sudden death, when the mind–body relationship at the gross level is still very firm, it is thought that there is a greater chance of carrying forward the acquired characteristics and memories, etc. Nonetheless, in both cases, the characteristics carried forward from a previous life are generally thought to be most strongly felt at an early stage of one's rebirth. This is because the personal characteristics of the previous life are thought, generally speaking, to be quickly overwhelmed by the developing characteristics inherited from the parents of the present life. Nonetheless, as I have mentioned, much depends in this respect on the individual's capacity for recall and this capacity for recall is dependent on a deepened retentive training acquired in this lifetime.

Now, let us look at the possible states of existence one can be born into. From the Buddhist perspective, rebirth in conditioned existence can take place in one of three realms: the formless realm, the form realm or the desire realm. The form and formless realms are fruits of subtle states of consciousness, attained upon the realisation of certain meditative concentrations. Our realm, the desire realm, is the most gross of these three. Six classes of beings are described as inhabiting the desire realm: gods (mundane celestial beings whose primary mental state is exaltation), antigods (who are predominantly hostile and jealous), human beings (who are influenced by all the five dissonant mental states), animals (who are under the sway of delusion), anguished spirits (who are under the sway of attachment and unsatisfied craving) and hell beings (who are overwhelmed by hatred, anger and fear). In the literature of Highest Yoga Tantra, the evolution of all the three realms of conditioned existence are described in terms of differing expressions or states of energy and, as I have mentioned, it is said that our fundamental ignorance is the root of conditioned existence and that karmic energy is its activating force. In the Buddhist view, therefore, it is the nature of our habitual tendencies that generates our future existence, driven by the natural law of cause and effect.

Further, when we observe the patterns of arising and subsiding that underlie the dynamic nature of the physical environment, the cycle of days and nights and the passing of the seasons, for example, and we observe how matter arises from insubstantial subatomic particles and we look at the patterns of causal connectedness in the arising and dissolution of our mental experiences from moment to moment, across the differing phases of deep sleep, dreams and our waking state, the notion of continuity of consciousness can come to be seen to be in accord with both the nature of our environment and the nature of our mental experience. Certainly, it has often been argued that one advantage of accepting the notion of continuity of consciousness is that it gives us a more profound ability to understand and to explain the nature of our existence and of the universe. In addition, this notion of continuity and causal interconnectedness reinforces a sense of consequences for our own actions, in terms of both the impact on ourselves and the impact on others and the environment.

So, in summary, when considering the notion of continuity of consciousness we must bear in mind that there are many different levels of greater or lesser subtlety in the states of consciousness. For example, we know of course that certain qualities of sensory perception are dependent on the physical constitution of the individual and that when the physical body dies, the states of consciousness associated with these sensory perceptions also cease. But, although we know that the human body serves as a condition for human consciousness, the question still remains: what is the nature of the underlying factor or essence that accounts for our experience of consciousness as having the natural quality of luminosity and awareness?

Finally, then, when considering the interrelationship between mind, body and the environment at the subtle level, we know that material things are composed of cells, atoms and particles and that consciousness is composed of moments. That is to say that mind and matter have distinctly different natures and therefore have different substantial causes. Material things come into being based on other material entities such as particles, atoms and cells and the mind comes into being based on a previous moment of mind, which is something that is luminous and has the capacity to be aware. Each moment of awareness therefore depends on a previous moment of awareness as its cause. This is the reasoning upon which Buddhist logic asserts that there is at the level of subtle mind and subtle wind a beginningless continuum of mind and matter.

It is through reflection on the above themes: the law of cause and effect, dependent origination, the dynamics of our physical environment, and, based on our analysis of the nature of mind, the mode of the arising and subsiding of thoughts, the shifts in the modalities of our consciousness between deep sleep, dreams and our waking state, etc., that the notion of continuity of consciousness may first become established as relevant to the understanding of our current condition. Once the notion of this continuity has been confirmed, through reflection and experience, then it becomes logical to prepare oneself for death and for future existences.

Now, as to the nature of the actual preparation itself, this will depend on each individual's depth of spiritual aspiration. For example, if an individual is simply seeking a favourable rebirth as a human being, there is no need to engage in a sophisticated meditative path related to the processes of death and rebirth. Simply to live a virtuous life is seen as sufficient. Similarly, in the case of those who are seeking personal liberation from conditioned existence and also in the case of those whose practice is confined to the sūtra level of the Mahāyāna path, their meditative preparation will be limited to ensuring the attainment of successive forms of existence that will be conducive to the continuation of their journey towards enlightenment. For these three kinds of individuals, no actual techniques for utilising the time of death as an essential element of the spiritual path have been set down in the classical Buddhist literature. Nevertheless, since the understanding of the processes of death, the intermediate state and rebirth are crucial to our understanding of the nature of existence, we do find extensive discussion of these three processes, even in the texts which relate to the aspirations of these three kinds of persons.

It is exclusively in tantra, however, and particularly in Highest Yoga Tantra, that the methods for utilising the processes of death, the intermediate state and rebirth are specifically taught as the basis for achieving liberation from cyclic existence. These methods involve the development of a skilful relationship with certain experiential stages that an individual actually induces with the intention of enhancing spiritual realisation and the fruition of their capacities as a human being.

Generally speaking, the practices of Highest Yoga Tantra present a spiritual path which enables the individual to attain complete buddhahood within a single lifetime, prior to the moment of death. Yet, for those who are unable to achieve this, it becomes crucial to use the transformative opportunities offered by the naturally occurring processes of death, the intermediate state and rebirth. Hence, in Highest Yoga Tantra, it is not merely the preparation for a more developed future rebirth which is important, but of more fundamental significance is the personal preparation for using one's own death and subsequent states as a means of achieving liberation.

In the literature of Highest Yoga Tantra, as I have mentioned, the three realms of conditioned existence into which a human being may be born are described in terms of differing expressions or modalities of energy (*rlung*) and it is said that our fundamental ignorance is the root of conditioned existence and that karmic energy is its activating force. Further, from the tantric perspective, death, the intermediate state and rebirth are also seen as nothing other than differing modalities of karmic energy. The point at which the gross levels of energy are completely dissolved and only the subtle energies remain is death. The stage at which these energies unfold into a more manifest form is the intermediate state, and the stage at which they eventually manifest substantially is called rebirth. Thus, all three states are differing manifestations of energy (*rlung*). Based on this understanding, since death is the state when all the gross levels of energy and consciousness have been dissolved, and only the subtle energies and consciousnesses remain, it is possible for an advanced yogin to meditatively induce a state which is almost identical to the actual experience of death. This can be achieved because it is possible to meditatively bring about the dissolution of the gross levels of energy and consciousness. When such a task is accomplished, the meditator gains an enormous potential to progress definitively in his or her spiritual practice. For at the stage, when the experience of fundamental inner radiance is genuinely effected through such a method, the yogin gains the capacity to actualise the illusory body of the meditational deity – thus ensuring the realisation of perfect buddhahood in this lifetime.

This achievement of perfect buddhahood entails the actualisation of the three dimensions or bodies of a buddha (*trikāya*). These fruitional bodies are related both to our ultimate natural state and to the emanational qualities of full enlightenment. Interestingly, we see exactly the same pattern of dimensions in our ordinary existence. Death is the point at which both the physical and mental fields dissolve into inner radiance and where both consciousness and energy exist at their most subtle non-dual level, as in deep sleep. This mode in its fruitional state is the Buddha-body of Reality (*dharmakāya*). Then, from within this essential or natural state, one enters into the intermediate state, where, although there is perceptual experience, the phenomenal forms are comparatively subtle and non-substantive, as in a dream. This mode in its fruitional state is the Buddha-body of Perfect Resource (*sambhogakāya*). Then, from this state, one assumes a grosser physical existence culminating in actual rebirth, as in our normal waking experience. This mode in its fruitional state is the Buddha-body of Emanation (*nirmāṇakāya*). Thus, we see a direct parallel between the three natural states of our existence and the three dimensions of a fully enlightened being.

Now, since actualisation of these three dimensions can be effected through the transformation of the three ordinary states of our existence, we find an array of practices which contain specific meditative techniques focusing on those attributes which the three ordinary states of existence and the three buddha-bodies have in common. Through these practices a continuity is developed between the ground or base (the ordinary state), the path, and the fruition (the buddha-bodies). In order to highlight the potential for liberation which exists in the skilful transformation of the ordinary states of existence, the great Indian Buddhist master Nāgārjuna uses the term '*kāya*' even when describing the three ordinary states. Thus, the dimension (*kāya*) of the moment of death is equated with the basic *dharmakāya*, the dimension (*kāya*) of the intermediate state with the basic *sambhogakāya* and the dimension (*kāya*) of the rebirth process with the basic *nirmāṇakāya*.[3] Thus, it is said, that through the meditative ability of an accomplished yogin, a genuine assimilation takes place at the actual moment of death, upon entering the intermediate state and upon beginning the process of rebirth.

With respect to training in these practices, a similitude of such an assimilation can be effected during the waking state, through generation stage practices, and during sleep, through dream yoga practices.

3. These relationships are vividly expressed in Chapter 11 of our text, 'The Great Liberation by Hearing', where specific instructions are given for recognising the spiritual opportunities that occur at the moment of death, that occur during the intermediate state of reality, and that occur as the processes of rebirth are experienced. Here the instructions speak of a recognition which assimilates the moment of death with the Buddha-body of Reality, the intermediate state of reality with the Buddha-body of Perfect Resource and the intermediate state of rebirth with the Buddha-body of Emanation. *Ed.*

In tantra the practice of imaginatively generating the meditational deity, that is to say, the practice of tantra's generation stage, is a unique path by which the three fruitional dimensions or buddha-bodies are brought into the path of one's practice. It is through understanding the profundity of this method that the tantric approach can be fully appreciated. The process of generating oneself as the meditational deity is the means by which the indivisible union of the realisation of emptiness and the realisation of perfect awareness is brought to fruition. This accomplishment directly counteracts the ordinary perceptions and apprehensions which underlie our ordinary dualistic experience. It is this accomplishment that culminates in the realisation of the ultimate nature of mind, the Buddha-body of Reality, the state beyond ordinary thought, where there is no longer any trace of the misapprehension of the nature of reality, of attachment or of aversion – only pure radiant awareness.

The practice of generating oneself as the meditational deity is found in all four classes of tantra. However, these methods are taught in their most sophisticated forms in the class of Highest Yoga Tantra. Depending on the spiritual capacities of the practitioner the tantras describe a graduated series of methods for generating oneself as the meditational deity. In the New Translation schools there is a systematisation according to four levels of capacity and in the Nyingma (or Old Translation) school the highest level of practice is further subdivided into three methods: Mahāyoga, Anuyoga and Atiyoga.

In the primary stages of tantric practice, in order to train oneself in the actualisation of the three buddha-bodies, as I have mentioned, the yogin first engages in the practices of the generation stage of meditation. The generation stage is like an imaginary rehearsal of the actual processes. Then, in the perfection stage of meditation, however, the experiences of entering the Buddha-body of Reality and actualising its emanational states, the Buddha-body of Perfect Resource and the Buddha-body of Emanation, are not imagined but real, and even involve certain physiological changes occurring in the yogin's body. Crucial to all these practices is the process of the dissolution of the gross consciousnesses and energies of the practitioner. Here, the practice of Highest Yoga Tantra underlines the importance of interrupting or cutting off the gross energy which serves as a vehicle for conceptual elaborations.

Thereby, hypothetically speaking, if the individual succeeds in interrupting the flow of karmic energy, then, even if the propensities for fundamental ignorance remain, they will be rendered impotent.

As I have noted above, if we observe carefully, we can see a basic pattern of emergence and dissolution which is common to both animate and inanimate phenomena. Among inanimate phenomena the processes of arising start from the very subtle and develop into the more gross. That is: there is an emergence from empty space, and a progression to movement or energy, to heat or light, to moisture or liquidity, and finally to solidity. The dissolution is the reverse of this sequence. This process of arising and dissolution also occurs in the body. In tantra, the process of dissolution of the physical elements which constitute a human body is described as beginning first with the dissolution of the earth element, followed by the water element, the fire element, the wind element and, finally, at the point at which only the space element is prominent, all the gross levels of energy and consciousness have dissolved. Then, in a further series of dissolutions, this stage gives rise to the experiences which are called: 'whitish appearance', followed by 'reddish increased appearance', 'blackish near attainment' and finally there is a culmination in the full experience of inner radiance called 'the attainment'.[4]

Because the stages of dissolution are natural processes, imagining these is of pre-eminent importance in the generation-stage practices of visualising the meditational deity.

Both in the New and Old Translation schools, the actualisation of inner radiance, the point at which all our gross consciousnesses and energies have been dissolved, is the primary intent. This is the essence of the Great Perfection (Dzogchen) practices[5] of the Nyingma tradition, of the Union of Emptiness and Luminosity Based on the Sameness of Saṃsāra and Nirvāṇa practices of the Sakya tradition, of the Great Seal (*Mahāmudrā*) practices of the Kagyu tradition and the Indivisible Union of Bliss and Emptiness practices of the Gelug tradition.

Now, when we speak of inner radiance, it is important to bear in mind that there are different levels at which this can be experi-

4. In our text these processes are described in Chapter 8. *Ed.*
5. The teachings presented in our text are based on the Great Perfection (Dzogchen) view. *Ed.*

enced and, in addition, there is one important difference between the Dzogchen view of inner radiance and that of the New Translation schools. As with that of emptiness, the experience of inner radiance can be of different types. The experience of inner radiance described in the New Translation schools is effected only subsequent to the dissolution of all the gross levels of conceptual elaboration. However, in the Dzogchen view, all states of awareness or consciousness are thought to be pervaded by inner radiance, just as a sesame seed is permeated by oil. Therefore, in Dzogchen, there exist refined instructions which allow the recognition of inner radiance even while all the gross levels of sensory activity are still active. This is where we come to the important distinction made in the Dzogchen teachings between the Tibetan terms '*sems*' and '*rig-pa*'. Our 'ordinary mind' (*sems*) refers to the gross dualising consciousness (*rnam-shes*), whereas 'pure awareness' (*rig-pa*) is free from the dualistic perceptions of subject and object. Following the practices of the Dzogchen teachings of the Nyingma school the student is directly introduced by an authentic spiritual teacher to the very nature of his or her mind as pure awareness. This is the focus of the 'Cutting through Resistance' (*khregs-chod*) aspect of the Dzogchen path and this is complemented by the All-surpassing Realisation (*thod-rgal*) practices which focus on eliciting and recognising the radiances of pristine cognition.[6] Irrespective of these differences of view and practice, however, a genuine experience of inner radiance is the realisation of the fundamental nature of our awareness, which is the inextricable union of emptiness and luminosity.

Now, when the subtle mind is completely pure, the body or energy aspect of the combination of subtle mind and subtle body arises as the five different coloured luminosities (white, blue, red, yellow and green) and in the form of buddha-bodies. All the different maṇḍalas, of the hundred deities, or the thousand deities, or whatever number, are all expressions of the five enlightened families, which are related to the purity of the five psycho-physical aggregates, the five elements and the five pristine cognitions. These

6. 'Cutting through Resistance' and the direct introduction to awareness are the subject matter of Chapter 4 of the present work. The introduction to the intermediate state of reality, in Chapter 11 of our text, is illustrative of the esoteric instructions on 'All-surpassing Realisation', which is the pinnacle of meditative practice according to the Nyingma school. *Ed.*

relationships form the core of the practices presented in Highest Yoga Tantra, as does the experiential cultivation of the nature of these deities through the daily practice.

So, in summary, by following in our practice the process of the natural dissolution of our gross forms of consciousness, and the natural arising from this state of the luminosities and bodies of the deities, first the actualisation of inner radiance is refined and this serves as the substantive cause for the arising of the Buddha-body of Perfect Resource and the Buddha-body of Emanation respectively. Thus the three bodies of a buddha are perfected, which is the fruition of the path of tantra.

Now, as for the forms of the meditational deity, which are generated in the practice of tantra, there are two principal types: peaceful deities and wrathful deities. In general terms, these are concerned with the transformation of the cognitive and emotional states associated with attachment and aversion respectively. The peaceful deities are quiescent and are expressions of the natural purity of attraction, that is the mind resting in its natural pristine state. The wrathful deities are the dynamic aspect of the peaceful deities and are expressions of the natural transformation of aversion. That is they represent the mind's active transformation of delusion into pristine cognition.[7]

As we now see, the path of Highest Yoga Tantra involves taking dissonant cognitive states, such as attachment and aversion, on to the path. In the path followed by pious attendants (*śrāvaka*) dissonant cognitive states are categorically perceived as something to be renounced. In the Mahāyāna path, however, there are two approaches which contrast with that of the pious attendants. According to the Mahāyāna sūtras, if a certain situation suggests a positive outcome in terms of benefiting others the voluntary use of desire or attachment is allowable. However, in the tantras it is not merely that desire or attachment is permissible when beneficial, here one deliberately utilises their energies as the path to purifying or consuming the dissonant states themselves.

Given that the practices of the tantras include the disciplined engagement of subtle physiological processes and the transforma-

7. The symbolism of each of the meditational deities associated with our text is described in Chapters 5, 6, 11 and 14 and in Appendix Two. *Ed.*

tion of the energies associated with attraction and aversion, before a practitioner can embark on the practices of tantra, he or she must find a spiritual teacher who meets the qualifications as set out in the authoritative literature and must receive empowerments and graduated instruction from that master. In addition, the practitioner should complete the preliminary practices and achieve a thorough grounding in the foundational paths of the sūtras, which includes the development of the altruistic intention to attain enlightenment (*bodhicitta*), the development of calm abiding – the stabilisation of attention on an internal object of meditation – and the development of penetrative insight – an analytical meditative state that dissects the nature of its object, its relationships, characteristics and function. The development of calm abiding and penetrative insight are the means by which the practitioner can cultivate his or her understanding of emptiness, which is an appreciation of the total absence of inherent existence and self-identity with respect to all phenomena. It is an essential prerequisite for beginning on the path of tantra that the practitioner achieve a profound appreciation of both non-substantiality and its interdependent relationship with phenomenal reality. The tantras presuppose this understanding, so it is in the sūtras therefore that we find the extensive elucidation of the methods for developing a complete understanding of emptiness.

Now, as to the nature of the understanding of emptiness presupposed by the tantras, the majority of masters of the Nyingma, Kagyu, Sakya and Gelug schools agree that this is the view of the Middle Way (*madhyamapratipad*) propounded in the sūtras and elucidated by Nāgārjuna in his works. In the Dzogchen view, however, there is also a unique method of explaining emptiness, which emphasises the inseparability of emptiness and inner radiance, but nonetheless, principally, this designation does refer to emptiness as presented in Nāgārjuna's Middle Way.

As far as the concept of emptiness or the ultimate nature of reality is concerned this is one area where there is an emerging convergence between the Buddhist understanding of the ultimate nature of existence and the evolving contemporary scientific view. This convergence relates to the unfindability of entities when these are analytically sought. In modern science the methods of analysis are principally applied to investigating the nature of material entities. Thus, the ultimate nature of matter is sought through a reductive process and the macroscopic world is reduced to the microscopic world of particles. Yet, when the nature of these particles is further examined, we find that ultimately their very existence as objects is called into question. This interface between non-substantiality and phenomena is a fundamental focus of Buddhist philosophical analysis and of experiential analysis through meditation on the nature of mind. As is now becoming more commonly known in the contemporary scientific field, a subtle understanding of the nature of the arising and dissolution of both individual thoughts and the cycles of existence lies at the heart of Buddhist literature and practice.

In summary, therefore, even though the stages of preparation for engaging in the practices of Highest Yoga Tantra are extensive, it is said that, since the mode of procedure in Highest Yoga Tantra follows a very close correspondence to the nature of existence, human beings of this world are regarded as having the perfect gross and subtle physiological basis for undertaking these practices successfully.

Normally in our lives, if we know that we are going to be confronted by a difficult or unfamiliar situation, we prepare and train ourselves for such a circumstance in advance, so that when this event actually happens we are fully prepared. As I have outlined, the rehearsal of the processes of death, and those of the intermediate state, and the emergence into a future existence, lies at the very heart of the path in Highest Yoga Tantra. These practices are part of my daily practice also and because of this I somehow feel a sense of excitement when I think about the experience of death. At the same time, though, sometimes I do wonder whether or not I will really be able to fully utilise my own preparatory practices when the actual moment of death comes!

A sense of uncertainty, and often fear, is a natural human feeling when thinking about the nature of death and the relationship between living and dying. It is perhaps not surprising therefore that the *Bar-do Thos-grol Chen-mo*, the *Tibetan Book of the Dead*, a treasure-text which focuses on this important subject, has become one of the best-known works of Tibetan literature in the West. Carrying out the first complete translation of this cycle of teachings has been an extraordinary accomplishment undertaken with great care over many years.

I hope that the profound insights contained in this work will be a source of inspiration and support to many interested people around the world, as they have been in my own culture.

Editor's Introduction

The *Tibetan Book of the Dead* includes one of the most detailed and compelling descriptions of the after-death state in world literature. It is not surprising therefore that when Chapter 11 of our text, 'The Great Liberation by Hearing', first appeared in English, in 1927, it caused a considerable stir and has remained one of the most well known of Tibet's literary works ever since. In our work, for the first time, we are presenting a complete translation of all twelve chapters of the compilation of texts known as the *Tibetan Book of the Dead*, which includes nine chapters not translated in W. Y. Evans-Wentz's original publication.

Our intention in carrying out this work was twofold. One was to present the entire original work, and the second was to compose the translation with the close support and participation of the contemporary masters and lineage holders of this tradition.

The complete *Tibetan Book of the Dead* is a comprehensive guide to both living and dying as originally taught by the great master from Oḍḍiyāna, Padmasambhava. Padmasambhava, along with Śāntarakṣita and King Trisong Detsen, formally established Buddhism in Tibet, during the eighth century, and most Tibetans revere him as a 'second Buddha'. The story of how this teaching was first given by Padmasambhava to King Trisong Detsen is presented in Gyurme Dorje's 'Brief Literary History', which follows.

The compendium of texts known as *The Tibetan Book of the Dead* contains exquisitely written guidance and practices related to transforming our experience in daily life, on how to address the processes of dying and the after-death state, and on how to help those who are dying. These teachings include: methods for investigating and cultivating our experience of the ultimate nature of mind in our daily practice (Chapters 2–7), guidance on the recognition of the signs of impending death and a detailed description of the mental and physical processes of dying (Chapter 8), rituals for the avoidance of premature death (Chapter 9), the now famous guide 'The Great Liberation by Hearing' that is read to the dying and the dead (Chapter 11), aspirational prayers that are read at the time of death (Chapter 12), an allegorical masked play that light-heartedly dramatises the journey through the intermediate state (Chapter 13), and a translation of the sacred mantras that are attached to the body after death and are said to bring 'Liberation by Wearing' (Chapter 14).

In addition, and at the advice of the late HH Dilgo Khyentse Rinpoche, we have also included two additional texts that are not usually included, namely Chapter 1, which poetically sets out the preliminary meditations and practices related to this cycle of teachings, and indeed to tantric practice in general, and Chapter 10, the instructions on methods for transferring consciousness at the point of death into an enlightened state, which are referred to in Chapter 11 and are an essential aspect of the practices related to dying.

Our second intention was to present the entire work in a way that, as honestly as we could, reflects the insights and intentions of the masters of the lineage and gives a sense of the elegance and moving, poetic beauty of the original work. In order to do this, as is described in the Acknowledgements, the translation has been based on the oral commentarial explanation of contemporary lineage holders and was carried out with the continuous advice of contemporary masters.

Given the above, there is very little to say with respect to offering further introduction to the meaning of the texts. It is our hope that with the help of HH the Dalai Lama's Introductory Commentary, the short introductions to each chapter, the notes and the glossary, the meaning will shine through as directly as was intended.

As I have been asked to do so, I will just say a few words about the psychological context of this material. It may seem somewhat woolly to many if it is said that the insights that are presented here come from those who have realised the ultimate nature of mind and thereby have experiential understanding of the processes of the mind in deep sleep, dreams, the waking state and throughout the processes of dying and beyond. But, as described by the Dalai Lama in the Introductory Commentary, the process of imagining and then actualising the stages of dissolution of consciousness that will occur naturally at the time of death lies at the heart of higher Tibetan Buddhist meditative practices, as do practices related to maintaining awareness during deep sleep and while dreaming.

As Gyurme Dorje describes in 'A Brief Literary History', this cycle of teachings is based on the *Guhyagarbha Tantra*. This text is described as having been received in a revelation from the primordial buddha Samantabhadra, transmitted through the agency of the meditational deities Vajrasattva and Guhyapati Vajrapāṇi. In other words, the source is Samantabhadra, who is the resonance of pure awareness, the natural purity of mental consciousness, transmitted through an embodiment of the insight, compassion and communicative skills (skilful means) of all the buddhas, that is to say of all those who abide in an unmoving realisation of the ultimate nature of mind.

As in all the major Buddhist tantric systems, the *Guhyagarbha Tantra* describes a maṇḍala, which is a visual representation of the components of the enlightened mind. Our chart of the maṇḍala of the Peaceful and Wrathful Deities (Appendix Two) sets out the core aspects of the symbolism of the maṇḍala associated with our text. As is always the case, this symbolism is based on the classical understanding of the nature of a person's psycho-physical components, as described in the Abhidharma literature, which is common to all forms of Buddhism. This analysis of the components of our being can be undertaken with our normal conceptual mind.

The actual experience of the luminosities which are said to underlie the maṇḍala is however only possible as a result of the accomplishment of very subtle meditative states, which are fruitional aspects of the path of Highest Yoga Tantra. As the Dalai Lama relates in his commentary, these luminosities only become apparent to the meditator once realisation of the ultimate nature of mind is achieved. This occurs during the processes of meditations, which are simulacra of the processes of dying and the re-emergence of consciousness from a non-conceptual inner radiance, the mind's ultimate nature. The processes of the dissolution of the coarse forms of consciousness into inner radiance and the emergence of consciousness from inner radiance also occur naturally at the time of death. In other words, according to Buddhist tradition, experiential access to the processes, which mirror those of dying and the re-emergence of consciousness after death, is achievable in the waking state.

When HH Dilgo Khyenste Rinpoche gave his commentary to the text he explained that the 'Introduction to the Intermediate State of Reality', the central section of 'The Great Liberation by Hearing', is an expression of the esoteric Thodgal practices of Dzogchen, the 'Great Perfection' teachings. Thodgal is the pinnacle of meditative practice according to the Nyingma school and it results in the direct experience during meditation of the luminosities and the maṇḍala of meditational deities that are described in Chapter 11. This arising of the five-coloured luminosities as a result of actualising the ultimate nature of mind is a phenomenon that has been described by all the great meditators of the four major Buddhist schools of Tibet and the pre-Buddhist Bon tradition. The point I am leading up to here is that the experiences described in our text relate to the modalities of our awareness from moment to moment, in our waking state, in deep sleep, in our dreams and also during the transition from life to death and beyond.

In this sense 'The Great Liberation by Hearing' can be read as a wonderful metaphorical narrative illustrating the processes of our cognitive state, whether in our waking state or in death.

Carl Jung in his commentary to Evans-Wentz's 1927 edition of the *Tibetan Book of the Dead* spoke about how compelling he found it to look at 'The Great Liberation by Hearing' backwards. From a psychoanalytical point of view this is indeed interesting, as our text can then be seen as providing a guide for tracing our confused and deluded states, back through our conditioned attraction and aversion to selected aspects of our experience, back through the weave of our habitual tendencies and mental constructs and a relentless series of voluntary or involuntary mental choices, back through the illusory comfort generated by our sense of ego, right back to a pure original cognitive event. This is something that we can explore during our own waking experience by analysing how our thoughts originate in the mind, interact with our mental constructs and guide our emotions and subsequent actions.

Chapter 4 of our text, 'The Introduction to Awareness', addresses this process of exploration directly. Here we find guidance for the meditator on how to recognise the mind's ultimate nature, the underlying, mirror-like pure awareness, free from dualistic elaboration, from which all our thoughts and perceptions arise and into which they always again dissolve. Chapter 11 then gives a symbolic description of how the pure radiances of our awareness, the ultimate nature of our pure psycho-physical components and elemental properties, arise as luminosities and meditational deities. At this critical point, either we recognise these luminosities and meditational deities as the embodiments of our own actual nature, and thereby remain in a state of pure perception, or, having failed to recognise their appearance as being a natural expression of the ultimate nature of all phenomena, we are then inexorably drawn into the clouded, dull impulses of dualistic experience. Once this occurs, the matrix of our habitual tendencies and mental constructs is activated and this generates our sense of independent, individual identity. By now our ego, which cannot accept the openness and clarity of the pristine perceptual state, is established and the mind functions purely on the basis of wanting to satisfy its conditioned expectations and impulses, from moment to moment.

In this ego-bound state our thoughts, speech and actions are then modulated by a process of inner judgement. As the text describes, death holds up an all-seeing mirror, 'the mirror of past actions', to our eyes, in which the consequences of all our negative and positive actions are clearly seen and there is a weighing of our past actions in the light of their consequences, the balance of which will determine the kind of existence or mental state we are being driven to enter. The 'life-review' aspect of this process, metaphorically described in our text as the weighing of white pebbles, representing our positive actions, against the weight of black pebbles, representing our negative actions, is wonderfully illustrated by the poet Heathcote Williams' phrase 'death develops life's photographs', which succinctly evokes the notion of our day-to-day obliviousness to the consequences of our actions being developed or processed in death so that we can experience them face to face.

Following the expansive process of the 'life-review', the mind is then driven into a new equilibrium, avoiding the chaos of dissociation. This twofold process of inner judgement, the 'life-review' followed by the coalescence of the mind into a new modality, is symbolically represented in our text by the actions of Yama, who is the embodiment of the infallible laws of cause and effect. In our waking state, this weighing and modulation of the momentum of our past thoughts, speech and actions is of course largely hidden, but we do experience this in our sense of 'conscience' at the time of thinking, speaking or acting. In death, as in life, the process of inner judgement is not of course a judgement by an external being but it is the result of our own mind's innate dynamic of manifesting the natural fruition of our own mental constructs and coalescing this ripening into a new equilibrium. At this stage, in particular, just as we are about to enter a changed emotive state, it is absolutely critical that we recognise the fundamental reality that we are experiencing the results of the mental states which we ourselves have generated and that we use this understanding to recognise the actual nature of our experience. In our day-to-day life we know that if we begin to feel angry, for example, this immediately creates an internal disturbance and this disturbance creates a shift in the way we perceive both others and our environment, which in turn affects the way in which others react to us, which then reinforces our initial anger and we feel confirmed in that new state. This is the cycle of experiencing the results of the mental states that we ourselves have generated, which can occur from moment to moment or according to our text from lifetime to lifetime.

Finally, if there is no recognition and as a culmination of this entire process, our text describes how, driven on by a relentless search for security and the urge to resolve our impulses and expectations, in a mental realm where our expectations and actual reality do not match, and based on the ever-present swinging back and forth of our attraction and aversion, we enter into an emotive state whose focus can be anywhere across the spectrum of elation, jealousy, pride, confusion, blankness, desire, craving, anger, hatred or fear. These states are depicted in our text as the realms of existence into which we may pass at birth.

Given the above, even if we do not accept the Buddhist understanding that the modalities of our consciousness in deep sleep, dreams and our waking state mirror those of death, we can still apply the advice given in 'The Great Liberation by Hearing' to our everyday experience. Giving up our compulsive attraction and aversion to aspects of our perceptual realm, glimpsing the causal dynamic of our actual condition and coming to the realisation that what we see is the product of our own mental constructs, and that we therefore do have the potential to view our experience more insightfully, is a powerful method of releasing us from the dissonant and perhaps even fearful qualities of our own self-made, perceptual landscape.

Chapters 1–7 provide us with a framework for achieving this release in our daily lives. Chapter 1 poetically evokes the perspectives that may lead us to realise that understanding our actual nature and understanding our current condition as human beings are worthwhile, Chapters 2–6 offer us methods for training our minds to instinctively recognise the actual nature of our being and existence, and Chapter 7 provides a framework for modulating and refining our motivation, perspectives and actions.

It is undeniably the case that in our society we do not easily accept that death is a natural part of life, which results in a perpetual sense of insecurity and fear, and many are confused at the time of the death of a loved one, not knowing what they can do to help the one that has passed away or how to address their own grief. Exploring ways of overcoming our fear of death and adopting a creative approach at the time of bereavement, that is, focusing one's energy on supporting the one that has passed away, are both extraordinary benefits of the insights and practices that are so beautifully expressed in the *Tibetan Book of the Dead*.

When I think of these things I often remember the Dalai Lama saying: 'When we look at life and death from a broader perspective, then dying is just like changing our clothes! When this body becomes old and useless, we die and take on a new body, which is fresh, healthy and full of energy! This need not be so bad!'

Graham Coleman
Thimpu, Bhutan

A Brief Literary History of the *Tibetan Book of the Dead*

by Gyurme Dorje

Since the publication in 1927 of Lama Kazi Dawa Samdup and W. Y. Evans-Wentz's pioneering English translation of three chapters from the cycle of texts known in the original Tibetan as *The Great Liberation by Hearing in the Intermediate States* (*Bar-do thos-grol chen-mo*), the chapters they translated, dealing with the nature of the after-death state, including the accompanying aspirational prayers, have attracted a compelling interest outside Tibet under the title the *Tibetan Book of the Dead*. Learned Tibetans today often express their surprise that this particular collection of meditative practices concerning methods for understanding the nature of mind and transforming our experiences throughout the round of life and death has become one of the most well known of all the works of Tibetan literature in translation. This renown is especially unexpected when one considers the esoteric origins of the text and its highly restricted transmission within Tibet until the mid-fifteenth century. It is on account of this widespread popular recognition however that the title coined by the editor of the first translation, Evans-Wentz, has been retained in all subsequent translations and related studies. Following in this tradition, we too have retained the title the *Tibetan Book of the Dead* to refer to the first complete English translation of *The Great Liberation by Hearing in the Intermediate States*, which includes translations of all twelve chapters of the original compilation.

EARLY ORIGINS

The Great Liberation by Hearing in the Intermediate States is an outstanding example of Nyingma literature. The Nyingmapa are the followers of the oldest of all the schools of Tibetan Buddhism, tracing their lineage back to the first wave of transmission of the Buddhist teachings to Tibet, to the royal dynastic period of Tibetan history in the eighth century, when great Indian masters such as Padmasambhava, Vimalamitra and Buddhaguhya initially introduced the three inner classes of tantra: Mahāyoga, Anuyoga and Atiyoga. These tantra texts are differentiated on the basis of their distinctive meditative techniques, known respectively as the generation stage, the perfection stage and the Great Perfection (Dzogchen).

All traditions of Tibetan Buddhism today share the inheritance of the canonical compilations of the Indian Buddhist scriptures and treatises contained in the *Kangyur* and *Tengyur*. The former contains those teachings of the Buddhas (vinaya, sūtras and tantras) that were translated from Sanskrit and other languages into Tibetan, mostly from the late tenth century onwards and compiled initially by Buton Rinchendrub (1290–1364). The latter includes the classical Indian commentaries that were also translated from Sanskrit into Tibetan. In a recently published and collated master edition of both the *Kangyur* and *Tengyur* these texts comprise 180 volumes.

At the same time, each school has its own distinctive writings. The particular literature of the Nyingma school comprises translations from Sanskrit and other languages, which are preserved in the twenty-six volume *Collected Tantras of the Nyingmapa* (*rNying-ma'i rgyud-'bum*), and a companion anthology of commentarial treatises, written by successive generations of Indian and Tibetan lineage holders. The latter, which has been faithfully handed down through a 'long lineage of oral precepts' (*ring-brgyud bka'-ma*), that is to say through an unbroken lineage of transmission from one generation of accomplished masters to the next, is continually growing and currently comprises 120 volumes in a recently published edition.

The *Collected Tantras of the Nyingmapa* has three main sections, corresponding to the compilations of Atiyoga, Anuyoga and Mahāyoga. Among them, the most influential single text is the *Guhyagarbha Tantra*, a revelation of the primordial buddha Samantabhadra, transmitted through Vajrasattva and Guhyapati Vajrapāṇi. The compendium of texts that we now know as the *Tibetan Book of the Dead* bases its symbolism and iconography on the *Guhyagarbha Tantra*. Founded on the classical Abhidharma view of the elements, psycho-physical aggregates, etc., this tantra text is the earliest known literary work to portray the natural purity and natural transformation of our mundane psychological states, respectively, as the maṇḍala of the forty-two peaceful deities and as the maṇḍala of the fifty-eight wrathful deities. Though generally and rightly classified as a Mahāyoga text, the *Guhyagarbha Tantra* has also been obliquely interpreted from the perspective of Dzogchen, most famously by Longchen Rabjampa (1308–63). The meditative techniques of both Mahāyoga and Dzogchen are clearly expressed among the chapters of our present work: the generation stage of meditation is emphasised in Chapters 5–7, and the Great Perfection in Chapters 4 and 11, these latter two chapters being based on the teachings of the two key aspects of the Great Perfection, namely Cutting through Resistance (*khregs-chod*) and All-surpassing Realisation (*thod-rgal*) respectively. Thus from the point of view of its theoretical foundation and practice, as well as in its iconography and symbolism, the *Tibetan Book of the Dead* echoes its roots in the *Guhyagarbha Tantra* but, in addition, vividly incorporates the classical teachings of Dzogchen.

The *Guhyagarbha Tantra* was initially compiled by King Indrabhūti and Kukkurāja of Sahor in north-west India (*circa* sixth century). The monarch, also known as King Dza, received the whole corpus of the Mahāyoga tantras in a vision from Vajrasattva, and Kukkurāja, a great accomplished master, divided this literature into eighteen books (*tantras*) – the most all-embracing of which is the *Guhyagarbha*. During the eighth century, the *Guhyagarbha Tantra* was translated into Tibetan from Sanskrit three times: initially by Buddhaguhya and Vairocana, secondly by Padmasambhava and Nyak Jñānakumāra, and definitively by Vimalamitra with Nyak Jñānakumāra and Ma Rinchen Chok. A much later indigenous Tibetan translation was also prepared in the fifteenth century by Tharlo Nyima Gyeltsen and Go Lotsāwa. The anthology of treatises related to the *Guhyagarbha Tantra* includes a large number of commentaries on this text, of both Indian and Tibetan origin, composed by illustrious masters such as Līlāvajra, Buddhaguhya, Rongzom Paṇḍita, Longchen Rabjampa and Lochen Dharmaśrī.

The iconography and symbolism of the hundred Peaceful and Wrathful Deities presented in the *Guhyagarbha Tantra* subsequently gave rise to a whole genre of literature in Tibet known as the Cycles of the Peaceful and Wrathful Deities (*zhi-khro*), among which our compilation of texts *The Great Liberation by Hearing in the Intermediate States* is the most influential.

THE CLOSE LINEAGE OF TREASURES

According to traditional accounts, when Padmasambhava introduced these teachings to Tibet in the eighth century he foresaw that the oral transmission of the 'long lineage' would be subjected over time to corruption and misapplication, and that the efficacy of the teachings would be diminished. To counteract this, through the agency of his consort Yeshe Tsogyal and other foremost disciples, he concealed a large number of 'treasure-teachings' (*gter-chos*), in the form of books and sacred artefacts, at power-places (*gnas*) throughout the Tibetan plateau, predicting that they would be rediscovered in future generations by their respective 'treasure-finders' (*gter-ston*) and promulgated for the sake of future generations. Prophecies were written, describing those who would have the power to unearth such revelations in the future – figures of the calibre of Nyangrel Nyima Ozer, Guru Chowang, and the discoverer of our text, Karma Lingpa. The term 'treasure-teachings' is generally extended to include not only concealed 'earth-treasures' (*sa-gter*), but also revelations discovered in a telepathic manner directly from the enlightened intention of buddha-mind (*dgongs-gter*), and pure visionary experiences (*dag-snang*).

This notion of the concealment of texts in the form of treasure had precedents in both Indian and Chinese Buddhism. Nāgārjuna, for example, is said to have received the *Prajñāpāramitā Sūtras* in the form of treasure from the ocean-depths, and, according to Nyingma doxographers, a recension of *Mahāyoga Tantras* was revealed to the eight teachers of Padmasambhava, at the Śītavana charnel ground near Vajrāsana. Similarly, the Chinese Buddhist tradition of elemental divination, which includes aspects of *Feng Shui* and *Yi Jing*, also recounts how the bodhisattva Mañjughoṣa concealed certain divinatory texts on Wang Hai Feng, the Eastern Peak of the sacred Mount Wutai Shan. Tibetan sources then describe how Mañjughoṣa subsequently revealed the *Precious*

Clarifying Lamp (*Rin-chen gsal-ba'i sgron-me*) to the Chinese master Dahura Nagpo.

Since the initial discoveries of the first Tibetan 'treasure-finder' Sangye Lama, in the eleventh century, a vast literature has been produced in Tibet by way of revelation through the 'close lineage of treasures' (*nye-brgyud gter-ma*), and redacted within the public domain. The *Collected Treasures* of the various treasure-finders are too voluminous to mention here, but many of their works are represented in the extensive nineteenth-century anthology known as the *Store of Precious Treasures* (*Rin-chen gter-mdzod*), which was recently republished in 76 volumes. Just as the anthology of the 'long lineage' contains many commentaries on the *Guhyagarbha Tantra*, a significant number of 'treasure-teachings' are also inspired by its portrayal of the hundred Peaceful and Wrathful Deities. Among them the most elaborate is the cycle discovered in the fourteenth century by Karma Lingpa – the *Peaceful and Wrathful Deities: A Profound Sacred Teaching, [entitled] Natural Liberation through [Recognition of] Enlightened Intention* (*Zab-chos zhi-khro dgongs-pa rang-grol*). The compendium of texts now known outside Tibet as the *Tibetan Book of the Dead* is an abridgement of this treasury of texts discovered by Karma Lingpa.

THE CONCEALMENT BY PADMASAMBHAVA

The extant cycle of texts that comprise Karma Lingpa's revelations includes a few short biographies and historical accounts of the work's original concealment and subsequent revelation, which were composed by later lineage holders. The following passage from the *Middle-length Empowerment* (pp. 61–4) describes the roots of this tradition:

> At the time when [Padmasambhava] was turning incalculable wheels of the teachings concerning the supremely secret vehicle [of Vajrayāna], he revealed, in accord with the individual capacities of the fortunate king [Trisong Detsen] and his subjects, many practices related to the generation and perfection stages of the Peaceful and Wrathful Deities; and these were [later] concealed, for the most part, as profound treasures, for the benefit of beings in the future.
>
> When Padmasambhava was nearing the completion of his direct

spiritual work and teaching in Tibet, the sovereign and his son [Prince Mutri Tsenpo], along with the translator Chokrolui Gyelsten and others, offered him a maṇḍala of gold and turquoise, and fervently made the following supplication: 'Although your compassion is always present and in the past you have held high the incalculable beacons of the teaching, according to the outer and inner vehicles, yet for the benefit of ourselves, the king, ministers, friends and subjects, and for future beings of the degenerate age, we request you to give a teaching which is the quintessence of all the teachings of the outer and inner vehicles; one through which buddhahood may be attained in a single lifetime; one which will bestow liberation by merely hearing it, a profound and concise teaching containing the essential meaning.'

Thus, [in response to their supplication] the Great Master replied, 'O! Sovereign King, Prince, Ministers, in accord with your wish, I do have a teaching which is the essential point of all the six million four hundred thousand tantras of the Great Perfection, which were brought forth from the enlightened intention of glorious Samantabhadra. By merely hearing this teaching, the doors leading to birth in inferior existences will be blocked. By merely understanding it you will arrive at the level of supreme bliss. Those who take its meaning to heart will reach the irreversible level of the spontaneously accomplished awareness-holders. It can bring great benefit for all those who are connected with it.

'Although I do possess such a teaching, since those who are of weak mind, or who are naturally inclined towards the Lesser Vehicle, or who lack good fortune, and harbour wrong views and doubts, may disparage this teaching and thereby fall into inferior existences, you should not proclaim [this teaching] to others, even [by whispering its name] into the wind. It should be concealed as a [buried] treasure for the sake of future beings of the degenerate age.'

So it was that he named this teaching, which essentialises all teachings, the *Peaceful and Wrathful Deities: A Profound Sacred Teaching, [entitled] Natural Liberation through [Recognition of] Enlightened Intention*, and he bestowed it on the translator, [Chokro]lui Gyeltsen, as his legacy [of good fortune]. Then, directing his enlightened intention towards living beings of the future degenerate age, who would be of meagre merit, he concealed it in the form of a treasure at Mount Gampodar in Dakpo, at a site which resembles a dancing god.

THE PROPHECY CONCERNING KARMA LINGPA

Padmasambhava's prophesies concerning the treasure-finder Karma Lingpa and his immediate successors are also recounted elsewhere within the cycle. The following verses are taken from Gendun Gyeltsen's fifteenth-century account, entitled *Padmasambhava's Prophecy of the Treasure-finder and the Series of Authentic Lineage Teachers* (pp. 22ff.). In particular, they offer a rationale for the original concealment of the texts and predictions regarding their subsequent discovery and secret transmission. It is clear that even in this early formative period the cycle of texts had acquired two distinct titles, *The Great Liberation by Hearing during the Intermediate States*, and *The Natural Liberation through Recognition of Enlightened Intention*, reflecting its shorter and longer versions.

It says in a prophetic declaration of Orgyan Rinpoche:
'In the future, during the final era, the degenerate age,
When monks [act] like pigs and make women pregnant,
When virtuous actions generate and sustain resentment,
When the most noble of monks takes a bride,
When factionalism and wars are widespread,
At that time there is no doubt that all those bereft of such instructions
Will fall into the inferior existences.
So to benefit the sentient beings of this degenerate age,
I have committed [this cycle of teachings] to writing,
And concealed them at Mount Gampodar.
In that age, a supremely fortunate son will be born.
His father will have the name Accomplished Master Nyinda,
And he will be the courageous "Karma Lingpa".
On his right thigh there will be a mole,
Resembling the eye of pristine cognition,
And he will be born in the dragon or snake year,
Into a heroic family line, the fruit of past good actions.
May that fortunate person encounter this [teaching]!

'But he [Karma Lingpa] should not publicly teach the cycles of
The *Peaceful and Wrathful Deities: Natural Liberation through [Recognition of] Enlightened Intention*
To anyone at all, even by whispering into the wind,
And so it should remain until the time of the third lineage holder.
Obstacles will arise if these [teachings] are publicly taught!
However, he should impart the cycle of the
Great Compassionate One: Lotus Peaceful and Wrathful Deities
To all of his fortunate students!

'If the oral instructions of the lineage issuing from the third generation lineage holder
Are kept secret for seven years, there will be no obstacles.
When seven years have passed,
That [third generation successor] may properly impart to others
The empowerments and practical application of the [abridged] cycle,
The *[Great] Liberation [by Hearing] during the Intermediate States.*
Then, when nine years have passed, the [complete] cycle of the
Natural Liberation through [Recognition of] Enlightened Intention
Should be imparted gradually, not all at once!

'These treasures will be extracted in the region of Dakpo, in Southern Kongpo,
And they will be concentrated for the sake of living beings,
In the region of Draglong, in Upper Kongpo.
Karma Lingpa's activity on behalf of living beings will ripen in the north!'

THE LIFE OF KARMA LINGPA

Although the exact dates of Karma Lingpa are unknown, his birth and death have been accurately placed within the fourteenth century. The following passages describing his life and those of his immediate successors are taken from Gyarawa Namka Chokyi Gyeltsen's fifteenth-century *Jewel Garland: An Abridged History*

Karma Lingpa

of the Lineage (pp. 40ff.). Of particular interest is the discovery of two distinct cycles of treasure-teachings, the well-known *Peaceful and Wrathful Deities: Natural Liberation of Enlightened Intention*, and the *Great Compassionate One: Lotus Peaceful and Wrathful Deities*. The latter is no longer extant in this form, although it appears to have been the source for the masked drama contained in Chapter 13 of the present work.

> [Revered as an emanation of the great translator Chokrolui Gyeltsen], Karma Lingpa was born at Khyerdrup, above Dakpo in Southern Tibet. He was the eldest son of the accomplished master Nyinda Sangye, an upholder of the mantra tradition and a treasure-finder in his own right.
>
> In his fifteenth year, the prophetic declaration and the auspicious coincidence came together. From Mount Gampodar, which resembles a dancing god, he extracted the *Peaceful and Wrathful Deities: Natural Liberation of Enlightened Intention*, along with the *Great Compassionate One: Lotus Peaceful and Wrathful Deities* and other treasures.
>
> Unfortunately others spoke ill of him because he did not form an auspicious relationship with the intended consort who had been prophesised for him in connection with his discovery of these treasure-teachings. He did have one son, but because he showed a yellow scroll [containing his treasures] to his student before the time when he was destined to impart the *Peaceful and Wrathful Deities: Natural Liberation of Enlightened Intention*, it is said he encountered life-threatening obstacles.
>
> Karma Lingpa was endowed with innumerable attributes, and dwelt as the very embodiment of unimpeded enlightened activity. So, knowing of his own untimely death, he said with prescience: 'In the near future, many marks in the form of lotus flowers will appear on my body!', and he also made numerous other clairvoyant statements. Then, the next year, when he was on the point of death, he granted the empowerments and transmissions of the *Peaceful and Wrathful Deities: Natural Liberation of Enlightened Intention*, to his son alone, and not to any others, saying 'You should entrust this teaching to a saintly person who maintains the commitments and has the name Nyinda. His actions for the welfare of living beings will be most extensive!' Making many such prophecies, Karma Lingpa passed away.

Thus the first lineage holder was Karma Lingpa's own son, Nyinda Choje, the author of Chapter 1 of the present work. The second-generation lineage holder, Lama Nyinda Ozer of Tsikar Monastery in Longpo, was born in 1409 (earth female ox year), and he is said to have written down the text contained in Chapter 1 of the present work. It is the third-generation lineage holder Gyarawa Namka Chokyi Gyatso who has the distinction of being the first person to publicly teach the treasures of Karma Lingpa. The transmissions of the *Peaceful and Wrathful Deities* and *The Great Liberation by Hearing in the Intermediate States* that eventually came to permeate the entire Tibetan plateau can all trace their roots back to his teaching activity, particularly at Menmo and Thangdrok monasteries in Kongpo.

The extensive dispersion of the lineage throughout Tibet and the Himalayan region that issued from Gyarawa has been recently documented, along with visual charts, by Bryan J. Cuevas in his work *The Hidden History of the Tibetan Book of the Dead*. We will not therefore describe this again here. However, one important figure, from the perspective of the literary history, is Rigdzin Nyima Drakpa (1647–1710), who in his later years, at Takmogang and Chakru, began transcribing and collating the various texts associated with Karma Lingpa's cycle. It is clear from the various extant lineage prayers that he was directly responsible for standardising the shorter anthology entitled *The Great Liberation by Hearing in the Intermediate States* in its present form.

Rigdzin Nyima Drakpa's lineage was particularly influential in the nomadic areas of Sok Dzong, where the mantrins of the Kabgye Lhakhang even now maintain the lineage of his teachings, and in Dzachuka, where his teacher Dzogchen Pema Rikdzin founded Dzogchen Monastery in 1685. He also formed a spiritual rapport with Terdak Lingpa, on account of which the transmissions of Tsele, Lhalung and Mindroling all converged in his own son Orgyan Tendzin. Subsequently, the teachings of the Karma Lingpa tradition were passed on from Mindroling to Dzogchen in the following line of transmission: Pema Gyurme Gyatso, Gyelse Ratna Vija, Dzogchen II Gyurme Thekchok Tendzin, Pema Kundrol Namgyel and Dzogchen III Ngedon Tendzin Zangpo. The last named was responsible for preparing the first xylographic edition of *The Great Liberation by Hearing in the Intermediate States*, at Dzogchen Monastery in the mid-eighteenth century.

EDITIONS AND CONTENT OF *THE GREAT LIBERATION BY HEARING IN THE INTERMEDIATE STATES*

The diverse strands of the lineage stemming from Karma Lingpa and Gyarawa, summarised above, ensured that their legacy would flourish throughout Tibet and in the neighbouring sub-Himalayan regions of Northern Nepal, Sikkim and Bhutan. The earliest texts which these spiritual successions imparted through the generations were handwritten manuscripts, including a great many local and anonymous supplements. Yet, as Bryan Cuevas has rightly observed, 'most of the available recensions of [Karma Lingpa's] *Peaceful and Wrathful Deities* come to us in the form of xylographic prints and facsimile reproductions from blocks carved only in the last two centuries'. Unfortunately, the scribal errors that have crept into many of these 'standard' editions subsequently acquired great currency.

At present, the most extensive extant version of the *Peaceful and Wrathful Deities: Natural Liberation of Enlightened Intention* is not a block-print, but the manuscript version from the library of the late *Kyabje* Dudjom Rinpoche, who in the 1960s had his scribe prepare an elegant three-volume edition on the basis of the two volumes in his possession, which were apparently of Katok provenance. This manuscript contains sixty-four distinct texts, which are arranged sequentially under the categories of history, empowerment, generation stage, perfection stage, introductions (according to the Great Perfection), path of skilful means, and protector liturgies. Although it is the most extensive version available, this manuscript is by no means exhaustive – for there are other, smaller published compilations, associated with Pelyul, Dzogchen and Nedo, containing texts that are excluded from the larger anthology. However, in our experience, and on the authority of Gene Smith, who generously made the Dudjom manuscript available on CD-ROM, the Dudjom manuscript is far more accurate than the many Indian and Bhutanese reprints that are more widely available and have provided the source for the recent partial translations of *The Great Liberation by Hearing in the Intermediate States*. Even the illuminated manuscript on which Kazi

Dawa Samdup's 1927 translation is based appears to perpetuate the same inaccuracies. After wrestling with the scribal errors, lacunae and inconsistencies that fill the various Indian reprints of *The Great Liberation by Hearing in the Intermediate States*, it was with considerable joy and relief that we were finally able to clarify obscure readings and eliminate many cumbersome and unnecessary annotations by basing our translation on the three-volume Dudjom edition of the *Peaceful and Wrathful Deities: Natural Liberation of Enlightened Intention*. Seldom have we opted for readings based on the two Indian reprints of *The Great Liberation by Hearing in the Intermediate States* at our disposal, the Delhi and Varanasi photo-offset publications, and when we have done so, we have indicated the reason for our choice in the notes. We have not, however, made reference to the new Amdo edition, compiled by Khenpo Dorje and just published in Hong Kong.

Readers wishing to understand the precise relationship between the chapters of the derivative *Great Liberation by Hearing in the Intermediate States*, and the larger cycle of the *Peaceful and Wrathful Deities*, are referred to Appendix One, where the correspondences are presented.

As stated above, this is the first complete English translation of *The Great Liberation by Hearing in the Intermediate States*, otherwise known to the outside world as the *Tibetan Book of the Dead*, and it is based on a version of the original text which has proven to be far more accurate than those used in previous translations. All the chapters of the anthology standardised by Nyima Drakpa and later published in woodblock form at Dzogchen Monastery are contained in this book. With the exception of Chapter 13, Part One, which may well derive from the non-extant *Lotus Peaceful and Wrathful Deities*, and Chapter 13, Part Two, which was composed by Gyarawa Namka Chokyi Gyatso, all the other chapters from Nyima Drakpa's compilation appear to have been taken from the original treasure-cycle of Karma Lingpa's *Peaceful and Wrathful Deities*.

In presenting our translation, we have sought to order the chapters according to the meaningful sequence of the intermediate states that arise in the course of life and death, and therefore the order of the chapters in this translation differs from the arrangement of Nyima Drakpa. In addition, we have included two further chapters from the *Peaceful and Wrathful Deities* that are not part of *The*

Great Liberation by Hearing in the Intermediate States. Chapter 1, outlining the preliminary practices of meditation, is attributed to Nyinda Choje and Nyinda Ozer, while Chapter 10, on consciousness transference, derives from Karma Lingpa's *Six Guidebooks of the Perfection Stage* of meditation. The first of these has been included because it provides an essential context to the later chapters, and the instructions on consciousness transference have been included because they are specifically mentioned in Chapter 11, as a necessary practice related to the intermediate state of the time of death.

THE TIBETAN BOOK OF THE DEAD

Contents

1. Natural Liberation of the Nature of Mind: The Four-session Yoga of the Preliminary Practice 5
2. A Prayer for Union with the Spiritual Teacher, [entitled] Natural Liberation, without Renunciation of the Three Poisons 23
3. Root Verses of the Six Intermediate States 29
4. The Introduction to Awareness: Natural Liberation through Naked Perception 35
5. The Spiritual Practice entitled Natural Liberation of Habitual Tendencies 59
6. Natural Liberation of Negativity and Obscuration through [Enactment of] the Hundredfold Homage to the Sacred Enlightened Families 93
7. Natural Liberation through Acts of Confession 113
8. Natural Liberation through Recognition of the Visual Indications and Signs of Death 151
9. Natural Liberation of Fear through the Ritual Deception of Death 183
10. Consciousness Transference: Natural Liberation through Recollection 197
11. The Great Liberation by Hearing 217
12. Aspirational Prayers 305
13. A Masked Drama of Rebirth 317
14. Liberation by Wearing: Natural Liberation of the Psycho-physical Aggregates 343

1

Natural Liberation of the Nature of Mind: The Four-session Yoga of the Preliminary Practice

CONTEXT

In its original Tibetan this preliminary practice is beautifully written in verse. In the monasteries and lay households of the practitioners of this cycle of teachings, it is usually sung melodically in the early morning, before any other practice or activity is begun. Often the young monks sing the opening verses of this poem as they go about their morning duties.

When engaging in a preliminary retreat, it is recommended that this meditation is done every day in four sessions: early morning till dawn, after sunrise until just before noon, from afternoon until just before sunset, and from sunset until late evening.

The practice essentialises the 'four common or outer preliminaries' and the 'five uncommon or inner preliminaries', which are described in the glossary. It is recommended that the inner preliminary practices are repeated 100,000 times as a prerequisite to receiving instruction on the 'generation stage' practices of the Vehicle of Indestructible Reality (*Vajrayāna*).

Herein is contained the *Natural Liberation of the Nature of Mind: The Four-session Yoga which is a Spiritual Practice of the Vehicle of Indestructible Reality, the Way of Secret Mantras,*[1] an extract from the *Peaceful and Wrathful Deities: A Profound Sacred Teaching, [entitled] Natural Liberation through [Recognition of] Enlightened Intention.*[2]

It would be excellent if one were to train one's mental continuum according to the [following] preliminary practices which are based on the *Peaceful and Wrathful Deities: A Profound Sacred Teaching, [entitled] Natural Liberation through [Recognition of] Enlightened Intention.*

COMMON PRELIMINARY PRACTICE

O, Alas! Alas! Fortunate Child of Buddha Nature,
Do not be oppressed by the forces of ignorance and delusion!
But rise up now with resolve and courage!
Entranced by ignorance, from beginningless time until now,
You have had [more than] enough time to sleep.
So do not slumber any longer, but strive after virtue with body, speech and mind!

Are you oblivious to the sufferings of birth, old age, sickness and death?
There is no guarantee that you will survive, even past this very day!
The time has come [for you] to develop perseverance in [your] practice.

For, at this singular opportunity, you could attain the everlasting bliss [of nirvāṇa].
So now is [certainly] not the time to sit idly,
But, starting with [the reflection on] death, you should bring your practice to completion![3]

The moments of our life are not expendable,
And the [possible] circumstances of death are beyond imagination.
If you do not achieve an undaunted confident security now,
What point is there in your being alive, O living creature?

All phenomena are [ultimately] selfless, empty, and free from conceptual elaboration.
In their dynamic they resemble an illusion, mirage, dream, or reflected image,
A celestial city, an echo, a reflection of the moon in water, a bubble, an optical illusion, or an intangible emanation.
You should know that all things of cyclic existence and nirvāṇa
Accord [in nature] with these ten similes of illusory phenomena.

All phenomena are naturally uncreated.
They neither abide nor cease, neither come nor go.
They are without objective referent, signless, ineffable, and free from thought.[4]
The time has come for this truth to be realised!

Homage to the spiritual teachers!
Homage to the meditational deities!
Homage to the ḍākinīs!
O, Alas! Alas! How needing of compassion are those living beings, tortured by their past actions,
[Who are drowning] in this deep chasm, the engulfing ocean of their past actions!
Such is the nature of fluctuating cyclic existence!
Grant your blessing, so that this ocean of sufferings may run dry!

How needing of compassion are those who are skill-less,[5]
Those who are tortured by ignorance and past actions,
Those who indulge in actions conducive to suffering –
Even though they desire happiness!
Grant your blessing, so that the obscuration of dissonant mental states and past actions may be purified!

How needing of compassion are the ignorant and the deluded,
[Bound] in this confining dungeon of egotistical attachment and the subject–object dichotomy,
Who, like wild game, are trapped in this snare, time after time!
Grant your blessing, so that cyclic existence may be stirred to its depths!

How needing of compassion are those beings who endlessly revolve [in the cycle of existence],
As if [circling] perpetually [on] the rim of a water-wheel,
In this six-dimensional city of imprisoning past actions!
Grant your blessing, so that the womb entrances to the six classes of existence may be barred!

We who are fearless and hard-hearted, despite having seen so many sufferings of birth, old age, sickness and death,
Are wasting our human lives, endowed with freedom and opportunity,[6] on the paths of distraction.
Grant your blessing, so that we may [continuously] remember impermanence and death!

Since we do not recognise that impermanent [things] are unreliable,
Still, even now, we remain attached, clinging to this cycle of existence.
Wishing for happiness, we pass our human lives in suffering.
Grant your blessing, so that attachment to cyclic existence may be reversed!

Our impermanent environment will be destroyed by fire and water,[7]
The impermanent sentient beings within it will endure the severing of body and mind.

The seasons of the year: summer, winter, autumn and spring, themselves [exemplify] impermanence.
Grant your blessing, so that disillusionment [with conditioned existence] may arise from the depths [of our hearts]!

Last year, this year, the waxing and waning moons,
The days, nights, and indivisible time moments are all impermanent.
If we reflect carefully, we too are face to face with death.
Grant your blessing, so that we may become resolute in our practice!

Though this [body] endowed with freedom and opportunity is extremely hard to find,
When the Lord of Death[8] approaches in the semblance of disease,
How needing of compassion are those who, bereft of the [sacred] teachings,
Return empty-handed [from this life]!
Grant your blessing so that [a recognition of] urgency may grow in our minds!

Alas! Alas! O Precious Jewel, embodiment of compassion!
Since you, the Conqueror, are endowed with a loving heart,
Grant your blessing, so that we and the six classes of beings
May be liberated, right now, from the sufferings of cyclic existence!

UNCOMMON PRELIMINARY PRACTICE

Refuge

(Then, the outer, inner, and secret refuges should be adopted in the following way:)

Outer Refuge

I bow down to and take refuge in the spiritual teachers
Whose enlightened intention, throughout the past, present and future,

Is uninterruptedly directed towards living beings,
The infinite sentient beings of the three world systems and six classes.

I bow down to and take refuge in the [perfect] buddhas,
The Transcendent Ones Gone to Bliss of the ten directions and four times,
Foremost of humankind, adorned by the major and minor marks,
Whose enlightened activities are inexhaustible, and as vast as space.

I bow down to and take refuge in the sacred teachings,
Including the doctrines of the ultimate truth, quiescent and desireless,
The irreversible path[9] of the three vehicles,
And the transmissions, esoteric instructions, and treatises
Of the transmitted precepts and treasures.

I bow down to and take refuge in the communities [of monks and nuns],
Who abide on the unerring path, forming a field of all supreme merits,[10]
Together with the assembly of Sublime Ones, set apart from the stains of dissonant mental states,
And the supreme upholders of the Teaching: bodhisattvas, pious attendants, and hermit buddhas.

Inner Refuge

I bow down to and take refuge in the spiritual teachers,
[Embodying] the essential nature of the buddhas of the three times,
The masters of all the secret and unsurpassed maṇḍalas,
Who guide all living beings with their blessings and compassion.

I bow down to and take refuge in the meditational deities,
Who, even though [they remain unmoving as] the Buddha-body of Reality,
Uncreated and free from the limits of conceptual elaboration,

Emanate in peaceful and wrathful forms for the sake of living beings,
And confer the supreme and common accomplishments.

I bow down to and take refuge in the assembly of ḍākinīs,
Who, moving with the energy of compassion through the space of reality,
Grant supreme bliss [as they arise] from their pure abodes,
And bestow accomplishments upon those who keep their commitments.

Secret Refuge

From within a state free from grasping and beyond intellect,
I take refuge in the nature of the great expanse of sameness and perfection,[11]
Atemporal emptiness, free from conceptual elaboration,
Primordially pure in essence, natural expression and compassionate energy.

From within [a state which is] non-conceptual, naturally radiant and stark,
I take refuge in the primordial embodiment of the five buddha-bodies,
Spontaneously and naturally present,
[Abiding] in the maṇḍala of the [unique] seminal point,
Which is [the union of] expanse and awareness, and of radiance and emptiness,
The indestructible chain of inner radiance, that is intrinsic awareness.

Throughout the three times, beginningless and endless,
I take refuge in the Compassionate Ones,
Unimpeded, naturally expressive, and all-pervasive,
The unimpededly arising and subsiding rays of light,
Which emanate through the expressive power of awareness,
Dispelling, non-conceptually, the darkness in the minds of living beings.

The Generation of an Altruistic Intention

(Then, the altruistic intention of the Greater Vehicle should be generated in the following way:)

Even though all phenomena are empty and selfless,
Sentient beings fail to realise this. Alas! How needing of compassion are they!
So that all those who are the focus of our compassion may attain enlightenment,
I must rouse my body, speech and mind to [the practice of] virtue!

For the benefit of all sentient beings of the six classes,
From now until enlightenment is attained,
Not just for my own sake but for the benefit of all,
I must generate the mind [aspiring] to supreme enlightenment!

How needing of compassion are those bereft of the [sacred] teachings,
Who have ensnared themselves within the unfathomable ocean of suffering.
So that all those who are the focus of our compassion may be established in happiness,
I must generate the mind [aspiring] to supreme enlightenment!

I myself and all infinite sentient beings
Are primordially of the nature of buddhahood.
So that we may [all] become supreme embodiments, who know this to be so,
I must generate the mind [aspiring] to supreme enlightenment!

The ocean of mundane cyclic existence is like an illusion.
All compounded things lack permanence.
Their essence is empty and selfless,
But these naive beings [right here] who do not realise this to be so

Roam through cyclic existence, [driven on] by the twelve links of dependent origination.
So that all beings gripped in this quagmire of name and form may attain buddhahood,[12]
I must rouse my body, speech, and mind to [the practice of] virtue!

I take refuge [from now] until enlightenment,
In the Buddha, the [sacred] teachings and supreme assembly.
Through the merit of practising generosity and the other [perfections],
May I attain buddhahood for the sake of [all] living beings!
May I become a spiritual teacher, [able to] guide infinite sentient beings,
As many as there are, without exception!

(Then, one should meditate on the four immeasurable aspirations as follows:)

May all sentient beings be endowed with happiness!
May they all be separated from suffering and its causes!
May they be endowed with joy, free from suffering!
May they abide in equanimity, free from attachment or aversion!

Purification of Negativity and Obscuration through the Repeated Recitation of the Hundred-syllable Mantra [of Vajrasattva]

(This should be done in the context of the following visualisation:)

At the crown of my head, on a lotus moon cushion,
Is my spiritual teacher, [resplendent] in the form of Vajrasattva.
His body is translucent, like crystal, and at his heart,
[Resting] on a moon-disc, is a syllable HŪṂ, surrounded by the Hundred-syllable Mantra.[13]

A stream of nectar then descends through my crown fontanelle,[14]
Purifying my violations [of the commitments], my negativities and obscurations.

May Vajrasattva, glorious transcendent one,
Anoint me at this very moment
With the nectar stream of pristine cognition,
So that the negativities and obscurations
Of myself and all sentient beings, without exception, are purified.

OṂ VAJRASATTVA SAMAYAMANUPĀLAYA VAJRASATTVA TVENOPATIṢṬHA DṚḌHO ME BHAVA SUPOṢYO ME BHAVA SUTOṢYO ME BHAVA ANURAKTO ME BHAVA SARVASIDDHIṂ ME PRAYACCHA SARVAKARMASU CA ME CITTAṂ ŚREYAḤ KURU HŪṂ HAHAHAHA HO BHAGAVĀN SARVA TATHĀGATA VAJRA MĀ ME MUÑCA VAJRABHAVA MAHĀSAMAYASATTVA ĀḤ[15]

Owing to my ignorance, delusion, and confusion,
I have transgressed the boundaries of the commitments, which I should have guarded.
O my protector and spiritual teacher, be my refuge!

You who are the supreme and glorious Vajra-holder,[16]
Embodying great compassion and love,
O Foremost of beings, be our refuge.
Assist us to purify and cleanse, without exception, this mass of flaws –
Our negativities, obscurations, transgressions, and downfalls.

By this virtuous activity,
May I swiftly attain [the state of] Vajrasattva, now,
And may all sentient beings, without exception,
Be swiftly established in that same state!
May we become exactly like you, Vajrasattva,
Exactly resembling you in body, retinue, lifespan, fields,
And in your supreme and exquisite major marks.[17]

The Maṇḍala Offering

(Then present the maṇḍala of offerings in the following way:)

OṂ VAJRA BHŪMI ĀḤ HŪṂ[18]
The base transforms into a powerful ground of gold.[19]
OṂ VAJRA REKHE ĀḤ HŪṂ[20]
The outer periphery becomes a jewelled fence of iron mountains,
And at the centre is Mount Sumeru, king of mountains,
Majestic and formed from the five precious substances,
Exquisitely beautiful in shape, and delightful to behold,
Encircled by seven [concentric] golden mountain ranges,
And seven [intervening] emanational oceans.
To the east is the continent Viratdeha,
And to the south is Jambudvīpa,
The west is adorned by Aparagodanīya,
And to the north is Uttarakuru.
[To either side of these continents are] the eight subcontinents:
Deha and Videha [to the east],
Cāmara and Aparacāmara [to the south],
Śāṭhā and Uttaramantriṇa [to the west],
And Kurava and Kaurava [to the north].
I offer this [world-system], along with the sun, moon, Rahu, Ketu,[21]
And the luxuriant resources and riches of gods and humans,
To you, my precious spiritual teachers, and to your retinues.
Through your compassion, please accept them for the benefit of all beings!

OṂ ĀṂ HŪṂ[22]
To my precious spiritual teachers and the fields of the Buddha-body of Emanation,
I offer all the inestimable resources of gods and humans,
Within the immeasurable palace of the animate and inanimate trichiliocosm,
[In the form of] a dense cloud of offerings, as numerous as atomic particles,
Together with Mount Sumeru and its continents.

Please accept [these offerings], with compassion and love!
May all beings be born into the fields of the Buddha-body of Emanation!

OṂ ĀḤ HŪṂ
To my precious spiritual teachers and the fields of the Buddha-body of Perfect Resource,
I offer this perfect purity of the sensory spectra and sensory activity fields,
Adorned by the five sense-faculties, radiant and brilliant,
Within the immeasurable palace of the pure energy channels of my body.
Please accept [these offerings], with compassion and love!
May all beings be born into the fields of the Buddha-body of Perfect Resource!

OṂ ĀḤ HŪṂ
To my precious spiritual teachers and the field of the Buddha-body of Reality,
I offer this primordially pure and innate pristine cognition
That abides within the immeasurable palace of the pure Buddha-body of Reality, which is mind's actual nature,[23]
Free from an objective referent, empty, radiant, and free from subjective apprehension.
Please accept [these offerings], with compassion and love!
May all beings be born into the field of the Buddha-body of Reality!

OṂ ĀḤ HŪṂ
By offering this exquisite and pleasing maṇḍala,
May no obstacles arise on the path to enlightenment!
May the enlightened intention of Those Gone to Bliss, past, present and future, be realised,
May I neither be bewildered in migratory existence,
Nor lulled by the solitary quiescence [of nirvāṇa]!
But may I liberate beings throughout the expanse of space!

OṂ ĀḤ HŪṂ MAHĀ GURU DEVA ḌĀKINĪ RATNA MAṆḌALA PŪJĀ MEGHA Ā HŪṂ[24]

Prayer to the Lineage Teachers

(Then, in order to cultivate union with the spiritual teacher, the prayer to the lineage should be recited as follows:)

I pray to the [direct] intentional lineage of the conquerors:
To Samantabhadra, primordial lord, Buddha-body of Reality,
To the Conqueror Vajradhara, embodiment of the sixth [enlightened family],
And to Vajrasattva, foremost of guides, the supreme buddha-mind.

I pray to the [symbolic] lineage of the awareness holders:
To the awareness holder Prahevajra, supreme among emanations,
To the spiritual teacher Śrī Siṃha, supreme son of the conquerors,
To the undying Padmākara, established in the Buddha-body of Indestructible Reality,
And to the ḍākinī [Yeshe] Tshogyalma, worthy recipient of the secret mantras.

I pray to the aural lineage of [authoritative] personages:
To Karma Lingpa, master of the profound treasures,
To the one named [Nyinda] Choje, supreme son of his buddha-mind,
And to the one named Sūryacandra [Nyinda Ozer], lord of living beings during this degenerate age.

I pray to the assembled deities of the three roots:
To all the genuine spiritual teachers of the core lineage,
Who form the connecting links [of this transmission],[25]
To the Peaceful and Wrathful meditational deities, in whom appearance and emptiness are indivisible,
And to the oceanic assembly of ḍākinīs and oath-bound protectors of the [sacred] teachings!

O you spiritual teachers who uphold the lineage of the oral transmission,[26]
And train each according to his or her needs!

If your teaching were to enter into decline,
The yogins of this era would be [utterly] disheartened.
Please, therefore, continue to guide all beings from this swamp of cyclic existence!

As we call out to you with mournful and tormented cries,
Bring to mind, now, the strict vows which you made in the past![27]
Reveal your faces from the expanse of space, endowed with major and minor marks!
Please guide all beings from this swamp of cyclic existence!
Let your Brahmā voice reverberate like a thousand peals of thunder![28]
Open [wide] the portals to the treasury of your buddha-mind!
Pour out the light rays of your discriminative awareness and compassion!
Please guide all beings from this swamp of cyclic existence!
Liberate now, without exception, all beings of this final era![29]
Anoint [us] now with the river of the four pure empowerments!
Liberate now the four continua, bewildered by dissonant mental states!
Please guide all beings from this swamp of cyclic existence!
Grant now the fruitional attainment of the four buddha-bodies of Those Gone to Bliss!
May I become a spiritual teacher, [able] to guide all the infinite sentient beings,
Who have been my parents, throughout space, without exception!
Please guide all beings from this swamp of cyclic existence!

Receiving the Four Empowerments

(Then the meditation to be adopted while receiving the four empowerments should be as follows:[30])

From the crown of the spiritual teacher in union with consort,
A white syllable OṂ, [radiating] rays of light,
Descends into the mid-point between my eyebrows,

The vase empowerment is thus received and the obscurations of the body are purified.
Please confer [upon me] the accomplishments of buddha-body!

From the throat of the spiritual teacher in union with consort,
A red syllable ĀḤ, [radiating] rays of light,
Descends into the sense faculty of my tongue,
The secret empowerment is thus received and the obscurations of speech are purified.
Please confer [upon me] the accomplishments of buddha-speech!

From the heart of the spiritual teacher in union with consort,
A blue syllable HŪṂ, [radiating] rays of light,
Descends into the centre of my heart,
The empowerment of pristine cognition is thus received, and the obscurations of mind are purified.
Please confer [upon me] the accomplishments of buddha-mind!

From the navel of the spiritual teacher in union with consort,
A red syllable HRĪḤ, [radiating] rays of light,
Descends into the centre of my navel,
The obscurations which [mundanely] differentiate between body, speech and mind are purified,
And the fourth empowerment of indivisible coemergence is received.

O glorious and precious root spiritual teacher!
Be indivisibly present, [seated] on the pistil of a lotus within my heart for ever!
Through your great kindness, favour me with your acceptance,
And please confer [upon me] the accomplishments of buddha-body, speech and mind!

May we become exactly like you, glorious spiritual teacher!
Exactly resembling you in body, retinue, lifespan, fields,
And in your supreme and excellent major marks.

These verses forming the preliminary practice of the *Peaceful and Wrathful Deities: A Profound Sacred Teaching, [entitled] Natural*

Liberation through [Recognition of] Enlightened Intention may be applied as a supplementary method in the context of mental purification.

This spiritual practice of the unsurpassed Greater Vehicle (Mahāyāna) is an oral teaching of [Nyinda] Choje Lingpa, the eldest son of the treasure-finder Karma Lingpa; and it was committed to writing by Guru Sūryacandraraśmi [i.e. Nyinda Ozer].

2

A Prayer for Union with the Spiritual Teacher, [entitled] Natural Liberation, without Renunciation of the Three Poisons

CONTEXT

This prayer to the spiritual teacher is generally recited immediately after the *Preliminary Practice*. It is also recommended that it be recited at the beginning of any ritual, or when thinking of the spiritual teacher or whenever the practitioner is about to enter into periods of meditation.

A correct perception of the spiritual teacher is considered vital for all practitioners of the Vehicle of Indestructible Reality (*Vajrayāna*). Further, it is considered essential that a practitioner receive spiritual inspiration, as transmitted through an unbroken lineage of masters, from a living teacher. First, however, before accepting anyone as a spiritual teacher, it is also regarded as essential that the practitioner examine and scrutinise the prospective teacher over a long period of time and accept him or her as a qualified teacher only when it is certain that the person meets the requirements of a spiritual teacher as set out in the authoritative sacred texts. Then, if they are sure that their own motivation is sincere, students should follow the advice of their chosen spiritual teacher with incontrovertible devotion.

Ultimately, the inspiration that is requested from the spiritual teacher is coming from the purity of the practitioner's own perception, altruistic intention and confidence.

Herein is contained *A Prayer for Union with the Spiritual Teacher, [Embodiment of] the Three Buddha-bodies, [entitled] Natural Liberation, without Renunciation of the Three Poisons,*[1] [which is an extract] from the *Peaceful and Wrathful Deities: A Profound Sacred Teaching, [entitled] Natural Liberation through [Recognition of] Enlightened Intention.*[2]

In the palace of reality's expanse, pure and pervasive,
Is my spiritual teacher, the Buddha-body of Reality –
Uncreated and free from conceptual elaboration.
To you, I pray with fervent devotion.
I request the primordially pure self-empowerment,
The blessings of the Buddha-body of Reality,[3]
So that naturally arising pristine cognition
Is uncontrived and spontaneously present,
Through natural liberation,
Without renunciation of ignorance and delusion.

In the palace of great bliss, which is pristine cognition, radiant and pure,
Is my spiritual teacher, the Buddha-body of Perfect Resource –
Unimpeded and supremely blissful.
To you, I pray with fervent devotion.
I request the spontaneously present self-empowerment,
The blessings of the Buddha-body of Perfect Resource,[4]
So that intrinsic awareness, which is pristine cognition,
Is naturally liberated in supreme bliss,[5]
Through natural liberation,
Without renunciation of desire and clinging.

In the palace of the lotus, untainted and pure,
Is my spiritual teacher, the Buddha-body of Emanation –
Naturally arising in unlimited forms, beyond determination.
To you, I pray with fervent devotion.
I request the naturally liberating self-empowerment,
The blessings of the Buddha-body of Emanation,
So that intrinsic awareness, which is naturally manifesting
Pristine cognition, naturally radiates,[6]
Through natural liberation,
Without renunciation of discordant views and aversion.

In the palace of intrinsic awareness, the genuine inner radiance,
Is my spiritual teacher, [the unity of] the three buddha-bodies –
Beyond spatial delineation, and supremely blissful.
To you, I pray with fervent devotion.
I request the supremely blissful self-empowerment,
The blessings of the Three Buddha-bodies,
So that naturally arising pristine cognition
Is spontaneously present as the three buddha-bodies,[7]
Through natural liberation,
Without renunciation of the subject–object dichotomy.

How needing of compassion are suffering sentient beings, right here,
Who are driven on through cyclic existence by delusion and confusion –
Because they do not understand that their own mind
Is the Buddha-body of Reality, free from extremes!
May they all actualise the Buddha-body of Reality!

How needing of compassion are mistakenly prejudiced sentient beings, right here,
Who are driven on through cyclic existence by attachment and craving –
Because they do not understand that their own awareness
Is the Buddha-body of Perfect Resource, imbued with supreme bliss!
May they all actualise the Buddha-body of Perfect Resource!

How needing of compassion are sentient beings with discordant views, right here,
Who are driven on through cyclic existence by aversion and dualistic perception –
Because they do not understand that their own mind
Is the Buddha-body of Emanation, arising and subsiding [naturally]!
May they all actualise the Buddha-body of Emanation!

How needing of compassion are all unenlightened living beings, right here,
Who, as a result of grasping, are obscured by dissonant mental states and [subtle obstructions to] knowledge –
Because they do not understand [that their own mind]
Is indivisible from the three buddha-bodies!
May they all actualise the three buddha-bodies!

These verses forming *A Prayer for Union with the Spiritual Teacher, [Embodiment of] the Three Buddha-bodies, [entitled] Natural Liberation, without Renunciation of the Three Poisons*, which are an extract from the *Peaceful and Wrathful Deities: A Profound Sacred Teaching, [entitled] Natural Liberation through [Recognition of] Enlightened Intention*, were composed by Padmākara, the preceptor from Oḍḍiyāna.

May [the influence of] this sacred teaching not be extinguished until cyclic existence has been emptied![8]

This prayer was brought forth from Mount Gampodar, which resembles a dancing god, by the accomplished master Karma Lingpa.

3

Root Verses of the Six Intermediate States

CONTEXT

According to this cycle of teachings, the circle of birth and death can be seen as being composed of six intermediate states. These six modalities of existence: our waking living state, dreaming, meditation, the time of death, and the two successive phases of the after-death state are defined in the glossary.

This poem emphasises the centrally important perspective that relates to each of these states. It is recommended that practitioners should memorise these verses and recite them repeatedly, while reflecting on their meaning, throughout their lives.

Herein is contained the *Root Verses of the Six Intermediate States*.[1]

I bow down to the Conquerors, the Peaceful and Wrathful Deities.

The root verses concerning the six intermediate states are as follows:

Alas, now as the intermediate state of living[2] arises before me,
Renouncing laziness, for which there is no time in this life,
I must enter the undistracted path of study, reflection and meditation.
Taking perceptual experience and [the nature of] mind as the path,
I must cultivate actualisation of the three buddha-bodies.
Now, having obtained a precious human body, this one time,
I do not have the luxury of remaining on a distracted path.

Alas, now as the intermediate state of dreams arises before me,
Renouncing the corpse-like, insensitive sleep of delusion,
I must enter, free from distracting memories, the state of the abiding nature of reality.
Cultivating [the experience of] inner radiance,
Through the recognition, emanation, and transformation of dreams,
I must not sleep like a beast,
But cherish the experiential cultivation which mingles sleep with actual [realisation].

Alas, now as the intermediate state of meditative concentration arises before me,
Renouncing the mass of distractions and confusions,
I must undistractedly enter a state,
Which is devoid of subjective apprehension, and free from the [two] extremes,
And attain stability in the stages of generation and perfection.
At this moment, having renounced activity,
And having attained a singular [concentration],
I must not fall under the sway of bewildering mental afflictions!

Alas, now as the intermediate state of the time of death[3] arises before me,
Renouncing [all] attachment, yearning and subjective apprehension in every respect,
I must undistractedly enter the path, on which the oral teachings are clearly understood,
And eject my own awareness into the uncreated expanse of space.
Immediately upon separation from this compounded body of flesh and blood,
I must know [this body] to be like a transient illusion.

Alas, now as the intermediate state of reality[4] arises before me,
Renouncing the merest sense of awe, terror or fear,
I must recognise all that arises to be awareness, manifesting naturally of itself.
Knowing [such sounds, lights and rays] to be visionary phenomena of the intermediate state,
At this moment, having reached this critical point,
I must not fear the assembly of Peaceful and Wrathful Deities, which manifest naturally!

Alas, now as the intermediate state of rebirth[5] arises before me,
I must with one-pointed intention concentrate my mind,
And resolutely connect with the residual potency of my virtuous past actions.

I must obstruct the womb entrance and call to mind the methods of reversal.
This is the time when perseverance and purity of perception are imperative.
I must give up all jealousy and meditate on my spiritual teacher with consort.

From the mouth of the accomplished masters come these words:
'O, [you], with your mind far away, thinking that death will not come,
Entranced by the pointless activities of this life,
If you were to return empty-handed now, would not your [life's] purpose have been [utterly] confused?
Recognise what it is that you truly need! It is a sacred teaching [for liberation]!
So, should you not practise this divine [sacred] teaching, beginning from this very moment?'

And it is also said,
'If I choose not to take the oral teachings of the spiritual teacher to heart,
Am I not the deceiver of myself?'

This completes the *Root Verses of the Six Intermediate States*.

4

The Introduction to Awareness: Natural Liberation through Naked Perception

CONTEXT

This chapter is the essence of the esoteric instruction by which the student is introduced to the ultimate nature of mind. Prior to entering into this practice, which focuses directly on the nature of mind itself, this introduction should be received from an accomplished lineage holder. Then, whilst in solitary retreat, it is recommended that this text be read repeatedly as a guide between meditation sessions.

Herein is contained *The Introduction to Awareness: Natural Liberation through Naked Perception*,[1] [which is an extract] from the *Peaceful and Wrathful Deities: A Profound Sacred Teaching, [entitled] Natural Liberation through [Recognition of] Enlightened Intention*.[2]

Homage to the deities [embodying] the three buddha-bodies, who are the natural radiance of awareness.

[Here], I shall present the teaching [known as] *The Introduction to Awareness: Natural Liberation through Naked Perception*, [which is an extract] from the *Peaceful and Wrathful Deities: A Profound Sacred Teaching, [entitled] Natural Liberation through [Recognition of] Enlightened Intention*. Thus, shall I introduce [to you the nature of] intrinsic awareness. So contemplate it well, O Fortunate Child of Buddha nature.

SAMAYA *rgya rgya rgya*

[THE IMPORTANCE OF THE INTRODUCTION TO AWARENESS]

EMAHO!

Though the single [nature of] mind, which completely pervades both cyclic existence and nirvāṇa,

Has been naturally present from the beginning, you have not recognised it.

Even though its radiance and awareness have never been interrupted,

You have not yet encountered its true face.
Even though it arises unimpededly in every facet [of existence],
You have not as yet recognised [this single nature of mind].
In order that this [single] nature might be recognised by you,
The Conquerors of the three times have taught an inconceivably [vast number of practices],
Including the eighty-four thousand aspects of the [sacred] teachings.
Yet, [despite this diversity], not even one of these [teachings] has been given by the Conquerors,
Outside the context of an understanding of this nature![3]
[And even] though there are inestimable volumes of sacred writings, equally vast as the limits of space,
Actually, [these teachings can be succinctly expressed in] a few words,[4] which are the introduction to awareness.

Here [is] the direct [face to face] introduction
To the enlightened intention of the Conquerors.
Here is the method for entering [into actual reality],
[In this very moment], without reference to past or future [events].

[THE ACTUAL INTRODUCTION TO AWARENESS]

KYE HO!
O fortunate children, listen to these words!
The term 'mind' is commonplace and widely used,
Yet there are those who do not understand [its meaning],
Those who falsely understand it, those who partially understand it,
And those who have not quite understood its genuine reality.
Thus there has arisen an inconceivably vast number of assertions [as to the nature of mind],
Posited by [the various] philosophical systems.[5]

Further, since ordinary persons do not understand [the meaning of the term 'mind'],

And do not intuitively recognise its nature,
They continue to roam through the six classes of sentient [rebirth] within the three world-systems,
And consequently experience suffering.[6]
This is the fault of not understanding this intrinsic nature of mind.

Even though pious attendants and hermit buddhas claim that they understand [this single nature of mind] as the partial absence of self,[7]
They do not understand it exactly as it is.
Furthermore, being fettered by opinions held in accordance with their respective literatures and philosophical systems,[8]
There are those who do not perceive the inner radiance [directly]:
The pious attendants and hermit buddhas are obscured [in this respect] by their attachment to the subject–object dichotomy.
The adherents of Madhyamaka are obscured by their attachment to the extremes of the two truths.
The practitioners of Kriyātantra and Yogatantra are obscured by their attachment to the extremes of ritual service and attainment.[9]
The practitioners of Mahāyoga and Anuyoga are obscured by their attachment to [the extremes of] space and awareness.[10]
All these [practitioners] stray from the point because they polarise the non-dual reality,
And since they fail to unify [these extremes] in non-duality, they do not attain buddhahood.
Thus, all of those beings continue to roam in cyclic existence,
Because they persistently engage in [forms of] renunciation,
And in acts of rejection and acceptance with regard to their own minds,
Where [in reality] cyclic existence and nirvāṇa are inseparable.

Therefore, one should abandon all constructed teachings,
And all [unnatural] states free from activity,
And, by virtue of this *[Introduction to] Awareness: Natural Liberation through Naked Perception*, which is presented here,
One should realise all things in the context of this great natural liberation.

So it is that all [enlightened attributes] are brought to completion within the Great Perfection.
SAMAYA *rgya rgya rgya*

[SYNONYMS FOR MIND]

As for this apparent and distinct [phenomenon] which is called 'mind':
In terms of existence, it has no [inherent] existence whatsoever.
In terms of origination, it is the source of the diverse joys and sorrows of cyclic existence and nirvāṇa,
In terms of [philosophical] opinion, it is subject to opinions in accordance with the eleven vehicles.
In terms of designation, it has an inconceivable number of distinct names:
Some call it 'the nature of mind', the 'nature of mind itself',
Some eternalists give it the name 'self',
Pious attendants call it 'selflessness of the individual',[11]
Cittamātrins call it 'mind',
Some call it the 'Perfection of Discriminative Awareness',
Some call it the 'Nucleus of the Sugata',
Some call it the 'Great Seal',
Some call it the 'Unique Seminal Point',
Some call it the 'Expanse of Reality',
Some call it the 'Ground-of-all',
And some call it 'ordinary [unfabricated consciousness]'.

[THE THREE CONSIDERATIONS]

The following is the introduction [to the means of experiencing] this [single] nature [of mind]
Through the application of three considerations:
[First, recognise that] past thoughts are traceless, clear, and empty,
[Second, recognise that] future thoughts are unproduced and fresh,

And [third, recognise that] the present moment abides naturally and unconstructed.

When this ordinary, momentary consciousness is examined nakedly [and directly] by oneself,

Upon examination, it is a radiant awareness,

Which is free from the presence of an observer,

Manifestly stark and clear,

Completely empty and uncreated in all respects,

Lucid, without duality of radiance and emptiness,

Not permanent, for it is lacking inherent existence in all respects,

Not a mere nothingness, for it is radiant and clear,

Not a single entity, for it is clearly perceptible as a multiplicity,

Yet not existing inherently as a multiplicity, for it is indivisible and of a single savour.[12]

This intrinsic awareness, which is not extraneously derived,

Is itself the genuine introduction to the abiding nature of [all] things.

For in this [intrinsic awareness], the three buddha-bodies are inseparable, and fully present as one:

Its emptiness and utter lack of inherent existence is the Buddha-body of Reality;

The natural resonance and radiance of this emptiness is the Buddha-body of Perfect Resource;

And its unimpeded arising in any form whatsoever is the Buddha-body of Emanation.

These three, fully present as one, are the very essence [of awareness] itself.

[CONSEQUENCES OF THE INTRODUCTION TO AWARENESS]

When the introduction is powerfully applied in accordance with the [above] method for entering into this [reality]:

One's own immediate consciousness is this very [reality]!

[Abiding] in this [reality], which is uncontrived and naturally radiant,

How can one say that one does not understand the nature of mind?
[Abiding] in this [reality], wherein there is nothing on which to meditate,
How can one say that, by having entered into meditation, one was not successful?
[Abiding] in this [reality], which is one's actual awareness itself,
How can one say that one could not find one's own mind?
[Abiding] in this [reality], the uninterrupted [union] of radiance and awareness,
How can one say that the [true] face of mind has not been seen?
[Abiding] in this [reality], which is itself the cogniser,
How can one say that, though sought, this [cogniser] could not be found?
[Abiding] in this [reality], where there is nothing at all to be done,
How can one say that, whatever one did, one did not succeed?
Given that it is sufficient to leave [this awareness] as it is, uncontrived,
How can one say that one could not continue to abide [in that state]?
Given that it is sufficient to leave it as it is, without doing anything whatsoever,
How can one say that one could not do just that?
Given that, [within this reality], radiance, awareness, and emptiness are inseparable and spontaneously present,
How can one say that, by having practised, one attained nothing?
Given that [this reality] is naturally originating and spontaneously present, without causes or conditions,
How can one say that, by having made the effort [to find it], one was incapable [of success]?
Given that the arising and liberation of conceptual thoughts occur simultaneously,
How can one say that, by having applied this antidote [to conceptual thoughts], one was not effective?

[Abiding] in this immediate consciousness itself,
How can one say that one does not know this [reality]?[13]

[OBSERVATIONS RELATED TO EXAMINING THE NATURE OF MIND]

Be certain that the nature of mind is empty and without foundation.
One's own mind is insubstantial, like an empty sky.
Look at your own mind to see whether it is like that or not.
Divorced from views which constructedly determine [the nature of] emptiness,
Be certain that pristine cognition, naturally originating, is primordially radiant –
Just like the nucleus of the sun, which is itself naturally originating.
Look at your own mind to see whether it is like that or not!

Be certain that this awareness, which is pristine cognition, is uninterrupted,
Like the coursing central torrent of a river which flows unceasingly.
Look at your own mind to see whether it is like that or not!

Be certain that conceptual thoughts and fleeting memories are not strictly identifiable,
But insubstantial in their motion, like the breezes of the atmosphere.
Look at your own mind to see whether it is like that or not!

Be certain that all that appears is naturally manifest [in the mind],
Like the images in a mirror which [also] appear naturally.
Look at your own mind to see whether it is like that or not!

Be certain that all characteristics are liberated right where they are,
Like the clouds of the atmosphere, naturally originating and naturally dissolving.
Look at your own mind to see whether it is like that or not!

There are no phenomena extraneous to those that originate from the mind.
[So], how could there be anything on which to meditate apart from the mind?
There are no phenomena extraneous to those that originate from the mind.
[So], there are no modes of conduct to be undertaken extraneous [to those that originate from the mind].
There are no phenomena extraneous to those that originate from the mind.
[So], there are no commitments to be kept extraneous [to those that originate from the mind].
There are no phenomena extraneous to those that originate from the mind.
[So], there are no results to be attained extraneous [to those that originate from the mind].
There are no phenomena extraneous to those that originate from the mind.
[So], one should observe one's own mind, looking into its nature again and again.

If, upon looking outwards towards the external expanse of the sky,
There are no projections emanated by the mind,
And if, on looking inwards at one's own mind,
There is no projectionist who projects [thoughts] by thinking them,
Then, one's own mind, completely free from conceptual projections, will become luminously clear.
[This] intrinsic awareness, [union of] inner radiance and emptiness, is the Buddha-body of Reality,
[Appearing] like [the illumining effect of] a sunrise on a clear and cloudless sky,

It is clearly knowable, despite its lack of specific shape or form.
There is a great distinction between those who understand and those who misunderstand this point.

This naturally originating inner radiance, uncreated from the very beginning,
Is the parentless child of awareness – how amazing!
It is the naturally originating pristine cognition, uncreated by anyone – how amazing!
[This radiant awareness] has never been born and will never die – how amazing!
Though manifestly radiant, it lacks an [extraneous] perceiver – how amazing!
Though it has roamed throughout cyclic existence, it does not degenerate – how amazing!
Though it has seen buddhahood itself, it does not improve – how amazing!
Though it is present in everyone, it remains unrecognised – how amazing!
Still, one hopes for some attainment other than this – how amazing!
Though it is present within oneself, one continues to seek it elsewhere – how amazing!

[INTRINSIC AWARENESS AS VIEW, MEDITATION, CONDUCT, AND RESULT]

EMA! This immediate awareness, insubstantial and radiant,
Is itself the highest of all views.
This non-referential, all-encompassing [awareness] which is free in every respect
Is itself the highest of all meditations.
This uncontrived [activity based on awareness], simply expressed in worldly terms,
Is itself the highest of all types of conduct.
This unsought [attainment of awareness], spontaneously present from the beginning,
Is itself the highest of all results.

[Now], the four great media, which are errorless, are presented:[14]

[First], the great medium of errorless view
Is this radiant immediate awareness –
Since it is radiant and without error, it is called a 'medium'.
[Second], the great medium of errorless meditation
Is this radiant immediate awareness –
Since it is radiant and without error, it is called a 'medium'.
[Third], the great medium of errorless conduct
Is this radiant immediate awareness –
Since it is radiant and without error, it is called a 'medium'.
[Fourth], the great medium of errorless result
Is this radiant immediate awareness –
Since it is radiant and without error, it is called a 'medium'.

[Now] the four great nails, which are unchanging, are presented:[15]

[First], the great nail of the unchanging view
Is this radiant immediate awareness –
Since it is firm throughout the three times, it is called a 'nail'.
[Second], the great nail of unchanging meditation
Is this radiant immediate awareness –
Since it is firm throughout the three times, it is called a 'nail'.
[Third], the great nail of unchanging conduct
Is this radiant immediate awareness –
Since it is firm throughout the three times, it is called a 'nail'.
[Fourth], the great nail of the unchanging result
Is this radiant immediate awareness –
Since it is firm throughout the three times, it is called a 'nail'.

Now follows the esoteric instruction which reveals the three times to be one:

Abandon your notions of the past, without attributing a temporal sequence!

Cut off your mental associations regarding the future, without anticipation!

Rest in a spacious modality, without clinging to [the thoughts of] the present.

Do not meditate at all, since there is nothing upon which to meditate.

Instead, revelation will come through undistracted mindfulness –
Since there is nothing by which you can be distracted.
Nakedly observe [all that arises] in this modality, which is without meditation and without distraction!
When this [experience] arises,
Intrinsically aware, naturally cognisant, naturally radiant and clear,
It is called 'the mind of enlightenment'.
Since [within this mind of enlightenment] there is nothing upon which to meditate,
This [modality] transcends all objects of knowledge.
Since [within this mind of enlightenment] there are no distractions,
It is the radiance of the essence itself.
This Buddha-body of Reality, [union of] radiance and emptiness,
In which [the duality of] appearance and emptiness is naturally liberated,
Becomes manifest [in this way], unattained by the [structured] path to buddhahood,
And thus Vajrasattva is [actually] perceived at this moment.

Now follows the instruction which brings one to the point where the six extreme [perspectives] are exhausted:[16]
Though there is a vast plethora of discordant views,
Within this intrinsic awareness or [single nature of] mind,
Which is the naturally originating pristine cognition,
There is no duality between the object viewed and the observer.
Without focusing on the view, search for the observer!
Though one searches for this observer, none will be found.
So, at that instant, one will be brought to the exhaustion point of the view.
At that very moment, one will encounter the innermost boundary of the view.
Since there is no object at all to be observed,
And since one has not fallen into a primordial vacuous emptiness,[17]
The lucid awareness, which is now present,
Is itself the view of the Great Perfection.
[Here], there is no duality between realisation and lack of realisation.

Though there is a vast plethora of discordant meditations,
Within this intrinsic awareness,
Which penetrates ordinary consciousness to the core,
There is no duality between the object of meditation and the meditator.
Without meditating on the object of meditation, search for the meditator!
Though one searches for this meditator, none will be found.
So, at that instant, one will be brought to the exhaustion point of meditation.
At that very moment, one will encounter the innermost boundary of meditation.
Since there is no object at all on which to meditate,
And since one has not fallen under the sway of delusion, drowsiness, or agitation,[18]
The lucid uncontrived awareness, which is now present,
Is itself the uncontrived meditative equipoise or concentration.
[Here], there is no duality between abiding and non-abiding.

Though there is a vast plethora of discordant modes of conduct,
Within this intrinsic awareness,
Which is the unique seminal point of pristine cognition,
There is no duality between the action and the actor.
Without focusing on the action, search for the actor!
Though one searches for this actor, none will be found.
So, at that instant, one will be brought to the exhaustion point of conduct.
At that very moment, one will encounter the innermost boundary of conduct.
Since, from the beginning, there has been no conduct to undertake,
And since one has not fallen under the sway of bewildering propensities,
The lucid uncontrived awareness, which is now present,
Is itself pure conduct, without having to be contrived, modified, accepted or rejected.
[Here], there is no duality between purity and impurity.

Though there is a vast plethora of discordant results,
Within this intrinsic awareness,
Which is the true nature of mind, the spontaneous presence of the three buddha-bodies,
There is no duality between the object of attainment and the attainer.
Without focusing on the attainment of the result, search for the attainer!
Though one searches for this attainer, none will be found.
So, at that instant, one will be brought to the exhaustion point of the result.
At that very moment, one will encounter the innermost boundary of the result.
Since, whatever the [projected] result, there is nothing to be attained,
And since one has not fallen under the sway of rejection and acceptance, or hope and doubt,
The naturally radiant awareness, which is now spontaneously present,
Is the fully manifest realisation of the three buddha-bodies, within oneself.
[Here], there is the result, atemporal buddhahood itself.

[SYNONYMS FOR AWARENESS]

This awareness, free from the eight extremes, such as eternalism and nihilism [and so forth],
Is called the 'Middle Way', which does not fall into any extremes.
It is called 'awareness' because mindfulness is uninterrupted.
It is given the name 'Nucleus of the Tathāgata'
Because emptiness is [naturally] endowed with this nucleus of awareness.
If one understands this truth, one reaches perfection in all respects,
For which reason, this [awareness] is also called the 'Perfection of Discriminative Awareness'.
Furthermore, it is called the 'Great Seal' because it transcends the intellect and is atemporally free from extremes,

And, further, it is called the 'Ground-of-all',
Because [this awareness] is the ground of all joys and sorrows associated with cyclic existence and nirvāṇa –
The distinction between these being contingent on whether or not this [awareness] is realised.
[Further], this radiant and lucid awareness is itself referred to as 'ordinary consciousness',
On account of those periods when it abides in its natural state in an ordinary non-exceptional way.
Thus, however many well-conceived and pleasant-sounding names are applied to this [awareness],
In reality, those who maintain that these names do not refer to this present conscious awareness,
But to something else, above and beyond it,
Resemble someone who has already found an elephant, but is out looking for its tracks [elsewhere].

Though one were to scan the [entire] external universe,
[Searching for the nature of mind], one would not find it.
Buddhahood cannot be attained other than through the mind.
Not recognising this, one does indeed search for the mind externally,
Yet, how can one find [one's own mind] when one looks for it elsewhere?
This is like a fool, for example, who, when finding himself amidst a crowd of people,
Becomes mesmerised by the spectacle [of the crowd] and forgets himself,
Then, no longer recognising who he is, starts searching elsewhere for himself,
Continuously mistaking others for himself.

[Similarly], since one does not discern the abiding nature,
Which is the fundamental reality of [all] things,
One is cast into cyclic existence, not knowing that appearances are to be identified with the mind,
And, not discerning one's own mind to be buddha, nirvāṇa becomes obscured.
The [apparent] dichotomy between cyclic existence and

nirvāṇa is due to [the dichotomy between] ignorance and awareness,
But there is [in reality] no temporal divide between these two, [even] by a single moment.

Seeing the mind as extraneous to oneself is indeed bewildering,
Yet bewilderment and non-bewilderment are of a single essence.
Since there exists no [intrinsic] dichotomy in the mental continuum of sentient beings,
The uncontrived nature of mind is liberated just by being left in its natural state.
Yet if you remain unaware that bewilderment [originates] in the mind,
You will never understand the meaning of actual reality.
So you should observe that which naturally arises and naturally originates within your own [mind].
[First], observe [the source] from which these appearances initially originated,
[Second, observe the place] in which they abide in the interim,
And [third, observe the place] to which they will finally go.
Then, one will find that, just as, for example, a pond-dwelling crow does not stray from its pond,
Even though it flies away from the pond,
Similarly, although appearances arise from the mind,
They arise from the mind and subside into the mind of their own accord.

This nature of mind, which is all-knowing, aware of everything, empty and radiant,
Is established to be the manifestly radiant and self-originating pristine cognition,
[Present] from the beginning, just like the sky,
As an indivisible [union] of emptiness and radiance.
This itself is actual reality.
The indication that this is [the actual reality] is that all phenomenal existence is perceived in [the single nature of] one's own mind;
And this nature of mind is aware and radiant.
Therefore, recognise [this nature] to be like the sky!

However, this example of the sky, though used to illustrate actual reality,
Is merely a symbol, a partial and provisional illustration.
For the nature of mind is aware, empty and radiant in all respects,
While the sky is without awareness, empty, inanimate and void.
Therefore, the true understanding of the nature of mind is not illustrated by [the metaphor of] the sky.
[To achieve this understanding], let the mind remain in its own state, without distraction!

[THE NATURE OF APPEARANCES]

Now, with regard to the diversity of relative appearances:
They are all perishable; not one of them is genuinely existent.
All phenomenal existence, all the things of cyclic existence and nirvāṇa,
Are the discernible manifestations of the unique essential nature of one's own mind.
[This is known because] whenever one's own mental continuum undergoes change,
There will arise the discernible manifestation of an external change.
Therefore, all things are the discernible manifestations of mind.
For example, the six classes of living beings discern phenomenal appearances in their differing ways:
Eternalistic extremists [and others] who are remote from [the Buddhist perspective],
Perceive [appearances] in terms of a dichotomy of eternalism and nihilism;
And [followers of] the nine sequences of the vehicle perceive [appearances] in terms of their respective views, [and so forth].
For as long as this diversity [of appearances] is being perceived and diversely elucidated,
Differences [as to the nature of appearances] are apprehended,
And consequently, bewilderment comes about through attachment to those respective [views].

Yet, even though all those appearances, of which one is aware in one's own mind,
Do arise as discernible manifestations,
Buddhahood is present [simply] when they are not subjectively apprehended or grasped.
Bewilderment does not come about on account of these appearances –
But it does come about through their subjective apprehension.
[Thus], if the subjectively apprehending thoughts are known to be [of the single nature of] mind, they will be liberated of their own accord.

All things that appear are manifestations of mind.
The surrounding environment which appears to be inanimate, that too is mind.
The sentient life-forms which appear as the six classes of living beings, they too are mind.
The joys of both the gods and humans of the higher existences which appear, they too are mind.
The sorrows of the three lower existences which appear, they too are mind.
The five poisons, representing the dissonant mental states of ignorance, which appear, they too are mind.
The awareness, that is self-originating pristine cognition which appears, it too is mind.
The beneficial thoughts conducive to attainment of nirvāṇa which appear, they too are mind.
The obstacles of malevolent forces and spirits which appear, they too are mind.
The deities and [spiritual] accomplishments which manifest exquisitely, they too are mind.
The diverse kinds of pure [vision] which appear, they too are mind.
The non-conceptual one-pointed abiding [in meditation] which appears, it too is mind.
The colours characteristic of objects which appear, they too are mind.
The state without characteristics and without conceptual elaboration which appears, it too is mind.

The non-duality of the single and the multiple which appears, it too is mind.
The unproveability of existence and non-existence which appears, it too is mind.[19]

There are no appearances at all apart from [those that originate in] the mind.
The unimpeded nature of mind assumes all manner of appearances.
Yet, though these [appearances] arise, they are without duality,
And they [naturally] subside into the modality of mind,
Like waves in the waters of an ocean.
Whatever names are given to these unceasingly [arising] objects of designation,
In actuality, there is but one [single nature of] mind,
And that single [nature of mind] is without foundation and without root.
[Therefore], it is not perceptible at all, in any direction whatsoever.
It is not perceptible as substance, for it lacks inherent existence in all respects.
It is not perceptible as emptiness, for it is the resonance of awareness and radiance.
It is not perceptible as diversity, for it is the indivisibility of radiance and emptiness.
This present intrinsic awareness is manifestly radiant and clear,
And even though there exists no known means by which it can be fabricated,
And even though [this awareness] is without inherent existence,
It can be directly experienced.
[Thus], if it is experientially cultivated, all [beings] will be liberated.

[CONCLUSION]

All those of all [differing] potential, regardless of their acumen or dullness,
May realise [this intrinsic awareness].
However, for example, even though sesame is the source of oil, and milk of butter,
But there will be no extract if these are unpressed or unchurned,
Similarly, even though all beings actually possess the seed of buddhahood,
Sentient beings will not attain buddhahood without experiential cultivation.
Nonetheless, even a cowherd will attain liberation if he or she engages in experiential cultivation.
For, even though one may not know how to elucidate [this state] intellectually,
One will [through experiential cultivation] become manifestly established in it.
One whose mouth has actually tasted molasses,
Does not need others to explain its taste.
But, even learned scholars who have not realised [this single nature of mind] will remain the victims of bewilderment.
For, however learned and knowledgeable in explaining the nine vehicles they may be,
They will be like those who spread fabulous tales of remote [places] they have never seen,
And as far as the attainment of buddhahood is concerned,
They will not approach it, even for an instant.

If this nature [of intrinsic awareness] is understood,
Virtuous and negative acts will be liberated, right where they are.
But if this [single nature] is not understood,
One will amass nothing but [future lives within] cyclic existence, with its higher and lower realms,
Regardless of whether one has engaged in virtuous or non-virtuous actions.

Yet, if one's own mind is simply understood to be pristine cognition, [utterly] empty [of inherent existence],
The consequences of virtuous and negative actions will never come to fruition –
For just as a spring cannot materialise in empty space,
Within [the realisation of] emptiness, virtuous and negative actions do not objectively exist.[20]

So it is that, for the purpose of nakedly perceiving the manifestly present intrinsic awareness,
This *Natural Liberation through Naked Perception* is most profound.
Thus, [by following this instruction], one should familiarise oneself with this intrinsic awareness.

Profoundly Sealed!

E-MA!
This *Introduction to Awareness: Natural Liberation through Naked Perception*
Has been composed for the sake of future generations, the sentient beings of a degenerate age.
[It integrates] in a purposeful concise abridgement,
All my preferred tantras, transmissions and esoteric instructions.
Though I have disseminated it at this present time,
It will be concealed as a precious treasure.
May it be encountered by those of the future,
Who have a [positive] inheritance of past actions.[21]
SAMAYA *rgya rgya rgya!*

This treatise concerning the direct introduction to awareness, entitled *Natural Liberation through Naked Perception*, was composed by Padmākara, the preceptor of Oḍḍiyāna. May [its influence] not be ended until cyclic existence has been emptied.

5

The Spiritual Practice entitled Natural Liberation of Habitual Tendencies

CONTEXT

This is the concise 'generation stage' practice associated with this cycle of teachings. Normally, after completing the preparatory philosophical studies and meditational practices over many years, the full generation stage practice entitled *The Natural Liberation of Feelings* would be done four times a day while in an extended solitary retreat. Following this retreat, the full generation stage practice should be done at least monthly. As a method for enhancing and sustaining an unbroken purity of perception, this concise practice, *The Natural Liberation of Habitual Tendencies*, should be done three times a day, in the morning, at midday and in the evening, throughout the practitioner's life. If this is not practical, then the concise practice should be done twice a day, in the morning and evening, or at least once a day in the morning, following the *Preliminary Practice* (Chapter 1).

The aim is to provide a means by which the practitioner can cultivate an unwavering recognition of the nature of the Peaceful and Wrathful Deities within his or her own mind and body. Thereby recognition of the natural purity of the practitioner's impure habitual tendencies is continuously developed. The measure of successful training is: the location and nature of the deities will be remembered even in the practitioner's dreams, and, the arising of a sustained recognition that all phenomena, sounds and thoughts are, in their essence, the body, speech and mind of the deities.

Herein is contained *The Spiritual Practice entitled Natural Liberation of Habitual Tendencies*,[1] [which is an extract] from the *Peaceful and Wrathful Deities: A Profound Sacred Teaching, [entitled] Natural Liberation through [Recognition of] Enlightened Intention.*[2]

I respectfully bow down to Samantabhadra and Mahottara,[3]
To the assembly of the Peaceful and Wrathful deities,
And to the assembly of the Hundred Sacred Enlightened Families!
Having been liberated in the intermediate states,
May all beings abide in the reality of the three buddha-bodies.

O You who are fortunate and auspiciously blessed,
Apply [yourself to] the meditations and recitations of this most lucid Spiritual Practice,
Which is a coalescence of the [full means of accomplishment] of the Peaceful and Wrathful Deities!
Never forget [to practise this] throughout the three times.

THE TEN-BRANCHED PRAYER FOR THE ACCUMULATION [OF MERIT]

[First], visualise in the space before you the Three Precious Jewels and the deities of the hundred enlightened families, and then recite as follows:

The Branch of Taking Refuge

OṂ ĀḤ HŪṂ
I respectfully take refuge, inseparably, from now until enlightenment,
In the infinitude of Peaceful and Wrathful Deities, the Conquerors Gone to Bliss,
The Three Precious Jewels, the meditational deities,
The ocean of ḍākinīs, and assembly of oath-bound protectors,
Within the infinite [buddha] fields, reaching to the limits of space.

The Branch of Invitation

I request the infinite Peaceful and Wrathful Deities
Of the ten directions and four times,
Compassionate emanations embodying discriminative awareness and skilful means,
Pervading the vast infinite space of reality's expanse,
To come to this place for the sake of [all] living beings.

The Branch of Requesting [the Deities] to be Seated

I request that [the meditational deities] be seated,
Here on sun, moon, and lotus cushions,
[Symbolising] skilful means, discriminative awareness, and their stainless [union],
Upon their bejewelled thrones [fashioned] in the form of lions and so forth,
In [an attitude of] unblemished supreme delight,
Within this maṇḍala of pristine cognition,
Which is the [natural] purity of phenomenal existence!

The Branch of Paying Homage

I bow down to the assembly of the Peaceful and Wrathful Conquerors,
To the father and mother deities, and [all] their offspring,
[Whose essence is] the pristine cognition of Samantabhadra,
Displayed as uncorrupted bliss in the secret womb of Samantabhadrī.

The Branch of Making Offerings

I request the Peaceful and Wrathful Conquerors, the oceans of Those Gone to Bliss,
To partake of these inestimable outer, inner, and secret offerings,
Both those actually arrayed and those mentally emanated,
Which are offered for the benefit of all living beings.

The Branch of the Confession of Negativity

I acknowledge and remorsefully confess all my negative obscurations
And all my habitual tendencies of body, speech and mind,
Beginninglessly influenced by the three poisons
Which are the accumulating causes for [rebirth]
Among the lower states [of suffering] in cyclic existence.

The Branch of Sympathetic Rejoicing

I rejoice with great delight in the [buddha] fields of supreme bliss,
Where all phenomenal existence is [recognised as] the pervasion of reality's expanse.
I rejoice in [all] compassionate acts, in their merits, and in their altruistic intention,
And in all [deeds that are] the source of merit and pristine cognition.

The Branch of Turning the Wheel of the [Sacred] Teachings

I exhort the teachers throughout the fields of the ten directions,
Who are as numerous as atoms,
To stir from their meditative commitments for the sake of all sentient beings,
And to turn the Wheel of the Sacred Teachings,
Thus [entirely] pervading the reaches of space.

The Branch of Requesting [the Buddhas] Not to Enter Nirvāṇa

I beseech you all, O teachers, infinite buddhas without exception,
To remain [present] and not to pass into nirvāṇa,
And to continue to enact deeds of extensive benefit for the sake of beings,
Until the world-systems of cyclic existence have been emptied!

The Branch of the Dedication [of Merit] to the Unsurpassed Greater Vehicle

[By the power of] whatever past, present and future virtues I accumulate,
May all sentient beings, throughout the furthest reaches of space,
Mature into worthy recipients of the unsurpassed Greater Vehicle,
And then swiftly attain the status of the infinite Peaceful and Wrathful Deities!

PURIFICATION

OṂ ĀḤ HŪṂ BODHICITTA MAHĀSUKHAJÑĀNA DHĀTU ĀḤ
OṂ RULU RULU HŪṂ BHYOḤ HŪṂ[4]

From the field of reality's expanse, uncreated and pure,
Within a celestial palace, which is a seminal point [of light], pure, unceasing, and radiant,
Through the natural expressive power of one's own mind, uncontrived and empty,
Intrinsic awareness, radiant and empty, arises in the form of Vajrasattva,
[Seated] upon a bejewelled throne adorned with lotus, sun and moon [cushions].
[Vajrasattva is] white, radiant, with one face, two arms, and a smiling countenance;
The right hand holds a vajra at the heart,

[Symbolising the union] of awareness and emptiness,
The left hand supports a bell [resting] on the hip,
[Symbolising the union] of appearances and emptiness;
And the head [is adorned with a garland of] perfect buddhas,
[Representing] the five enlightened families of Those Gone to Bliss.
Thus, [Vajrasattva] manifests in the form of the Buddha-body of Perfect Resource,
[Exquisitely] adorned with silks and jewels,
Seated in the posture of royal ease,
With the right leg extended, and the left drawn in.[5]

[Radiating] at the heart is the seed-syllable HŪṂ,
Surrounded by the Hundred-syllable Mantra:

OṂ VAJRASATTVA SAMAYAMANUPĀLAYA VAJRASATTVA TVENOPATIṢṬHA DṚḌHO ME BHAVA SUPOṢYO ME BHAVA SUTOṢYO ME BHAVA ANURAKTO ME BHAVA SARVASIDDHIṂ ME PRAYACCHA SARVAKARMASU CA ME CITTAṂ ŚREYAḤ KURU HŪṂ HAHAHAHA HO BHAGAVĀN SARVA TATHĀGATA VAJRA MĀ ME MUÑCA VAJRABHAVA MAHĀSAMAYASATTVA ĀḤ[6]

Having performed the twofold act of benefiting [self and others] through the emanation and reabsorption [of light from these syllables], the obscurations of conceptual thought are purified. Do not be distracted! Recite this quintessential [mantra] of the hundred sacred enlightened families as much as possible, so that the two obscurations may be cleansed.

MAIN PRACTICE

Having thus purified the [two] obscurations, one should visualise the assembled Peaceful and Wrathful Deities of the hundred sacred enlightened families as a maṇḍala [of deities] within one's body, and pray. It is in this context that the aspirational prayers of the intermediate states are recited. [The combined practice] is as follows:

Then, [maintaining the recognition of] oneself as Vajrasattva,
In the celestial palace of one's own precious heart,
One clearly discerns a seminal point [formed of] the five lights,
Whose nature is the five pure essences [of the five elements],
[And from this], the thirty-six peaceful buddhas[7] radiantly manifest,
Amidst a radiant and vibrant maṇḍala suffused by the five pristine cognitions,
Their bodies composed of five lights, the unimpeded [union of] emptiness and radiance,
[Seated] upon a tier of lotus, sun and moon [cushions],
Supported by lion, elephant, horse, peacock and cīvaṃcīvaka [thrones].

OṂ ĀḤ HŪṂ
Within the expanse of a seminal point located at the centre of one's heart,
The primordial lord, the unchanging buddha-body of light,
Samantabhadra, the Buddha-body of Reality, blue in colour,
And Samantabhadrī, the expanse of reality, white in colour,
Are indivisibly united, both in the posture of meditative equipoise,
Seated upon lotus, sun and moon cushions,
[Symbolising the union of] radiance and emptiness.
To you, the supreme ancestors of the buddhas of past, present and future,
I bow down, make offerings, take refuge and pray:
As soon as we die and begin to transmigrate,[8]
At that very moment, when the pure inner radiance of reality dawns,
May we be welcomed by the father Samantabhadra before us,
May we be supported by the mother Samantabhadrī behind us;
And thus [encircled] may we be guided to the indivisible level of Samantabhadra.[9]

OṂ ĀḤ HŪṂ
[In the channel centre of one's heart] is Vairocana in blissful union with Dhātvīśvarī,
White and radiant, holding a wheel and a bell,

Seated cross-legged, [symbolising the union of] radiance and emptiness,
[Amidst a mass of light, radiating the pristine cognition of reality's expanse].
To you, the principal [deities] of the central Buddha Family,
I bow down, make offerings, take refuge and pray:
As soon as we die and begin to transmigrate,
At that very moment, when the visions of the intermediate state of reality dawn,
And we roam [alone] in cyclic existence [driven] by deep-seated delusion,
May the Transcendent Lord Vairocana draw us forward,
Leading us on the path of radiant light,
Which is the pristine cognition of reality's expanse.
May the supreme consort [Ākāśa] Dhātvīśvarī support us from behind,
And thus [encircled] may we be rescued
From the fearsome passageway of the intermediate state,
And be escorted to the level of an utterly perfected buddha.[10]

OṂ ĀḤ HŪṂ
In the eastern channel branch of one's heart,
Is Vajrasattva, in blissful [union] with Buddhalocanā,
Blue and radiant, holding a vajra and a bell,
Seated cross-legged, [symbolising the union of] radiance and emptiness,
Amidst a mass of light radiating the mirror-like pristine cognition.
To the right is white Kṣitigarbha, holding a seedling and a bell,
To the left is white Maitreya, holding a blossoming orange bush and a bell,
To the front is white Lāsyā, holding a mirror and a bell,
And to the rear is white Puṣpā, holding a flower and seated with one leg extended and the other drawn in.
To you, the sixfold principal and encircling [deities] of the Vajra Family,
I bow down, make offerings, take refuge and pray:
As soon as we die and begin to transmigrate,

At that very moment, when the visions of the intermediate state of reality dawn,
And we roam [alone] in cyclic existence [driven] by deep-seated aversion,
May the Transcendent Lord Vajrasattva draw us forward,
Leading us on the path of radiant light,
Which is the mirror-like pristine cognition.
May the supreme consort Buddhalocanā support us from behind,
And thus [encircled] may we be rescued
From the fearsome passageway of the intermediate state,
And be escorted to the level of an utterly perfected buddha.

OṂ ĀḤ HŪṂ
In the southern channel branch of one's heart,
Is Ratnasambhava, in [blissful] union with Māmakī,
Yellow [and radiant], holding a jewel and a bell,
Seated cross-legged, [symbolising the union] of radiance and emptiness,
Amidst a mass of light, radiating the pristine cognition of sameness.
To the right is yellow Samantabhadra, holding a grain-sheath and a bell,
To the left is yellow Ākāśagarbha, holding a sword and a bell,
To the front is yellow Mālyā, holding a garland and seated with one leg extended and the other drawn in,
And to the rear is yellow Dhūpā, holding incense and [also] seated with one leg extended and the other drawn in.
To you, the sixfold principal and encircling [deities] of the Ratna Family,
I bow down, make offerings, take refuge, and pray:
As soon as we die and begin to transmigrate,
At that very moment, when the visions of the intermediate state of reality dawn,
And we roam [alone] in cyclic existence [driven] by deep-seated pride,
May the Transcendent Lord Ratnasambhava draw us forward,
Leading us on the path of radiant light,

Which is the pristine cognition of sameness.
May the supreme consort Māmakī support us from behind,
And thus [encircled] may we be rescued
From the fearsome passageway of the intermediate state,
And be escorted to the level of an utterly perfected buddha.

OṂ ĀḤ HŪṂ
In the western channel branch of one's heart,
Is Amitābha, in blissful union with Pāṇḍaravāsinī,
Red and radiant, holding a lotus and a bell,
Seated cross-legged, [symbolising the union of] radiance and emptiness,
Amidst a mass of light, radiating the pristine cognition of discernment.
To the right is red Avalokiteśvara, holding a lotus and a bell,
To the left is red Mañjuśrī, holding a sword and a bell,
To the front is red Gītā, holding a gong and seated with one leg extended and the other drawn in,
And to the rear is red Ālokā, holding a butter lamp, and [also] seated with one leg extended and the other drawn in.
To you, the sixfold principal and encircling [deities] of the Padma Family,
I bow down, make offerings, take refuge, and pray:
As soon as we die and begin to transmigrate,
At that very moment, when the visions of the intermediate state of reality dawn,
And we roam [alone] in cyclic existence [driven] by deep-seated attachment,
May the Lord Transcendent Lord Amitābha draw us forward,
Leading us on the path of radiant light,
Which is the pristine cognition of discernment.
May the supreme consort Pāṇḍaravāsinī support us from behind,
And thus [encircled] may we be rescued
From the fearsome passageway of the intermediate state,
And be escorted to the level of an utterly perfected buddha.

OṂ ĀḤ HŪṂ

In the northern channel branch of one's heart,
Is Amoghasiddhi, in blissful union with Samayatārā,
Green and radiant, holding a crossed-vajra and a bell,
Seated cross-legged, [symbolising the union of] radiance and emptiness,
Amidst a mass of light, radiating the pristine cognition of accomplishment.
To the right is green Sarvanivāraṇaviśkambhin, holding a book and a bell,
To the left is green Vajrapāṇi, holding a vajra and a bell,
To the front is green Gandhā, holding a conch and seated with one leg extended and the other drawn in,
And to the rear is green Nartī, holding a food-offering, and [also] seated with one leg extended and the other drawn in.
To you, the sixfold principal and encircling [deities] of the Karma Family,
I bow down, make offerings, take refuge, and pray:
As soon as we [die and] begin to transmigrate,
At that very moment, when the visions of the intermediate state of reality dawn,
And we roam [alone] in cyclic existence [driven] by deep-seated envy,
May the Transcendent Lord Amoghasiddhi draw us forward,
Leading us on the path of radiant light,
Which is the pristine cognition of accomplishment.
May the supreme consort Samayatārā support us from behind,
And thus [encircled] may we be rescued
From the fearsome passageway of the intermediate state,
And be escorted to the level of an utterly perfected buddha.

OṂ ĀḤ HŪṂ

In the channel branch at the eastern gate of one's heart,
Are white [Trailokya]vijaya and Aṅkuśā,
In [blissful] union, and dancing.
In the channel branch at the southern gate of one's heart,
Are yellow Yamāntaka and Pāśā,
In [blissful] union, and dancing.
In the channel branch at the western gate of one's heart,

Are red Hayagrīva and Spoṭhā,
In [blissful] union, and dancing.
In the channel branch at the northern gate of one's heart,
Are green Amṛtakuṇḍalin and Ghaṇṭā,
In [blissful] union, and dancing.
To you, the eight emanational gatekeepers, male and female,
I bow down, make offerings, take refuge, and pray:
As soon as we die and begin to transmigrate,
At that very moment, when the visions of the intermediate state of reality dawn,
And we roam [alone] in cyclic existence [driven] by deep-seated habitual tendencies,
May the four Mahākrodha male gatekeepers draw us forward,
Leading us on the path of radiant light,
Which is the four pristine cognitions combined.[11]
May the supreme consorts, the four female gatekeepers, support us from behind,
And thus [encircled] may we be rescued
From the fearsome passageway of the intermediate state,
And be escorted to the level of an utterly perfected buddha.

OṂ ĀḤ HŪṂ
Amidst an expanse of light in the channel branch of the energy centre of great bliss at one's crown,
Within a radiant and vibrant maṇḍala, that is a lustrous white seminal point,
[Stands] Śakra, sage of the god realms, white in colour, and playing a lute.
May he obstruct pride, which is the entrance to rebirth in the god realms!

Amidst an expanse of light in one's occipital channel, which resembles the horn of an ox,[12]
Within a radiant and vibrant maṇḍala, that is a lustrous green seminal point,
[Stands] Vemacitra, sage of the antigods, green in colour, bearing armour and a weapon,
May he obstruct envy, which is the entrance to rebirth in the antigod realms!

Amidst an expanse of light in one's 'life-force' channel, which resembles a crystal tube,[13]
Within a radiant and vibrant maṇḍala, that is a lustrous yellow seminal point,
[Stands] Śākyamuni, sage of human beings, yellow in colour, and carrying a mendicant's staff.
May he obstruct attachment, which is the entrance to rebirth in the human realms!

Amidst an expanse of light in the energy centre of one's navel,
Within a radiant and vibrant maṇḍala, that is a lustrous blue seminal point,
[Stands] Sthirasiṃha, sage of animals, blue in colour, and carrying a book.
May he obstruct delusion, which is the entrance to rebirth in the animal realms!

Amidst an expanse of light in the channel branch at one's bliss-sustaining secret place,[14]
Within a radiant and vibrant maṇḍala, that is a lustrous red seminal point,
[Stands] Jvālamukha, sage of the anguished spirits, red in colour, carrying a [wish-granting] casket.
May he obstruct miserliness, which is the entrance to rebirth among the anguished-spirit realms!

Amidst an expanse of light in the energy centre at the soles of one's feet,
Within a radiant and vibrant maṇḍala, that is a lustrous black seminal point,
[Stands] Yama Dharmarāja, sage of the hell beings, black in colour, and carrying a flame and water.
May he obstruct aversion, which is the entrance to rebirth among the hell realms!

To you, the six sages, the Buddha-bodies of Emanation,
Who act for the benefit of living beings,
I bow down, make offerings, take refuge, and pray:
As soon as we die and begin to transmigrate,

At that very moment, when the visions of the intermediate state of rebirth dawn,
And we roam [alone] in cyclic existence [driven] by deep-seated habitual tendencies,
May the three sages of the higher realms draw us forward,
Leading us on the path of radiant light,
Which is the four pristine cognitions combined.
May the three sages of the lower realms support us from behind,
And thus [encircled] may we be rescued
From the light paths of the six impure states [of existence],
And be escorted to the level of an utterly perfected buddha.

OṂ ĀḤ HŪṂ
The forty-two deities of the peaceful assembly blaze with rays of light:
Radiant, vibrant, resplendent, and naturally beautiful.
Their bodies are supple, slender, handsome, upright, and youthful,
Exquisitely ornamented and [splendidly] endowed with the major and minor marks.
To you, the assembled peaceful deities of the indestructible expanse,
I bow down, make offerings, take refuge, and pray:
As soon as we die and begin to transmigrate,
At that very moment, when the visions of the intermediate state of reality dawn,
And we roam [alone] in cyclic existence [driven] by the five deep-seated poisons,
May all the peaceful male deities draw us forward,
Leading us on the path of radiant light,
Which is the five pristine cognitions combined.
May the supreme female consorts, Queens of the Expanse, support us from behind,
And may the male and female gatekeepers support us from the perimeter,
And thus [encircled] may we be rescued
From the fearsome passageway of the intermediate state,
And be escorted to the level of an utterly perfected buddha.

OṂ ĀḤ HŪṂ

At this time when we dwell within the intermediate state of living,
The forty-two assembled peaceful deities,
Are radiantly present within the celestial palace of our own hearts,
Embodied in the form of a cluster of five-coloured lights.
Yet, as soon as we die and begin to transmigrate,
This assembly of peaceful deities will emerge from our hearts,
And fill the space before us.
Each of the innumerable central and peripheral forms
Will be [fully endowed with] the ornaments and attire [of the peaceful deities],[15]
Each composed of the five-coloured lights [indicative of the union] of radiance and emptiness,
And [encircled] by an expanse of rainbow light.
Vibrant beaming shafts of light, indicative of the five pristine cognitions,
Emanating five[-coloured] seminal points, sounds, lights and rays,
Radiant, vibrant, resplendent, clear, and naturally resonant,
Will beam out, as if piercing our hearts.
Concomitant with these lights of the five pristine cognitions,
The six light paths indicative of the six classes of deluded impure beings will also dawn before us.
At this moment, O compassionate assembly of peaceful deities,
Blessed Transcendent Ones, Beings of Compassion,
Do not withhold your compassion,
But draw us forward on the path [of radiant light],
Which is the four pristine cognitions combined,
And draw us back from the paths [of the dull lights],
Which are [the doors to] the six states of impure [existence]!

OṂ ĀḤ HŪṂ

In the celestial palace of perfect resource, within one's own throat,
Amidst an expanse permeated with rainbows and lights,
In the central channel branch of the energy centre of perfect resource,
Is Padmanaṭeśvara, the great Awareness Holder of Maturation,

Red and radiant, glowing in [an array of] five[-coloured] lights,
And embraced by the Ḍākinī of Pristine Cognition,
[Their union symbolising the coalescence of] bliss and emptiness.
[She holds] a blood-filled skull and a curved knife,
Raised in the gesture of pointing to the sky.
May the awareness holders of buddha-body protect all living beings!

OṂ ĀḤ HŪṂ
In the eastern channel branch of the energy centre of perfect resource, within one's throat,
Is the great Awareness Holder who Abides on the Levels,
White, radiant, smiling, and embraced by the White Ḍākinī.
[She holds] a blood-filled skull and a curved knife,
Raised in the gesture of pointing to the sky.
May the awareness holders of buddha-mind protect all living beings!

OṂ ĀḤ HŪṂ
In the southern channel branch of the energy centre of perfect resource, within one's throat,
Is the great Awareness Holder with Power over the Lifespan,
Yellow, radiant, smiling, and embraced by the Yellow Ḍākinī.
[She holds] a blood-filled skull and a curved knife,
Raised in the gesture of pointing to the sky.
May the awareness holders of buddha-attributes protect all living beings!

OṂ ĀḤ HŪṂ
In the western channel branch of the energy centre of perfect resource, within one's throat,
Is the great Awareness Holder of the Great Seal,
Red, radiant, smiling, and embraced by the Red Ḍākinī.
[She holds] a blood-filled skull and a curved knife,
Raised in the gesture of pointing to the sky.
May the awareness holders of buddha-speech protect all living beings!

OṂ ĀḤ HŪṂ
In the northern channel branch of the energy centre of perfect resource, within one's throat,
Is the great Awareness Holder of Spontaneous Presence,
Green, radiant, wrathful, smiling, and embraced by the Green Ḍākinī.
[She holds] a blood-filled skull and a curved knife,
Raised in the gesture of pointing to the sky.
May the awareness holders of buddha-activity protect all living beings!

OṂ ĀḤ HŪṂ
To you, the assembly of awareness holders, the heroes and ḍākinīs,
I bow down, make offerings, take refuge and pray:
As soon as we die and begin to transmigrate,
At that very moment, when the visions of the intermediate state of reality dawn,
And we roam [alone] in cyclic existence [driven] by deep-seated habitual tendencies,
May the heroic awareness holders draw us forward,
Leading us on the path of radiant light,
Which is the [luminance of] spontaneously arising pristine cognition.[16]
May the supreme female consorts, the assembly of ḍākinīs, support us from behind,
And thus [encircled] may we be rescued
From the fearsome passageway of the intermediate state,
And be escorted to the pure fields of the sky-farers.

OṂ ĀḤ HŪṂ
At this time when we dwell within the intermediate state of living,
The assemblies of awareness holders, both heroes and ḍākinīs,
Are radiantly present within the celestial palace of the energy centre of perfect resource within our own throats,
Embodied in the form of a cluster of five-coloured lights.
Yet, as soon as we die and begin to transmigrate,
This divine assembly of the awareness holders will emerge from the throat [centre],

And fill the space before us.
Amidst a plethora of musical sounds they will manifest in myriad dancing postures,
Pounding and vibrating throughout all world-systems,
[And generating] a vibrant beaming path of light,
Indicative of spontaneously arising pristine cognition.
Simultaneously, the [light] path of the animal realms, indicative of delusion,
Will [also] dawn before us.
O divine assembly of awareness holders, at that moment,
Do not withhold your compassion,
But draw us back from the [dull-light] path,
Which is the gateway to the deluded animal-realms,
And draw all beings along the path [of light],
Which is [the luminance of] spontaneously arising pristine cognition!
Seize us with your compassion,
[Ensuring] that we recognise [the characteristics of] the intermediate state!
Empower us so that we may become awareness holders, children of the Conquerors.

OṂ ĀḤ HŪṂ
At the crown-centre of onself, [visualised] as Vajrasattva,
In the celestial palace of the blazing skull, within one's brain,
Amidst an expanse of light composed of flaming seminal points of rainbow-light,
Is the assembly of blood-drinking deities,[17] standing in clusters.

OṂ ĀḤ HŪṂ
In the central channel branch of the skull, within one's brain,
Amidst an expanse of light, composed of flaming seminal points of rainbow-light,
[Stands] Samantabhadra in the form of Mahottara Heruka.
He has three faces: brown, white and red; and six arms:
The three right arms brandish a vajra, a khaṭvāṅga, and a small drum,
And the left hold a bell, a blood-filled skull, and a noose of entrails.

Mahottara Heruka is joyously and indivisibly embraced by Krodheśvarī.
May these two, the central male and female consorts, guide all beings [to liberation]!

OṂ ĀḤ HŪṂ
On a throne in the central channel branch of one's skull,
Amidst an expanse of light, composed of flaming seminal points of rainbow-light,
[Stands] Vairocana in the form of Buddha Heruka.
He has three faces: reddish brown, white and red; and six arms:
The three right arms brandish a wheel, an axe, and a sword,
And the left hold a bell, a ploughshare, and a blood-filled skull.
Buddha Heruka is joyously and indivisibly embraced by Buddhakrodheśvarī.
May these two, the blood-drinking deities of the Sugata Family, guide all beings [to liberation]!

OṂ ĀḤ HŪṂ
On [a throne in] the eastern channel branch of the skull, within one's brain,
Amidst an expanse of light, composed of flaming seminal points of rainbow-light,
[Stands] Vajrasattva in the form of Vajra Heruka.
He has three faces: dark blue, white and red; and six arms:
The three right arms brandish a vajra, a skull, and an axe,
And the left hold a bell, a blood-filled skull, and a ploughshare.
Vajra Heruka is joyously and indivisibly embraced by Vajrakrodheśvarī.
May these two, the blood-drinking deities of the Vajra Family, guide all beings [to liberation]!

OṂ ĀḤ HŪṂ
On [a throne in] the southern channel branch of the skull, within one's brain,
Amidst an expanse of light, composed of flaming seminal points of rainbow-light,

[Stands] Ratnasambhava in the form of Ratna Heruka.
He has three faces: dark yellow, white and red; and six arms:
The three right arms brandish a jewel, a khaṭvāṅga, and a club,
And the left hold a bell, a blood-filled skull, and a trident.
Ratna Heruka is joyously and indivisibly embraced by Ratnakrodheśvarī.
May these two, the blood-drinking deities of the Ratna Family, guide all beings [to liberation]!

OṂ ĀḤ HŪṂ
On [a throne in] the western channel branch of the skull, within one's brain,
Amidst an expanse of light, composed of flaming seminal points of rainbow-light,
[Stands] Amitābha in the form of Padma Heruka.
He has three faces: dark red, white and blue; and six arms:
The three right arms brandish a lotus, a khaṭvāṅga, and a mace,
And the left hold a bell, a blood-filled skull, and a small drum.
Padma Heruka is joyously and indivisibly embraced by Padmakrodheśvarī.
May these two, the blood-drinking deities of the Padma family, guide all beings [to liberation]!

OṂ ĀḤ HŪṂ
On [a throne in] the northern channel branch of the skull, within one's brain,
Amidst an expanse of light, composed of flaming seminal points of rainbow-light,
[Stands] Amoghasiddhi in the form of Karma Heruka.
He has three faces: dark green, white and red; and six arms:
The three right arms brandish a sword, a khaṭvāṅga, and a mace,
And the left hold a bell, a blood-filled skull, and a ploughshare.
Karma Heruka is joyously and indivisibly embraced by Karmakrodheśvarī.
May these two, the blood-drinking deities of the Karma Family, guide all beings [to liberation]!

OṂ ĀḤ HŪṂ

To you, the twelve central, male and female, blood-drinking deities,

I bow down, make offerings, take refuge, and pray:

As soon as we die and begin to transmigrate,

At that very moment, when the visions of the intermediate state of reality dawn,

And we roam [alone] in cyclic existence [driven] by deep-seated confused perceptions,

May the conquerors, the male wrathful blood-drinking deities, draw us forward,

Leading us on the path of radiant light,

Which is the five fully perfect pristine cognitions.

May the assembly of wrathful female deities, Queens of the Expanse, support us from behind,

And thus [encircled] may we be rescued

From the fearsome passageway of the intermediate state,

And be escorted to the level of an utterly perfected buddha.

OṂ ĀḤ HŪṂ

Amidst an expanse of light in the eastern channel branch of one's skull,

[Stands] Gaurī, white in colour, holding a human-corpse cudgel and a skull;

Amidst an expanse of light in the southern channel branch of one's skull,

[Stands] Caurī, yellow in colour, shooting an arrow from a bow;

Amidst an expanse of light in the western channel branch of one's skull,

[Stands] Pramohā, red in colour, holding a crocodile victory-banner;

Amidst an expanse of light in the northern channel branch of one's skull,

[Stands] Vetālī, black in colour, holding a vajra and a blood-filled skull;

Amidst an expanse of light in the south-eastern channel branch of one's skull,

[Stands] Pukkasī, red-yellow in colour, clutching and devouring entrails;

Amidst an expanse of light in the south-western channel branch of one's skull,
[Stands] Ghasmarī, green-black in colour, stirring a blood-filled skull with a vajra;
Amidst an expanse of light in the north-western channel branch of one's skull,
[Stands] Caṇḍālī, pale-yellow in colour, [clutching] a human corpse and eating its heart;
Amidst an expanse of light in the north-eastern channel branch of one's skull,
[Stands] Śmaśānī, blue-black in colour, tearing apart the head and body of a bloated corpse.

OṂ ĀḤ HŪṂ
To you, the Eight Mātaraḥ, beginning with Gaurī,
[Who are embodiments] of the [eight] classes [of consciousness],[18]
I bow down, make offerings, take refuge, and pray:
As soon as we die and begin to transmigrate,
At that very moment, when the visions of the intermediate state of reality dawn,
And we roam [alone] in cyclic existence [driven] by deep-seated confused perceptions,
May the four Mātaraḥ, beginning with Gaurī, draw us forward,
Leading us on the path of light,
Which is [the vibrance of] the sounds, lights and rays [of the eight classes of consciousness].
May the four Mātaraḥ, beginning with Pukkasī, support us from behind,
And thus [encircled] may we be rescued
From the fearsome passageway of the intermediate state,
And be escorted to the level of an utterly perfected buddha.

OṂ ĀḤ HŪṂ
Amidst an expanse of light in the outer eastern channel branch of one's skull,
[Stands] lion-headed Siṃhamukhī, brown-black in colour, carrying a corpse in her mouth;
Amidst an expanse of light in the outer southern channel branch of one's skull,

[Stands] tiger-headed Vyāghrīmukhī, red in colour, with her two arms crossed;
Amidst an expanse of light in the outer western channel branch of one's skull,
[Stands] fox-headed Śṛgālamukhī, black in colour, eating entrails;
Amidst an expanse of light in the outer northern channel branch of one's skull,
[Stands] wolf-headed Śvānamukhī, blue-black in colour, tearing apart a bloated corpse;
Amidst an expanse of light in the outer south-eastern channel branch of one's skull,
[Stands] vulture-headed Gṛdhramukhī, white-yellow in colour, carrying a human corpse draped over her shoulder;
Amidst an expanse of light in the outer south-western channel branch of one's skull,
[Stands] kite-headed Kaṅkamukhī, red-black in colour, carrying a large human corpse;
Amidst an expanse of light in the outer north-western channel branch of one's skull,
[Stands] crow-headed Kākamukhī, black in colour, brandishing a skull and a sword;
Amidst an expanse of light in the outer north-eastern channel branch of one's skull,
[Stands] owl-headed Ulūkamukhī, dark blue in colour,[19] holding a vajra.

[OṂ ĀḤ HŪṂ]
To you, the Eight Piśācī, beginning with Siṃhamukhī,
[Who are embodiments] of the [eight] sensory objects,[20]
I bow down, make offerings, take refuge, and pray:
As soon as we die and begin to transmigrate,
At that very moment, when the visions of the intermediate state of reality dawn,
And we roam [alone] in cyclic existence [driven] by deep-seated confused perceptions,
May the four Piśācī, starting with Siṃhamukhī, draw us forward,
Leading us on the path of pure [radiant] light,
Which is the purity of the naturally manifesting eight objects [of consciousness].

May the four Piśācī, starting with Gṛdhramukhī, support us from behind,
And thus [encircled] may we be rescued
From the fearsome passageway of the intermediate state,
And be escorted to the level of an utterly perfected buddha.

OṂ ĀḤ HŪṂ
In the channel branch at the eastern gate of the skull, within one's brain,
Is horse-headed [Aṅkuśā], white in colour, carrying an iron hook and a skull.
In the channel branch at the southern gate of the skull, within one's brain,
Is sow-headed [Pāśā], yellow in colour, holding a noose and a skull.
In the channel branch at the western gate of the skull, within one's brain,
Is lion-headed [Sphoṭā], red in colour, holding an iron chain and a skull.
In the channel branch of the northern gate of the skull, within one's brain,
Is snake-headed [Ghaṇṭā], green in colour, holding a bell and a skull.[21]
To you, the Four Female Gatekeepers, who are pristine cognition in emanational form,
I bow down, make offerings, take refuge, and pray:
As soon as we die and begin to transmigrate,
At that very moment, when the visions of the intermediate state of reality dawn,
And we roam [alone] in cyclic existence [driven] by deep-seated confused perceptions,
May Aṅkuśā and Pāśā draw us forward,
Obstructing the entrances to confusion through the four types of birth,
And opening the doors to the four rites of pure enlightened activity.
May Sphoṭā and Ghaṇṭā support us from behind,
And thus [encircled] may we be rescued
From the fearsome passageway of the intermediate state,
And be escorted to the level of an utterly perfected buddha.

OṂ ĀḤ HŪṂ
In the minor channels of the eastern outer courtyard of one's skull,
[Stand] the six Queens of Yoga who enact the rites of pacification:
Yak-headed Manurākṣasī, brownish white, and holding a vajra;
Snake-headed Brahmāṇī, yellowish white, and holding a lotus;
Leopard-headed Raudrī, greenish white, and holding a trident;
Weasel-headed Vaiṣṇāvī, bluish white, and holding a wheel;
Brown bear-headed Kaumārī, reddish white, and holding a short pike;
And black bear-headed Indrāṇī, white, and holding a noose of entrails.
O you, the six yoginī from the east, who enact the rites of pacification,
Perform the rites which pacify our fears of the intermediate state![22]

OṂ ĀḤ HŪṂ
In the minor channels of the southern outer courtyard of one's skull,
[Stand] the six Queens of Yoga who enact the rites of enrichment:
Bat-headed Vajrā,[23] yellow, and holding a razor;
Crocodile-headed Śāntī, reddish yellow, and holding a vase;
Scorpion-headed Amṛtā, reddish yellow, and holding a lotus;
Hawk-headed Saumī, whitish yellow, and holding a vajra;
Fox-headed Daṇḍī, greenish yellow, and holding a cudgel;
And tiger-headed Rākṣasī, blackish yellow, and drinking from a blood-filled skull.
O you, the six yoginī from the south, who enact the rites of enrichment,
Perform the rites which enrich pristine cognition during the intermediate state![24]

OṂ ĀḤ HŪṂ
In the minor channels of the western outer courtyard of one's skull,
[Stand] the six Queens of Yoga who enact the rites of subjugation:

Vulture-headed Bhakṣasī, greenish red, and holding a club;
Horse-headed Ratī, red, and holding a human torso;
Garuḍa-headed Rudhiramadī, pale red, and holding a cudgel;
Dog-headed Ekacāriṇī Rākṣasī, red, and holding a vajra;
Hoopoe-headed Manohārikā, red, and firing an arrow from a bow;
And deer-headed Siddhikarī, greenish red, and holding a vase.
O you, the six yoginī from the west, who enact the rites of subjugation,
Perform the rites which assure our independence during the intermediate state![25]

OṂ ĀḤ HŪṂ
In the minor channels of the northern outer courtyard of one's skull,
[Stand] the six Queens of Yoga who enact the rites of wrath:
Wolf-headed Vāyudevī, bluish green, and brandishing an ensign;
Ibex-headed Agnāyī, reddish green, and holding a firebrand;
Sow-headed Varāhī, blackish green, and holding a noose of fangs;
Crow-headed Cāmuṇḍī, reddish green, and holding an infant human corpse;
Elephant-headed Bhujanā, blackish green, and holding a bloated corpse;
And snake-headed Varuṇānī, bluish green, and holding a noose of snakes.
O you, the six yoginī from the north, who enact the rites of wrath,
Perform the rites which utterly destroy the confused perceptions of the intermediate state![26]

OṂ ĀḤ HŪṂ
At the [outer] eastern gate of one's skull is Vajrā [Mahākālī],
White, cuckoo-headed, and holding an iron hook;
At the [outer] southern gate of one's skull is Vajrā [Mahāchāgalā],
Yellow, goat-headed, and holding a noose;
At the [outer] western gate of one's skull is Vajrā [Mahākumbhakarṇī],

Red, lion-headed, and holding an iron chain;
And at the [outer] northern gate of one's skull is Vajrā [Lambodarā],
Dark green, snake-headed, and holding a bell.
O you, the four female gatekeepers, Queens [of Yoga] who enact the emanational rites,
Perform the rites which obstruct the doors [leading] to [mundane] rebirth from the intermediate state![27]

OṂ ĀḤ HŪṂ
To you, the Twenty-eight Īśvarī, Queens of Yoga,
I bow down, make offerings, take refuge, and pray:
As soon as we die and begin to transmigrate,
At that very moment, when the visions of the intermediate state of reality dawn,
And we roam [alone] in cyclic existence [driven] by deep-seated confused perceptions,
May the seven Īśvarī of the east draw us forward,
Leading us on the path of radiant light,
Which is [a vibrance of] sounds, lights and rays.
May the seven Īśvarī of the south support us from behind,
May the seven Īśvarī of the west support us from the perimeter,
And may the seven Īśvarī of the north destroy [and liberate] our enemies,
And thus [encircled] may we be rescued
From the fearsome passageway of the intermediate state,
And be escorted to the level of an utterly perfected buddha.

OṂ ĀḤ HŪṂ
At this time when we dwell within the intermediate state of living,
The assembly of the sixty blood-drinking deities[28]
Is radiantly present within the celestial palace of the skull, at the crown-centre, within one's brain –
Embodied in the form of a cluster of five-coloured lights.
Yet, as soon as we die and begin to transmigrate,
This assembly of blood-drinking deities will emerge from the brain,
And appear [before us], filling the entire trichiliocosm.

[Each of] the central and peripheral [forms]
Will be endowed with fearsome ornaments and attire.
[Resounding] within an immense space,
Vibrant with sounds, lights and rays,
The bodily demeanour of these wrathful deities
Will be elegant, heroic and terrifying,
Their roar wild, murderous and awesome,
Each blazing with compassion, wrath and fierce aversion,
Adorned by face markings of human ash, blood, and grease;[29]
Dressed in skirts of moist hide and flayed tiger skin;
Decorated with skull garlands and wreaths of snakes;
Resplendent in a blazing mass of fire which pounds
With the cries of 'HA HA HŪṂ PHAṬ strike! Slay!',
Reverberating like a thousand peals of thunder.
Fully arrayed with hand-emblems and multifarious faces,
Displaying the arts of transformation,
They will pulverise and rock the infinite trichiliocosm.
At that very moment when the fierce sounds, lights and rays
Dawn before us in terrifying manifestation,
O you, the compassionate assembly of wrathful blood-drinking deities,
O Beings of Compassion, do not withhold your compassion at that [time]!
As we roam [alone] in cyclic existence [driven] by deep-seated habitual tendencies,
May the assembly of wrathful blood-drinking [deities] draw us forward,
Leading us on the path of [radiant] light,
Which is free of fear and terrifying perceptions!
May the assembly of wrathful female deities, Queens of the Expanse, support us from behind!
May the assembly of the Mātaraḥ, Piśācī, and Female Gatekeepers support us from the perimeter!
May the Eight Great Projectresses [who propel beings to exalted rebirths],
Propel us from our [mundane] states [into higher rebirth]!
May the diverse animal-headed Īśvarī eliminate all obstacles!
May the four supreme Female Gatekeepers obstruct the entrance to [mundane] births;
And thus [encircled], may we be rescued

From the fearsome passageway of the intermediate state,
And be escorted to the level of an utterly perfected buddha.

OṂ ĀḤ HŪṂ
When we roam alone, separated from our loved ones,
And [myriad] images of emptiness arise, naturally manifesting,
May the buddhas [quickly] release the power of their compassion,
And may the fear of the awesome and terrifying intermediate state be annulled.
When the radiant light path of pristine cognition dawns,
May we recognise [its nature], without awe and without terror,
And as the [manifold] forms of the Peaceful and Wrathful Deities arise,
May we be fearlessly confident, and recognise [the characteristics of] the intermediate state.
When we experience suffering, as the result of negative past actions,
May our meditational deities utterly dispel all such misery,
And as the natural sound of reality reverberates like a thousand peals of thunder,
May [all sounds] be heard as the sacred resonance of the Greater Vehicle.
When we are driven on by past actions, without a refuge,
May the Great Compassionate One, Mahākāruṇika, protect us,
And as we experience suffering generated by habitual tendencies and past actions,
May the meditative stabilities of inner radiance and bliss [naturally] arise.
May the fields[30] *of the five elements not rise up as a hostile force,*
But may we see these as the buddha fields of the five enlightened families![31]

By the blessing of the spiritual teachers of the oral lineage,
By the compassion of the assembly of Peaceful and Wrathful Deities,
And by the force of the purity of my altruistic aspiration,

May all the aspirational prayers, here expressed,
Be immediately realised.

CONCLUSION

If one consistently perseveres in this *Spiritual Practice* of the Peaceful and Wrathful Deities, together with the recitation of the aspirational prayers, even the negativity and obscurations caused by past actions which involve the five inexpiable crimes will be purified. Even the very hell realms themselves [can] be stirred [by the power of this practice]. If this practice is followed, there is no doubt that one will be born as an awareness holder amongst the fields of the Conquerors. For it is said in the transmitted precepts of the Transcendent One Samantabhadra himself:

'One who respectfully pays homage to the maṇḍala
Of the Peaceful and Wrathful Deities of the *Magical Net*,
Will purify each and every transgression [of the commitments].
Even the negativity of the five inexpiable crimes will be purified.
Even the hell realms themselves may be stirred [by the force of this practice],
And one will become recognised as an awareness holder,
Among the fields of the Conquerors.'

The advantages which accrue from engaging in the *Spiritual Practice* as here set down, are extremely great. It is said that just by simply hearing, once, the names of the deities of this maṇḍala, one will avoid rebirth in the lower existences, and buddhahood will eventually be attained. Samantabhadra himself has said:

'If anyone hears, only once, the names of these deities of the maṇḍala, he or she will be saved from falling into the great hells.'

And:

'Anyone who respectfully pays homage
To the natural maṇḍala of the *Magical Net*,
Will purify each and every transgression [of the commitments].

The commitments will be repaired, and accomplishments attained.'

Therefore, since the advantages of following this practice are beyond expression, one should persevere with this *Spiritual Practice* and [consistently] visualise one's own body as the assembly of the Peaceful and Wrathful Deities. Thus, the supreme and common accomplishments will be attained in this very life; and after one has died, when the visions of the Peaceful and Wrathful Deities dawn during the intermediate state of reality, one will dissolve indivisibly with the meditational deities, and buddhahood will be attained.[32] Experientially cultivate this [*Spiritual Practice*]! Do not forget its words and meanings even if you were to be pursued by a hundred assassins. Embrace it! Hold it [to your heart]! Read it aloud! Comprehend it in its entirety! Keep it in mind, fully and accurately!

This most lucid *Spiritual Practice*, which is a coalescence of the [full means of accomplishment of the] Peaceful and Wrathful Deities is the experiential cultivation associated with the *Liberation by Hearing in the Intermediate States.*[33] It is the essence of the *Peaceful and Wrathful Deities: The Ritual Purification entitled Natural Liberation of Feelings.*[34] It is a supporting text to the *Natural Liberation of Awareness: Secret Empowerment of the Intermediate States,*[35] and it is the main practice associated with the *Reparation [of Commitments] and Confession: Natural Liberation of Transgressions.*[36] It is the path of liberation followed by fortunate beings. May [the influence of] this *Spiritual Practice: Natural Liberation of Habitual Tendencies* not be exhausted until cyclic existence has been emptied.

SAMAYA *rgya rgya rgya dge'o*

6

Natural Liberation of Negativity and Obscuration through [Enactment of] the Hundredfold Homage to the Sacred Enlightened Families

CONTEXT

This practice reinforces the previous meditation, taking the form of a physical prostration to each of the Peaceful and Wrathful Deities in turn. This *Hundredfold Homage* can be done on its own or immediately after the practice of the *Natural Liberation of Habitual Tendencies*. It can also be practised whenever feast-offerings are performed in conjunction with *The Natural Liberation of Feelings* or whenever the practitioner makes offerings of incense, flowers and butter-lamps to the deities.

Practitioners should make these prostrations while clearly visualising before them the form of the deity, in perfect detail, and while experientially cultivating the deity's nature and the inner meaning of the symbolism. Also, as the colophon recommends, the practitioner should concurrently: 'mentally admit and feel remorse for all one's negativities and obscurations, which have been, are being and will be accumulated.'

Herein is contained an ancillary chapter of the *Liberation by Hearing in the Intermediate States*,[1] entitled *Natural Liberation of Negativity and Obscuration through [Enactment of] the Hundredfold Homage*,[2] [which is an extract from] the *Peaceful and Wrathful Deities: A Profound Sacred Teaching, [entitled] Natural Liberation through [Recognition of] Enlightened Intention*.[3]

I respectfully bow down to Samantabhadra and Mahottara,
To the assembly of Peaceful and Wrathful Deities,
And to the assembly of the hundred sacred enlightened families.
Having purified all negativity and obscurations,
May I act so as to guide all beings to the pure buddha fields!

I [now] present this *Natural Liberation of Negativity and Obscuration through [Enactment of the Hundredfold] Homage*, a method for performing a hundredfold homage to the infinite Peaceful and Wrathful Deities of the hundred sacred enlightened families, by which negativity and obscuration may be purified. Cherish your zeal in this [practice] throughout the three times!

NAMO![4]
I bow down to[5] Samantabhadra, the Buddha-body of Reality,
Father of all buddhas, the natural purity of mental consciousness,
The primary buddha, unchanging body of light,
Sky [blue], and seated in the posture of meditative equipoise.

I bow down to Samantabhadrī, the supreme consort,
Natural purity of the sensory spectrum of phenomena,[6]

Stainless white, like crystal,
Mother of all buddhas of past, present and future,
Joyously embracing her consort, in supreme bliss.

I bow down to Vairocana, [manifestation of] supreme buddha-body,
The natural purity of the aggregate of form,
Pure without renunciation of delusion,
Conch [white], holding a wheel and a bell,
[Seated] on an exalted throne supported by lions,
The [resplendent] pristine cognition of reality's expanse.

I bow down to Vajrasattva, [manifestation of] supreme buddha-mind,
The natural purity of the aggregate of consciousness,
Pure without renunciation of aversion,
Azure [blue], holding a vajra and a bell,
[Seated] on an exalted throne supported by elephants,
The [resplendent] mirror-like pristine cognition.

I bow down to Ratnasambhava, [manifestation of supreme] buddha attributes,
The natural purity of the aggregate of feeling,
Pure without renunciation of pride,
Golden [yellow], holding a jewel and a bell,
[Seated] on an exalted throne supported by horses,
The [resplendent] pristine cognition of sameness.

I bow down to Amitābha, [manifestation of] supreme buddha-speech,
The natural purity of the aggregate of perceptions,
Pure without renunciation of attachment,
Copper [red], holding a lotus and a bell,
[Seated] on an exalted throne supported by peacocks,
The [resplendent] pristine cognition of discernment.

I bow down to Amoghasiddhi, [manifestation of supreme] buddha activities,
The natural purity of the aggregate of motivational tendencies,
Pure without renunciation of envy,

Turquoise [green], holding a crossed-vajra and a bell,
[Seated] on an exalted throne supported by *cīvaṃcīvaka* birds,
The [resplendent] pristine cognition of accomplishment.

I bow down to Dhātvīśvarī, the supreme consort,
The mother of the Buddha Family, natural purity of space,
Moonlike [white], holding a wheel and a bell,
Joyously embracing her consort, in supreme bliss.

I bow down to Buddhalocanā, the supreme consort,
The mother of the Vajra Family, natural purity of earth,
Beryl [blue], holding a vajra and a bell,
Joyously embracing her consort, in supreme bliss.

I bow down to Māmakī, the supreme consort,
The mother of the Ratna Family, natural purity of water,
Minium [orange], holding a jewel and a bell,
Joyously embracing her consort, in supreme bliss.

I bow down to Pāṇḍaravāsinī, the supreme consort,
The mother of the Padma Family, natural purity of fire,
Fire-crystal [red], holding a lotus and a bell,
Joyously embracing her consort, in supreme bliss.

I bow down to Samayatārā, the supreme consort,
The mother of the Karma Family, natural purity of wind,
Sapphire [green], holding a crossed-vajra and a bell,
Joyously embracing her consort, in supreme bliss.

I bow down to Kṣitigarbha, male bodhisattva who acts for the benefit of beings,
The natural purity of visual consciousness, transcendent of renunciation,
Snow-mountain [white], holding a seedling and a bell.

I bow down to Maitreya, male bodhisattva who acts for the benefit of beings,
The natural purity of auditory consciousness, transcendent of renunciation,
Cloud-white, holding a blossoming orange bush and a bell.

I bow down to Samantabhadra, male bodhisattva who acts for the benefit of beings,
The natural purity of olfactory consciousness, transcendent of renunciation,
Amber [yellow], holding a grain-sheath and a bell.

I bow down to Ākāśagarbha, male bodhisattva who acts for the benefit of beings,
The natural purity of gustatory consciousness, transcendent of renunciation,
Burnished golden [yellow], holding a sword and a bell.

I bow down to Avalokiteśvara, male bodhisattva who acts for the benefit of beings,
The natural purity of tactile consciousness, transcendent of renunciation,
Coral [red], holding a lotus and a bell.

I bow down to Mañjuśrīkumārabhūta, male bodhisattva who acts for the benefit of beings,
The natural purity of mental consciousness, transcendent of renunciation,
Minium [orange], holding a lily and a bell.

I bow down to Nivāraṇaviśkambhin, male bodhisattva who acts for the benefit of beings,
The natural purity of the 'ground-of-all' consciousness, transcendent of renunciation,
[Green] as the night-flowering lotus, holding a book and a bell.

I bow down to Vajrapāṇi, male bodhisattva who acts for the benefit of beings,
The natural purity of 'defiled' consciousness, transcendent of renunciation,
Emerald [green], holding a vajra and a bell.

I bow down to white Lāsyā, [female bodhisattva] whose offerings [delight]
The eyes of [all] Those Gone to Bliss, past, present and future,

The natural purity of visual phenomena, transcendent of renunciation,
Quartz [white], holding a mirror and a bell.

I bow down to white Puṣpā, [female bodhisattva] whose offerings delight
[The minds of all] Those Gone to Bliss, past, present and future,
The natural purity of past conceptual thoughts, transcendent of renunciation,
Pearl [white], holding a white lotus and a bell.

I bow down to yellow Mālyā, [female bodhisattva] whose gestures delight
[The minds of all] Those Gone to Bliss, past, present and future,
The natural purity of indeterminate conceptual thoughts, transcendent of renunciation,
Saffron [yellow], holding a garland and a bell.

I bow down to yellow Dhūpā, [female bodhisattva] whose offerings [delight]
The noses of [all] Those Gone to Bliss, past, present and future,
The natural purity of fragrance, transcendent of renunciation,
Golden [yellow] in colour, holding sweet-smelling incense and a censer.

I bow down to red Gītā, [female bodhisattva] whose offerings [delight]
The ears of [all] Those Gone to Bliss, past, present and future,
The natural purity of sound, transcendent of renunciation,
Marsh mallow [pink], and playing a lute.

I bow down to red Ālokā, [female bodhisattva] whose offerings [delight]
The eyes of [all] Those Gone to Bliss, past, present and future,
The natural purity of future conceptual thoughts, transcendent of renunciation,
Lotus [pink], and holding a glowing butter lamp.

I bow down to green Gandhā, [female bodhisattva] whose offerings [delight]
The bodies of [all] Those Gone to Bliss, past, present and future,
The natural purity of present conceptual thoughts, transcendent of renunciation,
Poppy [green], holding a perfume-filled conch.

I bow down to green Nartī, [female bodhisattva] whose offerings [delight]
The tongues of [all] Those Gone to Bliss, past, present and future,
The natural purity of taste, transcendent of renunciation,
Marine [green], holding a [deliciously] nutritious food-offering.

I bow down to [Trailokya-]Vijaya, [male gatekeeper] whose wrathful presence
Guards against obstacles at the eastern gate,
The natural purity of eternalist views, transcendent of renunciation,
White, holding a cudgel and a bell.

I bow down to Yamāntaka, [male gatekeeper] whose wrathful presence
Guards against obstacles at the southern gate,
The natural purity of nihilistic views, transcendent of renunciation,
Yellow, holding a skull-club and a bell.

I bow down to Hayagrīvarāja, [male gatekeeper] whose wrathful presence
Guards against obstacles at the western gate,
The natural purity of egotistical views, transcendent of renunciation,
Red, holding an iron chain and a bell.

I bow down to Amṛtakuṇḍalin, [male gatekeeper] whose wrathful presence
Guards against obstacles at the northern gate,

The natural purity of substantialist views,[7] transcendent of renunciation,
Green, holding a crossed-vajra and a bell.

I bow down to Vajrāṅkuśā, [female gatekeeper] whose immeasurable compassion
Guides the six classes [of beings] away from [their mundane] realms,
White, holding an iron hook that attracts,
She embraces her wrathful consort in blissful union.

I bow down to Vajrapāśā, [female gatekeeper] whose immeasurable loving kindness
Acts [ceaselessly] on behalf of beings,
Yellow, holding a noose that lassoes,
She embraces her wrathful consort in blissful union.

I bow down to Vajrasphoṭā, [female gatekeeper] whose immeasurable sympathetic joy
Embraces [each and every] living being,
Red, holding an iron chain that binds,
She embraces her wrathful consort in blissful union.

I bow down to Vajraghaṇṭā, [female gatekeeper] whose immeasurable equanimity
Transcends discrimination between living beings,
Green, holding a bell that summons,
She embraces her wrathful consort in blissful union.

I bow down to Indraśakra, [sage] whose emanational buddha form
Acts [ceaselessly] on behalf of beings,
The natural purity of pride, and guide of the god realms,
White and holding a lute.

I bow down to Vemacitra, [sage] whose emanational buddha form
Acts [ceaselessly] on behalf of beings,
The natural purity of envy, and guide of the antigod realms,
Green, holding armour and a weapon.

I bow down to Śākyamuni, [sage] whose emanational buddha form
Acts [ceaselessly] on behalf of beings,
The natural purity of attachment, and guide of the human realms,
Yellow, holding a begging bowl and staff.

I bow down to Sthirasiṃha, [sage] whose emanational buddha form
Acts [ceaselessly] on behalf of beings,
The natural purity of delusion, and guide of the animal realms,
Blue, and holding a book.

I bow down to the transcendent Jvālamukha, [sage] whose emanational buddha form
Acts [ceaselessly] on behalf of beings,
The natural purity of miserliness, and guide of the anguished-spirit realms,
Red, and holding a bejewelled casket.

I bow down to Dharmarāja, [sage] whose emanational buddha form
Acts [ceaselessly] on behalf of beings,
The natural purity of aversion, and guide of the hell realms,
Black, and holding a warming flame and cooling water.

I bow down to Mahottara Heruka, who has three faces,
Dark brown, white and red; and six arms:
A vajra, khaṭvāṅga, and small drum in his right hands,
And a bell, blood-filled skull, and noose of entrails in his left.

I bow down to Buddha Heruka, who has three faces,
Dark brown, white and red; and six arms:
A wheel, axe, and sword in his right hands,
And a bell, ploughshare, and blood-filled skull in his left.

I bow down to Vajra Heruka, who has three faces,
Dark blue, white and red; and six arms:
A vajra, blood-filled skull, and axe in his right hands,
And a bell, blood-filled skull, and ploughshare in his left.

I bow down to Ratna Heruka, who has three faces,
Dark yellow, white and red; and six arms:
A jewel, khaṭvāṅga, and mace in his right hands,
And a bell, blood-filled skull, and trident in his left.

I bow down to Padma Heruka, who has three faces,
Dark red, white and blue; and six arms:
A lotus, khaṭvāṅga, and cudgel in his right hands,
And a bell, blood-filled skull, and small drum in his left.

I bow down to Karma Heruka, who has three faces,
Dark green, white and red; and six arms:
A sword, khaṭvāṅga, and cudgel in his right hands,
And a bell, blood-filled skull, and ploughshare in his left.

I bow down to Krodheśvarī, wrathful Queen of [Reality's] Expanse,
Dark blue, holding a vajra,
Offering a blood-filled skull to her consort's mouth,
She joyously embraces him, in supreme bliss.

I bow down to Buddhakrodheśvarī, the Buddha Queen of [Reality's] Expanse,
Red-brown, holding a wheel,
Offering a blood-filled skull to her consort's mouth,
She joyously embraces him, in supreme bliss.

I bow down to Vajrakrodheśvarī, Vajra Queen of [Reality's] Expanse,
Pale blue, holding a vajra,
Offering a blood-filled skull to her consort's mouth,
She joyously embraces him, in supreme bliss.

I bow down to Ratnakrodheśvarī, Ratna Queen of [Reality's] Expanse,
Pale yellow, holding a jewel,
Offering a blood-filled skull to her consort's mouth,
She joyously embraces him, in supreme bliss.

I bow down to Padmakrodheśvarī, Padma Queen of [Reality's] Expanse,
Pale red, holding a lotus,
Offering a blood-filled skull to her consort's mouth,
She joyously embraces him, in supreme bliss.

I bow down to Karmakrodheśvarī, Karma Queen of [Reality's] Expanse,
Pale green, holding a crossed-vajra,
Offering a blood-filled skull to her consort's mouth,
She joyously embraces him, in supreme bliss.

I bow down to Gaurī of the eastern direction,
Acting on behalf of living beings as one of the Mātaraḥ,
Wrathful, white, and aloof on her throne of human corpses,
Brandishing a human corpse as a cudgel
To destroy the conceptual landscape of cyclic existence.

I bow down to Caurī of the southern direction,
Acting on behalf of living beings as one of the Mātaraḥ,
Wrathful, yellow, and aloof on her throne of human corpses,
Shooting an arrow from a bow
To bind indivisibly skilful means and discriminative awareness.

I bow down to Pramohā of the western direction,
Acting on behalf of living beings as one of the Mātaraḥ,
Wrathful, red, and aloof on her throne of human corpses,
Holding a crocodile victory-banner
To resist [the seductions of] cyclic existence.

I bow down to Vetālī of the northern direction,
Acting on behalf of living beings as one of the Mātaraḥ,
Wrathful, black,[8] and aloof on her throne of human corpses,
Holding a vajra and a blood-filled skull
[To sustain recognition of] the unchanging reality.

I bow down to Pukkasī of the south-eastern direction,
Acting on behalf of living beings as one of the Mātaraḥ,

Wrathful, red-yellow, and aloof on her throne of human corpses,
[Clutching and] devouring entrails
To draw [sentient beings] free from the dissonant realms.

I bow down to Ghasmarī of the south-western direction,
Acting on behalf of living beings as one of the Mātaraḥ,
Wrathful, green-black, and aloof on her throne of human corpses,
Drinking blood from a skull
To consume [the turning circle of] cyclic existence.

I bow down to Caṇḍālī of the north-western direction,
Acting on behalf of living beings as one of the Mātaraḥ,
Wrathful, pale yellow, and aloof on her throne of human corpses,
Tearing apart the head and body of a bloated corpse
To sever erroneous thoughts [at their roots].

I bow down to Śmaśānī of the north-eastern direction,
Acting on behalf of living beings as one of the Mātaraḥ,
Wrathful, blue-black, and aloof on her throne of human corpses,
Tearing apart [the head from] a human corpse
To sever the buttresses of cyclic existence.

I bow down to brown-black, lion-headed Siṃhamukhī,
Acting on behalf of living beings in the form of a Piśācī,
Carrying a corpse in her mouth, and shaking her mane
To stir cyclic existence to its depths.

I bow down to red, tiger-headed Vyāghrīmukhī,
Acting on behalf of living beings in the form of a Piśācī,
With her two arms crossed, and staring with bulging eyes
To overwhelm attachment to cyclic existence.

I bow down to black, fox-headed Śṛgālamukhī,
Acting on behalf of living beings in the form of a Piśācī,
Brandishing a razor, and devouring lungs and a heart
To purify dissonant mental states in their basic nature.

I bow down to blue-black, wolf-headed Śvānamukhī,
Acting on behalf of living beings in the form of a Piśācī,
Tearing apart a corpse, and staring with bulging eyes
To stir the pit of cyclic existence.

I bow down to white-yellow, vulture-headed Gṛdhramukhī,
Acting on behalf of living beings in the form of a Piśācī,
Clawing a bloated corpse, and extracting the entrails
To sever the three poisons from their roots.

I bow down to red-black, kite-headed Kaṅkamukhī,
Acting on behalf of living beings in the form of a Piśācī,
Carrying a bloated corpse, draped over her shoulder
To extract [beings] from the pit of cyclic existence.

I bow down to black, crow-headed Kākamukhī,
Acting on behalf of living beings in the form of a Piśācī,
Brandishing a sword, and drinking blood from a skull
To consume and liberate dissonant mental states.

I bow down to blue-black, owl-headed Ulūkamukhī,
Acting on behalf of living beings in the form of a Piśācī,
Holding an iron hook,[9] and carrying a blood-filled skull
To draw [beings] free from the false mentality of cyclic existence.

I bow down to horse-headed Aṅkuśā at the eastern gate,
Acting on behalf of living beings in the form of a female gatekeeper,
Horse-headed, white, and holding an iron hook,
The force of her immeasurable compassion
Guiding [those trapped in] cyclic existence away from the lower realms.

I bow down to sow-headed Pāśā at the southern gate,
Acting on behalf of living beings in the form of a female gatekeeper,
Sow-headed, yellow, and holding a noose,
The force of her immeasurable loving kindness
Constricting the false mentality [of beings].

I bow down to lion-headed Sphoṭā at the western gate,
Acting on behalf of living beings in the form of a female gatekeeper,
Lion-headed, red, and holding an iron chain,
The force of her immeasurable sympathetic joy
Shackling the dissonant mental states generated by ignorance.[10]

I bow down to snake-headed Gaṇṭhā at the northern gate,
Acting on behalf of living beings in the form of a female gatekeeper,
Snake-headed, green, and holding a bell,
The force of her immeasurable equanimity
Subduing the cognitive resonances of the five poisons.[11]

I bow down to the Projectress who Casts a Noose,[12]
Manifestation of the natural purity of reality,
Clothed in flayed hides, she unites the three levels of existence
With the [pure buddha] fields, however these may manifest,
And casts her noose of solar rays,
Projecting [beings of] the trichiliocosm into higher rebirths.

I bow down to the Projectress who Casts a Pike,[13]
[Holding] a blood-filled skull, and casting a pike,
She purifies the five dissonant mental states
To dispel permanently the diseases of conceptual thought,
The force of her compassion, rich in skilful means,
Projecting human beings into higher rebirths.

I bow down to the Projectress who Rings a Bell,[14]
Holding to her heart a blood-filled skull,
She subjugates the entire trichiliocosm
To secure ignorant sentient beings in [reality's] expanse,
The resonance of her charisma
Projecting [beings of] the chiliocosm into higher rebirths.

I bow down to the Projectress who Carries a Garuḍa,[15]
Her body an exquisite white-yellow,
[Signifying] her proficiency in the rites of pacification and enrichment.

Holding to her heart a blood-filled skull
To overpower the five sensory desires,
She carries a vajra and a large garuḍa,
Projecting the gods into higher rebirths.

I bow down to the Projectress who Casts a Shooting Star,[16]
Her awesome body an exquisite blue-black,
[Holding] a vajra and casting a shooting star
To avert the intensity of 'The Great Battle',[17]
She drinks blood from a skull,
Projecting the antigods into higher rebirths.

I bow down to the Projectress who Holds a Thunderbolt-garland,[18]
Her body part red and part black,
[Signifying proficiency in the rites of] subjugation and wrath,
Her facial expression fixed in domination.
To purify and ease outer and inner obscurations,
[She wields] a vajra and thunderbolt-garland,
Projecting anguished spirits into higher rebirths.

I bow down to the Projectress who Wields an Eagle-feathered Banner,[19]
Her body part white and part black,
[Signifying] her proficiency in the rites of pacification and wrath,
Drinking blood from a skull
To dissolve delusion [into emptiness],
[She holds] a vajra and wields an eagle-feathered banner,
Projecting animals into higher rebirths.

I bow down to the Projectress who Holds a Sword,[20]
Her body part yellow and part black,
[Signifying] her proficiency in the rites of enrichment and wrath,
Drinking blood from a skull
To dissolve the hells into emptiness,
[She holds] a vajra and a sword,
Projecting the hell-beings into higher rebirths.

I bow down to yak-headed Manurākṣasī,
The brownish white yoginī, holding a vajra and skull.

I bow down to snake-headed Brahmāṇī,
The yellowish white yoginī, holding a vajra and lotus.

I bow down to leopard-headed Raudrī,
The greenish white yoginī, holding a vajra and trident.

I bow down to weasel-headed Vaiṣṇāvī,
The bluish white yoginī, holding a vajra and wheel.

I bow down to brown bear-headed Kaumārī,
The reddish white yoginī, holding a vajra and pike.

I bow down to black bear-headed Indrāṇī,
The white yoginī, holding a vajra and noose of entrails.

I bow down to bat-headed Vajrā,[21]
The yellow yoginī, holding a jewel and razor.

I bow down to crocodile-headed Śāntī,
The reddish yellow yoginī, holding a jewel and vase.

I bow down to scorpion-headed Amṛtā,
The reddish yellow yoginī, holding a jewel and lotus.

I bow down to hawk-headed Saumī,
The whitish yellow yoginī, holding a jewel and vajra.

I bow down to fox-headed Daṇḍī,
The greenish yellow yoginī, holding a jewel and cudgel.

I bow down to tiger-headed Rākṣasī,
The blackish yellow yoginī, holding a jewel and blood-filled skull.

I bow down to vulture-headed Bhakṣasī,
The greenish red yoginī, holding a lotus and club.

I bow down to horse-headed Ratī,
The red yoginī, holding a lotus and human torso.

I bow down to garuḍa-headed Rudhiramadī,
The pale red yoginī, holding a lotus and cudgel.

I bow down to dog-headed Ekacāriṇī,
The red yoginī, holding a lotus and vajra.

I bow down to hoopoe-headed Manohārikā,
The red yoginī, holding a lotus and a bow and arrow.

I bow down to deer-headed Siddhikarī,
The greenish red yoginī, holding a lotus and vase.

I bow down to wolf-headed Vāyudevī,
The bluish green yoginī, holding a crossed-vajra and ensign.

I bow down to ibex-headed Agnāyī,
The reddish green yoginī, holding a crossed-vajra and firebrand.

I bow down to sow-headed Varāhī,
The blackish green yoginī, holding a crossed-vajra and a noose of fangs.

I bow down to crow-headed Cāmuṇḍī,
The reddish green yoginī, holding a crossed-vajra and an infant corpse.

I bow down to elephant-headed Bhujanā,
The blackish green yoginī, holding a crossed-vajra and a bloated corpse.

I bow down to snake-headed Varuṇānī,
The [bluish] green[22] yoginī, holding a crossed-vajra and a noose of snakes.

I bow down to cuckoo-headed Vajrā [Mahākālī],
The white gatekeeper, holding a vajra and iron hook.

I bow down to goat-headed Vajrā [Mahāchāgalā],
The yellow gatekeeper, holding a jewel and a noose.

I bow down to lion-headed Vajrā [Mahākumbhakarṇī],
The red gatekeeper, holding a lotus and an iron chain.

I bow down to snake-headed Vajrā [Lambodarā],
The blackish green gatekeeper, holding a crossed-vajra and a bell.

While reciting this prayer, all the male and female yogins present should remove their outer garments and, as they make [successive] full-length prostrations, they should respectfully pay homage [to the deities]. While respectfully narrating this eulogy in a melodious voice and enacting the hundredfold homage, one should mentally admit and feel remorse for all one's negativities and obscurations, which have been, are being and will be accumulated.

This *Natural Liberation of Negativity and Obscuration* is an extraordinary [method for] purifying obscurations, by enacting in full the one hundred and ten homages[23] to the Peaceful and Wrathful Deities. Whatever other [confessional] practices one may [generally] undertake, such as the *Reparation and Confession of the Hells*,[24] the merits accrued by one who practises in this manner are immeasurable. Therefore, one should persevere diligently with the enactment of this *Hundredfold Homage*.

May [the influence of this] *Natural Liberation of Negativity and Obscuration through [Enactment of] the Hundredfold Homage to the Hundred Sacred Enlightened Families of the Peaceful and Wrathful Deities* not be exhausted until cyclic existence has been emptied.

This most profound teaching is an ancillary chapter of the *Liberation by Hearing in the Intermediate States*, a supporting text to the *Reparation and Confession of the Hells*, and a synopsis of the three editions [long, medium and short] of the *Peaceful and Wrathful Deities: The Ritual Purification [entitled Natural Liberation of Feelings]*. It should be propagated everywhere and enacted energetically at all times without interruption.

7

Natural Liberation through Acts of Confession

CONTEXT

In addition to the experiential cultivation of the nature of the deity, as outlined in the previous two chapters, the act of confession plays an important role in purifying the negativity and obscuration that has, according to the Buddhist perspective, clouded our minds over a beginningless cycle of lifetimes.

In Buddhist practice this process of purification, which includes the reparation of commitments and vows, is enhanced by the engagement of the 'four antidotal powers'. In the context of this cycle of teachings the four powers are:

1. The power of reliance, which here refers to the visualisation of the hundred Peaceful and Wrathful Deities.
2. The power of the actual antidote, which here refers to the recitation of the *Natural Liberation through Acts of Confession*, together with the practice of the Hundred-syllable Mantra of Vajrasattva.
3. The power of remorse, which is the genuinely remorseful recollection of all negative acts previously committed.
4. The power of resolve, which is the pledge never to engage wilfully in such negative actions again.

Before beginning the confessional practice, it is recommended that the practitioner should make actual or mentally emanated offerings before his or her altar. Then, each afternoon, while sitting on the floor in front of the altar, the practitioner should engage in this practice, with the palms of the hands placed together, chanting the words lucidly and with conviction. For as long as practitioners have not gained full accomplishment in the practices of this cycle of teachings, inappropriate negative actions of body, speech and mind should be continuously confessed.

Herein is contained the *Natural Liberation through Acts of Confession, in the Presence of the Peaceful and Wrathful Deities*,[1] an extract from the *Peaceful and Wrathful Deities: A Profound Sacred Teaching, [entitled] Natural Liberation through [Recognition of] Enlightened Intention*.[2]

I respectfully bow down to Samantabhadra, Mahottara,
And the assembly of Peaceful and Wrathful Deities!
May the degenerations [of our commitments] be purified!

In order that the degenerations [of our commitments] may be naturally purified, without being renounced, the [following] *Natural Liberation through Acts of Confession, in the Presence of the Peaceful and Wrathful Deities*, which is an extract from the *Peaceful and Wrathful Deities: Natural Liberation through [Recognition of] Enlightened Intention*, is [now] presented. Be persevering in this regard, O Children of Posterity! SAMAYA!

This [confessional practice] is presented in six parts, namely: confession [in the presence] of the inexpressible truth, confession in the presence of the Peaceful Deities, confession in the presence of the Wrathful Deities, the plaintive confession of rampant egohood, confession in the presence of the view, and confession [in the presence] of all Those Gone to Bliss.

PRELIMINARIES

The invitation and request for [the confessional field] to be present

OṂ O, supreme buddha-body of pristine cognition,
Even though, like the [clarity of the] waxing moon,
You are free from conceptual elaboration in this natural maṇḍala,
Your compassion [radiates to all] without bias, like the rays of the sun.
Please be present here, and attend to us!

The homage to the three buddha-bodies, which compose the Peaceful and Wrathful Deities

I bow down to the three buddha-bodies of the Peaceful and Wrathful Deities:
To the Buddha-body of Reality, the inexpressible and unwavering discriminative awareness,
To the supremely blissful Buddha-body of Perfect Resource, the lords of the five enlightened families,
And to the Buddha-body of Emanation: extensive, compassionate and skilful.

The threefold offering of [outer] phenomena, [inner] cloud-masses, and secret [substances]

By arraying the vast and pure expanse of space,
With [billowing] clouds of unsurpassed Samantabhadra-like offerings,
Whether they be actually gathered together or imagined,
We dedicate [to you] oceans of outer, inner and secret offerings.[3]

The secret offering of supreme bliss

May [the deities] be delighted by the non-dual 'generative essence'[4]
Whose [blissful] single savour indicates a [pristine] state,
Where all the infinite maṇḍalas of the conquerors, without exception,
Are established, beyond conjunction or disjunction,
In the secret womb of Samantabhadrī.

The affirmation of vows within the modality of the view

Since the nature of mind is the great expanse of reality,
And all things are pure atemporal inner radiance,
This yoga is itself the inexpressible and inconceivable expanse.
Everlastingly we bow down to the mind of enlightenment,
Which is [the realisation of] sameness!

The call to the assembly of Peaceful and Wrathful Deities for attention

ĀḤ In the atemporal omnipresence of the Great Perfection, which is Samantabhadra,
Is [displayed] the maṇḍala of the outer, inner, and secret arrays.
Here, the expanse of male and female deities is the [natural] purity of mundane existence,
And the spontaneously perfect male and female consorts are the [natural purity] of past and future [events].
All of these are centred in the 'lotus of vast space', which is that of [Samantabhadrī],
She who embodies the most secret and most joyous of supreme forms.
Within this [space, the maṇḍala] radiates as a supreme non-dual seminal point,
And within this secret maṇḍala, where there is no conjunction or disjunction,
Is [arrayed] the buddha-body of the uncontrived nucleus of enlightenment, free from conceptual elaboration,

Where the immutable deities of supreme bliss manifest in myriad forms.
O, you manifold assembly of [peaceful] emanations, present within the indivisible expanse,
Including the male and female [buddhas] of the five enlightened families, who are the Great Embodiment,
The [sixteen] male and female bodhisattvas, and the six sages who instruct living beings,
Along with the eight emanational gatekeepers, male and female;
O, you manifold [wrathful] assembly of the emanational deities of pristine cognition,
[Including] the ten male and female wrathful conquerors,
Great and glorious [principals] of the five enlightened families,
Who preside over the indestructible matrix of female [wrathful] deities,
The [sixteen active] seals [who represent the natural transformation]
Of the classes of consciousness and their objects,
And the four gatekeepers;
O, you twenty-eight outer and inner ḍākinīs and yoginīs,
Who, with motherly loving kindness and sisterly affection,
Evaluate our good and bad [conduct],
And inspect our commitments;
And you oath-bound [protectors] of indestructible reality, who have been subjugated –
Please, [all of you], attend to us!

CONFESSION [IN THE PRESENCE] OF THE INEXPRESSIBLE TRUTH

HŪṂ We [aspiring] awareness holders, who are heirs to the compassionate lineage,
Strive to cultivate the mind of enlightenment for the sake of all living beings.
In order that the unsurpassed state may be attained,
We have repeatedly received and earnestly undertaken
[Both] the individual disciplines of the ocean-like teachings,[5]

And the supreme vows concordant with buddha-body, speech and mind, including:

The [appropriate] commitments of [the Vehicle of] Indestructible Reality,

Which are dangerous to transgress, and must be constantly maintained,

Together with all the general and particular higher commitments.

Yet, even though we strive neither to abandon nor to transgress [these commitments],

And we strive neither to deviate from the truth nor to allow our minds to fluctuate,

Since we idly think that we have the momentary luxury to sit back in relaxation,

We have not reached fulfilment and our mental energy has been faltering.

We have lacked alertness, and have been overpowered by carelessness.

If, therefore, under the sway of ignorance, consciously or unconsciously,

Our meditation has lacked perseverance,

And we have been distracted in our ritual service and means for attainment,

We will have contradicted the injunctions of the Teacher and contradicted our vows.

Further, it says in the [Buddha's] scriptures:

'A yogin should not associate, even for a moment, with one whose commitments have degenerated.'

Not being [continuously] cognisant of this, we have transgressed the secret approach [of the tantras],

And [consistently] we have had difficulty discriminating [between worthy and unworthy associates].

Lacking supernormal prescience, we have failed to recognise those that are unworthy.

Thus, now, with heartfelt remorse, we confess all our individual faults,

Which have already become the misfortunes of this life and will become the obscurations of future lives.

Whatever faults of degeneration and obscuration have tainted us,

Whether they be our own actual degenerations or those acquired through association with others by:
Mixing in assemblies with those whose [commitments] have degenerated,
Repairing [the commitments of] those who have degenerated,
Giving the [sacred] teachings to those who are degenerate and unworthy,
Or by committing the degenerate fault of not avoiding [the influence of] those who have degenerated, and so forth,
Do not permit the retribution of the sublime [protectors] to fall upon us!
Attend to us with the compassion of your loving kindness!
And make us secure, so that we never stray from the non-dual expanse.
Having inspired us to abide within the modality of non-referential equanimity,
Please grant us the purity of the non-dual truth!

In ultimate truth, inexpressible and without conceptual elaboration,
There is no objective referent to any conceptual thought whatsoever.
But if, by the power of illusion-like relative appearances, we should err,
[We acknowledge this and seek your forgiveness.]
We confess that we have deviated from the buddha-mind!
If we have committed transgressions, please forgive our deviations.

Throughout beginningless time and throughout the limits of cyclic existence,
We have roamed within these turning worlds driven on by the forces of [ripening] past actions –
[Endlessly] drinking the poisons of dissonant states and false perspectives on reality.
May The One Gone to Bliss, king among compassionate physicians,
Grant the medicine of liberation, the nectar of the genuine teachings,

To those [of us] who are severely afflicted by the [primal] disease, which is suffering!
May all the diseases caused by bewildering dissonant states be pacified!
May we be sustained in the nucleus of unsurpassed enlightenment!
We take refuge in you, O compassionate lord of loving kindness!
We confess that we have contradicted the buddha-mind!

If we have boasted of our high view and yet not understood the meaning of actual reality,
If we have not clearly visualised the meditational deity, owing to our meditations being excessively brief,
Or if we have made an inadequate number of recitations or spoken these defectively,
However we have deviated from the buddha-mind of the oceans of conquerors,
We confess our transgressions in the presence of the Peaceful and Wrathful Conquerors.
We make confession to you, O Compassionate Ones!
We make confession in the presence of the entire assembly of the deities of pristine cognition!

If we have failed to please our spiritual teacher, on account of the feebleness of our effort,
If we have failed to be well regarded by our spiritual brothers and sisters, on account of the feebleness of our devotion,
If we have divulged the oral teachings to another, on account of our flirtatious intentions,
Indeed, whatever extravagances, omissions, deviations or mistakes we have made,
With respect to the fundamental commitments of buddha-body, speech and mind,
Whilst swayed by the influence of ignorance, either consciously or unconsciously,
We confess all such transgressions in the presence of the Peaceful and Wrathful Conquerors.
We make confession to you, O Compassionate Ones!

We make confession to the oceanic assembly of the conquerors!
May all [the degenerations] that we now confess be cleansed and purified!
Please grant us the purity of the non-dual truth!
SAMAYA!

CONFESSION IN THE PRESENCE OF THE PEACEFUL DEITIES, THE EMBODIMENT OF [THE QUIESCENT NATURE OF] REALITY

The initial confession is that to Samantabhadra and Samantabhadrī, the father and mother consorts

HŪṂ We pray to you, father and mother, listen and attend to us!
Mind and phenomena are atemporally manifest buddhas,
But even though this [reality] is the expression of your enlightened intention,
O Samantabhadra and Samantabhadrī, father and mother, in union,
Due to our ignorance, we have not understood this to be so.
For whatever ways we have contradicted the buddha-mind
Of you, Samantabhadra and Samantabhadrī, father and mother,
We seek your forgiveness, O greatly compassionate ones!

Second is the confession to the five male buddhas of the enlightened families of the conquerors

We pray to you, the five [male buddhas] of the enlightened families of the conquerors, listen and attend to us!
The five psycho-physical aggregates are atemporally manifest buddhas,
But even though this [reality] is the expression of your enlightened intention,
O five [male buddhas] of the enlightened families of the conquerors,

Due to our ignorance, we have not understood this to be so.
For whatever ways we have contradicted the buddha-mind
Of the five [male buddhas of the] enlightened families of the conquerors,
We seek your forgiveness, O greatly compassionate ones!

Third is the confession to the five female buddhas of the enlightened families

We pray to you, the five female buddhas of the enlightened families, listen and attend to us!
The five elements are atemporally manifest buddhas,
But even though this [reality] is the expression of your enlightened intention,
O, five female buddhas of the enlightened families,
Due to our ignorance, we have not understood this to be so.
For whatever ways we have contradicted the buddha-mind
Of the five female buddhas of the enlightened families,
We seek your forgiveness, O greatly compassionate ones!

Fourth is the confession to the eight male bodhisattvas of the retinue

We pray to you, the eight male bodhisattvas, listen and attend to us!
The eight classes of consciousness are atemporally manifest buddhas,
But even though this [reality] is the expression of your enlightened intention,
O, eight male bodhisattvas, due to our ignorance, we have not understood this to be so.
For whatever ways we have contradicted the buddha-mind of the eight male bodhisattvas,
We seek your forgiveness, O greatly compassionate ones!

Fifth is the confession to the eight female bodhisattvas

We pray to you, the eight female bodhisattvas, listen and attend to us!
The eight objects of consciousness are atemporally manifest buddhas,

But even though this [reality] is the expression of your enlightened intention,
O, eight female bodhisattvas, due to our ignorance, we have not understood this to be so.
For whatever ways we have contradicted the buddha-mind of the eight female bodhisattvas,
We seek your forgiveness, O greatly compassionate ones!

Sixth is the confession to the six sages

We pray to you, the six sages, listen and attend to us!
The six dissonant mental states are atemporally manifest buddhas,
But even though this [reality] is the expression of your enlightened intention,
O, six sages, due to our ignorance, we have not understood this to be so.
For whatever ways we have contradicted the buddha-mind of the six sages,
We seek your forgiveness, O greatly compassionate ones!

Seventh is the confession to the four male gatekeepers

We pray to you, the four male gatekeepers, listen and attend to us!
The four immeasurable [aspirations] are atemporally manifest buddhas,
But even though this [reality] is the expression of your enlightened intention,
O, four male gatekeepers, due to our ignorance, we have not understood this to be so.
For whatever ways we have contradicted the buddha-mind of the four male gatekeepers,
We seek your forgiveness, O greatly compassionate ones!

Eighth is the confession to the four female gatekeepers

We pray to you, the four female gatekeepers, listen and attend to us!
The four extremes of eternalism and nihilism are atemporally manifest buddhas,

But even though this [reality] is the expression of your enlightened intention,
O, four female gatekeepers, due to our ignorance, we have not understood this to be so.
For whatever ways we have contradicted the buddha-mind of the four female gatekeepers,
We seek your forgiveness, O greatly compassionate ones!

Then the confession should be made to the [entire array of the] peaceful deities in the following way:

OṂ Since our minds are not endowed with pristine cognition, which is intrinsic awareness,
We have not correctly integrated the psycho-physical aggregates, the sensory spectra, and their activity fields,
Within the maṇḍala of the peaceful deities.
We seek the forgiveness of each of you, the forty-two peaceful deities!

Since our minds are not endowed with pristine cognition, which is intrinsic awareness,
We have not correctly integrated the five psycho-physical aggregates with the five [male buddhas] of the enlightened families,
And further still, our own minds, swayed by ignorance, have continued to be afflicted by egotism.
We seek the forgiveness of you, the assembly of Samantabhadra!

Since our minds are not endowed with pristine cognition, which is intrinsic awareness,
We have not correctly integrated the five elements with the five female buddhas,
And further still, our own minds, swayed by ignorance, have continued to be afflicted by egotism.
We seek the forgiveness of you, the assembly of Samantabhadrī!

Since our minds are not endowed with pristine cognition, which is intrinsic awareness,
We have not correctly integrated the four classes of

consciousness and four sense organs with the [eight] male bodhisattvas,
And further still, our own minds, swayed by ignorance, have continued to be afflicted by egotism.
We seek the forgiveness of you, the assembly of male bodhisattvas!

Since our minds are not endowed with pristine cognition, which is intrinsic awareness,
We have not correctly integrated the four objects of consciousness and four times with the [eight] female bodhisattvas,
And further still, our own minds, swayed by ignorance, have continued to be afflicted by egotism.
We seek the forgiveness of you, the assembly of female bodhisattvas!

Since our minds are not endowed with pristine cognition, which is intrinsic awareness,
We have not correctly integrated the six dissonant mental states with the [six] sages,
And further still, our own minds, swayed by ignorance, have continued to be afflicted by egotism.
We seek the forgiveness of you, the emanational buddha-bodies, the six sages!

Since our minds are not endowed with pristine cognition, which is intrinsic awareness,
We have not correctly integrated the four immeasurable [aspirations] with the [four] male gatekeepers,
And further still, our own minds, swayed by ignorance, have continued to be afflicted by egotism.
We seek the forgiveness of you, the wrathful male gatekeepers!

Since our minds are not endowed with pristine cognition, which is intrinsic awareness,
We have not correctly integrated the eternalist and nihilist [perspectives on] awareness with the [four] female gatekeepers,
And further still, our own minds, swayed by ignorance, have continued to be afflicted by egotism.
We seek the forgiveness of you, the wrathful female gatekeepers!

Since our minds are not endowed with pristine cognition, which is intrinsic awareness,
We have not correctly integrated mind and phenomena with Samantabhadra and Samantabhadrī, the father and mother,
And further still, our own minds, swayed by ignorance, have continued to be afflicted by egotism.
We seek the forgiveness of you, Samantabhadra and Samantabhadrī!

Since our minds are not endowed with pristine cognition, which is intrinsic awareness,
We have been afflicted by bewildering ignorance,
And have been alienated from the meditational deities
By the force of dissonant mental states and past [negative] actions.
Swayed by self-deception, we have disappointed our teachers,
Stirred by strong pride, we have agitated our spiritual brothers and sisters,
Distracted by vanity,[6] we have divulged the secret mantras,
Gripped by miserliness, we have been untimely in the dedication of offerings,
Entrapped by base friendships, we have violated the secret [precepts] of the rituals,
Weakened by feeble yogic discipline, we have failed to eradicate obstructing forces.
Thus, [our commitments] have degenerated due to either excessive or deficient determination and strength.

Throughout our lives, from beginningless time until the present [life],
In which we have assumed this body,
However much negativity and non-virtuous past actions we have accrued,
We seek your forgiveness for all these transgressions.

O you whose cognisance and knowledge spans [the three] times,
Since you are sublime beings, embrace us!
Since we are sentient beings, we are flawed and bewildered,

And, since [this separation] is an illusion, may our confession be granted!
Since you are accomplished in skilful means, bestow your purity upon us!

Then a remorseful confession should be made to the peaceful deities as follows:

OṂ Most precious Samantabhadra [in union], supreme buddha-mind,
Even though you are our father and hold mastery over the three world-systems,
And even though you are our mother and assimilate [all things] in the ultimate expanse,
By conceiving of our bodies [in a mundane way], we have dishonoured the illusory body.
Thus our commitments have degenerated and we have grown truly remorseful.
We seek your forgiveness, O Samantabhadra and Samantabhadrī, mother and father!

Most precious buddhas of the five enlightened families, [manifestations of] supreme buddha-mind,
Even though you are our fathers and hold mastery over the three world-systems,
And even though you are our mothers and assimilate [all things] in the ultimate expanse,
By conceiving of our bodies [in a mundane way], we have dishonoured the illusory body.
Thus our commitments have degenerated and we have grown truly remorseful.
We seek your forgiveness, O father and mother buddhas of the five enlightened families!

Most precious male and female bodhisattvas, [manifestations of] supreme buddha-mind,
Even though you are our fathers and hold mastery over the three world-systems,
And even though you are our mothers and assimilate [all things] in the ultimate expanse,

By conceiving of our bodies [in a mundane way], we have dishonoured the illusory body.
Thus our commitments have degenerated and we have grown truly remorseful.
We seek your forgiveness, O male and female bodhisattvas!

Most precious six sages, buddha-bodies of emanation, [and manifestations of] supreme buddha-mind,
Even though you hold mastery over all the sentient beings throughout the three world-systems,
And even though you emancipate their respective worlds into the ultimate expanse,
By conceiving of our bodies [in a mundane way], we have dishonoured the illusory body.
Thus our commitments have degenerated and we have grown truly remorseful.
We seek your forgiveness, O six sages, emanational buddha-bodies!

Most precious male and female gatekeepers, [manifestations of] supreme buddha-mind,
Even though you are our fathers and hold mastery over the three world-systems,
And even though you are our mothers and assimilate [all things] in the ultimate expanse,
By conceiving of our bodies [in a mundane way], we have dishonoured the illusory body.
Thus our commitments have degenerated and we have grown truly remorseful.
We seek your forgiveness, O male and female gatekeepers!

CONFESSION IN THE PRESENCE OF THE WRATHFUL DEITIES

The confession of faults in achieving meditative stability in reality is as follows:

OṂ As we have failed to liberate the egotism of the subject–object dichotomy,

Within the original maṇḍala of natural sameness,
We still have not realised the non-dual truth of the abiding nature.
O non-dual Buddha-body of Reality, we seek forgiveness![7]

The confession of faults in achieving the meditative stability which illuminates all that appears is as follows:

You open the portals which unimpededly illuminate the ultimate truth,
And [naturally] arise as the Buddha-body [of Perfect Resource], within an expanse of radiantly clear moonlight,
But we have let the light [emanating from] the seminal points of your 'generative essence' be diffused.
O Buddha-body [of Perfect Resource], which illuminates all that appears, we seek forgiveness![8]

The confession [of faults in achieving] the meditative stability of the causal basis [entailing the visualisation of] the tiered celestial palace and the seats [of the wrathful deities] is as follows:

From the expanse of space, which is the unborn ultimate truth,
There appears the buddha-body, the medium through which the fruitional attributes [of buddhahood] emerge.
Yet we have not even clearly visualised this powerful celestial palace,
The abode in which the supreme power [of buddha-body] is gradually generated.
In the presence of the blazing celestial palace, we seek forgiveness!

Confession to the five male herukas, the executors of buddha-body

Though you steadfastly [appear] as buddha-bodies, sealed within the nature of supreme bliss,
Holding in your hands the respective implements, emblematic of the six pristine cognitions,

We have not [even] achieved the experience of such [vividly] clear visualisation.
O five blood-drinking herukas, we seek forgiveness!

Confession to their consorts, the five krodheśvarī

O supreme mother-consorts, conjoined indivisibly with the [male] buddha-bodies,
We have let the light of your non-dual 'generative essence' be diffused,
Into the 'spacious expanse', which is the lotus seed of desire.
O five krodheśvarī deities, we seek forgiveness!

Confession to the eight mātaraḥ

O wrathful female deities of pristine cognition, born of buddha-mind,
[The natural transformation] of the eight classes of consciousness,
O Gaurī and accompanying [Mātaraḥ], ḍākinīs of pristine cognition,
For whatever ways we have contradicted your buddha-mind,
O eight mātaraḥ [who embody] the classes [of consciousness], we seek forgiveness!

Confession to the eight piśācī

O Siṃhamukhī and accompanying [piśācī],
Though you remain unwavering in a compassionate and quiescent state,
You emanate in blazing awesome forms, [endowed] with fangs and wings,[9]
To pacify misconceptions and substantialist views.
For whatever ways we have contradicted your buddha-mind,
O eight piśācī [who embody] the objects [of consciousness], we seek forgiveness!

Confession to the four female gatekeepers

O four female gatekeepers, at [the portals of] the ornate palatial maṇḍala,
You who summon [with the hook], bind [with the noose], shackle [with the chain] and insulate [with the bell],
O Horse-headed Aṅkuśā and accompanying [female gatekeepers],
For whatever ways we have contradicted your buddha-mind,
O seals of the four gatekeepers, we seek forgiveness!

Confession to the twenty-eight īśvarī

O Īśvarī, you who are accomplished in the rites of 'liberation',[10]
And hold mastery over [the judgement of] virtuous and non-virtuous actions,
O Īśvarī, assembly of mothers,
For whatever ways we have contradicted your buddha-mind,
O oceanic expanse of mothers and sisters, we seek forgiveness!

Confession to the awareness holders

[O awareness holders], though you never stray from a state of compassionate equipoise,
Within the maṇḍala of spontaneously present natural expression,
We have not achieved your [pristine] clarity of subtle meditative stability.
O you who maintain the enlightened attributes, we seek your forgiveness!

Confession of one's beginningless violation of the commitments

Throughout the beginningless succession of our births,
Until now, when we have assumed these, our present bodies,
We have revolved within the worlds of rebirth, swayed by ignorance,
And however many human births we have taken,

Wherever we have been born, we have engaged in all kinds of negative acts,
Including the five inexpiable crimes and the five approximate crimes –
Actually committing them, or inciting [others] to commit them,
And even rejoicing in committing and inciting them.
Please direct your enlightened compassion towards us!
Grant us purification, and bestow your [spiritual] accomplishments upon us!

Then the confession should be recited to the entire maṇḍala of wrathful deities, and the request for forgiveness made in the following way:

HŪṂ O herukas of pristine cognition, natural purity of the five poisons,
[Resplendent] amidst flames blazing like the fire at the end of an aeon,
United with the five krodhīśvarī, the great mothers of space;
O four inner ḍākinīs, Gaurī and your partners,
O outer yoginīs, Pukkāsī and your partners,
O fanged clusters of devourers, Siṃhamukhī and your partners,
O winged [clusters] of the intermediate directions, Gṛdhramukhī and your partners,
O twenty-eight īśvarī, of the blazing courtyard,
O four female gatekeepers, who summon, bind, shackle and insulate[11] at the four gates:
We who have not even clearly visualised the bodies of the assembly of wrathful herukas,
We who have failed to recite sufficient heart-mantras,
And failed to stabilise [the actualisation of] the seals,
We who have failed to offer adequate feast- and torma-offerings,
Request the entire assembly of wrathful deities for forgiveness!

Next, the following specific confessional prayers should be made to the maṇḍala of the wrathful deities:

OṂ Should we have broken our pledge, which is dangerous to transgress,
Having earlier taken upon us this supremely secret vow,
For whatever ways we have contradicted the buddha-mind of the five families of herukas,
We seek your forgiveness, O greatly compassionate ones!

Should we have been obscured by conceptual grasping,
Whilst engaged in the practices of the supreme sexual yoga,
For whatever ways we have contradicted the buddha-mind of the great mother Krodhīśvarīs,
We seek your forgiveness, O [mother] krodheśvarīs!

Should we have failed to actualise the sacred substances and the seals,
For whatever ways we have contradicted the buddha-mind of the carnivorous Gaurīs,
We seek your forgiveness, O eight mātaraḥ, embodiments of the classes [of consciousness]!

Should we have failed to array the offerings of flesh and blood,[12] in accordance with the textual descriptions,
For whatever ways we have contradicted the buddha-mind of the Piśācīs, Siṃhamukhī and her partners,
We seek your forgiveness, O ḍākinīs, embodiments of the objects [of consciousness]!

Should we have failed to differentiate between the four gates: east, south, west, and north,
For whatever ways we have contradicted the buddha-mind of the female gatekeepers, the horse-headed Aṅkuśā and her partners,
We seek your forgiveness, O four female gatekeepers of pristine cognition!

Should we have failed to subdue [attachment to] the six realms of cyclic existence,
Having accepted [vows], which are dangerous to transgress,
For whatever ways we have contradicted the buddha-mind of the seven mothers and four sisters,[13]
We seek your forgiveness, O eleven ḍākinīs!

Should we have allowed our resources to become exhausted and the first fruits of the feast-offerings to be spoiled,
For whatever ways we have contradicted the buddha-mind of the Īśvarī who monitor the first fruits [of the feast-offerings],
We seek your forgiveness, O twenty-eight īśvarī!

Should we have failed to remain unmovingly in the sacred abodes, but instead engaged in [distracted] activities,
For whatever ways we have contradicted the buddha-mind of the wardens of the sacred abodes,[14]
We seek your forgiveness, O great wardens of the sacred abodes!

Should we have failed to regard our personal [spiritual teacher] as our parent,
For whatever ways we have contradicted the buddha-mind of the vajra-master,
We seek your forgiveness, O regal vajra[-master]!

Should we have failed to master meditative stability,
And failed to distinguish [the characteristics of] the Peaceful and Wrathful Deities,
For whatever ways we have contradicted the buddha-mind of the assistant vajra-master,[15]
We seek your forgiveness, O lamp of the Buddhist teachings![16]

Should we have interrupted [the stabilisation of] the seals through our laziness,
For whatever ways we have contradicted the buddha-mind of the ritual officiant,
We seek your forgiveness, O master of ritual activities!

Should we have failed to reach the highest criteria when engaged in the practices of sexual yoga,
For whatever ways we have contradicted the buddha-mind of the female consorts, the embodiments of discriminative awareness,
We seek your forgiveness, O secret mother, consort who embodies awareness!

Should we have lacked the power to maintain meditative stability when engaging in rites of 'liberation',
For whatever ways we have contradicted the buddha-mind of the male 'liberating' avengers,
We seek your forgiveness, O [Citipati], master of 'liberating' avengers![17]

Should we have failed to please the buddha-mind of the wrathful female emanations,
For whatever ways we have contradicted the buddha-mind of the [gatekeeping] messengers who summon and guide,[18]
We seek your forgiveness, O [female gatekeepers], who swiftly enact the rites!

Should we have broken the continuous expression of love and affection through our laziness,
For whatever ways we have contradicted the buddha-mind of our brothers and sisters, [our companions] on the path to enlightenment,
We seek your forgiveness, O vajra-brothers and sisters!

Should we have allowed our commitments to degenerate out of trivial banter,
For whatever ways we have contradicted the buddha-mind of those [protectors] who determine the outer and inner [boundaries of our precepts],
We seek your forgiveness, O you [protectors] who keep vigil over the commitments!

Should we have consumed our resources [accumulated for the feast-offering],
And allowed the first fruits of the residual offering to be spoiled,

For whatever ways we have contradicted the buddha-mind of the subterranean goddesses within the outer retinue,
We seek your forgiveness, O greatly compassionate ones!

Please be patient [with us],
And bestow your pure spiritual accomplishments upon us!

PLAINTIVE CONFESSION OF RAMPANT EGOHOOD[19]

OṂ O great compassionate and transcendent lord Vajrasattva,
Whose supremely exquisite form, immaculate and white,
Is suffused by a pure inner radiance, glowing like a hundred thousand suns and moons,
[Emanating] heroic rays of light, which illuminate the chiliocosm,
You who are known as the guide and teacher of the three levels of existence,
The unique friend to all living beings of the three world-systems,
O lord of loving kindness, deity of compassion, please attend to us!

From beginningless time, without end, I have roamed throughout cyclic existence –
Led astray by the momentum of my mistaken past actions and improper past behaviour,
I have mistaken the path and become lost on the path.
I regret with powerful remorse the negative past actions I have committed, of any kind.
Drawn by the momentum of momentary yet violently resonant past acts,
I have sunk into this ocean of suffering, the sea of cyclic existence.
The fires of blazing hatred have unabatingly seared my mind,
The dense darkness of delusion has blinded my discriminative awareness,

The ocean coasts of desire have drowned my consciousness,
The mountain of fierce pride has entombed me in the lower existences,
The cruel whirlwind of envy has sucked[20] me into these turning worlds,
Where, entwined by the tight knot of egocentricity,
I have fallen into the pit of desire, this chasm of blazing fires.
Unbearably brutal misery has poured down on me like heavy rain.
[Damaged] by such extreme and unbearable suffering,
[Seared] by the blazing ferocious fires of my negative past actions,
The shoots of my consciousness and sense faculties have been blunted.
If my body, this illusory aggregate, can no longer withstand [all this pain],
How can you bear [to witness] this, O Compassionate Lord of Loving Kindness?[21]

Obscured fool [that I am, burdened by] the most negative, evil past acts,
Propelled by the momentum of these past actions,
I have taken birth as the personification of rampant egohood within this world-system of desire.
I regret having taken such birth, and am dismayed by my past acts!
Yet, regardless of my regret and my dismay, past actions cannot be re-made.
The momentum of past actions is as strong as a river's inexorable flow,
So how can the mighty river of past actions be reversed in a mere moment!
All that ripens is born from one's own past actions,
And I am one who has been swept along by the violent whirlwind of my past actions,
And accordingly have roamed over countless past aeons,
Lost within the dark prisons of cyclic existence.
O Lord of Loving Kindness, through the blessing of your compassion,

Purify the obscurations [generated by] my past actions and dissonant mental states,
And secure me in the presence of your mother-like loving kindness!

Here am I, continuously yearning for the sight of your compassionate face,
Which shines with a luminosity like that of the sun,
And radiates with a clarity like that of the moon.
Yet my darkened eyes, blinded by the cataracts[22] of beginningless ignorance,
Are unable to see you,
O Lord of Living Beings, where are you [now]?

When I am terrified by the utterly unbearable and virulent power of past actions,
And my hair stands on end, out of fear,
I call out this lament, in heartfelt passion,
And cry out [to you] in a voice of utter despair!
O Lord of Loving Kindness, if you do not attend [to me] with compassion now,
At the time of my death, when my mind and body separate,
When I am cut off from the company of spiritual friends, and dragged away by Yama,
At that time, when my relatives stay behind in the world,
Yet I alone am led away by the power of past actions,
At that time, I will be unprotected and without a refuge.
So, do not on any account hesitate or delay now,
But draw near to me at this very moment,
And enact the wrathful rites of 'liberation'.

Beings such as I, who are afflicted by past actions,
Have been subject to misconceptions since beginningless time.
As a result, we have not achieved release from the [turning] states of cyclic existence.
Indeed, beings such as I have assumed such a countless number of corporeal forms,
During countless births in countless aeons,
That if our flesh and bones were to be collected together,

Their accumulated mass would fill this world,
And if our pus and blood were to be collected together,
Their accumulated mass would fill a vast ocean,
And if the residue of our past actions were to be collected together,
Their extent would be beyond conception and inexpressible.
Though I have continued endlessly in a cycle of births and deaths,
Throughout the three world-systems,
The actions that I have committed have been pointless and unproductive.
Yet, from amongst all these many countless births,
The actions committed in the course of just a single lifetime
Could have been worthwhile if only I had trained well,
Pursued the path of unsurpassed enlightenment,
And thus attained the genuine final nirvāṇa.
But, swayed by the virulence of past actions and the great potency of dissonant mental states,
I have assumed bodies, these networks of flesh and blood, and roamed throughout cyclic existence,
Thrust into [a succession of] prison-like existences,
Where the suffering is hard to bear.
All my transgressions, resonant with such unbearably intense suffering,
Have been born out of my own past actions.
Please, through your great compassion, shatter the momentum of [these] past actions,
And reverse the vital energy of past actions, [generated by] dissonant mental states!

When, overpowered by the influence of perverse past actions [rooted in] fundamental ignorance,
I wander perpetually within the darkness of unknowing,
Why do you not release me, [suffusing me] with the lamplight of your pristine cognition?
When I can no longer bear the continuing fruition of my transgressions and past actions,
Why do you not embrace me with the enlightened activity of your great compassion?

When I fall into the abyss of error,
Why do you not catch me in the palm of your swift compassion?
When I am afflicted by the irresistible diseases of the three poisons,
Why do you not cure me with the medicine of your compassionate skilful means?
When the fires of my suffering – the continuing maturation of my own past actions – blaze,
Why do you not release a compassionate shower of cooling rains?
When I sink into the swamp of suffering in cyclic existence,
Why do you not draw me up with the hook of compassionate skilful means?

Were I to attain the resultant [states of enlightenment],
By training, again and again, in the three world-systems of cyclic existence,
What need would there be for your sublime compassion then?
Given that this [release] would be the potent inheritance of my [positive] past actions,
Would there be anyone to whom I would need to express my gratitude?
[But], O spiritual warrior, you who are endowed with the power of compassion,
Since the momentum of my [negative] past actions is so potent,
Do not be ineffective! Do not be indifferent! Do not be inactive!
From your heart, O compassionate conquering deity, gaze upon me now!
Draw me up from the swamp of cyclic existence!
Lead me swiftly to the supreme level of the three buddha-bodies.

CONFESSION IN THE PRESENCE OF THE VIEW

OṂ How mistaken is the view which dualises subject and object,
When the expanse of reality is free from conceptual elaboration!
How deluded we have been by our grasping at characteristics!
We confess this transgression within the expanse of supreme bliss,
Which is free from conceptual elaboration!

How debilitating is the view which dualises good and evil,
When Samantabhadra, [The Ever Perfect], is beyond good and evil!
How pitiful we are, clinging to purity and impurity!
We confess this transgression within the expanse,
Which is free from the duality of good and evil!

How mistaken is the view which sees buddhas [as great] and sentient beings [as small],
When, in the state of sameness, there is neither great nor small!
How deluded we have been in clinging to the dichotomy of great and small!
We confess this transgression within the expanse of supreme bliss, which is sameness!

How debilitating is the view which dualises this life and the next,
When the mind of enlightenment is free from birth or death!
How deluded we have been in clinging to the dichotomy of birth and death!
We confess this transgression within the deathless, immutable expanse!

How mistaken is the view which dualises form and material substance,
When the supreme seminal point is free from spatial dimensions!

How deluded we have been in clinging to the dichotomy of corners and angles!
We confess this transgression within the supreme seminal point, which is all-embracing in its symmetry![23]

How mistaken is the view which dualises beginning and end,
When the essential nature of the three times is unchanging!
How deluded we have been in clinging to the dichotomy of transitional processes!
We confess this transgression within the expanse of the three times, which is unchanging!

How debilitating is the view which dualises cause and effect,
When the naturally present pristine cognition arises effortlessly!
How deluded we have been in clinging to the dichotomy of effort and attainment!
We confess this transgression within the naturally present expanse, which arises without effort!

How pitiful is the view which dualises eternalism and nihilism,
When the pristine cognition of [intrinsic] awareness is free from eternalism and nihilism!
How deluded we have been in clinging to the dichotomy of existence and non-existence!
We confess this transgression within the expanse of pristine cognition, which is beyond eternalism and nihilism![24]

How debilitating is the view which oscillates between biased positions,
When the pure expanse of reality is free from middle and extremes!
How deluded we have been in clinging to the dichotomy of middle and extremes!
We confess this transgression within the pure expanse of reality, which is free from a middle or extremes!

How debilitating is the view which dualises outside and inside,
When the celestial palace is free from inner and outer dimensions!

How deluded we have been in clinging to the dichotomy of spaciousness and confinement!
We confess this transgression within the expanse [of the celestial palace],
Which is free from the duality of spaciousness and confinement, or of inner and outer dimensions!

How pitiful is the view which dualises 'higher and lower' [approaches],
When the sexual centre of the female consort is free from [the distinction between] higher and lower [energy centres]!
How deluded we have been in clinging to the dichotomy between higher and lower [energy centres]![25]
We confess this transgression within the expanse of the [consort's] secret place,[26]
Which is free from [the distinction between] higher and lower!

How debilitating is the view which dualises objects and mind,
When the Buddha-body of Reality is free from individuated distinctions!
How deluded we have been in clinging to the dichotomy between the environment and its inhabitants!
We confess this transgression within [the expanse of] the Buddha-body of Reality, which is unchanging!

How debilitating is the view which discriminates between individual thoughts,
When the dynamic of the male consort acts unconstrictedly!
How deluded we have been in clinging mistakenly to nominalism!
We confess this transgression within the expanse of the awareness holders, who are free from conceptual thoughts!

Since pristine cognition, which is intrinsic awareness, has not arisen within us,
How pitiful is this mind obscured by ignorance,
Which grasps immaterial phenomena as materially substantive!
We confess this transgression within the expanse of natural pristine cognition!

Since we have failed to understand the nature of uncreated truth,
How tormented is this intellect of a bewildered being,
Which apprehends the uncreated truth in terms of 'I' and 'mine'!
We confess this transgression within the expanse of supreme bliss, which is uncreated!

Since we have failed to mentally elucidate the nature of reality,
We have not understood that phenomenal appearances are illusory,
And thereby our minds have become attached to material wealth!
We confess this transgression within the uncreated reality, which is free from attachment!

Since we have failed to realise that cyclic existence is free from inherent existence,
We have grasped at the self-existence of things and their characteristics,
And thereby sought happiness through non-virtuous behaviour.
How deluded we have been in clinging to the dichotomy between hope and doubt!
We confess this transgression within the expanse of enlightenment, which is untainted!

Since we have failed to understand the truth of sameness with true equanimity,
We have mistakenly clung to the permanence of relatives and friends.
How totally mistaken is this mind of ignorant people [such as ourselves]!
We confess this transgression within the expanse of supreme bliss, which is sameness!

Since we have failed to encounter the true meaning of reality,
We have forsaken truth and persevered in non-virtuous acts.
We have forsaken the transmitted precepts of the Teacher and

have been deceived by the vagaries of [mundane] human doctrines!
We confess this transgression within the expanse of supreme bliss, which is reality!

Since we have failed to experience the natural liberation of pristine cognition, which is [intrinsic] awareness,
We have forsaken the modality of intrinsic awareness, and persevered in distracted acts.
Take pity on these sentient beings who are devoid of such truthful experience!
We confess this transgression within the expanse, which is free from distraction!

To the assembled deities of pristine cognition, to the protectors who uphold the commitments,
And to those yogins who have fulfilled their commitments in accordance with the textual elucidation,
We remorsefully confess all our own faults,
[We remorsefully confess] all our deviations and obscurations generated by our unrealised view!

CONFESSION IN THE PRESENCE OF ALL THOSE GONE TO BLISS

OṂ We pray to all Those Gone to Bliss, throughout the three times,
To you, the conquerors, and your retinues,
And to all who maintain the commitments of indestructible reality,
Please, each of you, attend to us!

Having initially generated the mind [aspiring] to supreme enlightenment,
In order to actualise the indestructible reality of buddha-body, speech and mind,
On the enlightened plain of an accomplished awareness holder,

We have adopted numerous secret commitments,
Relating to both the meditational deities and our vajra-masters,
And we have pledged not to transgress these injunctions, to which we are bound,
[For to do so] would lead to a birth in the hells,
Driven by our past actions and misfortunes.

[Nonetheless], swayed by attachment, aversion, delusion, pride, envy and so forth,
We have continued to err:
Should we have belittled the vajra-master in our hearts, the 'lamp of the teaching',
And thus allowed our commitments to degenerate,
And should we have harboured ill will and mistaken attitudes
Towards the vajra-companions who share our commitments,
For [whatever] such [harm we have thus created],
We confess all our degenerations of the commitments of buddha-body!

Should we have not clearly visualised the seals of the meditational deity,[27]
Should we have been deficient in our mantra recitations during our ritual service,
Should we have failed to carry out the rites through which both ritual service and attainment are fulfilled,
Especially with respect to the ritual offerings of six session [yoga],
And should we have been incapable of practising in accordance with the teachings and the texts,
We confess all such degenerations of the commitments of buddha-speech!

Should we have degraded the commitments, which the vajra-master imparted as an esoteric instruction of buddha-mind,
Commitments he orally seeded in our hearts, through the grace of his loving kindness,
And should we have even transgressed our secret name,[28] by divulging it carelessly,
We confess all such degenerations of the commitments of buddha-mind!

We [also] confess our degenerations of the ancillary commitments,
Caused by our failure to realise the essential sameness of phenomena.
We confess our degenerations of the commitments relating to ritual service and attainment,
Caused by our falling into the sleep of idleness and apathy.
We confess [each and every one of our] degenerations of the commitments of buddha-body, speech and mind,
Caused by our transgressions, enacted physically, verbally and mentally!

In the presence of our revered spiritual teachers,
We confess our inadequate utensils and resources.
In the presence of the assembled meditational deities,
We confess our prejudices towards their practices of visualisation.[29]
In the presence of the four classes of ḍākinīs,
We confess our degenerations of our commitments and pledges.
In the presence of the protectors of the [sacred] teachings,
We confess our [tardy] torma-offerings, whether years or months overdue.
In the presence of our parents of the three times,
We confess our failure to repay their kindness.
In the presence of our spiritual brothers and sisters,
We confess our inadequate fervour for upholding the commitments.
In the presence of the six classes of sentient beings,
We confess the inadequacy of our compassion and altruism.

We confess all our contradictions and degenerations:
Those relating to the *prātimokṣa* vows,
Those relating to the trainings cultivated by the bodhisattvas,
And those relating to the commitments upheld by the awareness holders.[30]
From now on we shall not conceal [such degenerations]
And we resolve to guard against any and every infraction!

As we confess all our negative obscurations born of indulging in the three poisons,
Please purify [all our obscurations]
And grant us the supreme and common accomplishments of buddha-body, speech and mind!

The Hundred-syllable Mantra [of Vajrasattva] should be recited [repeatedly] in conjunction with these verses and thus the confession will be effected.

This *Natural Liberation through Acts of Confession in the Presence of the Peaceful and Wrathful Deities*,
Which is a supporting text to the *Reparation and Confession: Natural Liberation of Degenerations*,[31] is thus presented.
Be persevering with regard to this practice, O Children of Posterity!
May this practice be encountered by all those of the future who have a [positive] inheritance of past actions!

This *Natural Liberation through Acts of Confession, in the Presence of the Peaceful and Wrathful Deities* was extracted from the *Tantra of Immaculate Confession* by Padmākara, the preceptor of Oḍḍiyāna. May [the influence of] this sublime teaching not be exhausted until all of cyclic existence is emptied!

May virtue prevail!
SAMAYA *rgya rgya rgya!*
gter-rgya! sbas-rgya! gtad-rgya![32]
A treasure of Karma Lingpa!

8

Natural Liberation through Recognition of the Visual Indications and Signs of Death

CONTEXT

Since the human body is regarded as an abode of deities, it is the responsibility of the practitioner to protect the body from the causes of harm, disease and premature death and to foster the conditions which support an active and unencumbered life up to the natural exhaustion of the lifespan.

This chapter describes six categories of signs indicative of the time of death, together with a variety of techniques for purposefully eliciting specific indications of death. Also described, in the section titled 'Signs of Extremely Near Death', are the experiential and outer signs that occur during the process of dying. Lastly, the signs that are indicative of the nature of the future rebirth, which occur at or after death, are described.

This chapter and the following chapter: *Natural Liberation of Fear through the Ritual Deception of Death* are inextricably interlinked. Should the predictive signs described in this chapter definitively arise, then it is expected that the appropriate practices described in the following chapter: *Natural Liberation of Fear through the Ritual Deception of Death* should be undertaken without delay.

The sophisticated description of the process of dying, contained in the section 'Signs of Extremely Near Death', concurs with the understanding of the process of death commonly found in classical Buddhist literature.* This section forms a component of the *Liberation by Hearing* (Chapter 11) and it is a vital aspect of the guidance to be given by a qualified spiritual teacher at the time of death.

The predictive signs of death, however, are more idiosyncratic and show influences from Tibetan folklore and traditional medicine. Further, in terms of the predictive signs of death, it is said that the

*For a detailed description of the processes of death, see also HH Dalai Lama, *Advice on Dying*.

subtler signs described here can only be accurately recognised by those who are continuously engaged in meditative practice.

The elicitation and analysis of the predictive signs is not a common practice today, except, in the case of certain signs, in the context of traditional medicine. Nonetheless, this text demonstrates a powerful sensitivity to impermanence and a sustained sensitivity to one's immediate experience.

Herein is contained the *Natural Liberation through [Recognition of] the Visual Indications and Signs of Death*,[1] an extract from the *Peaceful and Wrathful Deities: A Profound Sacred Teaching, [entitled] Natural Liberation through [Recognition of] Enlightened Intention*.[2]

I bow down to the naturally radiant Peaceful and Wrathful Deities,
[Manifestations of] the three buddha-bodies!

This natural liberation through [the recognition of] signs
Which is a technique for analysing [the onset of] death
Is presented as a supporting text to the *Natural Liberation by Hearing in the Intermediate States*.[3]
Study it repeatedly, O Child of Buddha Nature.
SAMAYA!

INTRODUCTION

Alas! This illusory and feeble aggregate of form,
Created from compounded past actions and conditions,
Like [the flame of] a butter lamp blowing in the wind, cannot last for ever.[4]
Nothing at all exists which is not subject to the conditioning of death,
And indeed, since it is uncertain when death will occur,
One should constantly be cognisant of the signs of [impending] death,
And strive after [the accumulation of] virtue.

There are two [primary] conditions responsible for the death of human beings:
[First] untimely death and [second] death due to the [natural] exhaustion of the lifespan.[5]
Untimely or sudden death may be averted,
By successful application of the *Ritual Deception of Death*,[6]
But death due to the [natural] exhaustion of the lifespan
Is like the burning out of a butter lamp,
So there is no way of averting this through 'ritual deception',
And thus, [if this is indicated], one should make preparations to depart.
In either case, [however], it is most important to engage in the following analysis.

This teaching [on the visual indications and signs of death]
Is presented in terms of six general topics, namely:
External, internal, and secret signs of death,
Signs of remote death, signs of near death,
And, lastly, miscellaneous signs of death.

When investigating [the time of] death,
First one should make offerings
To the [visualised] assemblies of spiritual teachers, meditational deities and ḍākinīs,
And please the protectors of the [sacred] teachings with torma-offerings.
Then, one should present feast-offerings to one's fellow practitioners,
And also engage in charitable acts.
Then, [the signs of] death should be examined in the following way.

EXTERNAL SIGNS OF DEATH

First, when the examination of external [signs] is made,
It is the bodily characteristics that should be investigated,
Because the signs of death will arise in relation to these [characteristics].
The body is composed of the four elements,

Thus the following portents of its demise
Will arise prior [to the time of death]:
Loss of appetite, dullness of the sense faculties,
A feeling of anger which consumes body, speech and mind,
Distracted or depressed thoughts,
Disturbed dreams, character changes, and fading complexion.
These are the portents [indicating] that life[-threatening] hindrances may arise.

More particularly, there are the following specifically physical signs of death:[7]
If the fingernails and toenails become bloodless or lustreless,
[This indicates] death after nine months, less half a day.
If the cornea of the eyes begin to cloud over,
[This indicates] death after five months.
If the hair on the nape of the neck grows upwards,
[This indicates] death after three months.

[Then again, more generally], if one urinates, defecates and sneezes simultaneously,
This too is an indication of death.
Also, if one's urine falls in two forks,
If one's muscles become utterly loose and flabby,
If faeces are excreted and semen ejaculated simultaneously,
If one's body odour changes dramatically,
If one's conduct changes dramatically,
If one blushes little and one's complexion becomes pallid,
If the tone of one's voice becomes thin, and one's eyes become sunken,
If the space above the bridge of the nose becomes exfoliated,
If the eyes do not clearly perceive forms,
Or else if they perceive incorrectly, and so forth,
If [the ears] do not hear, or else hear incorrectly,
If [the nose] does not smell, or else smells incorrectly,
If [the tongue] does not taste, or else tastes incorrectly,
If the point between the eyebrows is effaced,
Or evaporation ceases from the crown of the head,
These [signs] may all indicate that one has fallen into the hands of the Lord of Death.[8]

Furthermore, while in good health,
[The following technique for eliciting indications can also be applied]:
If, when the [closed] eyes are pressed with the fingers,
The [minute] circles of light which appear
Are absent from the lower part of the left eye,
[This indicates that] one may die after six months,
But if they are absent from the upper part [of that eye],
One may die after three months.
If these [same circles] are absent from the direction of the [left] nostril,
[This indicates that] one may die after one month.
If they are absent from the direction of the [left] ear,
[This indicates that] one may die after two months.

[Resuming this process, focusing on the right eye]:
If [the circles] are absent from the lower part of the right eye,
One should know that one may die after ten days.
If they are absent from the upper part [of the right eye],
[This indicates that] one may die after five days.
If they are absent from the direction of the [right] ear,
[This indicates that one may die] after three days;
And if they are absent from the direction of the [right] nostril,
One should know that one may die after two days, even if one is not sick.

Secondly, if when the ears are cupped with the fingers,
No humming sound is heard throughout an entire day,[9]
One should know that one might die after six years.
If it is absent for two days,
One may die after six years less two months.
Similarly, for each additional day [that the sound is absent],
[This indicates that] one may die, decrementally, after three fewer months.
That is, if [the sound] is absent for a third or fourth day,
Death may come after three [or six] fewer months, respectively.
It has also been said that the number of days [indicated] might not necessarily be definite.

There are also other [external] signs of death, such as:
If one feels [continuously] angry and short-tempered,
If one feels fearful, wherever one may be,
If one's positive perspective, devotion, and similar qualities ebb away,
If one feels aversion towards saintly beings,
If one feels depressed, wherever one may be, and [constantly] wishes to go [elsewhere],
If one wishes to be separated from sympathetic Buddhist companions,
If one delights in the social diversions and distracting activities of cyclic existence,
Or if one feels excessive attachment, aversion, pride, or envy,
These may all indicate that one has fallen into the hands of the Lord of Death.

These, [the above], are called 'the external signs of death',
Which, it is said, can be averted by the ritual deception of death.
The techniques, by which they are averted, should be studied,
By referring to the *Ritual Deception of Death* [chapter, which follows].

INTERNAL SIGNS OF DEATH

The investigation of the internal signs of death
Comprises the examination of vital breath and the examination of dreams.

Examination of the Vital Breath[10]

Around the time of the [vernal or autumnal] equinox,
At daybreak on the first day [of the lunar month],
One should sit upright, with the body in the seven-point posture of Vairocana.
Then, one should observe the vital breath, and note from which [nostril] this emerges.
If, at this time, the vital breath is moving through the left nostril,

Then, for a period of three days, the breath will continue to move exclusively through the left nostril,
But then on the fourth day it will change,
And proceed to move through the right nostril for three days.
Thus it will alternate in this way every three days between the two nostrils.

[Observe this process and] count the number of days diligently, and do not make a mistake.
If no error is made [in the counting], and if the breath moves successively in this way,
And then begins to move erratically after one and a half months,
It is said that one may die after [a further] six months.
If the breath begins to move erratically after one month,
It is said that severe misfortunes may occur.
If it begins to move erratically after two weeks,
[It is said that] serious illness may occur.
If it moves erratically after five days,[11]
[It is said that] slander and calumny may occur.
If [the breath] does not alternate [from one nostril to the other] over a ten-day period,
Then, as soon as it does change, one may die.
If it moves simultaneously through both nostrils and the mouth,
[This indicates that] one may die after half a day.
And if it ceases to move through the nose and instead moves only through the mouth,
It is said that one will die immediately.

Examination of the Signs of Death which Occur in Dreams[12]

[First, one should know that] those dreams which occur in the late evening or around midnight are unreliable,
But if one dreams between dawn and daybreak that:
One is riding a cat or a white monkey with a red face,
While moving further and further towards the east,
It is said that this is a sign of death caused by king spirits.[13]
If one dreams of riding a tiger, fox, or corpse,

Or of riding a buffalo, pig, camel, or donkey,
While moving further and further towards the south,
This is a sign of death [indicating that] one has fallen into the hands of Yama.

Furthermore, if one dreams of eating faeces,
Of wearing black clothes of yak hair, while plunging downwards,
Of being trapped in a wicker-basket or snare,
Of being bound with iron chains,
Or of copulating repeatedly with a black figure or animal,
These are [also] signs [which are indicative] of death.

If one dreams of being disembowelled by a fierce black woman,
And that one's entrails are spilling out,
Or that a black man arrives, wielding an iron mace,
And coming into one's presence, he tells you to depart,
Or [if one dreams] that one is being dragged along by a black rope attached to the neck,
Or that one is inside a lofty red-coloured castle,
Surrounded by a moat and perimeter wall,
Or [if one dreams] of being decapitated and having one's head carried off by another,
Or of being surrounded by crows, anguished spirits, or villains,
Or of being willingly led away, or leaving [home] in a bridal procession,
Of being naked, with one's hair cut off and beard shaved,
Of constantly associating with friends who have died,
Of being dragged along by a crowd of dead people,
Of jumping into water, sinking into mud, or being swallowed by fish,
Of entering a womb and falling asleep,
Of being overcome in a battle, in which the other side is victorious,
Of wearing red clothing, and being adorned with red garlands,
Of repeatedly picking red flowers,
Of climbing a mountain of red shellac,

Of having one's head wrapped in a red silk turban,
Of twigs growing on the crown of your head, and birds nesting there,
Of falling asleep repeatedly in a terrifying charnel ground,
Of being old, and carrying a heavy burden,
Of the sun and moon falling to the plains, leaving one shrouded in darkness,
Of jumping headlong into a pit,
Of dancing together with a host of ogres,
Or setting out, thinking one will roam to unfamiliar distant lands, never to return –
If such dreams and others like them occur when one is not sick, they are indefinite [with respect to the time of death],
And one may be released [from their indications] by means of the [appropriate] ritual service.
If, however, such dreams continually recur,
[This indicates that] one will die within a year.

If one should dream of the sun and moon being eclipsed,
Falling to the plains, or repeatedly setting,
One's father, mother, or teacher may die,
And it is said that if they are sick at the time,
Their death will be inevitable.

The above are called the 'internal signs of death',
Which are slightly more difficult [to avert]
Through ritual deception than the aforementioned [external signs].

SECRET SIGNS OF DEATH

The secret signs of death will [now] be described.
When the external and internal signs of death occur,
They can be averted by repeatedly performing the *Ritual Deception of Death*.
If, however, the external and internal signs are not [successfully] reversed,
One should then examine the secret signs in the following way:

Having first generated the mind [aspiring] to supreme enlightenment,[14]
And then taken refuge and offered prayers,
One should examine, on the morning of the first day of the month,
The flow of one's semen or menstrual blood.
It is said that if the semen of a man is blackish yellow,
Or if the menstrual blood of a woman is whitish,
Death may occur after two months.
If the semen of a man is reddish,
He may die or be subjected to slander after six months.
However, if its [natural] whiteness is undiminished,
[This indicates that] there is no obstacle [to life],
And [the semen] should be inhaled through the nose, while it is still warm.
This is itself a rite associated with the *Ritual Deception of Death*.

Furthermore, if semen flows without any [blissful] sensation,
And it is interspersed with quicksilver-like globules, the size of sesame seeds,
It is said that one will die [imminently].
If the flow of a woman's menstrual blood is unceasing,
And if at that time she dreams she is picking red flowers,
[This indicates that] death will [soon] follow.
Moreover, if a man has continual spermatorrhoea,
Even when not engaged in sexual intercourse,
It is said that he may die after four months.
If a black mole suddenly appears for the first time,
At the orifice of the glans penis,
Or if one has an undistracted and constant [sexual] desire, thinking only of women,
And one allows one's commitments in respect of the third empowerment to degenerate,[15]
These are not only signs of death,
But also omens that one will later proceed to [rebirth in] the indestructible hells.
[Therefore], if one does not confess [and repair] these [degenerations] fully,
One will experience the fierce sufferings of the hells.

In order for the confession to be effective, however,
You should perform the ritual deception pertaining to the secret [signs of] death,
Yet [death] will be harder to deceive than in the two preceding categories.

The above are called the 'secret signs of death'.

SIGNS OF REMOTE DEATH

The examination of the signs of death when it is [still] years or months away
Should be made by scrutinising the 'shadow of one's lifespan',
Optically projected onto the sky, in the way described below.
[These indications may show that] one will die, or that one will not die,
And that the averting [of death] will be possible, or impossible.[16]

[To begin], offerings should be made to the spiritual teacher, and the Three Precious Jewels,
Torma-offerings should be presented to the ḍākinīs and protectors of the [sacred] teachings;
And then, after going for refuge and offering prayers,
The examination should be made [as follows]:

In an isolated and delightful place,
In the morning or afternoon of the first day of the month,
Or in the evening or at dawn of the fifteenth day,[17]
When the sky is clear and there is no wind,
One should sit naked in a comfortable spot,
And there, after praying fervently,
One should repeat the following mantra one hundred times:
OṂ ĀYUṢE SAṂHĀRAKEŚVARE HŪṂ PHAṬ[18]
Then, standing up, naked, one should bow down seven times
To each of the gods of the [ten] directions,
And then, directly stretching out one's four limbs,
While holding in one's hand a rosary or suitable symbolic hand-implement,[19]

One should inscribe the letter A on the heart of one's shadow.[20]

[Next], without blinking, one should gaze fixedly at the letter A [drawn] at the heart [of the shadow],

And focus one's awareness upon [the letter A].

Then, once the eyes have grown numb [through strain],

One should look up into the centre of the cloudless sky,

At which time one's own form should become visible in the sky.

One should then know that if the head and body of this [reflected image] are intact, and [the image] is pale in colour,

This is an auspicious sign that there will be no obstacles and that one will not die [imminently].

If one's reflected image is not visible in the sky,

[First], perform the rite for affirmation of vows,

And, while sitting in the 'indestructible cross-legged posture',

With the hands in the 'gesture of meditative equipoise',[21]

Look [for the image again], in the above manner.

If [one's reflected image] still does not appear,

It may not be significant, as it may have been obscured by clouds or atmospheric winds,

In which case, the examination should be postponed until the sky is clear.

[When the reflected image does become visible, however,]

Its examination entails three considerations: of completeness, shape, and colour.

First, the completeness [of the reflected image] should be examined as follows:

When [assessing] the completeness of the image

In relation to the number of years [one is yet to live],

If the hand-held implement is missing,

This [indication] is called the 'separation from the deity on whom one has relied',[22]

And it indicates that one's life may end in seven years' time.

If the right hand is missing,

[This indicates that] one may die after five years.

If the left hand is missing,

[This indicates that] one may die after three years.

If the right leg is missing below the knee,
One may die after two years.
If the left leg is missing,
[This indicates that] one may die after one year.

Next, when [assessing] the completeness [of the image]
In relation to the number of months [one is yet to live]:
If the right part of the head is missing,
One may die after nine months.
If the left part of the head is missing,
One may die after seven months.
If the head is missing above the neck,
One may die after five months.
If the head and the neck are both missing,
One may die after three months.
If the upper trunk is missing,
One may die after two months.
If the lower trunk is missing,
One may die after one month.

Next, when [assessing] the completeness [of the image]
In relation to the number of days [one is yet to live]:
If the right side of the body is missing,
One may die in twenty-nine days.
If the left side [of the body] is missing,
One may die in twenty-one days.

Second, the [overall] shape [of the image] should be examined as follows:

If [the image] is square, one may die after five months.
If it is round, one may die after four months.
If it is semicircular, one may die after three months,
And if it is oblong, one may die after two months.
In all these cases, death may be averted by ritual deception.
However, if it is triangular, one will die after one month.
If it resembles a bundled corpse, one will die after half a month.
If it is upside down,[23] one will die after ten days.
In these last three cases, death cannot be averted and is absolutely inevitable.

Third, the colour [of the image] should be examined as follows:

If it is white in colour, and fades from the centre,

This is a sign that one has displeased serpentine water spirits, king spirits, and gods.

If it is black in colour, and fades from the right,

This is a sign that one has been overwhelmed by beguiling forces and imprecatory female spirits.

If it is red in colour, and fades from the left,

This is a sign that one has been seized by martial haunting spirits, and by one's own lifelong companion gods,

Or else that one will encounter woundings and diseases.

If it is yellow in colour, and fades from the head,

This is a sign that one has been seized by serpentine water spirits, king spirits and bewitchers.

If it is blue in colour, and fades from the legs,

This is a sign that one has been seized by serpentine water spirits and lake-dwelling medicinal spirits.

If it is hazy and diffuse,

This is a sign that one has been seized by imprecatory female spirits and the acolytes of Yama.

If it appears yellowish and uneven,

[This is a sign that one has been seized] by the spirit lords of the soil.

If it is garish, irregular, and variegated,

[This indicates that] one has been seized by the eight classes of spirits,

Comprising the diverse beguiling forces of death.

All these are [the signs] recognised with respect to the colours [of the reflected image].

When any of the above signs of death occur,

One should persevere with [the practices set down in] the *Ritual Deception of Death*,

And then re-examine [the image], in the manner described above.

If the limbs are complete,

[Death] may be ritually deceived.

But if the ritual deception of death fails to be effective, even after being applied three times,

This is a sign that the time has come for one's life to end.
Therefore, those of highest [potential] should maintain the view,
Which accords with the profound abiding nature [of reality],[24]
Those of average [potential] should meditate on the meditational deity, according to the generation and perfection stages,
And those of lowest [potential] should persevere with the accumulation [of merit].

The above is the analysis of the reflected image in the sky.

SIGNS OF NEAR DEATH

The analysis of the signs of near death is now presented.
The examination of [the signs] described so far should be made when one is in good health,
For [at that time] there are [still] many possibilities [for recovery], because the signs of a remote death can be ritually deceived.
Here, however, with regard to a sick person,
The signs indicative of [near] death arise as follows:

If one's gums grow grimy and black,
This is called the 'gathering of the personal demons of the elements',
And it indicates that one may die after nine days.
If the nostrils sag inwards and deflate,
This is called the 'blockage of the passageway of the vital breath',
And it indicates that one may die after nine days.
If the limbs are subject to repeated fits of expansion and contraction,
This is called the 'scaling of the mountain of the elements',
And it indicates that one may die after five days.
If the eyes stare fixedly, without blinking,
This is called the 'escape of the mother-like vital breath',[25]
And it indicates that one may die after three days.
If the cheeks sag inwards,

This is called the 'rupture of the edge of the earth element',
And it indicates that one may die at daybreak, ten days later.
If breathing is repeatedly agitated,
This is called the 'collision of vital energy and mind',
And it indicates that one may die after six days.[26]
If the tip of the nose inclines to the right or left,
This is called the 'cutting off of the bridge of the nose',
And it indicates that one may die after seven days.
If tears flow uncontrollably from the eyes,
This is called the 'impediment',
And it indicates that one may die after five days.
If the right or left cheek sags inwards,
This is called the 'cutting off of the intervening muscle',
And it indicates that [one may die] after one day.
If the upper and lower teeth become locked,
This is called the 'blockage of the path of the elements',
And it indicates that one may die after two and a half days.
If a black spot appears on the tongue,
It is certain that one will die after two days.
If the ears lie flat against the head,
This is called the 'blockage of the stairway of the ears',
And it indicates that one may die within half a day.
If the xiphoid of the chest sags inward,
This is called the 'rupture of the support of the water element',
And it indicates that one may die after two weeks.
If the hands shake for a prolonged time, when standing or sitting,
One should know that one may quickly die.

Other signs of [near] death should also be examined in the following way:
At noon one should face towards the south,
Placing the elbows on the knees,
Whereupon, lifting up one's hand,
One should place [the wrist] at the point between the eyebrows,
And focus both eyes upon one's hand.
[The image of the arm] will appear very thin, and if it then vanishes,

This is called the 'severing of the bond between atmosphere and earth',
And it indicates that one may die after nineteen days.

[Or else, one should position oneself at sunrise] with a pool or pond to the east,
And stand up and gaze at the surface of a wall towards the west.
Two superimposed shadows will appear, one above the other,
And if the upper shadow disappears,
This is called the 'fall of a rider on a white lioness from the slopes of Mount Sumeru',
And it indicates that one may die after fifteen and a half days.

[Alternatively, one should examine irregularities in one's urine specimen]:[27]
In the morning after a night when one has not engaged in sexual intercourse,
Drunk alcohol, or talked excessively,
One should fill a clay container with one's [first] urine, at sunrise, and examine it.
If [the urine] has a bluish or reddish vapour which then disappears,
This is called the 'vanishing of the froth of the ocean',
And it indicates that one will certainly die after nine days.
If the vapour is blackish and putrid,
[This indicates that] one will die after one day.
If the vapour is red and spotted, one may die after nine [days].

[Alternatively], one should defecate at sunrise,
And if no vapour arises from [the faeces],
This is called the 'ceasing of monks' smoke in the cities of the earth element',
And it indicates that one may die after nine days.

[Further], if, when the [closed] eyes are pressed, no circles of light appear,
This is called the 'setting of the unchanging sun at the summit of Mount Sumeru',[28]
And it indicates that one may die after three or seven days.

[Further], if, when the ears are cupped with the fingers,
The humming sound which is [normally] present is absent,
This is called the 'interruption of the natural sound of the ḍākinīs from within Mount Sumeru',[29]
And it indicates that one may die after seven or thirteen days.

[Alternatively], on a morning when the sun is shining,
One should turn one's back to the sun,
And if no evaporation [is seen to] rise from the crown of one's shadow,
This is called the 'rupturing of the Wish-granting Tree from the Summit of Mount Sumeru',[30]
And it indicates that one may die after five days.

[Also], if a single tuft of hair exceptionally rises upwards from the posterior fontanelles,
This is called 'the black lord of death, one-legged Yavati, arising as an enemy against the Wish-granting Tree',[31]
And it indicates that one may die after seven days.

Whichever of these [signs of] death occur,
They indicate the specific time-frame [of impending death].
Therefore, upon the occurrence of such [signs], the *Ritual Deception of Death* should be performed three times.
If this is carried out [successfully], untimely death will be averted.
One should [therefore] exert oneself and persevere in [applying] the practical instructions,
As [taught] in the *Natural Liberation of Fear through the Ritual Deception of Death*.
But if the ritual deception does not take effect,
Despite being performed on three occasions,
Death is definite, for one's lifespan is at its end.

MISCELLANEOUS SIGNS OF DEATH[32]

Here follows the presentation of the miscellaneous signs of death.
Regardless of whether one is sick or healthy,

If one cannot see the point of the nose with the eyes,
One may die after five months.
If one cannot see the tip of one's own tongue,
One may die after three days even if one is not sick.
If, when one gazes at the surface of a clear mirror,
One cannot see with one's left eye, one may die after seven months.
[Usually], when one breathes into the palm of one's own hand [from close by], it will feel warm,
And when one does so [from a distance] it will feel cold,
But if these [sensations] are reversed,
One should know that one might die after ten days.
If, when one looks for one's reflection in a vessel filled with water,
No reflections, images, or the like, are apparent,
This too is a sign of death.
If, when bathing, water does not cling to the area around the heart,
Or if the water dries out [quickly] around the heart, this may indicate death.
It is [also] said that if no sound is emitted when one snaps the fingers, this may indicate death;
And if the anklebones protrude from the legs,
It is said that one may die after one month.

[Furthermore], it is said that if one leaves no footprints in soft earth, this may indicate death,
And if one becomes weaker after having eaten nutritious food,
And if one's shadow changes [its shape unnaturally], this too may indicate death.

When lice and nits [suddenly] gather or leave, this may indicate death.
If a former temperament, peaceful or wrathful, is reversed,
And if a former pattern of behaviour, good or bad, changes,
These too are signs indicative of a person's death.
If one's image reflected in water or in a mirror lacks a head or limbs,
This too may be a sign of death.

If there is a retraction of the penis and protrusion of the testicles, or vice versa,
If a previously unheard pulmonary wheezing sound occurs,
And if one cannot sense the smell of a dying butter lamp,
These are said to be signs that one will certainly die [imminently].

In addition to such signs, the following may also occur:
A turbid confusion and darkening of normal consciousness,
A loss of one's former appetite,
Embarrassment and incapacity in undertaking virtuous acts,
A [restless] urge to leave, and an inability to stay in one place,
Discomfort in bed and inability to fall asleep,
Recurring amnesia and disorientation,
Recurring memories of one's former kindred, and the desire to be with them [again],
Death wishes and the desire to commit suicide,
The desire to roam and travel alone, without companions,
Inertia, faintheartedness, and character changes,
Poor physique and the convergence of many different illnesses,
Dreams which are disturbed and recurringly negative,
The welling up of powerful mental anxiety,
Impious behaviour, which does not avoid the five poisonous, dissonant mental states,
Lack of clarity and loss of faith in the [sublime] instructions,
And incontinence or constant secretion of generative fluids.

Such are the [miscellaneous] signs that death is near.
Examine and scrutinise them with awareness!
Then, [if the time of death has arrived],
The transference of consciousness should be performed![33]

SIGNS OF EXTREMELY NEAR DEATH

Now follows the presentation of the signs of extremely near death:
The five sense faculties dissolve sequentially,
And as a sign of this [imminent] demise of the sense faculties,

One will be unable to digest food and drink, and one may vomit.
Bodily warmth will diminish, the neck will not support the head,
And one will feel that the head is sinking downwards.

Then the five elements will dissolve as follows:[34]
The internal earth element comprises flesh and bone.
As an indication of its dissolution into the external earth element,
The body will grow heavy, and its skin will sag towards the ground,
Whereupon, as an internal sign, one will feel that the body is sinking into the earth.
Because the energy of earth will have dissolved into water,
One will be incapable [of supporting] one's physical form.
Bodily strength will slip away, and consciousness will become clouded.[35]

The internal water element comprises blood and serum.
As an indication of its dissolution into the external water element,
Saliva and nasal mucus will be secreted,
While the throat and the tongue will become dry.
Because the energy of water will have dissolved into fire,
The warmth of the body will slip away,
And consciousness will oscillate between clarity and dullness.[36]

The internal fire element comprises warmth.
As an indication of its dissolution into the external fire element,
The eyes will roll upwards, and one will no longer recognise people.
Because the energy of fire will have dissolved into wind,
The warmth [of the body] will converge.[37]

The internal wind element comprises breath.
As an indication of its dissolution into the external wind element,
The breath will become wheezy, and the limbs will quiver.

As an internal indication, consciousness will become turbulent,
While mirage-like flashing and fleeting [visions] will arise,
And [concurrently] all lice and nits will leave the body.[38]

[Then], the red 'generative essence' derived from one's mother will rise upwards,
And the phenomenon called 'redness' will occur,
Wherein all appearances are suffused by redness.
At that point, appearances will dissolve into the '[subtle mental consciousness of] increasing [redness]',
And the forty patterns of conceptual thought that originate from attachment will cease.[39]

[Then], the white 'generative essence' derived from one's father will fall downward,
And the phenomenon called 'whiteness' will occur,
Wherein all appearances are suffused by whiteness.
At that point, the 'increasing [redness]' will dissolve into the '[subtle mind of] attainment',
And the thirty-three patterns of conceptual thought that originate from aversion will cease.

[During this process, each exhalation of] breath will become increasingly protracted,
While all the blood of the body will converge in the 'life channel',[40]
And then a single drop of blood will form at the heart-centre.
In this way, the phenomenon called 'blackness' will occur,
Engulfing the suffocating mind in blackness,
And one will experience the sensation of falling into darkness, as if into an abyss.
At that point, 'attainment' will dissolve into the '[subtle mind of] near attainment',
And the seven patterns of conceptual thought that originate from delusion will cease.

[During this process], the mouth will open, and the eyes will roll upwards,
[Exposing] their pale underside.
External appearances [will fade], as during the setting of the sun,

And [finally] the sense faculties, memory, and perceptions will all cease,
Whereupon, all [external] appearances will be absorbed into blackness.
At that point, the [exhaled] breath will extend [from the body] by a cubit,
And [all] internal appearances will [also] come to resemble darkness.

Then, the blood in the heart will form two drops,
The head will stoop,
And the [exhaled] breath will extend [from the body] by an arrow-length.

Following this, the blood in the centre of the heart will form three drops,
And, with HIKA-like gasps, the [exhaled] breath will extend [from the body] by a double arm-span.[41]
[Then], the external breath will cease, and, engulfed by blackness, one will become unconscious.
Then, the white and red 'generative essences' will meet together at the heart,
And, as this occurs, one will swoon into a state of blissfulness.
Thus, consciousness dissolves into inner radiance,[42]
Engendering the experience of the 'co-emergent delight'.
[At this point], awareness dissolves into actual reality, at the centre of the heart, [like the meeting of] mother and child.[43]
[It is at this time that] the inner breath will [also] cease,[44]
And the vital energy and mind will rest in the central channel.

[At this moment], the inner radiance of the ground dawns upon all sentient beings,
And, in the case of a few yogins who have achieved realisation,
At this moment, the inner radiance of the path meets [the inner radiance of the ground],[45]
Like a [meeting of] a mother and child,
And [thus, now], instantaneously, in an ascending and core-penetrating manner,
These [yogins] will actualise the uncreated Buddha-body of Reality,

And through the Buddha-bodies of Perfect Resource and Emanation,
They will perform inestimable actions for the sake of all beings.
[Thus], the three buddha-bodies will be spontaneously present,
And buddhahood will have been attained.

Because of this, one should understand the significance of obtaining a human body,
And cherish the experiential cultivation of the profound [sacred] teachings.
For, even though the genuine inner radiance [of the ground] will [always] arise [at the moment of death],
In the case of all beings who have not [already] realised the [inner radiance of the path],
It will not be recognised.
The [past] births that one has assumed and left behind are countless and infinite,
And, although the inner radiance has indeed arisen an indescribable [number of times],
It has been obscured [again and again] by the dense [fog of] coemergent ignorance,
And [thereby], one has come to wander endlessly through cyclic existence.
This is why it is important to achieve such a secure level [of realisation in this life].

[SIGNS INDICATING THE PLACE OF SUBSEQUENT REBIRTH]

At the moment, [as described above], when the outer breath is about to cease,
Signs will also occur [which indicate] the place of subsequent rebirth.
If [when dying] the right hand quivers, one talks nonsensically,
And bodily warmth recedes from under the right armpit,
[This indicates that] one will be born as an antigod.

If nasal mucous and vital wind flow through the left nostril,
And bodily warmth recedes from the left eye,
[This indicates that] one will be born as a human being.
If animal sounds are emitted from the mouth, urine is secreted from the urethra,
And bodily warmth recedes from the genitals,
[This indicates that] one will be born as an animal.
If the skin turns yellowish and lustreless,
And there is salivation, accompanied by sensations of hunger,
While reproductive fluid is secreted,
[This indicates that] one will be reborn as an anguished spirit.
If the right leg shakes, defecation takes place,
Anger is felt, and bodily warmth recedes from the soles of the feet,
It is said that this person will be born in the hells.
If one experiences intense pride, bodily warmth recedes from the ears,
And consciousness is emitted via the ears,
[This indicates that] one will be born as a *yakṣa*.[46]

If good circumstances prevail [at the time of death],
And if there is minimal impairment of the vital organs, and clear mindfulness,
And if one's spiritual teacher and fellow practitioners gather together, with an inspired perspective,
And if serum and other signs appear at the crown of the head,
And consciousness is transferred from the crown of the head,
Then, it is said that one will achieve liberation, or take birth among the higher realms.[47]
Therefore, it is most important [to create] the right circumstances at the time of death.

Furthermore, there are indications and signs of a higher or lower rebirth
That arise after the death of a sentient being.
These relate to changes occurring in the sky, which should be examined over [an appropriate] number of days:
If the sky turns dark brown, or vaporous [clouds] well up,
Or if there are winds, chilling breezes, blizzards and so forth,

All these are indications that the [deceased] will be born among the hell realms.
If a lustreless mist hangs in the sky, and the sun and moon fade,
If there is no wind or breeze, and the sun is obscured,
Or if there are traces of rain, or else if it rains in the evening,
All these are indications that the [deceased] will be born among the realms of anguished spirits.
If the sky turns brownish, and there is unbroken black cloud,
Or if there is a mist and an unpleasantly brown sky,
All these are indications that the [deceased] will be born among the animal realms.
If the clouds in the sky turn yellowish black and assume terrifying forms,
And hurtle fiercely back and forth, driven by the wind,
Or if there is thunder and lightning, and the sun and moon become invisible,
All these are indications that the [deceased] will be born among the antigod realms.
If the sky is bright and the sun and moon are clearly visible,
[Or the atmosphere is] utterly clear, without wind or breeze,
All these are indications that the [deceased] will be born among the god realms.
If the sky is bright and clear, and fine white silken clouds appear,
Or if the sun and moon are encircled by aureoles of light,
All these are the indications that the [deceased] will be born among the human realms.

Whichever of the above indications arise,
They signify that the [deceased] will be born in one or other of the six [mundane] realms.
These [signs] will occur either two, three, or seven days after death,
As it is explained in the *Tantra of the Cremation of Corpses*.[48]

The indications that one has attained the three buddha-bodies with a pure rebirth,
Or that one has attained liberation in the manner of the sky-farers,

Are explained in the *Tantra of the Cremation of Corpses*, and in the *Liberation by Wearing*.[49]

One should therefore consult these sources in detail.

CONCLUSION

Since living beings do not know when they will die,
These signs of death should be looked for again and again.
When the signs occur, indicating that one is certainly to die,
Then one should renounce whatever possessions one has,
And clearly call to mind the spiritual teacher,
One's fellow practitioners, assembled around one, and the oral teachings.
Especially, one should prepare to apply the transference [of consciousness],[50]
And listen to and reflect on the teaching of the *Liberation by Hearing in the Intermediate States*.[51]

[However], when the external, internal, and secret signs of death do occur,
If one does not perform the *Ritual Deception of Death*,[52]
One will incur the downfall of abandoning the assemblies of the Peaceful and Wrathful Deities,
Who are the Conquerors, present within one's own body.[53]
As a result, one's commitments will degenerate, and one will proceed to the hells.
It is said that this is even more negative than the [five] inexpiable crimes.
Therefore one should diligently persevere in the practices of the *Ritual Deception of Death*.
[Furthermore], if consciousness is transferred [too soon],
When [only] one or other of the external or internal signs of death is present,
This is called the 'slaying of the deities'.
One must not allow this to occur, because the downfall will be extremely great.
But if all the signs of death are completely present, and cannot be averted,

Then, and only then, should one apply the instructions of consciousness transference.

It is said, in the tantras, with regard to the advantages of the timely application of consciousness transference,

That even one who has committed an inexpiable crime

Will proceed to higher rebirths and blissful states,

And can attain liberation, [through the timely application of the instructions on transference].

EMA! I have here presented the *Natural Liberation through [Recognition of] the Visual Indications and Signs of Death*,

Which is a supporting text to the teaching on the *Liberation by Hearing in the Intermediate States*,

An extract from the *Peaceful and Wrathful Deities: A Profound Sacred Teaching, [entitled] Natural Liberation through [Recognition of] Enlightened Intention.*

O yogins of posterity, comprehend this as it is!

SAMAYA! *rgya rgya rgya!*

May [this teaching] be encountered by fortunate beings,

Who possess a [positive] residue of past actions,

And who are intelligent, faithful, persevering, and compassionate.

May [the activities associated with this teaching],

The *Natural Liberation through [Recognition of] the Visual Indications and Signs of Death*, never be exhausted

Until cyclic existence has been emptied!

This is a treasure-teaching revealed by the accomplished master Karma Lingpa. May virtue prevail!

9

Natural Liberation of Fear through the Ritual Deception of Death

CONTEXT

This is the companion text to the previous chapter and it describes the practices to be followed in the event that definitive signs indicating death are discerned.

The general consolidated rite described in this chapter follows the classical structure of many *Vajrayāna* protective rituals. This consolidated rite, and similar rituals, are commonly performed in Tibetan Buddhist communities today by practitioners, both for their own benefit and for the benefit of others.* On the other hand, the specific rites, related to specific signs, are again idiosyncratic and are not commonly practised.

*For a selection of finely translated *Vajrayāna* protective rituals, see Stephen Beyer, *The Cult of Tārā*.

Herein is contained the *Natural Liberation of Fear through the Ritual Deception of Death*,[1] [an extract] from the *Peaceful and Wrathful Deities: A Profound Sacred Teaching, [entitled] Natural Liberation through [Recognition of] Enlightened Intention*.[2]

I bow down to the glorious transcendent one, [Vajra]kumāra, whose face frowns with wrath![3]

The methods by which death can be averted and postponed should now be explained in order that living beings might be released from suffering, and in order that all the unremitting and extremely bitter sufferings of death, [in particular], might be dispelled by Mahākāruṇika.[4] For, the sufferings of all such beings [who are afflicted by the discomforts associated with death] may be completely curtailed [through ritual means]. It is the case that, for some children of buddha nature, the signs of death will arise, [when looked for] as described in the previous chapter. The esoteric instructions for averting [the signs which indicate] the swiftly approaching year or month [of death] consist of both the general consolidated rite and specific rites.

GENERAL CONSOLIDATED RITE FOR AVERTING DEATH

The general rite for averting death is applicable in cases when the lifespan is threatened by obstacle-causing forces and [imbalanced] elemental forces. Now, the body of a person acts as a supporting frame for the five elements, and it naturally comprises five appendages, five sense-organs, five solid viscera, five hollow viscera, and five great energy channels. In each of these [anatomical] parts, the five elements circulate in a clockwise manner,[5] and the cessation of life can occur due to [external] circumstances, or one could die through the mingling of conflicting internal elements, or life could also cease through the agency of a severe obstacle-causing force. The [time of] death may be ascertained by actually observing the respective signs associated with these [three causes of death], as and when they manifest.

Immediately following the initial experience of such [signs], one should perform the [appropriate] rites for averting [death], which include ceremonies, services, and exorcisms.

In this regard, [one should know that] of the twelve months of the year, two are ruled by each of the [five] elements, while the two [remaining] months are ruled [by all five elements] in common. Also, within each of these months [of the year] there is a five-day period ruled by each of the [five] elements, while the five [remaining] days are ruled [by all five elements] in common. [The signs of death] cannot be averted, however, when an [imbalanced] elemental or malevolent force [completely] controls the body. Just as, for example, if fire breaks out in a tall fortress, it is more easily averted while it is first confined within the lower storey, but should it reach the top [of the fortress], the fire cannot be extinguished.

A person in whom the signs [of death] have manifested should first make preliminary offerings to the spiritual teacher, and to the Three Precious Jewels, and accumulate as much merit as possible. Then, the ritual for averting [an imbalance in the elements] should be effected through the agency of the wheels and seed-syllables of the elements. This should be done as follows: [First], draw a series of wheels [representing the elements] on Indian paper or palm leaf. The representation of the [green] wheel of the wind element[6] should depict four spokes and a circumference, with five YAṂ syllables inscribed, one on each spoke and one at the centre, and with the vowels and consonants [depicted] on the outer circumference.[7] The red wheel of the fire element should be similar [in design], with four spokes etc., but inscribed with five RAṂ syllables, placed as before, and the vowels and consonants on its circumference, [all placed] as before. Similarly, the yellow wheel of the earth element should be depicted with five LAṂ syllables, the white wheel of the water element with five KHAṂ syllables, and the azure wheel of the space element with five E syllables. [Then], on each of these inscribed wheels, one should visualise the deities who embody the nature of these elements, corresponding in colour to their respective wheels.[8]

Then one should make five offerings, [one] to [each of] these [deities], confess all negativity, and pray for one's desired purpose. After this, recite the seed-syllables of the individual [deities] the appropriate number of times, corresponding to the age of the person in years, and [visualise that] the [seed-syllables] are then absorbed into the [respective] deities.[9] Then [each of the depictions] of the [elemental] wheels should be placed inside containers made from two small bowls of dough, which are sealed together, and bound with threads of five colours, forming [the pattern of] a cross.

In addition, a dough effigy of the subject's human form should be prepared, one cubit in height. The dough should be mixed with wood, water, fire, earth, and the breath of different species of sentient beings.[10] [Depictions of] the [same] five seed-syllables should then be inserted into the five [corresponding] sense-organs [of this effigy].[11]

As for the substances to be used for the ritual deception of the malevolent forces [which cause death], create substitutes, which may be made either of red minium clay, or else from dough, which is then painted. These should all be equal finger-widths in size, black, red, yellow, white, green and multicoloured,[12] corresponding in number to the age of the subject. These should be mixed with the subject's grime, clothing, nasal mucus, saliva, tears, hair, fingernails, and so forth; as well as with ground jewels or precious substances. They should then be adorned with [five] coloured wool threads and various silks, and also decorated with many sorts of bird feathers, [which are indicative] of bad omens.[13] Each [substitute] should then have a torma-offering [prepared], corresponding to it in colour, and [it should be surrounded by] a number of dough *chang-bu* offerings, equalling the subject's age in years.

Then, consecrate all these with the six mantras and six gestures, and repeat the following words, 'Take them! Take them! O mighty [malignant] ones! Your craving! Your attachment! Your clinging! Your memories! Your grasping! Your thoughts! Your contact! Let go of them! Be pacified! And be free!'

Then, together with the [bowls containing the elemental] wheels, cast [these substitutes] into the torrent of a wide river. Death will thereby be averted for up to three years. It is best, therefore, if this rite is performed once every three years, even before the indications [of death] have occurred.

SPECIFIC RITES FOR AVERTING DEATH

I bow down to the deity Mahākāruṇika,
Who is a sanctuary of great bliss.

The methods employed in the specific rites for averting death are now presented.

[Ritual Averting of Signs of Near Death]

For all these rites, which follow, it is best if the subject's own spiritual teacher can be present, or alternatively a sympathetic friend. They should empower the five sense-organs [of the subject] with the seed-syllables of the elements.[14]

Then, in cases when the fingernails become lustreless, [as described in the previous chapter], a religious feast should be offered to seven monks. Donations should be offered, and one should receive the [Buddhist] vows, wearing yellow clothes. If one has already taken these vows, one should retake them. Thereby, [death] will be averted.

Similarly, in cases when the cornea of the eyes begins to fade, small terracotta imprints of white earth should be moulded, their number equalling the subject's own age in years. After seven circumambulations [of the terracotta imprints], cast these into a lake or river, and then [retreat], taking a number of paces equal to the subject's age in years, while reciting the Heart-mantra of Dependent Origination[15] and not looking back.

In cases when the hair of the nape of the neck grows upwards, one should prepare a dough with black seeds and [use this to] make a substitute effigy, one cubit in height. Into its heart, one should then insert a number of crushed berries, equalling the subject's age in years, and attach a label bearing the subject's own name. The hair should be made from the subject's cut hair. Blood should be drawn from the subject's body, and smeared on its face. It should then be wrapped in the subject's clothing and smeared with black pigment. Then, at one hundred and twenty-one paces from the subject's own dwelling, one should dig a triangular dark pit, and recite [RAṂ], the seed-syllable of the element fire, a number of times equalling the subject's age in years. Then repeat the following words three times, 'Black demon! Take this [effigy]! This is important! This is important!' Then, throw it into the pit, defecate upon it, cover it with earth and run away. Then, one should re-examine [the above sign of death]. If it persists as before, the rite will not have been effective [and need not be repeated]. However, there is no doubt that if other [associated signs] have not been [completely] averted by a single performance [of the rite], they will be successfully averted following three such performances.

In cases when the indication of [protruding] ankle bones appears, one should face westwards towards the sun when it is close to setting, and remove one's clothes. Then placing a dog's tail under you and some excrement in a heap in front, one should eat a mouthful and bark like a dog. This [rite] should be repeated three times.

Also in cases when other people are afflicted by illness: if the roots of their teeth grow grimy and black, such a person should wear a goat's skin, face the sunrise, and bleat three times like a goat. Similarly, in cases when the nostrils sag inwards, it will be beneficial if one visualises the syllable A on the tip of the subject's nose,[16] recites the syllable A twenty-one times, and bathes in various rivers.

In cases when the limbs are subject to repeated spasms, it will be beneficial if one draws a four-spoked wheel on each of the limbs with a solution of shellac, and bathes a number of times, equalling the subject's age in years, in [consecrated] water over which many *dhāraṇī* mantras have been recited.

In cases when the eyes stare fixedly, one should prepare a bountiful religious feast on behalf of the monastic community; and hold a party for a number of children, equalling the subject's age in years. One should also wear red clothing.

In cases when the right cheek sags inwards, [for the rites of the earth element], one should mould a number of small terracotta imprints, equalling the subject's age in years. For the rites of the water element one should make a number of water libations, equalling the subject's age in years; for the rites of the fire element one should make a number of burnt offerings, equalling the subject's age in years; for the rites of the wind element, one should erect a number of flags, equalling the subject's age in years; and for the rites of the space element, one should recite a number of syllables E, equalling the subject's age in years. Thereby, there is no doubt that [death] will be ritually deceived.

In cases when the breathing becomes agitated, it will be beneficial and [death] will be averted if one makes a concentrated paste of molasses over which [YAṂ], the seed-syllable of the wind element, has been recited.

In cases when the nose tilts to the right or left, one should visualise a white syllable HŪṂ on the tip of the nose. In cases when tears flow uncontrollably, one should visualise the syllable BHRŪṂ on the subject's eyes.[17] In cases when the left cheek sags inwards, one should visualise the syllable KṢA [on the cheek].[18] In cases when the teeth become locked, one should visualise the syllable HŪṂ [on the teeth]. If a black spot appears on the tongue, one should visualise the short syllable HŪṂ [on the tongue].[19] If the ears lie flat [against the head], one should visualise the syllable MĀṂ [on the ears].[20] If the xiphoid of the chest is sagging inwards, one should visualise the syllable MŪṂ [on the xiphoid].[21] In cases when the pulse of the carotid arteries[22] is missing, one should visualise the syllable HŪṂ [on those arteries]. These visualised syllables should be recited as many times as equals the subject's age in years; and they should also be drawn [on the appropriate point of the body], using vermilion and scented water.

[Ritual Averting of the Signs of Remote Death]

Similarly, when an examination is made of one's reflected image optically projected onto the sky: if the symbolic hand-held implement is missing, one should perform one hundred and eight feast-offerings on behalf of one's spiritual teacher. If the right hand is missing, one should prepare a dough effigy, one cubit in height, using seven kinds of grain. The head should be fashioned to resemble an open-jawed lion, and a number of gull feathers should be inserted into it, equalling the subject's age in years. The effigy should then be carried down a main street towards a royal manor, which is located to the north.

In cases when the left hand is missing, one should place the fang of a black-striped tiger and the fang of a black dog inside a weasel skin. On top of that one should place a dough effigy, kneaded together with the subject's own urine, and then ritually expel the effigy by throwing it into a river.

In cases when the right leg is missing below the knee, [death] will be averted if, at dusk as the sun is setting, one offers a number of acacia or juniper lamps, equalling the subject's age in years.

In cases when the left leg is missing, one should make an effigy of white earth, one cubit in height, and insert into its heart a birchwood stick, four finger-widths in length, marked with notches, equalling the subject's own age in number. It should be carried off at daybreak, and left in an empty quadrangle.

In cases when the right part of the head is missing, one should compound various kinds of inauspicious earth with the fruits of black wood trees, and [out of this mixture] make a black amulet, into which the subject's own hair and clothing fragments should be inserted, along with a label made from mountain willow wood, [inscribed] with the names of the twelve [animal] year-signs. Then the amulet should be sealed, and a number of thorns of different species should be attached to its upper face. If one can find as many differing types of thorn as equals the subject's age in years it would be best. Otherwise, if one cannot find [that many], one should insert as many [differing types] as one can find. Then at midnight, one should put on black clothing and carry the amulet to a cemetery.

In cases when the left part of the head is missing, one should make a dough effigy using twenty-five different types of grain, and insert [fragments of] human bones, horse bones and dog bones into its heart. Then, one should wrap the effigy in the subject's old clothing, and at twilight on the eleventh day [of the lunar month], one should give it to another person for insertion into a pit [which has been made] eighty paces to the south. At that time, one should cry out, proclaiming one's sorrows three times, and bury the effigy. Thereupon, [death] will be averted.

In cases when the head is missing above the neck, one should make a number of burnt offerings using thorn bushes, equalling the subject's age in years, and burn them in succession. While each of these is burning, the heart-mantra syllable of fire [RAṂ] should be recited, for a number of times equalling the subject's age in years.

In cases when the head and the neck are missing, one should blacken one's body with burnt charcoal, and bind one's hair up on the crown of the head. Then, on a piece of paper, four finger-widths in size, one should write the subject's age and the name of the present year, and around this in the four cardinal directions, one should inscribe the seed-syllables of the four elements. This [paper simulacrum] should then be attached to the nose, and at noon on the ninth day [of the lunar month], one should run in each of the four directions, shouting out uninterruptedly, 'You take this! You take this!' Then the paper should be buried in a charnel ground.

In cases when the upper trunk is missing, one should light a wood fire, and burn a label inscribed with the names of the twelve [animal] year-signs. In cases when the lower trunk is missing, it will suffice if one goes to a charnel ground, and uses the assorted bones one finds to make smoke.

In cases when the right side of the body is missing, [one should recite the *dhāraṇī* mantra of] Uṣṇīṣa[-vijayā], as many times as equals the subject's age in years, and one should [mould] a number of small terracotta imprints, equalling the subject's age in years. In cases when the left side [of the body] is missing, one should read aloud countless *dhāraṇī* mantras, and wear red clothing.

[Ritual Averting of Further Signs of Near Death]

In cases when the 'severing of the bond between atmosphere and earth' occurs, one should read aloud the extensive scriptures,[23] or complete a number of virtuous acts.

In cases when the 'fall of a rider on a white lioness' occurs, it will be beneficial if one performs as many maṇḍala rituals as equals the subject's age in years.

If the 'rupturing of the [Wish-granting] Tree' occurs, one should know the cures for each of the [ailments affecting] the solid and hollow viscera.[24]

In cases when urine scum appears reddish blue,[25] one should fashion a dough effigy of the twelve [animal] year-signs, with their elements,[26] and for each subsequent change in the colour [of the urine scum], one should make a single terracotta imprint, a single water libation, a single 'substitute effigy' of the subject, and a single burnt offering of birchwood. Then, at sunrise, one should carry these off to a cemetery in the north-east.

In cases when [the urine vapour] is blackish and putrid, one's purpose will be achieved if one mixes powdered iron and copper with various grains, and scatters this [mixture] in the four directions.

In cases when the vapour is red and spotted, one should make a number of substitutes, imbued with the subject's own body odour, equalling the subject's age in years, and attach a red silk flag and a porcupine quill to each. [Death] will be averted if one carries these off, together with assorted bones, to a main road in the east.

In cases when one's excrement has no vapour, one should face the west at a time when the sun is at its peak, and inscribe the elemental seed-syllables on the skull of a horse. [Death] will then be averted if one neighs as many times as possible.

In cases when the humming sound [normally heard] when the ears [are cupped] is absent,[27] one should prepare a number of torma-offerings of various foods, equalling one's age in years, and attach a label to each of these, bearing the names of the twelve [animal year-signs]. One's purpose will be achieved if one then conveys these [torma-offerings] to the foot of a palm tree.[28]

In cases when the [sign known as] '[one-legged Yavati] arising [as an enemy] against the leaves of the Wish-granting Tree' occurs, one will be liberated [from the indications of death], if one perseveres in the accumulation [of merit] and engages in virtuous activities.

[CONCLUSION]

After the rituals have been performed according to the above instructions, one should look again [for the visual indications of death]. If the nature of their appearance has altered, the indications will undoubtedly be averted if the rites are repeated from seven to twenty-one times, or a number of times equalling the subject's age in years.

This completes the esoteric instruction concerning the ritual aversion of death, which was composed by the master Padmasambhava, as a means of liberating sentient beings from their sufferings. May it be encountered by one of worthy past actions!

SAMAYA! *rgya rgya rgya!*

This is a treasure-teaching revealed by the treasure-finder Karma Lingpa.

10

Consciousness Transference: Natural Liberation through Recollection

CONTEXT

Practitioners of this cycle of teachings who commence with the *Preliminary Practice* (Chapter 1), and purify all their negativity and obscurations, generated by their past actions, through the practice of the *Natural Liberation of Habitual Tendencies*, the *Hundredfold Homage* and the *Confession* (Chapters 5–7), and who also experientially cultivate the practices described in the *Introduction to Awareness* (Chapter 4), will, in the best of cases, attain liberation from cyclic existence in this very lifetime.

However, those who are unable to realise this level of achievement should implement the instructions on consciousness transference described in this chapter at the time of their own death.

This wonderful practice is classed among the few that do not require previous experience of Vajrayāna meditational practices in order to be effective. Once guidance has been received from a qualified spiritual teacher, the practitioner should follow the course of training, outlined in this chapter, until the signs of accomplishment arise. Then, the practitioner should maintain this proficiency throughout his or her life.

It is regarded as extremely beneficial if those that are accomplished in this practice perform this consciousness transference in support of other people or animals when they are dying. This should be begun during the interval between the cessation of the outer respiration and the cessation of the inner respiration, at the point when the mind and body separate, and can be continued for an appropriate period after death.

As the text stresses, at the time of the practitioner's own death, it is critically important that this technique is only actually implemented at the exact moment of death.

Herein is contained an oral instruction entitled *Consciousness Transference: Natural Liberation [through Recollection]*,[1] which relates to the intermediate state of the time of death. This is the fourth topic in the *Guide to the Six Intermediate States according to the Perfection Stage*,[2] which is an extract from the *Peaceful and Wrathful Deities: A Profound Sacred Teaching, [entitled] Natural Liberation through [Recognition of] Enlightened Intention.*[3]

INTRODUCTION

This *Consciousness Transference: Natural Liberation through Recollection*, which is the fourth topic [in the *Guide to the Six Intermediate States according to the Perfection Stage*, and which specifically contains] guidance on the intermediate state of the time of death, will [now] be presented.[4]

This *Consciousness Transference: Natural Liberation through Recollection* is a powerful method, a means for attaining buddhahood which does not [necessarily] require meditation. This oral instruction through which buddhahood can be attained at the time of death is [therefore] most valuable for those who have not trained in the cycle of Cutting through Resistance, or [in the meditations of] the Illusory Body, Dream Yoga, and Inner Radiance, and have [therefore] not realised the truth of the four modes of liberation. In particular, [it is valuable] for ordinary persons, officials, householders and distracted individuals who have had no time to meditate, despite having received those [instructions]. That is, [it is valuable to all] those who have not engaged in experiential cultivation, even though they may have obtained profound teachings, and who, [as a consequence], may die in an ordinary frame of mind, having left the instructions as [unrealised] words, or having left [their relationship to] the [sacred] teachings as a [mere] theoretical understanding.

Now, anyone who is born is subsequently certain to die. Yet the time of death is unknown. Indeed, since one's death might be imminent, one should be constantly alert to [the signs which portend] death. In accordance with the *Natural Liberation through [Recognition of] the Visual Indications and Signs of Death*,[5] one should analyse the signs indicative of remote death, the signs indicative of near death, the signs indicative of uncertain death, and the signs indicative of inevitable death. One should also persevere with [the practices contained in] the *Ritual Deception of Death*, as these correspond to the signs of death which might appear.[6] If, on the other hand, one were to perform this consciousness transference, either when the signs of death are not fully present or even when the signs are fully present but without having [first] practised the ritual deception of death, then one would, in effect, incur the crime of slaying a deity, and the crime of committing suicide. This is an even greater misdeed than committing [one of the five] inexpiable crimes. Thus, it is essential that one should perform the general and specific ritual deceptions of death, whichever is appropriate, three times or as often as is required, in accordance with the *Natural Liberation of Fear through the Ritual Deception of Death*.[7] If, despite having performed the [appropriate] ritual deception of death on three occasions, the indications of death are unaltered, this demonstrates that death is certain to occur. It is at this time [only] therefore that one should begin to engage in the [actual practice of] consciousness transference.

Since it is said that [this practice may confer] higher rebirth or liberation even on one who has committed the five inexpiable crimes, the timely application of consciousness transference can be of extremely great benefit.

TRAINING IN CONSCIOUSNESS TRANSFERENCE

[The practice of] consciousness transference has two aspects: [namely] training and the actual application.

First, with regard to training: just as, for example, when a man faces the inevitability of the arrival of an external foe, before his enemy approaches, he will prepare armour, weapons, and arrows, and train in the arts [of warfare], but only don [and apply] these when the enemy [actually] arrives and strikes, so, in this context, the training takes place before the indications of death have arisen. Since one does not know when one will die, training should be undertaken from the present moment, for it is essential that [one is able] to complete the actual application [of consciousness transference] successfully, when death becomes certain.

Now, the training in consciousness transference may be undertaken [in two contexts]: at times when [general] guidance [on preliminary practices] is being given, or when specific guidance on consciousness transference is being given, whichever is appropriate.[8]

As found in the preliminary practices of the [general] guidance,[9] one should reflect upon the difficulty of obtaining [a human form endowed with] freedoms and opportunities [conducive to practice], and [one should reflect on] the sufferings of cyclic existence, and develop an attitude which is disillusioned with cyclic existence and desirous of renunciation. Furthermore, even though one has obtained [the above freedoms and opportunities], which are difficult to obtain, one should [always], from the depths of one's heart, remember death, which is never far away.

Then, sitting on a comfortable seat in the posture of the bodhisattvas, one should, in the following manner, close the orifices [of the body which lead to rebirth] within cyclic existence:

The body should be upright and erect. The hands should cover the knees, forming the earth-touching gesture,[10] and the shoulders should be drawn upwards. Then, in one's own heart one should visualise an azure blue syllable HŪṂ, blazing with light, from which a single syllable HŪṂ breaks away and descends to the rectum, precisely blocking the orifice through which the hells are entered. Another syllable HŪṂ breaks away and descends to the orifice of procreation, thereby blocking the entrance to [the realm of] the anguished spirits. Similarly, another syllable HŪṂ [breaks away and] blocks the entrance [to the world of] animals, which is in the urethra, while yet another syllable HŪṂ moves to the navel, and others to the mouth, the nostrils, the eyes, and the ears, each one precisely blocking its respective orifice.[11]

Then, on the crown of the head, one should visualise that the crown fontanelle is blocked by a downward-facing white syllable HAṂ.[12] [Further, one should visualise] the central channel, in the middle of the body, straight and erect, with a yellowish white lustre, like a taut air-filled sheep's intestine, with its lower extremity extending below the navel, and its upper extremity extending to the crown fontanelle. At the lower extremity below the navel, at a focal point where the three [main] channels converge,[13] one should visualise a brilliant white seminal point, which is the essence of awareness, radiant and clear, breathing rhythmically, continuously pulsating, and on the verge of ascending.

In the space above the crown of the head, one should visualise one's spiritual teacher, seated, full of joy, in the form of Vajradhara. Then, one's bodily weight should be [drawn in and] concentrated upwards, and the rectum forcefully closed. The eyes should be turned upwards, the tongue [lifted to] rest along the upper palate, and the hands firmly placed in the 'fist' gesture,[14] with the thumbs pressing down on the bases of the fourth fingers.

[Then], from below the navel, the seminal point is moved forcefully upwards, and, through the engagement of speech, it is elevated with the support of guttural gasps pronounced as 'HI-KA HI-KA'. Through the force of the vital energy below, the seminal point is unable to resist being accelerated upwards through the central channel. By this method, it is moved upwards, with seven HI-KA gasps, to the navel. Then, with a further seven HI-KA gasps it reaches the heart, with a further seven it reaches the throat, and with a further seven it reaches the space between the eyebrows. Then, uttering HI-KA, [a final time], the seminal point makes contact with the syllable HAṂ at the crown fontanelle, after which one should visualise that it spins downwards again and comes to rest below the navel as a white diffusion. Rest in that state for some time.

By simply repeating this exercise a few times, signs will emerge that this [training in] consciousness transference has taken effect: a sensation of warmth will well up at the crown fontanelle, and there will be sensations of prickliness, irritation, numbness, and swelling, while the crown of the head will seem to become supple and numb, and serous fluid, blood, and so forth will emerge at the crown fontanelle. When this occurs, the spiritual teacher should carefully examine the crown fontanelle: a peacock feather or stalk of grass should be inserted [into the fontanelle] so that it settles into [the fontanelle]. This [insertion] confirms that the training in consciousness transference has been successfully achieved.

If you do not stop at this point, your practice can limit your lifespan. Therefore, one should cease the visualisation and yogic exercises, and the crown of the head should be massaged with butter or grain-seed oil. If, on the other hand, the signs do not appear, [the seminal point] should be moved upwards many times by vigorous effort until the signs eventually do emerge.

Furthermore, swelling may occur on the crown of the head, and if [the seminal point] remains localised at the crown fontanelle [and the fontanelle is not breached], headaches and similar [uncomfortable sensations] will occur. Therefore, one should visualise that the syllable HAṂ at the crown fontanelle is opened up, and that the seminal point emerges vertically from the crown fontanelle, touches the feet of the spiritual teacher [visualised above], and then descends again through the fontanelle to rest motionless below the navel. By repeating this exercise, just a few times, the crown fontanelle will be opened, blood or serous fluid will certainly emerge, and the blade of grass can then be inserted.

After this, it is very important that the crown fontanelle be re-blocked by the syllable HAṂ, for not doing so could limit your lifespan.

Subsequently [in training], when manoeuvring the seminal point up and down within the central channel without the HI-KA breathing and yogic exercises, it remains very important to keep the crown fontanelle blocked with the syllable HAṂ.

The [training in] consciousness transference should be practised in the above manner.

However, because HI-KA is a mantra which reduces the lifespan, this should only be used until [training in] consciousness transference is successful. Otherwise, after [the training] has been successful, do not resort to the HI-KA breathing. If, on account of excessive exertion, one overdoes [the training in] consciousness transference, one will run the risk of lapsing into perpetual unconsciousness. In such cases, and if the consciousness has risen too precipitously, and one experiences vertigo and so forth, one should beat the soles of the feet with the fists and massage the crown of the head. Then, while focusing intensely on the visualisation of an extremely heavy golden stūpa on the soles of the feet, one should perform many yogic jumps, so that [the consciousness] is becalmed. These essential points are to be generally observed in the course of the practical training.

The 'consciousness transference of the training phase' which has just been described should be carefully practised while one is in good health, and before the signs of death emerge. SAMAYA!

THE ACTUAL APPLICATION OF CONSCIOUSNESS TRANSFERENCE AT THE TIME OF DEATH

[The Timing and Context]

Secondly, the application phase refers to the actual transference of consciousness, which is to be undertaken when the indications of death are unequivocally present and when, even after performing the [appropriate] ritual deception of death [practice] on three occasions, it is indicated that one will not recover. There are four [modes of actual consciousness transference], namely: consciousness transference into the Buddha-body of Reality; consciousness transference into the Buddha-body of Perfect Resource; consciousness transference into the Buddha-body of Emanation; and the consciousness transference of ordinary persons.

Concerning these, it is said [in the *Root Verses of the Six Intermediate States*]:[15]

Alas, now as the intermediate state of the time of death arises before me,
Renouncing [all] attachment, yearning and subjective apprehension in every respect,
I must undistractedly enter the path, on which the oral teachings are clearly understood,
And eject my own awareness into the uncreated expanse of space.

Now, when the signs of the onset of the intermediate state of the time of death are provoked by fatal illnesses, at this time, when the indications of death are completely present, there are oral instructions which bring clearly to mind that which may be obscured during the intermediate state of the time of death. [The clarity of these instructions] is likened to [the clarity of] an elegant lady looking into a mirror. These [instructions] are twofold: a clarification which is elucidated by another[16] and a clarification undertaken by oneself.

In the former context: regardless of whether or not one perceives the unequivocal presence of the signs of [one's own impending] death, these signs will be recognised by the physician and by the nurses, based on [their knowledge of] the behavioural changes which occur.[17] Nonetheless, if one's own mindfulness remains clear, one should also examine the indications of near death of one's own accord. In any case, when [it is thus ascertained that] one is dying, an invitation should be sent to one's root spiritual teacher if he or she lives nearby, and all one's possessions should be offered to the teacher, without even a single instant of attachment. If one remains even slightly attached [to worldly goods], one may be cast into inferior existences, as recounted in the story of the monk Barwasum.[18]

If an individual is unable to make such offerings in actuality, these should be offered mentally, and thereby a complete state of renunciation should be achieved. In particular, one should not leave any object at all close to [the dying person] which could give rise to attachment or aversion. This is the sense of the verse 'Renouncing [all] attachment, yearning and subjective apprehension in every respect.' At this time, renunciation should be generated stainlessly. As it is said in the *Tantra of the Coalescence of Sun and Moon*:[19]

> In particular, one should please with offerings and feasts
> One's own spiritual teacher, the monastic community,
> And the field of accumulated merits.[20]

Once the spiritual teacher has arrived, one should confess any former violations or breaches of the commitments, if any; and make amends for any transgressions or downfalls previously committed. If one holds any vows, these should be reaffirmed, and if no vows are held, these should be taken on the basis of the *Rite of Going for Refuge*.[21] Then, if one has had previous experience in [the practice of] consciousness transference, one should assume the appropriate bodily posture, and the visualisation should be repeatedly elucidated by one's spiritual teacher, in accordance with the [specific tradition] of consciousness transference one formerly practised.[22] Thereupon, it should take effect. As an indication of success, as soon as one has expired, the signs that this transference has been effective, such as blood or serous fluid [appearing] at a swelling on the crown of the head, will certainly emerge.

If these signs do emerge, there will be no need to elucidate the intermediate states. But if they do not appear, the spiritual teacher should place his or her lips close to the ear, or else place a bamboo reed or a hollow tube of paper close to the ear, and through it slowly elucidate the verses [describing] the intermediate states in succession, starting with the intermediate state of reality or inner radiance, in accordance with the *Liberation by Hearing*.[23] If this is done appropriately, it is certain that [these instructions] will be effective. [The reason for their effectiveness can be illustrated as follows]: If, for example, a powerful king were to dispatch a message through a reliable person, it would be impossible for that person to forget [the message]. He would communicate it absolutely, fearing that royal reproach would ensue if he were to forget. Similarly, in this context, too, fearing the abyss of the lower existences, one will certainly retain the instructions in mind, and thereby achieve certainty as to [the nature] of the intermediate state of reality.

If one's spiritual teacher is not present, the elucidation should be made by a spiritual friend holding the same teaching lineage [as oneself], or else by a fellow spiritual sibling whose commitments have not been dissipated, and whose view and conduct are sympathetic.

It is said in the *Tantra of the Coalescence of Sun and Moon*:

> At that time, the oral instructions of the spiritual teacher
> Should saturate one's mental continuum.
> These truths should be repeatedly elucidated.
> The elucidation should be made repeatedly by a spiritual teacher, spiritual friend, or by a fellow spiritual sibling.

Such is the form of the clarification which should be made by others [who are caring for a dying person].

Secondly, the clarification to be undertaken by oneself [at the time of one's own death] is applicable in cases where the spiritual teacher and fellow students have not gathered together, or where one dies alone in a hermitage, or when one already has a refined experience [of consciousness transference] and does not require an elucidation to be made by others. In such cases, one should bring clearly to mind the practices which one formerly experientially cultivated.

Consciousness Transference into the Buddha-body of Reality

Now, if one is a person who has some understanding of inner radiance, who has cultivated the view of emptiness, and encountered it directly in [one's own] awareness, the consciousness transference into the Buddha-body of Reality is the supreme [method].

Thus, when this is undertaken, one should first ensure, as above, that one is completely without a single possession which could generate attachment or aversion. If one is capable, one should secure one's body in the seven postures [of Vairocana], or sit upright. If this is not possible, one should lie on one's right side, with the head pointing north, and repeatedly think: 'Now that I am about to die, how fortunate am I to be able to effect the transference of consciousness based on a profound instruction such as this, while in the three realms of cyclic existence in general and in particular in this degenerate age. So today, I shall now recognise the inner radiance of death to be the Buddha-body of Reality, and consequently take birth as an inestimable number of emanations, in order to guide each in accord with his or her needs. I must act on behalf of sentient beings until cyclic existence has been emptied!' In this way, generate the altruistic intention [to attain enlightenment for the benefit of others] fervently and repeatedly. Then, one should think undistractedly, as follows: 'I must attend to [the words of] my spiritual teacher, and must [act] in accordance with the content of the profound teachings which I [formerly] received.' The whole point is that one should not be distracted from a state in which the oral instructions are clearly held in mind.

Then, without concocting thoughts, one should free oneself from the [dualistic] framework of the object, which is to be transmigrated, and the [subjective] act of consciousness transference. Intrinsic awareness should be uncontrived and clear, undistracted and distinct, stark in its [coalescence of] radiance and emptiness. Let [this experience] remain unmoving for a prolonged period. If one expires in this state, the mother and child inner radiances, that is to say the inner radiance of the ground and the inner radiance of the path which is the focus of one's current meditation, will encounter each other, like a stream meeting the main river. [Thus], one will attain the uncreated Buddha-body of Reality, in an upward-moving core-penetrating manner; and liberation will be instantaneous. This is called the 'pure consciousness transference into the Buddha-body of Reality' because those who have highly developed experience and realisation need repeat only this, again and again. It is the best of all modes of consciousness transference.

Now, in the case of those who have not recognised [intrinsic awareness] and who are without experience and realisation, though they may well try to apply this consciousness transference into the Buddha-body of Reality, [this would be ineffectual]. It would be [like trying] to show a material object to someone who has been blind from birth, or [like trying] to point out a [particular] star to a dog. It is very important, therefore, that the [method of] consciousness transference and the manner of its clarification correspond to the mental capacity of the individual.

If, however, the consciousness transference into the Buddha-body of Reality is effected in the above manner, as an 'outer sign', the sky will become clear and unclouded; and as an 'inner sign', the body will glow radiantly and its lustre will not fade for a long time. The 'secret signs' include the appearance of the white syllable AṂ and the azure syllable HŪṂ [among the cremated relics].[24]

Such is [the instruction on] the consciousness transference into the Buddha-body of Reality. SAMAYA!

Consciousness Transference into the Buddha-body of Perfect Resource

If one chiefly practises the generation stage [of meditation] and particularly if one has little certainty with regard to [the experience of] emptiness, one should undertake the consciousness transference into the Buddha-body of Perfect Resource. If one is capable of securing one's body in an upright position, adopting as suggested before the appropriate bodily posture, then one should sit upright and bring clearly to mind the visualisations of consciousness transference, as previously practised during one's training. In particular, one should clearly visualise above the crown of one's head, upon a lotus, sun and moon cushion, one's spiritual teacher [in the form of] the Buddha-body of Perfect Resource. [The teacher may be visualised as] the great Vajradhara, or Vajrasattva, Avalokiteśvara, and so forth, and especially as one's own particular meditational deity, following whichever [practices of] the generation stage one prefers. One should meditate clearly on the essence of intrinsic awareness as a white seminal point, [situated] below the navel at the lower extremity of the central channel within the body; or alternatively, [one should clearly visualise here] the seed-syllable of one's very own meditational deity: a white syllable AḤ, an azure syllable HŪṂ, a red syllable HRĪḤ, and so forth, as appropriate.[25] It will be best if one [also] clearly visualises that [each of] the orifices [of one's body] is blocked by the syllable HŪṂ; but if this is not visualised, one should focus one's consciousness single-pointedly within the central channel, without mentally engaging the orifices.

Then, one's bodily weight should be [drawn in and] concentrated upwards, and the rectum forcefully closed. The eyes should be turned upwards, and the tongue [lifted to] rest along the [upper] palate. The lower vital energy should be moved upwards, while focusing one's consciousness within the central channel. Then, in conjunction with a series of HI-KA HI-KA gasps, [the seminal point] should be moved successively upwards until it reaches the crown fontanelle. There, it breaks open the orifice of the crown fontanelle, which had been blocked by the syllable HAṂ, and shoots upwards, like an arrow, blazing with white light, and then it dissolves into the heart of the meditational deity [seated above]. One's awareness should then be focused upwards into the heart of the meditational deity, and without letting it descend, it should be repeatedly drawn in, and absorbed [into the deity's heart]. Then, finally, [the visualisation of] the meditational deity should also be dissolved into a non-referential state. If one's breath ceases while [resting] in that state, one will attain the status of an awareness holder, inseparable from the meditational deity; and achieve buddhahood in the Buddha-body of Perfect Resource.

If the consciousness transference into the Buddha-body of Perfect Resource does take effect in the above manner, as an 'outer sign', the sky will be filled with rainbows and light; and as an 'inner sign', blood or serous fluid will emerge from the crown fontanelle at the top of the head, or dew-like drops, swellings, and so forth will also appear. The 'secret signs' include the appearance of any one of the five types of bone relic, and the appearance of [bone relics] shaped like the physical form or hand-implement of a deity, and so forth.[26]

Such is the consciousness transference into the Buddha-body of Perfect Resource. SAMAYA!

Consciousness Transference into the Buddha-body of Emanation

As for the appropriate bodily posture, one should lay the body down on its right side, since [this position] will facilitate the departure of the vital energy from the left nostril. Then, one should request that a statue, relief, or drawing of the Buddha-body of Emanation be placed in front of oneself. This could be a representation of the Great Sage [Śākyamuni Buddha], the King of Medicine [Vaiḍūryaprabharāja], Maitreya, or Padmasambhava of Oḍḍiyāna; or it could be an image of one's own spiritual teacher or spiritual friend. Offerings should be extensively arrayed before the [image]. If no image is actually present, clearly visualise one, and make mentally imagined offerings.

Then, all those present, oneself and others, should make the following aspirational prayer, saying, 'Now, may I, consequent on my death, for the sake of all sentient beings, take birth in an emanational body; and may this be of extensive benefit to all living beings! May this emanational body also be endowed with the major and minor marks, and may there be no obstacles to its lifespan and enlightened activity! May I be reborn as a great awareness holder, holding the lineage of the buddhas of the three times!'

Mentally, too, one should retain this fervent aspiration [constantly], and visualise that within the utterly translucent central channel, the essence of one's awareness is located in a triangle below the navel, in the form of a white seminal point, tinged with red, which is glistening and concentrated, and on the verge of rising upwards. Immediately, the rectum should be closed and drawn in, so that there is no option but for the seminal point to be forced upwards by the power of the vital energy below. Then, by means of HI-KA HI-KA gasps, which should be performed to the best of one's ability, [the seminal point] should be moved upwards, and, as it reaches the orifice of the left nostril, the [motion of one's] awareness should be synchronised with [that of one's] respiration. Then, in an instant, like an arrow being fired, [one's awareness] should penetrate the heart of the Buddha-body of Emanation which is before one. Let the vital energy and awareness remain there, without reabsorbing them [into one's body]. This exercise should be repeated until one's consciousness does depart [the body]. Consequently, [the transference] is certain to take effect. Once consciousness does depart in that state, it is certain that one will subsequently take birth in an emanational body which will act for the benefit of sentient beings.

If the consciousness transference into the Buddha-body of Emanation does occur in the above way, as an 'outer sign', clouds or rainbows will appear in the sky, some resembling a wish-granting tree or unfurled white silk, or a shower of flowers, and so forth. As an 'inner sign', blood, serous fluid, or generative fluid will emerge from the left nostril; or else dew-like drops, and so forth may appear. The 'secret signs' include the appearance of many small relics, a complete unbroken skull, and [bones in the shape of] the hand-emblems of deities.[27]

Such is the consciousness transference into the Buddha-body of Emanation. SAMAYA!

Instantaneous Consciousness Transference

All the [above methods of consciousness transference are appropriate] in the context of a person whose death is gradual; but in the case of those who die suddenly, there will not be sufficient time to engage in meditations, such as those [just described]. In this case, therefore, the method of instantaneous consciousness transference becomes most important. Since it is unknown what the circumstances of one's death will be, one should, from this very moment, alternate one's training, sometimes practising the consciousness-transference technique of the training phase, [described earlier], and sometimes practising the instantaneous consciousness transference.

The [practice] should be undertaken in the following manner:

One should establish a clear and mindful resolution, thinking, 'If I die suddenly, my mental focus should be directed towards the crown of my head!' This resolution is extremely important. It is similar, for example, to the resolution of someone who thinks that one should get up and leave [home] when the moon rises on the twenty-second day [of the lunar month]. If [this mental focus] is continuously maintained during the evening of the [day before], one will [actually] awaken when the moon rises, just after midnight. In exactly this way, from this very moment onwards, one should practise projecting one's mental focus upwards to the crown of the head whenever strong fear arises.

Then, when 'sudden death' does occur, as when falling straight over a steep precipice, the thought will arise, 'I am dying!' As soon as this happens, it would be best if one were to fervently recall one's spiritual teacher, or recall one's particular meditational deity, [as being present, seated] on the crown of one's head. Even if there is not sufficient time to make this recollection, it is essential to project one's mental focus upwards towards the crown of one's head. The reason for doing so is that even [ordinarily] now, when strong fear arises, we tend to cry out, 'O father! spiritual teacher!' [Similarly] therefore, at the moment [of sudden death] also, it is certainly possible that one will recollect one's teacher, or [if one has trained in this practice] that one will focus one's awareness at the crown of one's head [instinctively]. This is the most profound crucial point.

Likewise, were one to be engulfed by a great fire, or swiftly carried away by a mighty river, or struck on the head by lightning, or pierced by an arrow through the heart, one must immediately recollect one's spiritual teacher, [as being seated] on the crown of the head, or alternatively one must [at least] direct one's awareness to the crown of the head. This is called the 'instantaneous consciousness transference', and it is also known as the 'forceful consciousness transference'. As this is most profound, one should train one's mind assiduously [in this technique].

Moreover, it is said that at times when ordinary people experience strong fears, there are many advantages when they simply cry out 'O father! spiritual teacher!' or invoke the name of a buddha, saying, 'O Orgyan!'[28] If this is so, the benefits of [additionally] directing one's mental focus towards the spiritual teacher, present on the crown of the head, are inconceivable.

There are, altogether, nine different pathways through which consciousness transference can occur, and these are associated with persons of superior, average, and inferior capacity. The aperture of the crown fontanelle is the pathway through which [consciousness] departs to the pure [realm of the] sky-farers. Given this, [it is said that] one will attain liberation if awareness exits through the [crown fontanelle]. Since this is the supreme pathway, it is extremely important that one trains in directing one's mental focus towards this [aperture]. Furthermore, if consciousness is transferred through the pathway of the eyes, [it is said that] one will be born as a universal monarch, and if it is transferred through the left nostril, one will obtain an unimpaired human body. These are the three optimum apertures [associated with those of superior capacity].

One will, however, be born as a *yakṣa* if [consciousness is transferred] through the right nostril, or as a god of the world-system of form if [it is transferred] through the ears, and as a god of the world-system of desire if [it is transferred] through the navel. These are the three medial apertures [associated with those of average capacity]. Lastly, one will be born as an animal if [it is transferred] through the urethra, as a anguished spirit if [it is transferred] through the sexual passage,[29] and as a hell being if it is transferred through the rectum. These are the three inferior apertures [associated with those of inferior capacity]. Given that there are such very great consequential differences between the various apertures through which consciousness transference may occur, there will be inestimable benefits in directing one's awareness to the crown of the head, at the time of death.

Such is the forceful consciousness transference. SAMAYA!

Consciousness Transference of Ordinary Beings

In the case of those who have not realised the meaning of emptiness, and who do not know the significance of the generation and perfection stages [of meditation], it is the consciousness transference of ordinary beings which should be applied as follows: The head [of the dying person] should point north, with the body lying down on the right side. A spiritual teacher or fellow practitioner should then remind [the dying person] to pay attention, and if health permits, he or she should be encouraged to take refuge, to cultivate an altruistic intention, and to confess negativity. Then, the teacher should confer the vows of the Buddhist laity, and if there is time, the empowerments of the way of secret mantras should be conferred. Consequently, by dying with a positive momentum of past actions, the individual who has [just received] these untainted commitments and vows, with respect to the nature of reality,[30] will be liberated from inferior existences, and there will be inestimable advantages.

In the case of a person who cannot do even that, one should slowly call out the name [of the dying one], saying, 'Lord Mahākāruṇika is present on the crown of your head! Be reverential!' One should stroke the crown of his or her head and gently pull the hair above the crown fontanelle. Thereby, the consciousness will [be encouraged to] exit from the crown fontanelle.

In the case of those who cannot do even that, and whose capacity is indistinguishable from that of animals, one should repeat the words, many times, 'Homage to Buddha Ratnaketu!', directing these [words] towards the head [of the dying person]. As a consequence, they will certainly be liberated from [rebirth in] the inferior existences, because, when in the past this buddha made his aspirational prayer, he did so, saying, 'May all who hear my name be liberated from [rebirth in] the inferior existences!' Alternatively, if one calls out the name of the [Medicine] Buddha Bhaiṣajyaguru Vaiḍūryaprabharāja, it is said that just by hearing his name, [the dying person] will be protected from the sufferings of inferior existences. Similarly, one may call out the name of whichever buddha one may know, and recite whichever blessed heart-mantra one may know, such as the Six-syllable Mantra.

In particular, if one has at hand the *Liberation by Wearing*,[31] one should read this aloud, and also recite the *Liberation by Hearing*,[32] repeating whichever aspirational prayers one may know. Since the positive momentum of [the dying person's] past actions can thereby be secured, this will be most advantageous. In the worst cases, it is said that simply by dying with the body lying down on the right side and the head pointing north, [that person] will not proceed into inferior existences.

CONCLUSION

In summary, since it is essential that all the advantages [that accrue from] practising the teachings should converge at the time of death, it is extremely important to become skilled [during one's lifetime] in the process of dying.

[This completes] the *Guide to the Intermediate State of the Time of Death* entitled *Consciousness Transference: Natural Liberation through Recollection*.

SAMAYA! *rgya rgya rgya!*

11

The Great Liberation by Hearing

CONTEXT

Traditionally, the procedures followed when a lama visits a dying or deceased person are intricate and prolonged, and will vary depending on whether the person is about to die, has just recently died, or has been dead for some days.

When a person is approaching death, it is customary for the relatives or close friends to seek the assistance of a fully qualified lama. The lama should be motivated by a sincere compassion for all sentient beings and should have mastered in his own mental continuum the direct experiential cultivation of the dying processes, as well as the consciousness transference practices.

It is very important that when coming in to the household, the attending lama is concentrated on the motivation to free the dying person from the sufferings of cyclic existence. Very often the mere presence of an accomplished lama can create a solid sense of calm and purposefulness, which inspires both the dying person and family.

The formal practice begins with the attending lama taking refuge in the Buddha, the sacred teachings, and the ideal spiritual community, on behalf of the dying person and all other sentient beings, including himself. At this point, the lama should visualise in the space in front of himself images of the three objects of refuge – the Buddha, sacred teachings and ideal community – forming a tree, whose branches like billowing clouds in the sky are adorned by buddhas, bodhisattvas and the spiritual masters of the lineage. Then he should visualise that the dying person, surrounded by all sentient beings, takes refuge by reciting the following verses three times:

I take refuge from now until enlightenment,
In the Buddha, the [sacred] teachings and the supreme assembly.

Through the merit of practising generosity and the other [perfections],
May I attain buddhahood for the sake of [all] living beings.

Maintaining this same visualisation, the lama should slowly recite with full concentration the four immeasurable aspirations, based on the cultivation of loving kindness, compassion, sympathetic joy, and equanimity.

May all sentient beings be endowed with happiness!
May they all be separated from suffering and its causes!
May they be endowed with joy, free from suffering!
May they abide in equanimity, free from attraction and aversion!

Up to this point, the preliminary procedures are common to all the traditions of Tibetan Buddhism. Next, the lama should enter into the practice of the *Natural Liberation of Habitual Tendencies*, as presented in Chapter 5. During the practice of the initial ten-branched prayer (contained in Chapter 5), the refuge tree is still visualised in the space in front. As the ten-branched prayer is concluded the lama visualises that all the objects of refuge melt into light and then gradually dissolve into the crowns of each of the attending persons, including the dying person and himself. So at this point the body, speech and mind of all enlightened beings, the objects of refuge, become indivisible from the lama's own body, speech, and mind and those of all others present. Like water poured into water they become inseparably one in nature. In this way, it is visualised that all those present are brought under the protection of the Three Precious Jewels.

Then, like a bubble emerging from water, the lama visualises himself arising out of emptiness in the form of Vajrasattva and he continues with the practice of the *Natural Liberation of Habitual Tendencies*. Once this practice is complete, extensive mental offerings should then be made to all the buddhas and bodhisattvas and the lama should slowly recite three or seven times the short prayer entitled an *Aspirational Prayer [Calling] to the Buddhas and Bodhisattvas for Assistance* (see Chapter 12), followed by the accompanying aspirational prayers. This is often followed by a series of more general recitations from the Buddhist canon, including the *Sūtra of the Three*

Heaps (*Triskandhakasūtra*, T 284), dedicated to the Thirty-five Buddhas of Confession, the recitation of the names of the thousand buddhas of this aeon, following the arrangement of Śākyaśrī of Kashmir, entitled *Ornate Garland of the Auspicious Aeon* (*Bhadrakalpikālaṃkāramālā*, T 1169), together with the recitation of the mantras given in the *Tantra of the Purification of All Lower Destinies* (*Sarvadurgatipariśodhanatantra*, T 483). Just to hear these names is said to make a powerful impact on the consciousness of the dying person.

At this point, the lama has to be very observant of the dying person. Excessive preoccupation with the completion of these recitations may distract him from seizing the moment when the dying person's consciousness actually leaves the body. Carefully observing the signs of death, as indicated in the *Natural Liberation through Recognition of the Visual Indications and Signs of Death* (Chapter 8), just before the person passes away, the lama should immediately begin the introduction to the intermediate state of the time of death (the first part of the present chapter), even if the previous recitations are unfinished. In certain circumstances, mouth to mouth resuscitation might be given, in accordance with the cycle entitled *Eight Transmitted Precepts: Oral Transmission of the Awareness Holder* (*bKa'-brgyad rig-'dzin zhal-lung*), which was revealed by the Fifth Dalai Lama, or an equivalent text. This may maintain life for a short period while final guidance is given.

Accordingly, the dying one should be guided through the processes of the dissolution of the elements (as set out in Chapter 8), before continuing with the introduction to the intermediate state of the time of death, as set out in this chapter. Usually, the dying person is addressed by name, or by the expression 'child of buddha nature' (*rigs-kyi bu*). One who is worthy of great respect is addressed by an expression such as 'venerable one', 'spiritual master', 'teacher', or 'your ladyship' and so forth. If it is someone from whom the attending lama has personally received teaching, he may use the expression 'lord of the refuge' (*skyabs-mgon*) or 'great lama' (*bla-chen*), and so forth. There are different modes of address.

The voice of the lama who calls out to the dying person should be very melodious, so that merely upon hearing the sound of the instructions the person feels soothed, elevated and attracted.

Following the outer dissolution of the four elements and the inner dissolution of the processes of conceptual thought into redness, whiteness and blackness, the lama should recite the verses describing the moment of the arising of the inner radiance of the ground. These words of introduction should be read aloud three times. If the dying person fails to recognise the first inner radiance and swoons into unconsciousness, the lama should proceed with the introduction to the second inner radiance followed by the introduction to the emergence of the Peaceful and Wrathful Deities during the intermediate state of reality.

Once the introduction to the intermediate state of reality has been completed, the attending lama should closely observe the body of the deceased and seek to determine whether he or she has attained liberation from rebirth in cyclic existence. If emancipation has occurred, the body will take on a certain glow, and while being in its presence, one will experience a sensation of happiness. The body will not smell. It will look just like a living person who is sleeping. These are signs that the consciousness of the deceased has attained liberation. In addition, external environmental signs may arise, as described in Chapter 8, including distinctive cloud formations and rainbows. If the deceased is a realised yogin, monk or layperson who has gained complete freedom at the time of death, then the attending lama may hear the sound of chanting and the music of sacred instruments, such as the skull drum or bell. On the other hand, if the consciousness of the deceased has not been emancipated, the complexion of the deceased will become disquieting and may inspire a sense of fear when it is seen. The face will become grey and dusty, and the body will begin to decompose very quickly.

If the consciousness of the deceased does not attain liberation while in the intermediate state of reality, the mental body assumed by the deceased will then immediately fall into the intermediate state of rebirth, at which time, the attending lama should recite the introduction to that phase, as presented in the latter part of this chapter.

Importantly, these introductions to the three intermediate states of the time of death, reality and rebirth should be supplemented, if appropriate, by the practice of the transference of consciousness, as presented in Chapter 10. If the internal and external signs are very good, consciousness transference will not be necessary and could even be potentially harmful.

The attending lama must take great care as to if and when consciousness transference should be practised. It is not only highly realised spiritual masters who remain in meditation during these intermediate states, but even ordinary men, women, and children may have achieved a settled state of mind, enabling them to remain in peaceful and deep meditation after death. If consciousness transference were performed in such cases, the deceased would be disturbed. Moreover, since the consciousness of the deceased has a tendency to leave the body from whichever point it is touched, the relatives, loved ones and the attending lama should refrain from touching the body or only tap the crown fontanelle in order to induce the consciousness to leave from that point.

If the attending lama decides that consciousness transference is the appropriate course of action, it should be repeated many times until certain indications occur, such as the emergence of mucus or blood from both nostrils. Further, in order to induce the consciousness to leave the body via the crown, which is the optimum gateway for the transference to take effect, the means of preventing the consciousness from leaving through other orifices as described in Chapter 10 should be applied. This is facilitated by visualising that the nine orifices of the body are each sealed by a single HŪṂ syllable, thus forcing the consciousness to exit via the crown fontanelle.

In any event, if the attending lama feels that the consciousness of the deceased has become confused and trapped, or if the corpse begins to decompose and lose its radiance, then consciousness transference should be immediately performed.

Once the introductions to the intermediate states of the time of death, reality, and rebirth have been concluded, the attending lama should then recite: the *Prayer for Union with the Spiritual Teacher* (Chapter 2), the *Natural Liberation of Habitual Tendencies* (Chapter 5), the *Hundredfold Homage* (Chapter 6), the *Confession* (Chapter 7), and the *Liberation by Wearing* (Chapter 14).

At this juncture the attending lama may read certain general prayers not included within the present cycle, such as the *Aspirational Prayer for Good Conduct* (*Bodhisattvapraṇidhānarāja*, T 1095), one of the many versions of the *Aspirational Prayer for Rebirth in Sukhāvatī* (contained in *bDe-smon Phyogs-sgrigs*), the *Aspirational Prayer of Maitreya* (*Maitreyapraṇidhāna*, T 1096), and the final chapter of the *Introduction to the Conduct of a Bodhisattva* (*Bodhisattvacaryāvatāra*, T 3871), which concerns the dedication of merit on behalf of all sentient beings.

These may be followed by a further recitation of prayers specific to the present cycle, namely the: *Root Verses of the Six Intermediate States* (Chapter 3) and the *Aspirational Prayers* (Chapter 12).

This completes the summary of the process through which the attending lama tends directly to the consciousness of the dying person and the deceased.

PART ONE

An Elucidation of the Intermediate State of the Time of Death and of the Appearance of the Peaceful Deities in the Intermediate State of Reality

Herein is contained the *Great Liberation by Hearing*,[1] an elucidation of the intermediate state of reality, [which is an extract] from the *Peaceful and Wrathful Deities: A Profound Sacred Teaching, [entitled] Natural Liberation through [Recognition of] Enlightened Intention*.[2]

I bow down to the spiritual teachers, [embodiment of] the Three Buddha-bodies:

To the Buddha-body of Reality, Infinite Light, Amitābha;

To the Buddha-body of Perfect Resource, the Peaceful and Wrathful Lotus Deities;

And to the Buddha-body of Emanation, Padmākara, protector of beings.

This *Great Liberation by Hearing*, the skilful means which liberates yogins of average ability during the intermediate states, has three parts, namely: the introduction, the main subject matter [of the text] and the conclusion.

INTRODUCTION

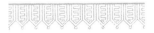

[All aspirants] should experientially cultivate the steps of guidance,[3] which are the means by which corporeal beings can achieve liberation. Those of highest acumen should certainly attain liberation [in their lifetime] through [the application of] that guidance. But if liberation does not occur thereby, [yogins] should implement, during the intermediate state of the time of death, [the appropriate procedure outlined in] the *Consciousness Transference: Natural Liberation through Recollection*.[4] Yogins of average ability should certainly be liberated by that. If liberation is not effected by the [application of consciousness transference], then [the recitation of] the following *Great Liberation by Hearing* should be persistently made during the intermediate state of reality.

First, therefore, yogins should examine the signs of death in accordance with the text entitled *Natural Liberation through [Recognition of] the Visual Indications and Signs of Death*, also known as the *Mirror which Clarifies the Visible Indications of Death*.[5] Thereupon, when the [inner] signs of the processes of death are definitively and completely present, [the appropriate procedure as outlined in] the *Consciousness Transference: Natural Liberation through Recollection* should be applied. Thus, if this transference is effective, there will be no need to read aloud the *Great Liberation by Hearing*.

If, however, the transference is ineffective, this *Liberation by Hearing* should be read aloud with correct pronunciation and clear diction, close to the corpse. If the corpse is not present, one should sit next to the bed or seat of the deceased. Then, having invoked the power of truth[6] and summoned the consciousness [of the deceased],[7] one should imagine him or her to be listening in one's presence and read aloud [this *Great Liberation by Hearing*]. At this time the relatives and close friends should [be advised to] show restraint because, at this stage, it is not appropriate to cry or dramatically express one's grief.[8]

If the deceased's body is present, then during the interval which follows the ceasing of respiration,[9] this *Great Liberation by Hearing* should be read aloud by a spiritual teacher, or by a spiritual sibling, sincere [practitioner], or a sympathetic friend, placing the lips [close] to the ear [of the deceased], without actually touching.[10]

THE MAIN SUBJECT MATTER

Now follows the actual exegesis of the *Liberation by Hearing*:

First, one should make extensive offerings to the Three Precious Jewels.[11] If these are unobtainable, one should make offerings by arraying whatever one has as a support for visualisation and mentally emanating an immeasurable [quantity of offerings]. Then one should recite, three or seven times, the *Aspirational Prayer [Calling] to the Buddhas and Bodhisattvas for Assistance*. After this, one should melodiously recite the *Aspirational Prayer which Protects from Fear of the Intermediate States*, the *Aspirational Prayer which Rescues from the Dangerous Pathways of the Intermediate States* and the *Root Verses of the [Six] Intermediate States*.[12]

Thereafter, this *Great Liberation by Hearing* is to be read aloud seven or three times, or [as many times] as the circumstances permit.

[The main subject matter of the *Great Liberation by Hearing*] comprises three sections: the introduction to inner radiance during the intermediate state of the time of death,[13] the great elucidation which introduces the intermediate state of reality[14] and a teaching on the means for obstructing the entrance to the womb during the intermediate state of rebirth.[15]

Introduction to Inner Radiance in the Intermediate State of the Time of Death

This introduction is made on behalf of those individuals who have good understanding, but do not yet have recognition [of inner radiance], as well as those who have gained recognition but have little familiarity, and all ordinary persons who have received little experiential guidance. By means of [this introduction], such beings will, upon recognising the inner radiance of the ground, attain the uncreated Buddha-body of Reality, in an ascending and core-penetrating manner, without [experiencing] the intermediate states.

Introduction to the Inner Radiance of the Ground

As for the method of making [this introduction], it is best if the root spiritual teacher from whom [the dying person] personally received guidance can be present. If he cannot be present, then a spiritual sibling with identical commitments[16] [should be called upon], or if none of these can be present, then a spiritual friend holding the same lineage[17] should attend; or if none of these at all can be present, someone who knows how to read aloud with correct pronunciation and clear diction should recite [the introductions] many times. Thereby, [the dying person] will remember that which had [formerly] been introduced by his or her spiritual teacher and immediately afterwards, being set face to face with the inner radiance of the ground, will undoubtedly attain liberation.

Concerning the time for making [this introduction]: after respiration has ceased, the vital energy is absorbed into the channel of pristine cognition[18] and the consciousness [of the deceased] naturally arises as a non-conceptual inner radiance. Later, the vital energy will be reversed and escape into the right and left channels and, as a result, the appearances of the [subsequent] intermediate state [of reality] will arise suddenly. Therefore, [the introduction to inner radiance at the time of death] should be made before [the vital energy] has escaped into the right and left channels. [Generally], the length of time during which the inner breath remains present within the central channel is just about the time taken to eat a meal.[19]

As regards the actual mode of making [this introduction], it is best if the consciousness transference is effected at that moment when the respiration is about to cease. If it is not, one should say the following words:

O, Child of Buddha Nature, (call the name of the dying person), *the time has now come for you to seek a path. As soon as your respiration ceases, [the luminosity] known as the 'inner radiance of the first intermediate state',*[20] *which your spiritual teacher formerly introduced to you, will arise. [Immediately] your respiration ceases, all phenomena will become empty and utterly naked like space. [At the same time], a naked awareness will arise, not extraneous [to yourself], but radiant, empty and without horizon or centre. At that moment, you should personally recognise this intrinsic nature and rest in the state of that [experience]. I too will introduce it [to you] at that time.*[21]

These words should be spoken audibly many times, impressing them on the mind [of the dying person] until respiration ceases.

Then, when the respiration is on the point of ceasing, one should lay [the dying person] on the right side, in the posture of the lion, and take the pulse.[22] Once the throbbing of the two carotid arteries has stopped, they should be firmly pressed [at their pressure points on the neck].[23] Then the vital energy, having entered the central channel, cannot reverse [and escape] and it will certainly emerge through the crown fontanelle.[24] The introduction should continue to be made at this time.

This phase in the process of death is called: 'the inner radiance of reality during the first intermediate state'. It is the unique and incontrovertible enlightened intention of the Buddha-body of Reality, which arises in the minds of all living beings. [At the moment of death], this coincides with the period when the vital energy is absorbed into the central channel, after respiration has ceased and before the ceasing of the inner breath. Ordinary people describe this state as 'loss of consciousness'.[25]

The duration of this [experience of inner radiance] is uncertain, [for it depends on] the health and characteristics of [the dying person's] physical constitution, and on the degree of [his or her proficiency in the practices related to] the vital energies and channels. For those who have considerable practical experience, or those who have achieved stability in the practice of calm abiding, or those who have healthy energy channels, this experience can be prolonged.[26] In striving to make this introduction, therefore, one should remind [the deceased] repeatedly [by giving the instruction as above and below], until serous fluid emerges from the apertures of the sense-organs.[27] For those persons of great negativity and those classes of beings with unhealthy channels this phase lasts no longer than a single snapping of the fingers. In others, it may last for as long as it takes to eat a meal. However, as most sūtras and tantras state that the period of unconsciousness [following the moment of death] may last for three and a half days, generally one should persevere for that length of time, in making this introduction to inner radiance.

As for the way in which this introduction is made: if capable, the dying person should facilitate this of his or her own accord by projecting a formerly cultivated [spiritual practice into the intermediate state]. If [the individual] is not capable of this, then a spiritual teacher, a student, or a spiritual sibling who was a close friend, should stay nearby and clearly remind [the dying person] of the signs [of death] in their correct sequence, saying:

Now, the sign of the dissolution of earth into water is present, of water into fire, fire into wind, wind into consciousness, and so forth [as set down in the text entitled *Natural Liberation through Recognition of the Visual Indications and Signs of Death*].[28]

Then, when the sequence of the signs is almost complete, [the attendant] should encourage the dying person to cultivate the following altruistic intention, beginning with the words: '*O, Child of Buddha Nature!*' or, if [the dying person] is a spiritual teacher, the attendant should gently say the following words into the ear:

O, Venerable One! I beg you not to be distracted from the cultivation of an altruistic intention!

If [the dying person] is a spiritual sibling or anyone else, [the attendant] should call to him or her by name and say the following words:

O, Child of Buddha Nature, that which is called death has now arrived. Therefore you should adopt an altruistic motivation and concentrate your thinking as follows: 'I have arrived at the time of death, so now, relying on the process of death, I will single-mindedly cultivate an altruistic intention. I will meditate on the generation of loving kindness, compassion and an altruistic intention to attain enlightenment. For the benefit of all sentient beings, who are as limitless as space, I must attain perfect buddhahood.' And in particular, [you should think]: 'At this moment, for the sake of all sentient beings, I must recognise [the time of] death as [the arising of] inner radiance, the Buddha-body of Reality, and while in that state, I must attain the supreme accomplishment of the Great Seal, and thereby act for the good of all sentient beings. If I do not achieve this accomplishment, then, recognising the intermediate state as it is, I will actualise the coalescent Buddha-body of the Great Seal during the intermediate state, and thereby, manifesting in order to instruct each in accordance with his or her needs, I will act for the benefit of all sentient beings, who are as limitless as space.' Without giving up the focus on cultivating an altruistic intention, in the above way, recollect the meditative experiences which you formerly developed on the basis of the oral teachings.

Those words should be clearly spoken, while placing the lips close to the ear [of the dying person]. Without permitting the attention [of the dying one] to be distracted even for an instant, [the attendant] should remind him or her of past meditative experiences.

Then, when the respiration has ceased, and the two carotid arteries have been firmly pressed, remind [the dying person] with the following words, if the individual was a spiritual teacher or a spiritual friend greater than oneself:

Venerable One! The inner radiance of the ground is now arisen before you. Recognise it, and concentrate directly on its experiential cultivation.

For all others, one should introduce [the inner radiance of the ground], with the following words:

O, Child of Buddha Nature, (call the name of the individual) *listen! Pure inner radiance, reality itself, is now arising before you. Recognise it! O, Child of Buddha Nature, this radiant essence that is now your conscious awareness is a brilliant emptiness. It is beyond substance, beyond characteristics and beyond colour, completely empty of inherent existence in any respect whatsoever. This is the female Buddha Samantabhadrī, the essential nature of reality. The essence of your own conscious awareness is emptiness. Yet, this is not a vacuous or nihilistic emptiness; this, your very own conscious awareness, is unimpededly radiant, brilliant and vibrant. This [conscious awareness] is the male Buddha Samantabhadra. The utterly indivisible presence of these two: the essence of your own awareness, which is empty, without inherent existence with respect to any substance whatsoever, and your own conscious awareness, which is vibrant and radiantly present, is the Buddha-body of Reality. This intrinsic awareness, manifest in a great mass of light, in which radiance and emptiness are indivisible, is the buddha [nature] of unchanging light, beyond birth or death. Just to recognise this is enough! If you recognise this brilliant essence of your own conscious awareness to be the buddha [nature], then to gaze into intrinsic awareness is to abide in the enlightened intention of all the buddhas.*

This introduction should be made three or seven times, with correct pronunciation and clear diction. Accordingly, [the deceased] will firstly recollect [the teachings] as they had been formerly given by his or her teacher, and secondly be introduced to inner radiance as a naked natural awareness. And then, thirdly, having recognised this, he or she will attain the Buddha-body of Reality, beyond conjunction or disjunction, and certainly achieve liberation. Recognition of the 'first inner radiance' [of the ground] takes place in this way.

[Introduction to the Inner Radiance of the Path]

If, however, it is feared that [the deceased] has not recognised the first inner radiance, the so-called 'second inner radiance' [of the path] will arise. [Again, it is said that this second inner radiance] lasts a little more than the time it takes to eat a meal, after the respiration has ceased. Specifically, it arises once the vital energy has escaped into the right or left channel, whichever is appropriate depending on the positive and negative past actions [of the deceased], and once the vital energy has emerged through one of the orifices of the body.[29] When this occurs, the consciousness suddenly becomes awake and lucid.

Although it is said that this second inner radiance also lasts [approximately] for as long as it takes to eat a meal, this actually depends, as before, on whether or not the energy channels are healthy and whether or not [the individual] has or lacks meditative experience.

Now, at this point, the consciousness emerges from the body and, [initially], the individual may not know whether or not he or she has died. The relatives are seen as before, and their cries of sorrow can be heard. During this period, before the harsh and bewildering experiences related to past actions have arisen, and before the terrifying experiences related to Yama have occurred, the oral teaching should be given.[30] This [oral teaching] concerns both the perfection stage and the generation stage [of meditation]. If [the deceased] was engaged in [the practices of] the perfection stage, one should call to him or her three times, by name, and repeat the above [instruction, which is] the introduction to inner radiance. If [the deceased] was engaged in [the practices of] the generation stage, one should read aloud the formal description of the individual's chosen meditational deity as set down in the corresponding meditative cycle. Then remind him or her with the following words:

O, Child of Buddha Nature! Meditate on this, your meditational deity. Do not be distracted! Concentrate intently on your meditational deity! Meditate that [the deity] appears, and yet is without inherent existence, like [the reflection of] the moon in water. Do not meditate on the deity as a solid corporeal form![31]

If [the deceased] was an ordinary person, without a specific practice, then preface the introduction with the following words:

Meditate on the Lord of Great Compassion![32]

By means of such an introduction, there is no doubt that even those who have not recognised [the nature of] the intermediate state will do so.

This, [the above] precise reminder, should be given by a spiritual teacher or sibling to those who, despite having already received this introduction from a spiritual teacher while they were alive, have an undeveloped meditative experience, and accordingly will not recognise the intermediate state by themselves. Equally, this instruction is of crucial importance in the case of those who, despite their meditative experience, are bewildered by serious illness at the moment of death and therefore cannot recall [their past meditative experiences]; and finally, it is particularly necessary in the case of those beings who, despite their former meditative experience, are at risk of falling into lower existences as a result of having broken their vows and having failed to maintain their basic commitments.[33]

[As stated above], it is best if [recognition] occurs during the first intermediate state. However, if it does not occur therein, awareness can be awakened and liberation attained during the second intermediate state. This second intermediate state is also called 'the pure illusory body'. [During this second phase], consciousness achieves an instance of clarity, even though the deceased may not know whether or not they are dead. If the teaching is given at this time, therefore, the mother and child aspects of reality can meet,[34] and [the deceased] will no longer be controlled by the force of past actions. Just as, for example, darkness is destroyed by the light of the sun, the controlling force of past actions is destroyed by this 'inner radiance of the path' and liberation is attained.

Now, this so-called 'second intermediate state' [occurring at that point when consciousness leaves the body] is one which suddenly appears to the 'mental body' [assumed by the deceased],[35] while the consciousness [of the deceased] retains the same range of hearing as before. If the above oral teaching is given at this time, its purpose can therefore be accomplished. Since the bewildering appearances generated by past actions have not yet arisen, [the deceased] is able to direct his or her attention anywhere. Therefore, even though [the individual] may not have attained recognition of the inner radiance of the ground, he or she will be liberated by the recognition of the inner radiance [of the path], which is the second intermediate state.

INTRODUCTION TO THE INTERMEDIATE STATE OF REALITY

If liberation is still not attained through the above [introductions], then the intermediate state of reality, also called 'the third intermediate state', will arise.[36] It is during this third phase that the bewildering apparitions, [which are the products] of past actions, emerge. Therefore, it is extremely important to read aloud the following *Great Introduction to the Intermediate State of Reality*[37] at this juncture. It is most powerful and beneficial.

At around this time, the bereaved relatives will be crying and expressing their grief. They will no longer be serving [the deceased's] share of food, they will have removed his or her clothes, and stripped down the bed, and so forth. Although [the deceased] can see them, they cannot see the deceased. Although the deceased can hear them calling out, they cannot hear the departed one calling back. So, [the deceased] may turn away in a state of despair.

At this time, three phenomena – sounds, lights and rays of light – will arise, and [the deceased] may faint with fear, terror or awe. Thus, during this period, the following *Great Introduction to the Intermediate State of Reality* should be given. Call the deceased by name and say the following words, with correct pronunciation and clear diction:

O, Child of Buddha Nature, listen very intently and without distraction. There are six kinds of intermediate state, namely: the intermediate state of living or natural existence, the intermediate state of dreams, the intermediate state of meditative stability or concentration, the intermediate state of the time of death, the intermediate state of reality, and the intermediate state of consequent rebirth.[38] *O, Child of Buddha Nature, [during and after death], you will experience three intermediate states: the intermediate state of the time of death, the intermediate state of reality and the intermediate state of rebirth. Of these three, it was the intermediate state of the time of death which you experienced until yesterday. Although the inner radiance of reality arose during that time, you did not recognise it. So now, [as a result], you have been compelled to wander here; and now you will experience the intermediate state of reality, followed by the intermediate state of rebirth. You must therefore recognise, without distraction, [the instruction and events] which I am now going to introduce to you.*

O, Child of Buddha Nature, that which is called death has now arrived. You are leaving this world. But in this you are not alone. This happens to everyone. Do not be attached to this life! Do not cling to this life! Even if you remain attached and clinging, you do not have the power to stay – you will only continue to roam within the cycles of existence. Therefore, do not be attached and do not cling! Think of the Three Precious Jewels!

O, Child of Buddha Nature, however terrifying the appearances of the intermediate state of reality might be, do not forget the following words. Go forward remembering their meaning. The crucial point is that through them recognition may be attained.

Alas, now, as the intermediate state of reality arises before me,
Renouncing the merest thought of awe, terror or fear,
I will recognise all that arises to be awareness, manifesting naturally of itself.
Knowing such [sounds, lights and rays] to be visionary phenomena of the intermediate state,
At this moment, having reached this critical point,
I must not fear the assembly of Peaceful and Wrathful Deities, which manifest naturally!

Go forward, reciting these words distinctly and be mindful of their meaning. Do not forget them! For it is essential to recognise, with certainty, that whatever terrifying experiences may arise, they are natural manifestations [of actual reality]. O, Child of Buddha Nature, when your mind and body separate, the pure [luminous] apparitions of reality itself, will arise: subtle and clear, radiant and dazzling, naturally bright and awesome, shimmering like a mirage on a plain in summer. Do not fear them! Do not be terrified! Do not be awed! They are the natural luminosities of your own actual reality. Therefore recognise them [as they are]!

From within these lights, the natural sound of reality will resound, clear and thunderous, reverberating like a thousand simultaneous peals of thunder. This is the natural sound of your own actual reality. So, do not be afraid! Do not be terrified! Do not be awed! The body that you now have is called a 'mental body', it is the product of [subtle] propensities and not a solid corporeal body of flesh and blood. Therefore, whatever sounds, lights or rays may arise, they cannot harm you. For you are beyond death now! It is enough that you simply recognise [the sounds and luminosities] to be manifestations of your own [actual reality]. Know that this is the intermediate state!

O, Child of Buddha Nature, if you do not now recognise [these phenomena] to be natural manifestations, whatever meditative practices you may have undertaken whilst in the human world, if you have not [previously] encountered this present instruction, you will fear the light, you will be awed by the sound and you will be terrified by the rays. If you do not now understand this essential point of the teaching, you will not recognise the sounds, the lights and the rays, and you will continue to roam within the cycles of existence.

O, Child of Buddha Nature, should you have moved on, [without recognition], after having been unconscious for [up to] three and a half days,[39] *you will awaken from unconsciousness and wonder, "What has happened to me?" So, recognise this to be the intermediate state! At this time, the aspects of the cycles of existence are reversed [into their own true nature] and all phenomena are arising as lights and buddha-bodies.*[40]

[On the first day of the intermediate state of reality],[41] *all space will arise as a blue light. At this time, from the central Buddha field called Pervasive Seminal Point,*[42] *the transcendent lord Vairocana will dawn before you, his body white in colour, seated on a lion throne, holding in his [right] hand an eight-spoked wheel and*

1. The assembly of the Forty-two Peaceful Deities (*zhi-ba'i lha-tshogs*).

2. (*above*) The male and female primordial buddhas Samantabhandra and Samantabhadrī in union. (*below*) Peaceful Deities of the Buddha family: the male buddha Vairocana, in union with the female buddha Ākāśadhātvīśvarī.

3. Peaceful Deities of the Vajra Family: (*centre*) the male buddha Akṣobhya-Vajrasattva, in union with the female buddha Buddhalocanā; (*left*) the male bodhisattva Kṣitigarbha; (*right*) the male bodhisattva Maitreya; (*top*) the female bodhisattva Puṣpā; (*bottom*) the female bodhisattva Lāsyā.

4. Peaceful Deities of the Ratna Family: (*centre*) the male buddha Ratnasambhava, in union with the female buddha Māmakī; (*left*) the male bodhisattva Samantabhadra; (*right*) the male bodhisattva Ākāśagarbha; (*top*) the female bodhisattva Dhūpā; (*bottom*) the female bodhisattva Puṣpā.

5. Peaceful Deities of the Padma Family: (*centre*) the male buddha Amitābha, in union with the female buddha Pāṇḍaravāsinī; (*left*) the male bodhisattva Avalokiteśvara; (*right*) the male bodhisattva Manjuśrīkumārabhūta; (*top*) the female bodhisattva Ālokā; (*bottom*) the female bodhisattva Gītā.

6. Peaceful Deities of the Karma Family: (*centre*) the male buddha Amoghasiddhi, in union with the female buddha Samayatārā; (*left*) the male bodhisattva Nivāraṇaviśkambhin; (*right*) the male bodhisattva Vajrapāṇi; (*top*) the female bodhisattva Nartī; (*bottom*) the female bodhisattva Gandhā.

7. The Six Sages: (*top left*) Indraśakra; (*top right*) Śākyamuni; (*centre left*) Vemacitra; (*centre right*) Sthirasiṃha; (*bottom left*) Jvālamukha; (*bottom right*) Yama Dharmarāja.

8. The Eight Gatekeepers: (*top left*) Yamāntaka in union with Pāśā; (*top right*) Hayagriva in union with Sphoṭā; (*bottom left*) Trailokyavijaya in union with Ankuśā; (*bottom right*) Amṛtakuṇḍalin in union with Ghaṇṭā.

9. The Assembly of Fifty-eight Wrathful Deities (*khro-bo'i lha-tshogs*).

10. The male and female primordial buddhas Mahottra Heruka and Krodheśvarī in union.

11. Wrathful Deities of the Buddha Family: Buddha Heruka in union with Buddhakrodheśvarī.

12. Wrathful Deities of the Vajra Family: (*top*) Vajra Heruka in union withVajrakrodheśvarī; (*centre*) the six yoginī of the east: Manurākṣaśi, Brahmāṇī, Raudrī, Vaiṣṇāvī, Kaumārī, and Indrāṇī; (*bottom*) the wrathful gatekeeper Vajratejasī, alongside the yoginī gatekeeper Vajrā [Mahākālī].

13. Wrathful Deities of the Ratna Family: (*top*) the wrathful gatekeeper Vajrāmoghā, alongside the yoginī gatekeeper Vajrā [Mahāchāgalā]; (*centre*) Ratna Heruka in union with Ratnakrodheśvarī; (*bottom*) the six yoginī of the south: Vajrā, Śāntī, Amṛtā, Saumī, Daṇḍī and Rākṣasī.

14. Wrathful Deities of the Padma Family: (*top*) the wrathful gatekeeper Vajralokā, alongside the yoginī gatekeeper Vajrā [Mahākumbhakarṇī]; (*centre*) Padma Heruka in union with Padmakrodheśvarī; (*bottom*) the six yoginī of the west: Bhakṣasī, Ratī, Rudhiramadī, Ekacāriṇī, Manohārikā, and Siddhikarī.

15. Wrathful Deities of the Karma Family: (*top*) Karma Heruka in union with Karmakrodheśvarī; (*centre*) the six yoginī of the north: Vāyudevī, Agnāyī, Varāhī, Cāmuṇḍī, Bhujanā, and Varuṇānī; (*bottom*) the wrathful gatekeeper Vajravetālī, alongside the yoginī gatekeeper Vajrā [Lambodarā].

16. Clusters of the Eight Mātaraḥ and the Eight Piśācī: (*top left*) the four Piśācī of the cardinal directions: Simhaṃukhī, Vyāghrīmukhī, Śṛgālamukhī, and Śvānamukhī; (*bottom left*) the four Mātaraḥ of the cardinal directions: Gaurī, Caurī, Pramohā, and Vetālī; (*top right*) the four Piśācī of the intermediate directions: Gṛdhramukhī, Kaṅkamukhī, Kākamukhī and Ulūkamukhī; (*bottom right*) the four Mātaraḥ of the intermediate directions: Pukkasī, Ghasmarī, Caṇḍālī and Śmaśānī.

embraced by his consort Ākāśadhātvīśvarī. A blue luminosity, radiant and clear, bright and dazzling, [indicative of] the pristine cognition of reality's expanse, which is the natural purity of your aggregate of consciousness, [will emanate] from the heart of Vairocana and his consort, and it will shine piercingly before you [at the level of your heart, with such brilliance] that your eyes cannot bear it. Together with this [luminosity], a dull white light, [indicative of the realm] of the gods, will also dawn directly before you [and touch your heart]. At this time, under the sway of negative past actions, you will [wish to] flee in fear and terror from the bright blue light, which is the pristine cognition of reality's expanse, and you will come to perceive the dull white light of the god [realms] with delight. At this moment, do not be awed by the blue luminosity, which is radiant and dazzling, clear and very bright. This is the supreme inner radiance [of pristine cognition]! Do not be terrified! This is the light ray of the Tathāgata, which is called the pristine cognition of reality's expanse.[43] *Have confidence in it! Be drawn to it with longing devotion! Pray, with devotion, thinking: 'This is the light ray of the transcendent lord Vairocana's compassion. I take refuge in it.' For this, in reality, is the transcendent lord Vairocana and his consort come to escort you on the dangerous pathway of the intermediate state. This is the light ray of Vairocana's compassion! Therefore do not delight in the dull white light of the god [realms]! Do not be attached to it! Do not cling to it! This dull white light is the inviting path created by your own habitual tendencies for deep delusion, which you yourself have generated.*[44] *If you become attached to it, you will roam within the god realms and be drawn into [the cycles of existence of] the six classes of beings. [This dull light] is an obstruction blocking the path to liberation. Do not look at it! Be devoted to the bright blue light! Focus intently on the transcendent lord Vairocana and repeat after me the following aspirational prayer:*

O, as I roam in cyclic existence [driven] by deep-seated delusion,
May the transcendent lord Vairocana draw me forward,
Leading me on the path of radiant light,
Which is the pristine cognition of reality's expanse.
May the supreme consort [Ākāśa]dhātvīśvarī support me from behind,

And, thus [encircled], may I be rescued
From the fearsome passageway of the intermediate state,
And be escorted to the level of an utterly perfect buddha.

By making this aspirational prayer with fervent devotion, you will dissolve into rainbow light in the heart of Vairocana and his consort, and you will attain buddhahood, as the Buddha-body of Perfect Resource, in the central Buddha field of the Dense Array (Ghanavyūha).

If, however, even after receiving this introduction, as the result of negative obscuration and aversion, [the deceased] are nonetheless overawed by the lights and rays, and turn away, and even if, after repeating the aspirational prayer, they remain bewildered, then, on the second day, Vajrasattva's assembly of deities will come to escort them, and, at that same time, the negative past actions which are conducive to a rebirth in the hell [realms] will also emerge.

Again, calling the deceased by name, the introduction should be given with the following words:

O, Child of Buddha Nature, listen without distraction. On the second day the purity of the entire element water will arise in the form of a white light. At that time, from the eastern Buddha field of Manifest Joy (Abhirati), the transcendent lord Akṣobhya-Vajrasattva will dawn before you, his body blue in colour, holding in his [right] hand a five-pronged vajra, seated on an elephant throne and embraced by his consort Buddhalocanā. They are encircled by two male bodhisattvas, Kṣitigarbha and Maitreya, and two female bodhisattvas, Lāsyā and Puṣpā, thus, six buddha-bodies will be shining before you from within a space of rainbow light.

A [brilliant] white light, [indicative of] the mirror-like pristine cognition, which is the natural purity of the aggregate of form, white and dazzling, radiant and clear [will emanate] from the heart of Vajrasattva and his consort and it will shine piercingly before you [at the level of your heart, with such brilliance] that your eyes cannot bear it. Together with this light of pristine cognition, a dull smoky light, [indicative of] the hell [realms], will also dawn before you [and touch your heart]. At that time, under the sway of aversion, you will [wish to] turn away in fear and terror from the bright white light and come to perceive the dull smoky light of the hell [realms] with delight. At that moment, you should fearlessly recognise the white light, white and dazzling, radiant and clear, to be pristine cognition. Have confidence in it! Be drawn to it with longing devotion! Pray with devotion, thinking: 'This is the light ray of the transcendent lord Vajrasattva's compassion. I take refuge in it.' This, in reality, is Vajrasattva and his consort come to escort you on the dangerous pathway of the intermediate state. This is the light-ray hook of Vajrasattva's compassion! Be devoted to it! Do not delight in the dull smoky light of the hell [realms]! This [dull light] is the inviting path of the negative obscurations created by your own deep aversion, which you yourself have generated. If you become attached to it, you will fall into the realms of hell, sinking into a swamp of unbearable suffering, from which there will be no [immediate] opportunity for escape. [This dull light] is an obstacle blocking the path to liberation. Do not look at it! Abandon your aversion! Do not be attached to it! Do not cling to it! Be devoted to the white light, radiant and dazzling! Focus intently on the transcendent lord Vajrasattva and recite the following aspirational prayer:

O, as I roam in cyclic existence [driven] by deep-seated aversion,
May the transcendent lord Vajrasattva draw me forward,
Leading me on the path of radiant light,
Which is the mirror-like pristine cognition.
May the supreme consort Buddhalocanā support me from behind,
And, thus [encircled], may I be rescued
From the fearsome passageway of the intermediate state,
And be escorted to the level of an utterly perfect buddha.

By making this aspirational prayer with fervent devotion, [you] will dissolve into rainbow light in the heart of the transcendent lord Vajrasattva, and you will attain buddhahood, as the Buddha-body of Perfect Resource, in the eastern Buddha field of Manifest Joy (Abhirati).

Yet, even after being introduced in this way, there are some individuals who will turn away in fear from the light-ray hook of compassion, being gripped by pride and powerful negative obscuration.[45] So it is that, on the third day, the transcendent lord Ratnasambhava's assembly of deities will come to escort [the deceased] and simultaneously the light path indicative of the human realm will emerge.

Again, calling the deceased by name, the introduction should be given with the following words:

O, Child of Buddha Nature, listen without distraction. On the third day, the purity of the entire element earth will arise in the form of a yellow light. At this time, from the yellow southern Buddha field of the Glorious (Śrīmat), the transcendent lord Ratnasambhava will dawn before you, his body yellow in colour, holding in his [right] hand a jewel, seated on a horse throne and embraced by his supreme consort Māmakī. They are encircled by two male bodhisattvas, Ākāśagarbha and Samantabhadra, and two female bodhisattvas, Mālyā and Dhūpā, thus, six buddha-bodies will be shining before you from within a space of rainbow light.

A yellow light [indicative of] the pristine cognition of sameness, which is the natural purity of the aggregate of feeling, yellow and dazzling, adorned by greater and lesser seminal points [of light], radiant, clear and unbearable to the eyes, [will emanate] from the heart of Ratnasambhava and his consort and will shine piercingly before you at the level of your heart [with such brilliance] that your eyes cannot bear it. Together with the light of pristine cognition, a dull blue light, [indicative of] the human realm, will also dawn before you and touch your heart. At that time, under the sway of pride, you will [wish to] turn away in fear and terror from the bright yellow light and you will come to delight in the dull blue light of the human realm and feel attachment towards it. At that moment, abandon your fear of the yellow light, and recognise it as pristine cognition, yellow and dazzling, radiant and clear! Let your awareness relax and abide directly within it, in a state of non-activity.[46] Again and again, have confidence in it! Be drawn to it with longing devotion! If you recognise it as the natural luminosity of your own awareness, even though you may feel no devotion towards it and have not recited the aspirational prayer, all the buddha-bodies and light rays will dissolve inseparably into you and you will attain buddhahood. If you are unable to recognise this [radiance] as being the natural luminosity of your own awareness, then pray with devotion, thinking: 'This is the light ray of the transcendent lord Ratnasambhava's compassion. I take refuge in it.' This, in reality, is the transcendent lord Ratnasambhava come to escort you on the fearsome dangerous pathway of the intermediate state. This is the light-ray hook of Ratnasambhava's compassion! Be devoted to it! Do not delight in the dull blue light of the human realm. This [dull light] is the inviting path created by your own habitual tendencies for deep-seated pride, which you yourself have generated. If you become attached to it, you will tumble down into the human realm, you will experience the sufferings of birth, old age, sickness and death, and there will be no [immediate] opportunity to escape from the swamp of cyclic existence. This [dull light] is an obstacle blocking the path to liberation! Do not look at it! Abandon pride! Abandon your habitual tendencies! Do not be attached to the dull blue light! Do not cling to it! Be devoted to the yellow light, golden and dazzling. Focus intently and single-mindedly on the transcendent lord Ratnasambhava and recite the following aspirational prayer:

O, as I roam in cyclic existence [driven] by deep-seated pride,
May the transcendent lord Ratnasambhava draw me forward,
Leading me on the path of radiant light,
Which is the pristine cognition of sameness.
May the supreme consort Māmakī support me from behind,
And, thus [encircled], may I be rescued
From the fearsome passageway of the intermediate state,
And be escorted to the level of an utterly perfect buddha.

By making this aspirational prayer with fervent devotion, you will dissolve into rainbow light in the heart of the transcendent lord Ratnasambhava, and you will attain buddhahood, as the Buddha-body of Perfect Resource, in the southern Buddha field of the Glorious (Śrīmat).

There is no doubt that if [the deceased] are receptive to this introduction, they will attain liberation, however weak their [individual] ability may be. Yet, even after being given this introduction many times, there are some whose positive opportunities have been exhausted by, for example, their great negativity or through not having maintained their commitments and so forth, who, even now, will not have accepted this introduction. These individuals will have turned away in fear of both the sounds and the luminosities and become agitated by desire and negative obscuration. So it is that, on the fourth day, the transcendent lord Amitābha's assembly of deities will come to escort them and, at that same time, the light path [indicative of the realm] of the anguished spirits, which is generated by desire and miserliness, will emerge.

Again, calling the deceased by name, the introduction should be given with the following words:

O, Child of Buddha Nature, listen without distraction. On the fourth day, the purity of the element fire will arise in the form of a red light. At that time, from the red western Buddha field of the Blissful (Sukhāvatī), the transcendent lord Amitābha will dawn before you, his body red in colour, holding in his [right] hand a lotus flower, seated on a peacock throne and embraced by the supreme consort Pāṇḍaravāsinī. They are encircled by two male bodhisattvas, Avalokiteśvara and Mañjuśrī, and two female bodhisattvas, Gītā and Ālokā, thus, six buddha-bodies will be shining before you from within a space of rainbow light.

A red light [indicative of] the pristine cognition of discernment, which is the natural purity of the aggregate of perceptions, red and dazzling, adorned by greater and lesser seminal points, radiant and clear, bright and dazzling, [will emanate] from the heart of Amitābha and his consort and will shine piercingly before you at the level of your heart [with such brilliance] that your eyes cannot bear it. Do not be afraid! Together with the light of pristine cognition, a dull yellow light, [indicative of the realm] of anguished spirits, will also dawn before you [and touch your heart]. Do not delight [in the dull yellow light]! Do not become attached to it and do not cling to it! At this time, under the sway of deep desire, you will [wish to] turn away in terror from the bright red light and you will come to delight in the dull yellow light of the anguished spirits and feel attachment towards it. At this moment, abandon your fear, and recognise the red light, bright and dazzling, radiant and clear, to be pristine cognition. Let your awareness relax and abide directly within it, resting in a state of non-activity. Have confidence in the radiant, red luminosity! Be drawn to it with longing devotion. If you recognise this radiance as the natural luminosity of your own awareness, even though you may feel no devotion towards it and have not recited the aspirational prayer, all the buddha-bodies and light rays will dissolve inseparably [into you] and you will attain buddhahood. If you are not able to recognise [the radiance] in this way, then pray with devotion, thinking: 'This is the light ray of the transcendent lord Amitābha's compassion. I take refuge in it.' This truly is the light-ray hook of the transcendent lord Amitābha's compassion! Be devoted to it! Do not turn away! Should you turn away, the luminosity will accompany you inseparably. Do not be afraid! Do not be attached to the dull yellow light of the anguished spirits! This is the inviting path created by your own habitual tendencies for deep-seated desire, which you yourself have generated. If you become attached to this [dull light], you will fall down into the realm of the anguished spirits and you will experience unbearable sufferings of hunger and thirst. This [dull light] is an obstacle blocking the path to liberation! Do not be attached to it! Abandon your attachment! Do not cling to it! Be devoted to the red light, which is radiant and dazzling, and focus intently and single-mindedly on the transcendent lord Amitābha and his consort, and recite the following aspirational prayer:

O, as I roam in cyclic existence [driven] by deep-seated desire,
May the transcendent lord Amitābha draw me forward,
Leading me on the path of radiant light,
Which is the pristine cognition of discernment.
May the supreme consort Pāṇḍaravāsinī support me from behind,
And, thus [encircled], may I be rescued
From the fearsome passageway of the intermediate state,
And be escorted to the level of an utterly perfect buddha.

By making this aspirational prayer with fervent devotion, you will dissolve into rainbow light in the heart of the transcendent lord Amitābha and his consort, and you will attain buddhahood, as the Buddha-body of Perfect Resource, in the western Buddha field of the Blissful (Sukhāvatī).

Although it is impossible not to be liberated by [the successful recognition of] this [introduction], there are nonetheless those who will be unable to give up their propensities due to habituation over long periods of time, even after receiving such an introduction. Under the sway of envy and negative past actions, they will become fearful and overawed by the sounds and luminosities. Failing to be caught by the light-ray hook of compassion, they roam downwards into the fifth day. So it is that, on the fifth day, the transcendent lord Amoghasiddhi's assembly of deities, resplendent with the light rays of compassion, will come to escort them and, at the same time, the light path indicative of [the realm of] the antigods, which is generated by the dissonant mental state of envy, will emerge invitingly.

Again, calling the deceased by name, the introduction should now be given with the following words:

O, Child of Buddha Nature, listen without distraction. On the fifth day, the purity of the entire wind element will arise in the form of a green light. At that time, from the green northern Buddha field [called] Matrix of Enlightened Activities (Karmaprasiddhi), the transcendent lord Buddha Amoghasiddhi with his retinue will dawn before you, his body green in colour, holding in his [right] hand a crossed-vajra, seated on a cīvaṃcīvaka bird throne and embraced by the supreme consort Samayatārā. These two are encircled by two male bodhisattvas, Vajrapāṇi and Nivāraṇaviṣkhambhin, and two female bodhisattvas, Gandhā and Nartī. Thus, six buddha-bodies will be shining [before you] from within a space of rainbow light.

A green light [indicative of] the pristine cognition of accomplishment, which is the natural purity of the aggregate of motivational tendencies, green and dazzling, radiant and clear, bright and awesome, adorned by greater and lesser seminal points, [will emanate] from the heart of Amoghasiddhi and his consort and it will shine piercingly before you at the level of your heart, [with such brilliance] that your eyes cannot bear it. Do not be afraid! This is the natural expressive power of your own awareness! Rest in a state of great equanimity, transcending activity, free from [the dichotomies of] attachment and aversion, based on [your feelings of] nearness and distance. Together with the light of pristine cognition, a dull red light, [indicative of the realm] of the antigods and formed by envy, will also dawn before you [and touch your heart]. Cultivate an equanimity toward this [dull light] which is free from attachment or aversion! Even if your mental capacity is diminished, at least do not delight in it. At this time, under the sway of deep envy, you will [wish to] turn away in terror from the bright and dazzling green luminosity and you will come to feel delight and attachment towards the dull red light of the antigods. At this moment, abandon your fear, and recognise the green luminosity, bright and dazzling, radiant and clear, to be pristine cognition. Let your awareness relax and abide directly within it, resting in a state of non-activity. Pray with devotion, thinking: 'This is the light ray of the transcendent lord Amoghasiddhi's compassion. I take refuge in it.' This, in reality, is the light-ray hook of the transcendent lord Amoghasiddhi's compassion, which is known as the pristine cognition of accomplishment. Be devoted to it! Do not turn away! Even if you do turn away, the luminosity will accompany you inseparably. So, do not be afraid! Do not be attached to the dull red light of the antigods. This is the inviting path of your past actions, which you yourself have engaged in, whilst motivated by deep envy. If you become attached to this dull light, you will fall into the realms of the antigods and experience the unbearable sufferings of [unrelenting] conflict and quarrelling. This [dull light] is an obstacle blocking the path to liberation! Do not be attached to it! Give up your yearning! Do not cling to it! Be devoted to the green light, which is radiant and dazzling, and focus intently and single-mindedly on the transcendent lord Amoghasiddhi and his consort, and recite the following aspirational prayer:

O, as I roam in cyclic existence [driven] by deep-seated envy,
May the transcendent lord Amoghasiddhi draw me forward,
Leading me on the path of radiant light,
Which is the pristine cognition of accomplishment.
May the supreme consort Samayatārā support me from behind,
And, thus [encircled], may I be rescued
From the fearsome passageway of the intermediate state,
And be escorted to the level of an utterly perfect buddha.

By making this aspirational prayer with fervent devotion, you will dissolve into rainbow light in the heart of the transcendent lord Amoghasiddhi and his consort, and you will attain buddhahood, as the Buddha-body of Perfect Resource, in the northern Buddha field [called] 'Matrix of Enlightened Activities' (*Karmaprasiddhi*).

By giving this introduction repeatedly in this way, however weak the [positive] residue of [a deceased individual's] past actions might be, he or she will [have the opportunity to] attain recognition at one point or another. As recognition occurs at any point, it will be impossible for liberation not to be achieved.

However, owing to a long association with myriad habitual tendencies and an unfamiliarity with pure vision and pristine cognition, even after being introduced repeatedly in this way, there are some who are nevertheless led backwards by negative propensities, despite this setting face to face having been given. Failing to be gripped by the light-ray hook of compassion, they will be overcome by awe and terror [upon the arising] of the lights and rays, and continue to wander downwards.

Thereupon, on the sixth day, the male and female deities of the five enlightened families, together with their retinues, will arise simultaneously, and at that very moment, the six [dull] lights, [indicative] of the six classes of living beings, will also arise simultaneously.

Therefore, calling the deceased by name, the introduction should be given with the following words:

O, Child of Buddha Nature, listen without distraction. Until yesterday the visions of the five individual enlightened families arose before you. Despite this, even though the [former] introduction was given, you experienced awe and terror; a response generated by your habitual tendencies. Consequently, you have remained in your present state, until now. If you had previously recognised [one of] the natural luminosities of the pristine cognitions of the five enlightened families as being a natural manifestation [of actual reality], you would have dissolved into rainbow light [at the heart] of [one of] these buddha-bodies of the five respective enlightened families, and attained buddhahood, in the Buddha-body of Perfect Resource. Yet, since you have been unable to recognise these [experiences] as being natural manifestations, you have wandered here. Therefore, listen now, without distraction. The vision of the entire [peaceful assembly] of the five enlightened families, together with that which is called: 'the vision of the four pristine cognitions combined',[47] *will now come to invite you. Recognise this!*

O, Child of Buddha Nature, [at this time] the four coloured lights, which are the pure forms of the four elements, will dawn before you; and, simultaneously, the buddha Vairocana and his consort will arise, as before, from the central Buddha field of the Pervasive Seminal Point [i.e. Akaniṣṭha-Ghanavyūha]. [At that same moment], the buddha Vajrasattva and his consort, surrounded by their retinue, will arise from the eastern Buddha field of Manifest Joy (Abhirati). The buddha Ratnasambhava and his consort, together with their retinue, will arise from the southern Buddha field of the Glorious (Śrīmat). The buddha Amitābha and his consort, together with their retinue, will arise from the western Buddha field of the Blissful (Sukhāvatī), and the buddha Amoghasiddhi and his consort, together with their retinue, will now arise before you from the northern Buddha field [called] Matrix of Enlightened Activities [i.e. Karmaprasiddhi], [all arising together] out of a space of rainbow light.

O, Child of Buddha Nature, encircling these male and female deities of the five enlightened families, the male gatekeepers, [Trailokya]vijaya, Yamāntaka, Hayagrīvarāja and Amṛtakuṇḍalin, will also arise, together with the female gatekeepers, Aṅkuśā, Pāśā, Sphoṭā and Ghaṇṭā. In addition, the six [emanational] sages who are transcendent lords, will also appear before you: Indraśakra who is the sage of the gods, Vemacitra who is the sage of the antigods, Śākyamuni who is the sage of humans, Sthirasiṃha who is the sage of the animals, Jvālamukha who is the sage of the anguished spirits, and Dharmarāja who is the sage of the hell beings. [Accompanying the above array], Samantabhadra and Samantabhadrī will also arise before you, [in the form called] Samantabhadra and Consort in Union, [the coalescence] which is the progenitor of all the buddhas.

These, the forty-two assembled deities of the Buddha-body of Perfect Resource, will emanate from within your heart and then appear before you. Recognise them! For they have arisen from within your own pure vision! O, Child of Buddha Nature, these buddha fields do not exist extraneously. They are the five aspects of your own heart; its four directions and centre. Emanating now from within your own heart, they have arisen before you. These buddha-bodies have not arisen extraneously. They have spontaneously arisen, atemporally, from the natural expressive power of your own awareness. Therefore recognise them as they are!

O, Child of Buddha Nature, these buddha-bodies [that you see before you] are neither large nor small, but perfectly proportioned, and they are [all adorned] with their respective ornaments, [costumes], colours, postures, thrones and hand-gestures. The array is made up of [central] couples [of male and female deities], forming five distinct clusters, and each cluster of five is encircled by an aura of five-coloured lights. All the male bodhisattvas of the [five] enlightened families who accompany the male [buddhas], all the female bodhisattvas of the [five] enlightened families who accompany the female [buddhas], and the entire maṇḍala will arise [before you], perfectly and simultaneously. So recognise them! They are your own meditational deities!

O, Child of Buddha Nature, from the hearts of the male and female buddhas of the five enlightened families, the light rays of the 'four pristine cognitions combined', very fine and clear, like a spider's web, will dawn before your heart, [like the] entwined light rays of the sun.

First, a sheet of radiant white[48] *light rays, bright and awesome, [indicative of] the pristine cognition of reality's expanse, will emanate from the heart of Vairocana, and touch your heart. Above*[49] *this sheet of light, a white seminal point resembling a mirror facing downwards will arise, emanating light rays, extremely radiant, bright and dazzling, adorned with five distinct seminal points of like nature, each of which in turn will be adorned by greater and lesser seminal points, [forming an array] with no centre or horizon.*

[Second], a sheet of radiant blue light, [indicative of] the mirror-like pristine cognition, [will emanate] from the heart of Vajrasattva. Above this, like a turquoise bowl facing downwards, a radiant blue seminal point will arise, [also] adorned by [an array of] greater and lesser seminal points.

[Third], a sheet of radiant yellow light, [indicative of] the pristine cognition of sameness, [will emanate] from the heart of Ratnasambhava. Above this, like a gold cup facing downwards, a radiant yellow seminal point will arise, [also] adorned by [an array of] greater and lesser seminal points.

[Fourth], a sheet of radiant red light, [indicative of] the pristine cognition of discernment, [will emanate] from the heart of Amitābha. Above this, like a coral bowl facing downwards, a radiant red seminal point will arise, extremely luminous and dazzling,

[resplendent] with the luminosity of pristine cognition. It too will be adorned with five distinct seminal points of like nature, each of which in turn will also be adorned by greater and lesser seminal points, [forming an array] with no centre or horizon. All of these [lights and seminal points] will indeed arise, and touch your heart.

O, Child of Buddha Nature, these [radiances] are arising out of the natural expressive power of your own awareness. They have not come from anywhere else. Therefore, do not be attached to them! Do not be afraid of them! Relax and rest in a non-conceptual state.[50] *[Abiding] in this state, all the buddha-bodies and light rays will merge into you, and buddhahood will then be attained.*

O, Child of Buddha Nature, [during the above series] the green light [indicative] of the pristine cognition of accomplishment will not arise. The reason for this is that the natural expressive power of pristine cognition, which is your own intrinsic awareness, is not yet perfected.[51]

O, Child of Buddha Nature, this [array of luminosities that you are now experiencing] is called: 'the vision of the four pristine cognitions combined'. It is [also] known as the 'hollow passageway of Vajrasattva'.[52] *At this time, therefore, you should recall the oral instructions, which your spiritual teacher formerly introduced to you. If you [successfully] recall this [former] introduction, you will have confidence in the visions that have already arisen, and you will recognise them, just as there is instant recognition at the meeting of a mother and her son, or just as one instantly recognises an old acquaintance the moment one sees them. Cutting through any doubt, you will recognise [these radiances] to be natural manifestations [of actual reality]. Achieving confidence, in this way, in the unchanging path of pure reality, and sustaining a continuous meditative stability,*[53] *you will dissolve into the buddha-body of great spontaneously present awareness*[54] *and irreversibly attain buddhahood in the Buddha-body of Perfect Resource.*

O, Child of Buddha Nature, together with the radiances of pristine cognition, the six [dull] lights [indicative] of the six classes [of beings] who are obscured by impure and bewildering perception, will also arise simultaneously. That is to say, the dull white light of the gods, the dull red light of the antigods, the dull blue light of the humans, the dull green light of the animals, the dull yellow light of the anguished spirits, and the dull smoky light of the inhabitants of the hells will arise alongside the radiances of pure pristine cognition. At that moment, do not seize upon, or become attached to, any [of these lights]! Relax and abide in a non-referential state. For if you are fearful of the pure radiances of pristine cognition and become attached to the impure lights of cyclic existence with its six classes [of beings], you will assume a body amongst [one of] these six realms, and you will be debilitated; for there will be no [immediate] opportunity for escape from cyclic existence, this vast ocean of suffering.

O, Child of Buddha Nature, if you are one who has not been introduced to the oral instructions of a spiritual teacher, you will be frightened and overwhelmed by these buddha-bodies and the radiances of pure pristine cognition, just described, and you will feel attachment towards the [dull] lights of impure cyclic existence. Do not do this! Be devoted to the bright and dazzling radiances of pure pristine cognition. Be full of devotion and think: 'The light rays of pristine cognition, which are the compassion of Those Gone to Bliss, the transcendent lords of the five enlightened families, have come to seize me with compassion. I take refuge in them.' Do not be attached to the bewildering lights of the six classes [of beings]. Do not cling to them! Focus one-pointedly on the male and female buddhas of the five enlightened families and recite the following aspirational prayer:

O, as I roam in cyclic existence [driven] by the five virulent poisons,
May the transcendent conquerors, [the male buddhas] of the five enlightened families, draw me forward,
Leading me on the path of radiant light,
Which is the four pristine cognitions combined.
May the five supreme female buddhas, [the purity of] the expanse, support me from behind,
And, thus [encircled], may I be rescued
From the light paths of the six impure classes [of beings]!
Released from the fearsome passageway of the intermediate state,
May I be escorted to the five utterly supreme and pure buddha fields.

By making this aspirational prayer, [the superior adept] will recognise [the radiances of pristine cognition] to be natural manifestations [of actual reality] and thereby, upon dissolving indivisibly with them, buddhahood will be attained. Those of average ability will achieve recognition on the basis of fervent devotion and thereby attain liberation, and even all [those of inferior ability] can, through the power of pure aspiration, close the womb entrances through which the six classes [of beings are born]. Thus, if the nature of 'the four pristine cognitions combined' is realised, [all of the above individuals] can attain buddhahood through 'the hollow passageway of Vajrasattva'. As a result of being introduced in such a clear and detailed way, the majority will attain recognition and many [individuals] will achieve liberation.

However, those most lowly individuals in the human world who totally lack the propensities for spiritual practice, and those who have broken their commitments and so forth, will continue to be bewildered, as a result of their [negative] past actions. Despite being introduced, they will continue to roam downwards, failing to achieve recognition.

So it is, that on the seventh day, the divine assembly of the Awareness Holders will arise from the pure realm of the sky-farers and come to escort [the deceased], as will, simultaneously, the light path to the animal realm, formed of the dissonant mental state, delusion.[55]

At this time, calling the deceased by name, the introduction should be given with the following words:

O, Child of Buddha Nature, listen without distraction. On the seventh day, a five-faceted multicoloured light, [which is indicative of] the purity of your habitual tendencies in the expanse [of reality], will arise before you. Simultaneously, the divine assembly of the awareness holders, arising from the pure realm of the sky-farers, will come forward to escort you.

In the centre of [this maṇḍala], suffused by rainbows and light, the unsurpassed [Vidyādhara] known as the 'awareness holder of maturation', Padmanarteśvara, will instantaneously arise, his body resplendent with the radiance of the five lights, embraced by his consort, a red ḍākinī, [who is dancing] with a blood-filled skull and a curved knife, raised in the gesture of pointing to the sky.

From the east of the maṇḍala, [the Vidyādhara] known as the 'awareness holder who abides on the levels' will instantaneously arise, his body white in colour, his face radiant and smiling. He is embraced by his consort, a white ḍākinī, who is dancing with a blood-filled skull and a curved knife, raised in the gesture of pointing to the sky.

From the south of the maṇḍala, [the Vidyādhara] known as the 'awareness holder with power over the lifespan' will instantaneously arise, his body yellow in colour and adorned by the exquisite [eighty] minor marks. He is embraced by his consort, a yellow ḍākinī, who is dancing with a blood-filled skull and a curved knife, raised in the gesture of pointing to the sky.

From the west of the maṇḍala, [the Vidyādhara] known as the 'awareness holder of the great seal' will instantaneously arise, his body red in colour, his face radiant and smiling. He is embraced by his consort, a red ḍākinī, who is dancing with a blood-filled skull and a curved knife, raised in the gesture of pointing to the sky.

From the north of the maṇḍala, [the Vidyādhara] known as the 'awareness holder of spontaneous presence' will instantaneously arise, his body green in colour, his face both wrathful and smiling. He is embraced by his consort, a green ḍākinī, who is dancing with a blood-filled skull and a curved knife, raised in the gesture of pointing to the sky.

Encircling these awareness holders, there will be inestimable crowds of ḍākinīs: the ḍākinīs of the eight charnel grounds, ḍākinīs of the four enlightened families, ḍākinīs of the three abodes, ḍākinīs of the ten directions, ḍākinīs of the twenty-four power-places, spiritual heroes and heroines, faithful retainers,[56] *and protectors of the [sacred] teachings – all wearing the six kinds of bone ornaments, playing drums, thigh-bone trumpets, and skull drums and [waving] banners made of the hide of 'ritually liberated' beings, canopies and streamers of human hide, [the entire display pervaded by] an incense cloud of burning human flesh, reverberating with the sound of countless and diverse musical instruments, the sound permeating all world systems, causing them to vibrate, tremble and quake. The crescendo will reverberate as if to split your head. Performing their diverse dances, this [array] will come to escort those who have kept their commitments and to bring to account those who have allowed their commitments to degenerate.*

O, Child of Buddha Nature, a five-coloured light, which is [indicative of] the purity of your habitual tendencies in the expanse [of reality] and of coemergent pristine cognition, composed of coloured threads [of light] twisted together, pulsing, shimmering, translucent, radiant, clear, bright and awesome, [will emanate] from the hearts of the five principal awareness holders and will shine piercingly before you, at the level of your heart [with such brilliance] that your eyes cannot bear it. At that moment, a dull green light, [indicative of] the realms of the animals, will arise simultaneously with the light of pristine cognition [and touch your heart]. At this time, bewildered and confused by your past habitual tendencies, you will be frightened by the five-coloured light, and wish to turn away. Instantly, you will be attracted to the dull light of the animal realms, so therefore, do not be frightened now by the bright and flashing five-coloured light! Do not be terrified! Recognise this [radiance] to be pristine cognition! Within the [five-coloured] light, all the natural sounds of the sacred teachings will resound like a thousand simultaneous peals of thunder. They will resound like a [violent] echo, an overwhelming reverberation, a tumultuous crescendo, a cacophony of war cries, and [pound with the roar of] wrathful mantras of terrifying ferocity. Do not be afraid! Do not turn away! Recognise these sounds and luminosities to be the naturally expressive power of your own awareness, manifesting naturally. Do not be attracted to the dull green light of the animals. Do not cling to it! If you become attached to it, you will fall into the obscured realms of the animals and be enveloped by the limitless sufferings of obfuscation, dumbness and servility, from which there will be no [immediate] opportunity for release. So do not be attached to that [dull green light]! Be devoted to the five-coloured light that is radiant and dazzling! Focus intently and one-pointedly on the divine assembly of the awareness holders, the transcendent lords and spiritual teachers, thinking: 'As you, the Awareness Holders together with your [attending] heroes and ḍākinīs have come forward to escort me to the pure realm of the sky-farers, I implore you, pity sentient beings such as myself who have failed to amass the accumulations [of merit and pristine cognition], and pity those such as I, who have not been rescued until now, even though we have been embraced by the compassion of all the assembled deities of the five enlightened families, Those Gone to Bliss, throughout the three times! Today may you, the divine assembly of awareness holders, not allow me to descend any further than this. Grasp me with the hook of your compassion, and lead me immediately to the pure realm of the sky-farers.' Focusing intently and one-pointedly on the divine [maṇḍala of] awareness holders, recite the following aspirational prayer:

O, as I roam in cyclic existence [driven] by deep-seated habitual tendencies,
May the divine assembly of awareness holders attend to me
And lead me on the path, with great love.
May the assembly of spiritual heroes and awareness holders draw me forward,
Leading me on the path of radiant light,
Which is [the luminance of] coemergent pristine cognition.
May the supreme consorts, the hosts of ḍākinīs, support me from behind,
And, thus [encircled], may I be rescued
From the fearsome passageway of the intermediate state,
And be escorted to the [sacred] pure realm of the sky-farers.

By making this aspirational prayer with fervent devotion, you will dissolve into rainbow light, in the heart of the divine assembly of the awareness holders, and thereafter, undoubtedly, be born into the pure-realm of the sky-farers.

All types of spiritual friend can attain recognition at this stage, and [thus] they will attain liberation. There is no doubt that even those with negative propensities can attain liberation at this point.

This concludes the first part of the *Great Liberation by Hearing*, the introduction to inner radiance in the intermediate state of the time of death and the introduction to the peaceful deities of the intermediate state of reality.

ITI! SAMAYA! *rgya rgya rgya!*

PART TWO

An Elucidation of the Appearance of the Wrathful Deities in the Intermediate State of Reality

Herein is contained *An Elucidation of the Arising of the Intermediate State of the Wrathful Deities.*[1]

INTRODUCTION

Now, the way in which the intermediate state of the wrathful deities arises should be presented. In the previous intermediate state of the peaceful deities there were seven successive [critical or] dangerous pathways. By receiving introduction to these sequentially, even though one might not have attained recognition at one [critical pathway], one should have attained recognition at another. Those who have achieved liberation [in this way] are countless.

Yet, although many have been liberated through such [introductions to the nature of reality], sentient beings are numerous. Evil past actions are very potent. Negative obscurations are dense. Habitual tendencies are long lasting. The cycle of ignorance and bewilderment is inexhaustible and undiminishing. Despite having received introduction in such detail, there are still a large number who roam downwards, not having achieved liberation.

Now, after the invitation of the assembly of the peaceful deities, and the divine assembly of the awareness holders and ḍākinīs, has passed, the blazing assembly of the fifty-eight wrathful blood-drinking deities, who are a natural transformation of the above assembly of peaceful deities, will arise. These deities will be very dissimilar [in appearance] to the peaceful deities. This is the intermediate state of the wrathful deities and, [consequently, as the deceased will be] overpowered by fear, terror or awe, recognition also becomes more difficult. Uncontrollably, awareness continually faints. But, nevertheless, if there is even the slightest recognition, liberation is easy. Should you ask why this is so – it is because once the awesome, terrifying and fearful appearances arise, the awareness does not have the luxury of distraction. The awareness is one-pointedly concentrated.

If, at this stage, oral instructions such as those which follow [have not been previously introduced, or] are not now introduced, even though one's studies may have been ocean-like, they will be of no benefit here. Even the preceptors [of monasteries] who uphold the monastic disciplines and great teachers of dialectics [who have not been previously introduced] will be bewildered on this occasion, and fail to attain recognition. Consequently, they will continue to roam in cyclic existence. This is even more so for ordinary persons: fleeing in awe, terror and fear, they will fall into the abyss of lower existences and suffer miserably. However, even the most inferior of yogins who has practised the way of secret mantra, will immediately, upon seeing the assembled blood-drinking deities, recognise them to be meditational deities, as if meeting old acquaintances. Trusting in them, the yogin will dissolve indivisibly [into the meditational deities] and attain buddhahood.

The crucial point is indeed that those in this world who have, [prior to death], meditated on the formal description of these blood-drinking buddha-bodies, and also made offerings and praises to them, or, at the very least, have simply seen their painted and sculpted images, may recognise the forms that arise here and attain liberation.

Moreover, when those preceptors who uphold the monastic disciplines and the teachers of dialectics [who have not been introduced] die, however great their perseverance was in religious conduct or however learned they were in their exegetical doctrines within the human world, no [auspicious] signs, such as major or minor bone relics or rainbow light, will appear.[2] Since they did not take the way of secret mantra to heart while they were alive, but instead deprecated the secret mantra, and failed to become acquainted [in life] with the assembled deities of the way of secret mantra, they will not recognise the [luminosities and deities] when they arise in the intermediate state. Suddenly seeing something they had not previously seen, they will develop an attitude of aversion and become hostile. Consequently they will proceed into lower existences. This [lack of familiarity and the arousal of aversion] is the reason why [auspicious] signs, such as major or minor bone relics, and rainbow light, do not occur in the case of those upholders of monastic discipline and dialectical philosophers, however excellent they may have been, who have not taken to heart and experientially cultivated the way of secret mantra.

On the other hand, practitioners of the way of secret mantra, even if they are the lowest of the low, however coarsely [they behaved] in the world, or however unrefined and uncultured they were, and however unseemly and inelegant their conduct, even if they have not been able to experientially cultivate the way of secret mantra successfully, will attain liberation in this instance, simply because they have not embraced a mistaken view, and are without doubt, and are devoted to the secret mantra. Even if such an individual's conduct in the human world was inelegant, at least one [auspicious] indication, such as major and minor relics, images or rainbow light, will occur at the moment of death. This is because the way of secret mantra carries an extremely great blessing.

Yogins of the way of secret mantra who are above average capacity, who have experientially cultivated the meditations of both the generation and perfection stages and [practised] the recitation of the heart-mantras, and so on, do not need to roam downwards this far into the intermediate state of reality. As soon as respiration ceases, they will certainly be invited to the pure realm of the sky-farers by the awareness holders, heroes and ḍākinīs. As an indication of this, [one or more of] the following signs will occur: the sky will become cloudless; [the body] will merge into rainbows and lights; a shower of flowers will fall; there will be the fragrance of perfume [in the air] and the sound of music in the sky; while rays of light, major and minor relics, images, rainbow lights, and so forth will appear [in the funeral pyre].[3]

So it is that, for the upholders of the monastic disciplines and teachers [of dialectics who have not been previously introduced], and for practitioners of the way of secret mantra whose commitments have degenerated, and for all ordinary persons, this *Great Liberation by Hearing* is indispensable.

Those serious meditators who have meditated on [the practices of] the Great Perfection and the Great Seal will recognise the inner radiance that dawns during the intermediate state of the time of death and will attain the Buddha-body of Reality. For these meditators there is absolutely no need to read this *Liberation by Hearing*.

[In summary], if individuals recognise the inner radiance during the intermediate state of the time of death, they will attain the Buddha-body of Reality. If they achieve recognition during this intermediate state of reality, when the visions of the Peaceful and Wrathful Deities arise, they will attain the Buddha-body of Perfect Resource. If they achieve recognition during the intermediate state of rebirth, they will attain the Buddha-body of Emanation. Alternatively, at the very least, [individuals who have heard this teaching] will be born into the higher existences, where, based on the residual potency of their past actions, they will again meet with, and be able to practise, this [sacred] teaching in the next life.

Since [this sacred teaching is based on recognition in the intermediate states] this *Great Liberation by Hearing* is the teaching whereby buddhahood can be attained without meditation. It is the teaching whereby liberation can be attained just by its being heard, it is the teaching whereby those that are the most negative are led onto the secret path,[4] it is the teaching whereby essential points [of discrimination] are instantly grasped, and it is the profound teaching whereby perfect buddhahood is instantaneously attained. Thus, it is impossible for those sentient beings who have been engaged by this teaching to fall into lower existences. This [*Liberation by Hearing*] and the [related] *Liberation by Wearing* should be read aloud together, since [their conjunction] is like a maṇḍala of gold, inlaid with turquoise ornaments.[5]

MAIN SUBJECT MATTER

Having outlined in this way the essential purpose of the *Liberation by Hearing*, [the deceased] should now be introduced to the arising of the intermediate state of the wrathful deities.

Again, you should call the deceased by name, three times, and say the following words:

O, Child of Buddha Nature, listen without distraction. Although the intermediate state of the peaceful deities did previously arise within you, you did not recognise it. So now you have wandered, [through the succession of pathways,] to here. Now, on the eighth day, the assembly of wrathful blood-drinking deities will arise. Recognise them and do not be distracted! O, Child of Buddha Nature, he who is called Great Glorious Buddha Heruka will [now] arise, vividly manifesting before you from within your own brain. His body, blazing in a mass of light, is dark brown in colour, having three heads, six arms and four legs, which are [firmly] set apart. His right face is white, the left red and the central face dark brown. His nine eyes are fixed in a fearsome wrathful gaze, his eyebrows are quivering like lightning, his fangs are bared and gleaming, and he is laughing loudly, uttering the sounds of Alala and Haha, and Shoo oo – like whistles, in loud piercing cries. The golden-auburn hair of his head blazes and rears upward, sun and moon-discs, black serpents and dry skulls adorn each of his heads, and black snakes and fresh skulls form a garland around his body. In his six hands he holds, on the right in the first hand, a wheel, in the middle one, an axe and in the last hand a sword and to the left, in his first hand, he holds a bell, in the middle one, a ploughshare and in the last a skull. The female consort Buddhakrodheśvarī is embracing his body, her right hand clasped around his neck and her left offering a skull-cup filled with blood to his mouth. Amidst loud pounding palatal sounds of 'Thuk-chom', and an [echoing] roar like the reverberation of thunder, the fire of pristine cognition blazes from the fiery indestructible pores of their bodies, and thus they stand together, [with one leg] extended and [the other] drawn in, on a throne supported by garuḍas.

Do not be afraid! Do not be terrified! And do not be awed! Recognise this to be the buddha-body of your own intrinsic awareness. These are your own meditational deities, so do not be terrified. This, in reality, is the transcendent lord Vairocana and his consort, so do not be afraid. Recognition and liberation will occur simultaneously!

If, upon hearing these words, [the deceased] recognises the meditational deities, he or she will dissolve indivisibly [within them] and thereby attain buddhahood in the Buddha-body of Perfect Resource.

Yet should [the deceased], once again, flee in awe and terror and thereby not attain recognition, then, on the ninth day, the Vajra family of blood-drinking deities will come to escort him or her.

Again, calling the deceased by name, the introduction should be given with the following words:

O, Child of Buddha Nature, listen without distraction. He who is called the transcendent lord Vajra Heruka, of the Vajra family of blood-drinking deities, will arise from the eastern direction of your brain and appear before you. His body is dark blue in colour, with three faces, six arms and four legs, [firmly] set apart. His right face is white, the left red and the central face is blue. In his six hands he holds, on the right in the first hand, a vajra, in the middle one, a skull-cup and in the last hand an axe, and to the left, in his first hand, he holds a bell, in the middle one, a skull-cup and in the last a ploughshare. The female consort Vajrakrodheśvarī is embracing his body, her right hand clasped around his neck and her left offering a skull-cup filled with blood to his mouth.

Do not be afraid! Do not be terrified! And do not be awed! Recognise this to be the buddha-body of your own awareness. These are your own meditational deities, so do not be terrified. This, in reality, is the transcendent lord Vajrasattva and his consort, so do not fear them. Be devoted to them! Recognition and liberation will occur simultaneously!

If, upon hearing these words, [the deceased] recognises the meditational deities, he or she will dissolve indivisibly [with them] and thereby attain buddhahood in the Buddha-body of Perfect Resource.

Yet, if those individuals who are greatly obscured by past actions, again flee in awe and terror and thereby do not attain recognition, then on the tenth day, the Ratna family of blood-drinking deities will come to escort them.

Again, calling the deceased by name, the introduction should be given with the following words:

O, Child of Buddha Nature, listen without distraction. On the tenth day, he who is called Ratna Heruka, of the Ratna family of blood-drinking deities, will arise from the southern direction of your brain and appear before you. His body is dark yellow in colour, with three faces, six arms and four legs, [firmly] set apart. His right face is white, the left red, and the central face is a burning dark yellow. In his six hands he holds, on the right in the first hand, a jewel, in the middle one, a khaṭvāṅga and in the last hand a club and to the left, in his first hand, he holds a bell, in the middle one, a skull-cup and in the last a trident. The female consort Ratnakrodheśvarī is embracing his body, her right hand clasped around his neck and her left offering a skull-cup filled with blood to his mouth.

Do not be afraid! Do not be terrified! And do not be awed! Recognise this to be the buddha-body of your own awareness. These are your own meditational deities, so do not be terrified. This, in reality, is the transcendent lord Ratnasambhava and his consort, so be devoted to them! Recognition and liberation will occur simultaneously!

If, upon hearing these words, [the deceased] recognises the meditational deities, he or she will dissolve indivisibly [with them] and thereby attain buddhahood [in the Buddha-body of Perfect Resource].

Yet, even after receiving this introduction, there are those who, owing to their negative habitual tendencies, will nevertheless flee in awe and terror. Not recognising their own meditational deities, they will perceive them as Yama and thereby the recognition will not occur. So it is that, on the eleventh day, the assembled deities of the Padma family of blood-drinking deities will come to escort the deceased.

Again, calling the deceased by name, the introduction should be given with the following words:

O, Child of Buddha Nature, [listen without distraction]. On the eleventh day, he who is called the transcendent lord Padma Heruka, of the Padma family of blood-drinking deities, will arise from the western direction of your brain, in union with his consort, and appear vividly before you. His body is dark red in colour, with three faces, six arms and four legs, [firmly] set apart. His right face is white, the left blue, and the central face is dark red. In his six hands he holds, on the right in the first hand, a lotus, in the middle one, a khaṭvāṅga and in the last hand a mace and to the left, in his first hand he holds a bell, in the middle one, a blood-filled skull and in the last a small drum. The female consort Padmakrodheśvarī is embracing his body, her right hand clasped around his neck and her left offering a skull-cup filled with blood to his mouth.

Do not be afraid! Do not be terrified! And do not be awed! Contemplate them with joy. Recognise this to be the buddha-body of your own awareness. These are your own meditational deities, so do not be terrified. This, in reality, is the transcendent lord Amitābha and his consort, so be devoted to them! Recognition and liberation will occur simultaneously!

If, upon hearing these words, [the deceased] recognises the meditational deities, he or she will dissolve indivisibly [with them] and thereby attain buddhahood [in the Buddha-body of Perfect Resource].

Yet, even after receiving this introduction, there are those who are held back by their negative habitual tendencies and there are those who will not recognise their meditational deities because they have fled in awe and terror. The recognition not having been attained, so it is that, on the twelfth day, the assembled deities of the Karma family of blood-drinking deities, followed by the Gaurī, the Piśācī, the Female Gatekeepers, and the Īśvarī, will come to escort the deceased. Since an even greater fear and terror will arise if these are not recognised, again, call the deceased by name, and offer the introduction in the following words:

O, Child of Buddha Nature, listen without distraction. When the twelfth day comes, he who is called the transcendent lord Karma Heruka, of the Karma family of blood-drinking deities, will arise from the northern direction of your brain, in union with his consort, and appear vividly before you. His body is dark green in colour, with three faces, six arms and four legs, [firmly] set apart. His right face is white, the left red, and the central face is an awesome dark green. In his six hands he holds, on the right in the first hand, a sword, in the middle one, a khaṭvāṅga and in the last hand a mace and to the left, in his first hand he holds a bell, in the middle one, a skull and in the last a plough-share. The female consort Karmakrodheśvarī is embracing his body, her right hand clasped around his neck and her left offering a skull-cup filled with blood to his mouth.

Do not be afraid! Do not be terrified! And do not be awed! Recognise this to be the buddha-body of your own awareness. These are your own meditational deities, so do not be terrified. This, in reality, is the transcendent lord Amoghasiddhi and his consort, so regard them with intense devotion! Recognition and liberation will occur simultaneously!

If, upon hearing these words, [the deceased] recognises the meditational deities, he or she will dissolve indivisibly [with them] and thereby attain buddhahood [in the Buddha-body of Perfect Resource].

Based on the spiritual teacher's [former] oral instruction, as one recognises these [visionary appearances] as the natural expressive power of awareness, naturally manifesting, liberation will occur. This is like one who recognises a stuffed lion-skin to be a stuffed lion. The nature of the stuffed lion is such that if its actual nature is not recognised it will generate awe and terror. But, as soon as someone points out what this really is, the façade is penetrated, and the fear dissolves. Similarly, here, when the assembly of blood-drinking deities arises, with their huge bodies and thick limbs, filling the whole of space, [the deceased] undoubtedly becomes awed and terrified. But, immediately upon hearing this introduction, the deceased will recognise the appearances to be natural manifestations [of actual reality], or to be their own meditational deities. [As this recognition occurs,] the two [aspects of inner radiance], the 'mother inner radiance', which was formerly [introduced] through the spiritual teacher's guidance, and the 'naturally arising child inner radiance', [the experience of] which emerges subsequently [as the result of practice], meet together – in other words, like meeting an old friend, [the inner radiance] that dawns face to face with oneself does so in a naturally liberating manner and one will be naturally freed within [the expanse of] naturally radiant intrinsic awareness.

If this introduction is not received, even good persons may turn away at this point and continue to roam within cyclic existence. [As this occurs] then, the female wrathful deities, the eight Gaurī, and the eight Piśācī, [the latter] having diverse [animal] heads, will emerge from within the brain [of the deceased], and appear before him or her. Again, calling the deceased by name, the introduction should be given in the following words:

O, Child of Buddha Nature, listen without distraction! The eight Gaurī will now be emerging from within your own brain and appearing before you. Do not be afraid! From the eastern direction of your brain the white Gaurī, holding a human corpse as a cudgel in her right hand and a blood-filled skull in her left hand, will arise before you. Do not be afraid! From the southern direction, the yellow Caurī, shooting an arrow from a bow; from the west, the red Pramohā, holding a crocodile victory-banner; and from the north, the black Vetālī, holding a vajra and a blood-filled skull, [will arise]. From the south-east, the red-yellow Pukkasī, holding entrails in her right [hand] and eating them with her left; from the south-west, the green-black Ghasmarī, holding a blood-filled skull in her left [hand], stirring this with a vajra in her right hand and drinking awesomely; from the north-west, the white-yellow Caṇḍālī, tearing apart the head and body [of a bloated corpse], holding the heart in her right hand and eating the body with her left; and from the north-east, the blue-black Śmaśānī, tearing a head and body apart and eating them, [will arise]. These eight Gaurī, who are indicative of the [eight] classes [of consciousness], will emerge from within your own brain, and surround the five blood-drinking deities and their consorts. Do not be afraid!

O, Child of Buddha Nature, listen without distraction! The eight Piśācī, who are indicative of the sense objects, will emerge, and appear before you, encircling this array. From the east, the dark brown Siṃhamukhī, lion-headed, her two arms crossed on her breast, carrying a corpse in her mouth and shaking her mane; from the south, tiger-headed, the red Vyāghrīmukhī, her two arms crossed, snarling and staring with bulging eyes; from the west, fox-headed, the black Śṛgālamukhī, holding a razor in her right hand, and entrails in her left, eating the entrails and licking the blood; from the north, wolf-headed, the black-blue Śvānamukhī, tearing apart a corpse with her two arms and staring with bulging eyes; from the south-east, vulture-headed, the white-yellow Gṛdhramukhī, carrying a large human corpse over her shoulder and holding a skeleton in [both] hands; from the south-west, kite-headed, the black-red Kaṅkamukhī, carrying a large corpse over her shoulders; from the north-west, crow-headed, the black Kākamukhī, holding a skull in her left [hand], a sword in her right, and eating a [human] heart and lungs; and from the north-east, owl-headed, the blue-black Ulūkamukhī, holding a vajra in her right [hand], wielding a sword in her left and eating flesh. These, the eight Piśācī, indicative of the sense objects, will emerge from within your brain and arise before you, encircling the five blood-

drinking deities and their consorts. Do not be afraid! Recognise all that arises as the natural expressive power of awareness, manifesting naturally.

O, Child of Buddha Nature, the four Female Gatekeepers will also emerge from within your brain and appear before you. Recognise them! From the eastern direction of your brain the white horse-headed Aṅkuśā, a blood-filled skull in her left hand; from the south, the yellow sow-headed Pāśā, holding a noose; from the west, the red lion-headed Sphoṭā, holding an iron chain; and from the north, the green snake-headed Ghaṇṭā, holding a bell, will instantaneously arise.[6] *These, the four Female Gatekeepers, will indeed emerge from within your brain and appear before you. Recognise them, as they are your own meditational deities!*

O, Child of Buddha Nature, on the periphery of these thirty deities, who are the wrathful Herukas [and their retinues], the twenty-eight Īśvarī will emerge from within your brain and appear before you. They will have diverse [animal] heads and bear diverse weapons. But, do not be afraid! Recognise all that arises as the natural expressive power of awareness, manifesting naturally. Now, at this most critical point, remember your spiritual teacher's oral instructions.

O, Child of Buddha Nature, from the east, the six yoginī of the east will emerge from within your brain and appear before you: the brownish white yak-headed Manurākṣasī, holding [a vajra and] a skull; the yellowish white snake-headed Brahmāṇī, holding a lotus; the greenish white leopard-headed Raudrī, holding a trident; the bluish white weasel-headed Vaiṣṇāvī, holding a wheel; the reddish white brown-bear-headed Kaumārī, holding a pike; and the white black-bear-headed Indrāṇī, holding a noose of entrails in her hand.[7] *Do not be afraid!*

O, Child of Buddha Nature, from the south, the six yoginī of the south will emerge from within your brain and appear before you: the yellow bat-headed[8] *Piṅgalā, holding a razor; the reddish yellow crocodile-headed Śāntī, holding a vase; the reddish yellow scorpion-headed Amṛtā, holding a lotus; the whitish yellow hawk-headed Saumī, holding a vajra; the greenish yellow fox-headed Daṇḍī, holding a cudgel, and the blackish yellow tiger-headed Rākṣasī holding a blood-filled skull in her hand.*[9] *Do not be afraid!*

O, Child of Buddha Nature, from the west, the six yoginī of the west will emerge from within your brain and appear before you:

the greenish red vulture-headed Bhakṣasī, holding a club; the red horse-headed Ratī, holding a large torso; the pale red garuḍa-headed mighty one [Rudhiramadī, consort of Mahābala], holding a cudgel; the red dog-headed [Ekacāriṇī] Rākṣasī, wielding a vajra-razor in her hand; the red hoopoe-headed Manohārikā, firing an arrow from a bow; and the greenish red deer-headed protectress of wealth, [Siddhikarī, consort of Vasurakṣita], holding a vase in her hand.[10] *Do not be afraid!*

O, Child of Buddha Nature, from the north, the six yoginī of the north will emerge from within your brain and appear before you: the bluish green snake-headed Vāyudevī, brandishing an ensign; the reddish green ibex-headed Agnāyī, holding a glowing fire-brand; the blackish green sow-headed Varāhī, holding a noose of fangs; the reddish green crow-headed Vajrā [Cāmuṇḍī], holding an infant human corpse; the blackish green elephant-headed Bhujanā, holding a club and drinking blood [from a skull]; and the bluish green snake-headed Varuṇānī, holding a noose of snakes in her hand.[11] *Do not be afraid!*

O, Child of Buddha Nature, the four yoginī who are the [four] female gatekeepers will emerge from within your brain and appear before you: from the east, the white cuckoo-headed Vajrā [Mahākālī], holding an iron hook; from the south, the yellow goat-headed Vajrā [Mahāchāgalā], holding a noose; from the west, the red lion-headed Vajrā [Mahākumbhakarṇī], holding an iron chain; and from the north, the black-green snake-headed Vajrā [Lambodarā], holding a bell in her hand. These four yoginī, the female gatekeepers, will indeed emerge from within your brain and appear before you. Do not be afraid!

Since these twenty-eight Īśvarī emanate naturally from the expressive power of the naturally arising deities, which are the wrathful Herukas – recognise them now!

O, Child of Buddha Nature, through the expressive power of emptiness, the Buddha-body of Reality has arisen as the peaceful deities, recognise this! Through the expressive power of radiance, the Buddha-body of Perfect Resource has arisen as the wrathful deities.[12] *Recognise this!*

At this time, when the assembly of the fifty-eight blood-drinking deities manifests from within your brain, you should recognise all that arises as the naturally arising luminosity of your own aware-

ness. Then, [if recognition occurs], you will immediately attain buddhahood, inseparable from the blood-drinking deities.

O, Child of Buddha Nature, if even now you do not recognise this [reality], and become afraid and turn away from the [visionary appearances], you will go on to experience yet further suffering. If recognition does not occur, all the blood-drinking deities will be perceived as Yama. You will be overwhelmed by fear, by awe and by terror at [the sight of] all the blood-drinking deities; and you will faint. Those [visionary appearances], which are natural manifestations [of actual reality], will [seem to] have become demons, and you will continue to roam in cyclic existence. But [even now], if you are not awed and not terrified, you will avoid the continued wandering within cyclic existence.

O, Child of Buddha Nature, the largest of the buddha-bodies of the Peaceful and Wrathful Deities will be as vast as the sky; the medium ones will be the size of Mount Sumeru; and even the smallest will be the size of eighteen of our bodies, standing one above the other.[13] *Do not be afraid! All phenomenal existence is now arising as luminosities and buddha-bodies. By recognising all the present visionary appearances to be the natural luminosity of your own intrinsic awareness, manifesting as lights and buddha-bodies, you will dissolve inseparably within the lights and buddha-bodies, and buddhahood will be attained. O Child of Buddha Nature, whatever fearsome and terrifying apparitions appear to you now, recognise them to be natural manifestations [of actual reality]. Do not be afraid! Recognise these [appearances] as inner radiance, your own natural luminosity. Upon recognition, you will undoubtedly attain buddhahood, right now. That which is called 'instantaneous perfect buddhahood' will occur at this very moment. Remember this, and hold it in your mind!*

Child of Buddha Nature, if you do not recognise [the visionary appearances] now, and continue to be afraid, then all the buddha-bodies of the peaceful deities will arise in the form of Mahākāla; all the buddha-bodies of the wrathful deities will arise in the form of Yama Dharmarāja; and then all of your perceptions will turn into malevolent forces. In this way, you will continue to wander in cyclic existence.

O, Child of Buddha Nature, if you do not recognise the present appearances as natural manifestations [of actual reality], even though you may have been learned in all the sūtras and tantras, which form the [Buddha's] transmitted precepts, and even though you may have practised these doctrines for an aeon, buddhahood will not be attained. Yet, if you recognise now the visionary appearances that are manifesting naturally, then, through [the understanding of] a single essential point, and through [the understanding of] a single word, you will attain buddhahood.

If, immediately after death, you do not recognise the appearances which manifest naturally, these appearances will [eventually] arise during the intermediate state of reality, in the forms of Yama Dharmarāja. The largest form assumed by Yama Dharmarāja is as vast as space; the medium form, the size of Mount Sumeru, filling this world-system. [Thus, Yama Dharmarāja will appear], his upper teeth biting into his lower lip, his eyes glassy, his hair tied up on the crown of his head, his belly bulging and his neck thin, brandishing in his hand the wooden slate [documenting] past actions – his mouth echoing with the cries of 'strike!', and 'kill!' – he is drinking brains, severing heads and ripping out internal organs. In this way, [it will appear as if his form] fills the entire world.

O, Child of Buddha Nature, when such visions arise, do not be afraid or terrified. Your body is a mental body, formed of habitual tendencies. Therefore, even if you are slain and cut into pieces, you will not die. You are, [in reality], a natural form of emptiness, so there is no need to be afraid. The forms of Yama Dharmarāja arise, too, from the natural luminosity of your own intrinsic awareness. They have no material substance. Emptiness cannot be harmed by emptiness. [Clearly] determine now that, other than arising from the natural expressive power of your own awareness, [whatever seems to appear to you] externally – the Peaceful and Wrathful Deities, the blood-drinking [Herukas], the diverse animal-headed deities, the rainbow lights, the frightening forms of Yama, etc. – these are all without substantial existence. If this is successfully determined, all fear and terror will be liberated [naturally], just where it is. You will dissolve inseparably [with the visionary appearances] and buddhahood will be attained.

Upon recognising [the visionary appearances] in this way, be fervently devoted, and think: 'These are my meditational deities. They have come to escort me on the dangerous pathway of the intermediate state. I take refuge in them.' Remember the Three

Precious Jewels! Remember your meditational deity, whichever it may be! Call to your meditational deity by name and pray with the following words: 'I am roaming in the intermediate state – come quickly to rescue me! Hold me in your compassion, O precious meditational deity!' Call to your spiritual teacher, by name, and pray with the following words: 'I am roaming in the intermediate state. Rescue me! Do not let your compassion forsake me!' Pray devotedly, yet again, to the assembled blood-drinking deities and recite this aspirational prayer:

O, as I roam in cyclic existence, [driven] by deep-seated habitual tendencies,
May the assembly of [male] Peaceful and Wrathful Deities, transcendent lords, draw me forward,
Leading me on the path of [radiant] light,
Through which [all] awesome and terrifying perceptions are left behind.
May the assembly of the wrathful female deities, Dhātvīśvarī [and so forth], support me from behind,
And, thus [encircled], may I be rescued
From the fearsome passageway of the intermediate state,
And be escorted to the level of an utterly perfect buddha.

Now, when I roam alone, separated from my loved ones,
And [myriad] images of emptiness arise, naturally manifesting,
May the buddhas [quickly] release the power of their compassion,
And may the fear of the awesome and terrifying intermediate state be annulled.

When the five radiant lights of pristine cognition dawn,
May I recognise them as my own [nature], without awe and without terror,
And as the [manifold] forms of the Peaceful and Wrathful Deities arise,
May I be fearlessly confident and recognise [the characteristics of] the intermediate state.

When I experience suffering as the result of negative past actions,
May the meditational deities dispel all such misery,

And as the natural sound of reality reverberates like a thousand peals of thunder,
May all [sounds] be heard as the resonance of the Six Syllables.

When I am driven on by past actions, unable to find a refuge,
May the Great Compassionate One, Mahākāruṇika, protect me.
And as I experience the suffering of habitual tendencies and past actions,
May the meditative stabilities of inner radiance and bliss [naturally] arise.

May the fields of the five elements not rise up as a hostile force,
And may I see [them as] the fields of the five enlightened families!

Recite this aspirational prayer with deep devotion. It is very important. As all fear and terror dissolve, you will assuredly attain buddhahood in the Buddha-body of Perfect Resource – so do not be distracted!

The above introduction should be given three or up to seven times. Even if the negativity of the deceased is very great and even if the inheritance of past actions is very bad, it is impossible for liberation not to occur – [if there is recognition]. Yet, regardless of how often these teachings are given, if recognition does not occur, [the deceased] will necessarily roam into the intermediate state of rebirth. The introduction to that [state] is presented below, in detail.

CONCLUSION OF THE INTRODUCTION TO THE INTERMEDIATE STATE OF THE TIME OF DEATH AND THE INTERMEDIATE STATE OF REALITY

Since it is generally the case that one will experience bewilderment at the time of death, this *Liberation by Hearing* is indispensable, whatever one's degree of familiarity with [meditative] practices. In the case of those who have considerable familiarity with [meditative] experience the recognition of the nature of reality can arise instantly, as soon as awareness separates from the material body. Therefore, it is essential to cultivate this experience [of reality] during one's lifetime. Those who have been introduced to [the nature of] awareness, directly, and who have cultivated [this aspect of meditative experience] during their lifetime, will have the greatest ability during the intermediate state of the time of death when the inner radiance arises. Additionally, those who during their lifetime emphasised meditation on the deity, according to the generation and perfection stages of the way of secret mantra, will have the greatest ability during the intermediate state of reality, when the visions of the Peaceful and Wrathful Deities arise.

Given the above, it is extremely important to train the mind particularly in this *Liberation by Hearing*, while one is alive. It should be embraced. It should be read aloud. It should be thoroughly comprehended. It should be taken to heart perfectly. It should be read aloud three times [a day], without fail. Its words and meaning should be so clearly impressed on the mind that, even were one to be pursued by a hundred assassins, its text and meaning would not be forgotten.

This being called the *Great Liberation by Hearing*, even those who have committed the five inexpiable crimes will attain liberation upon hearing [a recitation of its words]. Therefore, it should be read aloud in public places. It should be propagated. Since the awareness becomes many times clearer during the intermediate state, even if this teaching is sensed, as now, only once, and even if its meaning is not understood, it will be remembered at the time [of death], without a single word being forgotten. Therefore it should be read aloud to the ears of all during their lifetime. It should be read aloud across the pillows of all who are sick. It should be read aloud in the presence of all the bodies of the dead. It should be propagated, far and wide.

To meet with this [teaching] is a great good fortune. Except for those who have gathered the accumulations [of merit and pristine cognition], and purified their obscurations, it is difficult to encounter. Yet, once it is heard, liberation can be achieved just by avoiding a mistaken view.[14] Therefore it should be greatly cherished. It is the essence of all teachings.

This completes the introduction to the intermediate state of reality, which forms part of the *Great Liberation by Hearing in the Intermediate States*, the teaching on the intermediate states which liberates just by being heard, or just by being seen.

COLOPHON

This teaching was brought forth in secret by the accomplished master Karma Lingpa, the eldest son of the accomplished master Nyinda Sangye, from the sacred place of Mount Gampodar, which resembles a dancing god, and is located on the banks of the river Serden. The master Karma Lingpa entrusted its transmitted precepts and authorisation to his son, Choje Lingpa. The succession fell in turn to his [son] Guru Suryacandra [i.e. Lama Nyinda] and, in his presence, I Gaganadharmasamudra [i.e. Namka Chokyi Gyatso] received it with devotion.

PART THREE

An Elucidation of the Intermediate State of Rebirth

Herein is contained the *Great Liberation by Hearing*, an introduction to and elucidation of the intermediate state of rebirth, [which is an extract from] the *Peaceful and Wrathful Deities: A Profound Sacred Teaching, [entitled] Natural Liberation through [Recognition of] Enlightened Intention.*[1]

I bow with respect to the spiritual teachers, and assembled meditational deities.
May they effect liberation in the intermediate state!

From within the *Great Liberation by Hearing*, the intermediate state of reality has already been presented. Here then follows that which is known as the elucidation of the intermediate state of rebirth.

[INTRODUCTION TO THE MENTAL BODY]

Although the elucidation of the intermediate state of reality has already been given many times, with the exception of those who are greatly experienced in the meditations of the [sacred] teachings and those who have an excellent inheritance of past actions, it is difficult for those lacking familiarity with meditative experience and those with a negative disposition to attain recognition, on account of the fear and terror [induced by] negative past actions. Therefore, from the tenth day onwards, these individuals should once again be reminded [of the nature of this intermediate state], through the following words. As before, offerings should be made to the Three Precious Jewels, and the *Aspirational Prayer [Calling] to the Buddhas and Bodhisattvas for Assistance* should be repeated.[2] Then, one should read aloud the following, three or up to seven times, calling to the deceased by name:

O, Child of Buddha Nature, listen carefully and understand! Hell-beings, gods and those with the body of the intermediate state are born in a supernormal manner. Formerly, when the visions of the Peaceful and Wrathful Deities arose before you during the intermediate state of reality – you did not recognise them. Then, overwhelmed by terror, you would have fainted. Four and a half days later, upon awakening from this faint, your consciousness has again become clear and a body, resembling your former one, has arisen. This ['body'] is described in the tantras:[3]

> *Having the bodily form of one's past and emergent existences,*
> *Complete with all sense-faculties, and the power of unobstructed movement.*
> *Endowed with miraculous abilities derived from past actions,*
> *Visible to those similar in kind and through pure clairvoyance.*

Here, 'past and emergent'[4] *means that your [present] body [which is a product of] your past habitual tendencies will resemble a body of flesh and blood, but, like a body of the Auspicious Aeon (bhadrakalpa) it will also be radiant and possess certain of the major and minor marks. Since this [state] is an apparitional experience of the mental body, it is called 'the mental body of apparitional experience in the intermediate state'.*[5] *At this time, if you are to be born as a god, you will come to experience the apparitional field of the realm of the gods. Depending on whichever of the realms you are to take birth in, whether that of the antigods, humans, animals, anguished spirits or hell-beings, you will come to experience its particular apparitional field. Therefore, 'past' means that for three and a half days you will possess the bodily form [which is a product] of your past habitual tendencies and existences. And 'emergent' means that, after [three and a half days], the apparitional field of the next realm into which you are to be born, will 'emerge'. Hence, the expression 'past and emergent' [existences].*

Whatever apparitional fields emerge at this time, do not be drawn by them! Do not become attached to them! Do not cling to them! If you cling to them and become attached, you will continue to roam amongst the six classes [of beings] and be turning towards suffering. Although, until yesterday, the intermediate state of reality arose [within you], you did not recognise it. As a result you have been compelled to wander here. Now, just as was [formerly] introduced by your spiritual teacher, if you are able to cultivate, undistractedly, [a recognition of] the essential nature [of reality], if you can rest and abide without grasping and without activity, directly, in the unwavering, naked awareness, which is radiance and emptiness conjoined, you can attain liberation and avoid wandering, yet further, towards the womb entrances. If you are not able to achieve this recognition, then visualise your meditational deity, whichever it may be, or your spiritual teacher, as being [seated] on the crown of your head and be intensely and fervently devoted. This is most important. Again and again, do not be distracted.

If [the deceased] does indeed recognise this essential nature [of reality], he or she will attain liberation and avoid roaming further amongst the six classes [of beings]. But, on account of negative past actions, recognition is not easy to achieve, and therefore, one should reiterate [the introduction], in the following words:

O, Child of Buddha Nature, listen [carefully] yet again! The phrase, 'Complete with all sense-faculties, and the power of unobstructed movement'[6] *means that, even though you may have been blind, deaf or lame while you were alive, now, in the intermediate state, your eyes see forms, your ears hear sounds and all your sense-faculties are faultless, clear and complete. Hence [the tantra] says 'complete with all sense faculties'. Recognise this [sensory clarity], for it is a sign that you have died and are wandering in the intermediate state. Remember this oral instruction! O, Child of Buddha Nature, 'unobstructed' means that the body which you now have is a mental body. Your awareness is now separated from its physical support. Therefore, this is not a body of solid form. Accordingly, you now have the ability to move unobstructedly; penetrating to the core of all forms, you can pass through Mount Sumeru, and through dwellings, the earth, stones, boulders and mountains. Indeed, other than your mother's womb and the 'Indestructible Seat',*[7] *you can pass back and forth even through Mount Sumeru itself. Remember the advice of your spiritual teacher – for this [ability] is a sign that you are wandering in the intermediate state of rebirth. [Recognise this] and pray to the meditational deity Mahākāruṇika.*

O, Child of Buddha Nature, the phrase 'endowed with miraculous abilities derived from past actions'[8] *does not mean that you necessarily possess any enlightened attributes, or any miraculous ability in meditative stability, but that you have a miraculous ability which results from your past actions and accords with your past actions.*[9] *[Consequently], you will have the ability to circumambulate Mount Sumeru and the four continents, in an instant. Merely in the time it takes to withdraw or hold out an arm, you can travel instantly anywhere you wish, just by thinking of your desired destination. Do not be fascinated by these diverse and haphazard miraculous abilities. Do not indulge in them. Of all the things which you have the ability to recall, there is not one which you cannot make manifest. You have the ability now, to manifest [any aspect of your past], unimpededly. Therefore recognise this and pray to your spiritual teacher.*

O, Child of Buddha Nature, as for the phrase 'visible to those similar in kind and through pure clairvoyance',[10] *the words 'similar in kind' mean that in the intermediate state, those of a similar kind of birth will come to perceive one another. Thus, in the case of those 'similar in kind' who are to be born as gods, the gods [to be] perceive one another. Similarly, those that are 'similar in kind' to any of the six classes [of beings], will come to perceive one another. Do not become attached [at the sight of these beings]! Meditate on [the meditational deity] Mahākāruṇika. The words 'visible through pure clairvoyance' do not refer to the [clairvoyance] which results from the meritorious qualities of the gods and so forth, but they do refer to the pure clairvoyance with which those of genuine meditative concentration perceive.*[11] *However, this is not [a clairvoyance] that can perceive [the beings of the intermediate state] at all times. If you are intent on seeing [beings of like nature in this intermediate state] then they will be perceived. If you are not so intent, they will not be perceived. This [clairvoyance] will dissolve, as soon as your concentration is distracted.*

O, Child of Buddha Nature, with a body having qualities such as these just described, you will [once again] see your homeland and your relatives, as if in a dream. Yet, even though you call out to your relatives, they will not reply. You will see your family and relatives crying and realise: 'I am dead. What should I do now?' Thinking this, you will be overwhelmed by intense suffering – you will feel like a fish [expelled from the water], writhing on hot sand. Although you will suffer [on realising that you are dead], this is not helpful [to you now]. If you have a spiritual teacher, pray to your spiritual teacher! Pray to the meditational deity, Mahākāruṇika! Although you will feel attached to your relatives, this is not helpful [to you now]. Do not be attached! Pray to Mahākāruṇika, and be free of suffering, awe and fear.

O, Child of Buddha Nature, your [present] awareness, freed from its [physical] support, [is being blown] by the coursing vital energy of past actions. Choicelessly, riding the horse of breath, it drifts directionless, like a feather on the wind. To all those who are crying, you will call out: 'I am here! Do not cry!' But they will not hear you. Yet again, you will realise 'I am dead' and experience a very profound despair. Do not be absorbed by this suffering!

Continuously, there will be greyness, like autumn twilight, with neither day nor night. The intermediate states [between death and birth] will last for one week, or two, or three, or four, or five, or six or seven weeks – up to forty-nine days in all. It is said that suffering in the intermediate state of rebirth will last, generally speaking, for twenty-one days. However, since the duration [of this state] is based on past actions, a specific number of days is not certain.

O, Child of Buddha Nature, at this time the fierce, turbulent, utterly unbearable hurricane of past actions will be [swirling] behind you, driving you on. Do not be afraid! This is your own bewildered perception. Before you, there will be a terrifying, dense and unfathomable darkness, echoing with cries of 'Strike!' and 'Kill!' Do not be afraid! Moreover, in the case of very negative beings, a swarm of carnivorous ogres will arise, executors of the unfailing law of cause and effect,[12] *brandishing an array of weapons, and screaming out aggressively: 'Strike!' and 'Kill!' You will imagine that you are being pursued by terrifying wild animals. You will imagine that you are being pursued by hordes of people, and [that you are struggling] through snow, through rain, through blizzards and through darkness. There will be the sound of mountains crumbling, of lakes flooding, of fire spreading and the roar of fierce winds springing up. Terrified, you will try to flee wherever you can, but your path ahead will [suddenly] be cut off by three precipices: one white, one red and one black, all three awesomely frightening; you will feel as if on the verge of falling.*

O, Child of Buddha Nature, these are not truly precipices. They are aversion, attachment and delusion, respectively.[13] *Know now that this is the intermediate state of rebirth, and call to [the meditational deity] Mahākāruṇika, by name, and pray: 'O, lord Mahākāruṇika, Spiritual Teacher and Precious Jewel, save me* (say your name) *from falling into lower existences' [Pray with deep commitment in this way]; do not forget!*

At this stage, in the case of those individuals who have gathered the accumulations [of merit and pristine cognition] and have sincerely practised the teachings, one will be welcomed by [visions of] abundant riches and one will experience manifold blissful and happy states. [In the case of those individuals who are indifferent or deluded, who have been neither virtuous nor negative, one will experience neither pleasure nor pain, but only an apathetic delusion.][14] *Whichever of these happens, O, Child of Buddha Nature, whatever objects of desire or blissful or happy states appear before you, do not be attached to them. Do not cling to them! Be free from attachment and clinging and mentally offer these [experiences] to your spiritual teacher and to the [Three] Precious Jewels. Particularly, if these visions are of indifference, devoid of happiness or pain, abide in the experience of the Great Seal, where awareness is [naturally present], without meditation and without distraction. This is very important.*

O, Child of Buddha Nature, at this time, you will try to find shelter [from the hurricane of past actions] below bridges, in mansions, in temples or grass-huts or beside stūpas and so forth, but this [shelter] will be momentary, it will not last. Your awareness, now separated from your body, will not rest and you will feel reckless, angry and afraid. Your consciousness will be faltering, superficial, and nebulous. Again you will realise: 'Alas! I am dead, what should I do now?' Reflecting on this, your consciousness will grow sad, your heart will be chilled and you will feel intense and boundless misery. Your mind is being compelled to move on, without settling in one place. Do not indulge in all kinds of memories! Let your awareness rest in an undistracted state!

[The time will come when you will realise that] you have no food, except that which has been dedicated to you. As for companionship, [here], similarly, there will be no certainty. These

are both indications that the mental body is wandering in the intermediate state of rebirth. Your present feelings of happiness and sorrow are [now] driven by your past actions.

[Once again], seeing your homeland, circle of friends, relatives and even your own corpse, you will realise: 'I am dead! What should I do now?' You will feel deeply saddened [by your existence] in a mental body, and wish, 'O that I might obtain a physical body!' Consequently, you will experience roaming here and there in search of a body. You might even attempt, many times, to re-enter your own body, but a long time has already elapsed in the [previous] intermediate state of reality. In winter your body will have frozen, in summer it will have decayed. Alternatively, your relatives will have cremated it, buried it in a grave, or offered it to the birds and wild animals. Not finding a way back, you will feel utterly distressed, and you will certainly feel yourself [trying to] squeeze [into the crevices] between stones and rocks. Torments such as these will enfold you. This being the intermediate state of rebirth, so long as you search for a body, you will experience nothing but suffering. Therefore give up your clinging to a body and rest in a state of non-activity, [undistractedly].

Liberation can be obtained in the intermediate state, as a result of the above introduction. However, even though this introduction is given, due to negative past actions, recognition may not occur. So again, you should call to the deceased by name and say the following words:

O, Child of Buddha Nature, (call to the deceased by name), *listen [to me]. It is due to your own past actions that you are now suffering in this way. No one else is responsible – this is solely the result of your own past actions. Pray ardently now to the Three Precious Jewels. They will protect you. If you do not pray intensely now, especially if you do not know how to meditate on the Great Seal, or if you cannot meditate on a meditational deity, the 'innate good conscience' within you*[15] *will now gather together all your virtuous actions, counting them out with white pebbles, and the 'innate bad conscience' within you will gather together all your non-virtuous actions, counting them out with black pebbles. At this moment you will tremble with extreme fear, awe and terror. You will tell lies, saying, 'I have not committed non-virtuous actions!' But at this, Yama will say: 'I shall consult the mirror of past actions.'*[16] *In the mirror of past actions, [all your virtues and non-virtues] will be reflected vividly and precisely. Your attempts at deceit will be of no use. Tying a rope around your neck, Yama will drag you forward. He will sever [your head] at the neck, extract your heart, pull out your entrails, lick your brains, drink your blood, eat your flesh and suck your bones. Despite this, you will not die. Even as your body is [repeatedly] cut into pieces, it will be continuously revived. Experiencing being cut into pieces in this way, time after time, will cause enormous suffering. From the moment the counting of the pebbles begins, do not be afraid! Do not be terrified! Do not lie, and do not be afraid of Yama. The body which you now have is a mental body; therefore, even though you experience being slain and cut into pieces, you cannot die. [Recognise now, that] in reality, you need have no fear, because, [in truth], your [body] is a natural form of emptiness. The acolytes of Yama are also, [in reality], natural forms of emptiness – these are your own bewildered perceptions. Your body, formed of mental propensities, is [a natural form of] emptiness. Emptiness cannot harm emptiness. Signlessness cannot harm signlessness. Outside, and distinct from your own bewildering perceptions, Yama, gods, malevolent forces, the bull-headed Rakṣa and so on, do not substantially exist.*[17] *Recognise this! Recognise, now, that this is the intermediate state! Place your mind in the meditative stability of the Great Seal! If you do not know how to meditate, directly examine the essence of that which is producing your fear and terror. This [essence] is a stark emptiness, completely without inherent existence in any respect whatsoever! This [stark emptiness] is the Buddha-body of Reality. Yet, this emptiness is not a vacuous or nihilistic emptiness. The essential nature of this emptiness is an awesome, direct and radiant awareness, which is the enlightened intention of [the Buddha-body of] Perfect Resource. Indeed, emptiness and radiance are not separate: the essential nature of emptiness is radiance and the essential nature of radiance is emptiness. This indivisible, naked, unclouded and exposed awareness, present as it is right now in a natural uncontrived state, is the Buddha-body of Essentiality.*[18] *Furthermore, the natural expressive power [of this Buddha-body of Essentiality] is the compassionate Buddha-body of Emanation, which arises everywhere without obstruction.*

O, Child of Buddha Nature, listen [to me] now, and do not be distracted. By merely recognising [the essential nature of your experience] in the above way, you will attain perfect buddhahood, endowed with these four buddha-bodies. Do not be distracted! The division between buddhas and sentient beings is determined by this [recognition]. If you are distracted at this critical moment, the opportunity to escape from the swamp of suffering will be lost. It is said of this very moment:

> *In an instant, penetrating analysis is made.*
> *In an instant, perfect buddhahood is attained.*

Until yesterday, because you were distracted, even though so many aspects of the intermediate states have arisen, you did not attain recognition. [Up to this time], you have experienced so much fear and terror. Now, if you continue to be distracted, the lifeline of compassion, suspended to you, will be cut off and you will move on to a place where there is no [immediate] prospect of liberation. So be careful.

Through this introduction, even though [the deceased] may have failed to attain recognition previously, he or she will be able to do so at this stage and consequently attain liberation.

If, however, [the deceased] is a lay person, who does not know how to meditate, you should say the following words:

O, Child of Buddha Nature, if you do know how to meditate you should call to mind the Buddha, the [sacred] teachings, the [sublime] assembly of monks and nuns, and [the meditational deity] Mahākāruṇika and pray to them. Meditate on all the fearful and terrifying appearances as being [forms] of Mahākāruṇika, or your meditational deity. Remember your spiritual teacher and remember the name which you received during empowerment ceremonies in the human world.[19] *[Say this name to] Yama Dharmarāja and do not be afraid of him. [Know now, that] even if you were to plunge down over the precipices, you would not be harmed. So, abandon your fear and your terror.*

Even though liberation may not have been achieved previously, if the above introduction is accepted, [the deceased] will attain liberation at this juncture.

Yet, since there is the possibility that [the deceased] will not achieve recognition, even though the introduction has been given, it is very important to persevere. Therefore, once again, one should call to the deceased by name and say the following words:

O, Child of Buddha Nature, your present perceptions can, like a catapult, in a instant, cast you into the most awesome states; either blissful or full of suffering. Therefore, now, [it is critical that] your perceptions are not coloured by either attachment or aversion.

It may be that you are about to take birth in the higher realms, yet at the time when the perceptions of the higher realms occur, your living relatives, now left behind, are sacrificing and offering many animals on your behalf, dedicating [this activity] to you, the deceased. Corrupted perceptions will thus arise and consequently an intense aversion may well up [within you], and this will form a connecting link to a birth in the hell realms. Therefore, whatever activities occur in the place that you have left behind, meditate on loving kindness, and ensure that aversion does not arise!

Alternatively, your mind may grow attached to your wealth and possessions, now left behind, or else, knowing that your wealth and possessions are being enjoyed and owned by others, you may become both attached to those worldly goods and also hateful towards those left behind [who are using your possessions]. As a result of this, a connecting link will certainly be formed to a birth amongst the hell beings or amongst the anguished spirits, even though you may have been at the point of attaining birth in [one of] the higher realms. However attached you may be to the wealth now left behind, you do not have the ability to enjoy it. Since it is absolutely of no use to you, abandon your attachment and yearning for the wealth that you have left behind. Let it go! Be decisive! Regardless of who is enjoying your wealth, do not be possessive! Let it go! Cultivate devotion, and imagine that you are offering these [worldly possessions] to your spiritual teacher and to the [Three] Precious Jewels. Rest in a state free from attachment and free from clinging.

Once again, even when the Kaṅkaṇīdhāraṇī *incantation for the dead is being recited for you and the* Purification of the Lower Realms (Sarvadurgatipariśodhanatantra) *is being recited on your behalf, you may perceive, with your present subtle cognitive ability, that these [rites] are being performed impurely and distractedly, and that those [who are performing these rituals] are impure in both their commitments and vows and are careless in their conduct. As a result, you may have no confidence in them, you may form a bad opinion of them, and you may become fearfully and horribly aware of their negative past actions, etc., as well as of their impure practice of the [sacred] teachings and the rituals. Feeling this, you will experience the utmost sadness, and think: 'Alas, they have betrayed me! They have truly betrayed me!' As a consequence of your profound disenchantment, instead of maintaining purity of perception and [feelings of] respect, negative opinions and loss of confidence will arise within you. Thus, [these perceptions and feelings] will form a connecting link that will certainly propel you into the lower existences, and, in this way, [your subtle cognitive ability and the rituals recited on your behalf] will not have been of benefit, but rather of great harm.*

However impure may be the practice of the [sacred] teachings by your friends now left behind, you must maintain respect and purity of perception from the depths of your heart. Think to yourself: 'My own perception is so polluted! How could the speech of the buddhas be impure! These [impure perspectives] have arisen as a consequence of my own impure perception, and [will appear to me] just as the flaws on my face will be reflected in a mirror. As for these [individuals performing the rituals, in reality] their bodies are the [sublime] community of monks and nuns, their speech is the genuine [sacred] teaching, and their minds are the essence of the buddhas. Therefore, I take refuge in them.' Thinking thus, whatever activities occur in the place that you have left behind, they will certainly be beneficial to you. It is extremely important to maintain this purity of perception. Do not forget this!

Even if you are about to be born into the lower existences, [yet you do maintain purity of perception], and you perceive the relatives that you have left behind practising the virtuous teachings, unstained by negativity, and you see your spiritual teachers and masters purely practising the rituals with virtuous body, speech and mind, you will feel great joy. Simply through this [experience of great joy], even though you were about to fall into lower existences, this [joy] will form a connecting link, which will certainly turn you back towards the higher realms. Since there is such manifold benefit, do not now lapse into impure perception. It is extremely important to maintain purity of perception and to be unbiasedly devoted. So, be careful!

O, Child of Buddha Nature, in short, since your awareness during this intermediate state lacks any [material] support, it is light and volatile, and therefore, whatever virtuous or non-virtuous perceptions arise, these are very powerful. Do not be absorbed by non-virtuous thoughts! Call to mind the virtuous practices of your past! Even if you did not engage in virtuous practices [during your life], maintain purity of perception and deep devotion! Pray to your meditational deity or to Mahākaruṇika, and with a powerful longing repeat the following aspirational prayer:[20]

Now when I roam alone, separated from loved ones,
And [myriad] images of emptiness arise, naturally manifesting,
May the buddhas [quickly] release the power of their compassion,
And may the fear of the awesome and terrifying intermediate state be annulled.

When I experience suffering, as the result of negative past actions,
May the meditational deity [Mahākāruṇika] dispel all such misery,
And as the natural sound of reality reverberates like a thousand peals of thunder,
May all sounds be transformed into the resonance of the Six Syllables.

When I am driven on by past actions, unable to find a refuge,
May the Great Compassionate One, Mahākāruṇika, protect me,
And as I experience the suffering of habitual tendencies and past actions,
May the meditative stabilities of inner radiance and bliss [naturally] arise.

Say this aspirational prayer with ardent longing; it will certainly lead you on to the path. Be absolutely certain that this [aspirational prayer] will not deceive you. This is most important!

Through these words, [the deceased] will regain his or her focus, and recognition will occur. Then, liberation will be attained.

[OBSTRUCTION OF THE WOMB ENTRANCES]

Even though this introduction may have been given many times, due to the potency of strong negative past actions, recognition may be difficult. It is very beneficial, therefore, to repeat [the introduction] now, many times. Again, therefore, calling to the deceased by name, you should say the following words [at least] three times:

O, Child of Buddha Nature, if you have not taken to heart [the introduction] which has gone before, from now on, the body of your past life will grow more faint and the body of your next life will grow more vivid. At this, you will be dismayed, and you will think: 'I am experiencing such misery! Now I will look for whatever kind of body I can find.' Thinking in this way, you will move haphazardly and randomly towards whatever might appear and consequently the six lights indicative of the six realms of living beings will dawn; and, according to your past actions, [the light of the realm] into which you are to be born will shine the most of all. O, Child of Buddha Nature, listen! What are these six lights, you may ask? A dull white light indicative of the realm of the gods will arise. A dull red light indicative of the realm of the antigods will arise. A dull blue light indicative of the human realm will arise. A dull green light indicative of the animal realm will arise. A dull yellow light indicative of the realm of the anguished spirits will arise and a dull smoky light indicative of the realm of the hell-beings will arise. These six lights will emerge. And at this time, your [present] body will take on the colour of the light of the realm into which you are to be born. O, Child of Buddha Nature, at this juncture, the essential points of the oral instructions are extremely important.

Meditate now on the light [that dawns] as being Mahākāruṇika! Meditate on the thought that when the light dawns, it is Mahākāruṇika. This is the most profound crucial point. It is extremely important, because [this oral instruction] obstructs birth.

Alternatively, you should meditate for a long time on your meditational deity, whichever it may be. [Meditate on the deity] appearing like an illusion, completely free from inherent existence. This is called [the practice of] the 'pure illusion-like body'. Accordingly, dissolve [the form of] the meditational deity from the extremities [inwards], until it disappears completely, and abide in the [resultant] state of emptiness and radiance, where nothing at all substantially exists and where there is no subjective apprehension. Meditate yet again on the meditational deity. Meditate again on the inner radiance. Meditate alternately in this way, and after this, dissolve your awareness itself from the extremities [inwards, into emptiness and radiance]. Wherever there is space there is awareness. Wherever there is awareness there is the Buddha-body of Reality. Abide nakedly, therefore, in the state of the unimpeded Buddha-body of Reality, free from conceptual elaboration. [Abiding] in this state, birth will be obstructed and buddhahood will be attained.

Yet, those unfamiliar with meditative experience and those very weak in their practice will not be able to understand [and apply the above introductions]. Once again, overcome by confusion, they will wander towards the womb entrances. Thus, the teachings which obstruct the womb entrances become of great importance and you should, once again, call to the deceased by name and say the following words:

O, Child of Buddha Nature, if you have not attained recognition [as a result of the introductions] which have gone before, then, based on the potency of your past actions, the perception will arise that you are moving upwards, or moving horizontally or moving downwards.[21] *As this occurs, you should meditate on Mahākaruṇika. Remember this!*

Yet again, as described before, the experience will arise of being pursued by whirlwinds, blizzards, hail, or fog; and a crowd of people, and you will be trying to escape. Those who are lacking in merit will experience that they are fleeing towards a place of suffering. Those with merit will experience arriving at a place of happiness. O, Child of Buddha Nature, now, at this point, the signs of the environment into which you are to be born, on one amongst the four continents, will arise. Specifically for this moment, there are many profound essential points of oral instruction. Therefore listen, now, without distraction. Even though, previously, you have not taken to heart the essential instructions introduced to you, you can do so now, for even those whose practice is very weak can understand [and apply one of] the following essential instructions. So listen, now, without distraction.

At this stage, it is extremely important that you carefully employ the methods for obstructing the womb entrances. [Principally], there are two such methods of obstruction. These are: [first], the method which obstructs the person who is to enter the womb and, [second], the methods which obstruct the womb which is to be entered.

The oral teaching for the method which obstructs the person who is to enter the womb, is as follows:

O, Child of Buddha Nature, (call to the deceased by name) *visualise now your meditational deity, whichever it may be, with vibrancy. [Meditate on the deity] as [vividly] apparent, yet completely lacking in inherent existence, like [the reflection of] the moon in water. If you do not have a specific meditational deity, then visualise the lord Mahākāruṇika, again with great vibrancy. Then, [gradually], dissolve [the image of] the meditational deity from the extremities [inwards, until it disappears completely] and then meditate on the [resultant union] of inner radiance and emptiness, which is utterly free from any objective referent. This is the profound essential point. Meditate in this way, for it is said that by this means entry into a womb will be averted.*

Should even this [introduction] not cause obstruction and should [the deceased] continue to draw closer to the act of entering a womb, there are also the profound oral instructions which obstruct the womb entrances. These are as follows:

[O, Child of Buddha Nature,] listen [carefully]! In the recitation of the Root Verses of the [Six] Intermediate States, *the following lines are spoken. Repeat these, now, after me:*[22]

Alas, now as the intermediate state of rebirth arises before me,
I must with one-pointed intention concentrate my mind,
And resolutely connect with the residual potency of my virtuous past actions.
I must obstruct the womb entrances and call to mind the methods of reversal.
This is the time when perseverance and purity of perception are imperative.
I must give up all jealousy and meditate on my spiritual teacher with consort.

It is extremely important to clearly repeat these verses aloud, to arouse your memories [of past virtues], to meditate on this [prayer] and to experientially cultivate its meaning. The meaning of these verses is as follows: the line 'now as the intermediate state of rebirth arises before me'[23] *explains that you are now roaming in the intermediate state of rebirth. As an indication of this, if you look into water, you will not see your reflection. Your body does not even cast a shadow. These are both signs that you do not have a solid body of flesh and blood, but that you are roaming, with a [subtle] mental body, in the intermediate state of rebirth.*

Now, therefore, you 'must with one-pointed intention concentrate your mind',[24] *undistractedly. At this moment, this [singularity of] intention is by itself the most important factor. It is like a horse being controlled by the use of a bridle. Whatever your intention focuses upon, this will come about. Do not turn your mind to negative past actions! Call to mind, now, your connections in the human world with the [sacred] teachings and instructions, remember the empowerments and oral transmissions [previously received], remember [your connection with] this* Liberation by Hearing in the Intermediate States, *and so forth. It is extremely important that you 'resolutely connect with the residual potency of your virtuous past actions'.*[25] *Do not forget! Do not be distracted! The present moment is the dividing-line between progression and regression. The present moment is the time when, by lapsing into laziness, even for an instant, you will experience constant suffering. The present moment is the time when, by concentrating with a singular intention, you will achieve constant happiness. Concentrate your mind with a single-pointed intention.*

'Resolutely connect with the residual potency of your virtuous past actions.'

Now is the time when you must obstruct the womb entrances. It is said [in the verses] that you 'must obstruct the womb entrances and call to mind the methods of reversal. This is the time when perseverance and purity of perception are imperative'.[26] *You have now arrived at that stage. Your priority now is to obstruct the womb entrances. There are five methods which will bring about obstruction of the womb entrances, so keep them carefully in mind.*

O, Child of Buddha Nature, at this stage, the perception will arise of a male and a female engaging in sexual intercourse. Upon perceiving this, do not enter between the male and the female, but be mindful and 'meditate on' the male and the female as being your 'spiritual teacher with consort'.[27] *Prostrate yourself before them and make offerings, emanating these with your mind. Be intensely devoted and request instructions from [your spiritual teacher and consort]. Just by intently focusing your thought in this way, the womb entrances will certainly be obstructed.*

Should [the womb entrances] not be successfully obstructed through this method and you are nonetheless drawn ever nearer to entering the womb, then meditate now on the spiritual teacher and consort as being your personal meditational deities, whichever these may be, or [if you do not have a personal meditational deity], meditate on the spiritual teacher and consort as being Mahākāruṇika and his consort. Again, make offerings, emanating these with your mind and generate the thought very intently: 'I request [the attainment of your] spiritual accomplishment!' Thereby, the womb entrances will be obstructed.

Should even this not obstruct the womb entrances, and you are still drawn ever nearer to entering the womb, the third method, which reverses attachment and aversion, is now to be revealed to you. There are four modes of birth: birth from an egg, birth from a womb, supernormal birth, and birth from warmth and moisture.[28] *Among these, the birth from an egg and birth from a womb are very similar, in that in both cases you will see the male and the female engaged in sexual union, as [described] above. If, based on either attachment or aversion, you enter a womb at this time, you will be born as a horse, bird, dog, human, or whatever is appropriate. If you are to be born as a male, you will experience the perceptions of a male. You will feel intense aversion towards the father and you will feel jealousy and attachment towards the mother. If you are to be born as a female, you will experience the perceptions of a female. You will feel intense envy and jealousy towards the mother and you will feel intense attachment and affection towards the father. This [emotional arousal] will cause you to enter a womb. Here you will experience the 'coemergent delight', in the midst of the meeting between the sperm and the ovum. From that state of bliss you will faint into unconsciousness, and as time passes, the embryo will come to maturity in the womb, moving through [its various stages of development], that is, the clotting of the embryo, the oval elongation of the embryo,*[29] *and so forth until finally, you will emerge [from the womb] and open your eyes. Now, you will have turned into a puppy. Previously having been a human being, you will now have become a dog. So consequently, you will suffer in a dog-kennel, or similarly, in a pigsty, or an anthill, or a wormhole, or else you may be born as a baby bull, a goat, a sheep and so forth. There is no way back. You will experience all manner of sufferings in a state of great obscurity and delusion. Through this process you will continue to remain within the six classes of living beings, including the realms of the hell beings and the anguished spirits. You will be completely drained by boundless sufferings. There is nothing more awesome or frightening than this! Oh dear! This is truly terrifying! Oh dear, Oh dear, in this way, those who lack the oral instruction of a genuine spiritual teacher will indeed fall into the great abyss of cyclic existence and be tortured unbearably by continuous sufferings. Rather than this, listen to my words! Understand this instruction of mine. I will reveal now an oral instruction which obstructs the womb entrances, through the reversal of attachment and the reversal of aversion. Listen and understand this well! It is said [in the* Root Verses of the Six Intermediate States*]:*[30]

I must obstruct the womb entrances and call to mind the methods of reversal.
This is the time when perseverance and purity of perception are imperative.
I must give up all jealousy and meditate on my spiritual teacher with consort.

As is described [in the oral instruction] above, if you are to be born as a male, you will feel attachment towards the mother and aversion towards the father. If you are to be born as a female, you will feel attachment to the father and aversion towards the mother. Thus you will come to experience jealousy, [a conflict of attachment and aversion]. Specific to this stage, there is a profound oral instruction. O, Child of Buddha Nature, when the feelings of attachment and aversion arise, meditate as follows: 'Alas, sentient beings such as I, with such negative past actions, have, up until now, roamed in cyclic existence. I have continued to wander in this way, being driven on by my feelings of attachment and aversion. If, especially at this time, I continue to be influenced by attachment and aversion, there is a danger that I will roam into the limitlessly [diverse] states of cyclic existence and risk sinking into the ocean of suffering, for a very long time. Therefore, now, from the very beginning, I must not generate attachment or aversion. Oh dear, Oh dear! As of now, I shall never again be motivated by attachment or aversion.' By concentrating intently on this thought, as it is said in the tantras, the womb entrances will be obstructed by this [singular intent] alone. O, Child of Buddha Nature, do not be distracted! Concentrate your mind on this thought, with a one-pointed intention.

Yet if, even having done this, the womb entrances are still not obstructed and [the deceased] draws ever nearer to entering a womb, then the womb entrances should be obstructed by giving the oral instruction on the unreal and illusion-like nature [of all phenomena].[31]

[O, Child of Buddha Nature], meditate in the following way! 'Alas! The father and the mother [in sexual union], the rain, the blackness, the hurricane, the thunderous sound, the fearful and terrifying experiences, the nature of these and of all phenomena is illusion-like. In whatever form [phenomena] arise, they are not real. All substantial things are unreal and false, like a mirage. They are not permanent. They are not changeless. So what is the purpose of my attachment [to these perceptions]? What is the purpose of my awe and terror? That which is non-existent, I am seeing as existent! [In reality], all these things [that I perceive] are the perceptions of my own mind. Yet, the essential nature of mind is

primordially non-existent, like an illusion. So how is it possible for things to exist externally, in their own right? Since I have not understood this before, I have [always] regarded the non-existent as existent. I have regarded the unreal as real. I have regarded illusions as truth. This is why I have roamed in cyclic existence for such a long time. Now, yet again, if I do not realise that all these [phenomena] are illusions, I will continue to roam in cyclic existence, interminably, and without doubt, I will drown in a swamp of every manner of suffering. Now, [I must realise that] all these [phenomena] are completely devoid of substantial existence, even for a single instant. [In reality], they are like a dream, like an illusion, like an echo, like a celestial city, like a mirage, like a reflection, like an optical illusion, like the moon [reflected] in water. It is absolutely certain that these [phenomena] are not truly real, but that they are false. Through this singular resolve, I will blow apart my apprehension of their true existence. Through utter confidence in this [meditation], my apprehension of self-existence will be reversed.' By knowing from the depths of your heart that all these [phenomena] are unreal, the womb entrances will certainly be obstructed.

However, if, despite this [teaching] being given, the apprehension of true existence is not shattered, and the womb entrances are therefore not obstructed and [the deceased] draws ever nearer to entering a womb, then there is a [final] profound oral instruction:

O, Child of Buddha Nature, if, even after having engaged in the above [meditation], the womb entrances have still not been obstructed, now, according to the fifth [profound oral instruction], you must obstruct the womb entrances by meditating on inner radiance.[32] *The method of meditation is as follows: 'Alas! All [seemingly] substantial phenomena are [expressions of] my own mind. Yet, [in reality], this mind is of the nature of emptiness, it is beyond creation and beyond cessation.' By focusing your thought in this way, your mind should [naturally] return to an uncontrived and stainless state. Let the mind rest in this, its natural state, directly in itself, in the same way, for example, as water is poured into water. Let [the mind] rest in its natural flow, clear, unconstricted, uncontrived and relaxed.*[33] *[By following this method] you can be sure that the womb entrances to the four modes of birth will certainly be obstructed. Meditate again and again in this way, until the womb entrances are closed.*

Set down above are several profound and genuine instructions for effecting the obstruction of the womb entrances. For those with high, average or low ability, it is impossible not to be liberated by these [instructions]. This is because: first, consciousness in the intermediate state is endowed with an, albeit corrupt, supernormal cognitive ability. Therefore, whatever one says [to the deceased] is heard by the deceased. Second, even if the deceased was deaf or blind [while in the human world], now, [in the intermediate state], all the sensory faculties will be complete and therefore whatever is said will be apprehended. Third, since the deceased is continuously being overwhelmed by fear and terror, there is an undistracted concentration on what to do; therefore, what is said will be listened to. Fourth, since the consciousness has no [physical] support, it is easy to guide and it can penetrate to the essence of whatever is focused upon. [Additionally], since the power of retention is now many times clearer, even the mentally weak will have, in the intermediate state, a lucid awareness, by virtue of their past actions. Hence, they will have the gift of knowing how to meditate on that which is taught and the gift [to assimilate] such points [of instruction]. These are the reasons why the performance of rituals on behalf of the dead is beneficial. Indeed, it is extremely important to persevere in the reading aloud of this *Great Liberation by Hearing in the Intermediate States* for the entire forty-nine days. For if liberation is not achieved at one introduction, it can be achieved at another. This is the reason why, not just one, but many introductions should be given.

[CHOOSING A WOMB ENTRANCE]

Then again, there are several kinds [of persons] who do not achieve liberation, despite having received the above introductions and having been taught the above visualisation techniques. This [lack of ability] comes about through limited familiarity with virtuous past actions, extensive primal familiarity with non-virtuous past actions, and the potency and great force of negative obscurations.

So, at this stage, if the womb entrances have still not been [successfully] obstructed [as described] above, there is a profound oral instruction for choosing an [appropriate] womb entrance,[34] which should now be presented. Again, one should request the assistance of the buddhas and bodhisattvas, take refuge in [the Three Precious Jewels] and cultivate an altruistic intention. Then, as before, calling to the deceased by name, three times, one should say the following words:

O, Child of Buddha Nature, (repeat the name of the deceased), *listen [carefully]. Even though many [authentic] introductions to the instructions have previously been given to you, up until this stage, you have not taken these to heart. Now, if you have been unable to obstruct the womb entrances, the time has actually come for you to assume a body. There are [not just one, but] several different kinds of profound [and genuine] instructions which relate to your choice of an appropriate womb entrance. So comprehend these well. Do not be distracted. [Listen] without distraction! Understand, and maintain a firm intention!*

O, Child of Buddha Nature, now, [if you are to be born as a human] the indications and signs which relate to the environment into which you may be born, on one amongst the [four] continents, will arise. You must recognise these [indications]! Indeed, you must choose the continent based on [a careful examination of these] indications of the environment into which you may be born.

If you are to take birth on the Eastern Continent, Videha, you will see a lake, adorned by male and female swans. Do not be drawn towards this [place]! Call to mind the methods of reversal [and apply these]! For were you to go there, even though it is a happy and tranquil place, it is an environment where the [sacred] teachings do not flourish. So do not enter [this continent]!

If you are to take birth on the Southern Continent, Jambudvīpa, you will see grand and delightful mansions. If indeed you can enter here, do so!

If you are to take birth on the Western Continent, Aparagodanīya, you will see a lake adorned [around its shores] by male and female horses. Do not be drawn towards this place! Call to mind the methods of reversal [and apply these]! For even though it is a place of great wealth and [abundant] resources, it is an environment where the [sacred] teachings do not flourish. So do not enter [this continent]!

If you are to take birth on the Northern Continent, Uttarakuru, you will see a lake adorned [around its shores] by cattle or a lake adorned by trees. Recognise these appearances as indications of the birth that you are about to assume! Do not enter there! For even though this is a place where there is longevity and which has merit, it is an environment where the [sacred] teachings do not flourish. So do not enter [this continent]!

If you are to take birth as a god you will see delightful celestial palaces, many-storeyed and composed of diverse jewels. If indeed you can, you should enter here!

If you are to take birth as an antigod, you will see exquisite groves and spinning wooden torches [creating] wheels of fire. Do not enter there, under any circumstances! Call to mind the methods of reversal [and apply these]!

If you are to take birth as an animal, you will see rocky caverns, empty hollows and straw sheds, shrouded by mist. Do not enter there!

If you are to take birth as an anguished spirit, you will see tree-stumps, black protruding silhouettes, blind desolate gorges, or total darkness. Were you to go there, you would be born as an anguished spirit and experience the manifold sufferings of [insatiable] hunger and thirst. Do not enter there! Call to mind the methods of reversal [and apply these]! Be courageous and strong!

If you are to take birth as a hell being, you will hear the songs of those of negative past actions. Or, quite simply, you will feel powerless and compelled to enter. Whereupon, the perception will arise that you are moving into a land of darkness, where there are black and reddened houses, black earth-pits and black roads. Were you to be drawn to this place, you would enter the hells, and experience the [searing] unbearable sufferings of heat and cold. Be careful! Do not enter into the midst of this, for there will be no opportunity to turn back. Do not enter there, under any circumstances! As it is said [in the root verses]: 'You must obstruct the womb entrances and call to mind the methods of reversal.' These are [wholly] necessary now!

O, Child of Buddha Nature, although you do not wish to move forward, you are powerless not to do so. The avenging forces, who are the executors of the unfailing laws of cause and effect, will be pursuing you. You will have no choice but to move forward. Before you, the avengers and executors will be leading the way. The experience will arise of trying to flee from these forces, of trying to flee from the darkness, from the most violent windstorms, from the [thunderous] tumult, the snow, the rain, the hail and the turbulent blizzards, which swirl around you. [Frightened], you will set off to seek a refuge and you will find protection inside an enclosed space, such as within the mansions, just described, or in rock-shelters, or holes in the ground, or amongst trees, or within the bud of a lotus flower. Hiding here, you will be very hesitant to come out, and you will think: 'I should not leave here now.' You will be very reluctant to be separated from this protected place and you will become utterly attached to it. Then, because you are so very hesitant to go outside, where you would be confronted by the fears and terrors of the intermediate state, you will, because of this fear and awe, continue to hide away. Thus, you will assume a body, however utterly bad that may be, and you will, [in time], come to experience all manner of sufferings. This [experience of wanting to hide] is a sign that you are being obstructed by malignant forces and carnivorous ogres. Particularly related to this stage, there is a profound oral instruction. Listen, therefore, and understand!

At this time, when you are being pursued by avenging forces and you feel powerless [to escape] and you are terrified and frightened, you must, in an instant and with perfect recall, visualise the Transcendent Lord Mahottara Heruka, or Hayagrīva, or Vajrapāṇi, or else, if you have one, your personal meditational deity. [Visualise the deity] as having a huge buddha-body, with thick limbs, standing upright, in a terrifying wrathful manifestation, which pulverises every form of obstructing force. [By virtue of this practice], insulated from the avengers by the blessing and compassion [of the meditational deity], you will secure the ability to choose a womb entrance. This is a profound and genuine crucial point of the oral instructions. So, understand this now!

Moreover, O, Child of Buddha Nature, the gods [inhabiting the form realms] of meditative concentration, and similar beings [of the higher realms], take birth through the potency of their meditative stability.[35] *Also, certain classes of malevolent forces, including the anguished spirits, arise on the basis of the transformation of their mental body itself during this very [intermediate state], through a shift in their mode of perception. [In this way], they assume the forms of an anguished spirit, malign force or carnivorous ogre, capable of displaying diverse miraculous acts. The anguished spirits who reside in the ocean depths, the anguished spirits who move through space, the eighty thousand classes of obstructing forces, and so forth, all come into existence consequent on such a shift in their mode of perception, while [still] in the mental body.*

At this time, therefore, [while visualising the wrathful deity] it is essential that you hold in mind the meaning of emptiness, [the essence of] the Great Seal. If you are not able to practise in this way, you must cultivate your experience of the illusion-like natural expressive power [of actual reality]. If you are unable even to practise in that way, you should meditate on the meditational deity Mahākāruṇika, without allowing your mind to experience attachment, in any respect whatsoever. Through [practising this effectively], buddhahood will be attained in the Buddha-body of Perfect Resource, during this intermediate state.

O, Child of Buddha Nature, if, due to the potency of your past actions, you must at this stage enter a womb, a further teaching on the methods of choosing a womb entrance is now to be taught. Listen, [carefully], therefore! Do not just move towards whatever womb entrance appears to you. If, whilst being pursued by the avenging forces [of the laws of cause and effect], you are powerless [and unable to resist] the process of entering [a womb], then you must, at this time, meditate on Hayagrīva. Since you now possess a subtle supernormal cognitive ability, you will [clearly] apprehend all the [potential] birthplaces as they arise, in sequence. Therefore, make your choice, [based on the examination of the indications and based on the instructions]! There are two kinds of oral instruction [which can now be applied]: [first], the oral instructions for transferring the consciousness to the pure buddha fields[36] *and [second], the instructions for choosing a womb entrance within impure cyclic existence. Therefore, [listen carefully and] do as follows:*

First, the transference of consciousness to the utterly pure realms of the sky-farers is effected by those of highest ability, by directing their intention as follows. 'Alas! I am deeply sad that even after an infinite "incalculable aeon", I am still left behind in this swamp of cyclic existence. How dreadful it is, that while so many have attained buddhahood in the past, I have still not achieved liberation. Now, this cycle of existence disgusts me! It horrifies me! I have long been led astray by it! Now, the moment approaches for me to move forward! Now, I must take birth, miraculously, in the bud of a lotus flower, in the presence of the Buddha Amitābha, in the western Buddha field of the Blissful (Sukhāvatī)!' Focus your intention, concentratedly, on this thought! [It is essential that you make this effort!] Alternatively, you can focus your intention on whichever buddha field you wish. On Manifest Joy (Abhirati), on Dense Array (Ghanavyūha), on Alakāvatī, on Mount Potālaka, or [you may wish to focus] on coming into the presence of [Padmasambhava of] Oḍḍiyāna, in the celestial palace of Lotus Light, or indeed on whichever buddha field you wish to enter. Be single-minded! Do not be distracted! Immediately upon establishing [this intention], you will take birth in the [chosen] buddha field. Yet again, alternatively, if you wish to proceed into the presence of Maitreya in [the realm of] The Joyful (Tuṣita), think as follows: 'At this juncture in the intermediate state, the moment has come for me to proceed into the presence of the king of the [sacred] teachings, Maitreya, in [the realm of] The Joyful. Therefore, it is there that I will go!' If you focus your intention on this thought, you will take birth, miraculously, in the heart of a lotus, in the presence of Maitreya.

Alternatively, if you are unable to accomplish this [transference], or if you desire to enter a womb or you are obliged to enter one, then there are the following instructions on choosing a womb entrance within impure cyclic existence. Therefore, listen [carefully]. Utilising the supernormal cognitive ability which you now possess, examine the continents once again, as just described, and make your choice. You must enter a land where the [sacred] teachings flourish!

[Be warned, however!] It could be that, [in reality], you are about to take birth, by entering into a substance which is fetid and polluted, and yet that filthy mass will be perceived by you as sweet-smelling and you will be drawn towards it and take birth within it. Therefore, whatever such [attractive] appearances may arise, do not grasp at them as substantially real! Ensure that you remain utterly free from the symptoms of attachment and aversion, and on that basis choose an excellent womb entrance.

It is extremely important that your motivation is firmly concentrated [as you approach the womb entrance]. Therefore think as follows: 'Ah! For the sake of all sentient beings, I shall be born as a universal monarch, or [acting purely] like a great [dignified] sal tree, I shall be born into the brāhman class, or as the child of an accomplished master, or into a family which maintains an immaculate lineage of the [sacred] teachings, or into a family where the mother and father are deeply devout. Then, once I have taken on a body which is blessed with the merit of being able to act on behalf of all sentient beings, I shall [dedicate myself to] acting on their behalf!' You must concentrate your motivation on this thought and [thus] enter the womb.

As you enter the womb, consecrate it [by perceiving it] as a celestial palace of the deities.[37] *Be full of devotion. Ensure that you enter whilst praying to and imagining that you are receiving empowerments from the conquerors of the ten directions and from their sons, as well as from the meditational deities and, in particular, from Mahākāruṇika.*

[However be warned], for as you make this choice of a womb entrance, there is a risk of error. There is the risk of error when, through the potency of past actions, an excellent womb entrance is perceived as a bad one, and when a bad womb entrance is perceived as a good one. At this time, the essential points of the teaching are crucial. Therefore, once again, you should act as follows. Even though perceptions of an excellent [womb entrance] may occur, do not become attached to these. And [conversely] even though perceptions of a poor [womb entrance] may occur, do not feel aversion. The essential point of the profound and genuine [instructions] is that you enter the womb in a state of great equanimity, utterly free from [the dichotomies of] good and bad, acceptance and rejection, or attachment and aversion.

Nevertheless, with the exception of certain persons who have experience of this [equanimity] it is difficult [for beings] to sever themselves from the deep-seated and long-lasting disease of negative habitual tendencies. Therefore, if [the deceased] remains unable to be free from attachment and aversion, in the above manner, such negative beings who are of the lowest capacity may seek refuge in the animal realms or similar [kinds of inferior existences]. In order to counteract this, again calling to the deceased by name, you should speak as follows:

O, Child of Buddha Nature, if you do not know how to choose a womb entrance and you are unable to give up your attachment and your aversion, then, regardless of which of the above appearances arise, you must call out, by name, to the Three Precious Jewels. Take refuge in them! Pray to Mahākāruṇika! Go forward with your head held high. Recognise that this is the intermediate state! Give up your attachment and your clinging to the friends, sons, daughters and relatives that you have left behind. These [attachments] are not helpful [to you now]. Enter into the blue light of the human realm. Enter into the white light of the realm of the gods. Enter into the mansions of precious jewels and the gardens of delight.

This [introduction] should be enunciated up to seven times. Then one should pray to the buddhas and bodhisattvas, [reciting the *Aspirational Prayer Calling to the Buddhas and Bodhisattvas for Assistance*].[38] Then one should read aloud, up to seven times, the *Aspirational Prayer which Protects from Fear of the Intermediate States*, the *Root Verses of the [Six] Intermediate States*, and the *Aspirational Prayer which Rescues from the Dangerous Pathways of the Intermediate States*.[39] Then, one should also read aloud, clearly and with correct pronunciation, the *Liberation by Wearing: Natural Liberation of the Psycho-physical Aggregates*. And you should also read aloud the *Spiritual Practice: Natural Liberation of Habitual Tendencies*.[40]

CONCLUSION

Thus, [in summary], by acting correctly, yogins with high realisation will [successfully] effect the transference of consciousness at the moment of death, and, being spared the necessity of having to wander through the intermediate states, will attain liberation in an ascending and core-penetrating manner. Certain others, below these [yogins in ability], who have achieved [direct] meditative experience, will recognise the inner radiance of reality, at the culmination of the intermediate state of the time of death, [and will, similarly, attain buddhahood] in an ascending and core-penetrating manner. Others, below these, in accord with their inheritance of past actions and their particular level of ability, will attain liberation at one [moment] or at another, during the [respective] weeks [which follow the moment of death], as the visions of the Peaceful and Wrathful Deities gradually arise in the intermediate state of reality. Since there is a succession of dangerous passageways, recognition will occur at an appropriate juncture [during the intermediate state of reality] and liberation will follow.

However, those who have a very weak inheritance of [positive] past actions, those who are greatly clouded by negative obscuration and those who are burdened by the most non-virtuous past actions, will be obliged to roam downwards into the intermediate state of rebirth. Here, as before, since there are different levels of introduction, like the rungs of a ladder, recognition will occur, if not at one stage, then at another; and thereby liberation will follow.

But if those, just mentioned, who have a weak inheritance of [positive] past actions, do not achieve recognition and are accordingly overcome by fear and terror, then, there is a graded series of different forms of instruction [for obstructing, and] for choosing, the womb entrance. Thus, if recognition does not occur in the course of one such teaching, then, these individuals will be introduced to yet another [instruction] and upon understanding the [appropriate] visualisation technique they will achieve the inestimable bounty of the higher existences. Even if one is, like a beast, the lowest of the low, through the munificence of taking refuge, one will avoid birth in inferior existences and assume a precious human body, [blessed] with the benefits of freedom and favourable opportunities. Then, in the life to come, one will meet a spiritual teacher or spiritual friend, and one will receive the teachings, and thereby liberation will follow.

This [sacred] teaching, when encountered in the intermediate state of rebirth, is an [oral] instruction that connects [the deceased] with their residual inheritance of virtuous past actions. This is why it [is said to] resemble a connecting tube which [re-establishes continuity] when inserted into a broken water channel. Therefore, [based on the veracity of this method], it is impossible not to be liberated upon hearing this teaching, even for those of the greatest negativity. This is because, during the intermediate states, both the compassionate invitation of all the [Peaceful and Wrathful] Conquerors and the invitation of the manifestations of the malevolent and obstacle-causing forces arise simultaneously. As this occurs, merely by hearing this [sacred] teaching, the mode of perception [of the deceased] is transformed and liberation is thereby attained.

Further, this transformation is easy to effect because [the deceased] now possesses a [subtle] mental body and not a body of flesh and blood; the deceased continues to see and hear, with a subtle supernormal cognitive ability based on the potency of past actions, however far he or she has wandered into the intermediate states. [Thus], by sustaining mindfulness [of the teaching], the deceased is capable of transforming his or her perception in an instant. This is why [the reminder of the teaching] is extremely beneficial. Its impact is like that of a catapult machine; in other words, it resembles the way in which a huge tree-trunk, incapable of being lifted by a hundred men, can be easily steered wherever one wants in a moment, when it is floated in water. [In essence, the impact of hearing this doctrine] resembles the turning of a horse by its bridle.

All those who have died should be approached in the manner [here described]. If the corpse is present, then a friend should sit close to it and repeatedly read aloud this succinct reminder. This reading should continue [at least] until blood and serum emerge from the nostrils [of the deceased]; and until then, the corpse must not be disturbed.

The commitments which relate to this practice are as follows: no living creatures should be killed in dedication to the dead person; relatives and friends, whether oneself or others, should not cry, shout, mourn or wail in the presence of the corpse; and instead should engage in as much virtuous activity as possible.

Further, it would be extremely beneficial if this [sacred] teaching of the *Great Liberation by Hearing in the Intermediate States* is recited as a complement to [other systems of] meditative guidance, irrespective of the category of the [sacred] teachings to which they belong.

Further, this text should be recited constantly. Its words and meaning should be learnt by heart. Then, if one's health permits, when [the onset of] the intermediate state of the time of death becomes certain, and the signs of [approaching] death are recognised, one should read this text aloud to oneself, and reflect on its words and meaning. If one's health does not allow this, then entrust the book to a fellow Buddhist for him or her to read aloud. The reminder thus being made, there is no doubt that liberation will assuredly be attained.

This teaching, which does not necessarily require [prior] meditation practice, is the profound instruction which liberates by being seen, liberates by being heard and liberates by being read aloud. This profound instruction is one which can lead even those of the greatest negativity on the direct path [to liberation]. Ensure that its words and meaning are retained in the memory [such that] they are not forgotten, even if you were to be chased by seven [ferocious] dogs. This is a pith instruction for the attainment of buddhahood at the time of death. [Even if] all the buddhas of the past, present and future [were to search], they would not find a [sacred] teaching superior to this.

This completes the instruction on the intermediate state, which liberates corporeal beings, the profound, refined essence, entitled the *Great Liberation by Hearing in the Intermediate States*. It was brought forth from the mountain of Gampodar by the accomplished master Karma Lingpa, as a precious treasure.

MAṄGALAM!

12
Aspirational Prayers

CONTEXT

If possible, the dying person should recite these three aspirational prayers with intense longing at the time of death.

Otherwise, the attending lama should recite these prayers, also with intense longing, immediately before the *Liberation by Hearing* (Chapter 11) is read to the dying person. That is, following the taking of refuge in the Three Precious Jewels – the Buddha, the sacred teachings and the monastic community – and the making of offerings.

At this time, when it is likely that the dying person's consciousness is dimmed and the dying person may be feeling afraid, it is regarded as crucially important for the dying person to place their confidence in the buddhas and bodhisattvas and to request the buddhas and bodhisattvas to be their refuge and guide.

Herein is contained the *Aspirational Prayer [Calling] to the Buddhas and Bodhisattvas for Assistance.*[1]

I bow down to the Peaceful and Wrathful Conquerors!

This prayer should be recited at the time of one's own death, [or whenever appropriate]. First, make offerings, both actual and visualised, to the Three Precious Jewels. Then, while holding fragrant incense in one's hand, say the following words with fervent intensity:

O, buddhas and bodhisattvas, abiding in the ten directions, refuge of living beings, imbued with compassion, imbued with knowledge, imbued with clear vision and imbued with love, come to this place, by the power of your compassion and accept these displayed and visualised offerings! O, Compassionate Ones, as you are the fountain of all-knowing pristine cognition, of loving compassion, of effective activity, and of a power to grant refuge, beyond conception, [come to this place!]

O, Compassionate Ones, this human being, (say the name), *is leaving this world and journeying to another shore. He*[2] *is being cast off from this world and approaching the great transition of death. Suffering deeply, he is without a friend, without a refuge, without a protector and without a companion. His perception of this life is fading away. He is moving on to another world, entering a dense darkness and falling into an unfathomable abyss. Entering the thick forest of doubt, he will be driven on by the potency of past actions. He will be entering a great wilderness, borne away on a great ocean, and driven on by the vital winds of past actions. He will be moving in a direction where there is no firm ground, entering a great battlefield, being seized by great malevolent forces and becoming overwhelmed by fear and terror upon meeting the executors of the unfailing laws of cause and effect. In accord with his past actions, powerless [to resist], he may even, yet again, be entering the realms of rebirth. The time has come when he has no choice but to move on, alone, leaving his dear friends behind.*

O, Compassionate Ones, grant refuge now to this person (say the name), *who has no refuge! Protect him! Be his companion! Defend him from the great darkness of the intermediate state! Turn back the great hurricane of past actions! Protect him from the great fear and terror of the unfailing laws of cause and effect! Rescue him from the long and dangerous pathways of the intermediate state! O, Compassionate Ones, be unsparing in your compassion! Grant assistance to him! Do not allow him to be expelled into the three kinds of inferior existence. Without wavering from your ancient vows, swiftly release the power of your compassion. O, buddhas and bodhisattvas, for the sake of this person* (say the name), *be unsparing in your compassion, skilful means and ability! Seize him with your compassion! Do not allow [this] sentient being to fall under the power of negative past actions! O, Three Precious Jewels, protect us from the sufferings of the intermediate state!*

This *Aspirational Prayer [Calling] to the Buddhas and Bodhisattvas for Assistance* should be read aloud with intense devotion three times, by oneself and by all others present. May its impact not cease until cyclic existence has been emptied!

SAMAYA *rgya rgya rgya*! Let good auspices prevail!

Herein is contained the *Aspirational Prayer which Rescues from the Dangerous Pathways of the Intermediate States.*[3]

I bow down to the spiritual teachers, [meditational deities] and ḍākinīs,
May I be guided on the path by their great love.

O, as I roam in cyclic existence [driven] by deep-seated bewilderment,
May the spiritual teachers, holders of the oral lineages, draw me forward,
Leading me on the path of [radiant] light,
Which is undistracted study, reflection and meditation.
May the supreme consorts, the hosts of ḍākinīs, support me from behind,
And thus [encircled] may I be rescued
From the fearsome passageway of the intermediate state,
And be escorted to the level of an utterly perfect buddha.

O, as I roam in cyclic existence [driven] by deep-seated delusion,
May the transcendent lord Vairocana draw me forward,
Leading me on the path of radiant light,
Which is the pristine cognition of reality's expanse.
May the supreme consort [Ākāśa]dhātvīśvarī support me from behind,
And thus [encircled] may I be rescued
From the fearsome passageway of the intermediate state,
And be escorted to the level of an utterly perfect buddha.[4]

O, as I roam in cyclic existence [driven] by deep-seated aversion,
May the transcendent lord Vajrasattva draw me forward,
Leading me on the path of radiant light,
Which is the mirror-like pristine cognition.
May the supreme consort Buddhalocanā support me from behind,
And thus [encircled] may I be rescued
From the fearsome passageway of the intermediate state,
And be escorted to the level of an utterly perfect buddha.

O, as I roam in cyclic existence [driven] by deep-seated pride,
May the transcendent lord Ratnasambhava draw me forward,
Leading me on the path of radiant light,
Which is the pristine cognition of sameness.
May the supreme consort Māmakī support me from behind,
And thus [encircled] may I be rescued
From the fearsome passageway of the intermediate state,
And be escorted to the level of an utterly perfect buddha.

O, as I roam in cyclic existence [driven] by deep-seated attachment,
May the transcendent lord Amitābha draw me forward,
Leading me on the path of radiant light,
Which is the pristine cognition of discernment.
May the supreme consort Pāṇḍaravāsinī support me from behind,
And thus [encircled] may I be rescued
From the fearsome passageway of the intermediate state,
And be escorted to the level of an utterly perfect buddha.

O, as I roam in cyclic existence [driven] by deep-seated envy,
May the transcendent lord Amoghasiddhi draw me forward,
Leading me on the path of radiant light,
Which is the pristine cognition of accomplishment.
May the supreme consort Samayatārā support me from behind,
And thus [encircled] may I be rescued
From the fearsome passageway of the intermediate state,
And be escorted to the level of an utterly perfect buddha.

O, as I roam in cyclic existence [driven] by the five virulent poisons,
May the transcendent conquerors, [the male buddhas] of the five enlightened families, draw me forward,
Leading me on the path of radiant light,
Which is the four pristine cognitions combined.
May the five supreme female buddhas, [the purity of] the expanse, support me from behind,
And, thus [encircled], may I be rescued
From the light-paths of the six impure classes [of beings]
And be escorted to the five utterly supreme and pure buddha fields.

O, as I roam in cyclic existence driven by deep-seated habitual tendencies,
May the assembly of spiritual heroes and awareness holders draw me forward,
Leading me on the path of radiant light,
Which is the coemergent pristine cognition.
May the supreme consorts, the hosts of ḍākinī, support me from behind,
And thus [encircled] may I be rescued
From the fearsome passageway of the intermediate state,
And be escorted to the level of an utterly perfect buddha.

O, as I roam in cyclic existence driven by deep-seated bewildering perceptions,
May the assembly of Blood-drinking Wrathful Deities draw me forward,
Leading me on the path of radiant light,
Which is free of fear and terrifying perceptions.
May the assembly of the Krodheśvarī, Queens of the Expanse, support me from behind,
And thus [encircled] may I be rescued
From the fearsome passageway of the intermediate state,
And be escorted to the level of an utterly perfect buddha.

[OṂ ĀḤ HŪṂ][5]
May the elements of space not arise as a hostile force.
May I see them as the field of the blue buddha.

May the elements of water not arise as a hostile force.
May I see them as the field of the white buddha.
May the elements of earth not arise as a hostile force.
May I see them as the field of the yellow buddha.
May the elements of fire not arise as a hostile force.
May I see them as the field of the red buddha.
May the elements of wind not arise as a hostile force.
May I see them as the field of the green buddha.
May the [awesome] sounds, lights and rays not arise as a hostile force.
May I see them as the infinite fields of the Peaceful and Wrathful Deities.
May the rainbow-coloured elements not rise up as a hostile force.
May I see them as the fields of the manifold buddhas.

May I recognise all sounds as my own sounds.
May I recognise all lights as my own lights.
May I recognise all rays as my own rays.
May I spontaneously recognise [the characteristics of] the intermediate states.
May the fields of the three buddha-bodies be manifest.

SAMAYA!

Herein is contained the *Aspirational Prayer which Protects from Fear of the Intermediate States*.[6]

When my life's course is ended,
And I roam alone in the intermediate states,
The loved ones of this world can no longer help me.
So, [at this critical time], may the Conquerors, the Peaceful and Wrathful Deities,
[Quickly] release the power of their compassion,
And may the deep darkness of my ignorance be dispelled.

When I roam alone, separated from my loved ones,
And [myriad] images of emptiness arise, naturally manifesting,
May the buddhas [quickly] release the power of their compassion,
And may the fear of the awesome and terrifying intermediate states be annulled.

When the five radiant lights of pristine cognition dawn,
May I recognise them as my own [nature], without awe and without terror,
And as the [manifold] forms of the Peaceful and Wrathful Deities arise,
May I be fearlessly confident and recognise [the characteristics of] the intermediate states.

When I experience suffering, as the result of negative past actions,
May the Great Compassionate One dispel all such misery,

And as the natural sound of reality reverberates like a thousand peals of thunder,
May all sounds be heard as the teachings of the Greater Vehicle.

When I am driven on by past actions, unable to find a refuge,
May the meditational deities dispel all such misery,
And as I experience the suffering of habitual tendencies and past actions,
May the meditative stabilities of inner radiance and bliss [naturally] arise.[7]

When I am miraculously born into the intermediate state of rebirth,
May I not be beguiled by the perverse prophecies of Māra,[8]
And as I [freely] arrive at every place that I think of,
May the bewildering fear and terror, generated by my negative past actions, not arise.

When the roars of savage wild beasts echo around me,
May their cries be transformed into the sound of the sacred teachings, the Six Syllables,
And as I am engulfed by snow, rain, wind and darkness,
May I achieve the pure clairvoyance of radiant pristine cognition.

May sentient beings in the intermediate state, similar in kind to myself,
Be born into the higher realms, free from rivalry,
And as severe dissonant mental states generate insatiable hunger and thirst,
May the afflictions of hunger, thirst, heat and cold, be annulled.

When I see my future parents in union,
May I perceive them as Mahākāruṇika and consort,
And for the sake of others, being blessed with the power to choose a birthplace,
May I achieve an exalted body, adorned with the auspicious major and minor marks.

Once I have achieved birth in a supreme human form,
May I act so as to swiftly liberate all who see and hear me.
And may I not be influenced by my negative past actions,
But multiply and emulate my past merits.

Wherever I may be born, in whatever land it may be,
May I quickly encounter the meditational deity of my past lives.
Knowing, from immediately after birth, how to speak and walk,
May I remember my past lives and attain the power of non-forgetfulness.

May I easily come to master by study and reflection,
The manifold stages of learning – small, intermediate and great.
May the country into which I am born be auspicious,
And may all sentient beings be blessed with happiness.

O, Peaceful and Wrathful Conquerors, may I and all others
Become entirely at one with you, and come to resemble you,
In all your forms, your retinues, your lifespan and your buddha fields,
And in every quality of your supreme auspicious marks.

Through the compassion of Samantabhadra and the infinite Peaceful and Wrathful Deities,
By the power of the truth of pure reality,
And by the blessing of the mantrins who practise one-pointedly,
May [every wish of] this aspirational prayer be fulfilled.

This prayer entitled the *Aspirational Prayer which Protects from Fear of the Intermediate States* was composed by the preceptor from Oḍḍiyāna, Padmākara. May this profound sacred teaching not be extinguished until all the worlds of cyclic existence have been emptied.

SAMAYA *rgya rgya rgya!*

This is a treasure-text of *Tulku* Karma Lingpa.

13
A Masked Drama of Rebirth

CONTEXT

This allegorical play portrays the experiences of the archetypal evildoer Lakṣanāraka and the archetypal virtuous householder Śrījāta as they meet with Yama, the embodiment of the inexorable laws of cause and effect, in the intermediate state of rebirth. This lighthearted masked drama is still commonly performed today during public ceremonial occasions throughout Tibet, Bhutan and the Buddhist regions of the Himalayas. The play is staged, often to huge audiences, in the courtyards or public ceremonial areas of a monastery, often at the time of the annual 10th day sacred dances commemorating the life of Padmasambhava.

PART ONE

Herein is contained [a masked drama entitled] *Natural Liberation of the Intermediate State of Rebirth: A Teaching Revealing the Natural Expression of Virtue and Negativity, in the Intermediate State of Rebirth*;[1] which is an extract from the *Peaceful and Wrathful Deities: A Profound Sacred Teaching [entitled] Natural Liberation through [Recognition of] Enlightened Intention*.[2]

I respectfully bow down to the uncreated Buddha-body of Reality:
Samantabhadra and Samantabhadrī in union;
To the unceasing Buddha-body of Perfect Resource:
The Peaceful and Wrathful Lotus Deities;
And to the naturally arising Buddha-body of Emanation: Padmākara.
May [all beings] be liberated in the intermediate state!

Having earlier presented the empowerments and introductions
From the *Liberation by Hearing in the Intermediate States, An extract from the Peaceful and Wrathful Lotus Deities*,[3]
And having introduced the intermediate state of reality, which is the 'great liberation by seeing',[4]
Now I will present [a means of demonstrating] the introduction to the intermediate state of rebirth.[5]

THE SCENE

Here, having completed the previous introductions [to the intermediate states of the time of death and reality], I will present [in the form of a masked drama] the introduction to the intermediate state of rebirth. The spiritual teacher [should now appear fully attired] in the costume of Yama Dharmarāja, and wear a large wrathful mask, depicting Yama. He is carrying a large wooden slate in his right hand, and in his left he holds a large round mirror. Dressed in a silk brocade gown, he is seated on a great throne. In his retinue, there is a figure dressed as the black Ox-headed Rakṣa Demon,[6] *wearing an ox-head mask and holding a black lasso. Then, seated to the right, there is another figure dressed as the Monkey-headed Elemental Spirit,*[7] *with the face of a monkey, and holding a weight and measure in his hands.*[8] *Other figures also present include: one dressed as the Boar-headed Cemetery Spirit,*[9] *carrying a wooden slate; one dressed as the venomous Snake-headed Demon,*[10] *with the face of a snake and carrying a mirror; one dressed as the ferocious Bear-headed figure,*[11] *with the face of a bear and holding a bellows; one dressed as the awesome Lion-headed figure,*[12] *with the face of a lion and clutching a hammer; and one dressed as the Garuḍa-headed Bird figure,*[13] *with the face of a garuḍa and holding a saw. These figures with diverse [animal]-heads who are attired similarly to Yama, are dignified and standing in rows, to the right and left of Dharmarāja.*

The deity representing [the deceased's] good conscience[14] *is wearing a white peaceful mask and a white silk robe, and is carrying a bowl filled with white pebbles. The demon representing [the deceased's] bad conscience*[15] *is wearing a black wrathful mask and a black gown, and is carrying a bowl filled with black pebbles. Before Dharmarāja, on the right, is a long white carpet, which is rolled out like a white pathway, and at its end are two figures dressed in the costume of Mahākāruṇika, with one face and four arms, and bedecked with ornaments. They are seated at the end [of the white carpet] on a throne which is hidden by a curtain. On the left side is a long black carpet, which is rolled out like a black pathway, and it leads to the door of a dark room.*

Hidden elsewhere, in his home, is a person named the late Śrījāta ('gloriously born');[16] *while hidden somewhere in the corner [of the stage], is someone named the late Lakṣanāraka ('hundred thousand hells'),*[17] *who is a wrongdoing outcaste*[18] *of low birth.*

ACT ONE

DHARMARĀJA (*as he draws a cross on the wooden slate*): O! Ox-headed Rakṣa, it seems the time of death has come for a person in their home in the human world; the indication of this has appeared on my wooden slate.

OX-HEADED RAKṢA (*calling to the venomous Snake-headed Demon*): O, Venomous Snake-headed One! Look in your mirror! What is this deceased person's country? What is his family line? And what is his name? Please look!

VENOMOUS SNAKE-HEADED DEMON: O! The deceased whose time has come is from the country of Tāmradvīpa in India, and he lived in the city of Śāntikāla, which is a township of butchers. As for his family line, he belonged to the lowest social class of the four classes;[19] and his name is the wrongdoing Lakṣanāraka. His lifespan has come to an end, and [thus an indication of this] has appeared on the wooden slate. Now, go [and fetch him]!

(*Thereupon, the Ox-headed Rakṣa, the Boar-headed Cemetery Spirit, and the demon representing [the deceased's] bad conscience run off, while, in their wake, the deity representing [the deceased's] good conscience rushes to his assistance. As soon as they have found the 'wrongdoing one' in his house in the human world, they tie a black noose around his neck, and then Ox-headed [Rakṣa] and Boar-headed Cemetery Spirit both lead him away by the hands. The demon representing [the deceased's] bad conscience chases him from behind, carrying a load of black pebbles. Meanwhile, the deity representing [the deceased's] good conscience places [a mere] six white pebbles in the bowl for white pebbles, and, in embarrassment, tries to help. Holding a white scarf, with his hands folded in a gesture of supplication, he attempts to petition Ox-headed Rakṣa [on behalf of the deceased], but this is unsuccessful. Lakṣanāraka is then brought screaming into the presence of [Dharma-]rāja.*)

DHARMARĀJA (*interrogates him*): Hmm! Who are you, you black human being, carrying a weight and measure? Where are you from? Why do you not dare to look at me directly? You appear to have attained a human form, but what portion of your positive virtue is [now] left? Have you ever had any scruples about committing negative actions? What do you have to say about this? Speak quickly now!

THE WRONGDOING ONE [LAKṢANĀRAKA] (*lamentingly*): Alas! Alas! Permit me to speak in the presence of Yama Dharmarāja! I had an ordinary human form, my resources were few, my food and clothing poor. I have had many female dependants and thus little to eat. I had to take the lives of many beings and many years have passed since I ate rice, for I had nothing but warm [freshly slain] meat to eat. Many years have passed since I drank rice wine or pure liquor; for when thirsty I had to drink water and blood.

Nowadays in the populated areas of the world there are many who claim to be spiritual friends. They frequently teach about the defects of having committed negative actions and the benefits of having carried out positive actions. However, I did not go to them! Also, everyone would say, 'Don't persist in such negative actions, as one day death will come, and at that time you will go to the hells. You should renounce wrongdoing and perform virtuous actions!'

Even though they advised me by saying these things, I thought, 'I don't know whether I believe in the hells or not, and anyway there is no one who says they have been there, and then returned [to prove it].' So, I said to those people, 'Who has gone to the hells and then returned? If the hells exist, where are they? These are just the lies of clever-talking people. Under the ground, there is just solid earth and solid rock. There are no hells. Above, there is only empty sky. There are no buddhas. So now while I'm alive, if I kill for my food, it doesn't matter. When I die, my body will be taken to the charnel ground and it will be eaten by birds and wild animals. Not a trace will be left. My mind will vanish, so at that time who will be left to go to the hells.[20] HA! HA!'

So I did not believe in the hells and I committed negative acts. And I thought, 'Even if the hells do exist, they will only be set in some remote future life, so if I have sufficient food and clothing for now, the next life doesn't seem to matter.' So it was through this misunderstanding, this lack of awareness, and stupidity that I committed evil acts. It happened because I was not acquainted with the fact that you, Dharmarāja, [you] Ox-headed Rakṣa and [all you] others, actually exist. I did not knowingly do evil just out of contempt for all of you, who exist here in the world of the intermediate state. The fault lies with this misunderstanding and lack of awareness. So, now, all of you, lord and entourage, I request you not to pass judgement upon me. If I had known when I lived in the human world that this all actually existed, I would never have committed negative actions. Now I am stuck here under the influence of negative mental states. Alas! Alas!, since you are a King of Dharma, be merciful to me! Be my friend and supporter!

Underground there exists great suffering, Dharmarāja, so do not send me down there! Instead, please send me upward into the human world! Thereafter I will never perform evil actions again – only good ones!

THE DEITY REPRESENTING THE GOOD CONSCIENCE (*offering a white silk scarf*): O! Dharmarāja, listen to me! This outcaste butcher from Tāmradvīpa has committed evil deeds owing to his delusion and blinding ignorance, as a result of which he did not understand [the difference between] good and bad actions. Since he did not act knowingly or with understanding, I therefore petition you not to punish him. He has, after all, also carried out a small number of virtuous actions!

Once when six people were unable to escape from the current of a broad river, he saved all six – with a virtuous intent. As a mark of this, I have six white pebbles. And since there are also other virtuous actions, similar to this, which he has incidentally accumulated, Great Dharmarāja, I request your forgiveness on his behalf. (*As he says this, he prostrates three times [before Dharmarāja].*)

THE BLACK DEMON [REPRESENTING THE BAD CONSCIENCE]: HA, HA! Is this all you have to say, white deity [of good conscience]! Are you not embarrassed to carry this [almost] empty bowl! He, this low-caste butcher, has spent his life in evil deeds and has robbed himself of his share of virtue.

He has slain all the animals he has ever seen.
He has taken warm flesh for food,
And he has drunk warm blood as a beverage.
He has continuously spoken harshly [towards others].
In the upper valleys he has slain innocent wildlife;
In the lower valleys he has slain innocent fish;
And in between he has beaten innocent beggars.
He has defamed each and every spiritual teacher,
Burnt down a large temple,

Polluted a great lake with poison,
Burnt a vast mountain forest,
Beaten his parents, and destroyed a sacred reliquary.
Now in Tāmradvīpa, India,
There is no greater wrongdoer than he!
Look at the mound of black pebbles!
(*turning to Lakṣanāraka*)
In case you don't recognise yourself,
Your country is Tāmralipti, India,[21]
And your city is Śāntikāla.
Your father is the butcher, Tripon,[22]
Who came here eight years ago.
Your mother is the butcheress, Pelkyi,[23]
Who came here five years ago.
You are the offspring of these outcaste butchers.
Now you have come here – haven't you?
The year is the Water Female Pig,[24]
And this year your feeding [in the human world] has come to an end.
All those of eastern India
Call you 'Red-handed Butcher';
All those of southern India
Call you the 'wrongdoing Lakṣanāraka';
All those of western India
Call you 'Black Low-caste Butcher';
All those of northern India
Call you the 'Black Killer of All'.
Your caste is the black *caṇḍāla* caste
And your family line is that of wrongdoing butchers.
All generations of your family without exception
Will take the path to hell.
When you were killing, you seemed happy;
When you ate, it seemed tasty,
But does it taste so good now?
What use is your clever, slick-talking tongue [now]?
Now the time has come for you to experience suffering,
In retribution for the million animal lives [you have taken].
If you don't experience this suffering,
Then millions of creatures will have lost everything,
And you, Lakṣanāraka, will have gained everything.

As far as retribution for your crimes is concerned,
Even Dharmarāja with his mighty stature
Cannot stop the effects of your negative actions,
The greatest of which was burning down the temple,
And the smallest of which was the killing of lice.
This is why you have accumulated [all] these [black] pebbles.
So it is best if you prepare yourself to move on.
[Get ready to] go swiftly on this black path!
[There], the sealed copper cauldron [that awaits you] is wide and deep,
The waves of boiling bronze are fierce,
The fiery mass of past actions is intensely hot,
And the messengers of Yama have scant mercy.
Dharmarāja's attitude is extremely fierce,
The weapons of past actions are sharply pointed,
And the black winds of past actions are very powerful.
Now is the time for you to go to such a place!
Though I really do have compassion for you,
I am nonetheless very, very satisfied!
You must carry on your back the weight and measure,
Which you used as a fraudulent weight and measure!
You must wear at your side the weapons
With which you killed many sentient beings!
You cannot deny or misrepresent these things!
Now the time has come for you to go
To the citadels of the eighteen hells.
(*He begins to lead [Lakṣanāraka] away.*)

DHARMARĀJA:
Alas! How pitiful! How terrifying!
When one has obtained a human form,
One should proceed, with highly purposeful virtuous conduct,
On the path of liberation, where inferior rebirths are left behind;
And [thus] one is never separated from peace and happiness.
But on this occasion when you obtained a human life,
You threw away positive actions like dirt,
And seized upon negative actions,
For which reason you have wasted this highly meaningful human body,
Which is difficult to obtain.

Since you have done nothing at all, other than return empty-handed [from this life],
You are [only] carrying the burden of your negative acts! How sad!
Since the actions you have carried out must ripen upon yourself,
You cannot be protected even by the power of a thousand buddhas.
So I cannot respond to this, [your appeal], in any way!
Since the results of the premeditated negative acts,
Which you carried out when you had freedom,
Will all come to ripen upon you,
Even though you wail and lament,
No one at all should feel sorry for you.
Even though you have hopes in me,
I have no means to act in any way.
Since this mirror of past actions, which reflects phenomenal existence,
Truly depicts the natural expression of virtuous and negative acts,
How can it be that no past actions will appear in the case of wrongdoers?
When the deity who is your good conscience
And the demon who is your bad conscience
Compare the black and white pebbles of past actions,
Happy is the man who has accumulated virtue!
How very remorseful are you, who have accumulated evil!
On this dangerous red passageway traversed by all,
When you are brought to trial by the executors of Yama's rites,
Even though you may have been once very powerful,
Here, it will be of no avail!
Now is the time for the hearts and lungs of all great wrongdoers to be torn apart!
Since you have practised non-virtue,
This reckoning of your past actions
Will be quicker and more powerful than lightning,
So by fleeing you will not escape,
And by showing remorse, this will be of no help!
How pitiful are the human beings of Jambudvīpa

Who do not strive to practise the [sacred] teachings!
There will be no way of helping them.
This detailed accounting of positive and negative past actions
Forbids even the most minute negative deeds –
So what are those humans who have no scruples thinking of!
Though the white path of liberation leads to joy,
And the black path of inferior rebirth leads to suffering,
The humans of Jambudvīpa do not abandon negative actions,
Nor do they practise positive actions,
[And], even though they may feel sadness and remorse,
Past actions cannot be remade.
One's past actions accompany one's body like a shadow.
I hold all rewards in respect of positive virtues,
And I exact punishments in respect of negative deeds.
Judging the balance and counterbalance,
I examine good and bad actions.
So even though you have regrets, I cannot redo anything.
Now, even though I am very merciful, there is still no way that I can help you.
Once you take the black path to the hell realms,
You cannot be saved, even if you were to be engulfed by the compassion of the Sublime Ones.
So there is absolutely no way for me to do anything.
The Conqueror has said that sentient beings must reap [the fruits of] their own past actions.
So now the Ox-headed One will lead you away!
May your negativity and obscurations be quickly purified,
And may you then attain the ultimate level of the buddhas.

OX-HEADED RAKṢA: Since it is your own doing, even though you may have regrets, what is the use of that! As for us, we are not responsible [for your actions]! We have simply distinguished between truth and lies. If you had no responsibility for your past actions, then it would be meaningless for us to harm you. Now, as this is [the outcome of] your past actions, be off quickly!

(*Then he leads [Lakṣanāraka] away by a black noose, and the black demon [representing the bad conscience] drives him from behind, goading him along the path represented by the black carpet. Then in a dark room he is subjected to shouts of 'Strike! Kill!', which cause him to cry out in all sorts of ways.*)

THE SPIRITUAL TEACHER (*then makes a detailed elucidation, beginning with the words*): O, Children of Buddha Nature, those who have committed evil deeds will be singled out in this manner and their sufferings will be the same [as those described here]. You will definitely have such experiences. So, whether this core dilemma besets you at this time or not will depend on you yourselves. From now onwards, it is therefore important for you to strive after virtue, and avoid negativity, O, Children of Buddha Nature . . .

ACT TWO

DHARMARĀJA (*as he draws a cross on his wooden slate*): Alas! Ox-headed Rakṣa, there is someone from a household in the human world whose lifespan has come to an end. This sign has appeared on my wooden slate.

OX-HEADED RAKṢA (*calling to the venomous Snake-headed Demon*): O Venomous Snake-headed One, look in your mirror! Look and see where the deceased is!

VENOMOUS SNAKE-HEADED DEMON: The land of the one whose time has come, is in north-east India. The city is called Kāmarūpa.[25] His social class, among the four classes, is the mercantile class,[26] and his name is the householder, Śrījāta. His lifespan and merits have been exhausted, so the sign of this has appeared on the wooden slate. Now be off, quickly [and fetch him]!

(*So, all three, Ox-headed Rakṣa, Boar-headed Cemetery Spirit, and the demon representing [the deceased's] bad conscience run off, while in their wake, the deity representing [the deceased's] good conscience rushes to his assistance. As soon as they have found the householder, Śrījāta, in the human world at Kāmarūpa, the Ox-headed One leads him away and the Boar-headed One holds his arm, as the demon representing [the deceased's] bad conscience chases him from behind. Meanwhile, the deity representing the good conscience offers assistance as the deceased is brought into the presence of Dharmarāja, who questions him.*)

DHARMARĀJA: O, deceased Child of Buddha Nature, have you not come from the human world? There you had a human body endowed with freedom and favourable opportunities, which is difficult to acquire. You have encountered the Buddha's teachings, which are difficult to encounter; and you have been born as a man in Jambudvīpa, where it is difficult to take birth. What positive or virtuous past actions have you gathered? When you lived in the human world, did you practise the [sacred] teachings mindful of [cultivating] mental virtues and physical purity? What compounded virtues and attributes do you possess that would enable you to be saved [from rebirth in the hells]? Did you create [images, books and stūpas] representative of buddha-body, speech and mind? Did you commission the writing and recitation of the scriptures? Did you mould terracotta imprints? Did you offer water libations? Did you clear rocks from roads? Did you remove bothersome thorns from bad roads? Did you make offerings to those above? Did you bestow charity on those below? Did you scatter barley dough and grain at anthills? What other subtle acts of virtue did you accumulate, over and above these? Also, did you study, reflect and meditate [on the Buddhist teachings], and did you keep your one-day vows and fasts? Did you receive meditative instruction, empowerments and guidance? What other virtues of this type have you accumulated? Tell me quickly now! Negative past actions related to the body are killing, of which the greatest offence is the killing of one's parents and the smallest is the killing of lice and nits, stealing, improper sexual conduct and so forth. So what negative actions of body have you accumulated?

Then the negative actions related to speech are: meaningless gossip, harsh words, slander, lies and so forth. So what negative actions of speech have you accumulated?

The negative actions related to mind are: covetousness, harmful intent, distorted views, and so on. So what negative actions have you accumulated mentally?

Also, with regard to the five inexpiable crimes and the five approximate [crimes], what negative or non-virtuous actions have you accumulated, motivated through body, speech, or mind? Tell me now in clear detail!

THE HOUSEHOLDER ŚRĪJĀTA (*in a terrified and trembling voice*): May I speak in the presence of Dharmarāja! I am the householder Śrījāta, a citizen of the city of Kāmarūpa in the north-east of India. I also have female dependants. I was a humble person, self-sufficient in food and drink. I was a faithful devotee who made fulsome offerings to all the fine spiritual teachers who came to my district. I encouraged others to engage in virtuous actions. Motivated by virtue and good intent, I have restored ruined temples, saved many living creatures from certain death, and repeatedly received profound empowerments and guidance. When I travelled around, I cleared dangerous paths; when I stayed [at home] I recited the Six-syllable Mantra, and I kept my one-day vows and fasts. I am a householder who made offerings to the Three Precious Jewels above, and gave charity to those of unfortunate birth below. I am indeed a bodhisattva. This is why everyone calls me the householder Lakṣmin ('endowed with wealth'). Such is the unbroken sequence of my virtuous actions.

As for my negative past actions, although I had the intention not to harm even a single living being, since I was submerged in the perverse world which is cyclic existence, and I had a son, and in order for him to be able to join in matrimony, I took the lives of ten animals [for the wedding feast]. I confessed the negativity of this action, and recited the *Diamond Cutter*[27] one hundred times.

Then, when I and my neighbours took the lives of many living creatures in order to pay taxes in support of the village community, I too felt much remorse and made confession. Also, since I had lived as a worldly householder, I thought that I must have unintentionally killed [many insects] underfoot and by my hands, for which reason I often felt remorse.

Since the credentials of my virtuous and negative actions are established in these ways, I beg you to consider this conduct and favour me with your compassion.

DHARMARĀJA: Well then, if it is true what you have said, then you have thought well about virtuous and negative actions, and about cause and effect; but I shall consult the mirror of past actions because you human beings are clever liars! (*He shows him the mirror.*) Look, fortunate Child of Buddha Nature! This mirror of past actions in which phenomenal existence is clearly reflected is clearer than the omniscient eye that perceives the three times. When it manifestly reveals the natural expression of virtuous and negative past actions, whatever you have done in the human world, all the virtuous and negative actions you have committed in the human world, will visibly appear, immediately. So what lies and deceit have you spoken? Look at this mirror right now! (*Then, looking at the mirror*) Well, the virtuous and negative actions of which you have now spoken are not false. Well done! You will be sent on the white path.

THE BLACK DEMON [REPRESENTING THE DECEASED'S BAD CONSCIENCE]: Hey! May I speak in the presence of Dharmarāja! This bad person called the householder Śrījāta, has indulged his whole life in negative actions and has cared only for his own long-term selfish interests. His name is householder Śrījāta, and his nickname is 'monkey-head'. As for this faithless householder Śrījāta, his [birth] year is the year of the ox, his [birth]place is Kāmarūpa city, and his background is that of the mercantile class. He engaged in the following negative actions: Hurrying uptown, he killed his father and quarrelled; then rushing downtown, he fought with his neighbours, he threw stones at the camel belonging to his neighbour Śrībhadra and although he killed it, he denied his action and lied about it. He pushed the scribe Prajñāmati's young elephant over a cliff, and, although he killed it, he denied his action and lied about it. Now, we can compare the pebbles! How will it be possible for him to take the white path? It is utterly appropriate that he should go on the black path. (*He pours three handfuls of black pebbles in [to his bowl].*)

THE WHITE DEITY [REPRESENTING THE GOOD CONSCIENCE]: May I speak in the presence of Dharmarāja! The householder Lakṣmin [Śrījāta] is a most faithful devotee. He has strong interest in the [sacred] teachings and has avoided negative actions. When about five hundred miscreants were brought to trial in the presence of the Mahārāja, he offered five hundred *srang* of gold, and saved their lives. In the Indian city of Kāmarūpa, the householder Śrījāta alone is one who possesses great faith. Now, we can compare the pebbles! How will it be possible for him to take the black path? He should now set out, guided along the white path! (*He pours out about six measures of white pebbles [into his bowl].*)

THE MONKEY-HEADED ELEMENTAL SPIRIT: Deity and demon of conscience, both of you have no need to disagree, because when I raise my scale balance, the measures of virtue and negativity will be determined by the weights. Now, if you look, [the outcome] will be obvious. (*He weighs the pebbles, whereupon the white [container] is three times heavier.*)

DHARMARĀJA: Wonderful! Those who have obtained a human body, who delight in the [sacred] teachings, and fully realise their life's potential – as this [achievement] cannot be stolen or snatched by others – will themselves find happiness through their own virtues. With respect to this way of being, such as that of the householder Lakṣmin [Śrījāta] – how wonderful it would be if all sentient beings were to do the same! Supplicate Avalokiteśvara right now, and instantly travel the white path! (*Dharmarāja prays*) I pray to the meditational deity Mahākāruṇika, at the summit of Mount Potālaka in the east! Grant your blessing that we may realise the nature of mind to be the Buddha-body of Reality! (*He then recites the* Aspirational Prayer [Calling] to the Buddhas and Bodhisattvas for Assistance[28] *and then gives formal introduction to the methods for obstructing the womb entrances during the intermediate state [of rebirth] and for choosing a womb.*[29] *Lastly, he confers the introduction to the methods of transferring [consciousness] to the pure buddha-fields.*[30] *Immediately afterwards, the curtain is suddenly drawn back, and the form of Avalokiteśvara is vividly displayed. [The householder Śrījāta] is led along the path [of virtue] represented by the white carpet, clad in fine robes, and wearing fine ornaments.*)

DHARMARĀJA (*offering praise*): O, Child of Buddha Nature, this is how one should serve the purpose of obtaining a human body. Rejoice [in this]! (*Then, he recites the following aspirational prayer of Avalokiteśvara three times.*)

OṂ MAṆI PADME HŪṂ HRĪḤ![31]
May all sentient beings, including you Śrījāta,
Be guided on the path by the essence of the Six-syllable Mantra!
May cyclic existence with its three world-systems be churned to its depths,
And may the hells be exhausted and emptied!
(*He urges [all to recite] that Six-syllable Mantra.*)

THE SPIRITUAL TEACHER: O, Children of Buddha Nature, behold this distinction between the happiness and suffering experienced by the evil 'Red-handed Butcher' and the faithful householder Śrījāta, in consequence of their disparate accumulations of virtue and negativity! As we ourselves shall also encounter such experiences soon, it is most important that we strive after virtue and refrain from negativity! (*Then, [the spiritual teacher] should confer the empowerment [of the Peaceful and Wrathful Deities], recite the auspicious verses, and perform the aspirational prayer for the dedication of merit, followed by the concluding rite.*)

COLOPHON

How wonderful! I, Padmākara, having actually seen the hells, composed this [masked drama] as an adjunct to the teaching of the *[Great] Liberation by Hearing in the Intermediate States*, in order to benefit sentient beings of the future. May it be encountered by those who are fortunate!

This concludes the *Natural Liberation of the Intermediate State of Rebirth: A Teaching Revealing the Natural Expression of Virtue and Negativity*.[32] May all be auspicious![33]

PART TWO

Supplement to the Masked Drama of Rebirth

Herein is contained the *Supplement to the Teaching Revealing the Natural Expression of Virtue and Negativity in the Intermediate State of Rebirth, entitled Gong of Divine Melody;*[1] which is an extract from the *Peaceful and Wrathful Deities: A Profound Sacred Teaching, [entitled] Natural Liberation through [Recognition of] Enlightened Intention.*[2]

I bow down to Samantabhadra and the Peaceful and Wrathful Deities!

THE SCENE

(*In the context of [the masked drama entitled]* A Teaching Revealing the Natural Expression of Virtue and Negativity which is [associated with the] Introduction to the Intermediate State of Rebirth, *the one called 'the wrongdoing Lakṣanāraka' ('hundred thousand hells') is shown entering the inferior realms. Amidst the thunderous cries of 'Strike!' and 'Kill!' uttered by the executors of Yama's rites, he travels the black path, after which Dharmarāja teaches on the disadvantages of committing negative actions to the entire audience assembled there.*[3] *Following this, the deity representing the good conscience [should appear] in a state of sadness, and should urge [the audience to recite] the Six-syllable Mantra.*)

ACT ONE

THE DEITY REPRESENTING THE GOOD CONSCIENCE: Please recite the Six-syllable Mantra once on behalf of the deceased, the wrongdoing Lakṣanāraka! OṂ MAṆI PADME HŪṂ HRĪḤ! Please recite the Six-syllable Mantra once on behalf of all beings present within the intermediate state [of rebirth]! (*Then speaking to the assembled audience*) O listen! I am the one called deity of good conscience. This wrongdoing Lakṣanāraka has committed many negative actions, as a result of which, at this moment, in the whole world, I can only find six tiny white pebbles representing his virtuous actions, but there are innumerable pebbles [here] representing his non-virtuous past actions. [Now], by the power of his bad past actions, he has been led away to the hells by the executors of Yama's rites. Although I wanted to guide him to higher rebirths, I have been unable to find a way [to help him].

All of you who inhabit the human world of Jambudvīpa, and all of you gathered here, should not now engage in negative actions but practise only virtue. These following messages are the ones which we [now] send to you [from the intermediate state of rebirth]! (*Then, circumambulating the maṇḍala,*[4] *and chanting the Six-syllable Mantra in a melodious voice, he continues with a sad demeanour.*)

How wonderful! I pray to gracious Dharmarāja,
Glorious embodiment of the activities of the buddhas of the three times,
Who manifests for the benefit of beings!
Alas! Listen and be attentive, all you gathered here!
[Considering] the difficulties of obtaining a human form,
All those who commit non-virtuous and negative acts [while living in the world]
Will have missed the opportunity of escaping from this ocean of suffering.
All [such] beings living in this world,
Who are [all] powerless to remain [in the world] for long,
Will feel remorse when entering the jaws of the Lord of Death.
But [this remorse] will be of no benefit to them then –
For, despite their sorrows, they will be obliged to move on!

All peoples of the past have gathered family and wealth [around them],
Hoping these would last forever –
But, when [their own] impermanence and death arrive,
They set out alone, devoid of refuge or sanctuary.
The relatives and friends surrounding us in this life
Are like a gathering of shoppers at a market.
Although they seem close to us, they are not dependable.
When the market closes, the shoppers will disperse.
[Likewise,] this illusory aggregate of form,
Like a fallen cairn at the top of a pass,
Will be severed of all its flesh and bones.
This our body is not to be relied on!
Even though we have cherished this body,
[A collection] of pus, blood, serum, and sinews,
It is nonetheless [ever] on the verge of disintegration.
Even though we miss it, birds and dogs will devour it,
Even though we [try to sustain it by] engaging in ritual services,
It will be snatched away by Yama, the lord of death.
This body composed of the four elements will be left behind on the earth,
Our consciousness will travel as a wanderer through the intermediate states,
And the habitual tendencies of our negative past actions will follow like a shadow.
How pitiful that we have committed non-virtuous actions!
The deity and demon representing our good and bad conscience
Will compare the white and black pebbles of past actions,
And Dharmarāja will reveal all in the [all-seeing] mirror.
All great wrongdoers will suffer these torments.
Even though they should not commit even the slightest negative acts,
The human beings of Jambudvīpa are let down by wrongdoing!
It is by engaging in virtue that they will be reborn in the higher realms,
And by engaging in negativity that they will travel to the hells.
At this one time, when one has attained a human body,

But failed to return with at least some virtue,
What a pity it is that we carry the [alternative] burden of negativity,
And bring sufferings upon ourselves!
The hunters in the mountains,
The fishermen by the rivers,
And those who kill domestic livestock
Will transmigrate and be reborn in the eighteen hells.
Those who engage in deceit and deception,
Having adulterated measures and weights,
And those who steal, plunder or deceive
Will long roam through the three inferior existences.
Those bound to their wealth by the knot of miserliness,
Those who squander the property of others,
And those who appropriate donations made to the Three Precious Jewels,
Will long roam through the realms of anguished spirits.
This, the impact of non-virtuous past actions
Is like a thunderbolt, it is extremely powerful.
And even though we feel remorse, it will be of no help –
We will not be able to escape!
The punishment for negative actions is exacted by Yama.
In this dangerous passageway, traversed by all,
The executors of Yama's rites bring us to trial.
Pity those human beings who do not avoid negativity –
For there is no way to help them.
How severe is the attitude of Dharmarāja!
How precise is the accounting of the deity and demon of conscience!
How remorseful are the great wrongdoers!
Only by engaging in virtue, will one proceed to higher rebirths.
Alas! The body ages day by day.
The lifespan is consumed moment by moment.
Dying in turn, one after another,
Sentient beings of this errant degenerate age
Have lifespans shorter than the tail of a sheep!
All householders with many dependants, [such as this wrongdoer],
Will reap the fruits of their evil past actions in so many ways,

And even their relatives and friends will [one day] arise as their enemies.
In these bad times, keeping a household [can in itself] engender sorrow.
Now, [therefore], having attained a human body,
Endowed with freedom and favourable opportunities,
Direct your thought towards your own mind!
The critical point is to concentrate on the sacred teachings!
Then, you will be happy in this life and joyful in the next.

ACT TWO

(Then again, [in the masked drama of rebirth], when the householder Śrījāta is shown setting off for the realms of higher rebirth, he prays in the presence of Avalokiteśvara, and after [Dharmarāja] has finished reciting the aspirational prayer of Avalokiteśvara on behalf of Śrījāta, the householder is adorned with fine ornaments, and installed upon a throne. Then, before the multitude of the five hosts of ḍākinīs arrive to welcome him with music and song, at that time, the deity of good conscience should joyfully make the following prayer, telling of the advantages of abandoning negativity and practising virtue.[5])

THE DEITY REPRESENTING THE GOOD CONSCIENCE:
I pray to Samantabhadra and Samantabhadrī, the Buddha-body of Reality,
Who abide in Akaniṣṭha, the palace of reality's expanse!
I pray to Vajradhara, [lord of] the sixth [enlightened family],
Who abides in the Buddha field of the Dense Array.
I pray to the Teacher Vajrasattva,
Who abides in the Buddha field of Abhirati.
I pray to the awareness holder Prahevajra,
Who abides in the maṇḍala of spiralling rainbow lights![6]
I pray to the learned Śrī Siṃha,
Who abides in the assembly hall of Dhanakośa.
I pray to Padmākara of Oḍḍiyāna,
Who abides in the celestial palace of Lotus Light!
I pray to the ḍākinī Yeshe Tsogyal,
Who abides in the pure palace of the sky-farers!

I pray to the accomplished master Karma Lingpa,
Who abides in the buddha field of the Buddha-body of Emanation!
I pray to his spiritual son Nyinda Choje,
Who abides in the limitless palace of the [sacred] teachings!
I pray to the peerless Sūryacandra,
Who abides in the palace where the benefit of living beings is spontaneously accomplished!
I pray to the precious root spiritual teacher,
Seated on a sun and moon cushion above the crown of my head![7]
I pray to the infinitude of Peaceful and Wrathful meditational Deities,
Who abide in the maṇḍala of the Conquerors, which is one's own body![8]
I pray to the protectors of the [sacred] teachings Magon Chamdrel,
Who abide in the palace of the transmitted precepts and commitments!

How wonderful!
At this time when we have obtained a human body,
Endowed with freedom and favourable opportunities,
How amazing are our positive virtues!
At this time when our five sense-faculties are intact,
How amazing it is to be attracted by the [sacred] teachings!
At this time when we have encountered the Buddha's teaching,
How amazing it is to abandon non-virtue and negativity!
At this time when we possess illusory wealth and property,
How wonderful it is to offer these upwards to the Three Precious Jewels and downwards as charity!
Once we have abandoned negativity, there will be no more inferior rebirths.
How amazing is this householder Lakṣmin [Śrījāta], right here,
Who, having practised virtue, has obtained a higher rebirth!
How amazing is this householder Śrījāta, right here,
Who is now going [to higher rebirth] in a core-penetrating way,[9]
Without passing [further] through the intermediate state [of rebirth]!

How amazing is this householder Lakṣmin [Śrījāta],
Who has achieved happiness through the fruit of his virtue –
Śrījāta has reached the highest summit of his life's potential!

(*Thereupon, the hosts of welcoming ḍākinīs, adorned with the six kinds of bone ornaments, begin to dance, playing their ḍāmarus and bells, and, emerging from behind the door, they come to welcome him, singing* OṂ MAṆI PADME HŪṂ HRĪḤ *in a sweet melody.*)

THE HOSTS OF ḌĀKINĪS:
We have come from the land of the ḍākinīs.
We have come to invite the householder Śrījāta!
We have come from Oḍḍiyāna.
We have come to invite the householder Śrījāta!
We have come from Cāmaradvīpa.
We have come to invite the householder Śrījāta!
We have come from the Copper-coloured Mountain.
We have come to invite the householder Śrījāta!
We have come from Mount Potālaka.
We have come to invite the householder Śrījāta!
We have come from the pure realm of the sky-farers.
O, great householder Śrījāta,
Please come to the buddha fields!

(*The hosts of ḍākinīs encircle the householder, and he too begins to play the musical instruments [that he holds] in his hands and to dance with them. Then he exits together with the host of ḍākinīs.*)

This *Supplement to the Teaching Revealing the Natural Expression of Virtue and Negativity in the Intermediate State of Rebirth, entitled Gong of Divine Melody*, was composed by Namka Chokyi Gyatso on the third day of the ninth month of the sheep year at the retreat of Kharlateng, in front of the hermitage of Sangye Rinpoche, a place frequented by frontier tribes. By the power of virtue, may all beings be established on the level of Samantabhadra!

14

Liberation by Wearing: Natural Liberation of the Psycho-physical Aggregates

CONTEXT

As explained in the earlier chapters, this cycle of teachings contains a number of instructions which can effect liberation from cyclic existence, without prior experience of the meditations associated with the Vehicle of Indestructible Reality (*Vajrayāna*). Amongst these expressions of the sacred teachings is this *Liberation by Wearing*, which is said to effect liberation simply by its being worn as a mantra amulet on the body at the time of death or by its being heard at the time of death.

The text of this chapter expresses the enlightened intention of the Peaceful and Wrathful Deities in the form of mantra-letters. These mantra-letters are the resonance of the pure awareness of the deities expressed in the form of letter shapes and sounds.

Many practitioners of this cycle of teachings wear this mantra circle in an amulet throughout their lives. For others it is recommended that the mantra amulet should be worn at the time of death and not removed. It is also recommended that this text should be read aloud at the conclusion of each reading of the *Liberation by Hearing* (Chapter 11).

The Mantra Circle of the Peaceful and Wrathful Deities

Herein is contained the *Liberation by Wearing: Natural Liberation of the Psycho-physical Aggregates*,[1] an extract from the *Peaceful and Wrathful Deities: A Profound Sacred Teaching, [entitled] Natural Liberation through [Recognition of] Enlightened Intention.*[2]

I bow down to the primordial lords, Samantabhadra and Samantabhadrī,
And to the Peaceful and Wrathful Deities!

This [text] is the *Liberation by Wearing: Natural Liberation of the Psycho-physical Aggregates*,
In which [the mantras] of the Peaceful and Wrathful Deities, Those Gone to Bliss, are encompassed.

How wonderful! This is a great naturally arising [mantra circle].
The yogin who embraces this is immensely fortunate.
The yogin who encounters this is immensely fortunate.
The yogin who upholds this is immensely fortunate.
The yogin who reads this is immensely fortunate.
As it confers liberation by reading, there is no need for meditation.
As it confers liberation by wearing, there is no need for spiritual practice.
As it confers liberation through contact, there is no need for training.
As it confers liberation through feeling, there is no need for reflection.

This [mantra circle] confers natural liberation whenever it is encountered.

This is the natural liberation of the psycho-physical aggregates.

This is a field of experience of the fortunate!

[PART ONE]

How wonderful!

The enlightened intention of the father Samantabhadra

Manifests as the following naturally present mantra syllables of Atiyoga:

OṂ ĀḤ HŪṂ[3] EMA KIRI KIRI MASTABHALIBHALI SAMITASURUSURU KUNDHALIMASUMASU EKARILISUBHASTAYE CAKIRABHULITA CAYESAMUNTA CARYASUGHAYE BHITISANABHYAGHULIYE SAKARIDHUKANI MATARIBHETANA PARALIHISANA MAKHARTAKELANA SAMBHURATA MAIKACARATAMBA SURYAGHATARAYE BASHANA RANABHITI SAGHUTIPAYA GHURAGHURAPAGAKHARANALAṂ NARANARAYI THARAPAṬALAṂ SIRNASIRNABHESARASPALAṂ BHUDDHABHUDDHACHIŚASAGHELAṂ SASĀ ṚṜ ḶḸ IĪ MAMĀ RARĀ LAHA Ā[4]

This is the twenty-six line supreme essential mantra,

Through which the enlightened intention of Samantabhadra

Will naturally liberate mental apprehension in awareness,

As an indestructible chain of light, primordially pure and indivisible from Samantabhadra [when it is worn at the time of death],

While [externally] a cloudless sky will appear.

How wonderful!

The enlightened intention of the mother Samantabhadrī

Manifests as the following naturally present mantra-syllables of Atiyoga.

This is the essential mantra, liberating body, speech and mind in primordial purity:

OṂ ĀḤ HŪṂ EMA KIRI KIRI MASTABHALI SAMITASURUSURU KUNDHALIMASU EKARILISUBHASTAYE CATABHULITA CAYESAMUNTA CARYASUGHAYE BHITISANABHYAGHUYE KIRIDHAKINI

DHAKAMAHĀBHORI TANAPARALIHĪ SANAṆKHARATAKELAṂ SAMBHUDDARATA MEGACARAPATAṂ TAPASURYAGHATARA Ā MANAPARABHIHO TIṄGHURALA MASMINSAGHUTILA TAYA-GHURAGHURA RĀṆGAKHALARANALAṂ NARANARALAṂ ITHAR-PATALAṂ SIRNASIRNABHISARALAṂ SAKELAṂ SASĀ ṚṜ ḶḸ IĪ MAMĀ RARĀ[5]

This is the essential mantra through which the enlightened intention of Samantabhadrī liberates

The dynamic motion of awareness, encumbered by phenomenal characteristics, in unborn emptiness.

This is the twenty-nine line supreme essential mantra,

Through which liberation will occur in primordial purity, indivisible from Samantabhadrī, [when it is worn at the time of death],

While [externally] a clear and unobscured sky will appear.

How wonderful!

To symbolise the perfection of all enlightened attributes,

The [following] twenty-five mantras which reverse attachment are presented:[6]

To avert attachment to the sense-faculties,

[There is the mantra]: KARMA RAKṢA GHIHAṂTI.

[When it is worn at the time of death]

It will confer natural liberation by subduing the beguiling force of the dissonant mental states,

While [externally] a bright red rainbow will appear.

To avert attachment to the psycho-physical aggregates,

[There is the mantra]: BHIKARAṆA SO GAD GLING.

[When it is worn at the time of death]

It will confer natural liberation by subduing the beguiling force of the psycho-physical aggregates,

While [externally] a bright yellow rainbow will appear.

To avert attachment to all sense objects,

[There is the mantra]: BHUGARILABHADHUTRI.

[When it is worn at the time of death]

It will confer natural liberation by subduing the beguiling force of 'deva's son',
While [externally] a bright white rainbow will appear.

To let go of mental objects,
[There is the mantra]: RAMĀKALASAMIKHYE.
[When it is worn at the time of death]
It will confer natural liberation by subduing the beguiling force of the 'lord of death',
While [externally] a bright green rainbow will appear.

To sever past sensations, right where they are,
[There is the mantra]: MATAMPHAPHERAMITI.
[When it is worn at the time of death]
It will naturally liberate the ground-of-all [consciousness] in primordial purity,
While [externally] a bright blue rainbow will appear.

To recognise the appearance of compounded aggregations,
[There is the mantra]: KHAṬAREKṢASA MIG RLUNG.
[When it is worn at the time of death]
It will spontaneously liberate naturally manifesting appearances in primordial purity,
While [externally] a phenomenon like the unfolding of dazzling brocade will appear.

To enter the stronghold of awareness,
[There is the mantra]: EKARANABHECAKṢA.
[When it is worn at the time of death]
It will induce the attainment of the 'irreversible level',[7]
While [externally] *śarīraṃ* relics will appear [following the cremation].

To eradicate the continuum of bewilderment,
[There is the mantra]: YARIMUTRASAGHULI.
[When it is worn at the time of death]
It will naturally liberate the three world-systems in primordial purity,
While [externally] *churiraṃ* relics will appear [following the cremation].

To successively liberate the six classes of living beings,
[There is the mantra]: YASIRAṂ RLUNG PALAYA.
[When it is worn at the time of death]
It will naturally liberate beings of the six classes in primordial purity,
While [externally] *nyariraṃ* relics will appear [following the cremation].

To purge cyclic existence from its depths,
[There is the mantra]: MAMAKOLINAṂ SAMANTA.
[When it is worn at the time of death]
It will churn the depths of all lower existences,
While [externally] *pañcaraṃ* relics will appear [following the cremation].

To suppress apparitional reality,
[There is the mantra]: GHARILAṂBARIMAṂTI.
[When it is worn at the time of death]
It will guide [the deceased] to the genuine reality,
While [externally] *serriraṃ* relics will appear [following the cremation].

To let go of the 'source of the play [of phenomena]',
[There is the mantra]: BUGASIṄHAPHAṄGALA.
[When it is worn at the time of death]
It will liberate the phenomena that arise, right where they are,
While [externally] manifold shimmering rainbows will appear.

To sever the tethers of attachment,
[There is the mantra]: RAMISIPIKHETAPA.
[When it is worn at the time of death]
It will liberate objects of attachment in the expanse [of reality],
While [externally] a clear and bright sky will appear.

To focus on the chains [of light],
[There is the mantra]: BHIKHUMALABATAṂKE.
[When it is worn at the time of death]
It will induce the 'visionary appearance of increasing contemplative experience',[8]
While [externally] patterns will arise from the rainbow colours in the sky.

To view the seal of the deity,
[There is the mantra]: SAMANYIVADHERABA.
[When it is worn at the time of death]
It will induce the 'visionary appearance of reaching the limit of awareness',[9]
While [externally] the forms of the deities will appear.

To purify mistaken views and meditations,
[There is the mantra]: VAJRA SATTVA ṬIDHOME.
[When it is worn at the time of death]
Awareness will be naturally perfected,
While [externally] white rainbow lights will appear.

To simultaneously reach the levels and the paths,
[There is the mantra]: GHEPASUGHARNAMYE.
[When it is worn at the time of death]
The levels and paths will be simultaneously perfected,
While [externally] the natural sound of reality will resound.

To sever the basis of views which indulge in mental activity,
[There is the mantra]: DHARMAPATISAGHULI.
[When it is worn at the time of death]
Digressions will be liberated, right where they occur,
While [externally] white rays of light will appear.

To cause the three buddha-bodies to manifest as the path,
[There is the mantra]: RASMISAMAKHARGAD TSHE.
[When it is worn at the time of death]
The three buddha-bodies will arise as the path,
While [externally] perceptions of light will appear.

To cause the visionary appearances to genuinely arise,
[There is the mantra]: RŪPASAMIMITALI.
[When it is worn at the time of death]
A simultaneous, naked liberation will occur,
While [externally] winds and breezes will arise in the atmosphere.

To terminate attachment to sound,
[There is the mantra]: ṄATIBALAGILISA.
[When it is worn at the time of death]
Liberation will occur in the inexpressible, ineffable state,
While [externally] the number of rainbow lights that are seen will transcend recollection.

To master the levels of exalted meditative concentration,
[There is the mantra]: GHACCHAPAYAṂPA ETAṂ.
[When it is worn at the time of death]
The singular perfection of the levels and paths will be reached,
While [externally] the number of rainbow lights that are seen will induce non-conceptuality.

To extend buddha-activity to its limits,
[There is the mantra]: KARMĀ EKANUSA.
[When it is worn at the time of death]
Liberation will occur as essence, natural expression, and compassionate energy,[10]
While [externally] manifold subtle relics will appear [following the cremation.]

To avert expressed attachment to buddhahood,
[There is the mantra]: SANTRIMAMAKARMĀTA.
[When it is worn at the time of death]
The three buddha-bodies will be liberated in the space of primordial purity,
While [externally] a clear sky and shimmering rainbow will appear.

To discover the abodes of the Conquerors and their children,
[There is the mantra]: ṄALAKHEPAKILISA.
[When it is worn at the time of death]
It will liberate all beings who wear it and are touched by its breath,[11]
While [externally] rainbows and subtle relics will multiply.

How wonderful!
Since the unified enlightened intention of non-dual Samantabhadra and Samantabhadrī[12] is naturally present,

Each [of these individual mantras] has the capacity to confer liberation.
Thus they are [known as] the twenty-five seminal points, or mantra lines,
In which reality naturally resonates and naturally arises.
SAMAYA

[PART TWO]

How wonderful!
Then the male and female consorts [Samantabhadra and Samantabhadrī], having entered into non-dual union,
Emit multiple male and female emanations,
From which arises the maṇḍala of the hundred enlightened families of the Peaceful and Wrathful Deities.[13]

Within the naturally arising diffusive expanse of the enlightened intention of the Forty-two Peaceful Deities,
Like the sun emerging from the clouds,
This naturally arising enlightened intention then manifests as follows,
Within the field of experience of fortunate beings:

OṂ ĀḤ HŪṂ BODHICITTA MAHĀSUKHA JÑĀNADHĀTU ĀḤ is the unified enlightened intention of the Forty-two Peaceful Deities.
Thus[14] the mass of conceptual thoughts will be liberated in primordial purity,
As an expanse of supreme pristine cognition,
While [externally] the indestructible sound of these sixteen syllables
And inestimable rainbow lights and relics will appear.

How wonderful!
Then the individual enlightened intentions of the Forty-two Peaceful Deities naturally arise:

OṂ HŪṂ SVĀ ĀṂ HĀ
The mantra-letters of the naturally present causal basis[15] arise
In the form of these seed-syllables of the five male buddhas of the enlightened families.
Thus, the five psycho-physical aggregates will be naturally liberated,
And they will arise as the five pristine cognitions,
While [externally] five kinds of bone relic will appear [following the cremation].

MŪṂ LĀṂ MĀṂ PHYĀṂ TĀṂ
The mantra-letters of the naturally present causal basis arise
In the form of these seed-syllables of the five female buddhas of the enlightened families.
Thus, the five elements will be naturally liberated,
And they will arise inseparably from the five female buddhas,
While [externally] five-coloured rainbows will appear.

OṂ JINAJIK is the enlightened intention of Vairocana.
Thus the aggregate of form will be liberated in the pristine cognition of reality's expanse,
While [externally] white rainbow lights will shine,
And five-coloured *pañcaraṃ* relics, indicating attainment of the five buddha-bodies,
Will be retrieved from the heart [following cremation],
For which reason these are known as the 'supreme bone relics of the Tathāgata family'.

HŪṂ VAJRADHṚK is the enlightened intention of Vajrasattva.
Thus the aggregate of consciousness will be liberated in the mirror-like pristine cognition,
While [externally] blue rainbow lights will shine,
And blue-coloured *churiraṃ* relics, indicating an increase in enlightened attributes,
Will be retrieved from the blood [following cremation],
For which reason these are known as the 'supreme bone relics of the Vajra family'.

SVĀ RATNADHṚK is the enlightened intention of Ratnasambhava.
Thus the aggregate of feeling will be liberated in the pristine cognition of sameness,
While [externally] yellow rainbow lights will shine,
And yellow-coloured *seriraṃ* relics, indicating the fulfilment of all wishes,
Will be retrieved from the serous fluid [following cremation],
For which reason these are known as the 'supreme bone relics of the Ratna family'.

ĀṂ ĀROLIK is the enlightened intention of Amitābha.
Thus the aggregate of perception will be liberated in the pristine cognition of discernment,
While [externally] red rainbow lights will shine,
And red-coloured *śarīraṃ* relics, indicating attainment of the unborn reality,
Will be retrieved from the flesh [following cremation],
For which reason these are known as the 'supreme bone relics of the Padma family'.

HĀ PRAJÑĀDHṚK is the enlightened intention of Amoghasiddhi.
Thus the aggregate of motivational tendencies will be liberated in the pristine cognition of accomplishment,
While [externally] green rainbow lights will shine,
And green-coloured *nyariraṃ* relics, indicating the attainment of the emanational body,
Will be retrieved from the marrow [following cremation],
For which reason these are known as the 'supreme bone relics of the Karma family'.

MŪṂ DHĀTVĪŚVARĪ is the enlightened intention of [Ākāśa]dhātvīśvarī.
Thus the appearances of the space [element] will be naturally liberated,
While [externally] piercing white[16] rainbow lights will shine in the sky.

LĀṂ DVEṢARATI is the enlightened intention of Buddhalocanā.
Thus the earth element will be naturally liberated,
While [externally] piercing yellow rainbow lights will shine in the sky.

MĀṂ MOHARATI is the enlightened intention of Māmakī.
Thus the water element will be naturally liberated,
While [externally] piercing blue rainbow lights will shine in the sky.

PĀṂ RĀGARATI is the enlightened intention of Pāṇḍaravāsinī.
Thus the fire element will be naturally liberated,
While [externally] piercing red rainbow lights will shine in the sky.

TĀṂ VAJRARATI is the enlightened intention of Samayatārā.
Thus the wind element will be naturally liberated,
While [externally] piercing green rainbow lights will shine in the sky.

KṢIṂ MAI HŪṂ TRĀṂ HRĪḤ MŪṂ THLĪṂ JIṂ
The mantra-letters of the naturally present causal basis arise
In the form of these seed-syllables of the Eight Male Bodhisattvas.
Thus the eight classes of consciousness will be naturally liberated,
And arise inseparably from the eight male bodhisattvas,
While [externally] many subtle relics will appear [following the cremation].

KṢIṂ HI RĀJĀYA SVĀHĀ [is the enlightened intention of the male bodhisattva Kṣitigarbha].
Thus visual consciousness will be naturally liberated,
And arise inseparably from Kṣitigarbha.

MAI DHARAṆĪ SVĀHĀ [is the enlightened intention of the male bodhisattva Maitreya].
Thus auditory consciousness will be naturally liberated,
And arise inseparably from Maitreya.

HŪṂ SARĀJĀYA SVĀHĀ [is the enlightened intention of the male bodhisattva Samantabhadra].
Thus olfactory consciousness will be naturally liberated,
And arise inseparably from Samantabhadra.

TRĀṂ Ā GARBHAYAḤ SVĀHĀ [is the enlightened intention of the male bodhisattva Ākāśagarbha].
Thus gustatory consciousness will be naturally liberated,
And arise inseparably from Ākāśagarbha.

HRĪḤ HA HŪṂ PADMĀBHATAMAḤ SVĀHĀ [is the enlightened intention of the male bodhisattva Avalokiteśvara].
Thus tactile consciousness will be naturally liberated,
And arise inseparably from Avalokiteśvara.

MŪṂ ŚRĪ ĀṂ RĀGĀYA SVĀHĀ [is the enlightened intention of the male bodhisattva Mañjuśrī].[17]
Thus mental consciousness will be naturally liberated,
And arise inseparably from Mañjuśrī.

THLĪṂ NISĀRAMBHĀYA SVĀHĀ [is the enlightened intention of the male bodhisattva Nivāraṇaviṣkambhin].
Thus the ground-of-all consciousness will be naturally liberated,
And arise inseparably from Nivāraṇaviṣkambhin.

JIṂ KURUPĀṆI HRĪḤ SVĀHĀ [is the enlightened intention of the male bodhisattva Vajrapāṇi].
Thus the dissonant consciousness will be naturally liberated,
And arise inseparably from Vajrapāṇi.

Through these enlightened intentions of the Eight Male Bodhisattvas
The eight classes of consciousness will be naturally liberated,
And diverse, shimmering rainbow lights will appear.[18]

HŪṂ HŪṂ TRĀṂ JAḤ HRĪḤ VAṂ HOḤ ĀḤ
The mantra-letters of the naturally present causal basis arise
In the form of these seed-syllables of the Eight Female Bodhisattvas.
Thus mental constructs associated with the eight objects of consciousness will be naturally liberated,
[And arise inseparably from the eight female bodhisattvas],
While [externally], a shower of flowers will fall.

HŪṂ LĀSYE SAMAYAS TVAṂ [is the enlightened intention of Lāsyā].
Thus mental constructs associated with physical form will be naturally liberated,
And arise inseparably from Lāsyā.

HŪṂ PUṢPE ĀVEŚĀ [is the enlightened intention of Puṣpā].
Thus mental constructs associated with past events will be naturally liberated,
And arise inseparably from Puṣpā.

TRĀṂ MĀLYE SAMAYA HOḤ [is the enlightened intention of Mālyā].
Thus mental constructs associated with apparent phenomena will be naturally liberated,
And arise inseparably from Mālyā.

JAḤ DHŪPE PRAVEŚAYAS TVAṂ [is the enlightened intention of Dhūpā].
Thus mental constructs associated with objects of smell will be naturally liberated,
And arise inseparably from Dhūpā.

HRĪḤ GĪTI RĀGO'HAṂ [is the enlightened intention of Gītā].
Thus mental constructs associated with objects of sound will be naturally liberated,
And arise inseparably from Gītā.

VAṂ DĪPASUKHINĪ [is the enlightened intention of Ālokā].
Thus mental constructs associated with future events will be naturally liberated,
And arise inseparably from Ālokā.

HOḤ GANDHE CITTA HOḤ [is the enlightened intention of Gandhā].
Thus mental constructs associated with present events will be naturally liberated,
And arise inseparably from Gandhā.

ĀḤ NṚTI RĀGAYĀMI [is the enlightened intention of Nartī].[19]
Thus mental constructs associated with objects of taste will be naturally liberated,
And arise inseparably from Nartī.

Through these enlightened intentions of the Eight Female Bodhisattvas,
Mental constructs associated with the eight objects of consciousness will be naturally liberated,
While [externally], a shower of flowers and sounds of music will manifest, as the transfer of consciousness occurs.

KRIṂ PRAṂ TRUṂ KṢAṂ SRUṂ YE
The mantra-letters of the naturally present causal basis arise
In the form of these seed-syllables of the Six Sages.
Thus the six dissonant mental states will be naturally liberated,
The womb entrances of the six classes of beings will be obstructed,
And the Buddha-body of Emanation will continuously manifest for the benefit of sentient beings,
While [externally] manifold subtle relics will appear [following the cremation].

OṂ MUNI KRIṂ SVĀHĀ is the enlightened intention of Devendra Śakra.
Thus pride, the entrance to the god realms, will be obstructed.

OṂ MUNI PRAṂ SVĀHĀ is the enlightened intention of Vemacitra.
Thus envy, the entrance to the antigod realm, will be obstructed.

OṂ MUNI TRUṂ SVĀHĀ is the enlightened intention of Śākyamuni.
Thus desire, the entrance to the human realm, will be obstructed.

OṂ MUNI KṢAṂ SVĀHĀ is the enlightened intention of Sthirasiṃha.
Thus delusion, the entrance to the animal realm, will be obstructed.

OṂ MUNI SRUṂ SVĀHĀ is the enlightened intention of Jvālamukha.
Thus miserliness, the entrance to the anguished-spirit realms, will be obstructed.

OṂ MUNI YE SVĀHĀ is the enlightened intention of Dharmarāja.
Thus hatred, the entrance to the hell realms, will be obstructed.

Through these enlightened intentions of the Six Emanational Sages,
The entrances to the six imperfect classes of existence will be obstructed,
And the [altruistic] activities of the pure emanational bodies will manifest,
While [externally] shimmering rainbows will appear amidst the clouds.

HŪṂ HŪṂ HŪṂ HŪṂ JAḤ HŪṂ VAṂ HOḤ
The mantra-letters of the naturally present causal basis arise
In the form of these [seed syllables of] the Eight Male and Female Gatekeepers.
Thus, the entrances to the four types of birth will be obstructed,

And the four immeasurable aspirations will grow within the mental continuum,
While [externally] the four corresponding rainbow lights [white, yellow, red and green] will appear [following the cremation].

OṂ VAJRAKRODHA VIJAYA HŪṂ is the enlightened intention of Vijaya.
Thus mental constructs associated with eternalism will be naturally liberated,
And all acts of pacification will be accomplished.

OṂ VAJRAKRODHA YAMĀNTAKA HŪṂ is the enlightened intention of Yamāntaka.
Thus mental constructs associated with nihilism will be naturally liberated,
And all acts of enrichment will be accomplished.

OṂ PADMĀNTAKṚT HAYAGRĪVA HŪṂ is the enlightened intention of Hayagrīvarāja.
Thus mental constructs associated with egoism will be naturally liberated,
And all acts of subjugation will be accomplished.

OṂ VAJRAKRODHA AMṚTAKUṆḌALI HŪṂ is the enlightened intention of Amṛtakuṇḍalin.
Thus mental constructs associated with substantialism[20] will be naturally liberated,
And all acts of wrath will be accomplished.

Through these enlightened intentions of the Four Male Gatekeepers,
The four extremes, including eternalism and nihilism, will be naturally liberated,
And the four enlightened activities will be accomplished,
While [externally] the [four] corresponding rainbow lights – white, yellow, red and green, will appear.

OṂ VAJRĀṄKUŚĀ JAḤ is the enlightened intention of Aṅkuśā.
Thus the entrance to miraculous birth will be obstructed,
And immeasurable compassion will grow within the mental continuum.

OṂ VAJRAPĀŚĀ HŪṂ is the enlightened intention of Pāśā.
Thus the entrance to womb birth will be obstructed,
And immeasurable loving kindness will grow within the mental continuum.

OṂ VAJRASPHOṬĀ VAṂ is the enlightened intention of Sphoṭā.
Thus the entrance to egg birth will be obstructed,
And immeasurable sympathetic joy will grow within the mental continuum.

OṂ VAJRAGHAṆṬĀ HOḤ is the enlightened intention of Gaṇṭhā.
Thus the entrance to birth through heat and moisture will be obstructed,
And immeasurable equanimity will grow within the mental continuum.

[Through these enlightened intentions of the Four Female Gatekeepers,
The entrances to the four types of birth will be obstructed,
And the four immeasurable aspirations will grow within the mental continuum,
While [externally] the four corresponding rainbow lights [white, yellow, red and green] will appear.][21]

Through this expansive diffusion of the enlightened intention
Of the buddha-mind of the Forty-two Peaceful Deities,
The aggregate of conceptual thoughts is naturally liberated,
Causing bone-relics, small relics, and rainbow lights to appear.[22]

How wonderful!
Within the naturally arising diffusive expanse of the enlightened intention of the Sixty Herukas,
Like the sun emerging from the clouds,
This naturally arising enlightened intention then manifests as follows,
Within the field of experience of fortunate beings:

OṂ RULU RULU HŪṂ BHYOḤ HŪṂ
This mantra is the unified enlightened intention of the Sixty Herukas.
Thus mental constructs associated with dissonant mental states are liberated in primordial purity, as an expanse of supreme pristine cognition,
While [externally] the indestructible sound of the eight syllables of the RULU mantra will resound,
And manifold white fiery lights will shine [in the sky following the cremation].

How wonderful!
[Then], the enlightened intentions of all the Sixty Herukas naturally arise individually:

HŪṂ HŪṂ HŪṂ HŪṂ HŪṂ HŪṂ
The mantra-letters of the naturally present causal basis arise
In the form of these seed-syllables of the Six Male Herukas.
Thus the six dissonant mental states will be naturally liberated,
And arise inseparably from the Six Herukas,
While [externally] six-coloured flames will appear [during the cremation].

HŪṂ HŪṂ HŪṂ HŪṂ HŪṂ HŪṂ
The mantra-letters of the naturally present causal basis arise
In the form of these seed-syllables of the Six Īśvarī.
Thus mental constructs associated with the six objects will be naturally liberated,
And arise inseparably from the Six Īśvarī,
While [externally] six-coloured rainbow lights will appear [during the cremation].

OṂ MAHĀ KRODHA MAHĀŚRĪHERUKA HŪṂ PHAṬ is the enlightened intention of Mahottara Heruka.

Thus the dissonant mental state of ignorance will be liberated in primordial purity,

While [externally] dark brown flames will spiral to the right [during the cremation],

Unequivocally indicating an irreversible liberation, inseparable from Mahottara.

OṂ BUDDHA KRODHA MAHĀŚRĪHERUKA HŪṂ PHAṬ is the enlightened intention of Buddha Heruka.

Thus the dissonant mental state of delusion will be liberated in primordial purity,

While [externally] brilliant white flames will shoot upwards [during the cremation],

Unequivocally indicating liberation inseparable from Buddha Heruka,

[As the deceased will be born in the central Buddha field of the Dense Array].

OṂ VAJRA KRODHA MAHĀŚRĪHERUKA HŪṂ PHAṬ is the enlightened intention of Vajra Heruka.

Thus the dissonant mental state of hatred will be liberated in primordial purity,

While [externally] dark blue flames will shoot towards the east [during the cremation],

Unequivocally indicating [liberation] inseparable from Vajra Heruka,

As [the deceased] will be born in the [eastern] Buddha field of Manifest Joy.

OṂ RATNA KRODHA MAHĀŚRĪHERUKA HŪṂ PHAṬ is the enlightened intention of Ratna Heruka.

Thus the dissonant mental state of pride will be liberated in primordial purity,

While [externally] dark yellow flames will shoot towards the south [during the cremation],

Unequivocally indicating [liberation] inseparable from Ratna Heruka,

As [the deceased] will be born in the southern Buddha field of The Joyful.

OṂ PADMA KRODHA MAHĀŚRĪHERUKA HŪṂ PHAṬ is the enlightened intention of Padma Heruka.
Thus the dissonant mental state of desire will be liberated in primordial purity,
While [externally] dark red flames will shoot towards the west [during the cremation],
Unequivocally indicating [liberation] inseparable from Padma Heruka,
As [the deceased] will be born in the western Buddha field of The Blissful.

OṂ KARMA KRODHA MAHĀŚRĪHERUKA HŪṂ PHAṬ is the enlightened intention of Karma Heruka.
Thus the dissonant mental state of envy will be liberated in primordial purity,
While [externally] dark green flames will shoot towards the north [during the cremation],
Unequivocally indicating [liberation] inseparable from Karma Heruka,
As [the deceased] will be born in the northern Buddha field of the Matrix of Activity.

OṂ MAHĀ KRODHEŚVARĪ TVAṂ is the enlightened intention of Mahākrodheśvarī.
Thus mental constructs associated with apparent phenomena will be naturally liberated,
While [externally] smoke will spiral to the right [during the cremation],
Indicating liberation inseparable from Dhātvīśvarī.

OṂ BUDDHA KRODHEŚVARĪ TVAṂ is the enlightened intention of Buddhakrodheśvarī.
Thus mental constructs associated with physical objects will be naturally liberated,
While [externally] smoke will spiral upwards [during the cremation],
Indicating liberation inseparable from Buddhakrodheśvarī.

OṂ VAJRA KRODHEŚVARĪ TVAṂ is the enlightened intention of Vajrakrodheśvarī.
Thus mental constructs associated with objects of sound will be naturally liberated,
While [externally] smoke will spiral to the east [during the cremation],
Indicating liberation inseparable from Vajrakrodheśvarī.

OṂ RATNA KRODHEŚVARĪ TVAṂ is the enlightened intention of Ratnakrodheśvarī.
Thus mental constructs associated with objects of smell will be naturally liberated,
While [externally] smoke will spiral to the south [during the cremation],
Indicating liberation inseparable from Ratnakrodheśvarī.

OṂ PADMA KRODHEŚVARĪ TVAṂ is the enlightened intention of Padmakrodheśvarī.
Thus mental constructs associated with objects of taste will be naturally liberated,
While [externally] smoke will spiral to the west [during the cremation],
Indicating liberation inseparable from Padmakrodheśvarī.

OṂ KARMA KRODHEŚVARĪ TVAṂ is the enlightened intention of Karmakrodheśvarī.
Thus mental constructs associated with objects of touch will be naturally liberated,
While [externally] smoke will spiral to the north [during the cremation],
Indicating liberation inseparable from Karmakrodheśvarī.

Through the expansive diffusion of these naturally arising enlightened intentions of the Twelve Principal Herukas,
The host of mental constructs associated with the dissonant states will be naturally liberated,
While the five buddha fields will be mastered.

HA HA HA HA HA HA HA HA
The mantra-syllables of the naturally present causal basis arise
In the form of these seed-syllables of the Eight Mātaraḥ.
Thus mental constructs associated with the eight classes of consciousness will be naturally liberated,
While [externally] fiery sparks will spiral and shoot to the right [during the cremation].

OṂ VAJRA GAURĪ HA is the enlightened intention of Gaurī, the white female wrathful deity.
Thus mental constructs associated with the dissonant consciousness will be subdued.

OṂ VAJRA CAURĪ HA is the enlightened intention of Caurī, the yellow female wrathful deity.
Thus beings of the six classes will be propelled into higher rebirths.

OṂ VAJRA PRAMOHĀ HA is the enlightened intention of Pramohā, the red female wrathful deity.
Thus beings of the six classes will be steered away from cyclic existence.

OṂ VAJRA VETĀLĪ HA is the enlightened intention of Vetālī, the dark green female wrathful deity.
Thus liberation will occur in the enlightened intention of unchanging reality.

OṂ VAJRA PUKKASĪ HA is the enlightened intention of Pukkasī, the yellowish red female wrathful deity.
Thus beings will be propelled from dissonant mental states [into higher rebirths].

OṂ VAJRA GHASMARĪ HA is the enlightened intention of Ghasmarī, the green female wrathful deity.
Thus cyclic existence will be purified, right where it is,
While [externally] fiery sparks will spiral and shoot to the right during the cremation.

OṂ VAJRA CAṆḌĀLĪ HA is the enlightened intention of Caṇḍālī, the pale yellow female wrathful deity.
Thus dissonant mental states and erroneous thoughts will be severed.

OṂ VAJRA ŚMAŚĀNĪ HA is the enlightened intention of Smaśānī, the pale blue female wrathful deity.
Thus the buttresses of dissonant mental states will be severed.

Through these enlightened intentions of the Eight Mātaraḥ,
[The deceased] will be guided out of cyclic existence,
While [externally] fiery sparks will spiral and shoot forth [during the cremation].

HE HE HE HE HE HE HE HE
The mantra-letters of the naturally present causal basis arise
In the form of these seed-syllables of the Eight Piśācī.
Thus mental constructs associated with the eight objects of consciousness will be naturally liberated,
While [externally] fiery sparks will shoot forth in chains [during the cremation].

OṂ VAJRA SIṂHAMUKHĪ HE is the enlightened intention of Siṃhamukhī.
Thus cyclic existence will be purified in its primordial nature.

OṂ VAJRA VYĀGHRĪMUKHĪ HE is the enlightened intention of Vyāghrīmukhī.
Thus cyclic existence will be purified in its entirety.

OṂ VAJRA ŚṚGĀLAMUKHĪ HE is the enlightened intention of Śṛgālamukhī.
Thus dissonant mental states will be purified from their very roots.

OṂ VAJRA ŚVĀNAMUKHĪ HE is the enlightened intention of Śvānamukhī.
Thus the depths of cyclic existence will be churned.

OṂ VAJRA GṚḌHRAMUKHĪ HE is the enlightened intention of Gṛḍhramukhī.
Thus the three poisons will be severed from their roots.

OṂ VAJRA KAṄKAMUKHĪ HE is the enlightened intention of Kaṅkamukhī.
Thus beings will be guided from the pit of cyclic existence.

OṂ VAJRA KĀKAMUKHĪ HE is the enlightened intention of Kākamukhī.
Thus dissonant mental states will be purified in the creative play of [reality's] expanse.

OṂ VAJRA ULŪKAMUKHĪ HE is the enlightened intention of Ulūkamukhī.
Thus the buttresses of erroneous views will be severed.

Through these enlightened intentions of the Eight Piśācī,
Mental constructs associated with the eight objects will be naturally liberated.

JAḤ HŪṂ VAṂ HOḤ
The mantra-letters of the naturally present causal basis arise
In the form of these seed-syllables of the Four Female Gatekeepers [of the wrathful assembly].
Thus the entrances to the four types of birth will be obstructed,
And the four immeasurable aspirations will grow within the mental continuum.

OṂ VAJRĀṄKUŚĀ JAḤ is the enlightened intention of white horse-headed [Aṅkuśā Vajratejasī].
Thus beings will be pulled from the abodes of cyclic existence,
[And immeasurable compassion will grow within the mental continuum].

OṂ VAJRAPĀŚĀ HŪṂ is the enlightened intention of yellow sow-headed [Pāśā Vajrāmoghā].
Thus erroneous mental constructs will be securely tied,
[And immeasurable loving kindness will grow within the mental continuum].

OṂ VAJRASPHOṬĀ VAṂ is the enlightened intention of red lion-headed [Sphoṭā Vajrālokā].
Thus the dissonant mental state of ignorance will be firmly bound,
[And immeasurable sympathetic joy will grow within the mental continuum].

OṂ VAJRAGHAṆṬĀ HOḤ is the enlightened intention of green snake-headed [Gaṇṭhā Vajravetālī].
Thus mental constructs associated with the five poisons will be subdued,
[And immeasurable equanimity will grow within the mental continuum].

BHYOḤ BHYOḤ BHYOḤ BHYOḤ BHYOḤ BHYOḤ BHYOḤ
BHYOḤ BHYOḤ BHYOḤ BHYOḤ BHYOḤ BHYOḤ BHYOḤ
BHYOḤ BHYOḤ BHYOḤ BHYOḤ BHYOḤ BHYOḤ BHYOḤ
BHYOḤ BHYOḤ BHYOḤ BHYOḤ BHYOḤ BHYOḤ BHYOḤ
The mantra-letters of the naturally present causal basis arise
[In the form of these seed-syllables] of the Twenty-eight Īśvarī.
Thus the aggregates of bewildered thought will be purified,
While [externally] sounds, lights and rays will appear [during the cremation].

OṂ MANURĀKṢASĪ BHYOḤ is the enlightened intention of Manurākṣasī.[23]
OṂ BRAHMĀṆĪ BHYOḤ is the enlightened intention of Brahmāṇī.
OṂ RAUDRĪ BHYOḤ is the enlightened intention of Raudrī
OṂ INDRĀṆĪ BHYOḤ is the enlightened intention of Indrāṇī.
OṂ KAUMĀRĪ BHYOḤ is the enlightened intention of Kaumārī.
OṂ VAIṢṆĀVĪ BHYOḤ is the enlightened intention of Vaiṣṇāvī.
OṂ VAJRA PIṄGALĀ BHYOḤ is the enlightened intention of Vajra [Piṅgalā].
OṂ SAUMĪ BHYOḤ is the enlightened intention of Saumī.
OṂ AMṚTĀ BHYOḤ is the enlightened intention of Amṛtā.
OṂ DAṆḌĪ BHYOḤ is the enlightened intention of Daṇḍī.
OṂ RĀKṢASĪ BHYOḤ is the enlightened intention of Rākṣasī.
OṂ BHAKṢASĪ BHYOḤ is the enlightened intention of Bhakṣasī.

OṂ RATĪ BHYOḤ is the enlightened intention of Ratī.

OṂ RUDHIRAMADĪ BHYOḤ is the enlightened intention of Rudhiramadī.

OṂ EKACĀRAṆĪ BHYOḤ is the enlightened intention of Ekacāraṇī Rākṣasī.

OṂ MANOHĀRIKĀ BHYOḤ is the enlightened intention of Manohārikā.

OṂ SIDDHIKARĪ BHYOḤ is the enlightened intention of Siddhikarī.

OṂ VĀYUDEVĪ BHYOḤ is the enlightened intention of Vāyudevī.

OṂ MAHĀMĀRAṆĀ BHYOḤ is the enlightened intention of Mahāmāraṇā.

OṂ AGNĀYĪ BHYOḤ is the enlightened intention of Agnāyī.

OṂ VĀRĀHĪ BHYOḤ is the enlightened intention of Vārāhī.

OṂ CĀMUṆḌĪ BHYOḤ is the enlightened intention of Cāmuṇḍī.

OṂ BHUJANĀ BHYOḤ is the enlightened intention of Bhujanā.

OṂ VARUṆĀNĪ BHYOḤ is the enlightened intention of Varuṇānī.

OṂ MAHĀKĀLĪ BHYOḤ is the enlightened intention of Vajra Mahākālī.

OṂ MAHĀCHĀGALĀ BHYOḤ is the enlightened intention of Vajra Mahāchāgalā.

OṂ MAHĀKUMBHAKARṆĪ BHYOḤ is the enlightened intention of Vajra Mahākumbhakarṇī.

OṂ VAJRA LAMBODARĀ BHYOḤ is the enlightened intention of Vajra Lambodarā.

Through these enlightened intentions of the Twenty-eight Īśvarī,

The bewildering apparitions of the intermediate state will be naturally purified,

While [external] signs such as sounds, lights, rays and [bursts of] fire and smoke will appear as the transfer of consciousness occurs.

How wonderful!
The innermost heart[-mantras] of the Four Great Wrathful [Male Gatekeepers],
The subjugators who naturally liberate the four beguiling forces,
Appear as an unobstructed lion's roar,
Whose naturally arising enlightened intentions resound as follows:

OṂ VAJRA KRODHA KYEMA KYERI KARIMASTA BHALI BHALI ATA EKARASULI BHASATI ENILANILA KĀ EBINA ABHISIÑCA
This lion's roar which subdues the beguiling force of the psycho-physical aggregates,
[Is the enlightened intention of Mahābala Kumārakalaśa].
Thus one will dissolve indivisibly in the body of Buddha Kumārakalaśa,
And liberation will occur in the naturally present expanse.

OṂ VAJRA KRODHA MAHĀMUDRA JÑĀNA OJASVĀ HŪṂ SPHARAṆA PHAṬ SVĀHĀ
This lion's roar which subdues the beguiling force of the dissonant mental states,
[Is the enlightened intention of Yamāntaka Vajra Heruka].
Thus one will dissolve indivisibly in the body of Vajra Heruka,
And buddhahood will then be obtained.
One will be naturally liberated beyond the boundaries of the five poisons,
And emanations, and their emanations, will bring about the welfare of sentient beings.

OṂ VAJRA KRODHA AMṚTAKUṆḌALI HŪṂ CHINDHA CHINDHA BHINDHA BHINDHA HANA HANA DAHA DAHA PACA PACA HŪṂ PHAṬ
This lion's roar which subdues the beguiling force of 'deva's son',
[Is the enlightened intention of Amṛtakuṇḍalin].
Thus one will dissolve indivisibly in the body of Amṛtakuṇḍalin,
And buddhahood will then be obtained.
One will be freed from the sufferings of the lower existences,
And enlightened activities will be accomplished in all directions, without distinction.

OṂ VAJRA KRODHA HAYAGRĪVA HRĪḤ SARVA TATHĀGATA MAHĀPAÑCA OṂ ĀYURJÑĀNA MAHĀPUṆYE TIṢṬHA OṂ

This lion's roar which subdues the beguiling force of the lord of death,

[Is the enlightened intention of Hayagrīvarāja].

Thus Hayagrīvarāja's accomplishment of long-life will be attained,

And, abiding in the state of reality, which is supreme bliss,

Ignorance and other dissonant mental states will be uprooted,

The five poisons will be liberated, right where they are, without being renounced,

And the habitual tendencies of beginningless cyclic existence will be swept away.

[Through these innermost heart-mantras of the Four Great Wrathful Gatekeepers],

The four beguiling forces will be destroyed and liberated in the four buddha-bodies,

While [externally] bone relics, minor relics, and rainbow lights will appear [during the cremation].

[How wonderful!

Through the expansive diffusion of these enlightened intentions of the buddha-mind of the Sixty Herukas,

The mass of bewildered thoughts is naturally liberated,

While [externally] sounds, lights and rays, and bursts of fire or smoke, spiralling to the right of the pyre,

As well as rainbow lights, bone relics, and small relics, and other signs, will appear.][24]

[PART THREE]

How wonderful!

The enlightened intention of the unimpeded Buddha-body of Emanation

Arises as the following six syllables,

By which the six classes of sentient beings are naturally liberated into the expanse [of actual reality]:

'A A HA ŚA SA MA

Through this enlightened intention free from origination or cessation,
These six syllables which are the six naturally present seminal points [of light],
Will naturally liberate the six classes of sentient beings within the expanse [of reality],[25]
While [externally], numerous subtle relics and diverse rainbow lights will appear [during the cremation].

How wonderful!
The supreme enlightened intention of the Hundred Genuine Enlightened Families
Appears as the secret hundred syllable mantra,
Naturally arising within the heart of Vajrasattva, as follows:

OṂ VAJRASATTVA SAMAYAMANUPĀLAYA VAJRASATTVA TVENOPATIṢṬHA DṚḌHO ME BHAVA SUPOṢYO ME BHAVA SUTOṢYO ME BHAVA ANURAKTO ME BHAVA SARVASIDDHIṂ ME PRAYACCHA SARVAKARMASU CA ME CITTAṂ ŚREYAḤ KURU HŪṂ HAHAHAHA HO BHAGAVĀN SARVA TATHĀGATA VAJRA MĀ ME MUÑCA VAJRABHAVA MAHĀSAMAYASATTVA ĀḤ
Through this unified enlightened intention of the Hundred Enlightened Families,
Degenerations and breaches [of the commitments, and all] negativity and obscurations, will be naturally liberated, without renunciation,[26]
While [externally], bone relics, rainbows, lights and rays will appear [during the cremation],
And sounds will reverberate throughout the universe.

How wonderful!
The supreme innermost heart-mantra, unborn and liberating, arises in the form of the following naturally present syllables:
A Ā I Ī U Ū Ṛ Ṝ Ḷ Ḹ E AI O AU AṂ AḤ.
These sixteen unborn syllables, in eight pairs, will give rise to an indestructible resonance,
While [externally], they will produce a clear cloudless sky.

How wonderful!
The supreme innermost heart-mantra, unceasing and liberating, arises in the form of the following naturally present syllables:
KA KHA GA GHA ṄA CA CHA JA JHA ÑA ṬA ṬHA ḌA ḌHA ṆA TA THA DA DHA NA PA PHA BA BHA MA YA RA LA VA ŚA ṢA SA HA KṢA
These thirty-four unceasing syllables, in eight clusters, will give rise to an indestructible resonance,
Which is the enlightened intention of the unchanging [sacred] teachings,
While causing rainbow lights and relics to appear [in the pyre].

How wonderful!
The supreme innermost heart-mantra which liberates the enduring continuum [of phenomena] arises in the form of the following naturally present syllables:
[OṂ] YE DHARMĀ HETUPRABHAVĀ HETUN TEṢĀṂ TATHĀGATO HY AVADAT TEṢĀṂ CA YO NIRODHO EVAṂ VĀDĪ MAHĀŚRAMAṆAḤ SVĀHĀ[27]

These thirty-nine liberating mantra syllables, in twelve clusters, give rise to an indestructible resonance,
While [externally] multiplying relics and [shimmering] rainbow lights will appear.

The supplementary mantras which symbolise [the four] enlightened activities and [which are appended to the basic mantras above] arise in the form of the following naturally present syllables:

May diseases, possession by malignant forces,
And the eight fears, together with all negativity and obscurations,
Be pacified within the expanse of intrinsic awareness!
ŚĀNTIṂ KURUYE SVĀHĀ

May the lifespan [of beings] and all the fields of merit
Be enriched within the modality of [intrinsic] awareness!
PUṢṬIṂ KURUYE SVĀHĀ

May the Three Precious Jewels and all cyclic existence and nirvāṇa
Be controlled within the modality of [intrinsic] awareness!
VAŚAṂ KURUYE SVĀHĀ

May all hostile, obstructing forces,
The five poisons and the three poisons,
Be destroyed within the modality of [intrinsic] awareness!
MĀRAYA PHAṬ SVĀHĀ

May [all] these naturally present enlightened intentions,
Which are the unique offspring of all the teachings,
Naturally arise and manifest for the sake of sentient beings!

[CONCLUSION]

Through [the power of] this authentic precious jewel,
All one's needs and wishes in this life can be manifested,
And in the next life buddhahood can certainly be achieved.

This [mantra circle] should be accurately inscribed in a headed script,
On a sheet of fine blue paper,
The size of a four finger-width booklet,
Using refined gold, the colour of the Buddha,
And it should be rolled up in silk in the right way.[28]
[Then], on the eighth day of the lunar month,
Coinciding with the constellation Cancer,
A yogin with pure commitments should consecrate it,
And then it should be worn [continuously].[29]

Inexpressible virtues and negative actions may both greatly increase.
Therefore the [yogin] should persevere in the practice of virtue and act for the sake of sentient beings,
Avoiding even the most minute of negative acts.

One who does this in the correct manner,
Even if he or she has previously committed the five inexpiable crimes,
Cannot possibly fall into inferior existences, once this [mantra circle] has been encountered.

Since even those who have not practised the [sacred] teachings at all can attain buddhahood [in this way],
It is called the 'Liberation by Wearing'.
Since all who see this [mantra] circle can attain buddhahood,
It is called the 'Liberation by Seeing'.
Since all who touch it can attain buddhahood,
It is called the 'Liberation by Touching'.
Since all who hear it read aloud can attain buddhahood,
It is called the 'Liberation by Hearing'.
Since all who feel its breath can attain buddhahood,
It is called the 'Liberation by Feeling'.

Since there has never been a single buddha who did not see [this mantra circle],
It is indeed the nucleus of the [sacred] teachings.
All who see it being inscribed will attain buddhahood,
All who come into contact with it, by wearing it, will attain buddhahood.
All who hear it read aloud will attain buddhahood.
Therefore, it should be inscribed and worn [as an amulet].
It should be read aloud and contemplated in the appropriate way,
And it should be thoroughly comprehended in every respect!

Except for those fortunate ones, with appropriate past actions,
[This mantra circle] should be kept secret and concealed,
Because those who have not accumulated merit cannot comprehend [its meaning],
And if they were to defame this [mantra circle], they would proceed to the hells.
This is like an anguished spirit seeing [nutritious] food as an enemy!
Therefore, it should be kept as a secret, esoteric instruction.
[This mantra circle] is a field of experience of the fortunate.

It is extremely difficult to encounter this [mantra circle],
And once encountered, it is difficult to mentally comprehend.
Therefore, those who do encounter it should rejoice,
And embrace it with respect!

At the time of death [this mantra circle] should not be removed from the body,
And when cremation takes place it should not be removed from the corpse.
As a consequence, liberation may occur through seeing, hearing, recollection or contact.

This completes the *Liberation by Wearing: Natural Liberation of the Psycho-physical Aggregates*,
Which encompasses [the mantras of] the hundred enlightened families of the Peaceful and Wrathful Deities.

SAMAYA! *rgya rgya rgya a gter-rgya*

This is a discovered text extracted from Mount Gampodar by the treasure-finder Karma Lingpa.

ŚUBHAṂ

Appendix One: *Peaceful and Wrathful Deities* and the *Tibetan Book of the Dead*

A correspondence between the chapters of Karma Lingpa's *Peaceful and Wrathful Deities: A Profound Sacred Teaching, [entitled] Natural Liberation through [Recognition of] Enlightened Intention* (Dudjom Rinpoche three-volume edition, Delhi: Sherab Lama, 1975–6) and the chapters of this book

History (*lo-rgyus*)

1) *Memorandum* (*Them-byad zin-bris*), composed by Gyarawa Namka Chokyi Gyeltsen, Volume 1, pp. 1–6.

2) *Legend of King 'Gyod tshangs* (*'Gyod-tshangs rgyal-po'i lo-rgyus*). Volume 1, pp. 7–13.

3) *Legend of the Brahmin Dung-phreng* (*Bram-ze dung-phreng-gi lo-rgyus*). Volume 1, pp. 15–20.

4) *Padmasambhava's Prophecy of the Treasure-finder and the Series of Authentic Spiritual Lineage Holders* (*gTer-ston lung-bstan-dang khungs btsun-pa bla-ma brgyud-pa'i rim-pa-rnams*), composed by Gendun Gyeltsen. Volume 1, pp. 21–26.

5) *Abridged History of the Lineage entitled Jewel Garland* (*rGyud-pa'i lo-rgyus bsdus-pa nor-bu'i phreng-ba*), composed by Namka Chokyi Gyatso. Volume 1, pp. 27–48.

Empowerment (*dbang-bskur*)

1) *Natural Liberation through Encountering the Four Empowerments: The Extensive and Elaborate Empowerment of the Vase* (*dBang-bzhi 'phrad-tshad rang-grol-gyi spros-bcas bum-dbang chen-mo*). Volume 1, pp. 49–92.

2) *Natural Liberation through Encountering the Four Empowerments: The Extraordinary Profound Elucidation of the Three Higher Empowerments Including the Natural Liberation Through the Secret Empowerment of Great Bliss* (*dBang-bzhi 'phrad-tshad rang-grol-gyi gsang-dbang bde-chen rang-grol-la-sogs-pa'i dbang gong-ma gsum-gyi zab-gsal khyad-par-can*). Volume 1, pp. 93–125.

3) *Natural Liberation through the Propelling of the Six Classes of Beings into Higher Rebirth: The [Middle-Length] Empowerments of the Natural Liberation of Degenerated Commitments Through Reparation and Confession* (*sKong-bshags*

nyams-chags rang-grol-gyi dbang-bskur gnas-spar 'gro-drug rang-grol), Volume 1, pp. 127–160.

4) *Torma Empowerment: Meaningful to Touch* (*gTor-dbang reg-pa don-ldan*), composed by Namka Chokyi Gyatso. Volume 1, pp. 161–164.

5) *Natural Liberation through Encountering the Four Empowerments: Flower Elucidating the Concluding Sequences* (*dBang-bzhi 'phrad-tshad rang-grol-gyi rjes-kyi rim-pa gsal-ba'i me-tog*). Volume 1, pp. 165–168.

6) *Natural Liberation through Connecting with Practical Application: A Supplement to the Middle-length Maturational Empowerment entitled Natural Liberation of the Six Classes of Living Beings* (*sMin-byed sgo-'byed dbang-bskur 'bring-po 'gro-drug rang-grol-la kha-skong phyag-bzhes-kyis brgyab-pa 'brel-tshad rang-grol*). Volume 2, pp. 145–228.

7) *Minor Annotations on the Rites and Empowerments of the Binding to Higher Rebirth* (*gNas-lung-gi cho-ga-dang dbang-bskur sogs-la nye-bar mkho-ba'i zur-'debs phran-bu*). Volume 2, pp. 229–238.

Generation Stage of Meditation (*bskyed-rim*)

1) *Spiritual Practice entitled Natural Liberation of Habitual Tendencies* (*Chos-spyod bag-chags rang-grol*). Volume 1, pp. 169–200. **See Chapter 5.**

2) *Natural Liberation of the Nature of Mind: The Four-session Yoga of the Preliminary Practice* (*Chos-spyod thun-bzhi'i rnal-'byor sems-nyid rang-grol*), composed by Nyinda Ozer. Volume 1, pp. 201–216. **See Chapter 1.**

3) *Natural Liberation of Degenerated Commitments through Reparation and Confession: Preliminary Supplement to the Generation Stage of Ritual Purification* (*[sKang-bshags nyams-chags rang-grol-gyi] Las-byang bskyed-rim sngon-'gro lhan-thabs*), composed by Namka Chokyi Gyatso. Volume 1, pp. 217–232.

4) *Natural Liberation of Feelings: Primary Rosary of Ritual Purification according to the Assembly of Peaceful and Wrathful Deities*, in eighteen sections (*Zhi-khro 'dus-pa'i las-byang rtsa-phreng tshor-ba rang-grol spyi-don bco-brgyad-pa*). Volume 1, pp. 233–325.

5) *Natural Liberation of Feelings: Lesser [Rosary of] Ritual Purification*, in three essential sections (*Las-byang chung-ba tshor-ba rang-grol snying-po spyi-don gsum-pa*). Volume 1, pp. 327–352.

6) *Sequence of Meditation on the Peaceful and Wrathful Deities entitled Coemergent Pristine Cognition* (*Zhi-khro sgom-rim lhan-skyes ye-shes*). Volume 1, pp. 353–367.

7) *Natural Liberation of Negativity and Obscuration through [Enactment of] the Hundredfold Homage to the Sacred Enlightened Families* (*Dam-pa rigs-brgyar phyag-'tshal sdig-sgrib rang-grol*). Volume 1, pp. 369–390. **See Chapter 6.**

8) *Abridged Homage to the Peaceful and Wrathful Deities* (*Zhi-khro'i phyag-'tshal bsdus-pa*). Volume 1, pp. 391–396.

9) *Natural Liberation through Acts of Confession in the Presence of the Peaceful and Wrathful Deities* (*Zhi-khro'i klong-bshags brjod-pa rang-grol*). Volume 1, pp. 397–429. **See Chapter 7.**

10) *Natural Liberation of Degenerated Commitments through Reparation and Confession: The Sequence for the Fulfilment of Meditative Commitments* (*bsKang-

bshags nyams-chag rang-grol-gyi thugs-dam bskang-ba'i rim-pa), compiled by Namka Chokyi Gyatso. Volume 1, pp. 431–465.

11) *Natural Liberation of Degenerated Commitments through Reparation and Confession: The Natural Liberation of the Six Classes of Living Beings through the Guidance of the Deceased to Higher Rebirth* (*bsKang-bshags nyams-chag rang-grol-gyi tshe-'das gnas-spar/ 'dren 'gro-drug rang-grol spyi-don bcu-pa*). Volume 2, pp. 1–50.

12) *Natural Liberation through Enlightened Activity: The Burnt-offerings of the Ritual Purification* (*Las-byang sbyin-sreg phrin-las rang-grol*), composed by Namka Chokyi Gyatso. Volume 2, pp. 51–123.

13) *Natural Liberation through the Rite of Burnt Offerings: The Sequence of the Preliminary Practices* (*sByin-sreg phrin-las rang-grol-gyi sngon-'gro sta-gon-gyi rim-pa*). Volume 2, pp. 123–144.

14) *Abridged Notes on Ritual Service Elucidating the Meaning of Liberation* (*bsNyen-yig mdor-bsdus rnam-grol don-gsal*). Volume 2, pp. 239–253.

Perfection Stage of Meditation (*rdzogs-rim*)

1) *Contents entitled Natural Liberation of the Keys to the Chapters* (*Sa-bcad lde'u-mig rang-grol gsal-bar bkod-pa*), composed by Nyinda. Volume 2, pp. 255–265.

2) *Prayer entitled Natural Liberation in the Vast Expanse of the Three Buddha-bodies* (*gSol-'debs sku-gsum klong-yangs rang-grol*). Volume 2, pp. 267–272.

3) *A Prayer for Union with the Spiritual Teacher [entitled] Natural Liberation Without Renunciation of the Three Poisons* (*sKu-gsum bla-ma'i rnal-'byor-gyi gsol-'debs dug-gsum ma-spangs rang-grol*). Volume 2, pp. 273–276. **See Chapter 2.**

4) *Natural Liberation through Enlightened Intention: Guidance to the Experience of the Intermediate States: A Supplement on Mental Training in the Preliminary Practices* (*Bar-do'i nyams-khrid dgongs-pa rang-grol-gyi sngon-'gro rang-rgyud 'dul-byed-kyi lhan-thabs*), a teaching of Choje Lingpa, compiled by Nyinda Ozer and redacted by Namka Chokyi Gyatso. Volume 2, pp. 277–302.

5) *Natural Liberation through the Ground-of-all: A Manual of Guidance to the Intermediate State of This Life* (*sKyes-gnas bar-do'i khrid-yig kun-gzhi rang-grol*). Volume 2, pp. 303–340.

6) *Natural Liberation through Bewilderment: A Manual of Guidance to the Intermediate State of Dreams* (*rMi-lam bar-do'i khrid-yig 'khrul-pa rang-grol*). Volume 2, pp. 341–361.

7) *Natural Liberation through Awareness: A Manual of Guidance to the Intermediate State of Meditative Concentration* (*bSam-gtan bar-do'i khrid-yig rig-pa rang-grol*). Volume 2, pp. 363–377.

8) *Natural Liberation through Recollection: A Manual of Guidance to the Intermediate State of the Time of Death* (*'Chi-kha'i bar-do'i khrid-yig dran-pa rang-grol*). Volume 2, pp. 379–400. **See Chapter 10.**

9) *Natural Liberation through Vision: A Manual of Guidance to the Intermediate State of Reality* (*Chos-nyid bar-do'i khrid-yig mthong-ba rang-grol*). Volume 2, pp. 401–417.

10) *Natural Liberation through Rebirth: A Manual of Guidance to the Intermediate State of Rebirth* (*Srid-pa bar-do'i khrid-yig srid-pa rang-grol*). Volume 2, pp. 419–432.

Introductions (*ngo-sprod*)

1) *Preliminary Practice for All the Introductions entitled Exhortation on Impermanence, Based on Escorting a Corpse to a Cemetery* (*Ngo-sprod thams-cad-kyi sngon-'gro dur-khrod-du bam-ro bskyal-ba-la brten-nas mi-rtag-pa'i bskul-mar ngo-sprod-pa*). Volume 2, pp. 433–442.

2) *Introduction to the Origin, Emergence and Presence of Consciousness, Supported by the Human Body, from the Cycle of Introductions to the Great Perfection* (*rDzogs-pa chen-po ngo-sprod-kyi skor-las khams-pa'i mi-mo-la brten-nas rnam-shes 'byung-'jug-gnas gsum-gyi ngo-sprod*), redacted by Namgyel Zangpo. Volume 2, pp. 443–467.

3) *Introduction to Awareness: Natural Liberation through Naked Perception* (*Rig-pa mngon-sum-du ngo-sprod-pa gcer-mthong rang-grol*). Volume 2, pp. 469–488. **See Chapter 4.**

4) *Introduction to the Three Buddha-bodies in Accordance with the Great Perfection: A Supplement to the Liberation by Hearing* (*rDzogs-chen sku-gsum ngo-sprod bar-do thos-grol-gyi cha-lag*). Volume 2, pp. 489–493.

5) *Natural Liberation through Conscious Awareness: Introduction to the Six Lamps* (*sGron-ma drug-gi ngo-sprod shes-rig rang-grol*). Volume 3, pp. 1–20.

6) *Natural Liberation through Vision: Introduction by Means of a Crystal* (*Shel-rdo'i ngo-sprod mthong-ba rang-grol*). Volume 3, pp. 21–28.

7) *Supplement to the Introduction to the Inner Radiance of the Ground* (*gZhi'i 'od-gsal ngo-sprod-kyi lhan-thabs*), composed by Namka Chokyi Gyatso. Volume 3, pp. 29–36.

8) *Introduction by Means of a Butter Lamp* (*Mar-me'i ngo-sprod*), composed by Namka Chokyi Gyatso. Volume 3, pp. 37–40.

9) *Great Liberation by Hearing; Elucidating the Introduction to the Intermediate State of Reality* (*Chos-nyid bar-do'i ngo-sprod gsal-'debs thos-grol chen-mo*). Volume 3, pp. 41–114. **See Chapter 11, Parts One and Two.**

10) *Great Liberation by Hearing; Elucidating the Introduction to the Intermediate State of Rebirth* (*Srid-pa bar-do'i ngo-sprod gsal-'debs thos-grol chen-mo*). Volume 3, pp. 115–162. **See Chapter 11, Part Three.**

11) *Supplement to the Teaching Revealing the Natural Expression of Virtue and Negativity: An Introduction to the Intermediate State of Rebirth, entitled Gong of Divine Melody* (*Srid-pa bar-do'i ngo-sprod dge-sdig rang-gzugs ston-pa'i lhan-thabs dbyangs-snyan lha'i lhan-thabs*), composed by Namka Chokyi Gyatso. Volume 3, pp. 163–173. **See Chapter 13, Part Two.**

12) *Natural Liberation through Recognition of the Visual Indications and Signs of Death* (*'Chi-ltas mtshan-ma rang-grol*). Volume 3, pp. 175–204. See **Chapter 8.**

13) *Natural Liberation of Fear through the Ritual Deception of Death* (*'Chi-bslu 'jigs-pa rang-grol*) Volume 3, pp. 205–218. **See Chapter 9.**

14) *Developing the Greatness of the Teachings of the Liberation by Hearing during the Intermediate State of Dreams* (*rMi-lam bar-do thos-grol chos-kyi che-ba bskyed-byed*), composed by Nyinda Ozer. Volume 3, pp. 219–254.

15) *Liberation by Wearing: Natural Liberation of the Psycho-physical Aggregates, in which the Peaceful and Wrathful Deities are encompassed* (*Zhi-khro 'dus-pa'i btags-grol phung-po rang-grol*). Volume 3, pp. 255–286. **See Chapter 14.**

16) *An Abridgement of the Liberation by Wearing: Natural Liberation of the Psycho-physical Aggregates, entitled Nucleus of Natural Liberation* (*bTags-grol phung-po rang-grol-gyi don-bsdus rang-grol snying-po*). Volume 3, pp. 287–306.

17) *Chapter on the Means of Attaching a Diagram which Liberates by Wearing; from the Tantra of the Great Perfection: Natural Liberation of Cyclic Existence and Nirvāṇa* (*rDzogs-chen 'khor-'das rang-grol-gyi rgyud-las btags-grol bcang-thabs-kyi le'u*). Volume 3, pp. 307–313.

18) *Memorandum on the Actual Preparation of the Great Chart of the Liberation by Wearing* (*bTags-grol 'khor-lo chen-mo'i lag-len zin-bris*). Volume 1, pp. 467–492.

19) *Inventory for Insertion within the Casket* (*Glegs-bam bzhugs-pa'i dkar-chag*). Volume 1, pp. 493–499.

20) *Root Verses of the Six Intermediate States* (*Bar-do drug-gi rtsa-tshig*). Volume 3, pp. 316–318. **See Chapter 3.**

21) *Aspirational Prayer which Rescues from the Dangerous Pathways of the Intermediate States* (*Bar-do'i 'phrang-sgrol*). Volume 3, pp. 318–322. **See Chapter 12.**

22) *Aspirational Prayer which Protects from Fear of the Intermediate States* (*Bar-do'i 'jigs-skyobs-kyi smon-lam*). Volume 3, pp. 322–325. **See Chapter 12.**

23) *Natural Liberation of Fear: Aspirational Prayer [Calling] to the Buddhas and Bodhisattvas for Assistance* (*Sangs-rgyas byang-sems-rnams ra-mda' sbran-pa'i smon-lam 'jigs-pa rang-grol*). Volume 3, pp. 325–327. **See Chapter 12.**

Path of Skilful Means (*thabs-lam*)

1) *Natural Liberation through Desire: Most Profound Quintessence of Guidance on Supreme Bliss Pertaining to the Sexual Practices* (*'Og-sgo bde-ba chen-po'i khrid 'dod-chags rang-grol zhes-bya-ba yang-zab bcud-bsdus*). Volume 3, pp. 329–419.

2) *The Means of Establishing the Lineage by Carrying Desire onto the Path and the Means of Closing the Womb Entrances* (*'Dod-chags lam-khyer rigs-brgyud bzhag-thabs-dang mngal-sgo 'gag-thab khol-du phung-ba*). Volume 3, pp. 421–437.

3) *Natural Liberation through Supreme Bliss: A Profound Abridgement of the Guidance on Supreme Bliss Attained through the Sexual Practices* (*'Og-sgo bde-chen 'dod-chags rang-grol-gyi nyams-khrid gud-sbas don-bsdus zab-khrid bde-ba chen-po rang-grol zhes-bya-ba shin-tu zab-pa'i nying-khu*), composed by Nyinda Ozer. Volume 3, pp. 439–481.

Protector Rites (*bstan-srung*)

1) *Seven Classes of Oath-bound Protectors, Associated with the Peaceful and Wrathful Deities: Natural Liberation of the Venomous Hostile Malevolent Forces and Obstructors through Enlightened Activity* (*Zhi-khro bka'-srung dam-can sde-

bdun-gyi phrin-las dgra-bgegs gdug-pa rang-grol), composed by Nyinda Ozer. Volume 3, pp. 483–490.

2) *Seven Classes of Oath-bound Protectors, Associated with the Peaceful and Wrathful Deities: Natural Liberation of Venomous Forces through Reparation* (*Zhi-khro dam-can sde-bdun-gyi mdangs-bskang gdug-pa rang-grol*), Volume 3, pp. 491–498.

The Lotus Peaceful and Wrathful Deities (*Padma zhi-khro*)

1) *Natural Liberation of Rebirth: A Teaching Revealing the Natural Expression of Virtue and Negativity, through the Introduction to the Intermediate State of Rebirth* (*Srid-pa bar-do'i ngo-sprod dge-sdig rang-gzugs ston-pa'i gdams-pa'am me-long srid-pa rang-grol*), contained in the Delhi offset edition of the *Great Liberation by Hearing in the Intermediate States*, pp. 499–533. **See Chapter 13, Part One.**

Appendix Two: Symbolism of the Maṇḍala of the Peaceful and Wrathful Deities

The maṇḍala represents a perfected state of being, and the central deities within it symbolise the perfected states of the meditator's own awareness, psycho-physical aggregates, elemental properties, and sensory and mental processes. The peaceful deities represent the quiescent natural purity of these fundamental components of our being and the wrathful deities represent the transformative aspects of these energies, which bring about the natural transformation of the most enduring and deep-seated expressions of our mundane perceptual states. Last, the outer deities of the maṇḍala represent the modes of activity of an enlightened being.

The exact mapping of this symbolism does vary according to the lineage and class of the practice. In the chart presented below, the correspondences are based on Chapter 5 of the present work, supplemented by correspondences taken from other texts within the cycle, with certain common variances noted.

The Forty-two Peaceful Deities

The male and female primordial buddhas: Samantabhadra and Samantabhadrī in union represent the indivisible union of pure awareness and emptiness

	Location	Colour	Symbolising
Samantabhadra *kun-tu bzang-po*	Centre of the energy centre within the heart, embracing Samantabhadrī	Sky blue	The awareness aspect of the Buddha-body of Reality, the natural purity of mental consciousness, free from fundamental ignorance.
Samantabhadrī *kun-tu bzang-mo*	Centre of the energy centre within the heart, embracing Samantabhadra	Stainless white, like crystal	The emptiness aspect of the Buddha-body of Reality, the natural purity of the sensory spectrum of phenomena.

The five male buddhas: Vairocana, Akṣobhya-Vajrasattva, Ratnasambhava, Amitābha and Amoghasiddhi, represent the five pristine cognitions and the natural purity of the five psycho-physical aggregates

	Location	Colour	Symbolising	Enlightened family
Vairocana *rnam-par snang-mdzad*	Central channel within the heart, embracing Ākāśadhātvīśvarī	Conch white	The pristine cognition of reality's expanse, the natural purity of the aggregate of consciousness, free from delusion	Buddha

NB: In some sources, where Akṣobhya-Vajrasattva is placed at the centre of the maṇḍala and Vairocana in the east (e.g. Lochen Dharmaśrī, SDGG, pp. 81–6), Vairocana symbolises the aggregate of form. The distinction between these positions is related to the class of practice – the former corresponding to Atiyoga and the latter to a Mahāyoga interpretation of the *Guhyagarbha Tantra*.

(Akṣobhya-)Vajrasattva *mi-bskyod rdo-rje sems-dpa'*	Eastern channel branch of the heart, embracing Buddhalocanā	Azure blue	The mirror-like pristine cognition, the natural purity of the aggregate of form, free from aversion	Vajra
	NB: When placed at the centre of the maṇḍala, (Akṣobhya-)Vajrasattva represents the natural purity of the aggregate of consciousness. See above.			
Ratnasambhava *rin-chen 'byung-gnas*	Southern channel branch of the heart, embracing Māmakī	Golden yellow	The pristine cognition of sameness, the natural purity of the aggregate of feeling, free from pride	Ratna
Amitābha *snang-ba mtha'-yas*	Western channel branch of the heart, embracing Pāṇḍaravāsinī	Copper red	The pristine cognition of discernment, the natural purity of the aggregate of perceptions, free from attachment	Padma
Amoghasiddhi *don-yod grub-pa*	Northern channel branch of the heart, embracing Samayatārā	Turquoise green	The pristine cognition of accomplishment, the natural purity of the aggregate of motivational tendencies, free from envy	Karma

The five female buddhas: Ākāśadhātvīśvarī, Buddhalocanā, Māmakī, Pāṇḍaravāsinī and Samayatārā, represent the natural purity of the five elements

	Location	Colour	Symbolising	Enlightened family
Ākāśadhātvīśvarī *nam-mkha'i dbyings phyug-ma*	Central channel, within the heart, embracing Vairocana	Moon-like white	The natural purity of the space element	Buddha
Buddhalocanā *sangs-rgyas spyan-ma*	Eastern channel branch of the heart, embracing Akṣobhya-Vajrasattva	Beryl blue	The natural purity of the earth element	Vajra
	NB: In Chapter 11, Buddhalocanā is unusually identified with the natural purity of the water element, a role generally attributed to the female buddha Māmakī.			

	Location	Colour	Symbolising	Enlightened family
Māmakī *yum mā-ma-kī*	Southern channel branch of the heart, embracing Ratna-sambhava	Minium orange	The natural purity of the water element	Ratna
	NB: In Chapter 11, Māmakī is unusually identified with the natural purity of the earth element, a role generally attributed to the female buddha Buddhalocanā.			
Pāṇḍaravāsinī *yum-mchog gos-dkar-mo*	Western channel branch of the heart, embracing Amitābha	Fire-crystal red	The natural purity of the element fire	Padma
Samayatārā *yum dam-tshig sgrol-ma*	Northern channel branch of the heart, embracing Amoghasiddhi	Sapphire green	The natural purity of the element wind	Karma

The eight male bodhisattvas: Kṣitigarbha, Maitreya, Samantabhadra, Ākāśagarbha, Avalokiteśvara, Mañjuśrīkumārabhūta, Nivāraṇaviśkambhin and Vajrapāṇi, represent the eight classes of consciousness

NB: According to the *Guhyagarbha Tantra*, they also symbolise the four senses and four sense organs.

	Location	Colour	Symbolising	Enlightened family
Kṣitigarbha *sa'i snying-po*	Eastern channel branch of the heart, to the right of Vajra-sattva	Snow-mountain white	The natural purity of visual consciousness	Vajra
Maitreya *rgyal-ba byams-pa*	Eastern channel branch of the heart, to the left of Vajrasattva	Cloud-white	The natural purity of auditory consciousness	Vajra

Samantabhadra *byang-sems kun-tu bzang-po*	Southern channel branch of the heart, to the right of Ratna-sambhava	Amber yellow	The natural purity of olfactory consciousness	Ratna
Ākāśagarbha *nam-mkha'i snying-po*	Southern channel branch of the heart, to the left of Ratna-sambhava	Burnished golden yellow	The natural purity of gustatory consciousness	Ratna
Avalokiteśvara *spyan-ras gzigs*	Western channel branch of the heart, to the right of Amitābha	Coral red	The natural purity of tactile consciousness	Padma
Mañjuśrīkumāra-bhūta *'jam-dpal [gzhon--nur gyur-pa]*	Western channel branch of the heart, to the left of Amitābha	Minium Orange	The natural purity of mental consciousness	Padma
[Sarva] Nivāraṇavi-śkambhin *sgrib-pa rnam-par sel-ba*	Northern channel branch of the heart, to the right of Amoghasiddhi	Green as the night-flowering lotus	The natural purity of the 'ground-of-all' consciousness	Karma
Vajrapāṇi *phyag-na rdo-rje*	Northern channel branch of the heart, to the left of Amoghasiddhi	Emerald green	The natural purity of the defiled consciousness	Karma

The eight female bodhisattvas: Lāsyā, Puṣpā, Mālyā, Dhūpā, Gītā, Ālokā, Gandhā and Nartī, represent the four sense objects and the four phases of conceptual thought (past, present, future and indeterminate), or alternatively the eight objects of consciousness

	Location	Colour	Symbolising	Enlightened family
Lāsyā *lāsyā-ma*	The eastern channel branch of the heart, in front of Vajra-sattva	Quartz white	The natural purity of visual phenomena	Vajra
Puṣpā *puṣpe-ma*	The eastern channel branch of the heart, behind Vajrasattva	Pearl white	The natural purity of past conceptual thoughts	Vajra
Mālyā *mālyā-ma*	The southern channel branch of the heart, in front of Ratna-sambhava	Saffron yellow	The natural purity of indeterminate conceptual thoughts	Ratna
Dhūpā *dhūpe-ma*	The southern channel branch of the heart, behind Ratna-sambhava	Golden yellow	The natural purity of fragrance	Ratna
Gītā *ghirti-ma*	The western channel branch of the heart, in front of Amitābha	Marsh mallow pink	The natural purity of sound	Padma
Ālokā *āloka-ma*	The western channel branch of the heart, behind Amitābha	Lotus pink	The natural purity of future conceptual thoughts	Padma
Gandhā *ghandhe-ma*	The northern channel branch of the heart, in front of Amoghasiddhi	Poppy green	The natural purity of present conceptual thoughts	Karma
Nartī *nirti-ma*	The northern channel branch of the heart, behind Amoghasiddhi	Marine green	The natural purity of taste	Karma

The four male gatekeepers: Trailokyavijaya, Yamāntaka, Hayagrīva and Amṛtakuṇḍalin, represent the natural purity of the four extreme views and four aspects of enlightened activity

NB: According to Chapter 7, they represent the natural purity of the four immeasurable aspirations.

	Location	Colour	Symbolising	Enlightened family
Trailokyavijaya *khams-gsum rnam-rgyal*	The channel branch at the eastern gate of the heart, embracing Aṅkuśā	White	The natural purity of eternalist views and acts of pacification	Vajra
Yamāntaka *gshin-rje gshed*	The channel branch at the southern gate of the heart, embracing Pāśā	Yellow	The natural purity of nihilistic views and acts of enrichment	Ratna
Hayagrīva *rta-mgrin*	The channel branch at the western gate of the heart, embracing Spoṭhā	Red	The natural purity of egotistical views and acts of subjugation	Padma
Amṛtakuṇḍalin *bdud-rtsi 'khyil-ba*	The channel branch at the northern gate of the heart, embracing Gaṇṭhā	Green	The natural purity of substantialist views and acts of wrath	Karma

The four female gatekeepers: Aṅkuśā, Pāśā, Sphoṭā and Ghaṇṭā, represent the natural purity of the four types of birth and the four immeasurable aspirations

NB: According to Chapter 7, they represent the natural purity of the four extreme views.

	Location	Colour	Symbolising	Enlightened family
Aṅkuśā *lcags-kyu-ma*	The channel branch at the eastern gate of the heart, embracing Trailokyavijaya	White	The natural purity of miraculous birth and the immeasurable aspiration of compassion	Vajra
Pāśā *zhags-pa-ma*	The channel branch at the southern gate of the heart, embracing Yamāntaka	Yellow	The natural purity of womb birth and the immeasurable aspiration of loving kindness	Ratna
Sphoṭā *lcags-sgrogs-ma*	The channel branch at the western gate of the heart, embracing Hayagrīva	Red	The natural purity of egg birth and the immeasurable aspiration of empathetic joy	Padma
Ghaṇṭā *dril-bu-ma*	The channel branch at the northern gate of the heart, embracing Amṛtakuṇḍalin	Green	The natural purity of birth through heat and moisture, and the immeasurable aspiration of equanimity	Karma

The six sages: Indraśakra, Vemacitra, Śākyamuni, Sthirasiṃha, Jvālamukha and Yama Dharmarāja, represent the natural purity of the six dissonant mental states

	Location	Colour	Symbolising
Indraśakra *dbang-po brgya-byin*	In the channel branch of the energy centre of great bliss at the crown of the head	White	The natural purity of pride

Vemacitra *thag-bzang-ris*	In the occipital channel at the throat	Green	The natural purity of envy
Śākyamuni *shākya thub-pa*	In the 'life force' channel at the heart	Yellow	The natural purity of attachment
Sthirasiṃha *senge rab-brtan*	In the energy centre at the navel	Blue	The natural purity of delusion
Jvālamukha *kha-'bar-ma*	In the channel branch at the bliss-sustaining secret energy centre	Red	The natural purity of miserliness
Yama Dharmarāja *gshin-rje chos-kyi rgyal-po*	In the energy centre at the soles of the feet	Black	The natural purity of aversion

The Fifty-eight Wrathful Deities

The six peaceful male buddhas: Samantabhadra, Vairocana, Akṣobhya-Vajrasattva, Ratnasambhava, Amitābha and Amoghasiddhi are in their wrathful aspects respectively: Mahottara Heruka, Buddha Heruka, Vajra Heruka, Ratna Heruka, Padma Heruka and Karma Heruka, who represent the natural transformation of the six dissonant mental states

	Location	Colour	Symbolising	Enlightened family
Mahottara Heruka *che-mchog he-ru-ka*	In the central channel branch of the skull within the brain, embracing Krodheśvarī	Dark brown	The natural transformation of fundamental ignorance into pure awareness	
Buddha Heruka *buddha he-ru-ka*	In the central channel branch of the skull within the brain, embracing Buddhakrodheśvarī	Dark brown	The natural transformation of delusion into the pristine cognition of reality's expanse	Buddha

	Location	Colour	Symbolising	Enlightened family
Vajra Heruka *badzra he-ru-ka*	In the eastern channel branch of the skull within the brain, embracing Vajrakrodhīśvarī	Dark blue	The natural transformation of aversion into the mirror-like pristine cognition	Vajra
Ratna Heruka *ratna he-ru-ka*	In the southern channel branch of the skull within the brain, embracing Ratnakrodhīśvarī	Dark yellow	The natural transformation of pride into the pristine cognition of sameness	Ratna
Padma Heruka *padma he-ru-ka*	In the western channel branch of the skull within the brain, embracing Padmakrodhīśvarī	Dark red	The natural transformation of attachment into the pristine cognition of discernment	Padma
Karma Heruka *ka-rma he-ru-ka*	In the northern channel branch of the skull within the brain, embracing Karmakrodhīśvarī	Dark green	The natural transformation of envy into the pristine cognition of accomplishment	Karma

The six peaceful female buddhas: Samantabhadrī, Ākāśadhātvīśvarī, Buddhalocanā, Māmakī, Pāṇḍaravāsinī and Samayatārā in their wrathful aspects respectively are Krodheśvarī, Buddhakrodheśvarī, Vajrakrodheśvarī, Ratnakrodheśvarī, Padmakrodheśvarī and Karmakrodheśvarī, who represent the natural transformation of mental constructs associated with the six objects of consciousness

	Location	Colour	Symbolising	Enlightened family
Krodhéśvarī *kro-ti-sva-ri*	In the central channel branch of the skull within the brain, embracing Mahottara Heruka	Dark blue	The natural transformation of mental constructs associated with the sensory spectrum of phenomena	
Buddhakrodheśvarī *bde-gshegs dbyings-phyug-ma/ buddha kro-ti-sva-ri*	In the central channel branch of the skull within the brain, embracing Buddha Heruka	Red-brown	The natural transformation of mental constructs associated with physical objects [of sight]	Buddha

Vajrakrodhésvarī *yum ba-dzra kro-ti-sva-ri*	In the eastern channel branch of the skull within the brain, embracing Vajra Heruka	Pale blue	The natural transformation of mental constructs associated with objects of sound	Vajra
Ratnakrodheśvarī *yum ratna kro-ti-sva-ri*	In the southern channel branch of the skull within the brain, embracing Ratna Heruka	Pale yellow	The natural transformation of mental constructs associated with objects of smell	Ratna
Padmakrodheśvarī *yum padma kro-ti-sva-ri*	In the western channel branch of the skull within the brain, embracing Padma Heruka	Pale red	The natural transformation of mental constructs associated with objects of taste	Padma
Karmakrodheśvarī *karma yum kro-ti-sva-ri*	In the northern channel branch of the skull within the brain, embracing Karma Heruka	Pale green	The natural transformation of mental constructs associated with objects of touch	Karma

The eight Mātaraḥ: Gaurī, Caurī, Pramohā, Vetālī, Pukkasī, Ghasmarī, Caṇḍālī and Śmaśānī, represent the natural transformation of mental constructs associated with the eight classes of consciousness

	Location	Colour	Symbolising
Gaurī *ke'u-ri*	In the eastern channel branch of the skull within the brain	White	The natural transformation of mental constructs associated with visual consciousness, and the action of destroying the conceptual landscape of cyclic existence
Caurī *tsa'u-ri*	In the southern channel branch of the skull within the brain	Yellow	The natural transformation of mental constructs associated with auditory consciousness, and the action of propelling the six classes of beings into higher rebirth
Pramohā *pra-mo-hā*	In the western channel branch of the skull within the brain	Red	The natural transformation of mental constructs associated with olfactory consciousness, and the action of resisting [the seductions of] cyclic existence

	Location	Colour	Symbolising
Vetālī *vetālī*	In the northern channel branch of the skull within the brain	Green-black	The natural transformation of mental constructs associated with gustatory consciousness, and the action of [sustaining recognition of] the unchanging reality
Pukkasī *pu-kka-sī*	In the south-eastern channel branch of the skull within the brain	Red-yellow	The natural transformation of mental constructs associated with tactile consciousness, and the action of drawing [sentient beings] free from the dissonant realms
Ghasmarī *ghasmarī*	In the south-western channel branch of the skull within the brain	Green-black	The natural transformation of mental constructs associated with the mental consciousness, and the action of consuming [the turning circle of] cyclic existence
Caṇḍālī *gtum-mo*	In the north-western channel branch of the skull within the brain	Pale yellow	The natural transformation of mental constructs associated with the 'ground-of-all' consciousness, and the action of severing erroneous thoughts [at their roots]
Smaśānī *dur-khrod-ma*	In the north-eastern channel branch of the skull within the brain	Blue-black	The natural transformation of mental constructs associated with the deluded consciousness, and the action of severing the buttresses of cyclic existence

The eight Piśācī: Siṃhamukhī, Vyāghrīmukhī, Śṛgālamukhī, Śvānamukhī, Gṛdhramukhī, Kaṅkamukhī, Kākamukhī and Ulūkamukhī, represent the natural transformation of mental constructs associated with the objects of the eight classes of consciousness

	Location	Colour	Symbolising
Siṃhamukhī *seng-gdong-ma*	In the outer eastern channel branch of the skull within the brain	Brown-black	The natural transformation of mental constructs associated with visual objects, and the action of stirring cyclic existence to its depths

Vyāghrīmukhī *stag-gdong-ma*	In the outer southern channel branch of the skull within the brain	Red	The natural transformation of mental constructs associated with sounds, and the action of overwhelming attachment to cyclic existence
Śṛgālamukhī *sri-la gdong-ma*	In the outer western channel branch of the skull within the brain	Black	The natural transformation of mental constructs associated with smells, and the action of purifying dissonant mental states in their basic nature
Śvānamukhī *shva-na gdong-ma*	In the outer northern channel branch of the skull within the brain	Blue-black	The natural transformation of mental constructs associated with tastes, and the action of stirring the pit of cyclic existence
Gṛdhramukhī *rgod-gdong-ma*	In the outer south-eastern channel branch of the skull within the brain	White-yellow	The natural transformation of mental constructs associated with touch, and the action of severing the three poisons from their roots
Kaṅkamukhī *kang-ka gdong-ma*	In the outer south-western channel branch of the skull within the brain	Red-black	The natural transformation of mental constructs associated with mental phenomena, and the action of extracting [beings] from the pit of cyclic existence
Kākamukhī *khā-kha gdong-ma*	In the outer north-western channel branch of the skull within the brain	Black	The natural transformation of mental constructs associated with objects of the 'ground-of-all' consciousness, and the action of consuming and liberating dissonant mental states
Ulūkamukhī *hu-lu gdong-ma*	In the outer north-eastern channel branch of the skull within the brain	Dark blue	The natural transformation of mental constructs associated with objects of the deluded consciousness, and the action of drawing [beings] free from the false mentality of cyclic existence

The four Female Gatekeepers manifest as Vajratejasī, Vajrāmoghā, Vajralokā and Vajravetālī, respectively representing the closing of the doors to the four types of birth and the force of the four immeasurable aspirations

	Location	Colour	Symbolising	Enlightened family
Vajratejasī [*Aṅkuśā*] *lcags-kyu-ma*	In the channel branch at the eastern gate of the skull within the brain	White	The force of immeasurable compassion and the closing of the door to miraculous birth	Vajra
Vajrāmoghā [*Pāśā*] *zhags-pa-ma*	In the channel branch at the southern gate of the skull within the brain	Yellow	The force of immeasurable loving kindness and the closing of the door to womb birth	Ratna
Vajralokā [*Sphoṭā*] *lcags-sgrogs-ma*	In the channel branch at the western gate of the skull within the brain	Red	The force of immeasurable empathetic joy and the closing of the door to egg birth	Padma
Vajravetālī [*Ghaṇṭā*] *dril-bu-ma*	In the channel branch at the northern gate of the skull within the brain	Green	The force of immeasurable equanimity and the closing of the door to birth through heat and moisture	Karma

Twenty-eight Īśvarī, represent the purification of the aggregates of bewildered mental constructs and the enactment of enlightened activity

	Location	Colour	Symbolising	Enlightened family
The six yoginī of the east:	In the minor channels of the eastern outer courtyard of the skull		The activities of pacification	Vajra
Manurākṣasī		Brownish White		
Brahmāṇī		Yellowish White		
Raudrī		Greenish White		
Vaiṣṇāvī		Bluish White		
Kaumārī		Reddish White		
Indrāṇī		White		
The six yoginī of the south:	In the minor channels of the southern outer courtyard of the skull		The activities of enrichment	Ratna
Vajrā		Yellow		
Śāntī		Reddish Yellow		
Amṛtā		Reddish Yellow		
Saumī		Whitish Yellow		
Daṇḍī		Greenish Yellow		
Rākṣasī		Blackish Yellow		

	Location	Colour	Symbolising	Enlightened family
The six yoginī of the west:	In the minor channels of the western outer courtyard of the skull		The activities of subjugation	Padma
Bhakṣasī		Greenish Red		
Ratī		Red		
Rudhiramadī		Pale Red		
Ekacāriṇī Rākṣasī		Red		
Manohārikā		Red		
Siddhikarī		Greenish Red		
The six yoginī of the north:	In the minor channels of the northern outer courtyard of the skull		The activities of wrath	Karma
Vāyudevī		Bluish Green		
Agnāyī		Reddish Green		
Varāhī		Blackish Green		
Cāmuṇḍī		Reddish Green		
Bhujanā		Blackish Green		
Varunāṇī		Bluish Green		
The four yoginī gatekeepers:	At the [outer] eastern, southern, western and northern gates of the skull respectively		The closing of the four doors to the four types of birth, and the enactment of the four kinds of enlightened activity	
Vajrā Mahākālī		White		Vajra
Vajrā Mahāchāgalā		Yellow		Ratna
Vajrā Mahā-kumbhakarṇī		Red		Padma
Vajrā Lambodarā		Dark Green		Karma

Notes

List of Abbreviations

Derge Derge Parkhang xylographic editions, of the *Kangyur*, *Tengyur* and *Collected Tantras of the Nyingmapa* (NGB).

Disc. *gTer-ston*, discoverer of concealed teachings (*gter ma*).

DR *Zab-chos zhi-khro dgongs-pa rang-grol*, 3 vols. The most extensive and accurate version of Karma Lingpa's revelations (64 texts, 764 folios), a manuscript of Katok provenance, from the library of the previous Dudjom Rinpoche, published in photo-offset form (Delhi: Sherab Lama, 1975–76), reproduced on CD-ROM by TBRC, New York, Ref: 2330-2332.

GGFTC G. Dorje, *The Guhyagarbhatattvaviniścayamahātantra and its XIVth Century Tibetan Commentary Phyogs bcu mun sel.* 3 vols. Unpublished Ph.D. thesis, University of London, 1987. See also *The Guhyagarbha Tantra: Dispelling the Darkness of the Ten Directions* (forthcoming).

MTTWL P. Pfandt, *Mahāyāna Texts Translated into Western Languages.* Cologne: In Komission bei E. J. Brill, 1983.

NA Not available, not extant.

NGB The Derge xylographic edition of the *Collected Tantras of the Nyingmapa* (*rNying-ma'i rgyud-'bum*) in 26 vols.

NK *Collected Teachings of the Nyingmapa* (*rNying-ma'i bka'-ma*), compiled in 120 vols. by Khenpo Jamyang, Katok (1999).

NSTB Dudjom Rinpoche, *The Nyingma School of Tibetan Buddhism: Its Fundamentals and History*, translated by G. Dorje and M. Kapstein, Boston: Wisdom Publications, 1991. This volume contains two texts, *Gangs-ljongs rgya-bstan yongs-rdzogs-kyi phyi-mo snga-'gyur rdo-rje theg-pa'i bstan-pa rin-po-che ji-ltar byung-ba'i tshul-dag-cing gsal-bar brjod-pa lha-dbang gYul-las rgyal-ba'i rnga-bo-che'i sgra-dbyangs* (short title: *rNying-ma'i chos-'byung*), and the *gSang-sngags snga-'gyur rnying-ma-ba'i bstan-pa'i rnam-gzhag mdo-tsam brjod-pa legs-bshad snang-ba'i dga'-ston* (short title: *bsTan-pa'i rnam-gzhag*).

Redisc. Rediscoverer of twice-concealed teachings (*yang-gter*).

SDGG Lochen Dharmaśrī, *gSang-bdag dgongs-rgyan*, NK, Vol. 76.

T *A Complete Catalogue of the Tibetan Buddhist Canons*, ed. H. Ui *et al.*, Sendai: Tohoku University, 1934. This is a catalogue to the Derge xylographic edition of the *Kangyur* and *Tengyur*.

TBD *Tibetan Book of the Dead* (*Bar-do thos-grol chen-mo*).

TBD Amdo edition *Bar-do thos-grol chen-mo*, 303 pages, recently compiled by

Khenpo Dorje and published in Hong Kong, in Qinghai Buddhist Texts Series, Vol. 1 (n.d.).

TBD Delhi reprint *Bar-do thos-grol chen-mo*, 550 pages, Delhi (1985). Reproduced from a print of the Bhutanese Rinpung Dzong xylograph through the agency of HH Dilgo Khyentse Rinpoche.

TBD Varanasi reprint *Bar-do thos-grol chen-mo*, 122 pages, ed. Kalsang Lhundup, Varanasi (1969). Handwritten print based on the xylographic edition of HH Dilgo Khyentse Rinpoche, housed at Engon Monastery in Sikkim.

1 Natural Liberation of the Nature of Mind

1. Tib. *gSang-sngags rdo-rje theg-pa'i chos-spyod thun-bzhi'i rnal-'byor sems-nyid rang-grol.*
2. Tib. *Zab-chos zhi-khro dgongs-pa rang-grol.*
3. The practices concerning death (*'chi-ba*) are the analytical meditations on the nature of impermanence (*anitya*). See e.g. Paltrul Rinpoche, *The Words of My Perfect Teacher*, pp. 39–59; Sonam T. Kazi (trans.), *Kun-zang La-may Zhal-lung*, pp. 56–82; and Sgam.po.pa/H. V. Guenther (trans.), *The Jewel Ornament of Liberation*, pp. 41–54. The expression 'starting with' (*sogs-la*) implies that this will lead on to the other analytical meditations concerning past actions (*karma*) and the sufferings of cyclic existence (*saṃsāra*). On the application of the meditation on death by hermit buddhas who frequent charnel grounds in order to meditate in reverse on the twelve links of dependent origination (*pratītyasamutpāda*), see Dudjom Rinpoche, NSTB, pp. 228–9.
4. This description of phenomena accords with the account given by Nāgārjuna at the beginning of his *Root Stanzas of the Madhyamaka entitled Discriminative Awareness* (*Prajñā-nāma-mūlamadhyamakakārikā*). See the translation by D. Kalupahana, *Mūlamadhyamakakārikās*, Ch. 1.
5. i.e. lacking in skilful means, on which see glossary.
6. For a description of the eight freedoms (*dal-ba brgyad*) and the ten opportunities (*'byor-ba bcu*), see glossary.
7. On the dissolution of the physical environment (*lokadhātu*) by fire and water at the end of an aeon, see L. Pruden (trans.), *Abhidharmakośabhāṣyaṃ*, Ch. 3, The World, pp. 475–7, 489–95.
8. The 'Lord of Death' (*'chi-bdag*) is an epithet of Yama Dharmarāja. See glossary.
9. The expression 'irreversible path' (*phyir mi-zlog-pa'i lam*) refers to the sūtras of the second and third turnings of the wheel of the sacred teachings, which expound the definitive meaning. See glossary under definitive meaning.
10. Lit. 'accumulations' (Tib. *tshogs*). This refers to the accumulation of merit (*bsod-nams*), as opposed to the accumulation of pristine cognition (*ye-shes*). See glossary.
11. Tib. *mnyam-rdzogs klong-yangs chen-po'i rang-bzhin*. This expanse of sameness and perfection is synonymous with the Buddha-body of Reality. See Dudjom Rinpoche, NSTB, pp. 251–2.
12. Name and form (*nāmarūpa*) together comprise all the five psycho-physical aggregates (*pañcaskandha*) of which the mind-body complex is formed, viz.

form (*rūpa*), consciousness (*vijñāna*), feeling (*vedanā*), perception (*saṃjñā*), and motivational tendencies (*saṃskāra*). See glossary under aggregates.

13. The seed-syllable HŪṂ is that of Vajrasattva, symbolising buddha-mind. On its composition, see Paltrul Rinpoche, *The Words of My Perfect Teacher*, p. 272.
14. For an illustration depicting the crown fontanelle in its relation with the three main energy channels and ancillary vessels, see *Tibetan Medical Paintings*, p. 34.
15. See glossary under Hundred-syllable Mantra.
16. 'Vajra Holder' (*vajradhṛk*; Tib. *rdo-rje 'dzin-pa*), here referring to the deity Vajrasattva, is a title generally given to accomplished exponents of the Vehicle of Indestructible Reality (*Vajrayāna*).
17. This prayer for total union with the deity is repeated below, p. 21, at the end of the section on union with the spiritual teacher (*guruyoga*). As to the specified indications of this union, the body size (*kāya*; Tib. *sku'i tshad*) and lifespan of Vajrasattva (*āyuḥ*; Tib. *tshe*) are those of a buddha, on which see P. Williams, *Mahāyāna Buddhism*, pp. 181–4; his retinue (*parivāra*; Tib. *'khor*) comprises male and female bodhisattvas, on which see Ch. 5, p. 68; and his field (*kṣetra*; Tib. *zhing-khams*) is Abhirati on which see Ch. 11, p. 239. For the significance of the thirty-two major marks (*dvātriṃśasanmukhāpuruṣalakṣaṇa*; Tib. *skyes-bu dam-pa'i mtshan-bzang sum-cu rtsa-gnyis*), which are displayed on the buddha-body of form (*rūpakāya*), see glossary.
18. The initial mantra of the external maṇḍala of offerings: OṂ VAJRA BHŪMI ĀḤ HŪṂ indicates that the foundation or base of the symbolic maṇḍala is of the nature of indestructible reality (*vajra*; Tib. *rdo-rje*). Simultaneously, the practitioner sprinkles consecrated substances upon it. See Paltrul Rinpoche, *The Words of My Perfect Teacher*, p. 287; and Sonam T. Kazi (trans.), *Kun-zang La-may Zhal-lung*, p. 400.
19. The foundation of the maṇḍala is considered to be an immensely thick indestructible circle of wind, resting upon space, and surmounted by a circle of water and a sphere of gold. See L. Pruden (trans.), *Abhidharmakośabhāṣyaṃ*, Ch. 3, The World, pp. 451–2.
20. The second mantra of the maṇḍala of offerings: OṂ VAJRA REKHE ĀḤ HŪṂ indicates that the *cakravāḍa* or 'perimeter wall' of the maṇḍala is of the nature of indestructible reality. Simultaneously, the practitioner makes a clockwise circular motion with the right hand, and places a flower blossom on the surface of the maṇḍala, followed by the outer ring. See Paltrul Rinpoche, *The Words of My Perfect Teacher*, p. 287; and Sonam T. Kazi (trans.), *Kun-zang La-may Zhal-lung*, pp. 400–401.
21. On the perception of the sun (*sūrya*; Tib. *nyi-ma*) and moon (*candra*; Tib. *zla-ba*) from the perspective of Abhidharma, see L. Pruden (trans.), *Abhidharmakośabhāṣyaṃ*, pp. 460–62; and R. Kloetzli, *Buddhist Cosmology*, pp. 45–6. Rāhu (*sgra-gcan*) and Ketu (*dus-me*) are identified as the ascending and descending phases of the moon.
22. The syllables OṂ ĀṂ HŪṂ respectively symbolise buddha-body, speech and mind, for which reason, in the context of the present work, they frequently appear at the beginning of verses as an invocation. See Ch. 5, pp. 67ff. The three verses which follow respectively concern the outer, inner, and secret

maṇḍala of offerings which are made respectively to the Buddha-body of Emanation (*nirmāṇakāya*), the Buddha-body of Perfect Resource (*sambhogakāya*), and the Buddha-body of Reality (*dharmakāya*). On the construction of these three maṇḍalas, see Paltrul Rinpoche, *The Words of My Perfect Teacher*, pp. 288–95; and Sonam T. Kazi (trans.), *Kun-zang La-may Zhal-lung*, Pt. 2, pp. 403–4.

23. The ultimate nature of mind (*sems-nyid*) is identified with the Buddha-body of Reality (*dharmakāya*). For a detailed introduction to the nature of mind, within the context of the present work, see Ch. 4, pp. 38–57.

24. The concluding mantra of the maṇḍala of offerings OṂ ĀḤ HŪṂ MAHĀ GURU DEVA ḌĀKINĪ RATNA MAṆḌALA PŪJĀ MEGHA Ā HŪṂ indicates that a cloud of offerings is presented to the precious maṇḍala of the spiritual teachers, meditational deities, and ḍākinīs.

25. The spiritual teachers of the core lineage who are connected with this transmission (*'brel-tshad don-ldan rtsa-brgyud bla-ma-rnams*) are those in successive generations who have maintained the lineage of our text from the time of Nyinda Ozer down to the present. See 'A Brief Literary History', pp. xxxvi–xlviii.

26. The biographies of the important figures in the lineage of the oral transmission (*bka'-brgyud*) related to the teachings of the Nyingma school, are outlined in Dudjom Rinpoche, NSTB, pp. 601–739.

27. The strict vows made in the past (*sngon-gyi dam-bca' gnyan-po*) are those taken by buddhas and bodhisattvas in former lives pertaining to the propagation of the Buddhist teaching and the bodhisattva vow to remove the sufferings of all beings. See e.g. P. Williams, *Mahāyāna Buddhism*, pp. 49–54.

28. Listed among the eighty minor marks (*asītyanuvyañjana*), the Brahmā-like voice (*tshangs-pa'i gsung*) refers to one of the six modes of buddha-speech. See Longchen Rabjampa, GGFTC, pp. 703–4.

29. On the concept of cyclical time, see L. Pruden (trans.), *Abhidharmakośabhāṣyaṃ*, Ch. 3, The World, pp. 475–95; R. Kloetzli, *Buddhist Cosmology*, pp. 73–5. Each great aeon (*mahākalpa*) of cyclical time is said to comprise the four eras of creation (*vivartakalpa*), duration (*vivartasthāyikalpa*), dissolution (*saṃvartakalpa*), and non-duration (*saṃvartasthāyikalpa*). The expression 'final era' (*dus-mtha'*) refers to the period of dissolution.

30. On this conferral of the four empowerments, namely: the vase empowerment (*bum-dbang*), the secret empowerment (*gsang-dbang*), the empowerment of pristine cognition (*shes-rab ye-shes-kyi dbang*) and the fourth empowerment of indivisible coemergence (*dbyer-med lhan-skyes dbang bzhi-pa*) which respectively confer the accomplishment of buddha-body (*sku-yi dngos-grub*), the accomplishment of buddha-speech (*gsung-gi dngos-grub*), the accomplishment of buddha-mind (*thugs-kyi dngos-grub*), and the combined accomplishment of buddha-body, speech and mind (*sku-gsung-thugs-kyi dngos-grub*), see Paltrul Rinpoche, *The Words of My Perfect Teacher*, pp. 329–30; and Sonam T. Kazi (trans.), *Kun-zang La-may Zhal-lung*, Pt. 2, pp. 462–5.

2 A Prayer for Union with the Spiritual Teacher

1. Tib. *sKu-gsum bla-ma'i rnal-'byor gsol-'debs dug-gsum ma-spang rang-grol.*
2. Tib. *Zab-chos zhi-khro dgongs-pa rang-grol.*
3. The specific blessing which arises from the Buddha-body of Reality (*chos-sku'i byin-rlab*) is 'primordially pure' (*ka-dag*), indicating that in this context the Buddha-body of Reality is directly realised through the Atiyoga practice called 'Cutting through Resistance to primordial purity' (*ka-dag khregs-chod*), on which see Ch. 4; also Dudjom Rinpoche, NSTB, pp. 335–7.
4. This blessing is 'spontaneously present' (*lhun-grub*), indicating that the Buddha-body of Perfect Resource is directly realised through the Atiyoga practice called 'All-surpassing Realisation of spontaneous presence' (*lhun-grub thod-rgal*). See Dudjom Rinpoche, NSTB, pp. 337–45.
5. The pristine cognition of the Buddha-body of Perfect Resource, here referred to as 'naturally liberated in supreme bliss' (*bde-chen rang-grol*), comprises the mirror-like pristine cognition (*ādarśajñāna*), the pristine cognition of sameness (*samatājñāna*), and the pristine cognition of discernment (*pratyave-kṣanajñāna*). See glossary under pristine cognition.
6. The pristine cognition referred to here is the pristine cognition of the Buddha-body of Emanation, otherwise known as the pristine cognition of accomplishment (*kṛtyupasthānajñāna*). See glossary under pristine cognition.
7. The natural pristine cognition (*rang-byung ye-shes*) of the three buddha-bodies in union refers to the unity of all the five aspects of pristine cognition (*pañ-cajñāna*).
8. On the bodhisattva's altruistic aspiration not to enter nirvāṇa until all sentient beings have been liberated from cyclic existence (*saṃsāra*), see P. Williams, *Mahāyāna Buddhism*, pp. 49–54.

3 Root Verses of the Six Intermediate States

1. Tib. *Bar-do rnam-drug-gi rtsa-tshig*. These verses are reiterated in the context of other chapters of this cycle, e.g. Ch. 10, p. 205, and Ch. 11, pp. 235 and 288.
2. Chs. 1–7 of the present text relate to the intermediate state of living, including the intermediate states of dreaming and meditative concentration.
3. Chs. 8–10 of the present text relate to the intermediate state of the time of death.
4. The intermediate state of reality is the subject of Ch. 11.
5. The intermediate state of rebirth is the subject of Chs. 11 and 13.

4 Natural Liberation through Naked Perception

1. Tib. *Rig-pa ngo-sprod gcer-mthong rang-grol.*
2. Tib. *Zab-chos zhi-khro dgongs-pa rang-grol.*
3. The point is that all the inestimable 84,000 aspects of the sacred teachings, the nine vehicles, the three or four *piṭaka*, and so forth, depend upon the

primary understanding of intrinsic awareness. Cf. *Laṅkāvatārasūtra*, Ch. 2, v. 202: 'As long as sentient beings manifest, there will be no end to the vehicles. When the mind becomes transformed, there is neither vehicle nor mover.'

4. The Tibetan expression *tshig gsum* (lit. 'three words') is used colloquially to mean 'terse' or 'in few words'. Two alternative readings have been suggested: 1) The phrase 'three words' could refer to the three statements given on pp. 41–2, that 'past thoughts are traceless, clear and empty', that 'future thoughts are unproduced and fresh', and that 'the present moment abides naturally and unconstructed'. 2) A less likely view is that this expression may refer to the Atiyoga testament of Prahevajra (Tib. dGa'-rab rdo-rje), entitled *Three Points which Penetrate the Essential* (*tshig-gsum gnad-du brdeg-pa*). The three points contained in this latter work crystalise the process through which intrinsic awareness (*rang-rig*) is introduced. They are as follows: the 'direct introduction to the essence itself' (*ngo-rang thog-tu 'phrod-pa*), the 'direct determination of this unique state' (*thag-gcig thog-tu bcad-pa*), and the 'direct confidence in liberation' (*gdeng-grol thog-tu bca'-ba*). For the original text, see *Bi-ma sNying-thig*, Pt. 1, Vol. Ga, pp. 304–18, and Patrul Rinpoche's nineteenth-century commentary entitled *mKhas-pa'i shri rgyal-po mkhas-chos*. The background to the revelation of Prahevajra's testament is given in Dudjom Rinpoche, NSTB, pp. 490–94.

5. This verse derives from the *Guhyagarbha Tantra*, Ch. 13, v. 2: There are those of no understanding,/ And those of wrong understanding,/ Those of partial understanding,/ And those who have not [quite] understood genuine reality.

As explained by Longchen Rabjampa, GGFTC, pp. 988–97, those of no understanding (*ma-rtogs-pa*) are ordinary persons who adhere to the 'vehicles of gods and humans' (*devamanuṣyayāna*), striving after excellence and higher rebirths within cyclic existence (*saṃsāra*) through the practice of virtue. Those of misunderstanding (*log-rtogs-pa*) comprise the eternalistic and nihilistic extremist philosophers of ancient India, who adhere to the Nyayāyika, Vaiṣṇava, Sāṃkhyā, Vaiśeṣika, and Bārhaspatya standpoints. Those of partial understanding (*phyogs-tsam rtogs-pa*) comprise the pious attendants (*śrāvaka*) who realise the selflessness of the individual person (*pudgalanairātmya*) but fail to realise the selflessness of phenomena (*dharmanairātmya*), and the hermit buddhas (*pratyekabuddha*) who additionally realise the lack of inherent existence (*niḥsvabhāvatā*) with respect to external material phenomena, but fail to realise the lack of inherent existence in internal mental phenomena. Lastly, those who do not quite understand genuine reality (*yang-dag ji-bzhin-nyid-du ma-rtogs-pa*) comprise the adherents of the causal vehicles, who maintain the views of Cittamātra and Madhyamaka, realising respectively that phenomena are extensions of consciousness and that all phenomena, whether external or internal, are without inherent existence; yet not quite understanding that 'all things are identical in primordial buddhahood', or that 'neither renunciation nor acceptance is required because dissonant mental states themselves arise as pristine cognition'. At the same time, all these types are said to be 'meagre in their skilful means (*upāyakauśalya*)' and they 'accomplish their results with difficulty and toil over a long period of time'. Longchen Rabjampa concludes that only the adherents of the resultant vehicles (*phalayāna*) perceive genuine reality as it is, and among these, only Atiyoga is stated to be the 'naturally secret truth' (*rang-bzhin gsang-ba'i don*), while Kriyātantra and Ubhayatantra are referred to as 'disciplines' (*'dul-ba*), Yogatantra as 'enlightened intention' (*dgongs-pa*), and Mahāyoga as 'secrecy' (*gsang-ba*). These diverse classifications of Buddhist practitioners and vehicles are identified, one by one, in the following verses. For the Nyingma perspective of the non-Buddhist views 'of wrong understanding' (*log-rtogs-pa*) mentioned above, see also Dudjom Rinpoche, NSTB, pp. 64–7.

6. On the classifications of those ordinary persons 'of no understanding' *(ma-rtogs-pa)* who adhere to the 'vehicles of gods and humans' (*devamanuṣyayāna*), see Dudjom Rinpoche, NSTB, pp. 57–64.

7. The 'partial absence of self' (*phyogs-tsam bdag-med*) is that aspect of selflessness comprehended by pious attendants and hermit buddhas. See glossary under selflessness.

8. This passage, in which the texts (*gzhung*) and philosophical systems (*siddhānta*; Tib. *grub-mtha'*) of the diverse Buddhist schools are said to inhibit the perception of inner radiance, corresponds closely to a well-known quotation from the *Tantra of the All-accomplishing King* (*Kun-byed rgyal-po'i rgyud*, T 828), for a translation of which, see Dudjom Rinpoche, NSTB, pp. 295–7. The Buddhist and non-Buddhist spiritual and philosophical systems (*siddhānta*) are the subject of detailed analysis in many specialist treatises, among which the Nyingma presentations relevant to our present text include Longchen Rabjampa's *Treasury of Spiritual and Philosophical Systems* (*Grub-mtha' mdzod*), and Dudjom Rinpoche's *Fundamentals of the Nyingma School* (*bsTan-pa'i rnam-gzhag*).

9. According to the often-cited passage from the *Tantra of the All-accomplishing King* (*Kun-byed rgyal-po'i rgyud*, T 828) mentioned above, the weaknesses (*gol-sa*) of these three outer classes of tantra are respectively: maintaining the subject–object dichotomy in relation to purity (Kriyātantra), maintaining the duality of view and conduct (Ubhayatantra), and maintaining acceptance and rejection in relation to meditation (Yogatantra). In the present context, these are all subsumed in the weakness of excessive attachment to the so-called 'four branches of ritual service and attainment' (*bsnyen-sgrub yan-lag bzhi*), on which see the glossary.

10. The inner tantras of skilful means (*nang-pa thabs-kyi rgyud*), which are the subject of the present verse, are those of Mahāyoga, Anuyoga, and Atiyoga, for a detailed discussion of which, see Dudjom Rinpoche, NSTB, pp. 273–345, 357–72. Of these inner tantras of skilful means, only Atiyoga is considered to be free from weaknesses, while the *Tantra of the All-accomplishing King* (*Kun-byed rgyal-po'i rgyud*) refers to the weakness in Mahāyoga as 'excessive perseverance with regard to ritual service and attainment' (*sevāsādhana*); and to the weakness in Anuyoga as 'the duality of pure expanse or space' (*dag-pa'i dbyings*) identified with Samantabhadrī, and of pristine cognition or awareness (*jñāna*), which is identified with Samantabhadra. See NSTB, pp. 295–7. In the context of the present verse, these weaknesses are both subsumed in the dualistic notion of 'space and awareness' (*dbyings-rig*).

11. Our text at this point has the reading: *gdams-ngag gdams-ngag* ('oral teaching, oral teaching'). The meaningful reading: *gang-zag bdag-med* ('selflessness of the individual') is suggested by Zenkar Rinpoche.

12. The elimination of the dichotomy between 'singularity' (*gcig*) and 'multiplicity' (*du-ma*) is the subject of one of the great axioms of Madhyamaka dialectic,

known as the 'absence of the singular and the multiple' (*gcig-dang du-bral*), on which see M. D. Eckel, *Jñānagarbha's Commentary on the Distinction between the Two Truths*, pp. 80–85.

13. The innate presence of intrinsic awareness, without need for the elaborations of view (*lta-ba*), meditation (*sgom-pa*), conduct (*spyod-pa*), or result (*'bras-bu*), as expounded in these verses, is clearly discussed in the Atiyoga texts of Cutting through Resistance (*khregs-chod*). See e.g. Dudjom Rinpoche, NSTB, p. 335.
14. The adopting of these four media (*thig-bzhi*) is comparable to reaching the limits of awareness by the three presences (*sdod-pa gsum*), or the revealing of the limits of liberation by means of the four assurances (*gdeng-bzhi*), which consolidate the practices of the Great Perfection. On these Atiyoga terms, see Dudjom Rinpoche, NSTB, p. 343.
15. The riveting of these four nails (*gzer-bzhi*) is comparable to that of the three attainments (*thob-pa gsum*), which consolidate the practices of the Great Perfection. See Dudjom Rinpoche, NSTB, p. 343.
16. The two extremes of which the view is free are open and closed or high and low perspectives; the two extremes of which meditation is devoid are hope and doubt; the two extremes of which conduct is free are renunciation and acceptance; and the two extremes of which the result is free are beginning and end. These eight extremes may be reduced to six by omitting the category of the result.
17. On the view of vacuous emptiness (*stong-pa phyal-ba*) maintained by non-Buddhists, see Dudjom Rinpoche, NSTB, pp. 62–4, 66–7; and for a detailed discussion, the purpose of which is to indicate that the Buddhist view of emptiness is neither vacuous nor nihilistic, see ibid., pp. 178–216.
18. The nature of the delusion (*gti-mug*), drowsiness (*'thib-pa*), and agitation (*rgod-pa*), which obstruct the clarity of meditations such as calm abiding (*śamatha*), is discussed in L. Pruden (trans.), *Abhidharmakośabhāṣyaṃ*, Ch. 5, The Latent Defilements, pp. 767–868, and Ch. 8, The Absorptions, pp. 1215–82.
19. Existence and non-existence (*yod-med gang-du ma-grub*) form one binary subset within the four-point set (*catuṣkoṭi*) of propositions which are negated by Nāgārjuna in the *Root Stanzas of the Madhyamaka entitled Discriminative Awareness* (*Prajñā-nāma mūlamadhyamaka-kārikā*, T 3824). See D. Kalupahana (trans.), *Mūlamadhyamakakārikās*.
20. On the controversy concerning the emptiness which is devoid of virtuous and negative actions (*stong-pa-nyid-la dge-sdig yul-ma grub*), see the discussion on the view of the Great Perfection in NSTB, pp. 896–910.
21. The lives of the future treasure-finders (*gter-ston*) predicted by Padmasambhava, including that of Karma Lingpa, the treasure-finder associated with our present text, are recounted in NSTB, pp. 750–880, and on the prophecies found in the treasure-doctrines, ibid., pp. 934–5. On Karma Lingpa, see also 'A Brief Literary History', pp. xxxvi–xlviii.

5 Natural Liberation of Habitual Tendencies

1. Tib. *Chos-spyod bag-chags rang-grol.*
2. Tib. *Zab-chos zhi-khro dgongs-pa rang-grol.*
3. Samantabhadra (*kun-tu bzang-po*) and Mahottara (*che-mchog*) respectively represent the peaceful and wrathful aspects of the Buddha-body of Reality (*dharmakāya*).
4. The first of these mantras: OṂ ĀḤ HŪṂ BODHICITTA MAHĀSUKHAJÑĀNA DHĀTU ĀḤ is the unified enlightened intention of the forty-two peaceful deities. See below, Ch. 14, p. 354. The second mantra: OṂ RULU RULU HŪṂ BHYOḤ HŪṂ is the unified enlightened intention of the fifty-eight wrathful deities. See Ch. 14, p. 364.
5. Whereas the description of Vajrasattva given above, Ch. 1, pp. 15–16, focuses on the purificatory function of Vajrasattva, the present passage provides the formal description (*abhisamaya*; Tib. *mngon-rtogs*) for the visualisation of Vajrasattva, according to the generation stage (*utpattikrama*) of meditation.
6. For an explanation, see glossary under Hundred-syllable Mantra.
7. These comprise the ten male and female buddhas along with the sixteen male and female bodhisattvas. See Appendix Two.
8. An inserted annotation in the text adds that if this aspirational prayer is recited on behalf of a deceased person, the word 'we' should, on each occurrence, be replaced with 'the deceased'.
9. The level of Samantabhadra is the sixteenth buddha level, otherwise known as the Level of Unsurpassed Pristine Cognition (*ye-shes bla-ma*).
10. This and the following italicized verses are extracted from the *Aspirational Prayer which Rescues from the Dangerous Pathways of the Intermediate States*. See Ch. 12, pp. 310–13.
11. The four pristine cognitions combined are the first four of the five pristine cognitions, omitting the pristine cognition of accomplishment. See glossary. On the reason for the omission of the pristine cognition of accomplishment, see Ch. 11, p. 249.
12. The occipital channel, which resembles the horn of an ox, is adjacent to the energy centre of perfect resource at the throat (*mgrin-pa longs-spyod-kyi 'khor-lo*) of the subtle body.
13. The 'life-force' channel, which resembles a crystal tube, otherwise known as *katika*, is adjacent to the heart-centre (*snying-ga chos-kyi 'khor-lo*) of the subtle body.
14. The bliss-sustaining secret place (*gsang-ba bde-skyong-gi 'khor-lo*) is located at the genitalia of the subtle body.
15. The ornaments (*rgyan*) worn by the peaceful deities include the five silks (*dar-gyi chas-gos lnga*), i.e. scarves, pendants, blouse, skirt, and sleeves; and the eight jewels, i.e. crown, earring, throat necklace, shoulder ornament, mid-length necklace, long necklace, bracelets and anklets. On the symbolism of these ornaments, see T. Norbu, *The Small Golden Key*, pp. 77–8.
16. Tib. *lhan-skyes ye-shes.*
17. Tib. *khrag-'thung lha-tshogs*. A synonym for herukas or wrathful deities.
18. Tib. *gnas-kyi ke'u-ri-ma ma-mo brgyad*. Here *gnas* is equivalent to the eight

classes of consciousness (*rnam-shes tshogs-brgyad*). See Longchen Rabjampa, GGFTC, p. 1170.

19. Tib. *mthing-nag*. DR, p. 188. l. 6 reads *mthing-skya*, but see Ch. 6, p. 107, and Ch. 11, p. 264.
20. Tib. *yul-bdag sing-ha phra-men brgyad*.The eight sensory objects are the objects of the corresponding eight classes of consciousness. See Longchen Rabjampa, GGFTC, p. 1170.
21. These Four Female Gatekeepers of the wrathful assembly also have distinct names: the wrathful counterpart of Aṅkuśā is Vajratejasī, of Pāśā Vajrāmoghā, of Sphoṭā Vajralokā, and of Ghaṇṭā Vajravetālī.
22. This and the following verse concern the assembly of the twenty-eight Īśvarī (*dbang-phyug-ma nyer-brgyad*) on the outermost rings of the wrathful maṇḍala, who are collectively referred to as the 'emanational enactors of the four rites of enlightened activity'. Among these, the six yoginī from the east who enact the white rites of pacification (*shar-nas zhi-ba'i las-mdzad rnal-'byor dbang-phyug drug*) are sometimes depicted holding a vajra in addition to their individual hand-emblems, indicating that they belong to the retinue of Vajra Heruka in the east. Among them, Manurākṣasī in Ch. 5 is simply described as 'white' (*dkar-mo*) and in Ch. 11 as 'dark brown' (*smug-nag*). Also, in Ch. 11, Brahmāṇī is erroneously described as 'red-yellow' (*dmar-se*), Kaumārī as solely red (*dmar-mo*), and Vaiṣṇāvī as solely 'blue' (*sngon-mo*).
23. Vajrā is also known as Piṅgalā. See Ch. 11, p. 265.
24. The six yoginī from the south who enact the yellow rites of enrichment (*lho-nas rgyas-pa'i las-mdzad rnal-'byor dbang-phyug drug*) are sometimes depicted holding a jewel in addition to their individual hand-emblems, indicating that they belong to the retinue of Ratna Heruka in the south.
25. The six yoginī from the west who enact the red rites of subjugation (*nub-nas dbang-gi las-mdzad rnal-'byor dbang-phyug drug*) are sometimes depicted holding a lotus in addition to their individual hand-emblems, indicating that they belong to the retinue of Padma Heruka in the west. Among them, in Ch. 11, Ekacāriṇī is erroneously described as 'yellow' (*ser-mo*), Rudhiramadī as solely 'red' (*dmar-mo*), and Siddhikarī as solely 'green' (*ljang-khu*). The Sanskrit identifications for Rudhiramadī, the consort of Mahābala (*stobs-chen*), Siddhikarī, the consort of Vasurakṣita (*nor-srung*), and the *rākṣasī* Ekacāraṇī (*srin-mo*) are derived from Longchen Rabjampa, GGFTC, p. 1126.
26. The six yoginī from the north who enact the rites of wrath (*byang-nas drag-po'i las-mdzad rnal-'byor dbang-phyug drug*) are sometimes depicted holding a crossed-vajra in addition to their individual hand-emblems, indicating that they belong to the retinue of Karma Heruka in the north. Among them, in Ch. 11, Agnāyī and Cāmuṇḍī are described as solely 'red' (*dmar-mo*), Varāhī as solely 'black' (*nag-mo*), and Varunāṇī and Vāyudevī as solely 'blue' (*sngon-mo*). Also, in Ch. 11 (Varanasi reprint) Vāyudevī is depicted as 'snake-headed' instead of 'wolf-headed'.
27. This verse concerns the four yoginī who enact their emanational rites at the outermost gates of the skull (*sprul-pa'i las-mdzad dbang-phyug sgo-ma bzhi*), and who complete the group of twenty-eight Īśvarī. Note that while in our text all four of these gatekeepers are generally referred to by the collective name Vajrā (*rdo-rje-ma*), their distinctive names are found in Ch. 14, pp. 370–71, and in Longchen Rabjampa, GGFTC, pp. 1127–28.

28. These are the fifty-eight wrathful deities, with the addition of Mahottara Heruka and Krodhīśvarī.
29. The three smeared sacraments (*byug-pa'i rdzas gsum*) of the charnel ground, 'ashes, blood and grease' (*thal-chen rakta zhag-gi zo-ris*), indicate that they have subdued envy. The 'skirts of moist hide and flayed tiger-skin' (*ko-rlon gYang-gzhi stag-gi sham-thabs*) indicate that delusion, attachment and aversion are respectively subdued by the ten powers (*daśabala*), desireless compassion and wrathful compassion. The snakes indicate their subjugation of the five social classes. For a description of the symbolism of the wrathful deities in general, see T. Norbu, *The Small Golden Key*, pp. 78–84. In addition to the five herukas (*khrag-'thung khro-bo'i tshogs*), five krodhīśvarī (*dbying-phyug khro-mo'i tshogs*), eight mātaraḥ, eight piśācī, twenty-eight īśvarī (*dbang-phyug mgo-brnyan tshogs*), and four gatekeepers (*sgo-ma bzhi*) described in the previous verses, the wrathful maṇḍala also includes the eight great projectresses (*spor-byed chen-mo*), who propel the consciousness of the deceased to higher rebirths, and who are enumerated individually in Ch. 6, pp. 108–9.
30. Here 'fields' translates the Tibetan term *khams* ('sensory spectra') rather than *skye-mched* ('sensory activity fields').
31. This verse is derived from the *Aspirational Prayer which Protects from Fear of the Intermediate States* (*Bar-do phrang-grol-gyi smon-lam*), on which see Ch. 12, pp. 314–16.
32. On the attainment of buddhahood during the intermediate state of reality (*chos-nyid bar-do*), see below, Ch. 11, pp. 226–32.
33. Tib. *Bar-do thos-grol*. See below, Ch. 11, pp. 217–303.
34. Tib. *Zhi-khro'i las-byang tshor-ba rang-grol*. On this *sādhana* text, see Appendix One, p. 382.
35. Tib. *gSang-dbang rig-pa rang-grol*. This is one of the empowerment texts related to the cycle of the Peaceful and Wrathful Deities. See Appendix One.
36. Tib. *bsKong-bshags nyams-chags rang-grol*. See below, Ch. 7, pp. 113–50.

6 Natural Liberation of Negativity and Obscuration

1. Tib. *Bar-do thos-grol*.
2. Tib. *brGya-phyag sdig-sgrib rang-grol*.
3. Tib. *Zab-chos zhi-khro dgongs-pa rang-grol*.
4. A Sanskrit term, indicating obeisance or homage.
5. The Delhi reprint of *Bar-do thos-grol chen-mo* includes an annotation to the effect that when generating the visualisation of the maṇḍala in front rather than prostrating to an already clearly visualised assembly, the words 'I bow down to such and such a buddha-body' (*sku-la phyag-'tshal-lo*) should be replaced by the words 'such and such a buddha-body is primordially and radiantly present' (*sku-ni ye-nas gsal*).
6. Tib. *chos-kyi khams*.
7. Tib. *mtshan-'dzin*. Here substantialism refers to the grasping at characteristics, having failed to understand that they lack inherent existence.
8. DR here reads 'green-black' (*ljang-nag*), but see Ch. 5, p. 81, and Ch. 11, p. 264, where she is depicted as solely 'black'.

9. Note that Ulūkamukhī is described here as holding an iron hook (*lcags-kyu*), instead of a vajra, as in Ch. 5, p. 83, and Ch. 11, p. 264.
10. According to GGFTC, p. 1135, Sphoṭā may also have a bear-head (*dom-mgo*).
11. According to GGFTC, p. 1135, Ghaṇṭā may also have a wolf-head (*spyang-mgo*).
12. Tib. *Zhags-'phen-ma*.
13. Tib. *mDung-thung 'phen-ma*.
14. Tib. *sPor-byed dril-'khrol-ma*.
15. Tib. *sPor-byed khyung-thogs-ma*.
16. Tib. *sPor-byed skar-mda' 'phen-ma*.
17. This is a reference to the great mythological battle (*gYul-chen*) between the gods and antigods, on which see Antigods in glossary.
18. Tib. *sPor-byed rdo-rje glog-phreng 'dzin-ma*.
19. Tib. *sPor-byed glags-sha rdeb-ma*.
20. Tib. s*Por-byed ral-gri 'dzin-ma*.
21. Vajrā is more commonly known as Piṅgalā (*dga'-ba*). See Ch. 11, p. 265.
22. See Ch. 5, p. 86. DR reads 'green'.
23. The number 110 comprises the verses dedicated to the Hundred Peaceful and Wrathful Deities, with the addition of two verses dedicated to Mahottara Heruka and Krodheśvarī, as well as eight verses dedicated to the Projectresses (*spor-chen brgyad*).
24. Tib. *Na-rag bskang-bshags*. A celebrated treasure-doctrine (*gter-chos*) revealed during the thirteenth century by Guru Chowang, and included within his *Eight Transmitted Precepts: Consummation of All Secrets* (*bKa'-brgyad gsang-ba yongs-rdzogs*). On this text, see K. Dowman (trans.), 'Emptying the Depths of Hell', in *Flight of the Garuda*, pp. 53–61; also D. Christensen (trans.), *Na-rag bskang-bshags*.

7 Natural Liberation through Acts of Confession

1. Tib. *Zhi-khro'i klong-bshags brjod-pa rang-grol*.
2. Tib. *Zab-chos zhi-khro dgongs-pa rang-grol*.
3. The offerings and dedications of great magnitude attributed to the bodhisattva Samantabhadra are recounted in the *Avataṃsakasūtra*. See T. Cleary (trans.), *The Flower Ornament Scripture*, pp. 1135 ff.; and P. Williams, *Mahāyāna Buddhism*, pp. 125–7.
4. Tib. *gnyis-med byang-chub-sems*.
5. i.e. the monastic vows of the *prātimokṣa* (*so-sor thar-pa*) discipline, on which see glossary.
6. DR, p. 409, l. 2, reads: *srab-la 'phyar-bas* . . . Here we follow the Varanasi reprint: *'phyor-la gYeng-bas*. The Delhi reprint reads: *srog-la 'tshal-bas*.
7. In the context of the maṇḍala of wrathful deities, the Buddha-body of Reality is represented by Mahottara Heruka.
8. In the context of the maṇḍala of wrathful deities, the Buddha-body of Perfect Resource (*sambhogakāya*) is represented by the Five Herukas and their consorts.
9. The Four Piśācī situated in the cardinal directions of the wrathful assembly, namely, Siṃhamukhī, Vyāghrīmukhī, Śṛgālamukhī, and Śvānamukhī, as their

names suggest, possess fangs, while those of the intermediate directions: Gṛdhramukhī, Kaṅkamukhī, Kākamukhī, and Ulūkamukhī are winged figures.

10. Generally the Twenty-eight Īśvarī are associated with the complete four rites or aspects of enlightened activity (*las-bzhi*) and not only *abhicāra*.
11. DR, p. 412, l. 6, *'gugs-'ching-sdom-dgyes*. The Delhi reprint misreads *'gyed* for *'gyes*, while the Varanasi reprint misreads *'phying* for *'ching* and *dgyes* for *'gyes*.
12. Tib. *sha-khrag mchod-pa*. This refers to the offering of the five meats and five nectars, on which see G. Dorje, 'The Nyingma Interpretation of Commitment and Vow', in *The Buddhist Forum*, Vol. 2, pp. 71–95.
13. Tib. *ma-bdun sring-bzhi*. On this group of eleven peripheral ḍākinīs, who are classed as protectors in the retinue of Śrīdevī, see Jigme Lingpa, *dPal-chen 'dus-pa*.
14. The wardens of the secret abodes (*ti-ra gnas-nyul/ gnas-nyul chen-po*) are the protector deities associated with the sacred power-places or pilgrimage places of Tibet.
15. Tib. *rdo-rje rgyal-thab/thib*.
16. Tib. *bstan-pa'i sgron-me* is here used as an epithet of the assistant vajra-master. DR, p. 416, reads: *ston-pa'i sgron-ma*.
17. Tib. *sgrol-ging bdag-po* is an epithet of Citipati, an acolyte of Yama, Lord of Death.
18. i.e. the four female gatekeepers of the wrathful assembly, Vajratejasī, Vajrāmoghā, Vajralokā, and Vajravetālī, who 'summon and guide' (*'gug-'dren pho-nya*).
19. The rampant egohood which can result from improper application of Buddhist practices, particularly the tantras, is exemplified by the archetypal demonic form Rudra, who is compassionately 'liberated' by the wrathful deities. Accounts concerning the past lives of Rudra are to be found in the *mDo dgongs-pa 'dus-pa*, Chs. 22–31, 147.5.1ff.; in Yeshe Tshogyal, *The Life and Liberation of Padmasambhava*, Pt. I, pp. 26–47, and Longchen Rabjampa, GGFTC, pp. 1080–95.
20. Here we follow the Delhi reprint: *byings*. DR, p. 418, reads *gYeng*.
21. Tib. *byams-mgon thugs-rje-can*, i.e. Vajrasattva, to whom this entreaty is made.
22. lit. albugo (*ling-tog*).
23. Tib. *kun-nas zlum-po'i thig-le*.
24. Tib. DR, pp. 423–4, *gzung-'dzin gnyis-su 'dzin-pa nyon-re-mongs/ rig-pa ye-shes klong-du bshags-par bgyi*. Note that the Delhi reprint reads: *yod-dang med-par lta-ba nyon-re-mongs/ rtag-chad med-pa'i ye-shes klong-du bshags*.
25. On the practices pertaining to this distinction, see Longchen Rabjampa, GGFTC, pp. 900–914.
26. Tib. *bhaga*.
27. Tib. *yi-dam phyag-rgya*. On the linking of the seals of the deities and the recitation of mantra, see glossary under Seal and Mantras.
28. i.e. the secret name (*gsang-mtshan*) conferred by a vajra-master in the course of an empowerment ceremony.
29. Tib. *mngon-rtogs*.
30. The principal Nyingma text elucidating the integration of the vinaya, bodhisattva, and mantra vows expressed in this verse is Ngari Paṇchen's *Ascertainment of the Three Vows* (*sDom-gsum rnam-nges*).

31. Tib. *sKongs-bshags nyams-chags rang-grol.* This text, which is included within the wider cycle of *The Peaceful and Wrathful Deities: Natural Liberation [through Recognition] of Enlightened Intention*, comprises both empowerments and generation-stage practices. See Appendix One.
32. According to the tradition of the treasure-doctrines (*gter-chos*), there are four kinds of seal associated with the transmission of such teachings, namely: the seal of commitment (*samaya-rgya*), the seal of treasures (*gter-rgya*), the seal of concealment (*sbas-rgya*), and the seal of entrustment or succession (*gtad-rgya*). See Dudjom Rinpoche, NSTB, Vol. 2, p. 77.

8 Natural Liberation through Recognition of the Visual Indications and Signs of Death

1. Tib. *'Chi-ltas mtshan-ma rang-grol.* The recognition of the signs and portents of impending death is also discussed in the context of Tibetan medicine. See *Tibetan Medical Paintings*, pp. 47–52, and pp. 203–8.
2. Tib. *Zab-chos zhi-khro dgongs-pa rang-grol.*
3. Tib. *bar-do thos-pa rang-grol.* See Ch. 11.
4. For a discussion on the Buddhist phenomenological analysis of the aggregate of form (*rūpaskandha*), which constitutes the human body, see L. Pruden (trans.), *Abhidharmakośabhāṣyaṃ*, Ch. 1, The Dhātus, pp. 63ff.
5. Indications or symptoms of untimely death (*dus-min 'chi-ba*) may be treated by ritual purification, as recommended in this text, or by medical means, on which see *Tibetan Medical Paintings*, p. 85. On the course of the lifespan principle within the body, see *Tibetan Medical Paintings*, p. 39.
6. The ritual deception of death (*'chi bslu-ba*) is the subject of Ch. 9.
7. It should be stressed that the specificity of the external signs of impending death and the prognostications listed here are to be understood in the context of the spiritual practices outlined in other chapters of this cycle, since the examination cannot be undertaken in isolation from them.
8. Tib. *'chi-bdag lag-tu song-ba.* Lord of Death is an epithet of Yama.
9. i.e. one calendar day or lunar day (*tshes*), comprising twenty-four hours.
10. Vital breath is an aspect of vital energy (*rlung*; Skt. *vāyu*), on which see glossary under Vital Energy.
11. DR, Vol. 3, p. 181, l. 4, reads *zhag 'ga'* ('some days'), but we have taken the present reading from the Delhi reprint.
12. For an account of the examination of dreams from the perspective of Tibetan medicine, see *Tibetan Medical Paintings*, pp. 49–52, and 205–8.
13. Tib. *rgyal-pos srog-gcad.* Here we follow the Delhi reprint (p. 438, l. 3). DR, p. 182, l. 1, reads *rgyal-po'i srog-bcad.*
14. Tib. *byang-chub mchog-tu sems-bskyed.* See Ch. 1, pp. 14–15.
15. Tib. *dbang-gsum dam-tshig.* See glossary under Four Empowerments and Commitments.
16. See also *Tibetan Medical Paintings*, pp. 51–2; and for remote indications of death discernible to the physician approaching the residence of a patient, ibid., pp. 47–8. Note that DR, p. 186, l. 1, reads *gzungs* for *gzugs.*
17. i.e. the full-moon day of the lunar month.

18. This mantra is that of the 'lord who subsumes the lifespan'.
19. The other suitable hand-implements (*phyag-mtshan*) include the vajra and bell.
20. The letter A is symbolic of emptiness (*śūnyatā*).
21. This cross-legged posture (*rdo-rje skyil-krung*) and folded hand-gesture of meditative equipoise (*lag-pa mnyam-bzhag*) are both aspects of the seven-point posture of Vairocana (*rnam-snang chos-bdun*), on which see glossary.
22. Tib. *brtan-pa'i lha-dang bral-ba*.
23. Tib. *spyi-gtsug bzlog-na*. Our reading here follows the Delhi reprint (p. 450, l. 2). DR, p. 188, l. 6, has *spyi-gtsug 'dug-na*.
24. Tib. *gnas-lugs zab-mo'i lta-ba*.
25. Tib. *rlung-yum shor-ba*.
26. Note that DR (p. 191, l. 2) and the Indian reprints all read 'six months' (*zla-ba drug*).
27. For a discussion on the elaborate procedures for urinalysis in general, see *Tibetan Medical Paintings*, pp. 139–48, and 295–304.
28. On this portent known as 'setting of the unchanging sun at the summit of Mount Sumeru' (*ri-rab rtse-la mi-'gyur nyi-ma nub*), the method of ritually averting death is unspecified in Ch. 9. Note that the Delhi reprint has an annotation adding that: 'if, instead, there are small circles of light, this portends that the subject will fall ill'.
29. The Delhi reprint has an annotation adding that: 'if, instead, there is a slight humming sound, this portends that the subject will fall ill'.
30. On this portent known as 'rupturing of the Wish-granting Tree from the Summit of Mount Sumeru' (*ri-rab rtse-nas dpag-bsam ljon-shing chag*), the method of ritually averting death is unspecified in Ch. 9. Note that the Delhi version has an annotation adding that: 'if, instead, there is a slight trace of evaporation, this portends that the subject will fall ill'.
31. Yavati is more specifically identified as an acolyte of Mahākāla, or as an aspect of Pehar. The Delhi version has an annotation adding that: 'if, instead, the tuft of hair stands up alone for a short time, this portends that one will fall ill'. On the posterior and pterion fontanelles subsumed in the phrase *ltag-pa'i bdud-sgo-dag*, see *Tibetan Medical Paintings*, pp. 249–50.
32. Tib. *'chi-ltas thor-bu*. On this category of signs, which are also classified as 'sudden changes relating to death' (*glo-bur rnam-gyur-gyi 'chi-ltas*) within the Tibetan medical tradition, see *Tibetan Medical Paintings*, pp. 207–8.
33. See Chapter 10 for these practices.
34. As stated in Tsele Natsok Rangdrol, *The Mirror of Mindfulness*, p. 56, the sequence may alter as far as the dissolution of the outer elements is concerned.
35. At this juncture the secret sign of the impending luminosity appears like a mirage, and the subject's vision will become unclear. On this dissolution of the earth element into the water element, and its coincidence with the disintegration of the navel energy-centre of the body, see Tsele Natsok Rangdrol, *The Mirror of Mindfulness*, pp. 54–5.
36. At this juncture the secret sign of the impending luminosity appears like a misty smoke; and the subject's hearing will become unclear. On this dissolution of the water element into the fire element, and its coincidence with the disintegration of the heart energy-centre of the body, see Tsele Natsok Rangdrol, *The Mirror of Mindfulness*, p. 55.

37. At this juncture the secret sign of the impending luminosity appears like red fireflies, and the subject's ability to smell will cease. The location of the body from which the warmth recedes indicates the place of subsequent rebirth, as indicated on pp. 177–9. On this dissolution of the fire element into the air element, and its coincidence with the disintegration of the throat energy-centre of the body, see Tsele Natsok Rangdrol, *The Mirror of Mindfulness*, p. 55.
38. At this juncture the secret sign of the impending luminosity appears like a flaming torch, and the subject's ability to taste will cease. On this dissolution of the wind element into the space element or consciousness, and its coincidence with the disintegration of the sexual energy-centre of the body, see Tsele Natsok Rangdrol, *The Mirror of Mindfulness*, pp. 55–6. The five sense-faculties and the sensory spectra are also dissolved at this juncture. From this point onwards, death cannot be reversed.
39. Note that in other texts of this genre, the descent of whiteness precedes the ascent of redness. However, Jigme Lingpa in his *sKu-gsum zhing-khams sbyong-smon* follows the sequence outlined here, and according to Tsele Natsok Rangdrol, op. cit., p. 57, it is uncertain whether the whiteness or redness will manifest first.
40. Tib. *srog-rtsa*. The so-called 'black life channel' (*srog-rtsa nag-po*) is identified with the aorta, in Tibetan medicine, while the 'white life-channel' (*srog-rtsa dkar-po*) is identified with the spinal cord. See *Tibetan Medical Paintings*, pp. 191–2, and 197–8.
41. On the significance of the syllables HI KA in the transference of consciousness (*'pho-ba*), see Ch. 10, pp. 203–4.
42. On the dissolution of consciousness into inner radiance (*'od-gsal*; Skt. *prabhāsvara*) during the intermediate state of the moment of death (*'chi-kha'i bar-do*), see Ch. 11, pp. 227–34.
43. On the mother and child aspects of reality, otherwise known as the naturally occurring inner radiance of the ground and the cultivated inner radiance of the path, see Ch. 11, pp. 227–34. The latter is the intrinsic awareness cultivated by meditators during their lifetime.
44. The period following the cessation of the coarse outer breath (*phyi-dbugs*) and before the cessation of the subtle inner breath (*nang-dbugs*), also known as the life-sustaining wind (*srog-'dzin-gyi rlung*; Skt. *prāṇa*), is that during which the vital energy and mind are drawn together into the central channel, causing ordinary beings to lapse into unconsciousness. On this distinction between inner breath and outer breath, see also Ch. 11, p. 228.
45. The inner radiance of the path (*lam-gyi 'od-gsal*) is that experienced by practitioners and yogins through their spiritual practices prior to death. See glossary under Inner Radiance.
46. Tib. *gnod-sbyin*. Other texts suggest that this mode of rebirth is indicated by the emission of consciousness from the nose. See Lati Rinpoche and J. Hopkins, *Death, Intermediate State and Rebirth in Tibetan Buddhism*, p. 53; also A. Wayman, *The Buddhist Tantras*, p. 141. On the term *yakṣa*, see glossary.
47. On the transference of consciousness (*'pho-ba*) through the crown fontanelle, and the appearance of serum at the crown of the head as an indication of success in this practice, see below, Ch. 10, pp. 203–4.

48. Tib. *sKu-gdung 'bar-ba'i rgyud*. This text is one of the Seventeen Tantras of the Esoteric Instructional Class of the Great Perfection (*rdzogs-chen man-ngag sde'i rgyud bcu-bdun*), and is contained in NGB, Vol. 3.
49. Tib. *bTags-grol*. This text forms the subject matter of Ch. 14, pp. 347–79.
50. As explained in Ch. 10.
51. Tib. *Bar-do thos-grol*. This text is the subject matter of Ch. 11, pp. 225–303.
52. Tib. *'Chi-ba bslu-ba*. This text is the subject matter of Ch. 9, pp. 184–95.
53. The presence of the Peaceful and Wrathful Deities within the heart and the brain has already been explained in detail. See Ch. 5, pp. 67–88.

9 Natural Liberation of Fear

1. Tib. *'Chi-bslu 'jigs-pa rang-grol*. The *Tengyur* contains a number of ritual texts, similar to the present chapter, concerning the deception of death (*'chi-ba bslu-ba*; Skt. *mṛtyuṣṭhāpaka*), including those by Tathāgatarakṣita (T 1702), Vāgīśvarakīrti (T 1748), and Ajitamitragupta (T 2839). A hybrid Sanskrit title *Krodha amukha bhela* is also attributed to the present text.
2. Tib. *Zab-chos zhi-khro dgongs-pa rang-grol*.
3. The Varanasi reprint, p. 213, reads Vajrakumāra (*rdo-rje gzhon-nu*). DR, p. 206, l. 1, reads only *gzhon-nu*. Vajrakumāra is the subject of this invocation, being the embodiment of buddha-activity.
4. The earliest extant literature on guidance through the intermediate states appears to have a strong association with this particular bodhisattva. See e.g. *Kāraṇḍavyūhasūtra*, and M. Lalou, 'Chemins du mort dans les croyances de haute-asie', which includes a translation of an ancient Dunhuang manuscript entitled *Exposé du chemin du mort* (*gshin-lam bslan-ba*), where Avalokiteśvara is referred to particularly as a deity who guides and rescues those propelled towards hellish rebirths.
5. On the course of the lifespan principle (*tshe'i rtsa*), subsuming the five elements, over a monthly cycle, and the location of the vulnerable points of the body in relation to it, see *Tibetan Medical Paintings*, pp. 39–40.
6. Tib. *rlung-gi 'khor-lo*. On the meditative stabilities related to the five elements, and the relationship between the five colours, the five elements, and the five seed-syllables, see Longchen Rabjampa, GGFTC, pp. 619–20.
7. These are the vowels (*a-li*) and consonants (*ka-li*) of the Sanskrit alphabet, for the symbolism of which see Longchen Rabjampa, GGFTC, pp. 554–99.
8. The deities embodying the elements correspond to those of the Hindu pantheon, e.g. Pavana, who embodies the wind element, Agni who embodies the fire element, Varuṇa who embodies the water element, and Viṣṇu who embodies the earth element. For the Buddhist perspective, see Longchen Rabjampa, GGFTC, pp. 1124–8.
9. YAṂ is absorbed into Pavana, RAṂ into Agni, LAṂ into Viṣṇu, and KHAṂ into Varuṇa.
10. DR, p. 209, l. 3, adds an annotation, suggesting that these should include the breath of horses, elephants and buffaloes.
11. DR, p. 209, l. 4, adds an annotation to the effect that the syllable RAṂ is inserted into the effigy's eyes, the syllable KHAṂ into its ears, the syllable LAṂ into its tongue, the syllable YAṂ into its nose, and the syllable E into its neck.

12. DR, p. 209, l. 6, adds that the effigy should be black when offered to male malevolent forces (*bdud*), red when offered to martial haunting spirits (*btsan*) and hybrid serpentine haunting spirits (*klu-btsan*), yellow when offered to hybrid serpentine and plague-causing spirits (*klu-gnyan*) and malign goblins (*the'u-rang*), white when offered to the king spirits (*rgyal-po*), green when offered to the female malevolent forces (*bdud-mo*) and rural divinities (*yul-lha*), and multicoloured when offered to earth-ogres (*sa-srin*).
13. Tib. *ltas-ngan-gyi bya-sgrog*. Feathers of the owl in particular are deemed to be harbingers of ill-omens.
14. The sense organs are here consecrated with seed-syllables indicative of each of the five elements in turn, beginning with LAṂ, the seed-syllable of the earth element.
15. The Heart-mantra of Dependent Origination (*rten-'brel snying-po*), which liberates the enduring continuum of phenomena and induces the appearance of multiplying relics (*'phel-gdung*) and rainbow lights, is: YE DHARMĀ HETU-PRABHAVĀ HETUN TEṢĀṂ TATHĀGATO HY AVADAT TEṢĀṂ CA YO NIRODHO EVAṂ VĀDĪ MAHĀŚRAMAṆAḤ ('Whatever events arise from a cause, the Tathāgata has told the cause thereof, and the great virtuous ascetic has taught their cessation as well'). See also Ch. 14, p. 376; and S. Beyer, *The Cult of Tārā*, p. 146.
16. On the symbolism of the Sanskrit syllable A, indicative of emptiness, see GGFTC, pp. 559–63. This syllable is frequently utilised as a focal point for the meditations of calm abiding (*śamatha*), in which case it is visualised at the tip of the nose. There are recorded instances of the syllable actually manifesting on the tip of the nose of certain great meditation masters of the past. See e.g. the life of Kumārādza in NSTB, pp. 568–72.
17. On the seed-syllable BHRŪṂ, the first of the mantras through which the maṇḍala of the peaceful deities is generated, specifically referring to the creative visualisation of the celestial palaces of the deities, see Longchen Rabjampa, GGFTC, pp. 689–90.
18. On the seed-syllable KṢA, which is the final seed-syllable of the maṇḍala of the peaceful deities, specifically referring to Buddha Samantabhadra, see Longchen Rabjampa, GGFTC, p. 591.
19. The short syllable HŪṂ has a contracted *anusvāra*, in which the crescent and *nāda* are subsumed in the *bindu*.
20. The syllable MĀṂ is that of the female buddha Māmakī. See Longchen Rabjampa, GGFTC, pp. 691–2.
21. The syllable MŪṂ is that the female buddha Dhātvīśvarī. See Longchen Rabjampa, GGFTC, p. 691.
22. Tib. *rtsa gnyid-log*. See Ch. 11, p. 228.
23. On the diverse divisions of the Buddhist scriptures (*gsung-rab*) from the Nyingma point of view, see Dudjom Rinpoche, NSTB, pp. 73–87.
24. The rituals referred to here are somewhat unclear, but for the treatment of diseases pertaining to the five solid viscera and the six hollow viscera, see *Tibetan Medical Paintings*, pp. 101–2, and pp. 257–8.
25. The following series of signs of near death are observed in the urine specimen. Note that whereas here it is the urine scum (*spris-ma*) that appears blue or red, in Ch. 8, p. 170, these colours are attributed to the urine vapour (*rlangs-pa*). See

also the elaborate explanations of urinalysis given in *Tibetan Medical Paintings*, pp. 139–48, and pp. 295–304.

26. The combination of the five elements (*khams-lnga*) with the twelve animal year-signs is an important feature of elemental divination (*'byung-rtsis*), on which see G. Dorje, *Tibetan Elemental Divination Paintings*, pp. 66–86.
27. The Delhi reprint adds an annotation to the effect that this is also applicable if the humming sound disappears intermittently.
28. At this point, the various versions of our text include the following paragraph: 'In cases when [one's shadow] is missing from the neck upwards, one should visualise the syllable YAṂ in the subject's heart, and gaze upwards as high as one can. [Death] will then be averted if one performs ablutions from the crown downwards with water [empowered by] mantras of retention.' This observation appears to be misplaced, referring as it does to the analysis of the optically projected shadow rather than the humming of the ears.

10 Natural Liberation through Recollection

1. Tib. *'Pho-ba dran-pa rang-grol.*
2. Tib. *rDzogs-rim bar-do drug-gi khrid-yig.* This cycle has been translated into English by Alan Wallace. See *Natural Liberation.*
3. Tib. *Zab-chos zhi-khro dgongs-pa rang-grol.*
4. The six topics of the perfection stage (*sampannakrama*) respectively relate to the six intermediate states summarised in Ch. 3. Among them, the yoga of consciousness transference relates to the intermediate state of the time of death (*'chi-kha'i bar-do*), on which see also Ch. 11, pp. 225–34. At this point an annotation in the text refers to the importance of this chapter as 'an oral instruction which is like the giving of a royal injunction' (*rgyal-po bka'-them bskur-ba lta-bu*).
5. Tib. *'Chi-ltas mtshan-la rang-grol.* See Ch. 8, pp. 153–81.
6. On the ritual deception of death (*'chi-bslu*), see above, Ch. 9, pp. 184–95.
7. Tib. *'Chi-bslu 'jigs-pa rang-grol.* This is the subject matter of Ch. 9 above.
8. Consciousness transference may be taught in the context of general guidance (*khrid-kyi dus*), as in the case of the preliminary practices (*sngon-'gro*). See Paltrul Rinpoche, *The Words of My Perfect Teacher*, pp. 351–65; and Sonam T. Kazi (trans.), *Kun-zang La-may Zhal-lung*, Pt. 3, pp. 493–516. Manuals of particular guidance on consciousness transference (*'pho-ba'i sgos-khrid*) include the present chapter from Karma Lingpa's *Zhi-khro dgongs-pa rang-grol* and Tsele Natsok Rangdrol's *The Mirror of Mindfulness*, pp. 65–73.
9. Tib. *khrid kyi sngon 'gro.* See above, Ch. 1.
10. Tib. *sa-gnon-pa'i phyag-rgya* (Skt. *bhūmyākramaṇa*), here identified with the *bhūsparśamudrā.*
11. On the association of these other orifices with specific modes of rebirth, see p. 214.
12. On the crown or anterior fontanelle (*tshangs-pa'i bu-ga*), and its relationship to the central energy channel of the subtle body (*avadhūti*), see *Tibetan Medical Paintings*, pp. 33–40 and pp. 189–96.
13. On the relation between the central channel and those of the Rasanā to its right

and the Lalanā to its left, see also Longchen Rabjampa, GGFTC, pp. 1006 ff., and *Tibetan Medical Paintings*, pp. 33–4.

14. Tib. *khu-tshur.*
15. See Ch. 3, p. 33.
16. This refers to the recitation of Ch. 11 of the present work.
17. On these transformations, see Ch. 8, pp. 156–9 and 171–3.
18. This reference is unidentified.
19. Tib. *Nyi-zla kha-sbyor.* This text is contained in Vol. 4 of the *Collected Tantras of the Nyingmapa* (*rNying-ma'i rgyud-'bum*).
20. The 'field of accumulated merits' (*tshogs-bsags zhing*), to whom offerings are made, comprises one's parents, invalids or other disadvantaged persons, spiritual teachers, monks, and bodhisattvas.
21. Skt. *śaraṇagamana.* On the taking of refuge, see above, Ch. 1, pp. 11–13; and also glossary.
22. There are many diverse techniques of consciousness-transference within the Tibetan tradition, including those derived from *The Six Doctrines of Nāropā* (*Nāro chos-drug*), the *Innermost Spirituality of Longchenpa* (*Klong-chen snying-thig*), and the present cycle.
23. Tib. *thos-grol.* The words to be communicated in this context are contained below, Ch. 11, which includes descriptions of the three intermediate states of the time of death, reality, and rebirth. The intermediate state of reality (*chos-nyid bar-do*) is also known as the intermediate state of inner radiance (*'od-gsal*), on which see Ch. 11, p. 227ff.
24. Just as there are outer, inner, and secret signs of impending death (see Ch. 8, pp. 155–71) and outer and inner signs of the efficacy of the mantras utilised in 'liberation by wearing' (see Ch. 14, *passim*), so here, in the context of the various types of consciousness-transference, there are 'outer' signs observable in the atmosphere, 'inner' signs observable on the body of the deceased, and 'secret' signs observable in the relics that emerge after death. On the appearance of seed-syllables among the cremated relics of great spiritual teachers, see e.g. Dudjom Rinpoche, NSTB, p. 564.
25. The white syllable ĀḤ is the seed-syllable of Vajradhara, the azure syllable HŪṂ is that of Vajrasattva, and the red syllable HRĪḤ is that of Avalokiteśvara. See Longchen Rabjampa, GGFTC, Ch. 7, pp. 682–93.
26. The five types of bone-relic (Tib. *dung-rigs rnam-pa-lnga*), which appear following cremation, are associated with the five seed-syllables of the five male buddhas, and with five bodily constituents. See Ch. 14. On the appearance of cremation relics in the form of a deity's hand-implement (*phyag-mtshan*) or image (*sku-'dra*), see e.g. Dudjom Rinpoche, NSTB, pp. 572.
27. Here the emergence of fluids from the left nostril rather than the crown fontanelle is an indication that the consciousness-transference has taken effect into the Buddha-body of Emanation rather than into the Buddha-bodies of Reality or Perfect Resource. On the appearance of such signs, see Ch. 14, *passim*; and for a recorded instance of the whole skull being left as a cremation relic, see Dudjom Rinpoche, NSTB, p. 572.
28. Orgyan, i.e. an epithet of Padmasambhava.
29. Tib. *srid pa'i sgo zhes bya ba khams dang thig la dkar dmar 'gyu-ba'i lam.*
30. Tib. *de-kho-na-nyid-kyi dam-tshig-dang sdom-pa.* In general, all the commitments of the Vehicle of Indestructible Reality and all vows associated with

pious attendants and bodhisattvas may be termed commitments and vows taken with respect to the nature of reality. More specifically, however, this refers to the four commitments taken by practitioners of the Great Perfection: nothingness, evenness, uniqueness, and spontaneity, on which see R. Barron (trans.), *The Precious Treasury of the Way of Abiding.*

31. Tib. *btags-grol.* See Ch. 14.
32. Tib. *thos-grol.* See Ch. 11.

11 The Great Liberation by Hearing

Part One

1. Tib. *Thos-grol chen-mo.*
2. Tib. *Zab-chos zhi-khro dgongs-pa rang-grol.*
3. Tib. *khrid-kyi rim-pa.* This refers to all the levels of instruction received during the course of a person's lifetime, including those based on the sūtras and the tantras. The experiential cultivation of the 'great emptiness' (*stong-pa chen-po*) which the practitioner of Mahāyoga enters into in the course of daily practice brings about a dissolution of normal conceptual consciousness into a non-dual, non-conceptual awareness. The signs which accompany the successful actualisation of this meditative process are identical to those which occur at the time of death. The resulting familiarity with the process of the dissolution of consciousness allows the practitioner, at the time of death, to pass through an accustomed process and thereby to enter the non-conceptual inner radiance without confusion and to rest in its nature, with stability.
4. See above, Ch. 10.
5. See above, Ch. 8.
6. Tib. *bden-pa'i stobs.* This refers to an invocation prayer evoking the power of the truth of the ultimate nature of mind and phenomena embodied in the meditational deities, the sacred writings, and the community of sincere practitioners.
7. This esoteric meditative process, which is divulged only to fully qualified practitioners, is described in supplementary texts relating to the present cycle, such as *Guiding the Deceased to Higher Rebirths: The Natural Liberation of the Six Realms of Beings* (*Tshe-'das gnas-'dren 'gro-drug rang-grol*). See Appendix One.
8. The belief in the notion of the continuity of consciousness creates a very different perspective among the bereaved within Buddhist communities. Although grief is not repressed, the family members and friends are encouraged to support the consciousness of the deceased by being themselves strong in their spiritual practice and dedicating this effort to the deceased. Sympathy for the spiritual opportunities being presented to the deceased during and after the death process is strongly stressed. Clinging, attachment and extreme sorrow are discouraged, whilst creating an atmosphere of openness, compassion and acceptance of change is emphasised and highly valued.
9. On this interval following the cessation of outer respiration (*phyi-dbugs*) and preceding the cessation of inner respiration (*nang-dbugs*), see p. 228.
10. The injunction not to touch the body of the deceased extends from the moment

when the consciousness enters the central channel until the vital energy leaves the body; a period of time which can be just a few moments or up to three days. This injunction is often repeated in the present text and stressed by Tibetan lamas who explain that touching the body draws the mindfulness of the individual to the place being touched. Since the point on the body from which the consciousness exits is related to the quality of the mental realm into which it may enter, drawing the mindfulness by touching can be helpful or harmful. See above, Ch. 10, p. 214.

11. Traditionally, every Tibetan household has a shrine which is the focus of the household's daily ritual and devotional activity. At the time of a bereavement various ancillary rituals are also performed together with the reading of this *Great Liberation by Hearing*. Often a tent is erected in the garden and a large altar laid out. There is much activity, involving both the family and the attending monks, in making the preparations for the rituals. The sense of bewilderment at the death of a loved one is strongly tempered by the purposefulness in the activity directed at supporting and inspiring the consciousness of the deceased.

12. These prayers are read to the dying person in order to inspire a calm and dignified approach to death. For the full text of the *Aspirational Prayer Calling to the Buddhas and Bodhisattvas for Assistance* (*Sangs-rgyas-dang byang-chub sems-dpa'i-rnams-la ra-mda' sbran-pa'i smon-lam*); the *Aspirational Prayer which Protects from Fear of the Intermediate States* (*Bar-do 'jigs-skyob-ma'i smon-lam*), and the *Aspirational Prayer which Rescues from the Dangerous Pathways of the Intermediate States* (*Bar-do 'phrang-sgrol-gyi smon-lam*), see Ch. 12; and for the *Root Verses of the Six Intermediate States* (*Bar-do'i rtsa-tshig*), see above, Ch. 3. The attitude in which the dying person approaches death is regarded as the most essential factor in ensuring the continued well-being of the individual. For the dying individual to cultivate an attitude of compassion towards others during the process of death is regarded as primary. Remaining fearless and fully aware of the processes of dying, whilst also being prepared to recognise the qualities of awareness which naturally arise during and after the moment of death, is strongly encouraged.

13. Tib. *'chi-kha'i bar-do-la 'od-gsal ngo-sprod-pa*. This is the introduction to the radiance which arises immediately after the ceasing of respiration at the moment when the vital energies collect at the mid-point of the central channel, close to the heart. See also above, Ch. 8, pp. 173–7, and Ch. 10, pp. 205–9, where reference is also made to this intermediate state.

14. *Tib. chos-nyid bar-do-la 'od-gsal ngo-sprod-pa*. This is the introduction to the radiance experienced by the mental body of the deceased in the form of the Peaceful and Wrathful Deities. See pp. 234–72; also Tsele Natsok Rangdrol, *The Mirror of Mindfulness*, pp. 77–102.

15. Tib. *srid-pa bar-do-la mngal-sgo dgag-thabs bstan-pa*. The final section of this chapter describes five profound methods for avoiding uncontrolled rebirth in an unfavourable realm. See pp. 285–300; also Tsele Natsok Rangdrol, *The Mirror of Mindfulness*, pp. 105–28.

16. In this context, the advice is to invite to the bedside an individual who has followed the same meditational practices as the dying person.

17. In this context, the advice is to invite to the bedside an individual who has studied and practised within the same commentarial tradition.

18. i.e. the central energy channel of the body.
19. This period during which vital energy and consciousness are united in the central channel is also described as that in which the 'inner breath' (*nang-dbugs*) remains within the body. It is said to last approximately twenty minutes.
20. Tib. *bar-do dang-po'i 'od-gsal*, i.e. the inner radiance which arises at the culmination of the intermediate state of the time of death is the first of three successive 'intermediate states' that occur after death and prior to the rebirth process. They comprise the inner radiance of the ground, the inner radiance of the path, and the inner radiance of the Peaceful and Wrathful Deities in the intermediate state of reality. These three phases are not to be confused with the classical enumeration of the six intermediate states as described in Ch. 3 and in the glossary.
21. Throughout the death process and at each step in the reading of the *Great Liberation by Hearing*, the presiding lama should enter into those meditative states of awareness which the text describes and which the dying person is encouraged to cultivate. In this way, he serves as a support and anchor for the concentration of the dying and the deceased.
22. Tib. *rtsa rba-rlabs rtsis-ba*. Tibetan medicine describes diverse types of pulse which indicate impending death due to humoral imbalance, visceral failure and so forth. See *Tibetan Medical Paintings*, p. 137. On the procedures followed in pulse palpation, see ibid., p. 123.
23. Tib. *gnyid-log rtsa-gnyis*. The two carotid arteries 'which induce unconsciousness when pressed', are included among the body's most vulnerable points. See *Tibetan Medical Paintings*, pp. 33, 43. Pressure applied at the right moment is said to trap the vital energy and mind together in the central channel, with no possibility of regression or reversal. Correct training in this procedure is of crucial importance, and it is obviously essential that the carotids are not pressed until after the pulse has ceased.
24. On the crown or anterior fontanelle (Tib. *tshangs-bug*; Skt. *brahmarandhra*), which is the optimum point of exit for the consciousness of the dying individual, see Ch. 10, p. 214.
25. The period following the cessation of the coarse outer breath (*phyi-dbugs*) and before the cessation of the subtle inner breath (*nang-dbugs*), also known as the life-sustaining vital energy (Tib. *srog-'dzin-gyi rlung*; Skt. *prāṇa*), is that during which the vital energy and mind are drawn together into the central channel, causing ordinary beings to lapse into unconsciousness (*shes-pa brgyal*). This moment is also described in terms of the blackness induced by the merging of the white male and red female generative essences at the heart-centre of the central channel. See Ch. 8, p. 175.
26. The Tibetan biographical tradition cites many instances of great spiritual teachers who at the time of their demise enter into the prolonged experience of this intermediate state.
27. See Ch. 10, p. 203.
28. See Ch. 8, p. 173ff. An alternative description of this process is also given in medical texts. See *Tibetan Medical Paintings*, pp. 51–2: 'Upon the sinking of the earth element into the water element, the patient ceases to grasp the solidity of objects. Upon the sinking of the water element into the fire element, the sensory orifices dry up. Upon the sinking of the fire element into the wind

element, bodily heat disappears. Upon the sinking of the wind element into the space element, breathing stops. As far as the five sensory organs, born out of the five primordial elements, are concerned, the first to cease functioning is sight, then comes the ability to hear, followed by the senses of smell, taste and finally touch. Consequent on this tactile loss, life itself wanes; and all sensory functions dissolve into the life-sustaining breath, which itself vanishes into consciousness, destined for future rebirth.'

29. On the relationship between the various orifices from which serum is exuded and the realms inhabited by sentient beings, see Ch. 10, p. 214; also A. Wayman, *The Buddhist Tantras*, Ch. 12, pp. 139–50, whose account is based on the commentarial literature of the *Guhyasamāja Tantra*.
30. The harsh and bewildering experiences related to past actions (*las-kyi 'khrul-snang*) are those manifestations of sound, lights and rays of light which appear during the intermediate state of reality (*chos-nyid bar-do*), in contrast to the terrifying experiences related to Yama (*gshin-rje*) which occur during the intermediate state of rebirth (*srid-pa'i bar-do*). See p. 234ff and pp. 268–9.
31. Since the meditational deities are pure appearances inseparable from emptiness, they are said to 'appear and yet lack inherent existence' (*snang-la rang-bzhin med-pa*) and to be 'devoid of solid or corporeal forms' (*gdos-bcas med-pa*). See also Dudjom Rinpoche, NSTB, pp. 123–7, 279–80; Longchen Rabjampa, GGFTC, pp. 626–81.
32. i.e. Avalokiteśvara.
33. On the risk of inferior rebirth (*ngan-song*) which confronts those who have broken their vows (*sdom-pa shor-ba*) and failed to maintain their basic commitments (*rtsa-ba'i dam-tshig nyams*), see Ch. 7; also Longchen Rabjampa, GGFTC, pp. 1184–229.
34. On this convergence of the mother and child aspects of reality (*chos-nyid-ma-bu*), which are identified respectively with the inner radiance of the ground and the inner radiance of the path, the latter cultivated by the meditator during his or her lifetime, see also Ch. 8, pp. 176–7.
35. The experiences of the 'mental body' (*yid-kyi lus*) during the intermediate states of reality and rebirth are described below in detail. See pp. 273–85.
36. The intermediate state of reality is here referred to as the 'third intermediate state' (*bar-do gsum-pa*) when it is enumerated following the two phases of inner radiance of the ground and path that arise during the intermediate state of the time of death (*'chi-kha'i bar-do*).
37. Tib. *Chos-nyid bar-do'i ngo-sprod chen-mo*.
38. For a synopsis of the classical enumeration of the six categories of intermediate state: namely the intermediate state of the living or natural existence (*rang-bzhin skye-gnas-kyi bar-do*); the intermediate state of dreams (*rmi-lam bar-do*); the intermediate state of meditative stability (*ting-nge-'dzin bsam-gtan-gyi bar-do*); the intermediate state of the time of death (*'chi-kha'i bar-do*); the intermediate state of reality (*chos-nyid bar-do*); and the intermediate state of consequent rebirth (*lugs-'byung srid-pa'i bar-do*), see glossary. Tsele Natsok Rangdrol, *The Mirror of Mindfulness*, pp. 75–102, also discusses the diverse interpretations of the intermediate state of reality presented by the different schools of Tibetan Buddhism.
39. As stated above, p. 229, the intermediate state of the time of death is said to

last up to three and a half days, so that those who have failed to recognise the inner radiances of the ground and path remain unconscious for the same period of time. It is on being aroused from that unconscious state that the visions of the Peaceful and Wrathful Deities of the intermediate state of reality then arise. It is important to bear in mind that the use of the word 'day' in this context and those which follow is from the standpoint of the bereaved. From the perspective of the deceased, as Tsele Natsok Rangdol states, 'Few people, however, consider these to be actual solar days. Since they are . . . only meditation days, understand that for ordinary people they do not appear for more than a short moment' (*Mirror of Mindfulness*, p. 113).

40. On the reversal of cyclic existence and of all its aspects of mundane consciousness and sense-perception through the practices of the Great Perfection, see NSTB, p. 340, and GGFTC, pp. 395–97, 1001–5.

41. The events which unfold in the course of the intermediate states of reality and rebirth are held, in the view of the present text, to endure approximately for forty-nine days. Note however that this period of forty-nine days is not said to be fixed. See Tsele Natsok Rangdrol, *The Mirror of Mindfulness*, p. 22. It is recognised that the nature of the appearances in the intermediate state of reality will vary according to the meditative tradition followed. Tsele Natsok Rangdrol (ibid., pp. 98–100) does emphasise, on the other hand, that the pure psycho-physical aggregates, elements, sense-organs, and so forth, will manifest as sounds, lights and rays.

42. Tib. *dbus-su thig-le brdal-ba'i zhing-khams*. An epithet of the Akaniṣṭha-Ghanavyūha realm of Vairocana Buddha, on which see glossary.

43. Tib. *de-bzhin gshegs-pa'i 'od-zer chos-dbyings-kyi ye-shes zhes-bya-ba*. This luminosity is called the 'light ray of the Tathāgata' because Vairocana Buddha is said to preside over the Tathāgata or Buddha family. On the compassionate unfolding of the great light rays of the tathāgatas, see also Dudjom Rinpoche, NSTB, pp. 912–13.

44. Note that the text associates both the dull white light of the god-realms and the dull green light of the animal realms (see p. 253) with the propensities for delusion (*gti-mug*). More generally, delusion is recognised as the primary dissonant mental state giving rise to birth among the animals, and pride as the primary dissonant mental state giving rise to birth among the gods.

45. Note that pride is more generally associated with birth in the god realms, while it is attachment (*'dod-chags*) or a combination of all five dissonant mental states that is said to generate birth as a human being. See above, Ch. 5.

46. On the significance in Atiyoga of the 'state of non-activity' (*byar-med-kyi ngang*), see above Ch. 4; also NSTB, pp. 335–7, 896–910.

47. Tib. *ye-shes bzhi-sbyor-gyi snang-ba*.

48. This passage associates the white luminosity with the pristine cognition of reality's expanse and Vairocana, and the blue light with the mirror-like pristine cognition and Akṣobhya, reversing the earlier sequence. On this distinction, see Longchen Rabjampa, GGFTC, pp. 390–91.

49. DR, Vol. 3, p. 77, l. 3, reads *nang-du*.

50. Tib. *mi-rtog-pa'i ngang*. Along with bliss and radiance, this 'non-conceptual state' is considered to be one of the three concomitant experiences associated with the practice of the perfection stage (*sampannakrama*). See Longchen Rabjampa, GGFTC, pp. 827–8.

51. The green light associated with Amoghasiddhi is said not to arise until buddha-activities can be performed consequent on the attainment of perfect enlightenment.
52. This 'vision of the four pristine cognitions combined' (*ye-shes bzhi-sbyor-gyi snang-ba*) is said to occur in relation to the 'hollow passageway of Vajrasattva' (*rdo-rje sems-dpa' khong-gseng-gi lam*), a synonym for the central channel of the body, through which transference of consciousness (*'pho-ba*) is also effected. See Tsele Natsok Rangdrol, *The Mirror of Mindfulness*, p. 20.
53. Tib. *rgyun-gyi ting-nge-'dzin*; Skt. *sroto'nugatasamādhi*.
54. Tib. *rig-pa lhun-grub chen-po'i sku*. See glossary under Buddha-body.
55. On the conflation in this text of delusion (Skt. *moha*; Tib. *gti-mug*) with both the god-realm and the animal realm, see note 44.
56. On this class of faithful retainers (Tib. *ging*), who protect the maṇḍala from impediments, see also Ch. 7, note 17.

Part Two

1. Tib. *Khro-bo'i bar-do'i 'char-tshul bstan-pa bzhugs-so*.
2. See Ch. 14.
3. There are many specific instances of these indications symbolic of passage to the realm of the sky-farers (*dag-pa mkha'-spyod*) at the time of death, particularly in the context of the lineages of Atiyoga. See, for example, NSTB, p. 543 (the death of Bagom), p. 550 (the death of Dzeng Dharmabodhi), p. 561 (the death of Zhangton), p. 563 (the death of Nyibum), p. 564 (the death of Guru Jober), p. 568 (the death of Melong Dorje), p. 572 (the death of Kumārādza), and p. 594 (the death of Longchenpa). For a more detailed explanation of these phenomena, see Ch. 14, *passim*.
4. Tib. *gsang-lam*, i.e. the path of the secret mantras (*guhyamantra*).
5. The full text of the *Liberation by Wearing: Natural Liberation of the Psycho-physical Aggregates* (*bTags-grol phung-po rang-grol*) is contained below, Ch. 14, pp. 347–79.
6. The names of the four Female Gatekeepers of the wrathful assembly given here are identical to those given above, p. 247, in the context of the peaceful assembly. Their actual names are Vajratejasī in the east, Vajrāmoghā in the south, Vajralokā in the west, and Vajravetālī in the north, See, above, Ch. 5, p. 84.
7. The colours of Manurākṣasī, Brahmāṇī, Raudrī, Vaiṣṇāvī, and Kaumārī here accord with the descriptions in Ch. 5, p. 85, and Ch. 6, p. 110. DR, p. 103, depicts them respectively as dark brown, reddish yellow, dark green, blue, and red.
8. DR, p. 103, l.4, reads *phag-mgo* (pig-headed), but see Ch. 5, p. 85, and Ch. 6, p. 110.
9. Here the colours of Śāntī, Amṛtā, Saumī, and Daṇḍī accord with the descriptions in Ch. 5, p. 85, and Ch. 6, p. 110. DR, p. 103, depicts them respectively as red, red, white, and dark green.
10. Here the colours of Bhakṣasī and Rudhiramadī accord with the descriptions in Ch. 5, p. 86, and Ch. 6, pp. 110–11. DR, p. 104, depicts them respectively as dark green and white.

11. Here the colours of Vāyudevī, Agnāyī, Varāhī, Vajrā Cāmuṇḍī, and Varunāṇī accord with the descriptions in Ch. 5, p. 86, and Ch. 6, p. 111. DR, pp. 104–5, describes them respectively as blue, red, black, red, and blue.
12. On this distinction, see Longchen Rabjampa, GGFTC, pp. 397ff., and ibid., Ch. 15, pp. 1075ff.
13. On the variations in the size of the buddha-body, see R. Kloetsli, *Buddhist Cosmology*, p. 69, and on the varying sizes of the physical bodies of living beings within the three world-systems, see the chart in ibid., p. 38. The same work has much information on the dimensions of Mount Sumeru and its status within the world-system.
14. Mistaken views (*log-lta*) are principally those which disclaim an appropriate connection between virtuous causes and virtuous effects, and those which ascribe inherent existence in varying degrees to physical and mental phenomena.

Part Three

1. Tib. *Zab-chos zhi-khro dgongs-pa rang-grol las srid-pa bar-do'i ngo-sprod.*
2. Tib. *Sangs-rgyas-dang byang-chub sems-dpa'i-rnams-la ra-mda' sbran-pa'i smon-lam.* See Ch. 12, pp. 308–9.
3. These verses are found in Vasubandhu's *Treasury of the Abhidharma*, Ch. 3, vv. 13–14.
4. Tib. *sngon-'byung.*
5. Tib. *bar-do'i snang-ba yid-kyi lus.*
6. Tib. *dbang-po kun-tshang thogs-med rgyu.*
7. Vajrāsana, the 'indestructible seat' below the Bodhi Tree at present-day Bodh Gaya, the place where the buddhas of the 'auspicious aeon' are said to attain buddhahood.
8. Tib. *las-kyi rdzu-'phrul shugs-dang ldan.*
9. The miraculous ability based on past actions (*las-kyi rdzu-'phrul*) is an intensified perceptual state arising from past habitual tendencies (*vāsanā*), quite distinct from the four supports for miraculous ability (*ṛddhipāda*) or enlightened attributes (*guṇa*) indicative of buddhahood, on which see NSTB, Vol. 2, p. 138.
10. Tib. *rigs-mthun lha-mig dag-pas mthong.*
11. This 'pure clairvoyance' (*lha-mig dag-pa*), like the miraculous ability based on past actions (*las-kyi rdzu-'phrul*) described above, is a product of the intensified perception of the mental body, enabling those destined to one form of rebirth to perceive beings of their own kind. As such, it is differentiated from the clairvoyance possessed by the gods inhabiting the world-systems of form (*rūpadhātu*) and desire (*kāmadhātu*), but similar to that which is acquired in the course of meditation.
12. The carnivorous ogres (Tib. *srin-po*), acting as the executors of the unfailing law of cause and effect (*las-kyi sha-za*), are those who execute the rites of Yama (*gshin-rje'i las*). See Ch. 13, pp. 321ff.
13. The colours of the three precipices symbolic of the dissonant mental states (*kleśa*) – white, red, and black – are also respectively associated with the three enlightened families (*rigs-gsum*) through which they are purified, i.e. those of

Akṣobhya, who is the natural purity of aversion, Amitābha, who is the natural purity of attachment, and Vairocana, who is the natural purity of delusion. See Ch. 5, p. 97.

14. This sentence is omitted in DR, Vol. 3, f. 125, l. 1.
15. On the expression *lhan-cig skyes-pa'i lha*, here rendered as 'innate good conscience', and the expression *lhan-cig skyes-pa'i 'dre*, rendered here as 'innate bad conscience' see also Ch. 13, pp. 321ff.
16. On the 'mirror of past actions' (*las-kyi me-long*) in which Yama Dharmarāja is said to view the virtuous and non-virtuous actions of the deceased, see below, Ch. 13, pp. 321–2.
17. The 'bull-headed Rakṣa' (*rag-sha glang-mgo*) is the name of one of the acolytes of Yama Dharmarāja. See Ch. 13, pp. 321ff.
18. See glossary. For the Nyingma interpretation of the Buddha-body of Essentiality (*ngo-bo-nyid-kyi sku*; Skt. *svabhāvikakāya*), which some sources regard as the 'fourth' buddha-body, see Dudjom Rinpoche, NSTB, pp. 191ff.
19. On the significance of the 'name empowerment' (*ming-gi dbang*), see glossary under Four Empowerments.
20. The following verses derive from the *Aspirational Prayer which Protects from Fear of the Intermediate States* (*Bar-do'i 'jigs-skyobs smon-lam*). See below, Ch. 12, pp. 314–15.
21. Those experiencing the sensation of moving upwards (*gyen-la 'gro-ba*) have an affinity with rebirth in the god-realms, those moving horizontally (*'phred-la 'gro-ba*) have an affinity with the human realms, while those moving downwards (*mgo mthur-la brten-nas 'gro-ba*) have an affinity with the hells, anguished spirits and animals. See e.g. Longchen Rabjampa, GGFTC, pp. 493–4.
22. On these verses from the *Root Verses of the Six Intermediate States* (*Bar-do drug-gi rtsa-tshig*), see Ch. 3, pp. 33–4.
23. Tib. *bdag srid-pa bar-do 'char-dus 'dir.*
24. Tib. *mdun-pa rtse-gcig sems-la bzung-bya.*
25. Tib. *bzang-po las-kyi 'phro-la nan-gyis mthud.*
26. Tib. *mngal-sgo bkag-nas ru-log dran-par bya/ snying-rus dag-snang dgos-pa'i dus gcig yin.*
27. Tib. *bla-ma yab-yum.*
28. On the practices pertaining to the purification of the four modes of birth (*skye-gnas rigs bzhi*; Skt. *caturyoni*), namely: oviparous birth (*sgo-nga-nas skye-ba*; Skt. *aṇḍaja*), viviparous birth (*mngal-nas skye-ba*; Skt. *jārāyuja*), supernormal birth (*brdzus-te skye-ba*; Skt. *upapāduka*), and birth from warmth and moisture (*drod-sher-las skye-ba*; Skt. *saṃsvedaja*), see Dudjom Rinpoche, NSTB, p. 279. Note that the instructions given in our text at this juncture refer only to the first two categories.
29. The clotting of the embryo (*nur-nur-po*; Skt. *kalala*) and the oval formation of the embryo (*mer-mer-po*; Skt. *arbuda*) are the first two of the so-called five stages of embryonic development (*mngal-gyi gnas-skabs lnga*). For a more detailed, though slightly different, explanation, see *Tibetan Medical Paintings*, pp. 25–6 and 181–2.
30. See Ch. 3, p. 34.
31. Tib. *bden-med sgyu-ma lta-bu gdams-ngag.*

32. Tib. *'od-gsal sgoms-nas mngal-sgo 'gag.*
33. On this description of the mind resting in its natural state, which derives from the esoteric instructions of the Great Perfection on Cutting through Resistance (*rdzogs-chen khregs-chod*), see Ch. 4.
34. Tib. *mngal-sgo 'dam-pa'i gdams-ngag zab-mo.*
35. On the meditative stabilities (*samādhi*) or meditative concentrations (*dhyāna*) which give rise to birth in the world-system of form (*rūpadhātu*), see the chart in NSTB, pp. 14–15; and for a detailed discussion, see also L. Pruden (trans.), *Abhidharmakośabhāṣyaṃ*, Ch. 3, The World, pp. 365–495.
36. On the transference of consciousness to the pure buddha fields (*dag-pa sangs-rgyas-kyi zhing-du 'pho-ba*), see Ch. 10.
37. For a description of such consecration of the womb, see the life of Śākyamuni Buddha in Dudjom Rinpoche, NSTB, p. 416; also GGFTC, p. 474.
38. *Sangs-rgyas-dang byang-chub sems-dpa-rnams-la ra-mdar spran-pa'i smon-lam.* See below, Ch. 12, pp. 308–9.
39. For the text of the *Root Verses of the Six Intermediate States* (*Bar-do drug-gi rtsa-tshig*), see above, Ch. 3, pp. 32–4; and for that of the *Aspirational Prayer which Rescues from the Dangerous Pathways of the Intermediate States* (*Bar-do 'phrang-sgrol-gyi smon-lam*), see below, Ch. 12, pp. 310–13.
40. For the full text of the *Liberation by Wearing: Natural Liberation of Psycho-physical Aggregates* (*bTags-grol phung-po rang-grol*), see below, Ch. 14; and for that of the *Spiritual Practice: Natural Liberation of Habitual Tendencies* (*Chos-spyod bag-chags rang-grol*), see above, Ch. 5.

12 Aspirational Prayers

1. Tib. *Sangs-rgyas-dang byang-chub sems-dpa' rnams-la ra-mdar spran-pa'i smon-lam.*
2. Or she, as appropriate.
3. Tib. *Bar-do 'phrang-sgrol-gyi smon-lam.*
4. DR, pp. 320–21, inserts these verses after those dedicated to Amoghasiddhi.
5. This mantra, missing in DR, p. 321, l. 2, is inserted on the basis of its inclusion in the Delhi and Varanasi reprints.
6. Tib. *Bar-do'i smon-lam 'jigs-skyobs-ma.*
7. At this point the text inserts the following couplet, which has apparently been mis-transcribed out of context from the previous aspirational prayer:

    May the fields of the five elements not rise up as a hostile force.
    May I see them as the fields of the five buddhas.

8. An allusion to the beguiling prophecies of Māra, who sought to deceive Śākyamuni at the time of his attainment of buddhahood.

13 A Masked Drama

Part One

1. Tib. *Srid-pa bar-do'i ngo-sprod dge-sdig rang-gzugs ston-pa'i gdams-pa srid-pa bar-do rang-grol.* On the variant forms of the title, see Appendix One.
2. Tib. *Zab-chos zhi-khro dgongs-pa rang-grol.*
3. Tib. *Padma zhi-khro'i bar-do thos-grol.* On the cycles of *gter-ma* discovered by Karma Lingpa, and the various texts concerning empowerment (*dbang-bskur*) and introduction (*ngo-sprod*) contained within them, see above, 'A Brief Literary History', pp. xxxvi–xlviii, and Appendix One.
4. Here, the intermediate state of reality (*chos-nyid bar-do*) is described as such because the luminosities and the Peaceful and Wrathful Deities are directly seen, offering the potential for immediate liberation.
5. Although the introduction to the intermediate state of rebirth (*srid-pa'i bar-do*) has already been given (see Ch. 11, pp. 273–303), the drama presented here functions as a light-hearted didactic supplement to the previous introduction, and is directed specifically at the living rather than the deceased.
6. The acolytes of Yama include the Ox-headed Rakṣa Demon (*Rakṣa glang-mgo*).
7. Tib. *'Byung-po spre'u mgo.*
8. The *bre* is the standard Tibetan unit of dry measure, twenty of which equal one *khal*. The *srang* is the standard unit of weight measurement.
9. Tib. *Dur phag-mgo.*
10. Tib. *sDug-pa sbrul-mgo.*
11. Tib. *gTum-po dom-mgo.*
12. Tib. *srNgam-pa seng-mgo.*
13. Tib. *'Dab-chags khyung-mgo.*
14. Tib. *lhan-cig skyes-pa'i lha.* See also Ch. 11, p. 279.
15. Tib. *lhan-gcig skyes-pa'i 'dre.* See also Ch. 11, p. 279.
16. Tib. *dPal-skyes.*
17. Tib. *dMyal-ba 'bum.*
18. On the outcaste (*caṇḍāla*; Tib. *rigs-ngan gdol-pa*) community, traditionally excluded from Indian society for occupational reasons, see A. L. Basham, *The Wonder That Was India*, pp. 145–7.
19. The four classes of ancient Indian society comprise: the priestly class (*brāhmaṇavarṇa*); the princely class (*kṣatriyavarṇa*); the mercantile class (*vaiśya-varṇa*); and the labouring class (*śūdravarṇa*). See A. L. Basham, *The Wonder That Was India*, pp. 138–45.
20. On the currency of such materialistic and nihilistic philosophical views in ancient India, see Dudjom Rinpoche, NSTB, pp. 66–7; and see A. L. Basham, *The Wonder That Was India*, pp. 298–300.
21. Tāmralipti (*zangs-gling*) is identified with modern Tamluk on the Bengal coast. See NSTB, p. 455.
22. Tib. *shan-pa khri-dpon*; also translatable as 'myriarch of butchers'.
23. Tib. *shan-mo dpal-skyid.*
24. The year of the water pig is the last in the cycle of sixty years, according to

the calendrical system of elemental divination (*'byung-rtsis*), for which reason it will create a 'fin de siècle' notion in the minds of the audience.

25. Kāmarūpa in Assam is revered as one of the twenty-four sacred abodes of tantric Buddhist India. See NSTB, pp. 472 and 501.
26. Tib. *rje-rigs*; Skt. *vaiśya*. See above, note 19.
27. Tib. *rDo-rje gcod-pa* (*Vajracchedikā*, T 16). This sūtra is one of the best known of the shorter *Prajñāpāramitā* texts. Its Chinese version is said to be the world's oldest extant printed book.
28. See Ch. 12, pp. 308–9.
29. See Ch. 11, pp. 285–300.
30. See Ch. 10.
31. See glossary under Six-syllable Mantra.
32. Tib. *dGe-sdig rang-gzugs ston-pa'i gdams-pa ['am me-long] srid-pa [bar-do] rang-grol.*
33. Skt. *śubhaṃ bhavantu.*

Part Two

1. Tib. *Srid-pa'i bar-do'i ngo-sprod dge-sdig rang-gzugs ston-pa'i lhan-thabs dbyangs-snyan lha'i gaṇḍī.*
2. Tib. *Zab-chos zhi-khro dgongs-pa rang-grol.*
3. See pp. 326–8.
4. The maṇḍala of the Peaceful and Wrathful Deities would be constructed in two or three dimensions for the performance of this drama and the concomitant empowerment ceremonies.
5. See p. 333.
6. On the significance of the 'maṇḍala of spiralling rainbow lights' (Tib. *'ja'-'od 'khyil-ba'i dkyil-'khor*) for practitioners of the All-surpassing Realisation (*thod-rgal*) meditations of Atiyoga, see Dudjom Rinpoche, NSTB, pp. 337–43.
7. i.e. Namka Chokyi Gyelpo, the spiritual teacher of Gyarawa Namka Chokyi Gyatso, who composed this supplement.
8. See Ch. 5, pp. 67ff.
9. Tib. *zang-thal*. This expression indicates success in consciousness-transference or the direct realisation of inner radiance at death. See above, Ch. 10.

14 Liberation by Wearing

1. Tib. *bTags-grol phung-po rang-grol-gyi don-bsdus.*
2. Tib. *Zab-chos zhi-khro dgongs-pa rang-grol.*
3. OṂ ĀḤ HŪṂ are the essential mantras which liberate mundane body, speech, and mind in primordial purity.
4. This is the naturally resonant mantra of the Buddha Samantabhadra, written in the ḍākiṇī script of Oḍḍiyāna, in the form of a vajra-song. The ḍākiṇī script appears to be only remotely related to Sanskrit. The following interpretation of these syllables derives from the *Tantra of the Coalescence of Sun and Moon*

(*Nyi-zla kha-sbyor-gyi rgyud*, sDe-dge NGB, Vol. 4, p. 119a). For variant readings of the mantras, see also Namkhai Norbu, *The Dzogchen Ritual Practices*, pp. 132–6; and for its intonation, ibid., pp. 90–1. Following the tantra, the syllables are interpreted by Namkhai Norbu as follows: From the very beginning (EMA), intrinsic awareness has never been born, nor will it ever be born (KIRI KIRI). Self-arisen, it has never been interrupted (MAṢTA), nor will it ever be interrupted (BHALIBHALI). Since it is total vision, it has never been clarified, nor will it ever be clarified (SAMITASURUSURU). Being omnipresent, it has never been constructed, nor will it ever be constructed (KUNDHALIMASUMASU). Being unique it is perfectly realised in space through the methods of the four signs (EKARILISUBHASTAYE). It is natural liberation into the great expanse and it is supreme bliss (CAKIRABHULITA). Since it is the great expanse, it is habituated to supreme delight (CAYESAMUNTA CARYASUGHAYE). Relaxing the tension of this portion, which is relative existence, intrinsic awareness generates everything (BHITISANABHYAGHULIYE). And thus one transfers directly into the great inner radiance (SAKARIDHUKANI). Brilliant and wondrous, this light radiates (MATARIBHETANA), totally transcending everything, and it eliminates all errors (PARALIHISANA). In a state of being just as it is, it is free from all conceptions (MAKHARTEKELANA). Being perfect, it is like the light of the moon (SAMBHURATA MAIKACARATAMBA). Like the sunlight, it is luminous (SURYAGHATARAYE BASHANA). It is like a jewel, a mountain, a many-petalled lotus (RANABHITI SAGHUTIPAYA). It is the great resonance which has never been sounded, and never will be sounded (GHURAGHURAPAGAKHARANALAṂ). It is the primordial state which has never been created and never will be created (NARANARAYI THARAPAṬLAṂ). It is the great enlightened mind which was never adorned and never will be adorned (SIRNASIRNABHESARASPALAṂ). Self-originated and perfect, it will never become enlightened (BUDDHABUDDHA CHIŚASAGHELAṂ). Ten concluding syllables are focal points of bodily energy (SASĀ ṚṜ ḶḸ IĪ MAMĀ), while the other concluding syllables are associated with the buddha-bodies (RARĀ LAHA Ā).

5. This mantra in the form of a vajra-song is included in the *Tantra of the Coalescence of Sun and Moon* (*Nyi-zla kha-sbyor-gyi rgyud*, sDe-dge NGB, Vol. 4, pp. 119a–b). As before, it is written in the ḍākiṇī script of Oḍḍiyāna. The main verses are preceded by OṂ ĀḤ HŪṂ and concluded by the ten syllables of bodily energy (SASĀ ṚṜ ḶḸ IĪ MAMĀ), and those indicative of buddha-body (RARĀ). See Namkhai Norbu, *The Dzogchen Ritual Practices*, pp. 132–6.
6. These twenty-five mantras which follow are again rendered in the ḍākiṇī language of Oḍḍiyāna, as distinct from Sanskrit.
7. Tib. *phyir mi-ldog-pa'i sa*.
8. Tib. *nyams-gong 'phel-ba'i snang-ba*.
9. Tib. *rig-pa'i tshad-pheb-kyi snang-ba*.
10. Tib. *ngo-bo rang-bzhin thugs-rjer grol*.
11. Tib. *btags-cing dbugs-la sleb-pa'i tshad grol*.
12. The Delhi reprint (p. 225) comments that each of these preceding mantras encapsulates the natural sound of reality (*chos-nyid rang-sgra*) and is capable of conferring liberation. As such, these mantras are contrasted with the *vidyā*-

mantra and *dhāraṇīmantra*. See Namkhai Norbu, *The Dzogchen Ritual Practices*, pp. 128ff.

13. From this point onwards, the mantras are rendered in Sanskrit. On the 'hundred enlightened families of the Peaceful and Wrathful Deities' (*zhi-khro rigs-brgya*), see Appendix Two.
14. As in all the verses that follow, these events occur when the mantra circle is worn at the time of death.
15. The subtle wheel of vibrant mantra letters, vowels and consonants, from which the seed-syllables of the various deities are formed. See GGFTC, Ch. 4, pp. 544–74.
16. The text (p. 265, l. 3–4) reads 'blue' at this juncture.
17. The Varanasi reprint gives the alternative mantra for Mañjuśrī: VĀGĪŚVARĪ MUṂ ŚRĪ SVĀHĀ.
18. The abridged version of this text suggests that subtle relics rather than rainbow lights will appear at this juncture, in conformity with the opening verse of this section.
19. For Nartī, the alternative form 'Naivedyā' (Tib. *Zhal-zos-ma*) is also found.
20. Here substantialism (*mtshan-'dzin*) refers to the grasping at characteristics, having failed to understand that they lack inherent existence.
21. This verse is omitted in our text, but found in the abridged version.
22. For a more detailed explanation of the above mantras of the Forty-two Peaceful Deities, see Longchen Rabjampa, GGFTC, pp. 690–96.
23. The text does not add significant detail to the description of the mantras of the Twenty-eight Īśvarī. The actual mantras for this series are reproduced according to *rDor-rje me-long*, Peking Kangyur, Vol. 10, p. 20; but with the Sanskrit corrected in accordance with GGFTC, pp. 1124–8.
24. This verse is omitted in our text, but found in the abridged version. For a more detailed explanation of the above mantras of the sixty wrathful deities, including a number of variants, see Longchen Rabjampa, GGFTC, pp. 1144–56.
25. On the nature of these six syllables, which are associated with the six realms of existence according to the tradition of the Innermost Spirituality (*snying-thig*), see Namkhai Norbu, *The Dzogchen Ritual Practices*, p. 123.
26. On the Hundred-syllable Mantra of Vajrasattva, see glossary. On the breaches of the commitments, which it rectifies, see above, Ch. 7; and on the negativity and obscurations, which it purifies, see Ch. 1 and Ch. 6.
27. On this mantra, generally known as the Heart-mantra of Dependent Origination, see glossary.
28. Tib. *mgo-'jug ma-log*. Here this refers to the importance of folding the paper so that the heads and tails of the various letters are not inverted or wrongly positioned.
29. The booklet is then inserted within a golden casket, also known as *legs-'bam*, that may be tied in a top-knot on the yogin's head or worn around the neck.

Bibliography

For abbreviations used occasionally here, see pp. 403–4.

Section One: Canonical Texts

a) Anthologies

Kangyur (Tib: *bKa'-'gyur*; Eng: *Collected Translations of the Buddha's Teachings*). Several editions are extant including the authoritative Derge xylographic edition in 103 vols.

rNying-ma'i rgyud-'bum (Eng: *Collected Tantras of the Nyingmapa*). Several manuscript versions are extant, but only one xylographic edition at Derge in 26 vols.

b) Sūtras (*mdo-sde*)

Avataṃsakasūtra (Tib: *mDo-sde phal-po-che*; Eng: *Sūtra of the Great Bounteousness of the Buddhas*). T 44, MTTWL 197, translated by T. Cleary, *The Flower Ornament Scripture*, 3 vols. Boulder: Shambhala, 1984 onwards.

Kāraṇḍavyūhasūtra (Tib: *mDo-sde za-ma-tog*; Eng: *Sūtra of the Cornucopia of Avalokiteśvara's Attributes*), ed. P. L. Vaidya, Buddhist Sanskrit Texts, 17 (1961). T 116, MTTWL 90.

Laṅkāvatārasūtra (Tib: *mDo-sde laṅkar gshegs-pa*; Eng: *Sūtra of the Descent to Laṅkā*), ed. P. L. Vaidya, Buddhist Sanskrit Texts 3 (1963). T 107, translated by D. T. Suzuki, London: Routledge and Kegan Paul, 1932, 1956, etc.

Prajñāpāramitā (Tib: *Sher phyin*, Eng: *Transcendental Perfection of Discriminative Awareness*): a collective name for a whole genre of sūtras, including the three longest versions in 100,000 sections (T 8), 25,000 sections (T 9) and 8,000 sections (T 12). See MTTWL 208, 154 and 222 respectively. Extensively translated by E. Conze.

Ratnakūṭa (Tib: *dKon-mchog brtsegs-pa*; Eng: *Mound of Precious Gems*). T 45–93, MTTWL 122. Extensive selections are contained in G. C. C. Chang, *A Treasury of Mahāyāna Sūtras: Selections from the Mahāratnakūṭa*. Pennsylvania: Pennsylvania State University Press, 1983.

Sandhinirmocanasūtra (Tib: *dGongs-pa nges-par 'grel-pa theg-pa chen-po'i mdo*; Eng: *Sūtra of the Unravelling of Enlightened Intention*). T 106, MTTWL 197.

Partial translation in John Powers, *Jnanagarbha's Commentary on the Samdhinirmocana Sutra.*

Tathāgatagarbhasūtra (Tib: *De-bzhin gshegs-pa'i snying-po'i mdo*; Eng: *Sūtra of the Nucleus of the Tathāgata*). T 258, MTTWL 231.

Vajracchedikā (Tib: *rDo-rje gcod-pa*; Eng: *Diamond Cutter*), ed. P. L. Vaidya, Buddhist Sanskrit Texts 17 (1961), T 16, translated and edited by E. Conze, Serie Orientale Roma 13 (1957). Retranslated in Red Pine, *Diamond Sutra*, New York: Counterpoint, 2001.

c) Tantras

Buddhasamāyoga (Tib: *Sangs-rgyas mnyam-sbyor-gi rgyud*; Eng: *Tantra of Union in Equilibrium with the Buddhas*). T 366–7, Derge NGB Vols. 11–12.

Guhyagarbha Tantra (Tib: *rGyud gsang-ba'i snying-po*; Eng: *Tantra of the Secret Nucleus*). T 832, Derge NGB Vol. 9, ed. and translated in G. Dorje, GGFTC, 1987.

Guhyasamāja Tantra (Tib: *rGyud gsang-ba 'dus-pa*; Eng: *Tantra of the Secret Assembly*), ed. S. Bagchi, Buddhist Sanskrit Texts 9 (1965), ed. B. Bhattacharya, Gaekwad's Oriental Series, 53 (1967). T 442–3, Derge NGB Vol. 12. Translated by F. Fremantle in *A Critical Study of the Guhayasamāja Tantra*, Unpublished PhD thesis no. 774 271989, University of London.

Kun-byed rgyal-po'i rgyud (Eng: *Tantra of the All-accomplishing King*). T 828, Derge NGB Vol. 5. Translated in E. K. Neumaier-Dargyay, *Sovereign All-creating Mind*, Albany: SUNY (1992).

mDo dgongs-pa 'dus-pa (Eng: *Sūtra Which Gathers All Intentions*). T 829, Derge NGB Vol. 7.

Nyi-zla kha-sbyor (Eng: *Tantra of the Coalescence of Sun and Moon*). Derge NGB Vol. 4.

rDo-rje sems-dpa' sgyu-'phrul me-long (Eng: *Tantra of the Mirror of the Magical Net of Vajrasattva*). Derge NGB Vol. 11.

Sarvadurgatipariśodhanatantra (Tib: *Ngan-song sbyong-rgyud*; Eng: *Tantra of the Purification of the Lower Realms*). T 483, 485, ed. and translated T. Skorupski in *The Sarvadurgatipariśodhana Tantra: Elimination of All Evil Destinies*, Motilal Banarsidas, 1983.

sKu-gdung 'bar-ba'i rgyud (Eng: *Tantra of the Cremation of Corpses*). Derge NGB Vol. 3.

Section Two: Commentarial Literature

a) Anthologies

Tengyur (Tib: *bsTan-'gyur*; Eng: *Collected Translations of the Classical Treatises*). Again there are several extant versions, including the authoritative Derge xylographic edition in 213 vols.

rNying-ma'i bka'-ma (Eng: *Collected Teachings of the Nyingmapa*). The most extensive anthology of Nyingma commentarial literature, edited by Khenpo Jamyang at Katok (1999) in 120 vols.

b) Commentaries of Indic Origin

Ajitamitragupta, *'Chi slu-ba'i gdams-pa* (Eng: *Teachings on the Ritual Deception of Death*). T 2839.

Maitreya, *Abhisamayālaṃkāra* (Tib: *mNgon-rtogs rgyan*; Eng: *Ornament of Emergent Realisation*). T 3786, MTTWL 2–5. On this work see also Trangu Rinpoche, *Ornament of Clear Realization*, Auckland: Zhyisil Chokyi Ghatsal Publications, 2004, and Lati Rinbochay *et al.*, *Meditative States in Tibetan Buddhism*, London: Wisdom, 1982.

Nāgārjuna, *Prajñānāmamūlamadhyamakakārikā* (Tib: *dBu-ma rtsa-ba'i tshig-le'ur byas-pa shes-rab ces-bya-ba*; Eng: *Root Stanzas of the Madhyamaka entitled Discriminative Awareness*), ed. P. L. Vaidya, Buddhist Sanskrit Texts 10 (1960). T 3824, translated in F. J. Streng, *Emptiness: A Study in Religious Meaning*, Nashville/New York: Abingdon, 1967, and by K. Kalupahana, *Mūlamadhyamakakārikās*, Albany: SUNY, 1986.

Śāntarakṣita, *Tattvasaṃgraha* (Tib: *De-nyid bsdus-pa*; Eng: *Compendium of Topics*). T 4266, ed. D. Shastri, Baudha Bharati Series 1–2 (1968), translated by G. Jha, Gaekwad's Oriental Series 80 (1937), 83 (1939).

—— *Madhyamakālaṃkāra* (Tib: *dBu-ma rgyan*; Eng: *Ornament of the Middle Way*). T 3884, ed. and translated in Masamichi Ichigo, *Madhyamakālaṃkāra*, Kyoto: Kyoto Sangyo University, 1985.

Tathāgatarakṣita, *Mṛtyuṣādhāpaka* (Tib: *'Chi-ba bslu-ba*; Eng: *Ritual Deception of Death*). T 1702.

Tilopā, *Ṣaḍdharmopadeśa* (Tib: *Nāro chos-drug*; Eng: *The Six Doctrines of Nāropā*). T 2330. See H. V. Guenther, *The Life and Teaching of Nāropā*. Oxford: Clarendon Press, 1963.

Vāgīśvarakīrti, *Mṛtyuvañcanopadeśa* (Tib: *'Chi-ba bslu-ba*; Eng: *Esoteric Instructions on the Ritual Deception of Death*). T 1748.

Vasubandhu, *Abhidharmakośa* (Tib: *Chos-mgon pa'i mdzod*; Eng: *Treasury of the Abhidharma*), ed. D. Shastri, Baudha Bharati Series 5–8 (1970–72). T 4089, French translation by L. de la Vallee-Poussin, *L'Abhidharmakośa de Vasubandhu*, 6 vols., Paris, Paul Geuthner, 1923–36. English translation by L. Pruden, *Abhidharmakośabhāsyaṃ*, 4 vols. Berkeley: Asian Humanities Press, 1988.

c) Commentaries of Tibetan Origin

Dudjom Rinpoche, *bsTan-pa'i rnam-gzhag* (Eng: *Fundamentals of the Nyingma School*). Translated in NSTB.

Gampopa, *Dvags-po thar-rgyan* (Eng: *The Jewel Ornament of Liberation*). Translated by H. V. Geunther, Berkeley: Shambhala, 1971.

Gendun Gyeltsen, *gTer-ston lung-bstan-dang khungs-btsun-pa bla-ma brgyud-pa'i rim-pa-rnams* (Eng: *Padmasambhava's Prophecy of the Treasure-finder and the Series of Authentic Lineage Teachers*). Contained in DR, Vol. 1, pp. 21–6.

Gyarawa Namka Chokyi Gyeltsen, *rGyud-pa'i lo-rgyus bsdus-pa nor-bu'i phreng-ba* (Eng: *Jewel Garland: An Abridged History of the Lineage*). Contained in DR, Vol. 1, pp. 27–48.

Longchen Rabjampa, *Grub-mtha' mdzod* (Eng: *Treasury of Spiritual and Philosophical Systems*), ed. Dodrup Chen Rinpoche, Gangtok, Sikkim, *c.* 1969.

—— *gNas-lugs mdzod* (Eng: *Precious Treasury of the Way of Abiding*), trans. Richard Barron, Padma Publications, 1987.

Ngari Paṇchen, *sDom-gsum rnam-nges* (Eng: *Ascertainment of the Three Vows*). Contained in NK, Vol. 51. See HH Dudjom Rinpoche's commentary in *Perfect Conduct: Ascertaining the Three Vows*, Boston: Wisdom Publications, 1996.

Patrul Rinpoche, *mKhas-pa'i shri rgyal-po mkhas-chos*, in the *Collected Works of Patrul Orgyan Jigme Chokyi Wangpo* (*dPal-sprul gsung-'bum*), Vol. 5, pp. 206–25. On this text, see HH Dalai Lama, 'Hitting the Essence in Three Words', in *Dzogchen: The Heart Essence of the Great Perfection*, pp. 61–92, Snowlion, 2000; also Khenpo Palden Sherab and Khenpo Tsewang Dongyal, *Lion's Gaze*, Sky Dancer Press, 1999.

Tsele Natsok Rangdrol, *Bar-do spyi-don thams-cad rnam-pa gsal-bar byed-pa dran-pa'i me-long* (Eng: *Mirror of Mindfulness Clarifying All Aspects of the Intermediate States*), translated by Erik Schmidt Pema Kunsang in *The Mirror of Mindfulness*, Kathmandu: Rangjung Yeshe Publications, 1987.

d) Treasure-doctrines (*gter chos*)

Guru Chowang (disc.), *bKa'-brgyad gsang-ba yongs-rdzogs* (Eng: *Eight Transmitted Precepts: Consummation of All Secrets*). Contained in *bKa'-brgyad phyogs-bsgrigs*, 4 vols.

—— *bKa'-brgyad drag-po rang-byung-ba'i zhi-khro na-rag skong-bzhags-gyi cho-ga*, translated by K. Dowman, 'Emptying the Depths of Hell', in *Flight of the Garuda*, pp. 53–61.

Jamgon Kongtrul (redactor), *Rin-chen gter-mdzod* (Eng: *Store of Precious Treasures*), recently republished at Derge in 76 vols.

Jigme Lingpa (disc.), *Klong-chen snying-thig* (Eng: *Innermost Spirituality of Longchenpa*), contained in the *Collected Works of Jigme Lingpa*, Vols. 7–8, republished in 3 vols., New Delhi: Ngawang Sopa, 1973. Selections translated in Tulku Thondup, *The Dzogchen Innermost Essence Preliminary Practice* (ed. B. Beresford), Dharamsala: Tibetan Library of Works and Archives, 1982; *The Assemblage of the Knowledge-holders*, Shantiniketan, WB, 1980; and in *The Queen of Great Bliss*, Gangtok: Dodrup Chen Rinpoche, 1982.

—— *Rig 'dzin thugs-sgrub dpal-chen 'dus-pa*, contained in *Klong-chen snying-thig*, Vol. 1, pp. 616ff.

—— *sKu-gsum zhing-khams sbyong-ba'i smon-lam*, contained in *Klong-chen snying-thig*, Vol. 2, pp. 448–52.

Karma Lingpa (disc.), *Zab-chos zhi-khro dgongs-pa rang-grol* (Eng: *Peaceful and Wrathful Deities: A Profound Sacred Teaching, [entitled] Natural Liberation through [Recognition of] Enlightened Intention*). Several recensions are extant. B. J. Cuevas lists eighteen printed and manuscript versions of Tibetan and sub-Himalayan provenance. These include the most extensive and authoritative, DR, the full contents of which are listed in Appendix One, pp. 381–6.

—— *sKongs-bshags nyams-chags rang-grol [gyi dbang-bskur gnas-spar 'gro-drug rang-grol]* (Eng: *Natural Liberation through the Propelling of the Six Classes of*

Beings into Higher Rebirth: The [Middle-length] Empowerments of the Natural Liberation of Degenerated Commitments through Reparation and Confession), contained in DR, Vol. 1, pp. 127–60.

—— *dBang-'bring* (Eng: *Middle-length Empowerment*). See the previous entry.

—— *bsKang-bshags nyams-chag rang-grol-gyi tshe-'das gnas-'dren 'gro-drug rang-grol* (Eng: *Natural Liberation of Degenerated Commitments through Reparation and Confession: The Natural Liberation of the Six Classes of Living Beings through the Guidance of the Deceased to Higher Rebirth*), contained in DR, Vol. 2, pp. 1–50.

—— *rDzogs-rim bar-do drug-gi khrid-yig* (Eng: *Six Guidebooks of the Perfection Stage*), contained in DR, Vol. 2, pp. 303–432. Translated by Alan Wallace and Gyatrul Rinpoche in *Natural Liberation*.

—— *Bar-do thos-grol chen-mo* (Eng: *The Great Liberation by Hearing in the Intermediate States*, i.e. the *Tibetan Book of the Dead*), an abridgement of Karma Lingpa's revelations, extant in several editions – B. J. Cuevas lists eleven printed and manuscript versions of Tibetan and sub-Himalayan provenance. These include the Amdo edition, the Delhi reprint and the Varanasi reprint. The text is fully translated in the present work for the first time. Earlier partial translations were made by Kazi Dawa Samdup, in W. Y. Evans-Wentz, ed., *Tibetan Book of the Dead*, London/Oxford/New York: Oxford University Press, 1927; by Francesca Fremantle and Chogyam Trungpa, *Tibetan Book of the Dead*, Berkeley/London: Shambhala, 1975; by Robert Thurman, *Tibetan Book of the Dead*, Aquarian/Thorsons, 1994; and by Stephen Hodge and Martin Boord, *Illustrated Tibetan Book of the Dead*, New York: Godsfield Press, 1999.

—— *Thugs-rje chen-po padma zhi-khro* (Eng: *Great Compassionate One: Lotus Peaceful and Wrathful Deities*). NA, but extracts of a rediscovered treasure (*yang-gter*) of the same title, revealed by Jamyang Khyentse Wangpo, are found in the *Rin-chen gter-mdzod*, Vol. 34, pp. 235–432.

Longchen Rabjampa (disc./redisc.), *sNying-thig ya-bzhi* (Eng: *Four-part Innermost Spirituality*), containing the *Bla-ma yang-tig*, the *Bi-ma snying-thig*, the *mKha'-'gro yang-tig*, the *mKha'-'gro snying-thig*, and *Zab-mo yang-tig*. Derge xylographic edition in 4 vols., republished in Delhi by Sherab Gyaltsen Lama (1975) in 13 vols. Catalogue by S. Goodman in 'The Klong-chen snying-thig: An Eighteenth-century Tibetan Revelation', Appendix B.

Orgyan Lingpa (disc.), *Padma bka'-thang shel-brag-ma* (Eng: *The Injunctions of Padma, discovered at Crystal Rock*), Chengdu: Sichuan Nationalities Publishing House, 1987. Translated in G. C. Toussaint, *Le Dict de Padma*, Bibliothèque de l'Institut de Hautes Études Chinoises, Vol. 3, Paris: Libraire Ernest Leroux, 1933; and in K. Douglas and G. Bays, *Life and Liberation of Padmasambhava*, 2 vols., Emeryville, California: Dharma Publications, 1978.

Prahevajra (disc.), *Tshig-gsum gnad-du brdeg-pa* (Eng: *Three Points Which Penetrate the Essential*). Contained in *Bi-ma snying-thig*, Pt. 1, Vol. Ga, pp. 304–18.

Section Three: Secondary Sources

Basham, A. L., *The Wonder That Was India*, 3rd edn, London: Sidgwick & Jackson, 1967.

Beyer, S., *The Cult of Tārā*, Berkeley: University of California Press, 1978.

Blezer, H., *Kar gliṅ zi khro: A Tantric Buddhist Concept*, Leiden: Research School CNWS, 1997.

Chokyi Nyima Rinpoche, *The Bardo Guidebook* (trans. Eric Schmidt Pema Kunsang), Hong Kong: Rangjung Yeshe Publications, 1991.

Coleman, G. P. (ed.), *A Handbook of Tibetan Culture*, London: Rider, 1993.

Cuevas, B. J., *The Hidden History of the Tibetan Book of the Dead*, Oxford: Oxford University Press, 2003.

—— 'A Textual Survey of the *gter ma* of Karma-gling-pa: *Zab chos zhi khro dgongs pas rang grol* and *Bar do thos grol chen mo*', in *Tibetan Studies: Proceedings of the Eighth Seminar of the International Association for Tibetan Studies*, Bloomington: Indiana University Press (forthcoming).

HH Dalai Lama, *Dzogchen: The Heart Essence of the Great Perfection*, Ithaca, New York: Snowlion Publications, 2000.

—— *Advice on Dying and Living a Better Life*, London: Rider, 2002.

HH Dilgo Khyenste Rinpoche, *Pure Appearance* (trans. Ani Jinpa), Halifax: Vajra Vairochana Translation Committee, 1992.

Dorje, G., *The Guhyagarbhatattvaviniścayamahātantra and its XIVth-century Tibetan Commentary Phyogs bcu mun sel*, 3 vols., unpublished PhD thesis, University of London, 1987.

—— 'The Nyingma Interpretation of Commitment and Vow', in *The Buddhist Forum*, Vol. 2 (1991), pp. 71–95.

—— *Tibetan Elemental Divination Paintings: Illuminated Manuscripts from The White Beryl of Sangs-rgyas rGya-mtsho, with the Moonbeams treatise of Lo-chen Dharmaśrī*, London: Eskenasi and Fogg, 2001.

Dowman, K., *Flight of the Garuda*. Boston: Wisdom Publications, 1994.

HH Dudjom Rinpoche, *The Nyingma School of Tibetan Buddhism: Its Fundamentals and History*, translated by G. Dorje and M. Kapstein, Boston: Wisdom Publications, 1991.

—— *Counsels from My Heart* (translated by Padmakara Translation Committee), Boston: Shambhala, 2001.

Eckel, M. D., *Jñānagarbha's Commentary on the Distinction between the Two Truths*, Albany: SUNY, 1987.

Epstein, L., 'On the History and Psychology of the "das-log"', in *Tibet Journal*, 7.4 (1982), pp. 20–85.

Fremantle, F., *Luminous Emptiness: Understanding the Tibetan Book of the Dead*, Boston: Shambhala, 2001.

Germano, D., 'Dying, Death, and Other Opportunities', in D. S. Lopez Jr (ed.), *Religions of Tibet in Practice*, Princeton University Press, 1997.

Gethin, R., *The Foundations of Buddhism*, Oxford University Press, 1998.

Kazi, Sonam T. (trans.), *Kun-zang La-may Zhal-lung*, 2 vols., Englewood Cliffs, New Jersey: Diamond Lotus Publications, 1989.

Kloetzli, R., *Buddhist Cosmology*, Delhi: Motilal Banarsidas, 1983.

Kritzer, R., 'Antarābhava in the Vibhāṣā', in *Notom Domu Joshi Daigaku Kirisutokyo Bunka Kenkyujo Kiyo [Maranata]*, 3.5 (1997), pp. 69–91.

Lalou, M., 'Chemins du mort dans les croyances de haute-asie', in *Revue de l'Histoire des Religions*, 135.1 (1949), pp. 42–8.

Lati Rinpoche and J. Hopkins, *Death, Intermediate State and Rebirth in Tibetan Buddhism*, Ithaca, New York: Snowlion, 1979.

Mullin, G., *Death and Dying: The Tibetan Tradition*, Boston: Arkana, 1986.

Namkhai Norbu (trans. Brian Beresford), *The Dzogchen Ritual Practices*, London: Kailash Editions, 1991.

Norbu, T., *The Small Golden Key*, New York: Jewel Publishing House, 1977.

Orofino, G., *Sacred Tibetan Teachings on Death and Liberation*, Dorset: Prism Press, 1990.

Paltrul Rinpoche, *The Words of My Perfect Teacher* (trans. Padmakara Translation Committee), San Francisco: HarperCollins, 1994.

Parfionovitch, Y., Dorje, G., and Meyer, F., *Tibetan Medical Paintings*, London: Serindia, 1992.

Pommaret, F., *Les Revenants de l'au-dela dans le monde tibetain: Sources litteraires et tradition vivante*, Paris: Editions du Centre National de la Recherche Scientifique, 1989.

Reynolds, J. M., *Self-liberation through Seeing with Naked Awareness*, New York: Station Hill Press, 1989.

Sogyal Rinpoche, *The Tibetan Book of Living and Dying*, San Francisco: HarperCollins, 1992.

Tenga Rinpoche, *Transition and Liberation* (trans. Alex Wilding), Osterby: Khampa Buchverlag, 1996.

Tenzin Wangyal, *Wonders of the Natural Mind*, New York: Station Hill Press, 1993.

Wallace, A., and Gyatrul Rinpoche, *Natural Liberation: Padmasambhava's Teachings on the Six Bardos*, Boston: Wisdom Publications, 1998.

Wayman, A., *The Buddhist Tantras: New Light on Indo-Tibetan Esotericism*, London: Routledge and Kegan Paul, 1973.

Williams, P., *Mahāyāna Buddhism*, London/New York: Routledge, 1989.

—— *The Reflexive Nature of Awareness: A Tibetan Madhyamaka Defence*, Surrey: Curzon, 1998.

Glossary of Key Terms

(Words in bold type can be referenced elsewhere in the glossary; Tibetan and Sanskrit words are given in italics and text names in italics. For a description of the meditational deities forming the maṇḍala of the Peaceful and Wrathful Deities see Appendix Two.)

Abhidharma *mngon-pa'i chos*
This is a generic term referring to the classical Buddhist literature on phenomenology, psychology, epistemology, and cosmology.

Abhirati *mngon-par dga'-ba*, Skt. *Abhirati*
The eastern **buddha field** of Manifest Joy is the **pure realm** associated with the male **buddha** *Akṣobhya-**Vajrasattva***.

Abiding Nature of Reality *gnas-lugs*
The 'abiding nature of reality' is a synonym for **emptiness** as well as the **expanse of actual reality** (*dharmadhātu*).

Absence of Self-identity *bdag-med*, Skt. *nairātmya*
See **Selflessness**.

Accomplished Master *grub-thob*, Skt. *siddha*
An accomplished master is one who has fully developed the supreme and common spiritual **accomplishments**.

Accomplishment *dngos-grub*, Skt. *siddhi*
Spiritual accomplishments may be supreme or common. The former (*mchog-gi dngos-grub*) refers to the accomplishment of **enlightenment** or **buddhahood**. The latter (*thun-mong-gi dngos-grub*) are a series of mystical powers gained through meditative practices, which are based on ***mantra*** recitation in the context of specific rituals.

Accumulation *tshogs*, Skt. *sambhāra*
The Tibetan word *tshogs* generally has two senses, corresponding to the Sanskrit *sambhāra* and *gaṇa*. In the former case it refers to the two accumulations of **merit** (Tib. *bsod-nams-kyi tshogs*, Skt. *puṇyasambhāra*) and **pristine cognition** (Tib. *ye-shes-kyi tshogs*, Skt. *jñānasambhāra*), which are gathered by ***bodhisattvas*** on the path to **buddhahood**. The fulfilment of the 'two accumulations' constitutes the fruition of the entire path, according to the **Greater Vehicle** (*Mahāyāna*), resulting in the maturation of the **Buddha-body of Form** (*rūpakāya*) and the **Buddha-body**

of **Reality** (*dharmakāya*) respectively. For the second meaning of *tshogs*, see **Feast-offering.**

Accumulation of Merit *bsod-nams-kyi tshogs*, Skt. *puṇyasambhāra*
See **Merit.**

Actual Reality *chos-nyid*, Skt. *dharmatā*
According to the **Greater Vehicle** or *Mahāyāna* Buddhism, actual reality is a synonym for **emptiness** (*śūnyatā*), which refers to the ultimate nature of **reality.** See also **Apparent reality.**

Aeon *bskal-pa*, Skt. *kalpa*
The aeon is a fundamentally important concept in the traditional Indian and Buddhist understanding of cyclical time. According to ***Abhidharma*** literature, a great aeon (*mahākalpa*) is divided into eighty lesser or intervening aeons. In the course of one great aeon, the external universe and its sentient life-forms unfold and disappear. During the first twenty of the lesser aeons, the universe is in the process of creation and expansion (*vivartakalpa*); during the next twenty it remains created; during the third twenty, it is in the process of destruction or contraction (*samvartakalpa*); and during the last quarter of the cycle, it remains in a state of destruction.

Aggregate *phung-po*, Skt. *skandha*
A general philosophical term referring to the principal psycho-physical components which constitute the mind-body complex of a **sentient being.** Buddhist literature speaks of five such components, technically known as the five psycho-physical aggregates (*pañcaskandha*). These are: the **aggregate of form** (*rūpaskandha*), the **aggregate of feelings** (*vedanāskandha*), the **aggregate of perceptions** (*saṃjñāskandha*), the **aggregate of motivational tendencies** (*saṃskāraskandha*), and the **aggregate of consciousness** (*vijñānaskandha*). The Tibetan term *phung-po*, like its Sanskrit counterpart, literally means a 'heap' or a 'pile', an aggregate of many parts. **Sentient beings** in the **desire** and **form realms** manifestly possess all the five aggregates and those in the **formless realm** only the four mental aggregates.

Aggregate of Consciousness *rnam-par shes-pa'i phung-po*, Skt. *vijñānaskandha*
In the context of our text the aggregate of **consciousness** comprises the so-called **'eight classes of consciousness'** (*rnam-shes tshogs-brgyad*). These are: 1) the **ground-of-all consciousness** (*kun-gzhi rnam-par shes-pa*), which is an undifferentiated foundational consciousness underlying all the other aspects of consciousness in which are stored the imprints left by past experiences; 2) the deluded consciousness (*nyon-mong yid-kyi rnam-par shes-pa*), which is pervaded by fundamental ignorance and is responsible for our sense of selfhood and dualistic misapprehension of the true nature of phenomena; 3) the mental consciousness (*yid-kyi rnam-par shes-pa*), which objectively refers to mental constructs, thoughts and the experience of our senses; 4) visual consciousness (*mig-gi rnam-par shes-pa*); 5) auditory consciousness (*rna'i rnam-par shes-pa*); 6) olfactory consciousness (*sna'i rnam-par shes-pa*); 7) gustatory consciousness (*lce'i rnam-par shes-pa*); and 8) tactile consciousness (*lus-kyi rnam-par shes-pa*).

Aggregate of Feelings *tshor-ba'i phung-po*, Skt. *vedanāskandha*
The aggregate of feelings encompasses the pleasant, unpleasant, and neutral sensations which arise as an immediate reaction to objects of our senses.

Aggregate of Form *gzugs-kyi phung-po*, Skt. *rūpaskandha*
The aggregate of form includes both the subtle and manifest forms derived from the **elements** and experienced through the five senses, including, of course, our bodies and the environment. The aggregate of form is considered to have fifteen aspects, namely those related to the **elements**, earth, water, fire and wind; those related to the five sense objects, visual forms, sounds, smells, tastes, and contacts; those related to the five sense-organs, eye, ear, nose, tongue, and body, and, lastly, that aspect related to imperceptible forms which are said to be continuously present throughout past, present and future time.

Aggregate of Motivational Tendencies *'du-byas-kyi phung-po*, Skt. *saṃskāraskandha*
The aggregate of motivational tendencies, sometimes translated also as 'mental formations', refers to the array of specific types of causative mental states which give rise to our characteristic perspectives and emotions and which in turn condition our actions. These are the motivating impulses behind our thoughts, speech and actions which relate in specific ways to the perceived object. This aggregate includes the numerous modalities of the mind, such as the fifty-one **mental factors** listed in the ***abhidharma*** texts, as well as our habits, dispositions, and conceptualisation tendencies.

Aggregate of Perceptions *'du-shes-kyi phung-po*, Skt. *saṃjñāskandha*
The aggregate of perceptions recognises and identifies forms and objects. It differentiates one form/object from another and names them. This process includes extensive, minute, and mediocre modes of objectifying perception.

Akaniṣṭha *'og-min*
The central **buddha field** of *Akaniṣṭha* (lit. the 'Highest'), also known as the Dense Array (*Ghanavyūha*), is the pure realm associated with the male **buddha** *Vairocana*.

Alakāvatī *lcang-lo-can*
Alakāvatī is the name of the abode of the male ***bodhisattva Vajrapāṇi***.

All-surpassing Realisation *thod-rgal*, Skt. *vyutkrāntaka*
See under **Cutting through Resistance**.

Altruistic Intention to Attain Enlightenment *sems-bskyed*, Skt. *cittotpāda*
See ***Bodhicitta***.

Ancillary Commitments *yan-lag-gi dam-tshig*
See **Commitments**.

Anguished Spirits *yi-dvags*, Skt. *preta*
Among the **six classes of living beings**, the anguished spirits are characterised as being in a state of existence which, in terms of the degree of suffering, is intermediate to the animal and **hell** realms. Born as a result of a preponderance of miserliness in their past actions, they are characterised by unsatisfied craving.

Antigod *lha-ma-yin*, Skt. *asura*
One of **six classes of living beings** (*'gro-ba rigs-drug*). The mode of being and activity of the antigods is said to be engendered and dominated by envy, self-centred ambition and hostility. They are metaphorically described as being incessantly embroiled in a dispute with the **gods** (Skt. *deva/sura*) over the possession of a magical tree.

Anuyoga *rjes su rnal-'byor*
The eighth of the **nine vehicles**, and second of the three inner classes of ***tantra***, according to the ***Nyingma*** school of Tibetan Buddhism. *Anuyoga* emphasises the **perfection stage** of **meditation** (*sampannakrama*).

Apparent Reality *chos-can*, Skt. *dharmin*
According to the **Greater Vehicle**, the apparent reality of phenomena refers to the world of conventional truth characterised by duality, cause and effect and multiplicity. This is contrasted with the **actual reality**, which is the ultimate nature of phenomena. See **Two Truths**.

Arhat *dgra-bcom-pa*
A being who has attained freedom from the **cycle of existence** (*saṃsāra*) by eliminating the ***karmic*** tendencies and the **dissonant mental states** which give rise to compulsive existence in a cycle of death and rebirth. *Arhat*, literally 'worthy', is interpreted to mean 'Foe Destroyer', the foe in this context being the **dissonant mental states** which are at the root of our conditioned existence. The status of an *arhat* is the ideal goal to which practitioners of the **Lesser Vehicle** aspire. An individual person who becomes an *arhat* has still not become a fully **enlightened buddha**. This is because the attainment of **buddhahood** requires, in addition to the elimination of the **dissonant mental states**, a total overcoming of all the habitual tendencies imprinted upon our mental continuum by our long association with deluded states of **mind**. In other words, the attainment of full **enlightenment** requires the total overcoming of all personal limitations, which can be achieved only through a path that possesses the unification of the **skilful means** of universal **compassion** together with the **discriminative awareness** directly perceiving the actual nature of **reality**, at the most profound level.

Ascending and Core-penetrating *yar-gyi zang-thal*
According to *Atiyoga*, the attainment of the **Buddha-body of Reality** (*dharmakāya*) is described as 'ascending and core-penetrating' (*yar-gyi zang-thal*). Here, 'ascending' (*yar-gyi*) refers to the upward movement of **consciousness** through the **central channel** of the body and the consequent **'core-penetrating'** to the transformation of consciousness into the **pristine cognition** of **reality's expanse** (*dharmadhātujñāna*).

Atiyoga *shin-tu rnal-'byor*
The highest or ninth of the **nine vehicles**, and the third of the three inner classes of ***tantra***, according to the ***Nyingma*** school of Tibetan Buddhism, which is otherwise known as the **Great Perfection** (*rdzogs-pa chen-po*). See **Great Perfection**.

Attachment *'dod-chags*, Skt. *rāga*
One of the **'three poisons'** (*dug-gsum*) of the mind, along with **delusion** and **aversion**. In its extreme manifestation, in the form of insatiable craving, it is said to characterise the worlds of the **anguished spirits** (*pretaloka*).

Aural Lineage of Authoritative Personages *gang-zag snyan-brgyud*
One of the **six lineages** through which the Buddhist teachings are transmitted. The aural lineage of authoritative persons refers to the historical line of **accomplished masters** who have been responsible for aurally transmitting the Buddhist teachings through successive generations.

Auspicious Aeon *bskal-pa bzang-po*, Skt. *bhadrakalpa*
The name of the present **aeon** of time, during which one thousand **buddhas** are predicted to appear in succession. Among these, ***Śākyamuni Buddha*** is regarded as the fourth and ***Maitreya*** as the fifth.

Avalokiteśvara *spyan-ras gzigs dbang-phyug*
Avalokiteśvara is regarded as the embodiment of the compassionate aspect of the **mind** of all the **buddhas**, manifesting in the form of a **meditational deity**. He is revered as the patron deity of Tibet and has many different aspects, the most popular including the seated four-armed white form and 'thousand-armed' form ***Mahākaruṇika***. Our text refers to *Avalokiteśvara* as one of the eight principal male ***bodhisattvas***. See Appendix Two, pp. 390–91.

Aversion *zhe-sdang*, Skt. *dveṣa*
One of the '**three poisons**' (*dug-gsum*) of the mind. In Buddhist literature, the terms aversion and hatred are often used interchangeably with anger. In its subtle manifestation aversion is said to obstruct an individual from a correct perception of forms. In its extreme manifestation, as overwhelming hatred and fear, it is said to be characteristic of the worlds of the **hells** (*narakaloka*).

Awareness *rig-pa*, Skt. *vidyā*
As an ordinary verb, the Tibetan term *rig-pa* means 'to know' or 'to be aware'. When used as a noun, it has several distinct though not unrelated meanings, corresponding to the Sanskrit *vidyā*: 1) as a general term encompassing all experiences of **consciousness** and mental events, 2) as intelligence or mental aptitude, 3) as a science or knowledge-based discipline, 4) as a pure awareness. Our text generally assumes the last of these meanings, in which cases it is a synonym or abbreviation for **intrinsic awareness** (*rang-rig*). See under **Intrinsic Awareness**.

Awareness Holder *rig-'dzin*, Skt. *vidyādhara*
The awareness holders or knowledge holders are embodiments of the great **accomplished masters** who have attained the highest **realisations** of the ***tantras***. Amongst those whose accomplishments are classified as supramundane are ***Padmasambhava*** and *Vimalamitra*, who have transcended the span of human life, having attained the **rainbow body** through the practices of the **Great Perfection**. Five kinds of awareness holder are particularly identified, and their realisations are said to parallel those of the ***bodhisattva*** and **buddha** levels, namely the awareness holders of maturation, those with power over the lifespan, those abiding on the levels, those of the Great Seal, and those of spontaneous presence.

Basic Commitments *rtsa-ba'i dam-tshig*, Skt. *mūlasamaya*
See **Commitment.**

Beguiling Forces *bdud*, Skt. *māra*
See **Malevolent Forces.**

Being of Commitment *dam-tshig sems-dpa'*, Skt. *samayasattva*.
When deities are visualised in **meditation**, the form of the deity that is visually generated by the meditator is known as the Being of Commitment. This is differentiated from the **Being of Pristine Cognition** (*jñānasattva*, Tib. *ye-shes sems-dpa'*) or the actual **meditational deity**, which is invited to enter into the visualised form.

Being of Pristine Cognition *ye-shes sems-dpa'*, Skt. *jñānasattva*
See above under **Being of Commitment.**

Bewildered Perception *'khrul-snang*
The bewildering perceptions generated by the subject–object dichotomy.

Bewilderment *'khrul-pa*, Skt. *bhrānti*
Bewilderment is the confusion arising from the subject–object dichotomy and **fundamental ignorance**, on the basis of which rebirth in **cyclic existence** is perpetuated.

Bewitchers *'gong-po*
A class of malign spirits that are thought to frequent the atmosphere and the earth, many of whom were bound under an oath of allegiance to Buddhism by ***Padmasambhava*** during the eighth century. Their power to generate life-threatening obstacles, to assail bereaved persons, and so forth can be averted by counteracting rituals.

Bhaiṣajyaguru *sman-bla*
See **Vaiḍūryaprabharāja.**

Blessing *byin-rlabs*, Skt. *adhiṣṭhāna*
In the Buddhist context, the term blessing should not be understood in terms of grace as in the case of theistic religions. Rather, it relates to the sense of inspiration received from an external source, which transforms or awakens the potentials inherent within an individual's mental continuum. Thus, the Tibetan word *byin-rlabs* is interpreted to mean: 'to be transformed through inspiring magnificence'.

Blood-drinking [Heruka] *khrag-'thung [he-ru-ka]*, Skt. *heruka*
The Sanskrit word *heruka* is interpreted to mean 'one who delights in drinking blood' or 'one who holds a skull filled with blood', symbolising the wrathful dynamic transformation of the deep-seated **dissonant mental states.**

Blood-filled skull *dung-dmar*, Skt. *bhandha/bhāṇḍaka*
In tantric iconography, **meditational deities** are often depicted holding skull-cups filled with blood. The human skull symbolises mortality and impermanence while the blood represents the transmutation of **dissonant mental states** into **pristine cognition.**

Bodhicitta *byang-chub-kyi sems*
An altruistic intention or aspiration to attain full **enlightenment** for the benefit of all beings. *Bodhicitta* is cultivated on the basis of certain mental attitudes, principal among them being the development of **love** and great **compassion** towards all beings equally. The Tibetan tradition speaks of two major systems for training one's **mind** in the generation of *bodhicitta*: the first is *Atiśa*'s 'seven-point cause and effect' and the second is *Śāntideva*'s 'equality and exchange of oneself with others'. A genuine generation of *bodhicitta* is attained only when, through the training of the **mind,** the aspiration to attain full **enlightenment** becomes spontaneous and no longer requires any deliberate exertion. At that stage the individual becomes a ***bodhisattva.*** Literally, *bodhi* means '**enlightenment**', and *citta*, '**mind**'. The literature of the **Greater Vehicle** speaks of two types of *bodhicitta*: the conventional *bodhicitta* and the ultimate *bodhicitta*. The former refers to that aspect of *bodhicitta* defined above, whereas the latter refers to the **mind of enlightenment** i.e. the discriminative awareness directly realising **emptiness,** which is induced by the above altruistic

aspiration. The cultivation of an altruistic intention (*sems-bskyed*, Skt. *cittotpāda*) is included among the **preliminary practices** (*sngon-'gro*), in which context it is said to be an antidote for envy or self-centred ambition. In the ***tantras***, however, the term *bodhicitta* (*byang-sems*) specifically refers to the white/male and red/female **generative essences** of the body.

Bodhisattva *byang-chub sems-dpa'*
A spiritual trainee dedicated to the cultivation and fulfilment of the **altruistic intention to attain enlightenment**, who is gradually traversing the five *bodhisattva* **paths** (*pañcamārga*) and ten *bodhisattva* levels (*daśabhūmi*). An essential element of this commitment to work for others is the determination purposely to remain within **cyclic existence** instead of simply seeking freedom from **suffering** for oneself. Philosophically, the *bodhisattva* is said to have fully realised the two aspects of **selflessness,** with respect to **dissonant mental states** and the nature of all phenomena.

Bodhisattva Vows *byang-chub sems-dpa'i sdom-pa*, Skt. *bodhisattvasaṃvara*
See **Vows**.

Bon
An ancient spiritual tradition, considered by some scholars to be of Zoroastrian or Kashmiri Buddhist origin, which was widespread in Tibet, particularly in the far-western region of *Zhangzhung* prior to the official introduction and establishment of Buddhism. Although its literature clearly distinguishes it from both the indigenous shamanism or animism of Tibet and the Buddhist traditions, it has over the last several hundred years assimilated many of the Buddhist teachings and developed a neo-Buddhist theoretical foundation. The *Bon* tradition is particularly strong in the *Shang* valley of Western Tibet, in *Kongpo*, *Khyungpo* and the *Ngawa* region of *Amdo*.

Bone relics *gdung/ring-srel*
Within the tradition of the **Great Perfection** (*rdzogs-pa chen-po*), four kinds of relics are said to be left behind following the death of an **accomplished master**. These are: relics of the **Buddha-body of Reality** (*chos-sku'i ring-srel*), relics in the form of major and minor bone remains (*sku-gdung ring-srel*), relics in the form of clothing (*sku-bal ring-srel*), and relics of miniature size (*nyung-ngu lta-bu'i ring-srel*). Among these, the major bone relics (*gdung*) and minor bone relics (*ring-srel*) are retrieved from the funeral pyre. Biographical literature suggests that the veneration of such relics has been continuously observed within Buddhism from the time of ***Śākyamuni*** *Buddha*, whose own bone relics were interred within eight ***stūpas***. Five kinds of major bone relic are specifically enumerated. See Chapter 14.

Brāhman Class *bram-ze'i rigs*, Skt. *brāhmaṇavarṇa*
The priestly class, among the four traditional classes of Hindu society.

Buddha *sangs-rgyas*
The Sanskrit term buddha literally means 'awakened', 'developed', and 'enlightened'. The Tibetan equivalent *sangs-rgyas* is a combination of *sangs-pa* ('awakened' or 'purified'), and *rgyas-pa* ('developed'). These two words in this context denote a full awakening from **fundamental ignorance** (*avidyā*) in the form of the **two obscurations** (*dvayāvaraṇa*) and a full **realisation** of true knowledge, i.e. the **pristine cognition** (*jñāna*) of **buddha-mind**. A fully awakened being is therefore one who, as a result of training the mind through the ***bodhisattva*** **paths**, has finally realised his/

her full potential for complete **enlightenment** (*bodhi*), and has eliminated all the obscurations to true knowledge and **liberation.** Buddhas are characterised according to their five fruitional aspects of **buddha-body** (*kāya*), **buddha-speech** (*vāk*), **buddha-mind** (*citta*), **buddha-attributes** (*guṇa*), and **buddha-activities** (*kṛtyakriyā*), which are poetically described in some Tibetan literature as the 'five wheels of inexhaustible adornment' (*mi-zad-pa'i rgyan-gyi 'khor-lo lnga*).

Buddha-activities *phrin-las*, Skt. *kṛtyakriyā*
In general, it is said that the principal activity of the **buddhas** is to bring about the welfare of all **sentient beings**, an aim which initially motivated their aspiration to attain the fully enlightened state. The **Perfection of Discriminative Awareness** texts enumerate eighty inexhaustible buddha-activities, while some commentarial treatises mention twenty-one enlightened activities of the **buddhas**. With respect to the historical ***Buddha Śākyamuni***, the Buddhist texts list twelve principal deeds that exemplify his enlightened activities. These are in succession: 1) the descent from the celestial realm of ***Tuṣita***, 2) the entry into the womb, 3) birth, 4) displaying mastery in worldly arts and skills, 5) enjoying the women of the harem, 6) renouncing the worldly way of life, 7) undergoing severe physical penances, 8) meditating under the tree of enlightenment, 9) overcoming beguiling and **malevolent forces**, 10) attaining manifestly perfect **buddhahood**, 11) **turning the wheel of the sacred teachings**, and 12) entering the peaceful state of **final *nirvāṇa***. In terms of **skilful means**, buddha-activity may be focused through four modalities: pacification, enrichment, subjugation, and wrathful transformation. See **Four Aspects of Enlightened Activity**. Finally, according to the literature of the ***Nyingma*** school, there is an enumeration of five modes of buddha-activity when spontaneous or effortless activity is included along with these modalities.

Buddha-attributes *yon-tan*, Skt. *guṇa*
The attributes of a **buddha** may be subsumed as specific qualities of **buddha-body, speech** and **mind.** The attributes of **buddha-body** are those associated with the various 'dimensions' of **buddha-body**, described below, and more specifically with the **thirty-two major and eighty minor marks.** Those of **buddha-speech** are known as the 'sixty melodies of *Brahmā*', which implies that **buddha-speech** is soothing, gentle, firm, audible from a great distance, and so forth. The attributes of **buddha-mind** are threefold: **compassion, omniscience**, and **power**. Furthermore, in the literature of the ***tantras***, a classification of five resultant enlightened attributes is given, namely: the pure **buddha field**, the dimensionless **celestial palace**, the radiant and pure rays of light, the exalted thrones of the deities, and the possession of consummate resources.

Buddha-body *sku*, Skt. *kāya*
The term 'buddha-body' refers not only to the physical body of a **buddha**, but also to the varying 'dimensions' in which the embodiment of fully enlightened attributes is present. As such, the buddha-body can be categorised in different ways, corresponding to the different levels of the teaching. For example, ***sūtras*** of the **Lesser Vehicle** (*hīnayāna*) speak of the **Buddha-body of Reality** (*dharmakāya*) and the **Buddha-body of Form** (*rūpakāya*), while ***sūtras*** of the **Greater Vehicle** (*mahāyāna*) generally mention three buddha-bodies (*trikāya*), dividing the latter into the **Buddha-body of Perfect Resource** (*sambhogakāya*) and the **Buddha-body of Emanation** (*nirmāṇakāya*). See below. In the ***sūtras*** and treatises expounding **buddha-**

nature (*tathāgatagarbha*), such as ***Maitreya***'s *Supreme Continuum of the Greater Vehicle* (*Mahayanottaratantraśāstra*), an enumeration of **four buddha-bodies** (*catuḥkāya*) is mentioned. Here, the Buddha-body of Essentiality (*svabhāvikakāya*) is added to the above three buddha-bodies, to indicate either an active/passive distinction in the **Buddha-body of Reality**, or the underlying indivisible essence of the three buddha-bodies. In the ***tantras*** of the ***Nyingma*** school, there is an enumeration of **five buddha-bodies** (*pañcakāya*) where the Buddha-body of Awakening (*abhisambodhikāya*, Tib. *mngon-byang-gi sku*) refers to the apparitional modes of the three buddha-bodies, and the Buddha-body of Indestructible Reality (*vajrakāya*, Tib. *rdo-rje'i sku*) refers to their indivisible essence. Finally, in ***Atiyoga***, when the buddha-bodies are actualised, the **Buddha-body of Reality** is known as the youthful vase body (*gzhon-nu'i 'bum-pa'i sku*) and the **Buddha-body of Form** is known as the body of great transformation (*'pho-ba chen-po'i sku*).

Buddha-body of Emanation *sprul-sku*, Skt. *nirmāṇakāya*
The Buddha-body of Emanation is the visible and usually physical manifestation of fully enlightened beings which arises spontaneously from the expanse of the **Buddha-body of Reality**, whenever appropriate, in accordance with the diverse dispositions of sentient beings. The ***sūtras*** refer to three types of emanational body in relation to ***Śākyamuni Buddha***: (i) emanational birth in ***Tuṣita***, (ii) emanational art forms, and (iii) supreme emanation as one of the thousand **buddhas** of the **auspicious aeon**. From the distinctive ***Nyingma*** perspective, however, the three types of emanational body comprise: 1) natural emanations (*rang-bzhin sprul-sku*), which are the **buddhas** of the **five enlightened families** such as Vairocana in the forms they assume when appearing before ***bodhisattvas*** of the highest level; 2) supreme emanations (*mchog-gi sprul-sku*) such as ***Śākyamuni Buddha*** and the other **buddhas** of this aeon who initiate a new teaching, and 3) diversified emanations (*sna-tshogs sprul-sku*), including oases, food, medicine and other such material manifestations, which are of benefit to living beings, as well as emanational art forms (*bzo-bo sprul-sku*) and emanational births (*skye-ba sprul-sku*), such as those taken by ***Śākyamuni*** in previous lives, for example as Prince Satśvetaketu in the god realm of ***Tuṣita***.

Buddha-body of Form *gzugs-sku*, Skt. *rūpakāya*
According to the literature of the **Lesser Vehicle** (*hīnayāna*) the Buddha-body of Form refers to the thousand **buddhas** of the **auspicious aeon**, including ***Śākyamuni***. In the **Greater Vehicle**, however, the term includes both the **Buddha-body of Perfect Resource** and the **Buddha-body of Emanation**. According to *Atiyoga*, when the Buddha-body of Form is actualised through the practices of **All-surpassing Realisation**, a **rainbow-light body** is attained, and this realisation is known as the Buddha-body of Great Transformation (*'pho-ba chen-po'i sku*).

Buddha-body of Perfect Resource *longs-spyod rdzogs-pa'i sku*, Skt. *sambhogakāya*
The Buddha-body of Perfect Resource refers to the luminous, immaterial, and unimpeded reflection-like forms of the pure energy of enlightened mind, exemplified in the case of our text by the assembly of the forty-two peaceful deities and the fifty-eight wrathful deities (see Appendix Two), which become spontaneously present (*lhun-grub*) and naturally manifest (*rang-snang*) at very high levels of realisation, that is to say at the point at which the duality between subject and object

dissolves. The **intermediate state of reality** (*chos-nyid bar-do*) is considered to be an optimum time for the realisation of the Buddha-body of Perfect Resource.

Buddha-body of Reality *chos-sku*, Skt. *dharmakāya*
The Buddha-body of Reality is the ultimate nature or essence of the **enlightened mind**, which is uncreated (*skye-med*), free from the limits of conceptual elaboration (*spros-pa'i mtha'-bral*), empty of inherent existence (*rang-bzhin-gyis stong-pa*), naturally radiant, beyond duality and spacious like the sky. The **intermediate state of the time of death** (*'chi-kha'i bar-do*) is considered to be an optimum time for the realisation of the Buddha-body of Reality.

Buddha Family *de-bzhin gshegs-pa'i rigs*, Skt. *tathāgatakula*
One of the **five enlightened families** (*pañcakula*) into which the **meditational deities** of the **Buddha-body of Perfect Resource** are subdivided. The deities of the *Buddha* family include the peaceful aspects Vairocana and Dhātvīśvarī and the corresponding wrathful aspects Buddha Heruka and Buddhakrodheśvarī. See Appendix Two.

Buddha Field *zhings-khams*, Skt. *[buddha]kṣetra*
The operational fields or 'paradises' presided over by specific **buddhas**, which spontaneously arise as a result of their altruistic aspirations, are known as buddha fields. Such environments are totally free from **suffering**, both physical and mental, and they transcend the mundane **god** realms (*devaloka*) inhabited by **sentient beings** of the **world-systems** of desire, form, and formlessness. It is said that when sentient beings who have not yet been permanently released from the bondage of **cyclic existence** have an affinity with a specific **buddha** and are consequently born into a respective pure realm, they become temporarily free not only from manifest **sufferings** of the body and **mind** but also from the pervasive sufferings of past conditioning. Such fields or pure realms are regarded as conducive to the continuing cultivation of the path to **buddhahood**.

Buddhahood *sangs-rgyas nyid / sangs-rgyas-kyi go-phang*, Skt. *buddhatva/ buddhapada*
The attainment of a **buddha**, who has not only gained total freedom from karmically conditioned existence and overcome all the tendencies imprinted on the **mind** as a result of a long association with **dissonant mental states,** but also fully realised or manifested all aspects of **buddha-body, buddha-speech, buddha-mind, buddha-attributes** and **buddha-activities.**

Buddha-mind *thugs*, Skt. *citta*
The term buddha-mind is synonymous with **pristine cognition** (*jñāna*), five modes of which are differentiated. See **Pristine Cognition.** In the particular literature of the ***Nyingma*** school, these five modes are distinctively known as manifest enlightenment (*mngon-byang-gi thugs*), indivisible indestructible reality (*mi-phyed rdo-rje'i thugs*), great sameness (*mnyam-pa chen-po'i thugs*), great non-discursiveness (*mi-rtog chen-po'i thugs*), and liberator of sentient beings (*'gro-ba'i sgrol-ba'i thugs*).

Buddha Nature *rigs*, Skt. *gotra*
The seed of **enlightenment** inherent within the mental continuum of all sentient beings. It is this potential which makes it possible for every individual to realise the ultimate nature, given the application of appropriate methods. The notion of buddha nature is intimately linked with the Buddhist concept of the essential nature of **mind**, which according to Buddhism is considered to be pure, knowing and lumi-

nous. **Dissonant mental states** such as **attachment, aversion** and jealousy, which perpetually afflict our mind and give rise to **suffering,** are not the essential elements of our **mind** but adventitious and conditioned tendencies. Moreover, these dissonant states are all rooted in an ignorant state of mind which misapprehends the true nature of **reality.** Hence, through gaining genuine insights into the true nature of **reality,** misconceptions can be dispelled, thus cutting the root of all our **dissonant mental states** and allowing the buddha-nature within to manifest. The term **'nucleus of the *tathāgata*'** (*tathāgatagarbha*) is a synonym for this essence of **buddhahood.**

Buddha-speech *gsung*, Skt. *vāk*
The speech of the **buddhas** is, according to ***Nyingma*** literature, said to have five aspects in that the **buddhas** may communicate through 1) uncreated meaning (*skye-med don-gi gsung*), 2) **enlightened intention** and symbols (*dgongs-pa brda'i gsung*), 3) expressive words (*brjod-pa tshig-gi gsung*), 4) indivisible reality (*dbyer-med rdo-rje'i gsung*), and 5) the **blessings** of **awareness** (*rig-pa byin-labs-kyi gsung*). See **Buddha Attributes** and **Mantra.**

Burnt Offerings *sbyin-sreg*, Skt. *homa*
A **tantric** ritual in which many substances, such as wheat, sesame seeds, and mustard, etc., are burnt as offerings in a fire lit on a specifically designed hearth. There are different types of burnt-offering rituals corresponding to the enactment of the four rites related to the **four aspects of enlightened activity:** pacification, enrichment, subjugation and wrath.

Calm Abiding *zhi-gnas*, Skt. *śamatha*
Calm abiding is a meditative technique common to the entire Buddhist tradition, characterised by a stabilisation of attention on an internal object of observation conjoined with the calming of external distractions to the mind. Calm abiding is an essential basis for training one's mind in the generation of **penetrative insight** (*vipaśyana*), a true analytical insight into the more profound aspects of a chosen object, such as its **emptiness** or ultimate nature.

Cāmaradvīpa *rnga-yab gling*
The subcontinent *Cāmaradvīpa* is particularly associated, in ***Nyingma*** literature, with the **Copper-coloured Mountain** of ***Padmasambhava.*** See **Four Continents and Eight Subcontinents.**

Caryātantra *spyod-pa'i rgyud*
See **Ubhayatantra.**

Causal Vehicles *rgyu mtshan-nyid-kyi theg-pa*
See **Vehicle.**

Cause and Effect *rgyu-'bras*, Skt. *hetuphala*
In the context of Buddhist philosophy the term refers to the natural law that exists between a cause and its effect. Some of the principal features of the law are: 1) nothing evolves uncaused; 2) any entity which itself lacks a process of change cannot cause any other event; and 3) only causes which possess natures that accord with specific effects can lead to those effects. The term 'cause and effect' is often used to translate the Sanskrit word ***karma***, which literally means 'action'. See **Past Actions.**

Celestial Palace *gzhal-yas-khang*, Skt. *vimāna*
See **Maṇḍala.**

Central Channel *rtsa dbu-ma*, Skt. *avadhūti*
See **Energy Channels.**

Chang-bu Offerings *chang-bu*, Skt. *piṇḍa*
Finger-pressed strands of dough, which are made as offerings to assuage **anguished spirits** and to appease negative forces.

Channel Branch *rtsa-'dab*
According to the ***tantras*** and related medical traditions, there are five **energy centres** located along the **central channel** of the body at the focal points of the crown, throat, heart, navel and genitalia. A specific number of channel branches (*rtsa-'dab*) emerges from each of these energy centres, and these in turn conduct **vital energy** throughout the body through a network of 72,000 minor channels. See **Energy Channels.**

Channel of Pristine Cognition *ye-shes-kyi dhūti*
According to the ***tantras***, the channel of pristine cognition is a synonym for the **central channel** of the body. See **Vital Energy.**

Chiliocosm *stong dang-po 'jig-rten-gyi khams*, Skt. *sahasralokadhātu*
According to traditional Indian Buddhist cosmology, the world of the **four continents** surrounding **Mount** ***Sumeru*** when multiplied one thousand times forms a chiliocosm of parallel worlds (*stong dang-po*). The chiliocosm when multiplied one thousand times forms a larger *dichiliocosm* (*stong gnyis-pa*), which in turn when multiplied one thousand times forms an even larger trichiliocosm (*stong gsum-pa*). This evolution of expanding worlds continues to enlarge incrementally until the inconceivably vast number of multiple worlds is reached, in which a single supreme **Buddha-body of Emanation** is said to function simultaneously.

Citipati *dur-khrod bdag-po bdag-mo*
The *Citipati* are a pair of male and female acolytes of ***Yama***, lord of death, who are depicted as two skeletons in dancing posture, symbolising the rites of the charnel ground.

Cittamātra *sems-tsam-pa*
One of the four major Buddhist philosophical schools of ancient India, also known as *Vijñānavāda*, and associated in some respects with the *Yogācāra* tradition. The *Cittamātra* (lit. 'mind only') school founded by the fourth-century Indian master *Asaṅga* propounds an idealist or phenomenalistic view of the world. Its main tenet is that all phenomena are either actual mental events or extensions of the mind and the mind is regarded as existing as a substantially real entity. In addition, the school propounds that there exists no atomically composed material world external to, or independent of, our perceptions. According to the *Cittamātra* school consciousness itself is considered to be eightfold, with the **ground-of-all consciousness** as the foundation. See **Aggregate of Consciousness.**

Cittamātrin *sems rtsam-pa-po*
A follower of the ***Cittamātra*** school.

Cīvaṃcīvaka *shang-shang*
A mythical creature with the head, arms, and torso of a human being, and the wings and legs of a bird. The throne of the male **buddha** Amoghasiddhi assumes the form of a *cīvaṃcīvaka* bird.

Coemergent Delight *lhan-cig skyes-pa'i dga'-ba*, Skt. *sahajasukha/sahajānanda*
The coemergent delight is one of the **four delights** (*dga'-ba bzhi*) experienced during the **perfection stage** (*sampannakrama*) of meditation. See **Four Delights**. It is said that the coemergent delight is also naturally experienced at the moment of death (see Chapter 8) and at the moment of conception (see Chapter 11).

Coemergent Ignorance *lhan-cig-skyes-pa'i ma-rig-pa*, Skt. *sahajāvidyā*
See **Fundamental Ignorance**.

Coemergent Pristine Cognition *lhan-skyes ye-shes*, Skt. *sahajajñāna*
The natural emergence of pristine cognition that occurs during the perfection stage of meditation, when vital energy is absorbed within the central channel of the subtle body.

Commitment *dam-tshig*, Skt. *samaya*
A sacred commitment or pledge taken by a practitioner which is a prerequisite for the practice of the ***tantras***. The Tibetan '*dam-tshig*' literally means 'binding word', indicating that the person becomes bound by a solemn oath. Each class of ***tantra*** has its own categorisation of basic and ancillary commitments, which complement the ***prātimokṣa*** and ***bodhisattva* vows** taken by those who uphold the ***vinaya*** and the ***sūtra*** tradition of the **Greater Vehicle** respectively. See **Vows**. *Samaya* may entail the observation of specific precepts which are common to a whole class of ***tantra***, or individual precepts, which must be observed in relation to a particular **meditational deity**. When such commitments are broken they must be restored through appropriate tantric ritual practices, for their degeneration may cause serious hindrances to progress on the path. See Chapter 7.

Commitments of Indestructible Reality *rdo-rje dam-tshig*, Skt. *vajrasamaya*
A synonym for the **commitments** in general which are undertaken in the context of the **Vehicle of Indestructible Reality** (*Vajrayāna*).

Commitments Undertaken in Respect of Reality *de-kho-na-nyid-kyi dam-tshig*
A synonym for the four commitments specific to the practice of ***Atiyoga***.

Compassion *snying-rje/thugs-rje*, Skt. *karuṇā*
In Buddhist literature, the term 'compassion' is often used as a synonym for 'great compassion' (*mahākaruṇā*), which refers to a totally unbiased mind that aspires to the **liberation** of all **sentient beings** from **suffering**, equally. Compassion is said to become 'great' only when, through proper training of the **mind**, such an altruistic aspiration becomes spontaneous and no longer requires any conscious effort for its arising. The measure of having realised such a state is that one spontaneously feels a sense of intimacy and compassion towards all others, with the same degree of commitment and intensity that one feels towards one's most beloved. It is worth bearing in mind that in Buddhism, compassion should not be understood in terms of pity, which may imply a feeling of superiority toward the object of compassion.

Conceptual Elaboration *spros-pa*, Skt. *prapañca*
Conceptual elaboration refers to the presence of discursive or conceptual thought processes, the absence of which (Skt. *niṣprapañca*, Tib. *spros-bral*) is characteristic of the realisation of **emptiness** or **actual reality**.

Confession of Negativity *sdig-pa'i gshags-pa*, Skt. *pāpadeśanā*
A spiritual practice which involves the disclosure and purification of accumulated

negative actions. The successful application of confession must be undertaken within the framework of what are known as the four antidotal powers. For an explanation of these see the introductory context to Chapter 7.

Conqueror *rgyal-ba*, Skt. *jina*
In Buddhist literature, this term is an epithet for a **buddha**, indicating the victory attained by a **buddha** over **cyclic existence** (*saṃsāra*). In particular in the context of this book, the **Buddha-body of Perfect Resource** in the ***maṇḍala*** of the **Peaceful and Wrathful Deities** is described as represented by the '**five enlightened families** of the conquerors' (*rgyal-ba rigs-lnga*), where the five male **buddhas**, in both peaceful and wrathful forms, are known as the five conquerors. ***Vajradhara***, an aspect of the primordial ***buddha Samantabhadra***, who represents the **Buddha-body of Reality**, is also known as the 'sixth conqueror' (*rgyal-ba drug-pa*) or 'lord of the sixth **enlightened family**'. More generally, in its Tibetan form, this same epithet is frequently used as an honorific title before the names of highly venerated beings, e.g. *Gyalwa Yizhin Norbu* (for HH the ***Dalai Lama***), or *Gyalwa Karmapa*.

Consciousness *rnam-par shes-pa*, Skt. *vijñāna*
In Buddhism, consciousness is defined as 'an awareness which is knowing and luminous'. It is not physical and thus lacks any resistance to obstruction. It has neither shape nor colour; it can be experienced but not externally perceived as an object. In short, it includes both the conscious cognitive events and the subconscious aspects of the mind through which we know and perceive the world, as well as the emotions. A distinction is made between the mundane consciousness (*vijñāna*) of sentient beings, and the **pristine cognition** (*jñāna*) of the **buddhas**. See **Pristine Cognition** and **Aggregate of Consciousness**.

Consciousness Transference *'pho-ba*, Skt. *saṃkrānti*
A unique tantric practice undertaken to transfer the **consciousness** at the time of death, ideally to the unconditioned state of the realisation of the **Buddha-body of Reality**, or to a realm of existence with a favourable migration, ideally the **pure realm** of a **meditational deity**. See Chapter 10.

Continuum of the Ground *gzhi'i rgyud*, Skt. *āśrayatantra*
The continuum of the ground is identified with the primordially present **intrinsic awareness**, and the **actual reality** or **emptiness**, which is in harmony with the fruitional aspects of **buddhahood**. According to the ***tantras***, the continuum of the ground (*gzhi'i rgyud*) is the basis through which the **continuum of the path** (*lam-gyi rgyud*) fully manifests as the **continuum of the result** (*'bras-bu'i rgyud*).

Continuum of the Path *lam-gyi rgyud*, Skt. *mārgatantra*
According to the ***tantras***, the continuum of the path is the means through which the **continuum of the ground** (*gzhi'i rgyud*) becomes fully manifest as the **continuum of the result** (*'bras-bu'i rgyud*).

Continuum of the Result *'bras-bu'i rgyud*, Skt. *phalatantra*
According to the ***tantras***, the continuum of the result is the fruition or conclusion attained when the **continuum of the ground** (*gzhi'i rgyud*) becomes fully manifest through the **continuum of the path** (*lam-gyi rgyud*).

Copper-coloured Mountain *zangs-mdog dpal-ri*, Skt. *Tāmraśrīparvata*
A sacred abode located on the subcontinent ***Cāmaradvīpa*** (*rnga-yab gling*), where ***Padmasambhava*** is said to currently reside in an awesome rainbow-light form.

Core-penetrating *zang-thal*
See **Ascending and Core-penetrating.**

Cutting through Resistance *khregs-chod*
According to the pith or esoteric instructions (*man-ngag-gi sde*) of the **Great Perfection** (***Atiyoga***) there are two meditative techniques, which are engaged in successively. The first, Cutting through Resistance (*khregs-chod*) focuses on the recognition of **primordial purity** (*ka-dag*), the nature of **awareness** (*rig-pa*), through which the **Buddha-body of Reality** is attained. The second, **All-surpassing Realisation** (*thod-rgal*), focuses on the recognition of **spontaneous presence** (*lhun-grub*), eliciting and recognising the radiances of **pristine cognition** and the purity of our psycho-physical **aggregates** and **elements**, through which the rainbow-like **Buddha-body of Form** is attained. In **All-surpassing Realisation** practice, once a stable realisation of the nature of **awareness** has been attained through Cutting through Resistance, all phenomenal appearances are liberated through a spontaneous realisation of their essential modality as **inner radiance.** Cutting through Resistance is the subject matter of Chapter 4 of the present work. The introduction to the **intermediate state of reality**, in Chapter 11 of our text, is illustrative of the esoteric instructions on **All-surpassing Realisation**, which is the pinnacle of meditative practice according to the ***Nyingma*** school.

Cyclic Existence *'khor-ba*, Skt. *saṃsāra*
A state of existence conditioned by **dissonant mental states** and the imprint of **past actions** (*karma*), characterised by suffering in a cycle of life, death and rebirth, in which the **six classes of sentient beings** (*ṣaḍgati*; Tib. *'gro-ba rigs-drug*) rotate. Cyclic existence emerges from **fundamental ignorance** (*avidyā*) through a process known as the **twelve links of dependent origination** (*dvādaśāṅga-pratītya-samutpāda*). When **fundamental ignorance**, identified as the misapprehension of the nature of **actual reality** (*dharmatā*), is reversed, cyclic existence is itself reversed, and the contrasting state of ***nirvāṇa*** is attained, free from suffering and the processes of rebirth. See **Dependent Origination** and Nirvāṇa.

Ḍākinī *mkha'-'gro-ma*
Ḍākinī are female ***yoginī*** who have attained either mundane or supramundane spiritual **accomplishments** (*siddhi*), the latter referring to the realisations of **buddhahood.** They may be human beings who have achieved such attainments, or manifestations of the enlightened activity of **meditational deities**. The Tibetan equivalent *mkha'-'gro* literally means 'space voyager', space metaphorically implying **emptiness,** and voyager indicating someone immersed in its experience. The *ḍākinī* are said to confer enlightened or **buddha-activities** on the meditator, in contrast to the **spiritual teacher** who confers **blessings** and the **meditational deity** who confers **accomplishments.**

Ḍākinī of Pristine Cognition *ye-shes mkha'-'gro*, Skt. *jñānaḍākinī*
The female consorts of the principal **awareness holders** of maturation, power over the lifespan, the Great Seal and spontaneous presence.

Ḍākinī of the Three Abodes *gnas-gsum mkha'-'gro*
The *ḍākinī* of the three abodes are those of **buddha-body, speech** and **mind.**

Dalai Lama *rgyal ba yid-bzhin nor-bu/rin-po-che*
The temporal and spiritual leader of Tibet. The *Dalai Lama's* temporal reign began at the time of the fifth *Dalai Lama* in the 17th century. Since then the country has been ruled, periodically, by a succession of *Dalai Lamas*, until China's occupation in the 1950s. The *Dalai Lamas* are chosen according to a strict traditional procedure of observation and examination initiated following the death of the previous *Dalai Lama*. The present *Dalai Lama* is the fourteenth in the succession of this lineage. The title *Dalai Lama* was originally offered to *Sonam Gyatso*, the third *Dalai Lama*, by the then Mongol prince *Altan Qan*. The Mongol word *da-lai* (Tib. *rgya-mtsho*) means 'ocean (of wisdom)'.

Ḍāmaru *ḍā-ma-ru*
A hand-held double-sided drum, frequently identified with the **wrathful deities** and the ***ḍākinī***, and generally utilised as a ritual instrument in conjunction with the bell. The *ḍāmaru* is said to proclaim 'the sound of great bliss'.

Dedication of Merit *bsngo-ba*, Skt. *pariṇāma*
An important element of Buddhist practice enacted normally in the form of a recitation of verses of dedication at the conclusion of a spiritual practice. In all Buddhist practices, the establishment of the correct motivation at the beginning and the altruistic dedication at the end are regarded as highly significant. The most popular objects of the dedication are the flourishing of the **sacred teachings** of Buddhism throughout the universe and the attainment of full **enlightenment** by all **sentient beings.**

Definitive Meaning *nges-don*, Skt. *nītārtha*
The ***sūtra*** teachings of the **buddhas** are classified as being of either definitive meaning or provisional meaning (*neyārtha*) depending on whether they do not or do require further interpretation. In general, ***sūtras*** of provisional meaning concern the nature of **cyclic existence** (*saṃsāra*) and its antidotes, as expounded by ***Śākyamuni Buddha*** in the first **turning of the wheel of the sacred teachings.** By contrast, those ***sūtras*** of definitive meaning concern either the nature of **emptiness,** as expressed in the second **turning of the wheel of the sacred teachings,** or the explications on **buddha nature** and **buddha-attributes,** as expressed in the third **turning of the wheel of the sacred teachings.** There are divergent views in the various schools of Tibetan Buddhism as to which of the ***sūtras*** of the second and third turnings should be regarded as definitive or provisional.

Degenerate Age *snyigs-ma'i dus*, Skt. *kaliyuga*
According to the prevailing view of Indian cosmology, a period of cosmic or cyclical time (**aeon,** Skt. *kalpa*) comprises fourteen secondary cycles (Skt. *manvantara*), each of which lasts 306,720,000 years. Each secondary cycle is said to contain seventy-one 'great ages' (Skt. *mahāyuga*), and each of these is further subdivided into four ages (Skt. *caturyuga*) which are of decreasing duration, and known respectively as the Perfect Age (*kṛtayuga*), the Third Age (*tretāyuga*), the Second Age (*dvāpara-yuga*), and the Black or Degenerate Age (*kaliyuga*). Since these four ages represent a gradual decline in meritorious activities, special meditative practices and spiritual antidotes are associated with each in turn. Specifically, the Perfect Age is most suited

to the practice of the ***Kriyātantra***; the Third Age to that of the ***Caryātantra***; the Second Age to that of the ***Yogatantra***; and the present Black or Degenerate Age to that of the **Unsurpassed *Yogatantra***.

Deity *yi-dam*, Skt. *iṣṭadevatā*
See under **Meditational Deity**.

Delusion *gti-mug*, Skt. *moha*
One of the **three poisons** (*dug-gsum*) along with **aversion** and **attachment**, or **five poisons** (*dug-lnga*) along with **aversion**, **attachment**, pride, and envy, which perpetuate the **sufferings of cyclic existence**. Delusion is the obfuscating mental factor which obstructs an individual from generating knowledge or insight, and it is said to be characteristic of the animal world in general.

Dense Array *gtug-po bkod-pa*, Skt. *Ghanavyūha*
The Dense Array is a synonym for the central **buddha field** of ***Akaniṣṭha***. See under **Akaniṣṭha**.

Dependent Origination *rten-'brel*, Skt. *pratītyasamutpāda*
The doctrine of dependent origination can be said to be the most fundamental metaphysical view of Buddhist thought and it is intimately linked with the Buddhist notion of causation. The principle of dependent origination asserts that nothing exists independently of other factors, the reason for this being that things and events come into existence only by dependence on the aggregation of multiple causes and conditions. In general, the processes of **cyclic existence**, through which the external world and the **sentient beings** within it revolve in a continuous cycle of **suffering**, propelled by the **propensities** of **past actions** and their interaction with **dissonant mental states**, are said to originate dependent on twelve successive links, which are known as the **twelve links of dependent origination** (*dvādaśāṅga-pratītya-samutpāda*). These comprise: 1) **fundamental ignorance**, 2) **motivational tendencies**, 3) **consciousness**, 4) name and form, 5) **sensory activity fields**, 6) contact, 7) **sensation**, 8) **attachment**, 9) grasping, 10) rebirth process, 11) birth, 12) ageing and death. Although, in the ultimate sense there is no beginning to the continuum of **mind**, a relative beginning can be spoken of on the basis of a single instance of rebirth within **cyclic existence**. Every instance of birth in **cyclic existence** must have a cause and such causes are ultimately rooted in our **fundamental ignorance**, which misapprehends the true nature of **actual reality**. For an ordinary **sentient being** all the twelve links are interconnected and each component of the chain contributes to the perpetuation of the cycle. It is only through deliberate reversal of **fundamental ignorance** that one can succeed in bringing the whole cycle to an end. **Fundamental ignorance** (*avidyā*) gives rise to conditioning or tendencies (*saṃskāra*) which are stored in the substratum or **ground-of-all consciousness** (*ālayavijñāna*). Following the moment of a sentient being's conception, this inheritance of past actions from a previous life gives rise to name and form (*nāmarūpa*), i.e. to the five psycho-physical **aggregates** (*pañcaskandha*), which are products of that dualising consciousness. Then, the sensory activity fields (*āyatana*) provide the subjective and objective framework for sensory activity in its initial stages of development; while contact (*sparśa*) refers to the maturation of sensory perception as an unborn child develops a sensitivity to its environment inside the womb. Thereafter, sensation (*vedanā*), **attachment** (*tṛṣṇā*), grasping (*ādāna*), rebirth process (*bhava*), and actual birth (*jāti*)

together indicate the emergence of a **sentient being** within the living world; and these in turn lead inevitably to old age and death (*jarāmaraṇa*).

Desire *'dod-chags*, Skt. *rāga*
See **Attachment**.

Desire Realm, Skt. *kāmadhātu*
See **Three World-systems.**

Dhanakośa *dha-na-ko-sa*
The name of an island lake situated in the country of ***Oḍḍiyāna***, generally identified in the Tibetan tradition with the Swat Valley of modern Pakistan, where many of the Buddhist ***tantras*** were once disseminated and practised. It is considered to have been the birthplace of both ***Prahevajra***, the first human **lineage holder** of ***Atiyoga***, and of ***Padmasambhava***.

Dharmarāja *chos-rgyal*
See under **Yama Dharmarāja.**

Discriminative Awareness *shes-rab*, Skt. *prajñā*
The Sanskrit term *prajñā* is formally defined as 'the discriminative awareness of the essence, distinctions, particular and general characteristics, and advantages and disadvantages of any object within one's own perceptual range, at the conclusion of which doubts are removed'. In other words, this is the faculty of intelligence or discriminating awareness inherent within the mental continuum of all living creatures which enables them to examine the characteristics of things and events, thus making it possible to make judgements and deliberations. The term *prajñā* has commonly been translated into English as 'wisdom', largely following the example of Edward Conze, who translated a voluminous series of texts devoted to the **Perfection of Discriminative Awareness** (*Prajñāpāramitā*). According to the ***abhidharma*** of the **Lesser Vehicle**, *prajñā* is one of the five mental factors of ascertainment which arise during all mental events of a veridical nature. According to the **Greater Vehicle**, the perfection of this faculty of discriminative awareness (*prajñāpāramitā*) leads a ***bodhisattva*** to a total overcoming of all types of doubt and ignorance and to the realisation of the **emptiness** of all things. Here, in conjunction with **skilful means** (*upāya*), the term *prajñopāya* refers to the integration of the two principal aspects of the path to **enlightenment**. In this context *prajñā*, or true insight into the **emptiness** of all phenomena, is united in perfect union with **skilful means.** In tantric traditions, the union of *prajñopāya* is often depicted iconographically in the union of the male and female deities, and in the symbolic hand-implements such as the ***vajra*** and the bell.

Dissonant Mental States *nyon-mongs*, Skt. *kleśa*
The essentially pure nature of **mind** is obscured and afflicted by the various psychological defilements known as the dissonant mental states. The Tibetan word *nyon-mongs* implies a mental event whose arising causes psychological afflictions within the **mind**, thus destroying its peace and composure. According to ***abhidharma*** literature in general, there are six primary dissonant mental states: **fundamental ignorance, attachment, aversion,** pride, doubt, and afflicted or dissonant views; and an enumeration of twenty subsidiary mental states (Skt. *upakleśa*), which comprise: anger, malice, dissimulation, fury, envy, miserliness, dishonesty, deception, arrogance, mischief, indecorum, indecency, obfuscation, agitation, distrust, laziness,

carelessness, forgetfulness, distraction, and inattentiveness. Even more wide-ranging are the 84,000 dissonant mental states for which the 84,000 aspects of the **sacred teachings** are said to provide distinctive antidotes. At the root of all these psychological afflictions lies the **fundamental ignorance** which misapprehends the true nature of **reality**.

Downfalls *ltung-ba*, Skt. *āpatti*
See **Transgressions**.

Dream Yoga *rmi-lam*
Meditative techniques for utilising and transforming dream consciousness within the context of **Unsurpassed *Yogatantra*** practice. These include: meditative techniques for retaining awareness during the dream state; multiplying and transforming the contents of dreams and recognising their actual nature; and the dispelling of obstacles which prevent maintaining awareness in the dream state.

Dualism *gnyis-snang*, Skt. *ubhayābhāsa*
Any level of perception of duality. Buddhist thought describes various forms of dualism, principal amongst these being: 1) a dualistic perception of subject and object; 2) all appearances of **inherent existence**; 3) all appearances of conventionalities; and 4) all forms of conceptuality. A genuine direct **realisation** of **emptiness** is non-dual, in that it is free from all the above forms of dualism.

Dzogchen *rdzogs-chen*, Skt. *mahāsandhi*
See **Great Perfection**.

Eight Charnel Grounds *dur-khrod brgyad*
The eight charnel grounds are the great cemeteries of ancient India, which are regarded as inspirational places for the practice of meditation. These are respectively known, in Tibetan translation, as Tumdrak (*gtum-drag*), Tsangtsing Trikpa (*tshang-tshing 'khrigs-pa*), Bar Trikpa (*'bar 'khrigs-pa*), Kengruchen (*keng-rus-can*), Silbutsel (*bsil-bu-tshal*, Skt. *Śītavana*), Munpa Nagpo (*mun-pa nag-po*), Kili Kilir Dradrokpa (*ki-li ki-lir sgra-sgrog-pa*), and Haha Godpa (*ha-ha rgod-pa*).

Eight Classes of Consciousness *rnam-shes tshogs/gnas-brgyad*
See under **Aggregate of Consciousness**.

Eight Classes of Spirits *sde-brgyad*
A classification of the malign forces that can be appeased by specific offerings and rituals. Diverse enumerations of these malign forces have been made by *Nubchen Sangye Yeshe*. Accordingly, there is an outer eightfold group (*phyi-yi sde brgyad*), an inner eightfold group (*nang-gi sde brgyad*), a secret eightfold group (*gsang-ba'i sde brgyad*), a supreme eightfold group (*mchog-gi sde brgyad*), an emanational eightfold group (*sprul-pa'i sde brgyad*), and a phenomenal eightfold group (*snang-srid sde brgyad*).

Eight Extremes *mtha'-brgyad*, Skt. *aṣṭānta*
The eight extremes from which **intrinsic awareness** is free are those enumerated by ***Nāgārjuna*** in the *Root Stanzas of the Madhyamaka entitled Discriminative Awareness* (*Prajñānāma mūlamadhyamakakārikā*, T 3824), namely: cessation

(*'gag-pa*), creation or production (*skye-ba*), **nihilism** (*chad-pa*), **eternalism** (*rtag-pa*), coming (*'ong-ba*), going (*'gro-ba*), diversity (*tha-dad-pa*), and singularity (*gcig-pa*).

Eight Freedoms and Ten Opportunities *dal-ba brgyad dang 'byor-ba bcu*
Birth as a human being with the freedom and opportunity to follow the Buddhist path is regarded as difficult to attain and a precious circumstance. In the **preliminary practices** of the ***tantra*** path, in order to establish an appreciation for the significance of human rebirth, the freedom one has from eight unfavourable rebirths is a focus of contemplation, together with contemplation of the ten favourable opportunities. The eight freedoms are the freedoms from the following eight states: birth in the **hells**, birth as an **anguished spirit**, birth as an animal, birth as an uncivilised or barbarous person, birth as a long-living **god**, birth into a society that holds mistaken beliefs, birth in an age devoid of Buddhism, and birth with limited faculties. Among the ten favourable opportunities, there are five which are personally acquired and five which are contingent on external factors. The former comprise the favourable opportunities of being born as a human being, in a civilised society, with perfect sense-faculties, not being engaged in a conflicting lifestyle, and having confidence in Buddhism. The latter comprise the favourable opportunities of being born in an **aeon** when a **buddha** has appeared, when the sacred teachings have been taught, when they are still being practised, and when one actively engages in their practice, and finds a qualified **spiritual friend** (*kalyāṇamitra*). See Chapter 1.

Eight [Great] Fears *'jigs-pa brgyad*, Skt. *aṣṭabhaya*
These are variously enumerated but often include: drowning, fires, thieves, captivity, lions, snakes, elephants, and spirits.

Eight Great Projectresses *spor-byed chen-mo brgyad*
The eight great projectresses are female deities representing forces that propel various classes of **sentient beings** to exalted rebirths during the **intermediate state of reality**. See Chapter 6.

Eight Objects [of Consciousness] *[rnam-shes-kyi] yul brgyad*
These are the objects of the eight classes of consciousness, i.e. deep-seated **habitual tendencies** (ground-of-all consciousness), **dissonant mental states** (deluded consciousness), thoughts (mental consciousness), sights (visual consciousness), objects of taste (gustatory consciousness), sounds (auditory consciousness), smells (olfactory consciousness) and physical objects (tactile consciousness). See under **Aggregate of Consciousness.**

Eight Sensory Objects *yul brgyad*
See **Eight Objects of Consciousness.**

Eighteen Hells *dmyal-ba bco-brgyad*, Skt. *aṣṭadaśanaraka*
States of existence within the cycle of rebirth, conditioned by our past actions, where the experience of **suffering**, arising from hatred, anger and fear, is most intense and extended. ***Abhidharma*** literature mentions two main types of such hell-like existences, characterised by the dominance of either freezing coldness or burning heat. These two are in turn divided into eighteen subcategories.

Eighty Minor Marks *dpe-byad brgyad-cu*, Skt. *asītyanuvyañjana*
See **Major and Minor Marks.**

Eighty-four Thousand Aspects of the [Sacred] Teaching *chos-sgo brgyad-khri bzhi stong*
The **Buddha**'s teachings are said to comprise eighty-four thousand aspects or approaches, when they are classified according to their function as an antidote. It is said that there are eighty-four thousand **dissonant mental states**, comprising twenty-one thousand aspects respectively of **attachment** (*rāga*), **aversion** (*dveśa*), **delusion** (*moha*), and their combination; and there is an antidote within the **Buddha**'s teachings corresponding to each of these **dissonant mental states.**

Elemental Forces *'byung-po*, Skt. bhūta
A category of forces associated with the elements: earth, water, fire, wind and space, which are said to move through the body in a monthly cycle and to whom certain illnesses and paediatric disorders are attributed in Tibetan medicine. These may be appeased or brought back into balance by the application of medicinal antidotes, or by the counteracting rituals prescribed in the ***tantras***, as outlined in Chapter 9.

Elements / Elemental Properties *'byung ba*, Skt. *bhūta*
See **Five Elements.**

Eleven Vehicles *theg-pa bcu-gcig*
See **Vehicle.**

EMA *e-ma*
Identical to *EMAHO*.

EMAHO *e-ma-ho*
An exclamation of great wonder or astonishment.

Empowerment *dbang-bskur*, Skt. *abhiṣeka*
A ritual ceremony performed by accomplished **spiritual teachers** and **lineage holders** to empower prospective trainees, prior to their engaging in the various vehicles and specific practices of the ***tantras***. The meditative processes of the empowerment ritual are intended to activate the potentials inherent within the body, speech and mind of the trainee, in other words to awaken the seed of the natural ability to engage in the practice. Such empowerment ceremonies are an essential prerequisite for the practice of ***tantra*** in the Buddhist tradition. See also Four Empowerments.

Emptiness *stong-pa-nyid*, Skt. *śūnyatā*
The ultimate nature of **reality**. According to the ***Madhyamaka*** school it is the total absence of **inherent existence** and self-identity with respect to all phenomena. Its synonyms include **ultimate truth** (Skt. *paramārthasatya*), **actual reality** (Skt. *dharmatā*), and suchness (Skt. *tathatā*). Though presented in the scriptures of both the **Lesser Vehicle** and the **Greater Vehicle**, the theory of emptiness is most systematically developed in the writings of the second-century Buddhist thinker ***Nāgārjuna***, the founder of the ***Madhyamaka*** school. According to this view, all things and events, both external and internal, are devoid of any independent, intrinsic reality that constitutes their essence. Nothing can be said to exist independently from the complex network of factors that gives rise to their origination, nor are phenomena independent of the cognitive processes and conceptual designations (mental constructs) that make up the conventional framework within which their identity and existence are posited. It is our deeply ingrained tendency to conceive of things as materially existing in their own right that conditions and compels us to perceive

and grasp at a substantial reality of things and our own existence. In turn, when all levels of conceptualisation dissolve and when all forms of dichotomising tendencies are quelled through deliberate meditative deconstruction of **conceptual elaborations**, ***Nāgārjuna*** argues, the ultimate nature of reality – the emptiness – will finally become manifest to the person. Although the term is known also in the literature of the **Lesser Vehicle**, it is in the philosophical tenets of the ***Madhyamaka*** school that the different interpretations of emptiness were greatly elaborated. See **Madhyamaka**.

Energy Centre *rtsa-'khor*, Skt. *cakra*
According to the ***tantras*** and related medical traditions, there are five energy centres within the **subtle body**. These are located at the crown, throat, heart, navel and genitalia, where the right and left channels are said to loop around the central channel (*avadhūti*), forming knots (*rtsa-mdud*) which obstruct the flow of subtle energy into the central channel. At each of the five energy centres, there are a diverse number of **channel branches** (*rtsa-'dab*), through which vital energy is conducted throughout the body.

Energy Channels *rtsa*, Skt. *nāḍī*
In the ***tantras*** and related medical traditions, it is said that there are 72,000 vein-like channels through which flow the **vital energies** or subtle winds (*rlung*, Skt. *vāyu*) that sustain life and which also give rise to various conceptual states within the individual's mind. Three main channels run vertically from the crown fontanelle of the head down to the genitalia, intersecting at the five **energy centres** (Skt. *cakra*) of the crown, throat, heart, navel and genitalia. All the minor energy channels branch off from these **energy centres** to permeate the body. Among the three main channels, the one to the left is known as the *rkyang-ma* (Skt. *lalanā*), the one to the right as the *ro-ma* (Skt. *rasanā*), and the central channel as the *dbu-ma* (Skt. *avadhūti*).

Enlightened Family *rigs*, Skt. *gotra/kula*
This term may render either the Sanskrit *gotra*, in which case it is synonymous with **buddha nature**, or the Sanskrit *kula*, in which case it refers to the five families (Skt. *pañcakula*) into which the **Peaceful and Wrathful Deities** are grouped. See the individual entries under **Buddha Family, Vajra Family, Ratna Family, Padma Family** and **Karma Family** and Appendix Two.

Enlightened Intention *dgongs-pa*, Skt. *abhiprāya*
In the context of our text, enlightened intention refers to the unimpeded, non-conceptual and compassionate intention of the **buddhas**, whether or not it is clearly discerned by an observer.

Enlightenment *byang-chub*, Skt. *bodhi*
In the Buddhist context, 'enlightenment' refers to an individual's awakening to the mind's actual nature. The Tibetan equivalent *byang-chub* implies the **purification** (*byang*) of **obscurations** and the perfection (*chub*) of **omniscience**. The process of attaining enlightenment therefore proceeds in conjunction with the dispelling of the **dissonant mental states** which obscure the perception of **actual reality**. On the ***bodhisattva*** path, thirty-seven distinct aspects of enlightenment are sequentially cultivated. A fully enlightened being is a **buddha** who is totally free from all obstruction to true knowledge and the state of **liberation**, and is hence **omniscient** in the knowledge of **reality**.

Enrichment *rgyas-pa'i las*, Skt. *puṣṭikriyā*
See **Four Aspects of Enlightened Activity** and **Buddha-activities.**

Envy *phrag-dog*, Skt. *īrṣā*
Envy, which includes all the various forms of self-cherishing ambition, is one of the **five poisons** of the mind (*dug-lnga*), along with **aversion**, **delusion**, pride, and **attachment.** In its extreme manifestation, of persistent hostile competitiveness, it is said to characterise the worlds of the **antigods** (*asuraloka*).

Equanimity *btang-snyoms*, Skt. *upekṣā*
Equanimity is one of the **four immeasurable aspirations**, along with **loving kindness**, **compassion** and empathetic joy, which are cultivated in the **preliminary practices** and commonly repeated before engaging in daily practice. Equanimity is an essential element of the cultivation of the **altruistic intention to attain enlightenment** for the benefit of others, in the context of which the practitioner cultivates an unbiased attitude towards all **sentient beings**, regarding them as being completely equal and thus overcoming any sense of partiality towards them. Normally one's attitude towards other persons, for example, is strongly prejudiced by one's classification of others into seemingly incompatible groups of friends, enemies or those regarded with indifference. See also under ***Bodhicitta***.

Esoteric Instructional Class *man-ngag-gi sde*, Skt. *upadeśavarga*
See under **Great Perfection.**

Essence, Natural Expression and Compassionate Energy *ngo-bo rang-bzhin thugs-rje*
In the terminology of the **Great Perfection**, the essence (*ngo-bo*) is the modality of the **Buddha-body of Reality**, natural expression (*rang-bzhin*) is the modality of the **Buddha-body of Perfect Resource**, and compassionate energy or spirituality (*thugs-rje*) is the modality of the **Buddha-body of Emanation.** These three modalities may be cultivated through the techniques known as **Cutting through Resistance** (*khregs-chod*) and **All-surpassing Realisation** (*thod-rgal*). The term **natural expression** (*rang-bzhin*) also has another distinctive usage in the context of the present work, where it frequently refers to the attributes represented by the twenty-eight *Īśvarī* among the assembly of the fifty-eight **wrathful deities.** See **Natural Expression.**

Eternalist *mu-stegs-pa*, Skt. *tīrthika*
In general Buddhist usage, the term 'eternalist' refers to the four so-called eternalistic schools of ancient India, namely *Sāṃkhya*, Vaishnavism, Shaivism and Jainism, which posit the existence of an independent self or soul (*ātman*, Tib. *bdag*). By contrast, Buddhist schools identify the self in terms of the five psycho-physical **aggregates** (*pañcaskandha*), and therefore do not accept the notion of self in the sense of an eternal, unchanging, independently existing entity. Both eternalism and **nihilism** are regarded as the two extreme views, which are to be avoided when seeking an insight into **emptiness**, the true nature of **reality**, by means of the **Middle Way** (*madhyamapratipad*). Here all apprehensions of **inherent existence** constitute falling into the extreme of eternalism, and a total denial of the laws of **cause and effect** in association with past and future lives constitutes falling into nihilism.

Expanse of [Actual] Reality *chos-dbyings*, Skt. *dharmadhātu*
The expanse of actual reality is a synonym for the expanse of **emptiness.** As such,

it indicates both the dimension of the **Buddha-body of Reality**, and the **pristine cognition** of **reality's expanse** (*dharmadhātujñāna*).

Extremes *mtha'*, Skt. *anta*
From the perspective of the **Greater Vehicle**, the **Buddha-body of Reality** is said to be free from the dualistic extremes of creation and cessation (*skye-'gag*), **eternalism** and **nihilism** (*rtag-chad*), existence and non-existence (*yod-med*), and appearance and **emptiness** (*snang-stong*).

Feast-offering *tshogs [kyi 'khor-lo]*, Skt. *gaṇacakra*
The Tibetan word *tshogs* generally has two senses, corresponding to the Sanskrit *sambhāra* and *gaṇacakra*. In the latter case it refers to the feast-offerings which are a unique tantric method for conferring **accomplishment** and pacifying obstacles. In general, feast-offerings are frequently held to commemorate important events in the Buddhist calendar, such as the tenth-day feast-offering, dedicated to ***Padmasambhava***. The overall purpose is to distribute **merit** and **pristine cognition** in the context of a specific **tantric** ritual. See also under **Accumulation**.

Final Nirvāṇa *yongs-su mya-ngan-las 'das*, Skt. *parinirvāṇa*
The expression 'final *nirvāṇa*' refers specifically to the passing away of **buddhas**, such as ***Śākyamuni***, and it is considered to be the last of the twelve principal deeds, exemplified by the death of ***Śākyamuni*** at *Kuśinagara*. See also under **Nirvāṇa** and **Buddha activities**.

Five Aggregates *phung-po lnga*, Skt. *pañcaskandha*
See the separate entries, under **Aggregate of Consciousness, Aggregate of Form, Aggregate of Feelings, Aggregate of Perceptions**, and **Aggregate of Motivational Tendencies**.

Five Appendages *yan-lag lnga*, Skt. *pañcāṅga*
The head and the four limbs.

Five Approximating Crimes *nye-ba'i mtshams-med lnga*, Skt. *pañcopāntarīya*
The five crimes which approximate the **five inexpiable crimes** (*mtshams-med lnga*) in their severity are: to rape a female ***arhat*** (*dgra-bcom-ma-la 'dod-log spyod-pa*), to kill one who abides on the level of a genuine ***bodhisattva*** (*byang-sems nges-gnas gsod-pa*), to kill a trainee monk (*slob-pa'i dge-'dun gsod-pa*), to misappropriate the income of the **monastic community** (*dge-'dun-gyi 'du-sgo 'phrog-pa*), and to destroy a ***stūpa*** (*mchod-rten bshig-pa*).

Five Buddha-bodies *sku lnga*, Skt. *pañcakāya*
The **Buddha-body of Reality, Buddha-body of Perfect Resource, Buddha-body of Emanation**, Buddha-body of Awakening, and Buddha-body of Indestructible Reality. See **Buddha-body** and individual entries.

Five Degenerations *snyigs-ma lnga*, Skt. *pañcakaṣāya*
The five degenerations comprise: degeneration of the lifespan (*ayuḥkaṣāya*), degeneration in terms of views (*dṛṣṭikaṣāya*), degeneration in terms of **dissonant mental states** (*kleśakaṣāya*), degeneration of **sentient beings** (*sattvakaṣāya*), and degeneration of the present age (*kalpakaṣāya*).

Five Elements *'byung-ba lnga / khams lnga*, Skt. *pañcabhūta/ pañcadhātu*
According to the Indo-Tibetan system, as expounded in the ***tantras***, and in medical

and astrological texts, the five elements – earth, water, fire, wind, and space – are five basic components that make up our environment, our bodies, and, at their subtle levels, modalities of the mind. At the subtlest level, the elemental properties exist as the pure natures represented by the five female **buddhas** (*Ākāśadhātvīśvarī*, *Buddhalocanā*, *Māmakī*, *Pāṇḍaravāsinī* and *Samayatārā*) and these manifest as the physical properties of earth (solidity), water (fluidity), fire (heat and light), wind (movement and energy), and space – in other words as all the qualities that constitute the physical forms that we experience through our senses. A proper understanding of the elements and the way in which their properties permeate the nature of mind, the body and our environment is fundamental to the practice of Buddhist ***tantra***. See Chapters 8 and 11 and Appendix Two.

Five Enlightened Families *rigs lnga*, Skt. *pañcakula*
See **Buddha Family, Vajra Family, Ratna Family, Padma Family,** and **Karma Family** and Appendix Two.

Five Hollow Viscera *snod-lnga*
According to the traditions of Tibetan medicine, the five hollow viscera are those of the stomach, the large intestine, the small intestine, the bladder, the gall bladder, and the reservoir of reproductive fluid (*bsam-se'u*).

Five Inexpiable Crimes *mtshams-med lnga*, Skt. *pañcānantarīya*
The five inexpiable crimes, which are regarded as the most severe and consequently the most difficult to overcome by reparation, are: matricide (*ma gsod-pa*), arhatcide (*dgra-bcom-pa gsod-pa*), patricide (*pha gsod-pa*), creating a schism in the **monastic community** (*dge-'dun-gyi dbyen-byas-ba*), and intentionally wounding a **buddha** (*de-bzhin gshegs-pa'i sku-la ngan-sems-kyis khrag 'byin-pa*).

Five Poisons *dug-lnga*, Skt. *pañcakleśa*
The five poisons comprise five of the most basic **dissonant mental states** (*kleśa*) – all of which are grounded in **fundamental ignorance** (*avidyā*). They are: **delusion** (*moha*), **attachment** (*rāga*), **aversion** (*dveṣa*), pride (*abhimāna*), and envy/self-cherishing ambition (*īrṣā*).

Five Precious Substances *rin-chen lnga*
Gold, silver, turquoise, coral and pearl.

Five Pristine Cognitions *ye-shes lnga*, Skt. *pañcājñāna*
See under **Pristine Cognition.**

Five Sense-faculties/organs *dbang-po rnam-lnga*, Skt. *pañcendriya*
The five sense-faculties or sense-organs comprise: the eyes (*cakṣurindriya*), ears (*śrotrendriya*), nose (*ghrāṇendriya*), tongue (*jihvendriya*), and body (*kāyendriya*).

Five Solid Viscera *don-lnga*
According to the traditions of Tibetan medicine, the five solid viscera are the heart, lungs, liver, kidneys, and spleen.

Form Realm and Formless Realm
See **Three World-systems.**

Formal Description *mngon-rtogs*, Skt. *abhisamaya*
While practising the **generation stage** (*utpattikrama*) of meditation, the **deities** are visualised in accordance with their formal descriptions which are set down in the

texts of the appropriate **means for attainment** (*sgrub-thabs*, Skt. *sādhana*). In other contexts the term '*abhisamaya*' conveys the sense of 'emergent or clear realisation', as in ***Maitreya***'s *Ornament of Emergent Realisation* (*Abhisamayālaṃkāra*).

Four Aspects of Enlightened Activity *las-bzhi*, Skt. *catuṣkarman*
These are specific ritual functions based on the dynamic modes of a **buddha**'s activity, namely: pacification (*śāntikriyā*, Tib. *zhi-ba'i las*), which includes the pacification of obstacles to spiritual practice, illness and the causes of harm to society and the environment; enrichment (*puṣṭikriyā*, Tib. *rgyas-pa'i las*), which includes increasing the lifespan and prosperity; subjugation (*vaṣitakriyā*, Tib. *dbang-gi las*), which includes the controlling of negative and hostile forces; and wrath or transformation (*maraṇakriyā*, Tib. *drag-po'i las*), which includes the elimination of **malevolent forces**. The ritual enactment of these four rites is often undertaken in the context of a **burnt offering** ritual (*homa*).

Four Aspects of Ritual Service and Means for Attainment *bsnyen-sgrub yan-lag bzhi*, Skt. *caturāṅgasevāsādhana*
Whenever any **means for attainment** (Skt. *sādhana*) is practised, it will comprise the 'four aspects of ritual service and means for attainment'. The four branches are: ritual service (*sevā*), further ritual service (*upasevā*), means for attainment (*sādhana*) and great means for attainment (*mahāsādhana*), which respectively entail 1) ***mantra*** recitation and one-pointed visualisation of the **meditational deity**, 2) prayers that the **blessing** of the deity will descend to transform mundane body, speech and mind into **buddha-body, speech** and **mind**, 3) the absorption of accomplishments from the actual deity into the visualised deity and thence into oneself, and 4) the realisation of **primordial purity** experienced when body, speech and mind are identical to those of the deity.

Four Aspects of Sensory Contact *reg-bzhi*
These are sensory contact, along with its subject, object and actual sensation.

Four Buddha-bodies *sku-bzhi*, Skt. *catuḥkāya*
See under **Buddha-body**.

Four Classes of Ḍākinī *mkha'-'gro sde-bzhi.*
The four classes of ***ḍākinī*** comprise those born in sacred abodes or pure lands (*zhing-skyes mkha'-'gro*), those born in consequence of ***mantra*** recitation (*sngags-skyes mkha'-'gro*), those who are naturally born (*lhan-skyes mkha'-'gro*), and those born of **pristine cognition** (*ye-shes mkha'-'gro*).

Four Continents and Eight Subcontinents *gling bzhi-dang gling-phran brgyad*
According to traditional Indian Buddhist cosmology, the world has **Mount *Sumeru*** as its central axis, surrounded by seven concentric oceans divided from one another by seven successive ranges of golden mountains: *Yugandhara*, *Īṣadhāra*, *Khadirika*, *Sudarśana*, *Aṣvakarna*, *Vinataka*, and *Nimindhara*. The entire world is girded by a perimeter of iron mountains known as the *Cakravāla*. In each of the four cardinal directions of **Mount *Sumeru***, there is located a continent, along with two satellites or subcontinents. Among these, the eastern continent *Viratdeha* (*lus-'phags*; 'sublime in body') is semicircular and it has two subcontinents: *Deha* (*lus*) and *Videha* (*lus-'phags*). The southern continent *Jambudvīpa* (*'dzam-bu gling*; 'rose-apple continent') is triangular and its two subcontinents are ***Cāmaradvīpa*** (*rnga-yab gling*) and *Aparacāmara* (*rnga-yab gzhan*). The western continent, *Aparagodanīya* (*ba-*

lang spyod; 'rich in cattle'), is circular and its two subcontinents are *Śāṭhā* (*gYo-ldan*) and *Uttaramantriṇa* (*lam-mchog 'gro*). Lastly, the northern continent *Uttarakuru* (*sgra-mi-snyan*; 'unpleasant sound') is square and its two subcontinents are *Kurava* (*sgra mi-snyan*) and *Kaurava (sgra mi-snyan-gyi zla*). Among the four, *Jambudvīpa* is unique in that it is here that the **sacred teachings** of the **buddhas** are said to flourish. See Chapter 11, Part Three with respect to instructions for choosing a birthplace and Chapter 1 with respect to visualising the ***maṇḍala* of offerings.**

Four Delights *dga'-ba bzhi*
In the **perfection stage** (*sampannakrama*) of meditation, when the practices of sexual yoga (*sbyor-ba*) are applied in order to bring about a coalescence of bliss and **emptiness**, the **generative essence** (*thig-le*) of the body descends through the **central channel** and the four delights are sequentially experienced. As it descends from the **energy centre** of the crown fontanelle to the throat centre, the **pristine cognition** of delight (*dga'-ba*) is experienced. When it descends from the throat centre to the heart centre, the **pristine cognition** of supreme delight (*mchog-dga'*) is experienced. When it descends from the heart centre to the navel centre the **pristine cognition** of the absence of delight (*dga'-bral*) is experienced. And when it descends from the navel centre to the secret centre of the genitalia, the **coemergent delight** (*lhan-skyes dga'-ba*) is experienced. Thereafter, the **generative essence** is retained within the body and drawn upwards through the central channel, permeating each of the **energy centres** of the body in turn with unceasing bliss and non-conceptual **pristine cognition.** See also under **Coemergent Delight.**

Four Elements *'byung-ba bzhi*, Skt. *caturbhūta*
Earth, water, fire and wind. See **Five Elements.**

Four Empowerments *dbang-bskur bzhi*, Skt. *caturabhiṣekha*
The four **empowerments** of the **Unsurpassed *Yoga tantras***, including ***Mahāyoga***, are: the vase empowerment (*bum-dbang*), which purifies the ordinary body and its **energy channels** into the **Buddha-body of Emanation** (*nirmāṇakāya*); the secret empowerment (*gsang-dbang*), which purifies ordinary speech and its **vital energy** into the **Buddha-body of Perfect Resource** (*sambhogakāya*); the empowerment of discriminative **pristine cognition** (*shes-rab ye-shes-kyi dbang*) which purifies ordinary mind and its **seminal point** (*bindu*) into the **Buddha-body of Reality** (*dharmakāya*); and the empowerment of word and meaning (*tshig-don-gi dbang*), which purifies these three equally into the Buddha-body of Essentiality (*svabhāvikakāya*). See also **Empowerment.**

Four Extreme Views *mu-bzhi*
In the context of the present work, these are the four extreme views of permanence, decay, self, and **substantialism.**

Four Formless Meditative Absorptions *gzugs-med snyoms-'jug bzhi*, Skt. *catuḥsamāpatti*
The four formless meditative absorptions which lead to birth in the world-system of formlessness, at the summit of **cyclic existence**, are those known as: infinite as the sky (*ākāśānantyāyatana*), infinite consciousness (*vijñānānantyāyatana*), nothing-at-all (*akiṃcanyāyatana*), and neither perception nor non-perception (*naivasaṃjñānasaṃjñāyatana*). See **Three World-systems.**

Four Immeasurable Aspirations *tshad-med bzhi*, Skt. *catvāryapramāṇāni*
Immeasurable **compassion, love,** empathetic joy and **equanimity.** The cultivation of the four immeasurable wishes, which is normally accompanied by the recitation of a short prayer (see Chapter 1), is a common preliminary to daily practice. This contemplation establishes correct motivation and provides a strong impetus to the cultivation of the **altruistic intention to attain enlightenment** for the sake of all sentient beings.

Four Malevolent Forces *bdud-bzhi*, Skt. *caturmāra*
See **Malevolent/Beguiling Forces.**

Four Modes of Liberation *grol-lugs bzhi*
The four modes of liberation, according to Atiyoga, comprise: primordial liberation (*ye-grol*), **natural liberation** (*rang-grol*), direct liberation (*cer-grol*), and further liberation (*yang-grol*) or liberation from extremes (*mtha'-grol*). These are attained in connection with the **intermediate state of meditative concentration** (*bsam-gtan bar-do*).

Four Noble Truths *bden-pa bzhi*, Skt. *caturāryasatya*
The teaching on the four noble truths forms the basis of the first promulgation of Buddhism, since it is the very first formal discourse given by ***Śākyamuni*** in *Sarnath* following his attainment of **buddhahood** at *Bodh Gaya.* The four truths are: the truth of **suffering,** the truth of its origins, the truth of its cessation, and the truth of the path leading to such cessation. The doctrine of four truths lays the foundation upon which the entire structure of the path to **buddhahood** is built and the understanding of these four truths is therefore an indispensable basis for a successful practice of the Buddhist path. The first two truths constitute one inter-relationship of **cause and effect** and the remaining two, another. Without proper insight into the first inter-relationship no genuine aspiration to seek freedom from **cyclic existence** will arise. Similarly, without insight into the second, no genuine release from the bondage of **karmically** conditioned existence can be achieved.

Four Preliminaries
See **Preliminary Practices.**

Four Times *dus-bzhi*
Past, present, future, and indefinite time. In some contexts the four times refer to different phases of conceptual thought, in which case they are enumerated as past thoughts, present thoughts, future thoughts and indeterminate thoughts (*so-sor rtog-pa*).

Fundamental Ignorance *ma-rig-pa*, Skt. *avidyā*
The most fundamental misapprehension of the nature of **actual reality,** which is the source of all **dissonant mental states** and the **twelve links of dependent origination.** Divergent views exist among Buddhist thinkers about the specific character and nature of fundamental ignorance. For example, the fourth-century master *Asaṅga* conceives this ignorance to be a state of unknowing, ignorant of the actual nature of **reality.** In contrast, for masters like ***Nāgārjuna*** and especially *Dharmakīrti*, it is an active state of mis-knowing, i.e. it understands the existence of one's own self and the world in a fundamentally distorted manner. In the classical Indian Buddhist texts, two principal forms of fundamental ignorance are identified – (i) ignorance pertaining to the actual nature of **reality** and (ii) ignorance pertaining to the law of

cause and effect. The ***Nyingma*** master *Dudjom Rinpoche* explains the evolution of **bewilderment** from fundamental ignorance in three phases: first, the fundamental ignorance of **self-identity** (*bdag-nyid gcig-pu'i ma-rig-pa*) is not recognised to be false; second, the **coemergent ignorance** (*lhan-skyes ma-rig-pa*) ensures that the consciousness of **self-identity** and non-recognition of **actual reality** coincide; and, third, the fundamental ignorance of the imaginary (*kun-btags ma-rig-pa*) generates **bewilderment**, through which one's own bewildering perceptions are externally discerned in terms of the subject–object dichotomy, giving rise to all the **sufferings** of **cyclic existence**.

Garuḍa *khyung*
A mythical bird normally depicted with an owl-like sharp beak, often holding a snake, and with large and powerful wings. References to this bird can be also found in Hindu literature where it is often mentioned as the flying mount of powerful mundane **gods** (*deva*). In Buddhism, the symbolism of the *garuḍa* is generally associated with **pristine cognition** (it is said that the *garuḍa* can fly as soon as it is hatched) and with the consuming of **dissonant mental states** (the holding of a snake in its beak). In a Buddhist context, the *garuḍa* is also associated with ***Vajrapāṇi*** and certain wrathful forms of ***Padmasambhava*** through its power to subdue snakes, **serpentine water spirits**, and subterranean creatures, and, according to the ***Nyingma*** school, the *garuḍa* is sometimes revered as a guardian of **treasures** (*gter-bdag*) or even as a repository of **treasures** (*gter-kha*).

Gelug *dge-lugs*
One of the four main traditions or schools of Tibetan Buddhism. Founded by the great fourteenth-century philosopher *Tsongkhapa* and his foremost students, it quickly established itself as a dominant tradition of Tibetan Buddhism with its monasteries extending from the far west of Tibet to *Chamdo*, *Dartsedo*, and *Amdo* in the east. Following the Third ***Dalai Lama***'s visit to Mongolia, it became the state religion in Mongolia and the Buriat regions of the Soviet Union, and during the seventeenth century its hierarchy became the dominant political force in Central Tibet when the Fifth ***Dalai Lama*** assumed both spiritual and temporal power with the assistance of Mongol armies. 'Gelug' literally means the tradition of the virtuous path and is named after the monastery called *Geden* or *Ganden*, founded by *Tsongkhapa* in 1409.

Generation Stage *bskyed-rim*, Skt. *utpattikrama*
According to the traditions of the ***tantras***, the main practices of **meditation** which follow the successful conclusion of the **preliminary practices** (*sngon-'gro*) include the generation stage and the **perfection stage** (Skt. *sampannakrama*). Both the generation and **perfection stages** of meditation are related to transforming our mundane experiences of each of the phases of life and death, namely: the **intermediate states of the time of death, of reality, of rebirth**, and **of living**. The generation stage is characterised by the meditative processes of the practitioner's gradual identification with the form and **pristine cognition** of the **meditational deity** and it is during this stage that, with the support of ***mantra*** recitation, the elaborate visualisation of the deity is gradually generated and stabilised. This process, known as self-generation, is a simulacrum of bringing the three **buddha-bodies** on to the path and is composed therefore of three principal aspects: dissolution into **emptiness** (**Buddha-body of Reality**), arising into a subtle form such as a **seed-syllable** or

symbol (**Buddha-body of Perfect Resource**), and full emergence into the deity's form (**Buddha-body of Emanation**). See the Introductory Commentary by HH the Dalai Lama and **Perfection Stage.**

Generative Essences *byang-sems/thig-le*, Skt. *bodhicitta/bindu*
In the ***tantras*** and in Tibetan medicine, the generative essences or fluids are considered as arising from a supreme **seminal point** (*thig-le chen-po*) located in the middle of the heart centre. From the perspective of the ***tantras*** this supreme **seminal point** is regarded as the seed of **buddhahood** and from the perspective of Tibetan medicine it is regarded as the basis of both physical and mental health. This supreme **seminal point** at the heart is considered to be the size of a small pea or large mustard seed and it incorporates the pure essences (*dvangs-ma*) of the five elements, the presence of which is indicated by its five-coloured glow. From the perspective of the ***tantras*** the very subtle **vital energy**, known as the life-bearing wind or breath, dwells inside this **seminal point** and at the culmination of the **intermediate state of the time of death** all vital energies ultimately dissolve into it and the **inner radiance** of the ground dawns. During life, a single **seminal point** abides in each of the five **energy centres** and each seminal point is whiter at the top and redder at the bottom. At the crown centre the whiter element predominates and at the level of the genitalia the redder element predominates. According to Tibetan medicine, white generative fluids are said to produce bone tissue in the embryo, and it is from the bone marrow that both semen and breast milk are said to be produced. Red generative fluids are said to produce blood, flesh and skin. At their least subtle level, therefore, the former are identified with semen and the latter with menstrual blood. See also under **Seminal Point.**

Gods *lha*, Skt. *deva*
One of the **six classes of living beings** (*'gro-ba rigs-drug*). The mode of being and activity of the gods is said to be engendered and dominated by exaltation, indulgence and pride. The gods exist in realms higher than that of the human realm in the world-system of desire (*kāmadhātu*), and also in the world-systems of form (*rūpadhātu*) and formlessness (*ārūpyadhātu*). See **Three World-systems.**

Gods of the Ten Directions *phyogs-bcu'i lha*, Skt. *daśadikpāla*
The gods who traditionally are said to preside over the **ten directions** of space are otherwise known as the protector deities of the ten directions, viz.: *Indra*, *Yama*, *Varuṇa*, *Yakṣa*, *Agni*, *Rākṣasa*, *Vāyu*, *Bhūta*, *Brahmā*, and *Vanadevī* or *Sthāvarā*.

Great Bliss *bde-chen*, Skt. *mahāsukha*
In the context of **Unsurpassed *Yogatantra***, 'great bliss' refers to the blissful states experienced when the meditator enters into union with a partner (either in visualisation at the beginner's level or in actuality at an advanced stage). In both cases, the experiences, to be valid, have to arise as a result of the dissolution of mental conceptuality and the vital energies which support these conceptual states. Such a blissful state of **mind**, when generated within a direct experience of **emptiness**, free from attachment, becomes what is known as the union of bliss and **emptiness.**

Great Perfection *rdzogs-pa chen-po*, Skt. *mahāsandhi*
Great Perfection is a synonym for ***Atiyoga***, the highest of the **nine vehicles** according to the ***Nyingma*** tradition. ***Atiyoga*** is known as the Great Perfection because both the **generation** and **perfection stages** of **meditation** are effortlessly present. 'Perfection'

(*rdzogs*) implies that the enlightened attributes of the **Three Buddha-bodies** are effortlessly perfected in the stabilisation of the meditator's **intrinsic awareness** (*rang-rig*). Here the **Buddha-body of Reality** (*dharmakāya*) is the **essence** or **emptiness** (*ngo-bo stong-pa*) of **intrinsic awareness**; the **Buddha-body of Perfect Resource** (*sambhogakāya*) is its **natural expression** and radiance (*rang-bzhin gsal-ba*); and the **Buddha-body of Emanation** (*nirmāṇakāya*) is its all-pervasive unimpeded compassionate energy (*ma-'gags thugs-rje*) expressed in physical form. 'Great' (*chen*) implies that this perfection is the underlying nature of all things. The ***tantra*** texts and instructions of ***Atiyoga***, contained in the *Collected Tantras of the Nyingmapa*, are divided into three classes: the Mental Class (*sems-sde*), which emphasises the radiance (*gsal-ba'i cha*) of the nature of mind (*sems-nyid*); the Spatial Class (*klong-sde*) which emphasises the **emptiness** (*stong-pa'i cha*) of **reality's expanse** (*dharmadhātu*); and the **Esoteric Instructional Class** (*man-ngag-gi sde*), in which these aspects are given equal emphasis and in which the meditative techniques of **Cutting through Resistance** (*khregs-chod*) and **All-surpassing Realisation** (*thod-rgal*) lead respectively to the realisation of the **Buddha-body of Reality** and the **Buddha-body of Form.**

Great Seal *phyag-rgya chen-po*, Skt. *mahāmudrā*
According to the tradition of the ***sūtras***, the expression 'Great Seal' refers to the comprehension of **emptiness** as the all-encompassing ultimate nature of **reality. Emptiness** is called the great seal, for nothing extraneous to it exists, and all phenomena, both physical and mental, are in their ultimate natures empty of **inherent existence.** According to the tradition of the ***tantras*** in general, the practice of the Great Seal is considered in terms of ground, path and result. As a 'path', it comprises a sequence of systematic advanced **meditations** on **emptiness** and pure appearance, integrating the techniques of **calm abiding** and **penetrative insight,** which focuses on the nature of the meditator's own **mind.** This type of **meditation** is popular in both the ***Kagyu*** and ***Gelug*** schools of Tibetan Buddhism. As a 'result', the expression 'Great Seal' refers to the state of **buddhahood,** the conclusive result or supreme spiritual **accomplishment.** According to the ***Nyingma*** school, within the context of ***Mahāyoga*** in particular, the term refers to the great seal of **buddha-body** which secures the **ground-of-all consciousness** (*ālayavijñāna*) as the mirror-like **pristine cognition.** A distinction is also drawn between the supreme accomplishment of the Great Seal (*phyag-rgya chen-po mchog-gi dngos-grub*), which is to be attained in the course of the meditator's lifetime, and the coalescent Buddha-body of the Great Seal (*zung-'jug phyag-rgya chen-po'i sku*), which is identified with the **inner radiance** of the **Buddha-body of Reality.**

Greater Vehicle *theg-pa chen-po*, Skt. *mahāyāna*
When the Buddhist teachings are classified according to their power to lead beings to an enlightened state, a distinction is made between the teachings of the **Lesser Vehicle** (*hīnayāna*) and those of the Greater Vehicle. In terms of motivation, the practitioner of the Lesser Vehicle emphasises the individual's own freedom from **cyclic existence** as the primary motivation and goal and the practitioner of the Greater Vehicle emphasises altruism and has the **liberation** of all **sentient beings** as the principal objective. As the term 'Greater Vehicle' implies, the path followed by ***bodhisattvas*** is analogous to a large carriage which can transport a vast number of people to **liberation,** as compared to a smaller vehicle for the individual practitioner. In terms of philosophy, the principal philosophical schools of the Lesser Vehicle are

Vaibhāṣika and *Sautrāntika* and those of the Greater Vehicle are ***Cittamātra*** and ***Madhyamaka***. In terms of the path, the Lesser Vehicle emphasises complete renunciation of **dissonant mental states** and the practice of the **four noble truths** and the **twelve links of dependent origination**, while the Greater Vehicle allows the taking on to the path of **dissonant mental states** and emphasises the practice of the **six perfections**. According to the Greater Vehicle, the entire path towards the attainment of **buddhahood** is presented within the framework of two main systems or **vehicles** (*yāna*), those of the ***sūtras*** (*sūtrayāna*) and the ***tantras*** (*tantrayāna*). The former, also known as the **vehicle of *bodhisattvas*** (*bodhisattvayāna*), entails a progression from **fundamental ignorance** to **enlightenment** which may take place over an immeasurable number of lifetimes. The latter, also known as the **Vehicle of Indestructible Reality** (*Vajrayāna*) or the **vehicle of secret *mantras*** (*guhyamantrayāna*), includes the **preliminary practices** and the **generation** and **perfection stages** of meditation through which it is said that enlightenment can be achieved in a single lifetime.

Ground *gzhi*
See under **Continuum of the Ground.**

Ground-of-all *kun-gzhi*, Skt. *ālaya*
According to the **Great Perfection**, the ground-of-all is identified with the **continuum of the ground**. This ground-of-all is therefore contrasted with the **ground-of-all consciousness** (Skt. *ālayavijñāna*). See **Aggregate of Consciousness.**

Ground-of-all Consciousness *kun-gzhi'i rnam-par shes-pa*, Skt. *ālayavijñāna*
See under **Aggregate of Consciousness.**

Guhyagarbhatantra *rGyud gsang-ba'i snying-po*
The most all-embracing of the eighteen ***Mahāyoga tantras***, focusing specifically on the ***maṇḍala*** of the forty-two **peaceful deities** and the fifty-eight **wrathful deities**. There are three distinct versions of the *Guhyagarbhatantra*, respectively in 82, 46 and 22 chapters, and it is the last of these that is most widely studied. All of these versions are included within the general cycle of the *Tantra of the Magical Net (Māyājālatantra)*. See under **Magical Net** and Gyurme Dorje's 'Brief Literary History'.

Habitual Tendencies *bag-chags*, Skt. *vāsanā*
The deep-seated propensities and habitual tendencies inherited from our **past actions**. This concept of habitual tendencies is critical to the Buddhist understanding of the causal dynamics of karmic actions as well as its understanding of the process of conditioning. For example, when a person commits an act, such as the negative act of killing, the act itself does not last. So that which connects the committing of this act and the experiencing of its consequence in the future, in some instances in a future life, is the habitual tendencies imprinted upon one's psyche by the act committed. Similarly, when a strong emotion such as a powerful feeling of hatred arises, although the actual emotion may subside after a while, the experience leaves a mark or an imprint, which will continue to have an impact on the person's attitudes and emotions as well as behaviour. It is the collection of such countless habitual tendencies imprinted in our psyche by **dissonant mental states** that constitutes the obscuration of misconceptions concerning the known range of phenomena

(Skt. *jñeyāvaraṇa*), the total eradication of which occurs only when one achieves full awakening or **buddhahood**. See **Obscuration.**

Hand-gestures *phyag-rgya*, Skt. *mudrā*
See **Seal.**

Hatred *zhe-sdang*, Skt. *dveṣa*
See **Aversion.**

Hayagrīva *rta-mgrin*
The name of a wrathful deity, usually red in colour, with a green horse's head and neck (*rta-mgrin*) protruding from amongst the hair on his head. The teachings and the texts associated with *Hayagrīva* belong within the *sādhana* class of ***Mahāyoga***, where they are known as the ***tantras*** of buddha-speech. In this respect, *Hayagrīva* is considered to be the wrathful counterpart of ***Avalokiteśvara***. More generally, as in our text, he is depicted as a gatekeeper of certain ***maṇḍalas*** and sacred shrines. See Appendix Two.

Heart-mantra *snying-po*, Skt. *hṛdaya*
See **Mantra.**

Heart-mantra of Dependent Origination *rten-'brel snying-po*, Skt. *pratītya-samutpādahṛdaya*
The heart-mantra of **dependent origination,** YE DHARMĀ HETUPRABHAVĀ HETUN TEṢĀṂ TATHĀGATO HY AVADAT TEṢĀṂ CA YO NIRODHO EVAṂ VĀDĪ MAHĀŚRA-MAṆAḤ, can be translated as 'Whatever events arise from a cause, the Tathāgata has told the cause thereof, and the great virtuous ascetic also has taught their cessation as well.' See **Mantra** and **Dependent Origination.**

Hell [Realms] *na-rag dmyal-ba'i gnas/dmyal-ba*, Skt. *naraka*
See **Eighteen Hells.**

Hermit Buddha *rang-rgyal*, Skt. *pratyekabuddha*
The practitioners of the **Lesser Vehicle** (*hīnayāna*) include both **pious attendants** (*śrāvaka*) and hermit buddhas. Among these, the hermit buddhas are those who pursue the path to **liberation** without relying on a teacher, following a natural predisposition. According to ***Maitreya***'s *Ornament of Emergent Realisation*, the accomplishment of the hermit buddhas is considered to surpass that of the **pious attendants** in the sense that they realise the **emptiness** of external phenomena, composed of atomic particles, in addition to realising the **emptiness** of the individual personality (*pudgala*). However, unlike ***bodhisattvas*** they are said not to realise that the internal phenomena of **consciousness** too are without **inherent existence.** The **realisation** of a hermit buddha relies not only on the **renunciation** or monastic discipline, which is also undertaken by **pious attendants,** but on their comprehension of the **twelve links of dependent origination** and ability to reverse these through the power of **meditation.**

Hero *dpa'-bo*, Skt. *vīra*
See **Spiritual Hero.**

Heruka *khrag-'thung/he-ru-ka*
In general, the term *heruka* is an epithet for all **wrathful** male **meditational deities,** although in specific contexts it may refer exclusively to the **meditational deity**

Śrīheruka and related meditational deities such as *Cakrasaṃvara*. In the context of the present work, the term refers only to the six wrathful male **buddhas:** *Mahottara Heruka*, *Buddha Heruka*, *Vajra Heruka*, *Ratna Heruka*, *Padma Heruka*, and *Karma Heruka*. Literally, the term can be interpreted as 'blood-drinker', **'blood-drinking hero'**, 'delighting in blood', or 'holding a **blood-filled skull'**. See Appendix Two.

Higher Existences *gnas mtho-ris*, Skt. *svarga*
The three higher realms of the **gods, antigods**, and humans.

Highest Yoga Tantra *bla-med rgyud*, Skt. *yoganiruttaratantra*
See **Unsurpassed *Yogatantra*.**

Hundred Sacred Enlightened Families *dam-pa rigs-brgya*
Those of the forty-two **peaceful deities** and the fifty-eight **wrathful deities**. See Appendix Two.

Hundred-syllable Mantra *yig-brgya*
The hundred-syllable ***mantra*** of ***Vajrasattva*** may be interpreted as follows: 'OṂ Vajrasattva! Protect my commitments! Vajrasattva! Let them be firm! Let me be steadfast! Let me be satisfied! Let me be nourished! Let me be loved! Bestow all accomplishments upon me! With regard to all my past actions, make my mind virtuous! HŪṂ (seed-syllable of buddha-mind)! HA (four immeasurables)! HA (four empowerments)! HA (four delights)! HA (four buddha-bodies)! HOḤ (joyous laughter)! Transcendent One! Indestructible Reality of all the Tathāgatas! Do not forsake me! Make me into indestructible reality! Great Being of Commitment! ĀḤ (non-dual union).' The recitation of this ***mantra***, in conjunction with the visualisation of ***Vajrasattva*** and the confession of negativity, is an essential component of the **preliminary practices** (*sngon-'gro*). See Chapter 1 and **Vajrasattva.**

Ignorance *ma-rig-pa*, Skt. *avidyā*
See under **Fundamental Ignorance.**

Illusion-like Body *sgyu-ma'i lta-bu lus*
See under **Illusory Body.**

Illusory Body *sgyu-lus*
A specific ***Vajrayāna*** concept, the term 'illusory body' refers to a unique embodiment in which an advanced ***yogin*** arises at a high level of the **perfection stage** according to the **Unsurpassed *Yogatantras***. The arising of the ***yogin*** in the form of the illusory body occurs when an indivisible unity of buddha-body, speech and mind has been actualised at the conclusion of the **generation** and **perfection stages** of meditation. The attainment of the illusory body is divided into two stages; the attainment of the impure illusory body (*ma dag-pa'i sgyu-lus*) and then attainment of the pure illusory body (*dag-pa'i sgyu-lus*). The first stage is called impure because the ***yogin*** is still not totally free from all **habitual tendencies** that obstruct subtle knowledge. When the ***yogin*** attains the pure illusory body, which is in union with inner radiance, this marks the attainment of the highest union that is the full awakening of **buddhahood**, the attainment of the **Buddha-body of Perfect Resource**. According to the **perfection stage** of meditation, there are distinctive meditations which focus on the impure illusory body and the pure illusory body. In the former case, the meditation focuses on all physical phenomena as being dream-like and illusory in manner, without **inherent existence**. In the latter case, the meditation focuses on the ***maṇḍala*** of

deities visualised according to the so-called twelve similes of illusion (*sgyu-ma'i dpe bcu-gnyis*).

Impermanence *mi-rtag-pa*, Skt. *anitya*
Impermanence, along with **suffering** and the absence of **self-identity**, is regarded in Buddhism as one of the three marks or characteristics of causally conditioned phenomena. Although Buddhist literature mentions various degrees of impermanence, in general it can be defined as the moment by moment changing nature of all things. Nothing endures through time without change, and the process of change is dynamic and never ending, reflecting the nature of flux and fluidity in conditioned existence. This fundamental quality of impermanence extends to both the external world and the perceiving **mind**.

Imprecatory Female Spirits *ma-mo*, Skt. *mātaraḥ*
The imprecatory female spirits are generally depicted as ugly, ferocious, dark-complexioned, and half-naked with emaciated breasts and matted hair. They invoke curses and imprecations, inflicting plague (*dal-yams*) on living beings. The mundane imprecatory female spirits of Tibet were subdued by ***Padmasambhava*** on Mount *Chuwori*, while the supramundane category includes the protectress *Śrīdevī* (Tib. *dpal-ldan lha-mo*) in the form Rematī, and the eight *mātaraḥ* (*ma-mo brgyad*) headed by *Gaurī*, who form one subcategory of the fifty-eight **wrathful deities**. See Appendix Two. One of the eight principal **meditational deities** of the ***Mahāyoga*** *sādhana* class is known as Imprecatory *Mātaraḥ* (*ma-mo rbod-gtong*).

Incalculable Aeon *grangs-med bskal-pa*, Skt. *asaṃkhyeyakalpa*
The expression incalculable aeon indicates a period of time equivalent to 10 to the power of 59 lesser **aeons**.

Indestructible Chains of Inner Radiance *'od-gsal rdo-rje lu-gu-rgyud*
The appearance of indestructible chains of light or **inner radiance** occurs through the meditative technique known as **All-surpassing Realisation** (*thod-rgal*), according to the **Great Perfection** (*rdzogs-pa chen-po*). The arising of these chains of light is an indication of the **natural expression** (*rang-bzhin*) of **intrinsic awareness** (*rang-rig*), through which the **Buddha-body of Perfect Resource** becomes manifest.

Indestructible Cross-legged Posture *rdo-rje'i skyil-krung*, Skt. *vajrāsana*
Contrasted with the 'lotus posture' (Skt. *padmāsana*), this 'indestructible posture' is formed by crossing the legs with the feet upturned and folded along the thighs. In the case of the indestructible posture the right leg is folded above the left, whereas in the lotus position the left leg is folded over the right. This is one of the optimum recommended meditation postures, included in the **Seven-point Posture of** *Vairocana*.

Indestructible Expanse *rdo-rje'i dbyings*, Skt. *vajradhātu*
Generally a synonym for the **expanse of reality** (Skt. *dharmadhātu*) or **emptiness**. In certain contexts it also refers to the name of the central figures of the *Vajradhātu* ***maṇḍala*** of the ***Yogatantras***.

Indestructible Hell *rdo-rje dmyal-ba*, Skt. *vajranaraka*
A synonym for the hell of ultimate torment (Skt. *Avīci*), which relates to the admonition that those who violate their **commitments** in respect of the **Vehicle of Indestructible Reality** are reborn there. See **Eighteen Hells**.

Indestructible Reality *rdo-rje*, Skt. *vajra*
The fully enlightened **buddha-body, speech** and **mind** are described as indestructible reality. This suggests that the fruitional attributes of **buddhahood** are adamantine and indivisible, for they are invulnerable to all degrees of physical, verbal and mental defilement.

Individual Disciplines *so-sor thar-pa*, Skt. *prātimokṣa*
See under **Prātimokṣa.**

Inherent Existence *rang-ngo-bo-nyid*, Skt. *svabhāvatā*
The term 'inherent existence' refers to the ontological status of phenomena, according to which phenomena are attributed with existence in their own right, inherently, in and of themselves, objectively, and independent of any other phenomena such as our conception and labelling. The ***Madhyamaka*** schools of thought refute such a nature of existence and argue that nothing exists inherently, for nothing can be found to exist independently from conceptuality and labelling when scrutinised through an ultimate analysis. The ***Madhyamaka*** schools hold that things exist only conventionally and their existence can be validated only within a relative framework of conventional **reality**. Absence of such an ontological reality, i.e. the absence of the inherent existence of all phenomena, is defined as the true nature of **reality, emptiness**, by the ***Madhyamaka*** schools and by the ***tantras***.

Inner Radiance *'od-gsal*, Skt. *prabhāsvara*
Sometimes also translated as 'clear light', the Tibetan term *'od-gsal*, which has been rendered here as 'inner radiance', refers in the context of the **perfection stage** of **meditation** (Skt. *sampannakrama*) to the subtlest level of mind, i.e. the fundamental, essential nature of all our cognitive events. Though ever present within all **sentient beings**, this inner radiance becomes manifest only when the gross mind has ceased to function. Such a dissolution is experienced by ordinary beings, naturally, at the time of death, but it can also be experientially cultivated through the practices of **Unsurpassed *Yogatantra***. A fundamental distinction is made between the inner radiance of the ground (*gzhi'i 'od-gsal*) and the inner radiance of the path (*lam-gyi 'od-gsal*). The former, which is also known as the 'mother inner radiance' (*'od-gsal ma*), occurs naturally at the time of death, when it indicates the presence of the **Buddha-body of Reality** (*dharmakāya*), but which may not be accompanied by an awareness of its nature. The latter, which is also known as the 'child inner radiance' (*'od-gsal bu*) is an awareness of the ultimate nature of mind cultivated by the meditator in life, i.e. the realisation of the nature of the 'mother inner radiance' as it is developed in meditation. **Buddhahood** is achieved when the 'mother inner radiance' and 'child inner radiance' conjoin. See Chapters 8, 10 and 11. Chapter 11, in particular, differentiates three successive phases of inner radiance which are experienced at the time of death and immediately thereafter: the primary inner radiance (*bar-do dang-po chos-nyid 'od-gsal*), which is identified with the inner radiance of the ground, the secondary inner radiance (*bar-do 'od-gsal gnyis-pa*), which is identified with the inner radiance of the path, and the tertiary inner radiance (*bar-do 'od-gsal gsum-pa*), which is identified with the subsequent arising of the **Peaceful and Wrathful Deities** during the **intermediate state of reality** (*chos-nyid bar-do*).

Inner Tantras of Skilful Means *nang thabs-kyi rgyud*
The collective name for the ***tantras*** of ***Mahāyoga***, ***Anuyoga*** and ***Atiyoga***. See also under **Vehicle**.

Intentional Lineage of the Conquerors *rgyal-ba dgongs-pa'i brgyud-pa*
According to the ***Nyingma*** school, the Buddhist teachings are said to have been transmitted through six **lineages** (*brgyud-pa drug*). Among these, the first, which is known as the 'intentional lineage of the conquerors', refers to the **enlightened intention** (*dgongs-pa*) of ***Samantabhadra***, which confers the realisation of the atemporal **Buddha-body of Reality**, as a blessing upon the male and female **buddhas** of the **Buddha-body of Perfect Resource**.

Intermediate State *bar-do*, Skt. *antarābhava*
The original usage of the term within the literature of classical Buddhist ***abhidharma*** suggests that it referred exclusively to the period between the time of death and the time of rebirth. According to the ***Nyingma*** and ***Kagyu*** schools, however, the term 'intermediate state' refers to key phases of life and death identified as: the **intermediate state of living** (*rang-bzhin bar-do*), the **intermediate state of meditative concentration** (*bsam-gtan bar-do*), the **intermediate state of dreams** (*rmi-lam bar-do*), the **intermediate state of the time of death** (*'chi-kha'i bar-do*), **the intermediate state of reality** (*chos-nyid bar-do*) and the **intermediate state of rebirth** (*srid-pa'i bar-do*). During each of these phases, the consciousness of a **sentient being** has particular experiential qualities, and corresponding to these qualities of experience there are specific meditative techniques conducive to realisation of the ultimate nature of mind and phenomena. See Chapter 3 and individual entries below.

Intermediate State of Dreams *rmi-lam bar-do*
The intermediate state of dreams begins from the moment of falling asleep and ends when we awake. This intermediate state offers the opportunity for the practitioner to recognise the similarity between the illusory nature of dreams and that of our waking state. This practice is cultivated in the context of **dream yoga** where the ability to maintain awareness of the ultimate nature of mind and phenomena during both deep sleep and dreaming is refined.

Intermediate State of Living *rang-bzhin bar-do*
The intermediate state of living begins at the time of birth and continues until the time of death. Having obtained a precious human form with the ability to recognise our actual condition, the opportunity arises to adopt a way of life and to engage in the practices that lead to **buddhahood**. See Chapters 3 and 1, 2, 4, 5, 6 and 7.

Intermediate State of Meditative Concentration *bsam-gtan bar-do*
The intermediate state of meditative concentration entered during the waking state provides the opportunity for the practitioner to cultivate **meditative equipoise** (*samāhita*, Tib. *mnyam-bzhag*) and thereby to achieve stability in the **generation** and **perfection stages** of meditation. This in turn deepens an unbroken awareness of the ultimate nature of mind and phenomena in post-meditative activities and prepares the meditator for the **intermediate state of the time of death**. See Chapters 3 and 1, 2, 4, 5, 6 and 7.

Intermediate State of Reality *chos-nyid bar-do*
The intermediate state of actual reality arises after the **intermediate state of the time of death** (*'chi-kha'i bar-do*) and before the **intermediate state of rebirth** (*srid-pa'i*

bar-do). Here the opportunity occurs, based on the practices adopted during one's lifetime, to recognise the **natural purity** and **natural transformative** qualities of the ultimate nature of mind in the form of luminosities, rays, sounds and **meditational deities**. See Chapters 3 and 11.

Intermediate State of Rebirth *srid-pa'i bar-do*
The intermediate state of rebirth is entered after the **intermediate state of reality** when the consciousness arises in the form of a **mental body**, conditioned by the individual's inheritance of **past actions**, and the individual begins to experience both the surroundings where he or she died and the unfolding of experiential states driven by the momentum of **past actions**. If **liberation** from **cyclic existence** is not achieved during this intermediate state it comes to an end at the moment of conception. Since consciousness is said to possess certain heightened qualities during this period there is a potential to achieve **liberation**, or at the very least a favourable rebirth, at various key stages as this state is traversed. See Chapters 3 and 11.

Intermediate State of the Time of Death *'chi-kha'i bar-do*
The intermediate state of the time of death is entered at the time when the process of dying definitively begins, and ends with the onset of the **intermediate state of reality**. It includes the gradual dissolution of the five elements and their associated modes of consciousness and culminates with the arising of the **inner radiance** of the ground (*gzhi'i 'od-gsal*). The natural arising of **inner radiance** immediately after respiration ceases is regarded as a supreme opportunity to realise the **Buddha-body of Reality**. See Chapters 3, 8, 10 and 11.

Intrinsic Awareness *rang-rig*, Skt. *svasaṃvitti/svasaṃvedana*
According to Indian Buddhist epistemology, and particularly in the writings of the great logicians *Dignāga* and *Dharmakīrti*, the term *svasaṃvedana* refers to the apperceptive or reflexive faculty of consciousness, for which reason it is sometimes rendered as 'reflexive awareness' or 'apperceptive awareness'. However, in the view of the **Great Perfection** (*rdzogs-pa chen-po*) and in the context of the present work, the same term refers to the fundamental innate mind in its natural state of spontaneity and purity, beyond the alternating states of motion and rest and the subject–object dichotomy. It is therefore rendered here as 'intrinsic awareness'. As such, intrinsic awareness gives the meditator access to **pristine cognition** or the **buddha-mind** itself, and it stands in direct contrast to **fundamental ignorance** (*avidyā*), which is the primary cause of rebirth in **cyclic existence** (*saṃsāra*). The direct **introduction** to intrinsic awareness is a distinctive teaching within the ***Nyingma*** school and the principal subject matter of Chapter 4. This practice is a central component of the **Esoteric Instructional Class** (*upadeśa*) of ***Atiyoga***, where it is known as **Cutting through Resistance** (*khregs-chod*). See also **Awareness** and **Mind**.

Intrinsic Awareness which is Pristine Cognition *rang rig-pa'i ye-shes*
Generally this term refers to the **pristine cognition** arising from the direct realisation of **emptiness** by a **sublime being** (*ārya*, Tib. *'phags-pa*) in the context of deep **meditative equipoise**. This is so called because the nature and qualities of that experience can never be fully conveyed by means of language and words but remains totally evident to the *yogin* himself. In the context of the **Great Perfection** however, as exemplified by our text, the fusion of the meditator's intrinsic awareness with the pristine cognition of **buddha-mind** indicates not only that intrinsic awareness

provides access to **buddha-mind**, but that the identity of the two has been fully realised. See also **Intrinsic Awareness** and **Pristine Cognition**.

Introduction *ngo-sprod*
A genre of pith instructions in which the nature of **actual reality** or **intrinsic awareness** is formally introduced (*rig-pa'i ngo-sprod*), in a clear immediate manner, by a qualified **spiritual teacher**. See Chapter 4.

Invitation *spyan-'dren-pa*, Skt. *upanimantraṇa*
The term 'invitation' refers to the meditative process of the ***tantras***, whereby the actual **meditational deity** or **Being of Pristine Cognition** (*jñānasattva*, Tib. *ye-shes sems-dpa'*) is formally invited by the meditator to enter into the previously visualised form, known as the **Being of Commitment** (*samayasattva*, Tib. *dam-tshig sems-dpa'*).

Jambudvīpa *'dzam-bu gling*
See under **Four Continents and Eight Subcontinents**.

Kagyu *bka'-brgyud*
One of the four main traditions or schools of Tibetan Buddhism. The *Kagyu* lineage tradition stems from the great **accomplished masters** (*mahāsiddha*) of India such as *Tilopa*, *Naropa* and *Maitripa* through to *Khyungpo Neljor*, who founded the *Shangpa Kagyu* lineage, and *Marpa Lotsāwa*, who formed the *Dagpo Kagyu* lineage. The latter comprises four major sub-schools, namely the *Karmapa*, the *Tshalpa*, the *Barompa* and the *Phagmodrupa*, the last of which is further divided into the branches of the *Drigungpa*, *Taglungpa*, *Drukpa*, *Yazang*, *Trophu*, *Shugseb*, *Yelpa*, and *Martshang*. These traditions integrate practices derived from both the ***sūtras*** and the ***tantras***. There is a particular emphasis on the **Great Seal** (*Mahāmudrā*) system of practice and on **perfection stage** practices such as the Six Yogas of *Naropa*.

Kāmarūpa *ka-ma ru-pa*
A traditional name corresponding to parts of modern *Assam* in north-east India and the adjacent *Sylhet* region of Bangladesh.

Kangyur and Tengyur *bka'-bstan rnam-gnyis*
The *Kangyur* is the Tibetan Buddhist canon containing the original ***sūtras*** and ***tantras*** translated from Indian sources. The *Kangyur*, as we now know it, was formalised as a complete collection by the great fourteenth-century Tibetan scholar and encyclopaedist *Buton Rinchendrub*. *Buton* was also instrumental in the compilation of the *Tengyur*, the canonical collection containing translations of authoritative Indian commentarial works. Many manuscript versions of these anthologies were prepared over the centuries, and important xylographic editions were published at *Narthang*, *Derge*, *Lhasa*, *Litang*, *Cho-ne*, and *Beijing*. '*Kangyur*' (*bka'-'gyur*) literally means the translated sacred words or transmitted precepts of the **buddhas**, and '*Tengyur*' (*bstan-'gyur*), the translated commentaries.

Kaṅkaṇīdhāraṇī *kaṅ-ka-ṇī gzungs*
The name of an incantation text associated with *Akṣobhya-Vajrasattva*, through which offerings are made on behalf of the deceased.

Karma *las*
See **Past Actions**.

Karma Family *las-kyi rigs*, Skt. *karmakula*
One of the **five enlightened families** (*pañcakula*) into which the **meditational deities** of the **Buddha-body of Perfect Resource** are subdivided. The deities of the *Karma* family include the peaceful **buddhas** *Amoghasiddhi* and *Samayatārā* and the corresponding wrathful aspects *Karma Heruka* and *Karmakrodheśvarī*. See Appendix Two.

Karma Lingpa *karma gling-pa*
Karma Lingpa (*fl.* fourteenth century) is the **treasure-finder** who extracted from Mt *Gampodar* in *Dakpo* the cycle of teachings known as the *Peaceful and Wrathful Deities: A Profound Sacred Teaching, [entitled] Natural Liberation through [Recognition of] Enlightened Intention* (*Zhi-khro dgongs-pa rang-grol*), to which our present text belongs. See Gyurme Dorje's 'Brief Literary History'.

Karmaprasiddhi *byang-phyogs las-rab brtsegs-pa'i zhing-khams*
The northern **buddha field** of the 'Mound of Excellent Activities' (*Karmaprakūṭa*), otherwise known as the 'Matrix of Enlightened Activities' (Tib. *las-rab grub-pa*, Skt. *Karmaprasiddhi*), is the paradise presided over by the male ***buddha*** *Amoghasiddhi*. See Appendix Two.

Kāya *sku*
See **Buddha-body**.

Khaṭvāṅga *khaṭ-vāṅga*
Literally meaning 'bedpost', the *khaṭvāṅga* is a tantric staff, comprising a long eight-sided shaft of white sandalwood, sealed with a half-***vajra*** at its base, and a crossed-***vajra*** at its top, replete with streamers and surmounted by stacked skulls and human heads, indicative of the energy centres of body, speech and mind within the **subtle body**. In general, the *khaṭvāṅga* symbolises the union of great bliss and emptiness.

King Spirits *rgyal-po*
A class of male spirits who are said to have assumed their particular forms through a preponderance of anger and hatred. Their many mundane forms are to be differentiated from the five supramundane forms of the **protector** deity Pehar (*rgyal-po sku lnga*), which are respectively known as the kings of body, speech, mind, attributes and activities.

Kriyātantra *bya-ba'i rgyud*
The first of the three outer classes of ***tantra***, which form one subcategory of the six classes of ***tantra***, and the fourth of the **nine vehicles**, according to the ***Nyingma*** school of Tibetan Buddhism. *Kriyātantra* emphasises outer ritual practices such as the making of offerings, prostration, and praises to the **meditational deity** visualised in the space before one.

KYE HO *kye-ho*
An exclamation of astonishment or wonder.

Lake-dwelling Medicinal Spirits *mtsho-sman/'tsho-sman*
A group of five, seven or nine female spirits of the *sman-mo* class who dwell in lakes, and who are differentiated from the sky-dwelling medicinal spirits (*nam-mkha'i sman-mo*), the earth-dwelling medicinal spirits (*sa'i sman-mo*), and the hybrid serpentine-medicinal spirits (*klu-sman*). In general, the *sman-mo* are a category

of indigenous Tibetan spirits, to whom medicinal ***torma*-offerings** (*sman-gtor*), compounded of medicines, nectars and blood, are made. Foremost among them are the five sisters of longevity (*tshe-ring mched-lnga*), who are embodied in the five main snow peaks of the Everest range. The most powerful of these medicinal spirits are said to have been bound under an oath of allegiance by ***Padmasambhava*** at Silma in Tsang.

Lay Vows *dge-bsnyen-gyi sdom-pa*, Skt. *upāsakavrata*
See **Prātimokṣa** and **Vows**.

Lesser Vehicle *theg-dman*, Skt. *hīnayāna*
See **Greater Vehicle, Hermit Buddhas** and **Pious Attendants**.

'Liberating' Avengers *sgrol-ging*
This is the name of a class of male sword-wielding spirits, collectively known as the *skyes-bu ging-chen*, who are invoked in order to enact the wrathful **rites of 'liberation'**.

Liberation *grol-ba/sgrol-ba*, Skt. *mokṣa*
In a Buddhist context, the term liberation refers specifically to freedom from **cyclic existence**, the karmically conditioned cycle of death and rebirth, and consequently to freedom from all forms of physical and mental **suffering**. Such a liberation can be attained only through the total elimination of **fundamental ignorance** and the **dissonant mental states**, including **attachment** and **aversion**, which afflict the mind and perpetuate the cycle of existence.

Lifelong Companion Gods *'go-ba'i lha*
This is a category of spirits who are said to accompany an individual throughout his or her life, like a shadow, protecting the vitality (*bla*) of the individual. Five types of lifelong companion god (*'go-ba'i lha lnga*) are specifically identified: the gods of the life-essence (*srog-gi-lha*), the gods of masculinity (*pho-lha*), the gods of femininity (*mo-lha*), the gods of the countryside (*yul-lha*), and the gods of inimical force (*dgra-lha*).

Lineage *brgyud-pa*, Skt. *paraṃparā*
An unbroken line of successive teachers through whom the Buddhist teachings are transmitted. According to the ***Nyingma*** tradition, six forms of lineage are described: 1) the **intentional lineage of the conquerors** (*rgyal-ba'i dgongs-brgyud*), through which the **Buddha-body of Reality** communicates the teachings to the **Buddha-body of Perfect Resource**; 2) the **symbolic lineage of awareness holders** (*rig-'dzin brda'i brgyud-pa*), through which non-human and human **awareness holders** of the highest **spiritual accomplishments** symbolically receive the teachings from ***bodhisattvas*** of the tenth level; 3) the aural lineage of authoritative personages (*gang-zag snyan-khung-gi brgyud-pa*), through which **accomplished masters** orally transmit the teachings from one generation to the next; 4) the lineage empowered by enlightened aspiration (*smon-lam dbang-bskur-gyi brgyud-pa*), through which a **treasure-finder** of concealed texts is identified by their concealer's solemn affirmation, 5) the lineage of prophetically declared spiritual succession (*bka'-babs lung-bstan-gyi brgyud-pa*), through which a **treasure-finder** of concealed texts is identified from the authoritative prophesies of ***Padmasambhava***, and 6) the lineage of the ***ḍākinī***'s seal of entrustment (*mkha'-'gro gtad-rgya'i brgyud-pa*), through which a **treasure-finder** is

granted codified teachings by the lords of the **treasure** in fulfilment of the concealer's former aspiration.

Lineage Holder *brgyud-pa'i 'dzin-pa*, Skt. *paraṃparādhara*
One who maintains any of the six **lineages** and takes responsibility for their continued **transmission** from one generation to the next. See previous entry.

Longchen Rabjampa *klong-chen rab-'byams-pa*
A prolific writer (1308–63), regarded as one of the greatest masters of the ***Nyingma*** school, *Longchen Rabjampa* is renowned for his systematic commentaries on the **nine vehicles**, the perspective of ***Atiyoga***, and his revelation of the texts and practices contained in the *Four-part Innermost Spirituality* (*sNying-thig ya-bzhi*). His commentary on the **Guhyagarbhatantra**, entitled *Dispelling the Darkness of the Ten Directions* (*Phyogs-bcu'i mun-sel*), is an important source, clarifying the ***maṇḍala*** of the forty-two **peaceful deities** and the fifty-eight **wrathful deities** from the perspectives of the **ground**, **path**, and result.

Lotus *padma*
In Buddhist poetry and the visual arts the lotus, particularly the variety which grows in water, is often used as a symbol of purity. The lotus grows from an unclean mire, yet it is clean and unpolluted by the mire surrounding it. One finds the lotus depicted as the cushion or seat of many **meditational deities** in Buddhist **tantric** iconography. Among the **five enlightened families**, the ***Padma*** or Lotus family (*padma'i rigs*) is that of the ***buddha*** *Amitābha*.

Lotus Light Palace *padma 'od-kyi pho-brang*
The palace or operational field of ***Padmasambhava***. See under **Maṇḍala**.

Love/Loving Kindness *byams-pa*, Skt. *maitrī*
In a Buddhist context, loving kindness is defined as a **mental factor** characterised by a sincere wish that others enjoy happiness. According to this definition, love is one of the eleven 'wholesome **mental factors**' categorised in the ***abhidharma*** literature. However, in the case of the **four immeasurable aspirations**, the word love is used as an abbreviation for 'great love' (*byams-pa chen-po*, Skt. *mahāmaitrī*) which refers to an altruistic mental attitude that is unbiased in its love towards all beings and is also spontaneous and natural. It is said that such a spontaneous sense of universal or unqualified love can only arise as a result of a systematic meditative training and an understanding of **emptiness**.

Lower Existences *ngan-song*, Skt. *durgati*
The realms of the animals, **anguished spirits**, and **hells**.

Lower Vital Energy *'og-gi rlung*
The vital energy located at the lower extremity of the central **energy channel** within the **subtle body**. See **Vital Energy**.

Madhyamaka *dbu-ma*
Derived from the Sanskrit expression *madhyamapratipad*, meaning the 'Middle Way' between the extremes of **eternalism** and **nihilism**, which was expounded by ***Śākyamuni Buddha*** in the earliest ***sūtras***, *Madhyamaka* (*dbu-ma*) is the name of one of the most influential among the four classical schools of Indian Buddhist philosophy. Within the context of the *Madhyamaka* school, the Middle Way refers to the doctrine of **emptiness** (*śūnyatā*), which is held to be the ultimate nature of all

things. According to this view, all phenomena, whether mental or physical, cannot be found to possess any independent or self-validating natures, and their existence and identity are regarded as valid only within a relative framework of worldly convention. Further, it is propounded that not only do phenomena exist solely in dependence upon causes and conditions, but even their identities depend on conceptions and labelling. Nevertheless, this school holds that, unlike mere fantasies, such as unicorns for example, phenomena do exist conventionally and their ontology must be accepted as valid. Such a metaphysical position is designated the 'Middle Way' in that it is the mid-point between the extremes of total non-existence of **reality**, or **nihilism**, and the positing of an absolute, independent existence of **reality**, or **eternalism**. Founded by ***Nāgārjuna*** in the second century AD, the *Madhyamaka* school later evolved two sub-divisions: *Prāsaṅgika* and *Svātantrika*, based on the different interpretations of *Nāgārjuna*'s views which were made by *Buddhapālita* (later elucidated by *Candrakīrti*) and *Bhavaviveka* respectively. The Tibetan tradition, while recognising *Bhavaviveka*'s important contribution to Buddhist logic and philosophy, considers the *Prāsaṅgika* technique of *reductio ad absurdum* to be the most refined logical method in Buddhism for establishing the view of **emptiness**. The distinctive feature of the *Prāsaṅgika* school is its total denial of any ontology implying **inherent existence** of either external objects or subjective **consciousness**. There is also, according to some Tibetan interpretations, the tradition known as the Great *Madhyamaka* which in the course of meditative insight distinguishes between the intrinsic **emptiness** of phenomena (*rang-stong*) and the extrinsic **emptiness** of pure **buddha attributes** (*gzhan-stong*).

Magical Net *sgyu-'phrul drva-ba*, Skt. *Māyājāla*
The most all-embracing cycle of texts among the eighteen ***Mahāyoga tantras***, focusing specifically on the ***maṇḍala*** of the forty-two **peaceful deities** and the fifty-eight **wrathful deities**, and including within its corpus the ***Guhyagarbhatantra***. As such, it is the basis for all subsequent expositions of this particular ***maṇḍala***, including the present work. See Gyurme Dorje's 'Brief Literary History'.

Magon Chamdrel *ma-mgon lcam-dral*
An epithet of the protectress *Ekajaṭī* and *Dorje Lekpa*, who are revered as the foremost supramundane **protector** deities, according to the ***Atiyoga*** tradition of the ***Nyingma*** school.

Mahākāla *mgon-po nag-po*
The supramundane **protector** deity *Mahākāla* is a **wrathful** manifestation of ***Avalokiteśvara***. The meditative practices associated with this protector are popular in all four traditions of Tibetan Buddhism.

Mahākaruṇika *thugs-rje chen-po*
The thousand-armed form of ***Avalokiteśvara***. See **Avalokiteśvara**.

Mahāyāna *theg-pa chen-po*
See **Greater Vehicle**.

Mahāyoga *rnal-'byor chen-po'i rgyud*
The seventh of the **nine vehicles**, and first of the three inner classes of *tantras*, according to the ***Nyingma*** school. *Mahāyoga* emphasises the **generation stage** of meditation (*utpattikrama*) and the gradual visualisation of elaborate ***maṇḍalas*** of deities. It comprises eighteen basic ***tantras***, such as ***Guhyagarbha***, *Guhyasamāja*,

and *Buddhasamāyoga*, as well as a vast number of ***tantra*** texts associated with the so-called eight classes of **means for attainment** (*sgrub-pa bka'-brgyad*), which focus respectively on the deities *Yamāntaka*, *Hayagrīva*, *Śrīheruka*, *Vajrāmṛta*, *Vajrakīla*, *Mātaraḥ*, *Lokastotrapūjā* (*'jig-rten mchod-bstod*), and *Vajramantrabhiru* (*rmod-pa drag-sngags*). These texts are all contained in the *Collected Tantras of the Nyingmapa* (*rNying-ma'i rgyud-'bum*), and a small but important selection of them is also contained in the ***Kangyur***.

Maitreya *rgyal-ba byams-pa*
Maitreya is the embodiment of the great **loving kindness** (*mahāmaitrī*) of all the **buddhas**, as visualised in the form of a **meditational deity**. *Maitreya* therefore represents the perfected state of the faculty of **love/loving kindness** inherent within each individual's mental continuum. In addition, *Maitreya* is also revered as an eminent historical figure, a ***bodhisattva*** who was one of the eight principal ***bodhisattva*** disciples of ***Śākyamuni Buddha***. It is to him that the *Five Works* of *Maitreya* (*Byams-chos sde-lnga*) are attributed. According to the classical ***sūtra*** literature it is the ***bodhisattva*** *Maitreya* who is the coming **buddha**, fifth in the line of one thousand **buddhas** (**Śākyamuni** being the fourth) who will descend to this world during the **auspicious aeon**. Currently he is said to be residing in the **god** realm of ***Tuṣita***. He is also one of the four outer male ***bodhisattvas*** among the forty-two **peaceful deities**. See Appendix Two.

Major and Minor Marks *mtshan-dpe*, Skt. *lakṣaṇānuvyañjana*
The **Buddha-body of Supreme Emanation** is characterised by thirty-two major marks (Skt. *dvātriṃśan-mahāpuruṣalakṣaṇa*) and eighty minor marks (Skt. *asītyanuvyañjana*), which are all enumerated in ***Maitreya***'s *Ornament of Emergent Realisation* (*Abhisamayālaṃkāra*, T 3786, vv. 13–17 and 21–32). These include an array of perfected features of body and speech, which according to the commentaries are the specific results of diverse aspects of a **buddha**'s conduct.

Malevolent/Beguiling Forces *bdud*, Skt. *māra*
Buddhist literature speaks of four kinds of beguiling influences which are the obstacles that impede one's spiritual transformation. These are the influence of: our impure psycho-physical **aggregates** (*skandha*); our **dissonant mental states** (*kleśa*); deva's son (*devaputra*), which refers to sensual desires and temptations; and the lord of death (*mṛtyupati*), which refers to ordinary death, at the point of which rebirth in cyclic existence continues rather than the attainment of **buddhahood**. As recorded in the life of ***Śākyamuni Buddha***, these archetypal forces projected images of desire and terror which were designed to interrupt his **meditative equipoise**, just prior to his attainment of manifestly perfect **buddhahood** at *Bodhgaya* in India.

Maṇḍala *dkyil-'khor*
The Sanskrit word '*maṇḍala*' conveys a number of meanings – circle, wheel, circumference, totality, assembly or literary corpus. In the context of ***Anuyoga*** and ***Atiyoga***, the expression 'three *maṇḍalas*' specifically refers to the scope of **buddha-body, speech** and **mind**. Then, in a more general usage, this term indicates the central (*dkyil*) and peripheral (*'khor*) deities described in the ***tantra*** texts. These deities reside within a celestial palace (*vimāṇa*), which generally has a perfectly symmetrical design – with four gateways and four main walls composed of five layers of different colours, each of the features corresponding to a particular aspect of the principal deity's, and thereby to the meditator's, pure **awareness** and purity of perception.

The *maṇḍala* thus represents a perfected state of being and perception encompassing all phenomena. The celestial palace itself and the deities within it symbolise the perfected states of the meditator's own **awareness**, psycho-physical **aggregates**, elemental properties, sensory and mental processes, etc. When such *maṇḍalas* are represented symbolically, they may take the form of a two-dimensional image on painted cloth, or they may be made of coloured sand, or else constructed as a three-dimensional structure, carved from wood or other materials. The visualisation of *maṇḍalas* in their three-dimensional form plays a crucial role in the **generation stage** of meditation. Here, these 'abodes of the deity' are never perceived of as independently existing universes but as manifestations of the **pristine cognition** of the principal **meditational deity** being meditated upon. The symbolism of the *maṇḍala* of forty-two **peaceful deities** and fifty-eight **wrathful deities**, as it relates to our text, is given in Appendix Two.

Maṇḍala of Offerings *mchod-pa'i maṇḍal*
The *maṇḍala* of offerings is one of the **preliminary practices** (*sngon-'gro*), in which offerings are visualised and offered to the **spiritual teacher**, **meditational deity** or **Three Precious Jewels**. In general, there are outer, inner, and secret *maṇḍala* offerings, corresponding to the **Three Buddha-bodies** of **emanation**, **perfect resource** and **actual reality**. In the first, the entire external material universe, symbolised by Mount ***Sumeru*** and the **four continents**, etc., is offered, usually using a circular metal base on which are arranged small heaps of rice; second, the inner *maṇḍala* of offerings comprises the **subtle body**, complete with its **energy channels**, currents of **vital energy** and **seminal points**; and, third, the secret *maṇḍala* of offerings is that of **actual reality** or the ultimate nature of **mind**. In the **preliminary practices** all these are offered one hundred thousand times as an antidote for **attachment**.

Mañjuśrī *'jam-dpal*
Mañjuśrī is the embodiment of the **discriminative awareness** of all the **buddhas**, manifesting in the form of a **meditational deity**. He is normally depicted in his seated posture, holding a sword in his right hand (representing **discriminative awareness**) and a sacred text in his left hand (indicating his mastery of all knowledge). *Mañjuśrī* is also revered as an eminent historical figure who was one of the eight principal ***bodhisattva*** disciples of the ***Buddha***; and he is also one of the four outer male ***bodhisattvas*** among the forty-two **peaceful deities**. See Appendix Two.

Mantra *sngags*
The Sanskrit word *mantra* is an abbreviation of two syllables *mana* and *traya*, respectively meaning 'mind' and 'protection'. Hence '*mantra*' literally refers to 'protection of the mind'. The essential indication here is the protection of the mind from the overwhelming influence of ordinary perceptions and conceptions, which give rise to deluded states of existence, thus inhibiting the full expression of **buddha nature**. More specifically, *mantra* refers to the pure sound which is the perfected speech of an **enlightened** being. The aim of the **generation stage** practices is the cultivation of the mode of being of the **meditational deity**, that is to say the transformation of mundane body, speech and mind into **buddha-body**, **speech** and **mind**. This is supported in ritual practice by the enactment of the hand-gestures or **seals** (*mudrā*), which are the resonance of **buddha-body**, by *mantra* recitation, which is the resonance of **buddha-speech**, and by visualisation, which is the resonance of **buddha-mind**. In general, three types of *mantra* are differentiated: *mantras* of

retention (Skt. *dhāraṇī*, Tib. *gzungs-sngags*), gnostic *mantras* (Skt. *vidyāmantra*, Tib. *rig-sngags*), and secret *mantras* (Skt. *guhyamantra*, Tib. *gsang-sngags*). Among these, the first comprises the *mantras* associated with the ***sūtras*** which are designed to intensify **discriminative awareness**, the second are associated with specific deities of the outer ***tantras***, and designed to intensify **skilful means**, while the third are associated with the inner *tantras*, and are designed to intensify the **generation stage** of meditation. The term 'secret *mantra*' is also utilised as a synonym for the **Vehicle of Indestructible Reality** (*Vajrayāna*).

Mantrin *sngags-pa*
An adept of the vehicle of secret ***mantra*** (*mantrayāna*) in general. However, the word *ngakpa* (*sngags-pa*) is popularly used to denote those practitioners of ***tantra*** who choose to maintain a family life, passing on their teachings through a familial lineage, in contrast to the celibate life of a monk or nun.

Māra *bdud*
See under **Malevolent / Beguiling Forces.**

Martial Haunting Spirits *btsan*
A class of ghostly or haunting spirits, often depicted as armour-clad, who cause colic and intestinal disorders. Foremost among them are *Tsimara*, the protector of *Samye* monastery, and *Yamshu Marpo*. They are generally depicted as red in colour, brandishing a red lance with a red flag in the right hand and throwing a red-coloured snare (*btsan-zhags*) with the left hand, while riding a red horse.

Means for Attainment *sgrub-thabs*, Skt. *sādhana*
The literature of the Buddhist ***tantras*** is classified into ***tantra*** texts and means for attainment manuals. The former are general expositions concerning the **continua of the ground, path and result** associated with a particular ***maṇḍala*** of deities, while the latter are specific manuals derived from and inspired by the former as the detailed means for attainment, or meditative realisation, of a specific ***maṇḍala*** of deities. Such practices have four phases, which are often known as the **four aspects of ritual service and means for attainment** (*bsnyen-sgrub yan-lag bzhi*).

Meditation *sgom*, Skt. *bhāvanā*
Meditation is defined as a disciplined mental process through which a person cultivates familiarity with a chosen object, be it an external object like an image, or even a trivial object such as a pebble, etc., or an internal object such as one's own mind or personal identity. According to the ***sūtras***, there are two main types of meditation, one emphasising the faculty of stability and single-pointedness of mind and the other emphasising analysis and discrimination. The first type of meditation is absorptive, and produces a quality of mental placement and tranquillity, known as **calm abiding**, and the latter, known as **penetrative insight**, generates a deeper insight into the profound natures of the chosen object. In the context of the ***tantras***, meditation additionally includes the techniques of the **generation** and **perfection stages**, as well as those of the **Great Perfection**.

Meditational Deity *yi-dam*, Skt. *iṣṭadevatā*
Forms or resonances of fully manifest **buddhahood** whose characteristics are defined or revealed by the specific tantric practices on the basis of which they are visualised. After receiving **empowerment** and guidance concerning an appropriate meditational deity or ***maṇḍala*** of deities from an authoritative **spiritual teacher**, the practitioner

of the ***tantras*** seeks to experientially cultivate union with the qualities of **buddha-body, speech** and **mind** through the practice of the **generation stage** of meditation related to a specific meditational deity or ***maṇḍala*** of deities. It is essential that the meditational deities should not be perceived as externally existing or independent beings but rather as forms or resonances of **buddha-mind** itself. Union with the meditational deity is said to confer supreme **accomplishment** on the meditator, in contrast to meditation on the spiritual teacher, which confers **blessings**, and meditation on the ***ḍākinī***, which confers enlightened or **buddha activities**.

Meditative Commitment *thugs-dam*
This refers to a resolute period of **meditative equipoise**, and the **commitments** pertaining to meditative equipoise. Note that the same term is also used as the honorific equivalent of *yi-dam* (meditational deity).

Meditative Concentration *bsam-gtan*, Skt. *dhyāna*
Meditative concentration is defined as the one-pointed abiding in an undistracted state of mind free from the taint of **dissonant mental states** (*kleśa*). It is an advanced form of **calm abiding**, where often both **calm abiding** and **penetrative insight** may be present in perfect union. In the ***sūtras*** and ***abhidharma*** literature of the **Lesser Vehicle**, four states of meditative concentration are identified as being conducive to birth in the seventeen levels of the **form realm**. These are characterised, in their proper order, by a temporary sojourn from: 1) physical sensations of pain; 2) mental unhappiness; 3) mental excitements related to pleasure; and 4) mundane experiences of joy as a whole. In the context of the **Greater Vehicle**, meditative concentration is the fifth of the **six perfections** (Skt. *ṣaṭpāramitā*).

Meditative Equipoise *mnyam-par bzhag-pa*, Skt. *samāhita*
Meditative equipoise refers to a one-pointed placement of the mind on a meditation object or a theme, such as the **selflessness** of the individual personality (Skt. *pudgala-nairātmya*) and the **selflessness** of phenomena (Skt. *dharmanairātmya*), which invariably occurs in the context of prolonged **meditative stability** (Skt. *samādhi*). It is contrasted with periods of post-meditation (Skt. *pṛṣṭalabdha*, Tib. *rjes-thob*) during which the meditator arises from meditative equipoise, and engages with his or her environment.

Meditative Stability *ting-nge-'dzin*, Skt. *samādhi*
The Sanskrit term *samādhi* literally means 'union' or 'combination', and its Tibetan equivalent *ting-nge-'dzin* means 'adhering to that which is profound and definitive'. However, the term has several different meanings in different contexts. For example, in ***abhidharma*** texts it sometimes refers to a mental factor that is part of a group of mental factors present in every veridical cognition, whereas in the context of meditation, it can be synonymous with **meditative concentration**. In many instances, *samādhi* refers to specific meditative states such as diamond-like meditation, lion's majestic pose meditation and others enumerated in the ***sūtras*** and ***tantras*** of the **Greater Vehicle**. More specifically, in the ***Mahāyoga tantras***, the term meditative stability refers to the three phases of the **generation** and **perfection stages** of meditation. These are: the **meditative stability of reality** (*de-bzhin nyid-kyi ting-nge-'dzin*), the **meditative stability which illuminates all that appears** (*kun-tu snang-ba'i ting-nge-'dzin*), and the **meditative stability of the causal basis** (*rgyu'i ting-nge-'dzin*), which respectively and sequentially focus on great **emptiness**, great **compassion** and the **seals** of the **meditational deities**. In the **Unsurpassed**

Yogatantras, somewhat different terminology is used in the contexts of the **generation stage** and the **perfection stage.** In the generation stage, the practice of the **means of attainment** takes place within the framework of (i) the initial meditative stability (*dang-po sbyor-ba'i ting-nge-'dzin*), (ii) the meditative stability of the victorious rite of the ***maṇḍala*** (*dkyil-'khor rgyal-chog-gi ting-nge-'dzin*), and (iii) the meditative stability of the victorious rite of enlightened activity (*las rgyal-chog-gi ting-nge-'dzin*). In the context of the **perfection stage,** however, these same terms refer to an advanced level of realisation.

Mental Body *yid-lus*, Skt. *manokāya*
The non-corporeal body assumed during the **intermediate state of rebirth,** which is said to have an initial similitude to the physical body of the previous life. See Chapter 11.

Mental Factor *sems-byung*, Skt. *caitasika*
See **Mind.**

Merit *bsod-nams*, Skt. *puṇya*
Merit refers to the wholesome tendencies imprinted in the mind as a result of positive and skilful thoughts, words, and actions that ripen in the experience of happiness and well-being. According to the **Greater Vehicle,** it is important to dedicate the merit of one's wholesome actions to the benefit of all **sentient beings,** ensuring that others also experience the results of the positive actions generated.

Middle Way *dbu-ma'i lam*, Skt. *madhyamapratipad*
See **Madhyamaka.**

Mind *sems,* Skt. *citta*
In Buddhism, mind is defined as a dynamic process, which is simply the awareness of an object or event. In its technical usage mind is contrasted with fifty-one **mental factors,** which are enumerated in the ***abhidharma*** literature. In the context of this differentiation the primary function of 'mind' is to be aware of the referent object as a whole, whereas the modalities which relate to the specific aspects of the object are defined as '**mental factors**'. It is important to understand that mind in Buddhism should not be conceived of as a static thing or as something composed of a spiritual substance. Although some Buddhist philosophical schools of thought do identify mind as the essence of being or personal identity, the notion of self or person is not an essential component of the Buddhist concept of mind. In the ***Dzogchen*** teachings an important distinction is made between the Tibetan terms '*sems*' and '*rig-pa*'. Here, our 'ordinary mind' (*sems*) is the gross dualising **consciousness** (*rnam-shes*) whereas pure **awareness** (*rig-pa*) is free from the dualistic perceptions of subject and object. See **Awareness, Intrinsic Awareness,** and **Consciousness.**

Mind of Enlightenment *byang-chub sems*
See ***Bodhicitta*.**

Mindfulness *dran-pa*, Skt. *smṛti*
Mindfulness is the faculty which enables the **mind** to maintain its attention on a referent object, thus allowing for the development of familiarity with the object and also the ability to retain its imprint within memory for future recollection. Together with mental alertness, it is one of the two indispensable **mental factors** for the development of **calm abiding.** It is mindfulness which counteracts the arising of

forgetfulness, and forgetfulness is one of the greatest obstacles to a successful cultivation of **meditative stability**.

Monastic Community *dge-'dun*, Skt. *saṅgha*
In its classical Buddhist usage, the term refers mainly to the spiritual communities of ordained practitioners, both monks and nuns (Skt. *bhikṣu/ bhikṣuṇī*). The actual *saṅgha*, when viewed as an object of **refuge** in the context of the **Three Precious Jewels**, is a highly realised, 'supreme assembly' of those who have gained a direct insight into the true nature of **reality – emptiness** (i.e. those who have attained the path of insight).

Monastic Preceptor *mkhan-po*, Skt. *upādhyāya*
The term monastic preceptor specifically indicates one who presides over the monastic ordination ceremony of new monks. However, in some Tibetan traditions, the word '*khenpo*' (*mkhan-po*) suggests an ordained professor of Buddhist philosophy, in which case it is equivalent to the term *geshe* (*dge-shes*) in its later usage. See **Spiritual Friend**. The same term can also be used to refer to the abbot of a monastery, in which case it often takes the honorific form *mkhan rin-po-che*, the precious abbot.

Monastic Vows *sdom-pa*, Skt. *saṃvara*
See **Vows**.

Mother and Child Aspects of Reality *chos-nyid ma-bu*
The 'mother' and 'child' aspects of reality are those associated respectively with the **inner radiance** of the ground and the **inner radiance** of the path. See **Inner Radiance**.

Motivational Tendencies *'du-byas*, Skt. *saṃskāra*
See **Aggregate of Motivational Tendencies**.

Mount Gampodar *sgam-po-gdar-gyi ri-bo*
Mount *Gampodar* in *Dakpo* is the **treasure**-site (*gter-kha*) from which the cycle of the *Peaceful and Wrathful Deities: Natural Liberation through [Recognition of] Enlightened Intention* (*Zhi-khro dgongs-pa rang-grol*) was unearthed as **treasure** (*gter-ma*) by ***Karma Lingpa*** during the fourteenth century. See Gyurme Dorje's 'Brief Literary History'.

Mount Potālaka *ri-bo po-ta-la-ka*
Mount *Potālaka*, the abode of ***Avalokiteśvara***, is reputedly identified with a mountain in modern Karnataka State, South India, according to the classical Indian Buddhist tradition. However, in the Chinese Buddhist tradition, it is identified with the eastern island of *Putuo Shan* in the bay of *Hangzhou*.

Mount Sumeru *ri-rab*
Mount *Sumeru* is the *axis mundi* of Indian cosmology, the centre of the world. In terms of the Hindu, Jain, Buddhist and Bon pilgrimage traditions, it is widely identified with the sacred Mount *Kailash* in far-west Tibet. See **Four Continents and Eight Subcontinents**.

Nāgārjuna *klu-sgrub*
A pre-eminent second-century AD Indian scholar and the founder of the ***Madhyamaka*** philosophical school of Buddhist thought.

Natural Expression *rang-bzhin*, Skt. *svabhāva*
While the term *svabhāva* conveys other meanings, such as **self-identity** and **inherent existence** in the contexts of ***Madhyamaka*** philosophy and ***sūtra***-based literature in general, here in the specific terminology of the ***Nyingma*** school, it is rendered as 'natural expression' because it describes the dynamic of the **Buddha-body of Perfect Resource.** As such, it is contrasted with the essence – the dynamic of the **Buddha-body of Reality**, and compassionate energy – the dynamic of the **Buddha-body of Emanation.** The **Buddha-body of Perfect Resource** is said to be endowed with seven aspects of natural expression: 1) ripening in the nature of **reality**, 2) **buddha attributes** which are spontaneously present, 3) dimensionless **pristine cognition**, 4) intrinsic rather than external manifestation, 5) unqualified sameness, 6) freedom from single and multiple concepts, and 7) inseparability at all times. In the context of the present work, the term 'natural expression' also refers to the modalities of the twenty-eight wrathful *Īśvarī*, when contrasted with the '**natural purity**' (*gnas-dag*) of the **peaceful deities** and the '**natural transformation**' (*gnas-gyur*) of the **wrathful deities.**

Natural Liberation *rang-grol*
According to the terminology of the ***Nyingma*** school and in the context of the title of our text *Peaceful and Wrathful Deities: Natural Liberation through [Recognition of] Enlightened Intention* (*Zhi-khro dgongs-pa rang-grol*) the term 'natural liberation' refers to a natural process of recognition of the actual nature of the object, which is free from any form of renunciation or antidote. *Dudjom Rinpoche* explains the term 'natural liberation' (*rang-grol*) to mean that recognition or awareness is 'uncontrived by any antidote, and all that arises is liberated without reference to other liberating activities'. This accomplishment is a distinctive feature of the resultant **vehicles**, such as ***Atiyoga***, in contrast to the causal **vehicles**, in which the application of antidotes and **renunciation** are required.

Natural Pristine Cognition *rang-byung ye-shes*
This term denotes the presence of **intrinsic awareness which is pristine cognition** as an uncultivated seed, said to abide atemporally in the mental continua of all sentient beings. See **Intrinsic Awareness** and **Pristine Cognition**.

Natural Purity *gnas-su dag-pa/rnam-par dag-pa*
According to the terminology of the ***Nyingma*** school and in the context of the present work, the term 'natural purity' refers to the quiescent naturally abiding purity of the psycho-physical **aggregates, elemental properties**, and sensory and mental processes as represented by the forty-two **peaceful deities** of the ***maṇḍala.*** 'Natural purity' indicates the presence of the assembly of peaceful deities in the **continuum of the ground.** See Appendix Two.

Natural Transformation *gnas gyur-pa*
In contrast to the term '**natural purity**', the term 'natural transformation' refers to the transformative energies of the fifty-eight **wrathful deities** of the ***maṇḍala***, which bring about the active transformation of the conditioned **psycho-physical aggregates, elemental properties**, and sensory and mental processes. 'Natural transformation' indicates the presence of the assembly of **wrathful deities** in the **continuum of the ground**. See Appendix Two.

Naturally Manifest *rang-snang*
In the terminology of the ***Nyingma*** school, the term 'naturally manifest' or 'intrinsically manifest' (*rang-snang*) refers to the non-dual mode in which the natural radiance (*rang-gsal*) of **pristine cognition** (*ye-shes*) arises as **intrinsic awareness** (*rang-rig*). See **Intrinsic Awareness.** An important distinction is also made between the **Buddha-body of Perfect Resource,** which manifests naturally or intrinsically, and the **Buddha-body of Emanation,** which manifests extraneously (*gzhan-snang*), for the sake of sentient beings.

Negativity *sdig-pa*, Skt. *pāpa*
The negativity arising from the performance of **non-virtuous past actions,** which, along with negative **obscurations** (*sgrib*) and their **habitual tendencies** (*bag-chag*), all have their basis in **delusion, attachment,** and **aversion.** Negativity, therefore, generates a momentum towards a less favourable rebirth within **cyclic existence.**

New and Old/Ancient Translation Schools *gsar-ma-dang rnying-ma*
See **Nyingma.**

Nihilist *chad-lta-ba/mur-stug-pa*, Skt. *naiṣṭhika*
Nihilism and **eternalism** are the two extreme views which must, according to Buddhist thought, be transcended in order for any philosophical position to be considered well-founded. Nihilism in general refers to the view that denies the existence of objects, laws of **cause and effect** and the principle of **dependent origination.** However, based on one's metaphysical position with regard to the nature of **reality,** the criteria of what constitutes a denial of the existence of phenomena or the law of **cause and effect** may differ. In ancient India the nihilist view was characteristic of the *Carvāka* and *Bārhaspatya* materialist schools. See **Eternalist** and **Madhyamaka.**

Nine Sequences of the Vehicle *theg-pa'i rim-pa dgu*
See under **Nine Vehicles.**

Nine Vehicles *theg-pa dgu*, Skt. *navayāna*
In the ***Nyingma*** school, the Buddhist teachings are systematised according to a hierarchy of the three outer or causal **vehicles** (those of the **pious attendants, hermit buddhas** and ***bodhisattvas***), those of the three outer classes of ***tantra*** (***Kriyātantra, Ubhayatantra*** and ***Yogatantra***), and those of the three inner classes of ***tantra*** (***Mahāyoga, Anuyoga*** and ***Atiyoga***). See the nine individual entries.

Nirvāṇa *myang-'das*
Nirvāṇa (lit. 'state beyond sorrow') refers to the permanent cessation of all **suffering** and the **dissonant mental states** which cause and perpetuate suffering, along with all misapprehension with regard to the nature of **emptiness** (Skt. *śūnyatā*). *Nirvāṇa* is therefore the antithesis of **cyclic existence** (Skt. *saṃsāra*). Since it is through the misapprehension of the nature of **actual reality** (Skt. *dharmatā*) that our conscious states of delusion arise, a total elimination of these **dissonant mental states** can only be effected by generating a genuine insight into the true nature of **actual reality.** All the ***bodhisattva*** **paths** expounded in the ***sūtras*** and all the aspects of the **continuum of the path** which are expounded in the ***tantras*** are regarded as the means by which *nirvāṇa* might be attained. Classical Buddhist literature mentions three types of *nirvāṇa*: 1) *nirvāṇa* with residue, i.e. the initial state of *nirvāṇa* when the person is still dependent on his or her karmically conditioned psycho-physical **aggregates**

(*skandha*); 2) *nirvāṇa* without residue, i.e. an advanced state of *nirvāṇa* where the former aggregates have also been consumed within emptiness; and 3) non-abiding *nirvāṇa*, i.e. a state that has transcended both the extremes of conditioned **cyclic existence** and also the isolated peace or quiescence of *nirvāṇa*.

Non-virtuous Action *mi-dge-ba*, Skt. *akuśala*
See **Virtuous Action.**

Nucleus of the Sugata/Tathāgata *bde-gshegs snying-po / de-gshegs snying-po*, Skt. *sugatagarbha/tathāgatagarbha*
Both *Sugata* (One Who Has Gone to Bliss) and *Tathāgata* (One Who Has Thus Gone) are epithets of **Buddha.** However, the expression 'nucleus of the *sugata*' or 'nucleus of the *tathāgata*' refers to the seed of **buddha nature** present but uncultivated in the mental continuum of all sentient beings, and without which the attainment of **enlightenment** or **buddhahood** would be impossible. See **Buddha nature.**

Nyinda Choje *nyin-zla chos-rje*
The name of the son of ***Karma Lingpa***. See Gyurme Dorje's 'Brief Literary History'.

Nyinda Ozer *nyin-zla 'od-zer*
The name of a second-generation lineage-holder of ***Karma Lingpa***. See Gyurme Dorje's 'Brief Literary History'.

Nyingma *rnying-ma*
The oldest school of Tibetan Buddhism, based on the teaching traditions and texts introduced to Tibet during the earliest phase of Buddhist propagation, which coincided with the reigns of the Buddhist kings of the *Yarlung* dynasty in the eighth to ninth centuries. These traditions were introduced from India by ***Padmasambhava***, *Vimalamitra* and others, and maintained in Tibet by the twenty-five disciples of ***Padmasambhava***. The distinction between the old and new schools of Tibetan Buddhism is made on the basis of the interregnum which followed the persecution of Buddhism during the ninth century and preceded the second or later phase of Buddhist propagation when a further corpus of Buddhist literature was introduced from India by *Marpa*, *Drokmi Lotsāwa*, *Atiśa*, *Rinchen Zangpo* and others during the eleventh century. Lineages derived from the earlier phase and works translated before the interregnum are known as *Nyingma*, or the 'Ancient Translation school', in contrast to those which emerged thereafter and are known as *Sarma*, or the 'New Translation schools'.

Nyingthig *snying-thig*
The teachings known as the 'Innermost Spirituality' or 'Heart-Essence' (*snying-thig*) are the most important and essential pith instructions within the esoteric instructional class (*upadeśavarga*) of ***Atiyoga***, including the techniques of **Cutting through Resistance** and **All-surpassing Realisation.** Two distinct lineages of these teachings were introduced from India by ***Padmasambhava*** and *Vimalamitra*, and then transmitted with great secrecy in Tibet until the time of **Longchen Rabjampa** (fourteenth century), who integrated them in his *Four-part Innermost Spirituality* (*sNying-thig ya-bzhi*), from which time they were widely disseminated and practised. Diverse traditions of *Nyingthig* are practised within the **treasure** (*gter-ma*) traditions of the ***Nyingma*** school, the most influential in more recent times being the *Innermost Spirituality of Longchenpa* (*Klong-chen snying-thig*), which was revealed during the eighteenth century by *Rigdzin Jigme Lingpa* on the basis of his inspirational

visions of *Longchen Rabjampa*, and which has since become the most popular recension of *Nyingthig* teachings throughout Tibet.

Oath-bound Protectors *dam-can*
A class of **protectors** of the **sacred teachings** who are considered to have been originally indigenous Tibetan spirits, bound under an oath of allegiance to Buddhism by ***Padmasambhava*** during the eighth century.

Obscuration *sgrib-pa*, Skt. *āvaraṇa*
There are two main categories of obscurations (*sgrib-pa*), namely: the **dissonant mental states** (*nyon-sgrib*, Skt. *kleśāvaraṇa*) which are the obscurations to **liberation**, and the subtle propensities of these mental states as well as that of **fundamental ignorance**, which constitute the obscurations to **omniscience** (*shes-sgrib*, Skt. *jñeyā-varaṇa*). As the terms themselves indicate, the first category of obscurations obstruct the individual from gaining total freedom from **karmically** conditioned **cyclic existence**, and the latter from attaining a direct and non-deceptive realisation of all aspects of **reality**. The obscurations to **liberation** include not only the conscious states of our **deluded mind**, such as desire, hatred, jealousy, harmful intent, etc., but also the psychological **habitual tendencies** which are imprinted by these states, which serve as seeds for their continuity and recurrence. The second category of obscurations refers to the 'propensities for bewildering dualistic appearance' (*gnyis-snang khrul-pa'i bag-chags*), the subtle dispositions and latent tendencies which are deeply ingrained within an individual's psyche and which are the origins of our **dualistic** perceptions of the phenomenal world and of our own consciousness. A total overcoming of both obscurations (Tib. *sgrib-gnyis*) marks the attainment of **buddhahood.**

Obstacle-causing Spirits *bar-cad-kyi gdon*
The various classes of spirits (*gdon*) who cause obstacles to individuals and pollute the environment, which are said to impede certain localities, the physical body and human activities. In particular, there is an enumeration of eighteen such spirits to whom paediatric diseases are attributed by the Tibetan medical tradition.

Obstructing Forces *bgegs*, Skt. *vighna*
A class of forces which obstruct spiritual practice, but whose obstacles may be considered psychologically as cathartic in that their emergence may suggest that one's own negative **past actions** are ripening and therefore their negative impact is finally maturing and coming to an end. Often when **means for attainment** are performed in accordance with the ***tantras***, a ***torma*-offering** is dedicated to such obstructing forces prior to the commencement of the **generation stage** of meditation.

Oḍḍiyāna *o-rgyan*
Oḍḍiyāna, the birthplace of ***Padmasambhava***, is the name of an ancient kingdom, probably situated in the remote north-west of the Indian subcontinent, where a large corpus of tantric literature is said to have been propagated in the human world for the first time. The land of *Oḍḍiyāna* is associated with a number of great **accomplished masters** (*siddha*), including ***Padmasambhava***, *Kambalapāda*, and *Līlāvajra* in particular. On the basis of traditional Tibetan pilgrimage accounts, such as that written by *Orgyenpa Rinchenpel*, modern writers identify *Oḍḍiyāna* as having been in the region of the *Swat* valley in Pakistan. The Tibetan form of *Oḍḍiyāna*, *Orgyen*, is also by extension a name for ***Padmasambhava*** himself.

Offering *mchod-pa*, Skt. *pūjā*
In a Buddhist context, this refers to offerings made to the **meditational deity**, the **spiritual teacher** or other appropriate objects of veneration. In general, there are offerings associated with body, speech and mind. Thus, an offering can be of material substance such as flowers, scented water and food, or a verbal offering, such as the recitation of songs of praise, or a mental offering, such as the offering of the positive potentials which one may have accumulated as a result of having engaged in wholesome deeds beneficial to others. More specifically, the ***tantras*** identify four kinds of offering which are to be made, namely, outer, inner, secret and definitive offerings. The outer offerings of enjoyment (*phyi nyer-spyod-kyi mchod-pa*) are the eight associated with the eight offering goddesses, including water for the mouth, water for the feet, flowers, incense, light, perfume, food, and sound, as well as song, dance, and meditation. Inner offerings of commitment (*nang dam-rdzas-kyi mchod-pa*) refer to the pure essences of semen, blood and flesh, transformed through the *yoga* of the **energy channels**, currents and **seminal points** within the **subtle body**. Secret offerings are those of sexual union and 'liberation' (*gsang-ba sbyor-sgrol-gyi mchod-pa*) related to the esoteric rites and practices which transform the **five poisons** into the five **pristine cognitions**, and definitive offerings are those of great sameness (*de-kho-na-nyid mnyam-pa chen-po'i mchod-pa*), namely the union of bliss and **emptiness**.

Omniscience *thams-cad mkhyen-pa-nyid*, Skt. *sarvajñatā*
In a Buddhist context the word is reserved only for the all-knowing **pristine cognition** of the **buddhas**. Although the original Sanskrit and Tibetan terms, like their English equivalent, do carry with them the literal connotation of all-knowingness, the principal meaning of the term should be understood in terms of a direct and simultaneous perception of the dual aspects of **reality**, i.e. of the phenomenal aspects (valid only within the relative framework of our ordinary perceptions) and their ultimate nature, **emptiness**. In other words the term refers primarily to a non-conceptual simultaneous perception of the **two truths** within a single mental act.

One-day Vows *bsnyen-gnas-kyi sdom-pa*, Skt. *upavāsasaṃvara*
See **Prātimokṣa** and **Vows**.

Pacification *zhi-ba'i las*, Skt. *śāntikriyā*
See under **Four Aspects of Enlightened Activity**.

Padma Family *padma'i rigs*, Skt. *padmakula*
One of the **five enlightened families** (*pañcakula*) into which the **meditational deities** of the **Buddha-body of Perfect Resource** are subdivided. The deities of the *Padma* family include the peaceful **buddhas** *Amitābha* and *Pāṇḍaravāsinī*, and the corresponding wrathful aspects *Padma Heruka* and *Padmakrodheśvarī*. See Appendix Two.

Padmākara *padma'i 'byung-gnas*
See **Padmasambhava**.

Padmasambhava, *padma sam-bha-va*
Padmasambhava, also generally known as *Guru Rinpoche* and *Padmākara*, is revered as the master from **Oḍḍiyāna** who, along with **Śāntarakṣita** and King ***Trisong Detsen***, formally established Buddhism in Tibet during the eighth century. In particular, he is renowned for his suppression and conversion of malevolent

spirits and hostile non-Buddhist forces, as well as for introducing to Tibet many oral transmissions and texts of ***Mahāyoga*** and ***Atiyoga***, including the teachings contained in our text, the *Peaceful and Wrathful Deities: Natural Liberation through [Recognition of] Enlightened Intention* (*Zhi-khro dgongs-pa rang-grol*). To practitioners of the ***Nyingma*** school, and all those who follow the practices of the ***Nyingma*** **lineages**, he is revered as a 'second **buddha**', and there are many systems of meditation based on the visualisation of his rainbow-like form. Tibetan literature contains a number of biographical accounts, which describe his life in the form of eight or twelve different manifestations. See Gyurme Dorje's 'Brief Literary History'.

Palace *pho-brang/gzhal-yas-khang*, Skt. *vimāna*
See under **Maṇḍala.**

Paradise *zhings-khams*, Skt. *buddhakṣetra*
See **Buddha Field.**

Past Actions *las*, Skt. *karma*
The technical term '*karma*' refers to the dynamic relationship between actions and their consequences. It includes in its causal aspect both the actual actions (physical, verbal and mental) and the psychological imprints and tendencies created within the mind by such actions. After the performance of an action a causal chain is maintained within the mental continuum which continues through the present and successive rebirths. Such a karmic potential is activated when it interacts with appropriate circumstances and conditions, thus leading to the fruition of its effects. This dynamic of past actions has two main features: 1) one never experiences the consequences of an action not committed; and 2) the potential of an action once committed is never lost unless obviated by specific remedies. It is also worth bearing in mind that the idea of 'past actions' in Buddhism cannot be equated with the notion of causality as understood in a strictly deterministic sense.

Path *lam*, Skt. *mārga*
The means of spiritual practice (view, meditation, conduct and so forth) by which the resultant goal of any of the **nine vehicles** might be attained.

Peaceful and Wrathful Deities *zhi-khro*
See Appendix Two.

Penetrative Insight *lhag-mthong*, Skt. *vipaśyanā*
This is an analytical meditative state, penetrating the nature, characteristics or function of the chosen object of **meditation,** which is accompanied by physical and mental suppleness and generated on the basis of mental tranquillity or **calm abiding.** The object of such an insight can be mundane, such as the topics of **impermanence** and **suffering,** or supramundane, such as **emptiness,** the ultimate nature of **reality.** This 'penetrative insight' can be attained only in union with **calm abiding,** and many **meditation** manuals state that the **realisation** of '**calm abiding**' is an essential prerequisite for the cultivation of 'penetrative insight'. However, in **Unsurpassed *Yogatantra*** there exist advanced techniques which enable practitioners to attain '**calm abiding**' and 'penetrative insight' simultaneously.

Perception *'du-shes*, Skt. *saṃjñā*
See under **Aggregate of Perceptions.**

Perfection of Discriminative Awareness *sher-phyin*, Skt. *prajñāpāramitā*
Often translated also as 'perfection of wisdom', the Sanskrit word *prajñāpāramitā* refers to the sixth of the **six perfections** (Skt. *ṣaṭpāramitā*) which are cultivated by ***bodhisattvas***. The term 'perfection of discriminative awareness' has three different applications: firstly, it may refer to the resultant, perfected discriminative awareness (*'bras-bu sher-phyin*) of a **buddha**, which is totally non-dual, free of all **obscurations**, and perceives spontaneously in a single mental act the dual aspects of all phenomena. See **Two Truths**. Secondly, it may refer to the ***bodhisattva paths*** which lead to the above perfection of discriminative awareness (*lam sher-phyin*), blending together at the most profound level the discriminative awareness of **emptiness** (*śūnyatā*) and the **skilful means** of great **compassion** (*mahākaruṇā*). Thirdly, it may denote the literature of the *Prajñāpāramitā* subdivision of the ***sūtras*** of the **Greater Vehicle**, which outline the essential aspects of those paths and results (*gzhung sher-phyin*). Iconographically, *Prajñāpāramitā* is depicted in the form of a female **meditational deity** and the Sanskrit ***sūtras*** themselves are invariably entitled *Transcendent Lady who is the Perfection of Discriminative Awareness* (*Bhagavatīprajñāpāramitā*). See also under **Discriminative Awareness**.

Perfection Stage *rdzogs-rim*, Skt. *sampannakrama*
Following the meditative generation of the form of the **meditational deity** and an approximation of the **pristine cognition** of the **meditational deity** during the **generation stage** (Skt. *utpattikrama*), the perfection stage employs techniques for controlling the **energy channels**, **vital energies** and **seminal points** within the practitioner's transmuted body. The purpose is to make manifest the **inner radiance** induced by the ever-deepening realisation of the four kinds of **emptiness** or 'dissolution stages' and of the **coemergent pristine cognition** induced by the **four delights**. The factor that marks the transition from **generation stage** to perfection stage is the ***yogin***'s ability to draw the **vital energies** (Skt. *vāyu*) into the **central channel**. See also **Great Perfection**.

Perfections *pha-rol-du phyin-pa*
See under **Six Perfections**.

Pious Attendant *nyan-thos*, Skt. *śrāvaka*
The practitioners of the **Lesser Vehicle** (*hīnayāna*) include both pious attendants and **hermit buddhas** (Skt. *pratyekabuddha*). The primary differences between them are the focus and modalities of their practice on the path towards **liberation** from **cyclic existence**. The pious attendant places greater emphasis on destroying the mistaken belief in personal identity (*pudgala*) by overcoming the primary and secondary **dissonant mental states**, while the **hermit buddha** additionally comes to realise that objective phenomena are devoid of **inherent existence**. Characteristically, the pious attendants depend on oral instructions when both receiving teachings and when giving guidance to others on the path. See **Hermit Buddha**.

Posture of the Bodhisattvas *sems-dpa'i skyil-krung*, Skt. *sattvaparyaṅka*
Also known as the posture of royal ease (*mahārājalīlāsana*), this is the posture in which seated male and female ***bodhisattvas*** are commonly depicted iconographically or visualised in meditation in which the right leg is extended and the left leg drawn in. The extended right leg and foot symbolises the abandonment of all negative defects, and the drawn in left leg symbolises the deity's understanding and cultivation of all positive attributes. As the combined purity of the deity's

compassionate **skilful means** (extended right leg) and **discriminative awareness** (drawn in left leg), this posture also represents the abandonment of the two extremes of **cyclic existence** and ***nirvāṇa***.

Posture of the Lion *seng-ge'i 'dug-stangs*, Skt. *siṃhāsana*
The posture of the lion is the posture assumed by ***Śākyamuni Buddha*** at the time of his passing, lying on the right side with his right arm bent at the elbow and his palm supporting the head.

Posture of Royal Ease *rgyal-chen rol-pa'i skyil-krung*, Skt. *mahārājalīlāsana*
See under **Posture of the Bodhisattvas.**

Power *stobs*, Skt. *bala*
In general, spiritual power is classified, along with **discriminative awareness** and **compassion**, as one of the three principal attributes to be cultivated by ***bodhisattvas***, symbolised in this case by the form of the ***Bodhisattva Vajrapāṇi***. More specifically, ***bodhisattvas*** cultivate ten spiritual powers (*daśabala*) with respect to their reflections, higher aspirations, practice, **discriminative awareness**, aspirational prayers, diverse **vehicles**, modes of conduct, emanational abilities, **enlightenment**, and teaching of the sacred doctrine. Distinct from these are the so-called ten powers of the **buddhas** (*daśatathāgatabala*), which are all included among the categories of **buddha attributes. Buddhas** are said to be endowed with spiritual power because they have: (i) the power of knowing the positive and negative contingencies of all things, (ii) the power of knowing the maturation of **past actions**, (iii) the power of knowing diverse volitions, (iv) the power of knowing diverse **sensory spectra**, (v) the power of knowing those who are of supreme ability and those who are not, (vi) the power of knowing all spiritual paths – wherever they lead, (vii) the power of **omniscience** with respect to **meditative concentration, liberation, meditative stability, meditative equipoise,** and purification of **dissonant mental states,** (viii) the power of recollecting past abodes, (ix) the power of knowing where consciousness is transferred at the time of death and rebirth, and (x) the power of knowing that the entire flow of corrupt **past actions** has ceased.

Prahevajra *dga'-rab rdo-rje*
More commonly known in the Tibetan form *Garab Dorje*, *Prahevajra* is regarded as the first human **lineage holder** of ***Atiyoga***.

Prāsaṅgika *thal-'gyur-ba*
See **Madhyamaka.**

Prātimokṣa *so-sor thar-pa*
An individual's practice of ethical discipline which acts as a firm foundation for the aspirant's spiritual endeavour whilst on the path towards the attainment of **liberation** from **cyclic existence.** There are eight types of *prātimokṣa* vows: 1) **one-day vows** (Skt. *upavāsa/upavāsī*), a lay person's vow of abstinence, taken only for a twenty-four hour period, from killing, sexual misconduct, stealing, lying, alcohol, frivolous activities, eating after lunch, and using high seats or beds; 2–3) the five vows of a lay man and a lay woman (Skt. *upāsaka/ upāsikā*) which are not to kill, lie, steal, be intoxicated, or commit sexual misconduct; 4–5) the vows of the novice monk and novice nun (Skt. *śrāmaṇera/ śrāmaṇerikā*); 6) the vows of a probationary nun (Skt. *śiksamāṇa*); 7) the 253 vows of a fully ordained monk (Skt. *bhikṣu*); and 8) the 364 vows maintained by fully ordained nuns (Skt. *bhiksuṇī*). *Prātimokṣa*

literally means 'individual **liberation**', or the initial stage of release from the impulsive force of **non-virtuous** habits. '*Prāti*' means 'individually' or 'first', and '*mokṣa*', 'release', 'freedom', or '**liberation**'. See also under **Vows.**

Preceptor *mkhan-po*, Skt. *upādhyāya*
See **Monastic Preceptor.**

Precious Jewels *dkon-mchog*, Skt. *ratna*
See under **Three Precious Jewels.**

Preliminary Practices *sngon-'gro*
The preliminary practices are those undertaken by an aspiring practitioner of the ***tantras***, prior to engaging in the main practices of the **generation** and **perfection stages** of meditation. There are both outer, or common, preliminaries, and inner, or uncommon, preliminaries. The former are the four analytical meditations which turn the mind of the practitioner away from worldly distractions and towards the **sacred teachings**, namely those focusing: on the nature of the precious opportunities afforded by human birth; on death and **impermanence** (*anitya*); on the dynamics of **past actions** (*karma*) and their consequences; and on the **sufferings** of beings within **cyclic existence** (*saṃsāra*). The latter are the five purificatory practices, each of which is performed one hundred thousand times, namely: the taking of **refuge** in the **Three Precious Jewels**, in conjunction with the act of **prostration** (which purifies pride); the cultivation of the altruistic intention to attain enlightenment for the sake of others, in conjunction with the recitation of the appropriate verses (which purifies envy and mundane ambition); the recitation of ***Vajrasattva***'s **Hundred-syllable Mantra** (which purifies **aversion**); the **offering** of the ***maṇḍala*** (which purifies **attachment**); and the cultivation of union with the enlightened attributes of the **spiritual teacher** (*guruyoga*), in conjunction with the appropriate ***mantra*** recitation (which purifies **delusion**). See Chapters 1 and 2.

Primordial Purity *ka-dag*
See **Spontaneous Presence.**

Pristine Cognition *ye-shes*, Skt. *jñāna*
The modality of **buddha-mind.** Although all **sentient beings** possess the potential for actualising pristine cognition within their mental continuum, the psychological confusions and deluded tendencies which defile the **mind** obstruct the natural expression of these inherent potentials, making them appear instead as aspects of mundane **consciousness** (*vijñāna*). Buddhist literature mentions five types of pristine cognition which are the quintessential perfected states of our own mental faculties and which are identified with the five male **buddhas** of the ***maṇḍala*** of **Peaceful and Wrathful Deities.** See Appendix Two. The pristine cognition of **reality's expanse** (*dharmadhātujñāna*) is the natural purity of the **aggregate of consciousness,** free from **delusion**; the mirror-like pristine cognition (*ādarśajñāna*) is the mind to which all the objects of the five senses appear spontaneously as in a mirror, it is the natural purity of the **aggregate of form,** free from **aversion**; the pristine cognition of sameness (*samatājñāna*) is the mind that experiences the three different types of feelings (good, bad and indifferent) as of one taste, it is the natural purity of the **aggregate of feeling,** free from pride; the pristine cognition of discernment (*pratyavekṣaṇajñāna*) is the mind that accurately identifies names and forms, it is the natural purity of the **aggregate of perceptions,** free from **attachment**; and the

pristine cognition of accomplishment (*kṛtyupasthānajñāna*) is the mind that accords with awakened activities and their purposes, it is the natural purity of the **aggregate of motivational tendencies**, free from envy and self-centred ambition.

Propensities *bag-chags*, Skt. *vāsanā*
See **Habitual Tendencies.**

Prostration *phyag-'tshal-ba*
A common gesture of reverence in the practice of Tibetan Buddhism. During the **preliminary practices** (*sngon-'gro*) of the ***tantras***, the act of paying homage through prostration is undertaken, in conjunction with the recitation of the prayer of **refuge**, as a means of reducing and eliminating **pride.**

Protectors of the [Sacred] Teachings *chos-skyong/srung-ma*, Skt. *dharmapāla*
There are two main categories of protectors: 1) supramundane protectors, such as *Mahākāla*, *Ekajaṭī*, *Dorje Lekpa*, and *Rāhula*, who are the **wrathful** manifestations of **enlightened** beings; and 2) worldly protectors, many of whom were originally **malevolent forces** who were subdued by **accomplished masters** such as ***Padmasambhava*** and then assigned to protect the teachings. In both cases their activity is to protect the **sacred teachings** and its sincere practitioners from obstacles.

Provisional Meaning *drang-don*, Skt. *neyārtha*
See under **Definitive Meaning.**

Pure Illusory Body *dag-pa'i sgyu-lus*
See **Illusory Body.**

Pure Realm
See **Buddha Field.**

Pure Realm of the Sky-farers *dag-pa'i mkha'-spyod-kyi zhing*, Skt. *khecarīkṣetra*
The pure realm or fields of the sky-farers represents the level on which the **awareness-holders** (*vidyādhara*) are said to abide.

Pure Vision/Perception *dag-pa'i snang-ba*
In the terminology of the ***Nyingma*** school, the expression 'pure vision' frequently refers to a type of revelation, through which **meditational deities** or **accomplished masters** of the past appear in a vision to impart their teachings. This mode of pure vision, therefore, has some affinity with the revelations of the **treasures** (*gter-ma*). More generally, 'pure vision' denotes the purity of perception of **meditational deities**, symbolically represented by their respective ***maṇḍalas***, which is cultivated in the **generation stage** of meditation. However, the Tibetan equivalent *dag-pa'i snang-ba* is also used colloquially to mean a 'positive perspective' or 'positive outlook' on life.

Purification *sbyong-ba*, Skt. *śodhana*
The verb 'to purify' has two distinct meanings in a Buddhist context. Firstly, purification can refer simply to the purification of **non-virtuous** habits or **dissonant mental states**, etc., in which the objects of purification are, without qualification, totally eradicated from one's mental continuum. In the second meaning, which arises more in the context of ***tantra***, the term 'purification' has rather different implications. Here, the significance of the word is understood in terms of transmutation from an impure, polluted state into an unstained, purified state. This process

is exemplified by the practices related to *Carrying the Three Buddha-bodies on to the Path* (*sKu-gsum lam-'khyer*). In this context, the phases of ordinary death, **intermediate state**, and rebirth when experienced choicelessly as a result of one's **past actions**, are the bases of purification. The meditations on the **Three Buddha-bodies** are the purifying paths and the accomplishments of the **Buddha-body of Reality**, the **Buddha-body of Perfect Resource**, and the **Buddha-body of Emanation** are the purified results.

Purification of the Lower Realms *ngan-song sbyong-ba*, Skt. *durgatipariśodhana*
This is the *Tantra of the Purification of the Lower Realms* (*Sarvadurgatipari-śodhanatantra*), which is recited to assist the deceased in avoiding the pitfalls of rebirth as a sentient being trapped in the three **lower existences**.

Quiescence *zhi-ba*, Skt. *śānti*
This is a synonym for the quiescent state of ***nirvāṇa***, in which all **dissonant mental states** and misconceptions concerning **actual reality** have ended, and rebirth in **cyclic existence** no longer occurs. As such, it is the antithesis of the rebirth process (*srid-pa*). See also under **nirvāṇa**.

Rainbow Light [Body] *'ja'-lus*
The appearance of rainbow light at the time of death is indicative of the deceased's adeptness in the practices of the **Great Perfection** (*rdzogs-pa chen-po*) or in certain other **perfection stage** practices. There are many incidents recorded in Tibetan biographical literature concerning the attainment of the rainbow-light body at the time of death. On occasions when this attainment is residual, the physical body will shrink dramatically or vanish into light, leaving only the hair or fingernails of the deceased's physical form behind. However, when there is no residue, the entire physical form will vanish into light. In these latter cases, the body of rainbow light (*'ja'-lus*) or body of light (*'od-kyi sku*) is equivalent to the attainment of the **Buddha-body** of Great Transformation (Skt. *mahāsaṃkrāntikāya*, Tib. *'pho-ba chen-po'i sku*). See **Buddha-body**.

Ratna Family *rin-chen rigs*, Skt. *ratnakula*
One of the **five enlightened families** (*pañcakula*) into which the **meditational deities** of the **Buddha-body of Perfect Resource** are subdivided. The deities of the *Ratna* family include the peaceful **buddhas** *Ratnasambhava* and *Māmakī* and the corresponding wrathful aspects *Ratna Heruka* and *Ratnakrodheśvarī*. See Appendix Two.

Realisation *rtogs-pa*, Skt. *adhigama*
This refers to the spiritual experiences that a practitioner gains through insight into and transformation of the mental continuum whilst on the path to **enlightenment**, and to the resultant attainment of **liberation** or **buddhahood**.

Reality *chos-nyid*, Skt. *dharmatā*
In our text the term 'reality' has been used interchangeably with 'actual reality'. See **Actual Reality**.

Reality's Expanse *chos-dbyings*, Skt. *dharmadhātu*
See **Expanse of [Actual] Reality**.

Refuge *skyabs-'gro*, Skt. *śaraṇagamana*
This term in Buddhist usage indicates the act of entrusting one's spiritual growth and well-being to the **Three Precious Jewels**. The **Three Precious Jewels** are the

objects of refuge, and the nature of the refuge sought from each of the three differs. In the **Buddha**, the fully **enlightened** teacher, guidance on a correct path to **buddahood** is sought; in the **sacred teachings**, the **realisations** of the path are sought; and in the **monastic/supreme community** (*saṅgha*) perfect companionship on the path to **buddhahood** is sought. The successful taking of refuge in the **Three Precious Jewels** requires the following two conditions: a) a genuine anxiety in the face of the potential for future **suffering** and b) a genuine confidence in the capacity of the **Three Precious Jewels** to offer protection from these potential **sufferings**. In the context of our text, the act of going for refuge constitutes the first of the five uncommon **preliminary practices** (*thun-min sngon-'gro*). Here, the three levels of refuge are recognised: the outer refuge (*phyi'i skyabs-'gro*), which is taken in the **Buddha**, the **sacred teachings** and the **monastic community**; the inner refuge (*nang-gi skyabs-'gro*), which is taken in the **spiritual teacher**, the **meditational deity** and the ***ḍākinī*** and the secret refuge (*gsang-ba'i skyabs-'gro*), which is taken in the **Buddha-body of Reality**, the **Buddha-body of Perfect Resource** and the **Buddha-body of Emanation**.

Relative Truth *kun-rdzob bden-pa*, Skt. *samvṛtisatya*
See under **Two Truths**.

Relics *gdung/ring-srel*
See under **Bone Relics**.

Renunciation *nges-'byung/spang-ba*, Skt. *naiṣkramya/prahāṇa*
The English term renunciation translates both the Tibetan terms *nges-'byung* and *spang-ba*. In the former sense, renunciation refers to ***Śākyamuni Buddha***'s renunciation of the household life and it is defined as a mental attitude free from impulsive clinging to all worldly attributes such as wealth, fame, position and the thought of a favourable rebirth in a future life. It is only on the basis of such an attitude that the practitioner can spontaneously generate a genuine wish to be free from **cyclic existence**. Hence the real meaning of renunciation lies not just in mere physical separation from objects of desire but more importantly in a quality of mental **liberation** which is free from even the slightest degree of craving for mundane values. The Tibetan word *nges-'byung* literally means a 'definite emergence', indicating a definite emergence from the bonds of our normally narrow-minded attachment to worldly pleasures. In the latter sense (Skt. *prahāṇa*), renunciation refers to the four correct trainings which are included among the thirty-seven aspects of the path to enlightenment (*bodhipakṣikadharma*) cultivated by those aspiring to enlightenment, namely: 1) to not develop **non-virtuous actions** which have not arisen, 2) to renounce non-virtuous actions which have arisen, 3) to develop **virtuous actions** which have not arisen, and 4) to not renounce virtuous actions which have arisen.

Rinpoche *rin-po-che*
This term literally means 'high in value or esteem', and in ordinary language indicates a precious jewel. By extension, in Tibetan Buddhism, the term has come to refer to an incarnate master who is 'high in value' or 'most precious'. Accordingly, the title '*Rinpoche*' is widely used by Tibetans to refer to any incarnate **spiritual teacher**. See ***Tulku***.

Rite for Affirmation of Vows *'bogs-chog*
The rite for the affirmation of vows is that through which the ability to fulfil

and restore impaired **commitments** taken in association with the ***tantras*** is transferred.

Rites of Enrichment, Pacification, Subjugation and Wrath *zhi rgyas dbang drag-gi las*
See **Four Aspects of Enlightened Activity.**

Rites of 'Liberation' *sgrol-ba*
The rites of 'liberation' refers to practices, only to be applied by **accomplished masters** who have attained proficiency in **consciousness transference**, which end the life of a hostile being who is wholly intent on vicious negative activities. The consciousness of the harmful being is compassionately transferred to a realm of higher rebirth thus freeing him or her from the inevitable consequences of their future and **past actions.**

Ritual Officiant *las-mkhan*, Skt. *karmācārya*
The ritual officiant is the one who leads the students into the presence of a **spiritual teacher** at the time when **empowerment** is conferred, covering the students' eyes with a red blindfold and placing a flower and a ***vajra*** in their hands.

Ritual Service *bsnyen-pa*, Skt. *sevā*
See **Four Aspects of Ritual Service and Means for Attainment.**

Rosary *phreng-ba*, Skt. *mālā*
The Tibetan rosary generally has one hundred and eight beads, and is used for the counting of ***mantra*** recitations.

Rudra *ru-dra*
As expounded, for example, in the *Sūtra which Gathers All Intentions* (*mDo dgongs-pa 'dus-pa*) and later **treasure** (*gter-ma*) revelations as well, *Rudra* is the embodiment of rampant egohood, a being who assumed a powerful malevolent form, having misapplied the practice of the ***tantras*** in a previous life, and who was consequently subdued by the **wrathful** means of the **buddhas *Hayagrīva*** or ***Mahottara Heruka***. The metaphor illustrates the origins of the outer attributes of the **wrathful deities**, who are in essence the **peaceful deities**, but who adopted the outer terrifying characteristics of *Rudra* in order to actively confront deep-seated egohood. The metaphor illustrates that the **wrathful deities** represent the spontaneous process of transformation of the outer deluded state to its actual or enlightened nature.

Sacred Substances *rdzas*, Skt. *dravya*
According to the ***tantras***, ritual substances or articles are employed in order to symbolise the bond between the practitioner and the **meditational deity** and in some cases these actually symbolise the **meditational deities** or their attributes. In the context of an **empowerment** ceremony, symbolic implements, such as the ***vajra*** and bell, or diadem, vase and so on are known as sacred substances of empowerment (*dbang-rdzas*).

[Sacred] Teachings *[dam-pa'i] chos*, Skt. *[sad]dharma*
The Sanskrit term *dharma* carries a very broad range of meanings, derived from the Sanskrit word *dhṛ*, meaning 'to hold'. The Tibetan equivalent *chos* literally means 'change' or 'transformation', and refers both to the process of spiritual transformation and to the transformed result. Ten classical definitions of *dharma* are given

by *Vasubandhu* in his *Rational System of Exposition* (*Vyākhyāyukti*), namely: phenomenon, path leading to enlightenment, attainment of enlightenment, object of consciousness, merit, living thing, scripture, material thing, regulation, and spiritual tradition. In terms of the spiritual tradition of Buddhism, the term refers specifically to the second of the **Three Precious Jewels** (Skt. *triratna*), i.e. to the sacred teachings. See **Transmission.**

Sakya *sa-skya*
One of the four principal schools of Tibetan Buddhism, named after a monastery of the same name which was founded by *Khon Konchok Gyalpo* in the eleventh century in western Tibet, at a site which has a slightly whitish rock surface. *Sakya* literally means 'pale earth'. The widespread influence of the early *Sakya* masters soon evolved into a whole new school of Tibetan Buddhism, the school reaching its full maturity during the time of the *Sachen Gongma Nga*, the five great founders of *Sakya*, and in particular through the influence of perhaps the greatest of these, *Sakya Paṇḍita Kunga Gyaltsen.* The essence of the *Sakya* school's thought and practice is enshrined in the sets of instructions called 'the path and its fruit' (*lam-'bras*).

Śākyamuni Buddha *śākya thub-pa*
Our historical **buddha,** who is considered to have been the fourth supreme **Buddha-body of Emanation** to have appeared during this particular **aeon** (in which context ***Maitreya*** is regarded as the fifth or future **buddha**). The *Buddha Śākyamuni* is considered by historians to have lived in the sixth century BC and is credited, according to Buddhist tradition, as the progenitor of all the contemporary Buddhist lineages relating to the ***sūtras*** and certain of those related to the ***tantras***, and for the establishment of the early Buddhist **monastic community**.

Śākyasiṃha *śākya senge*
An epithet of ***Śākyamuni Buddha***.

Sal Tree *shing sā-la*
A tall tree (*Vatica robusta*) indigenous to the Indian subcontinent, with wide branches and thick foliage.

Samantabhadra *kun-tu bzang-po*
The male **buddha** *Samantabhadra* is the foremost figure in the assembly of the forty-two **peaceful deities.** It is important to differentiate the male **buddha** *Samantabhadra* from the male ***bodhisattva Samantabhadra.*** See below and Appendix Two.

Samantabhadra (bodhisattva) *byang-sems kun-tu bzang-po*
The male ***bodhisattva*** *Samantabhadra* is one of the four outer male ***bodhisattvas*** among the forty-two **peaceful deities.** See Appendix Two.

SAMAYA ***rgya rgya rgya***
Certain chapters of the present work end with these words of admonition that the **seal** of **commitment** (*samayamudrā*), through which **buddha-mind** is secured, is to be resolutely applied by those who receive the teaching. See **Seal** and **Commitment.**

Saṃsāra *'khor-ba*
See **Cyclic Existence.**

Śāntarakṣita *zhi-ba'i 'tsho / mkhan-po bo-dhi-sattva*
A **monastic preceptor** and exponent of ***Madhyamaka*** philosophy from *Zahor*, who officiated at the great *Nālandā* Monastic University in India before his arrival in Tibet at the invitation of King ***Trisong Detsen*** during the eighth century. In Tibet, he was responsible together with King ***Trisong Detsen*** and ***Padmasambhava*** for the construction of *Samye* Monastery, the first Buddhist monastery to be built in Tibet. King ***Trisong Detsen***, ***Padmasambhava*** and *Śāntarakṣita* jointly established Buddhism as the state religion of Tibet. *Śāntarakṣita* is the author of a highly influential encyclopaedic work on classical Indian philosophies entitled *Tattvasaṃgraha* and a short, but influential, work on *Madhyamaka* known as *Ornament of the Middle Way* (*Madhyamakālaṃkāra*).

Seal *phyag-rgya*, Skt. *mudrā*
According to the ***sūtras***, the word 'seal' denotes a secure **realisation** of **emptiness**. In the ***tantras*** it refers to the various hand-gestures which accompany the recitation of ***mantras***, and by extension refers also to the **meditational deity**'s symbolic hand-emblem (*phyag-mtshan*) – the ***vajra***, bell and so forth. In this context therefore the seals are the resonance of **buddha-body**. Furthermore, in the ***Yogatantras***, in particular, there are four seals which secure the aspects of mundane **consciousness** (*vijñāna*) as their corresponding aspects of **pristine cognition** (*jñāna*): among them, the **great seal** (*mahāmudrā*) of **buddha-body** secures the **ground-of-all consciousness** (*ālayavijñāna*) as the mirror-like **pristine cognition** (*ādarśajñāna*); the seal of the **sacred teachings** (*dharmamudrā*) of **buddha-speech** secures the mental consciousness (*manovijñāna*) as the **pristine cognition** of discernment (*pratyavekṣaṇajñāna*); the seal of commitment (*samayamudrā*) of **buddha-mind** secures the deluded consciousness (*kliṣṭamanovijñāna*) as the **pristine cognition** of sameness (*samatājñāna*); and the seal of action (*karmamudrā*) of **buddha-activity** secures the five sensory consciousnesses (*pañcadvāravijñāna*) as the **pristine cognition** of accomplishment (*kṛtyupasthānajñāna*). Then, according to ***Mahāyoga***, in the **perfection stage** of **meditation**, when the practices of sexual yoga (*sbyor-ba*) are applied in order to actualise the union of **great bliss** (*mahāsukha*) and **emptiness**, the term 'action seal' (*karmamudrā*) denotes an actual sexual partner, while the term 'seal of pristine cognition' (*jñānamudrā*), by contrast, denotes a mentally visualised consort. For a description of the meditative tradition known as *Mahāmudrā* see under **Great Seal**.

Secret Mantra *gsang-sngags*, Skt. *guhyamantra*
See **Mantra**.

Seed-syllable *yig-'bru*, Skt. *bījākṣara*
Generally this refers to Sanskrit syllables or letters visualised as the quintessential basis from which arise the forms of **meditational deities** in the practices of the **Vehicle of Indestructible Reality**. Often these letters or syllables are the first letter of the name of the deities themselves, or syllables or letters that are associated with specific **enlightened families**. So, for example, in the case of many of the deities belonging to the ***Vajra*** **family** of *Akṣobhya*, they are visualised as arising from the letter HŪṂ, while for deities belonging to the ***Padma*** **family**, the letter ĀḤ is often utilised, and so on.

Self *bdag-nyid*, Skt. *ātman*
For an introduction to the concept of 'self' as it applies to our text, see the Introductory Commentary by HH the Dalai Lama. See also under **Selflessness**.

Self-empowerment *rang-dbang*, Skt. *svādhiṣṭhāna*
A spiritual practice in which the **four empowerments** are received directly by the meditator from a visualised **spiritual teacher**, as presented in Chapter 2 of the present work. See **Empowerment.**

Self-identity *rang-bzhin*, Skt. *svabhāva*
This term refers to the **inherent existence** which the **eternalist** philosophies of Hinduism and Jainism project onto phenomena. Elsewhere, the Sanskrit term *ātman* (Tib. *bdag*), referring to the notion of an independent or substantial self, has also sometimes been translated as 'self-identity'.

Selflessness *bdag-med*, Skt. *nairātmya*
Selflessness in Buddhist philosophy is understood to imply the lack of **inherent existence** both in the personality and in physical and mental phenomena. The **Lesser Vehicle** schools such as *Vaibhāṣika* and *Sautrāntika* expound the doctrine of selflessness only in terms of personal identity. They propound that selflessness refers to the absence of an independently existing 'self' or 'I', emphasising that the self is neither substantial nor self-sufficient. Nowhere among the aggregates of the person, either individually, collectively, or even in their continuity can one find a substantial or solid being. Material objects are nothing but a series of indivisible atomic particles, and consciousness is nothing but a series of indivisible time moments. However, the ***Cittamātra*** and ***Madhyamaka*** schools extend this notion of selflessness to embrace all physical and mental phenomena. All such phenomena are equated with **emptiness** (*śūnyatā*), and these **Greater Vehicle** philosophical schools therefore speak of both the selflessness of persons (*pudgalanairātmya*) and the selflessness of phenomena (*dharmanairātmya*). Nevertheless, substantial philosophical differences exist between the two **Greater Vehicle** schools in their views on what it is that is being negated by the doctrine of **emptiness.**

Seminal Point *thig-le*, Skt. *bindu*
The Tibetan term *thig-le* conveys a wide range of meanings. It refers to: 1) the pure white/male and red/female **generative essences** of the body, which along with the **energy channels** and **vital energies** flowing through the channels, form an important aspect of human physiology according to the ***tantras*** and related medical traditions; 2) a synonym for the **Buddha-body of Reality** (*dharmakāya*), known as the 'unique seminal point' (*thig-le nyag-gcig*); and 3) the seminal points of light which appear during the **All-surpassing Realisation** (*thod-rgal*) practices of the **Great Perfection** (***Atiyoga***), and also during the **intermediate state of reality**. See Chapter 11, Part One.

Sense-faculties *dbang-po*, Skt. *indriya*
See under **Sense-organs.**

Sense-organs *dbang-po*, Skt. *indriya*
According to the analysis of ***abhidharma***, these comprise: the eye (*cakṣurindriya*), the ear (*śrotrendriya*), the nose (*ghrāṇendriya*), the tongue (*jihvendriya*), and the physical body (*kāyendriya*).

Sensory Activity Fields *skye-mched*, Skt. *āyatana*
The operational fields or contexts in which sensory perception is said to occur. ***Abhidharma*** sources identify twelve sensory activity fields (Skt. *dvādaśāyatana*), six of which are designated as external and the remainder as internal, divided into pairs

as follows: the activity field of the eye (*cakṣurāyatana*) and the activity field of form (*rūpāyatana*), the activity fields of the ear (*śrotrāyatana*) and of sound (*śabdāyatana*), the activity fields of the nose (*ghrāṇāyatana*) and of smell (*gandhāyatana*), the activity fields of the tongue (*jihvāyatana*) and of taste (*rasāyatana*), the activity fields of the body (*kāyāyatana*) and of touch (*spraṣṭāyatana*), and, lastly, the activity fields of the mind (*mana āyatana*) and of mental objects or phenomena (*dharmāyatana*).

Sensory Spectra *khams*, Skt. *dhātu*
A broad term denoting each and every aspect of sensory perception, including the sensory subject, object and their interaction. ***Abhidharma*** sources identify eighteen distinct sensory components or psycho-physical spectra (Skt. *aṣṭadaśadhātu*), grouped as follows: those of the eye, form and visual **consciousness**; those of the ear, sound, and auditory **consciousness**; those of the nose, smell, and olfactory **consciousness**; those of the tongue, taste, and gustatory **consciousness**; those of the body, touch, and tactile **consciousness**; and those of the mind, phenomena, and mental **consciousness**.

Sentient Being *sems-can/'gro-ba*, Skt. *sattva/ gati*
In a Buddhist context, the expression 'sentient being' has a technical usage which contrasts with the concept of a **buddha**. The term refers to beings in **cyclic existence** and also those who have attained **liberation** from it but who have not attained the non-abiding ***nirvāṇa*** of fully manifest **buddhahood**. The Sanskrit term *gati* (Tib. *'gro-ba*) literally means 'goer', and *sattva*, a 'living being'. The Tibetan equivalent of the latter, *sems-can*, literally means 'sentient' or 'a being with **mind**', as it does in English. See **Six Classes of Sentient/Living Beings**.

Serpentine Water Spirits *klu/klu-mo*, Skt. *nāga/nāginī*
Male or female water spirits, often depicted as half human and half serpentine, who reside in oceans, rivers, lakes and springs, and who are described in Buddhist literature as custodians or repositories of submerged spiritual or material **treasure**. It is considered important that their environment should be kept pristine and clean; otherwise, agitation or pollution can result in the emergence of water spirits that engender leprosy, consumption and various skin ailments.

Seven Emanational Oceans *rol-pa'i rgya-mtsho bdun*
See **Four Continents and Eight Subcontinents**.

Seven Golden Mountain Ranges *gser-gyi ri-bo bdun*
See **Four Continents and Eight Subcontinents**.

Seven-limbed Practice *yan-lag bdun-pa*
A **preliminary practice** which is normally undertaken as a prelude to the **generation stage** of meditation. The seven limbs together constitute a comprehensive practice for purifying negative potentials and accumulating **merit**, thus laying a stable basis for a successful meditational session. The seven limbs in their proper sequence are: 1) paying homage through **prostration**, 2) making **offerings**, 3) purifying **non-virtuous** habits, 4) rejoicing in the wholesome actions of others and oneself, 5) requesting the **buddhas** to teach, 6) appealing to the **buddhas** not to enter into ***nirvāṇa***, and 7) the **dedication of merit**. Our Chapter 5 includes an additional three.

Seven-point Posture of Vairocana *rnam-snang chos-bdun*
This is a metaphor for the ideal or recommended meditation posture, in which the legs are crossed in the '**indestructible posture**' (*vajrāsana*), the back straight, the hands in the gesture of **meditative equipoise**, the eyes focused on the tip of the nose, the chin slightly tucked in, the lips and teeth set in their natural positions, and the tip of the tongue touching the palate.

Sexual Yoga *sbyor-ba*
See under **Four Delights**.

Signlessness *mtshan-ma med-pa*, Skt. *nirlakṣaṇa*
Signlessness, along with **emptiness** (Skt. *śūnyata*) and aspirationlessness (Skt. *nir-praṇidhāna*), is regarded as one of the three approaches to liberation (*rnam-thar sgo gsum*) which are the hallmarks of the teachings on the **perfection of discriminative awareness** (Skt. *prajñāpāramitā*). Signlessness is the antithesis of **substantialist views** (*mtshan-'dzin*) – the perspective that grasps at the inherent existence of things by means of their characteristics such as colours, forms and other properties.

Single Nature of Mind *sems gcig-po*
In Chapter 4 of our text the phrase 'the single nature of mind' is a synonym for the ultimate nature of mind (*sems-nyid*), or the **actual reality** of mind.

Six Classes of Sentient/Living Beings *'gro-ba rigs-drug*, Skt. *ṣaḍgati*
A birth in **cyclic existence** is characterised as occuring among one or other of the six classes of living beings, depending on the nature and maturity of an individual's **past actions**. The six classes are: 1) **gods** (*deva*), mundane celestial beings whose primary mental state is one of pride or exaltation, 2) **antigods** (*asura*), who are predominantly hostile and jealous, 3) human beings, who are influenced by all five **dissonant mental states**, 4) animals, who are under the sway of instinct and obfuscation, 5) **anguished spirits** (*preta*), who are under the sway of **attachment** and unsatisfied craving, and 6) the denizens of the **hells** (*naraka*), who are overwhelmed by hatred, anger and fear. Since all five dissonant mental states have influence on human beings, it is not inappropriate to look upon all of these conditions also as extrapolations of human psychological states. In our text the primary causes of rebirth in each of these six realms are respectively identified as: pride, jealousy, **attachment**, **delusion**, miserliness and hatred. See also **Three World-systems**.

Six Dissonant Mental States *nyon-mongs drug*, Skt. *ṣaṭkleśa*
In certain instances in our text when the context relates to rebirth among the six classes of beings, this enumeration does not refer to the well-known ***abhidharma*** category of the six primary **dissonant mental states**: **fundamental ignorance**, **attachment**, **aversion**, pride, doubt, and dissonant or afflictive views, but to the six poisons (*dug-drug*) that are said to generate rebirth among the six classes of living beings, namely: pride, jealousy, **attachment**, **delusion**, miserliness and hatred.

Six [Emanational] Sages *sprul-sku thub-drug*
See under **Six Sages**.

Six Intermediate States *bar-do drug*
See under **Intermediate States**.

Six Kinds of Bone Ornament *rus-pa'i rgyan drug*
The six kinds of bone-ornament worn by the **wrathful deities**, which symbolise the transcendence of death and **dissonant mental states**, comprise: necklaces (*mgul-rgyan*), bracelets (*gdu-bu*), earrings (*rna-cha*), crowns (*dbu-rgyan*), bandoleers (*mchod phyir-thogs*), and human ashes (*thal-chen*).

Six Lineages *brgyud-pa drug*
See under **Lineage**.

Six Mantras and Six Gestures *sngags-drug-dang phyag-rgya drug*
A series of ***mantras*** and gestures used for the empowerment of substitutes or offerings made to harmful or obstructive forces. This process of consecration is effected by means of the following six **hand-gestures** (*phyag-rgya drug*) and six corresponding ***mantras*** (*sngags-drug*): 1) The **hand-gesture** of the **expanse of reality** is conjoined with the ***mantra*** OṂ SVABHĀVA ŚUDDHĀḤ SARVA DHARMĀḤ SVABHĀVA ŚUDDHO 'HAṂ, which purifies the ritual object. 2) The **hand-gesture** of the jewelled casket is conjoined with the ***mantra*** NAMAḤ SARVA TATHĀGATEBHYO VIŚVA MUKHEBHYAḤ SARVATHĀ KHAṂ UDGATE SPHARAṆA IMAṂ GAGANA KHAṂ SVĀHĀ, which expands the effigy to fill all of space. 3) The **hand-gesture** of swirling nectar is conjoined with the ***mantra*** OṂ VAJRA AMṚTA KUṆḌALI HANA HANA HŪṂ PHAṬ, which transforms the effigy into a vessel filled with nectars. 4) The **hand-gesture** of vast potency is conjoined with the ***mantra*** NAMAḤ SARVATATHĀGATA AVALOKITE OṂ SAMBHARA SAMBHARA HŪṂ, which empowers the effigy to gratify all the senses. 5) The **hand-gesture** of the comet of knowledge and bestowal of gifts is conjoined with the ***mantra*** OM JÑĀNA AVALOKITE SAMANTA SPHARAṆA RAŚMIBHAVA SAMAYA MAHĀMAṆI DURU DURU HṚDAYA JVALANI HŪṂ, which empowers the effigy to fulfil the hopes of all, without contention. 6) Lastly, the **hand-gesture** of the universal monarch is conjoined with the ***mantra*** NAMAḤ SAMANTA BUDDHĀNĀṂ GRAHEŚVARA PRABHĀ JYOTENA MAHĀSAMAYE SVĀHĀ, which ensures that the effigy will pacify, subjugate or transform all inimical forces, and bring about a successful outcome for the ritual as a whole.

Six Perfections *pha-rol-tu phyin-pa drug*, Skt. *ṣaṭpāramitā*
In the ***sūtra*** system of the path to **buddhahood**, the entire ***bodhisattva***'s way of life or conduct is founded upon the practice of the six perfections which comprise: generosity (*dāna*), ethical discipline (*śīla*), patience (*kṣānti*), perseverance or joyous effort (*vīrya*), **meditative concentration** (*dhyāna*), and **discriminative awareness** (*prajñā*). These six are known as 'perfections' when, for example, the practice of generosity is: 1) motivated by the **altruistic intention to attain enlightenment** for the sake of all beings; 2) undertaken within a sixfold combination of all the perfections; and 3) performed with an awareness of the **emptiness** (*śūnyatā*) of the agent, the act, and the object in question. As an aspiration, the word *pāramitā* is used to denote a means to perfection; but when describing the perfected result, at the attainment of **buddhahood**, it means 'transcendent perfection', in accord with its literal meaning, 'gone beyond'.

Six Pristine Cognitions *ye-shes drug*
The six arms of the ***herukas***, among the fifty-eight **wrathful deities** (see Appendix Two), symbolise the six **pristine cognitions**. These comprise the **Pristine Cognition** of pure expanse (*dag-pa'i dbyings-kyi ye-shes*), in addition to the standard enumeration of the five **pristine cognitions**. See **Pristine Cognition**.

Six Realms
See **Six Classes of Sentient/Living Beings.**

Six Sages *sprul-sku thub-drug*
The six sages are aspects of the **Buddha-body of Emanation** (*nirmāṇakāya*) which manifest in the realms of the **six classes of living beings**, namely: *Indraśakra*, the sage of the **gods** (*lha'i thub-pa dbang-po brgya-byin*), *Vemacitra*, the sage of the **antigods** (*lha ma-yin-gyi thub-pa thag-bzang-ris*), ***Śākyasiṃha*** or ***Śākyamuni***, the sage of humans (*mi'i thub-pa shākya seng-ge*), *Sthirasiṃha*, the sage of animals (*byal-song thub-pa seng-ge rab-brtan*), *Jvālamukha*, the sage of the **anguished spirits** (*yi-dvags-kyi thub-pa kha-'bar-ma*), and ***Yama Dharmarāja***, the sage of the **hells** (*dmyal-ba'i thub-pa chos-kyi rgyal-po*). See Appendix Two.

Six-syllable Mantra *yi-ge drug-pa*, Skt. *ṣaḍakṣara*
The six-syllable ***mantra*** (OṂ MAṆI PADME HŪṂ) is that of ***Avalokiteśvara.***

Sixty Wrathful Deities *kho-bo drug-cu*
A collective name for the assembly of fifty-eight **wrathful deities**, with the addition of the two aspects representing the **Buddha-body of Reality**: *Mahottara Heruka* and *Krodheśvarī*, who are respectively the wrathful counterparts of ***Samantabhadra*** and *Samantabhadrī*. See Appendix Two.

Skilful Means *thabs*, Skt. *upāya*
The concept of skilful means is central to the understanding of the **Buddha**'s enlightened deeds, including his teaching of the many scriptures. From a very early stage, Buddhism developed a hermeneutics of reading many of the scriptures attributed to the **Buddha** from the perspective of skilful means, that is to say from the perspective that the truths revealed in a specific teaching may be contingent on the needs, interests and mental dispositions of specific types of individuals. This idea of skilful means, especially in the context of acting for the welfare of others, such as through the giving of teachings, was applied also in relation to the altruistic deeds of the ***bodhisattvas***. According to the **Greater Vehicle**, training in skilful means (Skt. *upāyakauśalya*, Tib. *thabs-la mkhas-pa*) refers to the first five of the **six perfections**: generosity, discipline, patience, perseverance, and **meditative concentration**; when integrated with **discriminative awareness**, the sixth perfection, they form a union of **discriminative awareness** and means (Skt. *prajñopāya*). The perfection of skilful means is also separately enumerated among the ten perfections, where it indicates the inestimable result acquired by dedicating the **merit** of one's virtuous deeds, however small, for the benefit of all sentient beings in general and for the sake of great unsurpassed **enlightenment** in particular. In the ***tantras***, the technical term 'path of skilful means' (*thabs-lam*) refers to the practices in which the internal **sexual yoga** (*sbyor-ba*) of the **energy channels**, **vital energies** and **seminal points** is refined within the **subtle body**. Also, the three **inner classes of *tantra*** according to the ***Nyingma*** school are sometimes referred to as the 'vehicles of overpowering means' (*thabs dbang-bsgyur-ba'i theg-pa-rnams*), in the sense that they carry on the path all the **dissonant mental states** which are renounced in the lower paths.

Sky-farer *mkha'-spyod-ma*, Skt. *khecarī*
See **Pure Realm of the Sky-farers.**

Spacious Expanse *mkha'-dbyings*
A metaphor for the secret centre of the female deity or female consort.

Spirit Lords of the Soil *sa-bdag*, Skt. *bhūmipati*
According to Sino-Tibetan elemental divination, the spirit lords of the soil are a class of geomantic forces whose position rotates – in some cases according to the years of the sexagenary calendar, and in others according to the months of the year, the days of the month, and the hours of the day. It is regarded as important that the subterranean locations of the spirit lords should be known at the time of constructing a building or ***maṇḍala***, and before entering into specific activities.

Spiritual Accomplishment *dngos-grub*, Skt. *siddhi*
See under **Accomplishment**.

Spiritual Friend *dge-ba'i bshes-gsnyen/dge-bshes*, Skt. *kalyānamitra*
The term 'spiritual friend' refers to a **spiritual teacher** (Skt. *guru*) who can contribute to an individual's progress on the spiritual path to **enlightenment** and who acts wholeheartedly for the welfare of his or her students, adopting a renunciate lifestyle. In Tibet, during the eleventh and twelfth centuries, the term became synonymous with the great masters of the *Kadam* school, who combined a scrupulously renunciate lifestyle and deep humility with profound scholarship and meditative resolve. In later centuries, the Tibetan abbreviation *geshe* came to have an academic usage in the ***Gelug*** school, where it now identifies a scholar-monk with a doctorate title in traditional Buddhist studies, and is similar to the modern usage of the term '*khenpo*' (*mkhan-po*) in other traditions. See also under **Monastic Preceptor**.

Spiritual Hero *dpa'-bo*, Skt. *vīra*
A synonym for **awareness holder** and for *ḍāka*, the male equivalent of the ***ḍākinī***.

Spiritual Sibling *mched-grogs/rdo-rje spun-sring*
In the context of the ***tantras***, six types of spiritual sibling are identified: 1) universal spiritual siblings, i.e. all sentient beings who from beginningless time have been one's parents; 2) spiritual siblings who share the Buddhist teachings; 3) harmonious spiritual siblings, who are similar in view and conduct; 4) dear spiritual siblings, who share the same **spiritual teacher**; 5) close spiritual siblings, who receive teaching together; and 6) intimate spiritual siblings, who receive **empowerment** together.

Spiritual Teacher *bla-ma*, Skt. *guru*
The original Sanskrit word '*guru*' literally means 'heavy' or 'weighty', and by extension a 'venerable teacher'. The Tibetan equivalent '*bla-ma*' (pronounced *lama*) means 'unsurpassed' or 'supreme', indicating that the *guru* is unsurpassed in terms of being the perfect object towards which meritorious activity should be directed. However, it is important to note that specific qualifications are necessary in order to be considered as a spiritual teacher. These qualifications differ according to the level of spiritual practice at which a teacher is adopted. In the context of the ***tantras***, the spiritual teacher is said to confer **blessings** on the meditator, in contrast to the **meditational deity**, who confers supreme **accomplishment** and the ***ḍākinī***, who confer enlightened or **buddha activities**. Ultimately, the *guru* is one's own **buddha nature**.

Spontaneous Presence *lhun-grub*, Skt. *anābhoga*
In the esoteric instructional class of the **Great Perfection** (***Atiyoga***), the term primordial purity (*ka-dag*) refers to the ultimate essence of **buddhahood**, the **Buddha-body of Reality**, the realisation of which is approached through the practices of **Cutting through Resistance** (*khregs-chod*), as described in Chapter 4, and spontaneous

presence refers to the expressive nature of the **Buddha-body of Reality** as the **Buddha-body of Form**, the realisation of which is approached through the practices of **All-surpassing Realisation** (*thod-rgal*), as indicated in the emergence of the luminosities described in Chapter 11. More generally, this term refers to spontaneous or effortless activity, the fifth of the five kinds of **buddha activity**, according to the ***Mahāyoga*** texts.

Śrī Siṃha *shri sing-ha*
The name of an early exponent of the ***Atiyoga*** teachings, who was a native of *Shokyam* in Central Asia.

Śrīmat *dpal-dang ldan-pa'i zhing-khams*, Skt. *Śrīmat*
The southern **buddha field** of 'The Glorious' is the pure realm presided over by the male **buddha** *Ratnasambhava.*

Stūpa *mchod-rten*
A sacred object representative of **buddha-mind.** *Stūpas* were originally a symbol of the **Buddha-body of Reality**, constructed in a dome-shape to hold the remains of ***Śākyamuni Buddha***. The veneration of *stūpas* is closely connected to the earliest phase of the **Greater Vehicle** in ancient India, where the original *stūpa* design developed within the central monastic assembly hall (Skt. *caitya*). The *stūpas* commonly seen in Tibetan cultural areas are constructed to a specific architectural design, usually in the shape of a dome, raised on a square base of several layers, from which rises a multilayered spire. In monasteries and sacred sites, a series of eight *stūpas* is frequently constructed, symbolising different events in the life of ***Śākyamuni Buddha***. Others are extraordinarily large, like those of *Baudhanāth* and *Svayambhū* in Nepal, or *Sanchi* in India and *Borabudor* in Indonesia, and some enclose within them entire ***maṇḍalas*** of deities, such as the *Pelkhor Chode* at *Gyantse* in *Tsang* and the Memorial *Chorten* in *Thimphu*, Bhutan. The symbolism of the *stūpa* is complex, representing the progression to **buddhahood**, the **five elements**, the five **pristine cognitions**, and so forth. Smaller reliquary *stūpas* are frequently built as a funerary memorial to important **spiritual teachers**, often enshrining their sacred ashes or embalmed remains.

Subduer *rtsad-du gcod-pa*
According to the terminology of the ***Nyingma*** school, the six ***herukas*** of the assembly of fifty-eight **wrathful deities** are given the title 'subduer', referring to their activity of **natural transformation** with respect to the **dissonant mental states**. See Appendix Two.

Subjugation *dbang-gi las*, Skt. *vaṣitakriyā*
See **Four Aspects of Enlightened Activity.**

Sublime One *'phags-pa*, Skt. *ārya*
A sublime being is one who has entered into a direct realisation of the actual nature of reality, in other words the lack of **self-identity** of both oneself and phenomena. The level of experience of an *ārya* is stratified in relation to the resultant stage of the **vehicle** being followed.

Substantialist Views *mtshan-'dzin*, Skt. *lakṣaṇagrahaṇa*
The mistaken apprehension that the form, colour and other characteristics assumed by any particular entity have **inherent existence**.

Subterranean Goddesses *brtan-ma*
An important class of twelve indigenous Tibetan spirits who personify the mighty snow ranges of Tibet and who are gathered within the outer retinue (*phyi-'khor*) of the fifty-eight **wrathful deities**. Foremost among them are *Kongtsun Demo* (associated with Mt *Namchak Barwa*), *Machen Pomra* (associated with Mt *Amnye Machen*), *Dorje Chenchikma* (associated with Mt Everest), *Do-rje Kundrakma* (associated with Mt *Nyenchen Tanglha*), and *Dorje Kuntizang* (associated with Mt *Nojin Gangzang*).

Subtle Body *phra-ba'i lus* Skt. *sūkṣmakāya*
In contrast to our gross physical body, which is composed of flesh, bones and blood, the subtle body comprises a network of subtle **energy channels, vital energies** and **seminal points** of energy. This form arises as a natural expression of the interaction of the subtle **mind** and the subtle **vital energies** on which it depends. See the Introductory Commentary by HH the Dalai Lama. The most advanced level of subtle body, known in the ***tantras*** as the pure **illusory body** (*sgyu-lus*), is experienced only when an indivisible unity of **buddha-body, speech** and **mind** has been actualised at the conclusion of the **generation** and **perfection stages** of meditation. A similitude of such a subtle body can be experienced during the practice of **dream yoga**, when the level of consciousness is relatively subtle and deep, due to the temporary cessation of active sensory processes. The **mental body** (*yid-lus*) experienced during the **intermediate state of rebirth** is also a form of subtle body.

Suffering *sdug-bsngal*, Skt. *duḥkhatā*
In a Buddhist context, the term 'suffering' is used in a broad sense and includes not only physical sensations but also mental experiences, that is to say all the essentially unsatisfactory experiences of life in **cyclic existence**. The various forms of suffering can be categorised into three groups: 1) the suffering of suffering (*duḥkhaduḥkhatā*), 2) the suffering of change (*vipariṇāmaduḥkhatā*), and 3) the suffering of pervasive conditioning (*saṃskāraduḥkhatā*). The first category refers to all our physical sensations and mental experiences which are self-evident to us as suffering and towards which we have spontaneous feelings of aversion. The second category includes all our experiences which are normally recognised as pleasant and desirable, but which are nonetheless suffering in that persistent indulgence in these always results in the changed attitude of dissatisfaction and boredom. It is only through reflection that the unsatisfactory nature of such experiences can be realised. The third category refers to a basic level of suffering which underlies the round of birth, sickness, old age and death. This suffering serves as the cause of our experiences of the two other classes of suffering. It is called pervasive because it extends to all forms of life in cyclic existence, irrespective of whether or not life-forms are endowed with bodily existence. Suffering is identified as the first of the **four noble truths** (Skt. *caturāryasatya*), which were taught by ***Śākyamuni Buddha*** in the course of his first discourse, and the entire path of Buddhism, embracing all its **vehicles** (*yāna*), may be seen as the ways of eliminating suffering, thus bringing an end to **cyclic existence** itself.

Sugata Family *bde-bar gshegs-pa'i rigs*, Skt. *sugatakula*
A synonym for the ***Buddha*** **family**. See **Buddha Family**.

Sukhāvatī *bde-ba-can-gyi zhing-khams*
The western **buddha field** of 'The Blissful' is the pure realm presided over by the **buddha** *Amitābha*.

Supernormal Cognitive Power *mngon-shes*, Skt. *abhijñā*
Supernormal cognitive power is considered to be a by-product of advanced **meditation**, but similitudes of these powers are said to arise during the **intermediate state of rebirth** (*srid-pa'i bar-do*). Six powers are specifically enumerated: clairvoyance (*lha'i mig-gi mngon-shes*, Skt. *divyacakṣurabhijñā*); clairaudience (*lha'i rna-ba'i mngon-shes*, Skt. *divyaśrotrābhijñā*); knowledge of the minds of others (*gzhan-sems shes-pa'i mngon-shes*, Skt. *paracittābhijñā*); miraculous abilities (*rdzu-'phrul-gyi shes-pa'i mngon-shes*, Skt. *ṛddhyabhijñā*); knowledge of past lives (*sngon-gnas rjes-su dran-pa'i mngon-shes*, Skt. *pūrvanivāsānusmṛtyabhijñā*); and knowledge that the flow of all corrupt past actions has ceased (*zag-pa zad-pa'i mngon-shes*, Skt. *āsravakṣayābhijñā*). Among these, the first five are said to be mundane powers, whereas the sixth is possessed by **buddhas** alone.

Supreme Assembly *tshogs-chen*
In this context, a synonym for **Monastic Community.**

Sūtra *mdo*
The original discourses which ***Śākyamuni Buddha*** taught publicly to his disciples as a fully ordained monk, consequent to his attainment of **buddhahood.** In the context of the three successive **turnings of the wheel of the sacred teachings,** the **Buddha** expounded respectively 1) the discourses on the doctrine of the **four noble truths** (Skt. *caturāryasatya*), 2) the **Perfection of Discriminative Awareness** (*Prajñāpāramitā*), *Ratnakūṭa* and related *sūtras* which emphasise **signlessness,** aspirationlessness and **emptiness,** and 3) the *Nucleus of the Tathāgata* (*Tathāgatagarbha*) and related *sūtras,* as well as the *Sūtra of the Unravelling of Enlightened Intention* (*Sandhinirmocanasūtra*), which emphasise **buddha nature** and the thorough analysis of **buddha attributes.** Among these the first category is the corpus of the **Lesser Vehicle** *sūtras* and the last two are the **Greater Vehicle** *sūtras.* The scriptural **transmissions** of the **sacred teachings** of Buddhism comprise the canonical *sūtras* and ***tantras,*** as well as their commentarial literature.

Sūtrayāna *mdo-sde'i theg-pa*
A term referring collectively to the first three of the **nine vehicles** when contrasted with the six vehicles of the ***tantras.*** See also under **Greater Vehicle.**

Symbolic Lineage of Awareness Holders *rig-'dzin brda'i brgyud-pa*
The **lineage** through which non-human and human **awareness holders** of the highest **spiritual accomplishments** symbolically receive the teachings from ***bodhisattvas*** of the tenth level. More specifically, this refers to the **transmission** of advanced ***bodhisattvas*** such as ***Mañjuśrī***, ***Avalokiteśvara***, and ***Vajrapāṇi*** who communicated with their respective disciples (**gods, serpentine water spirits** and **mountain or sylvan spirits**) by means of symbolic gestures rather than words. It also refers to the mode in which the earliest human progenitors of the ***Atiyoga*** **lineage** received and transmitted their highest teachings.

Tantra *rgyud*
The Sanskrit word *tantra* and its Tibetan equivalent *rgyud* literally mean a 'continuum' or 'unbroken stream' flowing from **fundamental ignorance** to **enlightenment.** *Tantra* has two basic meanings in Buddhism – it refers to the **continua of ground, path and result,** and to the literature or *tantra* texts which expound these continua in the context of the classes of *tantra* (see below). The former is the

actual meaning of *tantra*. Through the **continuum of the path** (*lam-gyi rgyud*) the primordially present **continuum of the ground** (*gzhi'i rgyud*) is realised or fully manifested as the **continuum of the result** (*'bras-bu'i rgyud*). Because *tantra* includes sophisticated techniques which, unlike the ***sūtra*** path, enable dissonant mental states, such as desire/**attachment** and hatred/**aversion**, to be transmuted into states of **realisation**, without renunciation or rejection, the practitioner can cultivate an uninterrupted continuum between the practitioner's ordinary initial mind, the advanced mind on the path, and the resultant fully **enlightened mind** of the **Buddha**. In the ***Nyingma*** school the literature which expounds this dynamic is divided into a sixfold classification of the three outer *tantras*, namely: ***Kriyātantra***, ***Ubhayatantra***, and ***Yogatantra***, and the three inner *tantras*, namely: ***Mahāyoga***, ***Anuyoga*** and ***Atiyoga***. These six classes represent stages of ever-decreasing emphasis on external ritual and ever-increasing subtlety of internal **meditation** together with an ever-increasing subtlety of the **dissonant mental states**, attachment in particular, that can be transformed into a blissful experience conjoined with the **realisation** of the actual nature of **reality**. It is said that on the basis of the fulfilment of the **generation** and **perfection stages** of the three inner *tantras* fully manifest **buddhahood** can be attained in a single lifetime.

Tathāgata *de-bzhin gshegs-pa*
A synonym for **buddha**, used frequently in the ***sūtras***, which literally means 'One Who Has Thus Gone'. The expression is interpreted in different ways, corresponding to the different classes of ***sūtras*** and ***tantras***, but in general it implies 'one who has departed in the wake of the **buddhas** of the past', or 'one who has manifested the supreme **enlightenment** dependent on the **reality** that does not abide in the two extremes of existence and **quiescence**'.

Ten Directions *phyogs-bcu*, Skt. *daśadik*
The four cardinal and four intermediate directions, as well as the zenith and nadir.

Ten Opportunities *'byor-ba bcu*
See **Eight Freedoms and Ten Opportunities.**

Ten Similes of Illusory Phenomena *shes-bya sgyu-ma'i dpe-bcu*
The ten similes which illustrate the illusory nature of all things are: illusion (*sgyu-ma*), mirage (*smig-rgyu*), dream (*rmi-lam*), reflected image (*gzugs-brnyan*), a celestial city (*dri-za'i grong-khyer*), echo (*brag-ca*), reflection of the moon in water (*chu-zla*), bubble of water (*chu-bur*), optical illusion (*mig-yor*), and an intangible emanation (*sprul-pa*).

Terracotta Imprints *tsha-tsha*
Small votive images moulded with clay fashioned in the form of miniature ***stūpas*** or bas-relief **meditational deities**. They are usually empowered, in the context of appropriate rituals, and frequently interred within a larger ***stūpa*** or kept by devotees as an object of veneration.

Third Empowerment *dbang gsum-pa*
The third of the four empowerments. See **Four Empowerments.**

Thirty-two Major Marks *mtshan sum-cu-so-gnyis*, Skt. *dvātriṃśanmahāpuruṣalakṣaṇa*
See **Major and Minor Marks.**

Those Gone to Bliss *bde-bar gshegs-pa*, Skt. *sugata*
An epithet of the **buddhas**. The expression 'those gone to bliss of the three times' (*dus-gsum bde-gshegs*) refers to the **buddhas** of the past, present, and future, exemplified respectively by *Dīpaṃkara*, ***Śākyamuni***, and ***Maitreya***.

Thread-cross *mdos*
In its simplest form a thread-cross can be two crossed sticks or a simple wooden frame (*nam-mkha'*) around which coloured threads (*rgyang-bu*) are arranged in a diamond or other more complex pattern. Thread-crosses vary in size and complexity depending on the type of ritual for which they are constructed. In essence, they represent a 'trap' for negative and malevolent forces, where the trap symbolises and is empowered with all the qualities that can satisfy the negative or malevolent force. Thus, the design of the thread-cross can closely mirror that of a ***stūpa*** or three-dimensional ***maṇḍala*** and represent the purity of the psycho-physical **aggregates, elemental properties**, and sensory and mental processes, etc. On some occasions these complex thread-crosses can be enormous structures up to tens of feet high.

Three Buddha-bodies *sku-gsum*, Skt. *trikāya*
The Three Buddha-bodies comprise the **Buddha-body of Reality**, the **Buddha-body of Perfect Resource**, and the **Buddha-body of Emanation**. Jointly, they form the secret object of **refuge**. See their individual entries, and also under **Refuge**.

Three Levels of Existence *srid-pa gsum*, Skt. *tribhava*
The three levels of existence are those of celestial, terrestrial and subterranean beings.

Three Lower Existences *ngan-song gsum*, Skt. *tridurgati*
See **Lower Existences**.

Three Poisons *dug-gsum*
Attachment, aversion and **delusion**. See their individual entries.

Three Precious Jewels *dkon-mchog gsum*, Skt. *triratna*
The Three Precious Jewels comprise the **Buddha** (*sangs-rgyas*); the **sacred teachings** (Skt. *saddharma*, Tib. *dam-pa'i chos*); and the **monastic community** of monks and nuns (Skt. *saṅgha*, Tib. *dge-'dun*). Together these three form the outer objects of **refuge** (see Chapter 1). They are regarded as the perfect objects in which **refuge** can be sought from the unsatisfactory nature of life in **cyclic existence** in general, and particularly from the potential **suffering** of unfavourable future existences. They are called 'precious jewels' because, like the wish-fulfilling jewels of Indian classical literature, in their metaphorical sense, they possess the wish-fulfilling capacity to provide protection from the perils of **cyclic existence**. See their individual entries and also under **Refuge**.

Three Roots *rtsa-ba gsum*, Skt. *trimūla*
The three roots jointly form the inner object of **refuge**, according to the ***tantras*** (see Chapter 1). They comprise the **spiritual teacher** (Skt. *guru*, Tib. *bla-ma*), who confers **blessing** (Skt. *adhiṣṭhāna*), the **meditational deity** (Skt. *iṣṭadevatā*, Tib. *yi-dam lha*) who confers **accomplishments** (Skt. *siddhi*); and the ***ḍākinī*** (Tib. *mkha'-'gro*) who confer the actualisation of **buddha activities** (Skt. *kṛtyakriyā*). See their individual entries and also under **Refuge**.

Three Times *dus-gsum*
The three times are those of past, present, and future.

Three Vehicles *theg-pa gsum*, Skt. *triyāna*
See **Vehicle.**

Three World-systems *'jig-rten-gyi khams gsum*, Skt. *tridhātu*
According to Buddhism, **cyclic existence** includes three world-systems, namely: the world-system of desire (Skt. *kāmadhātu*), the world-system of form (Skt. *rūpadhātu*), and the world-system of formlessness (Skt. *ārūpyadhātu*). Among them, the world-system of desire is a state of existence dominated by sensual experiences, particularly the sensations of suffering and pleasure. It is inhabited by all **six classes of sentient beings**, including humans and six categories of **gods** (*kāmadevaṣaṭkula*). The world-system of form, in which beings have a comparatively subtle level of consciousness, temporarily devoid of gross sensations of pain and pleasure, is regarded as a state beyond ordinary human existence and inhabited only by gods. Birth in such a realm requires the attainment of one or all of the four **meditative concentrations** (Skt. *caturdhyāna*), in past lives. ***Abhidharma*** literature mentions twelve ordinary realms of form and five 'pure abodes' (*pañcaśuddhanivāsa*), above them, where birth can be taken consequent on these four concentrations. Lastly, the world-system of formlessness is regarded as the highest level of rebirth within **cyclic existence** and a state where an individual's physical faculties exist only as potencies and the individual functions only at the level of consciousness. It is said to be inhabited by those who have mastered the **four formless meditative absorptions** (Skt. *catursamāpatti*).

Torma-offering *gtor-ma*, Skt. *naivedya/bali*
Torma-offerings are cakes, usually made of dough and often decorated with colourful butter sculptures. Sometimes they are embodiments of the **meditational deities** associated with particular ritual practices, or they may be food-offerings presented to various deities or **protectors** visualised in the context of meditation. Yet again, *tormas* may act as physical symbols into which diverse aspects of negativity are absorbed, transformed, and removed through ritual practices.

Transcendent Lord *bcom-ldan-'das*, Skt. *bhagavān*
According to the Tibetan interpretation, the Sanskrit honorific term '*bhagavān*', which has often been translated as 'Blessed Lord', indicates a **buddha** who has: 1) 'destroyed' (*bcom*) the four **malevolent/beguiling forces** (*caturmāra*) comprising the influence of the psycho-physical **aggregates** (*skandha*), **dissonant mental states** (*kleśa*), sensual temptations and mundane death; 2) come to 'possess' (*ldan*) the six excellences (*ṣaḍguṇa*) of lordship, form, glory, fame, **pristine cognition** and perseverance; and 3) 'transcended' (*'das*) the **sufferings** of **cyclic existence.**

Transgressions *nyes-byas*, Skt. *duṣkṛta*
The **vows** maintained by Buddhist monks and nuns include the avoidance of primary downfalls (Skt. *āpatti*) and secondary transgressions. The term transgression (*nyes-byas*) is used in a technical sense to refer to a whole host of secondary precepts in the context of the **monastic vows** of individual liberation (***prātimokṣa***), and in the context of the ***bodhisattva*** and tantric vows. The list of these transgressions differs according to the context. See **Commitment, Prātimokṣa** and **Vows.**

Transmission *lung*, Skt. *āgama*
The Buddhist **sacred teachings** (*Skt. saddharma*) comprise both experiential **realisations** (*adhigama*; Tib. *rtogs-pa*) and authoritative transmissions. The latter include both the oral teachings and sacred scriptures (Skt. *pravacana*, Tib. *gsung-rab*), imparted by the **buddhas**, as well as the associated commentaries or **treatises** (Skt. *śāstra*, Tib. *bstan-bcos*), which have been transmitted in an uninterrupted **lineage** or succession from ancient times. In Tibetan Buddhism, it is regarded as essential that a transmission of both the text and its oral commentary is formally received from an authoritative **lineage holder**, if any significant spiritual experience is to be cultivated, since a mere theoretical understanding of these topics is not regarded as sufficient.

Transmitted Precepts *bka'-ma*, Skt. *pravacana*
From the perspective of the ***Nyingma*** school, the scriptures and oral teachings of Buddhism have been transmitted in two distinct ways: through the long oral lineage of transmitted precepts (*ring-brgyud bka'-ma*), which have been handed down from one generation of accomplished teachers to the next since ancient times, and through a close lineage of revealed teachings or **treasures** (*nye-brgyud gter-ma*), whose origin is more recent.

Treasure-finder *gter-ston*
An **accomplished master** holding an authentic **lineage** who successfully reveals a hidden **treasure**-text or sacred object, in accordance with the prophesies made by ***Padmasambhava*** or a specific concealer of **treasure**-texts. See under **Treasures**.

Treasures *gter-ma*, Skt. *nidhi*
The Sanskrit *nidhi* (Tib. *gter-ma*), translated in English as 'treasure' or 'revealed teaching' (*gter-chos*), refers to those sacred Buddhist texts and objects which were concealed in the past in order that they might be protected and revealed in the future for the benefit of posterity. The notion of the revelation of concealed texts as treasure is extremely ancient in India and China. Within Indian Buddhism, it is well known that the **Perfection of Discriminative Awareness** (*Prajñāpāramitā*) ***sūtras*** were reputedly revealed when ***Nāgārjuna*** received them in the form of treasure from the **serpentine water spirits** (*nāga*). A recension of the *sādhana* class of ***Mahāyoga tantras***, classified as *gter-chos* by ***Nyingma*** doxographers, is also said to have been revealed to eight great masters, including ***Nāgārjuna***, in the *Śītavana* charnel ground near *Vajrāsana*. In Tibet, the tradition of the treasures was introduced by ***Padmasambhava*** and his students, who concealed texts and sacred objects at geomantic power-places in the landscape, entrusting them to their respective custodians or treasure-lords (*gter-bdag*) or to ***ḍākinī*** for safe keeping, with the prediction that these would be discovered at some future time by a prophesied **treasure-finder** (*gter-ston*). Accordingly, it is believed that the students of ***Padmasambhava*** have continued to emanate in the form of **treasure-finders** in successive centuries in order to reveal these treasure-teachings. Other kinds of treasure-teachings revealed directly from the **enlightened intention** of **buddha-mind** in a telepathic manner (*dgongs-gter*), or in a pure visionary experience (*dag-snang*), are also recognised. There are many such lineages extant today, including that of the present text, and they are maintained mostly, but by no means exclusively, by the ***Nyingma*** school.

Treatise *bstan-bcos*, Skt. *śāstra*
The term treatise (*śāstra*) in the Buddhist context generally refers to authoritative works written by **accomplished masters** elucidating the profound meaning of the **Buddha**'s scriptures (*pravacana*). Treatises are contrasted with scriptures (both ***sūtras*** and ***tantras***), the latter being attributed to the **Buddha**. See **Kangyur** and **Tengyur.**

Trichiliocosm *stong-gsum 'jig-rten-gyi khams*, Skt. *trisahasralokadhātu*
See **Chiliocosm.**

Trisong Detsen *khri-srong lde'u btsan*
The thirty-eighth king of Tibet and son of King *Tride Tsukten*. Despite his accession to the throne at a tender age and the opposition of ministers who were ***Bon*** sympathisers he established Buddhism as the state religion of Tibet. He invited both ***Śāntarakṣita*** and ***Padmasambhava*** to construct Tibet's first monastery at *Samye* and to transmit the diverse Indian lineages of the ***vinaya***, ***sūtras*** and ***tantras***. He became a realised practitioner of the ***tantras*** in his own right, under the guidance of ***Padmasambhava***, and actively sponsored the education and projects of his highly organised translation teams. According to traditional accounts, it was King *Trisong Detsen* who requested ***Padmasambhava*** to give the teachings that are presented in our text. See Gyurme Dorje's 'Brief Literary History'.

Tulku *sprul-sku*, Skt. *nirmāṇakāya*
In its philosophical and classical usage the term refers to the **Buddha-body of Emanation**. However, based on this concept of emanation, a different usage developed in Tibet following the inception of a tradition to formally recognise the incarnations of high spiritual teachers after their death. The first such ***tulku*** to be given formal recognition was *Karma Pakshi*, the second, *Karmapa* (1204–83). Later, other important ***tulku*** institutions emerged, such as that of the ***Dalai Lama*** and *Panchen Lama*, and the system of recognising successive generations of ***tulkus*** became commonly established throughout Tibet and the Himalayan region.

Turning of the Wheel of the [Sacred] Teachings *chos-kyi 'khor-lo bskor-ba*, Skt. *dharmacakrapravartana*
This metaphor refers to the promulgation of the Buddhist teachings by the **Buddha** and continues to be used metaphorically with regard to the teaching activity of successive **lineage holders**. The ***Buddha Śākyamuni*** is recognised to have promulgated three sequential 'turnings of the wheel'. The association with the concept of a wheel derives from a comparison with the 'wheel of sharp weapons' said to be held in the hand of a **universal monarch**. Within the context of this comparison the **sacred teachings** are composed of ethical discipline (the central axis), analytic **discriminative awareness** (the sharp spokes) and **meditative concentration** (the stabilising perimeter). See also ***Sūtra***.

Tuṣita *dga'-ldan*
Tuṣita is the name of the fourth of the six **god** realms, which are said to be located within the **world-system** of desire (Skt. *kāmadhātu*). It is regarded as the current abode of the future **buddha** ***Maitreya***.

Twelve Links of Dependent Origination *rten-'brel bco-gnyis*, Skt. *dvādaśāṅga-pratītyasamutpāda*
See under **Dependent Origination.**

Twenty-four Power-places *yul nyi-shu rtsa-bzhi*, Skt. *caturviṃśatmahāsthāna*
The twenty-four power-places are the following regions of the ancient Indian subcontinent, which are associated with the ***tantras*** of the *Cakrasaṃvara* and ***Heruka*** classes: *Jālandhara, Oḍḍiyāna, Paurṇagiri, Kāmarūpa, Mālava, Sindhu, Nagara, Munmuni, Kāruṇyapāṭaka, Devīkoṭa, Karmārapāṭaka, Kulatā, Arbuda, Godāvarī, Himādrī, Harikela, Lampāka, Kāñcī, Saurāṣṭra, Kaliṅga, Kokaṇa, Caritra, Kośala,* and *Vindhyākaumārapaurikā*.

Two Accumulations *tshogs-gnyis*, Skt. *sambhāradvaya*
See under **Accumulations.**

Two Extremes *mtha' gnyis*, Skt. *antadvaya*
The two extremes of eternalism and nihilism. See under **Eternalist** and **Nihilist.**

Two Truths *bden-pa gnyis*, Skt. *satyadvaya*
All Buddhist philosophical schools of thought formulate their ontology within the framework of the two truths, the conventional or relative truth (Skt. *samvṛtisatya*, Tib. *kun-rdzob bden-pa*) and the ultimate truth (Skt. *paramārthasatya*, Tib. *don-dam bden-pa*). However, the definition of the two truths differs according to their different epistemological interpretations. The ***Cittamātra*** and ***Madhyamaka***, the two **Greater Vehicle** schools of thought which emphasise the doctrine of the two truths, define the ultimate truth as a synonym of **emptiness**, the ultimate nature of phenomena, while the conventional truth is defined as the empirical aspect of reality as conventionally experienced through our perceptions. Such an aspect of reality is true only within the relative framework of our own veridical experiences. However, according to the various ***tantra*** **vehicles** there are increasing degrees of subtlety in the interpretation of the two truths.

Ubhayatantra *gnyis-ka'i rgyud*
Ubhayatantra, also known as *Caryātantra*, is the second of the three outer classes of ***tantra***, which form one sub-category of the six classes of ***tantra***, and the fifth of the **nine vehicles**, according to the ***Nyingma*** school of Tibetan Buddhism. *Ubhayatantra* places an equal emphasis on both external ritual and internal meditation.

Ultimate Truth *don-dam bden-pa*, Skt. *paramārthasatya*
See under **Two Truths.**

Unique Seminal Point *thig-le nyag-gcig*
According to ***Atiyoga***, this expression is a synonym for the **Buddha-body of Reality.** For the range of meanings conveyed by the Tibetan term *thig-le*, see **Seminal Point.**

Universal Monarch *khor-lo bsgyur-ba*, Skt. *cakravartin*
In the context of Indo-Tibetan Buddhism, the concept of the benign universal monarch or emperor who rules in accordance with the law of the **sacred teachings** of Buddhism is one that has permeated Buddhist literature since the time of *Aśoka*. Their appearance in the world is considered a unique and rare event, just as the appearance of a **buddha** is considered to be unique and rare.

Unsurpassed Yogatantra *bla-med rgyud*, Skt. *Yoganiruttaratantra*
The highest among the four classes of ***tantra***, the other three being: ***Kriyā***, ***Caryā***, and ***Yoga tantra***. The differences between the four classes of ***tantra*** represent stages of ever-decreasing emphasis on external ritual and ever-increasing subtlety of internal **meditation.** *Niruttara* means 'unsurpassed' or 'highest' and it is in

the *Yoganiruttara* ***tantras*** that the meditative techniques for realising the **Three buddha-bodies** are the most subtle and refined. There are two distinct phases in the dissemination of the Unsurpassed *Yogatantras* in Tibet, which are reflected in two differing ways of classifying them. According to the ***Nyingma*** school, the earlier phase of dissemination, they are classified into ***Mahāyoga***, ***Anuyoga*** and ***Atiyoga***, whereas the later schools classify them into Father, Mother and Non-dual or Indivisible ***tantras***.

Uṣṇīṣavijayā *gtsug-gtor rnam-rgyal-ma*
One of the three principal meditational deities associated with longevity practices and the subject of five principal ***dhāraṇī*** incarnations, *Uṣṇīsavijayā* generally assumes a slightly wrathful appearance, with three faces (white, yellow and pale blue) and eight arms holding diverse symbolic implements. She is seated with her legs folded, in the **indestructible posture**.

Vaiḍūryaprabharāja *sang-rgyas sman-bla*
The **Buddha** of Medicine, the principal figure in the Buddhist medical ***tantras***, who is regarded as the progenitor of the *Four Tantras of Medicine* (*rGyud-bzhi*). According to certain sources ***Śākyamuni Buddha*** is believed to have assumed a specific form when teaching the medical ***tantras*** and that aspect of the **Buddha** is called *Vaiḍūryaprabharāja*, the 'King of Blue Beryl Light'. He is normally depicted in paintings as being blue in colour and holding in his left palm an alms bowl filled with the fruits of a medicinal plant, chebulic myrobalan. According to the **lineage** of the medical ***tantras***, there are eight different aspects of the Medicine **Buddha**, of which *Vaiḍūryaprabharāja* is the foremost.

Vajra *rdo-rje*
In the sense of *rdo-rje pha-lam* (pronounced '*dorje phalam*'), this term means the diamond, literally 'the sovereign among all stones'. In Buddhism however *rdo-rje* indicates the indestructible reality of **buddhahood**, which is defined as both imperishable (*mi-gshigs*) and indivisible (*ma-phyed*). The emblem symbolic of this indestructible reality is also known as *rdo-rje* or *vajra*. This is a sceptre-like *tantric* ritual object which is held in the right palm usually whenever playing a ritual bell. The sceptre symbolises **skilful means** and the bell **discriminative awareness**. Holding these together in the two palms represents the perfect union of **discriminative awareness** and **skilful means**. *Vajrā*, also known as *Piṅgalā* (*dmar-mo*), is the name given to the first of the six ***yoginī*** from the south, a subcategory of the twenty-eight *Īśvarī*. See Appendix Two.

Vajra-brothers and sisters *rdo-rje ming-sring*
The most intimate of spiritual siblings (*mched-grogs*), with whom one shares **empowerments** and **commitments**. See **Spiritual Sibling**.

Vajra Family *rdo-rje'i rigs*, Skt. *vajrakula*
One of the **five enlightened families** (*pañcakula*) into which the **meditational deities** of the **Buddha-body of Perfect Resource** are subdivided. The deities of the *Vajra* family include the peaceful **buddhas** *Akṣobhya-Vajrasattva* and *Buddhalocanā* and the corresponding wrathful aspects *Vajra Heruka* and *Vajrakrodheśvarī*. See Appendix Two.

Vajra-master *rdo-rje slob-dpon*, Skt. *vajrācārya*
The 'master of indestructible reality' who presides over **empowerment** ceremonies

and the related ritual dances of the great **means for attainment** (Skt. *mahāsādhana*, Tib. *sgrub-chen*), embodying the central **meditational deity** of the ***maṇḍala***.

Vajradhara *rdo-rje 'chang*
Vajradhara (lit. 'vajra-holder') is an expression of the **Buddha-body of Reality**, spontaneously arising from the pure, pristine expanse of **inner radiance**, in a form complete with all the characteristics of the **Buddha-body of Perfect Resource**. *Vajradhara* is thus regarded as the root of all the **five enlightened families** and consequently he is also known as the lord of the sixth **enlightened family**. Many ***tantra*** texts and **lineages** attribute their origin directly to the **Buddha-body of Reality** – represented in the form of either ***Samantabhadra*** or *Vajradhara*. Other ***tantra*** texts and **lineages** claim that *Vajradhara* is a form assumed by ***Śākyamuni Buddha*** when giving esoteric teachings on ***tantra***. *Vajradhara* is said to become manifest when one has totally overcome all dualistic conceptions and actualised **buddhahood**. He is usually depicted as seated and holding a ***vajra*** and bell in his crossed palms.

Vajrakīla *rdo-rje phur-ba*
One of the eight foremost **meditational deities** according to the '**means for attainment**' class of ***Mahāyoga***. *Vajrakīla* is dark blue in colour with three faces and six arms, the central pair of hands holding a ritual dagger (Skt. *kīla*). Often the lower part of his body is also visualised in the form of a ritual dagger, the three facets of the pyramidal blade representing the transformation of **delusion**, **attachment** and **aversion**. *Vajrakīla* is representative of the natural expression of **buddha activity**.

Vajrakumāra *rdo-rje gzhon-nu*
An aspect of the **meditational deity** ***Vajrakīla***. See under **Vajrakīla**.

Vajrapāṇi *phyag-na rdo-rje*
The embodiment of the spiritual **power** (*bala*) and **skilful means** of all the **buddhas** as visualised in the form of a **meditational deity**. *Vajrapāṇi* is generally depicted as being **wrathful** in aspect, holding a ***vajra*** in his right upraised hand and a skull-cup in his left. In peaceful form *Vajrapāṇi* is also one of the eight male ***bodhisattvas*** among the forty-two **peaceful deities**. See Appendix Two.

Vajrasattva *rdo-rje sems-dpa'*
Vajrasattva, or in literal translation 'the spiritual hero of indestructible reality', has two principal forms. Firstly, in the context of the ***Guhyagarbha tantra***, and related texts, he is identified with the peaceful male **buddha** *Akṣobhya-Vajrasattva*. See Appendix Two. Secondly, in the context of the **preliminary practices** (*sngon-'gro*) of **meditation**, the recitation of *Vajrasattva*'s **Hundred-syllable Mantra** (*yig-brgya*) purifies **negativities**, **obscurations**, **transgressions**, and **downfalls** (see Chapter 1). In this latter context, *Vajrasattva* is visualised as white in colour, dressed in the silken garments and ornaments of a ***bodhisattva***, and holding a ***vajra*** in his right palm close to the heart and a bell in his left hand close to the left side of his hip. Sometimes, both forms of *Vajrasattva* are integrated in a single practice, as in Chapter 5 of the present work, where practitioners first visualise the white form of *Vajrasattva*, before visualising the forty-two **peaceful deities**, including *Akṣobhya-Vajrasattva*, within their hearts. As a **lineage holder**, *Vajrasattva* is credited with the transmission of ***Atiyoga*** into the human world, appearing in the form of the *deva Adhicitta* (*lhag-sems-can*) before ***Prahevajra*** (*dga'-rab rdo-rje*) in a vision. According to the

Great Perfection, *Vajrasattva* is sometimes used synonymously to indicate the **Buddha-body of Reality**, and as such is identical to ***Samantabhadra***.

Vajrayāna *rdo-rje'i theg-pa*
See **Vehicle of Indestructible Reality**.

Vehicle *theg-pa*, Skt. *yāna*
The term 'vehicle' suggests a dynamic momentum leading to the attainment of ***nirvāṇa***. Although from one standpoint there may be as many vehicles as there are thoughts arising in the mind, the **sacred teachings** are classified into distinct vehicles according to their power. Accordingly, the expression 'two vehicles' refers to the distinction between the **Lesser Vehicle** and the **Greater Vehicle**, the expression '**three vehicles**' or 'three causal vehicles' refers to the vehicles of **pious attendants**, **hermit buddhas** and ***bodhisattvas***. The division into '**nine vehicles**', which corresponds to the ***Nyingma*** classification, includes the three causal vehicles of the **pious attendants**, **hermit buddhas** and ***bodhisattvas***, and the six resultant vehicles of ***Kriyātantra***, ***Ubhayatantra***, ***Yogatantra***, ***Mahāyoga***, ***Anuyoga*** (*rjes-su rnal-'byor-gyi theg-pa*), and ***Atiyoga*** (*shin-tu rnal-'byor-gyi theg-pa*).

Vehicle of Indestructible Reality *rdo-rje'i theg-pa*, Skt. *Vajrayāna*
The Vehicle of Indestructible Reality comprises, in the ***Nyingma*** classification, the six resultant vehicles of the ***tantras***, so-called because the indestructible and imperishable realities of **buddha-body**, **speech** and **mind** are fully realised and manifested when the **continuum of the ground** is transformed into the **continuum of the result** by means of the **continuum of the path**. See under **Tantra**. It is also known as the Vehicle of **Secret *Mantras*** (Skt. *Guhyamantrayāna*) because engaging in this path ensures the protection of the mind from dualistic perceptions and conceptions. See ***Mantra***.

Vidyādhara *rig-'dzin*
See under **Awareness Holder**.

Vinaya *'dul-ba*
The Sanskrit term *vinaya*, literally meaning 'discipline', refers to the monastic discipline maintained by members of the Buddhist community, including the ethical codes which regulate the life of fully ordained monks and nuns, as well as probationary nuns, novice monks and nuns, and male and female laity. The collection of ***Śākyamuni Buddha***'s discourses which elucidate and define the principles of these ethical codes (including the administrative guidelines for running a monastery) is known as the *vinayapiṭaka*, which is one of the three primary collections of discourses comprising the Buddhist canon (Skt. *tripiṭaka*). Based on different interpretations relating to the subtler points of the **Buddha**'s discourses on *vinaya*, there emerged, in ancient India, several distinct schools, including the *Sthaviravāda*, *Sarvāstivāda*, *Mahāsaṅghika* and *Sammitīya*. The *vinaya* tradition which became predominant in Tibet is that of the *Sarvāstivādins*. See **Vows** and ***Prātimokṣa***.

Virtuous Action *dge-ba*, Skt. *kuśala*
Both virtue and its opposite, non-virtue (Skt. *akuśala*, Tib. *mi-dge-ba*) are defined in terms of both motivation and the consequences of the action. In order for an action to be defined as either virtuous or non-virtuous, there are certain prerequisite features which must be present. These are: motivation, the actual execution of the

act, and the conclusion. An act is non-virtuous if it is: 1) motivated by negative intentions; 2) committed by the agent in a sane mind and with full knowledge; and 3) the person derives a sense of satisfaction from having accomplished the act. Such actions can be physical, verbal, or mental. Broadly speaking, non-virtuous actions are categorised into the following ten types: killing, stealing, and sexual misconduct (which are the three physical actions); lying, divisive speech, harsh speech, and meaningless gossip (which are the four verbal actions); and covetousness, harmful intent, and distorted views (which are the three mental actions). An act is considered virtuous if it either passively refrains from the ten recognised types of non-virtuous action, or actively engages in acts for the sake of others with an altruistic motivation.

Visionary Appearances *snang-ba*
According to the terminology of the **Great Perfection**, there are four successive visionary appearances experienced through the practice of **All-surpassing Realisation** (*thod-rgal*). These are: the visionary appearance of the direct perception of **reality** (*chos-nyid mngon-sum-gyi snang-ba*), the visionary appearance of increasing contemplative experience (*nyams gong-'phel-ba'i snang-ba*), the visionary appearance of reaching the limit of **awareness** (*rig-pa tshad-phebs-kyi snang-ba*), and the visionary appearance of the cessation of clinging to reality (*chos-nyid-du 'dzin-pa zad-pa'i snang-ba*).

Vital Energy *rlung*, Skt. *vāyu*
In the ***tantras*** and related medical traditions, it is said that there are ten kinds of vital energy or subtle winds which flow through the 72,000 **energy channels** (Skt. *nāḍī*) of the body. These sustain life and include the energies which support various conceptual states within the individual's mind. At the subtlest level, subtle mind and vital energy are thought of as a single entity. The ten kinds of vital energy comprise: five inner vital energies (*nang-gi rlung lnga*) which influence the body's inner motility, and five outer vital energies (*phyi-'i rlung lnga*) which have specific effects on the outward motility of the body. The former are the vital energies associated with the **five elements** (earth, water, fire, wind, space) and their respective colour-tones (yellow, white, red, green, blue). The latter comprise life-breath (Skt. *prāṇa*, Tib. *srog-'dzin*), muscular movement (Skt. *vyāna*), digestion (Skt. *samāna*), semiotic/vocal movement (Skt. *udāna*), and reproduction/waste disposal (Skt. *apāna*). The movement of vital energy through the **energy channels** of the **subtle body** is refined in the context of the **perfection stage** of meditation. Ordinarily, in the case of individuals who have not cultivated such practices, both vital energy and subtle mind are diffused via the right and left **energy channels** and thereby come to permeate the entire network of the body's minor channels. This dissipated vital energy is known as the vital energy of past actions (*las-kyi rlung*) because it is activated by **dissonant mental states**, and the influence of **past actions** predominates, obscuring the **inner radiance** of the subtle mind. However, when the practices of the **perfection stage** of meditation are applied, the knots which block their combined movement through the **energy centres** (Skt. *cakra*) located on the central **energy channel** are untied and both vital energy and subtle mind enter, abide and dissolve within the central **energy channel** of the body (Skt. *avadhūti*) and then the non-conceptual **inner radiance** arises, for which reason it becomes known as the **vital energy** of **pristine cognition** (*ye-shes-kyi rlung*). On a physical level, it is important,

according to the Tibetan medical tradition, that vital energy remains in balance with bile and phlegm, which are collectively known as the three humours, if sound health is to be maintained.

Vows [of Buddhism] *sdom-pa*, Skt. *saṃvara*
Sets of precepts or injunctions voluntarily adopted in the course of Buddhist practice which facilitate an individual's progress on the path to **enlightenment**. These include short-term vows, such as the one-day vows, lifelong vows, such as the monastic vows of a fully ordained monk or nun, and perpetual vows associated with the **Greater Vehicle**, which are to be maintained over a succession of lifetimes. All such vows may be subsumed within three categories: the monastic vows of the ***prātimokṣa***, the special vows of the ***bodhisattvas***, and the special **commitments** (Skt. *samaya*) undertaken by practitioners of the ***tantras***. See ***Prātimokṣa*** and **Commitment**. The special vows of the ***bodhisattvas***, exemplified by the *Sūtra of Ākāśagarbha*, extol that ***bodhisattvas*** must be careful to maintain their altruistic vows, expressed in the verses of the **four immeasurable aspirations**, and to avoid nineteen specifically enumerated root **downfalls** (Skt. *mūlāpatti*) and forty-six **transgressions** (Skt. *duṣkṛta*). In all schools of Tibetan Buddhism, the ***prātimokṣa*** and ***bodhisattva*** vows and the **commitments** of the ***tantras*** are fully integrated.

Vows of the Buddhist Laity *dge-bsnyen-gyi sdom-pa*
See under **Prātimokṣa.**

Water Libation *chu-gtor*
A specific purificatory offering of water, the rites of which were introduced to Tibet from India by *Atiśa* during the eleventh century.

Way of Secret Mantras *gsang-sngags[kyi theg-pa]*, Skt. *Guhyamantrayāna*
The 'way of **secret *mantras***' is a synonym for the **Vehicle of Indestructible Reality** (Skt. *Vajrayāna*).

Wind *rlung*, Skt. *vāyu*
See **Vital Energy.**

World-system *'jig-rten-gyi khams*, Skt. *lokadhātu*
See **Three World-systems.**

Wrath *drag-po'i las*, Skt. *maraṇakriyā*
One of the **four aspects of enlightened activity**. The concept of wrath in the context of Buddhist ***tantra*** should not be understood in terms of even the subtlest egocentric violence or fierceness. Wrath here refers to the natural transformative process of **buddha-mind**, the aggressive **natural transformation** of the deep-seated conditioning which underlies mundane deluded consciousness and the concomitant psycho-physical **aggregates, elemental properties**, and sensory and mental processes. See **Four Aspects of Enlightened Activity** and Appendix Two.

Wrathful Deities *khro-bo'i lha-tshogs*
See Appendix Two.

Yakṣa *gnod-sbyin*
A class of spirits of Indian origin who assume both male (*yakṣa*) and female (*yakṣiṇī*) forms. Frequently depicted as holding choppers, cleavers, and swords, they are said to inhabit mountainous areas and sylvan groves, and if propitiated in the context

of a **means for attainment** (Skt. *sādhana*), they may confer the common **accomplishment** of swift-footedness. The Tibetan equivalent *gnod-sbyin* literally means 'granting harm', emphasising their more malign attributes.

Yama *gshin-rje*
See under **Yama Dharmarāja.**

Yama Dharmarāja *gshin-rje chos-kyi rgyal-po*
The embodiment of the forces of **impermanence** and the infallible laws of **cause and effect.** His fierce form is iconographically depicted holding the wheel of life's rebirth processes (*bhavacakra*, Tib. *srid-pa'i 'khor-lo*) within his jaws, indicating that the nature of **cyclic existence** is in its entirety bound by **impermanence** and the laws of **cause and effect.** In the context of the **intermediate state of rebirth** (*srid-pa'i bar-do*) he personifies the process of confronting in death the nature of one's past life's actions and, based on the natural laws of **cause and effect,** he personifies the process of 'judgement' that determines the consequential outcome of such **past actions.** See Chapters 11 and 13 and the Introduction. *Yama Dharmarāja* is also the sixth of the **six sages** (*thub-pa drug*), who form one subcategory within the assembly of the forty-two **peaceful deities.** See Appendix Two.

Yeshe Tsogyal *ye-shes mtsho-rgyal*
Padmasambhava's innermost Tibetan consort who became accomplished in the ***maṇḍala*** of **Vajrakīla.** She compiled many of ***Padmasambhava***'s oral teachings and concealed them throughout Tibet in the form of **treasures** (*gter-ma*) to be discovered by later generations.

Yoga *rnal-'byor*
The Sanskrit word *yoga*, literally meaning 'union', is interpreted in Tibetan to mean 'union with the fundamental nature of **reality**'. In Buddhism, therefore, *yoga* refers to the methods through which the meditator unites with the qualities of the **meditational deity** in the context of the **generation stage,** and the nature of fundamental **reality** during the **perfection stage,** of **meditation.** In terms of the latter, it includes mental and physical practices, which refine the **energy channels,** and mature control of the **vital energies** and **seminal points** within the **subtle body.** These practices cultivate **discriminative awareness,** and the coalescence of **emptiness** respectively with the **four delights,** with **inner radiance,** and with non-conceptualisation.

Yogatantra *rnal-'byor-gi rgyud*
The third of the three outer classes of ***tantra***, which form one subcategory of the six classes of ***tantra***, and the sixth of the **nine vehicles,** according to the ***Nyingma*** school of Tibetan Buddhism. *Yogatantra* emphasises meditation, rather than external ritual, and here, the meditator progressively refines an identification with the **meditational deity.**

Yogic Exercises *khrul-'khor*, Skt. *yantra*
A series of vigorous exercises, including yogic jumps (*'bebs*), performed in conjunction with specific visualisations and breathing techniques, which enable the meditator to develop the physical flexibility necessary for the subtle meditative practices of the **perfection stage** of **meditation.**

Yogic Jumps *'bebs*
See under **Yogic Exercises.**

Yogin *rnal-'byor-pa*
According to the Tibetan definition, a *yogin* is defined as 'one who seeks to unite with the fundamental nature of **reality**'. In other words, a *yogin* is one who intensively follows the spiritual paths outlined in the **generation** and **perfection stages** of **meditation**, as well as the **Great Perfection**.

Yoginī *rnal-'byor-ma*
A female ***yogin***. In the context of the present work, the term most frequently refers to the twenty-eight *Īśvarī* who form one sub-category of the fifty-eight **wrathful deities**. See Appendix Two.

Thematic Index by Chapter

Chapter One
Natural Liberation of the Nature of Mind: The Four-session Yoga of the Preliminary Practice 8–22

COMMON PRELIMINARY PRACTICE 8–11

Meditation on the Four Themes that Turn the Mind Toward the Search for Liberation 8–11

UNCOMMON PRELIMINARY PRACTICE 11–21

Refuge 11–13

Outer Refuge 11–12

Inner Refuge 12–13

Secret Refuge 13

Generation of an Altruistic Intention 14–15

Recitation of the Hundred-syllable Mantra of Vajrasattva 15–16

The Maṇḍala Offering 17–18

Prayer to the Lineage Teachers 19–20

Receiving the Four Empowerments 20–21

Chapter Two
A Prayer for Union with the Spiritual Teacher, [entitled] Natural Liberation, Without Renunciation of the Three Poisons 26–8

PRAYER FOR UNION 26–7

With the Buddha-body of Reality 26

With the Buddha-body of Perfect Resource 26

With the Buddha-body of Emanation 27

With the Three Buddha-bodies in Union 27

ASPIRATIONAL WISHES 27–8

Chapter Three
Root Verses of the Six Intermediate States 32–4

Intermediate State of Living 32

Intermediate State of Dreams 32

Intermediate State of Meditative Concentration 33

Intermediate State of the Time of Death 33

Intermediate State of Reality 33

Intermediate State of Rebirth 33–4

Chapter Four
The Introduction to Awareness: Natural Liberation through Naked Perception 38–57

THE IMPORTANCE OF THE INTRODUCTION TO AWARENESS 38–9

THE ACTUAL INTRODUCTION TO AWARENESS 39–42

Synonyms for Mind 41

The Three Considerations 41–2

CONSEQUENCES OF THE

INTRODUCTION TO AWARENESS 42–4
OBSERVATIONS RELATED TO EXAMINING THE NATURE OF MIND 44–6
INTRINSIC AWARENESS AS VIEW, MEDITATION, CONDUCT, AND RESULT 46–50
Four Great Media 46–7
Four Great Nails 47
Unity of the Three Times 47–8
Exhaustion of the Six Extreme Perspectives 48–50
SYNONYMS FOR AWARENESS 50–53
THE NATURE OF APPEARANCES 53–5
CONCLUSION 56–7

Chapter Five
The Spiritual Practice entitled Natural Liberation of Habitual Tendencies 62–91

THE TEN-BRANCHED PRAYER FOR THE ACCUMULATION OF MERIT 62–5
Branch of Taking Refuge 63
Branch of Invitation 63
Branch of Requesting the Deities to be Seated 63
Branch of Paying Homage 63
Branch of Making Offerings 64
Branch of the Confession of Negativity 64
Branch of Sympathetic Rejoicing 64
Branch of Turning the Wheel of the Sacred Teachings 64
Branch of Requesting the Buddhas Not to Enter Nirvāṇa 65
Branch of the Dedication of Merit to the Unsurpassed Greater Vehicle 65
PURIFICATION 65–6
Visualisation of Vajrasattva 65–6
Recitation of the Hundred-syllable Mantra of Vajrasattva 66
MAIN PRACTICE 66–90
Visualisation, Prostration, Offerings, Refuge and Prayer to the Peaceful Deities 66–75
Samantabhadra and Samantabhadrī 67
Vairocana and Dhātvīśvarī 67–8
Vajrasattva and Buddhalocanā, encircled by Kṣitigarbha, Maitreya, Lāsyā and Puṣpā 68–9
Ratnasambhava and Māmakī, encircled by Samantabhadra, Ākāśagarbha, Mālyā and Dhūpā 69–70
Amitābha and Pāṇḍaravāsinī, encircled by Avalokiteśvara, Mañjuśrī, Gītā and Ālokā 70
Amoghasiddhi and Samayatārā, encircled by Sarvanivāraṇaviśkambhin, Vajrapāṇi, Gandhā and Nartī 71
Eight Male and Female Gatekeepers 71–2
Six Sages 72–4
Forty-two Assembled Peaceful Deities 74–5
Visualisation, Prostration, Offerings, Refuge and Prayer to the Assembly of Awareness Holders 75–8
Visualisation, Prostration, Offerings, Refuge and Prayer to the Twelve Principal Wrathful Deities 78–81
Mahottara Heruka and Krodheśvarī 78–9
Buddha Heruka and Buddhakrodheśvarī 79
Vajra Heruka and Vajrakrodheśvarī 79
Ratna Heruka and Ratnakrodheśvarī 79–80
Padma Heruka and Padmakrodheśvarī 80
Karma Heruka and Karmakrodheśvarī 80
Visualisation, Prostration, Offerings, Refuge and Prayer to the Peripheral Wrathful Deities 81–7
Eight Mātaraḥ 81–2

Eight Piśācī 82–4
Four Female Gatekeepers 84
Twenty-eight Īśvarī 85–7
Prayer to the Assembly of Sixty Wrathful Deities 87–9
Aspirational Prayers 89–90
CONCLUSION 90–91

Chapter Six
Natural Liberation of Negativity and Obscuration through [Enactment of] the Hundredfold Homage to the Sacred Enlightened Families 96–112
Homage to Samantabhadra and Samantabhadrī 96–7
Homage to the Five Peaceful Male Buddhas 97–8
Homage to the Five Peaceful Female Buddhas 98
Homage to the Eight Male Bodhisattvas 98–9
Homage to the Eight Female Bodhisattvas 99–101
Homage to the Four Male Gatekeepers 101–2
Homage to the Four Female Gatekeepers 102
Homage to the Six Sages 102–3
Homage to the Six Herukas 103–4
Homage to the Six Krodheśvarī 104–5
Homage to the Eight Mātaraḥ 105–6
Homage to the Eight Piśācī 106–7
Homage to the Four Female Gatekeepers 107–8
Homage to the Eight Projectresses 108–9
Homage to the Twenty-eight Īśvarī 110–12

Chapter Seven
Natural Liberation through Acts of Confession 116–50
PRELIMINARIES 117–19
Invitation and Request for the Confessional Field to be Present 117
Homage to the Three Buddha-bodies, which Compose the Peaceful and Wrathful Deities 117
Threefold Offering of Outer Phenomena, Inner Cloud-masses, and Secret Substances 117
Secret Offering of Supreme Bliss 118
Affirmation of Vows within the Modality of the View 118
Call to the Assembly of Peaceful and Wrathful Deities for Attention 118–19
CONFESSION IN THE PRESENCE OF THE INEXPRESSIBLE TRUTH 119–23
CONFESSION IN THE PRESENCE OF THE PEACEFUL DEITIES 123–30
To Samantabhadra and Samantabhadrī 123
To the Five Male Buddhas 123–4
To the Five Female Buddhas 124
To the Eight Male Bodhisattvas 124
To the Eight Female Bodhisattvas 124–5
To the Six Sages 125
To the Four Male Gatekeepers 125
To the Four Female Gatekeepers 125–6
To the Entire Array of the Peaceful Deities 126–9
Further Remorseful Confession to the Peaceful Deities 129–30
CONFESSION IN THE PRESENCE OF THE WRATHFUL DEITIES 130–38
Confession of Faults in Achieving Meditative Stability in Reality 130–31
Confession of Faults in Achieving the Meditative Stability which Illuminates All That Appears 131
Confession of Faults in Achieving the Meditative Stability of the Causal Basis 131
Confession to the Five Herukas 131–2

To the Five Krodheśvarī 132
To the Eight Mātaraḥ 132
To the Eight Piśācī 132
To the Four Female Gatekeepers 133
To the Twenty-eight Īśvarī 133
To the Awareness Holders 133
Confession of One's Beginningless Violation of the Commitments 133–4
Confession to the Entire Maṇḍala of Wrathful Deities and the Request for Forgiveness 134
Specific Confessional Prayers to the Maṇḍala of the Wrathful Deities 135–8
PLAINTIVE CONFESSION OF RAMPANT EGOHOOD 138–42
CONFESSION IN THE PRESENCE OF THE VIEW 143–7
CONFESSION IN THE PRESENCE OF ALL THOSE GONE TO BLISS 147–50
Confession of Degenerated Commitments and Infractions 147–50
Recitation of the Hundred-syllable Mantra of Vajrasattva 150

Chapter Eight
Natural Liberation through Recognition of the Visual Indications and Signs of Death 155–81

INTRODUCTION 155–6
EXTERNAL SIGNS OF DEATH 156–9
INTERNAL SIGNS OF DEATH 159–62
Examination of the Vital Breath 159–60
Examination of the Signs of Death which Occur in Dreams 160–62
SECRET SIGNS OF DEATH 162–4
SIGNS OF REMOTE DEATH 164–8
Analysis of the Reflected Image in the Sky 164–8
SIGNS OF NEAR DEATH 168–71
MISCELLANEOUS SIGNS OF DEATH 171–3
SIGNS OF EXTREMELY NEAR DEATH 173–7
Dissolution of the Five Sense Faculties and the Five Elements 173–5
Movement of the Generative Essences 175–6
Dawning of Inner Radiance 176–7
SIGNS INDICATING THE PLACE OF SUBSEQUENT REBIRTH 177–80
CONCLUSION 180–81

Chapter Nine
Natural Liberation of Fear through the Ritual Deception of Death 186–95

GENERAL CONSOLIDATED RITE FOR AVERTING DEATH 186–9
SPECIFIC RITES FOR AVERTING DEATH 189–94
Ritual Averting of the Signs of Near Death 189–91
Ritual Averting of the Signs of Remote Death 191–3
Ritual Averting of Further Signs of Near Death 193–4
CONCLUSION 194–5

Chapter Ten
Consciousness Transference: Natural Liberation through Recollection 200–216

INTRODUCTION 200–201
TRAINING IN CONSCIOUSNESS TRANSFERENCE 201–5
ACTUAL APPLICATION OF CONSCIOUSNESS TRANSFERENCE AT THE TIME OF DEATH 205–15
The Timing and Context 205–8
Consciousness Transference into the Buddha-body of Reality 208–9
Consciousness Transference into the

Buddha-body of Perfect Resource 209–11
Consciousness Transference into the Buddha-body of Emanation 211–12
Instantaneous Consciousness Transference 212–14
Consciousness Transference of Ordinary Beings 214–15
CONCLUSION 216

Chapter Eleven
The Great Liberation by Hearing 225–303

PART ONE: AN ELUCIDATION OF THE INTERMEDIATE STATE OF THE TIME OF DEATH AND OF THE APPEARANCE OF THE PEACEFUL DEITIES IN THE INTERMEDIATE STATE OF REALITY 225–54
INTRODUCTION 225–6
INTRODUCTION TO INNER RADIANCE IN THE INTERMEDIATE STATE OF THE TIME OF DEATH 227–31
Introduction to the Inner Radiance of the Ground 227–32
Introduction to the Inner Radiance of the Path 232–4
INTRODUCTION TO THE INTERMEDIATE STATE OF REALITY 234–54
Introduction to the Arising of Sounds, Lights and Rays 235–6
Appearance of the Peaceful Deities 236–54
White Vairocana and Ākāśadhātvīśvarī appear within Blue Luminosity 236–8
Blue Akṣobhya-Vajrasattva and Buddhalocanā appear within White Luminosity, Encircled by Four Bodhisattvas Kṣitigarbha, Maitreya, Lāsyā and Puṣpā 238–9
Yellow Ratnasambhava and Māmakī appear within Yellow Luminosity, Encircled by Four Bodhisattvas Ākāśagarbha, Samantabhadra, Mālyā and Dhūpā 239–41
Red Amitābha and Pāṇḍaravāsinī appear within Red Luminosity, Encircled by Four Bodhisattvas Avalokiteśvara, Mañjuśrī, Gītā and Ālokā 241–3
Green Amoghasiddhi and Samayatārā appear within Green Luminosity, Encircled by Four Bodhisattvas Vajrapāṇi, Nivāraṇaviṣkhambhin, Gandhā and Nartī 243–6
Entire Peaceful Assembly of the Five Enlightened Families Appears Together with the Vision of the Four Pristine Cognitions Combined 246–51
Divine Assembly of Awareness Holders and Ḍākinīs appears within Five-coloured Luminosity 251–4
PART TWO: AN ELUCIDATION OF THE APPEARANCE OF THE WRATHFUL DEITIES IN THE INTERMEDIATE STATE OF REALITY 255–70
Introduction 255–8
Arising of the Intermediate State of the Wrathful Deities 258–66
Buddha Heruka and Buddhakrodheśvarī 258–9
Vajra Heruka and Vajrakrodheśvarī 259–60
Ratna Heruka and Ratnakrodheśvarī 260–61
Padma Heruka and Padmakrodheśvarī 261–2
Karma Heruka and Karmakrodheśvarī 262–3
The Eight Gaurī, the Eight Piśācī, the Four Female Gatekeepers, and the Twenty-eight Īśvarī 263–6
Consequences of Recognition and Lack of Recognition 266–8

Aspirational Prayers 268–70
CONCLUSION OF THE INTRODUCTION TO THE INTERMEDIATE STATE OF THE TIME OF DEATH AND THE INTERMEDIATE STATE OF REALITY 270–72
PART THREE: AN ELUCIDATION OF THE INTERMEDIATE STATE OF REBIRTH 273–300
INTRODUCTION TO THE MENTAL BODY 273–85
Characteristics of the Mental Body 274–6
Characteristics of the Intermediate State of Rebirth 276–9
The Meeting with Yama Dharmarāja, Embodiment of the Infallible Laws of Cause and Effect 279–81
The Power of Perceptions 282–4
Prayer to Mahākaruṇika 284
OBSTRUCTION OF THE WOMB ENTRANCES 285–93
CHOOSING A WOMB ENTRANCE 293–300
Transferring the Consciousness to Pure Buddha Fields 297–8
Choosing a Womb Entrance within Impure Cyclic Existence 298–300
CONCLUSION 300–303

Chapter Twelve
Aspirational Prayers 308–16
Aspirational Prayer Calling to the Buddhas and Bodhisattvas for Assistance 308–9
Aspirational Prayer which Rescues from the Dangerous Pathways of the Intermediate States 310–13
Aspirational Prayer which Protects from Fear of the Intermediate States 314–16

Chapter Thirteen
A Masked Drama of Rebirth 320–41

PART ONE: *NATURAL LIBERATION OF THE INTERMEDIATE STATE OF REBIRTH: A TEACHING REVEALING THE NATURAL EXPRESSION OF VIRTUE AND NEGATIVITY IN THE INTERMEDIATE STATE OF REBIRTH* 320–34
THE SCENE 320–21
Act One: The Meeting of the Wrongdoing One Lakṣanāraka with Yama Dharmarāja 322–9
Act Two: The Meeting of the Virtuous Householder Śrījāta with Yama Dharmarāja 329–33
PART TWO: SUPPLEMENT TO *A TEACHING REVEALING THE NATURAL EXPRESSION OF VIRTUE AND NEGATIVITY IN THE INTERMEDIATE STATE OF REBIRTH*, ENTITLED *GONG OF DIVINE MELODY* 335–41
THE SCENE 335
Act One: Exhortation by the Deity of Good Conscience following the Entry into the Hells of the Wrongdoing One Lakṣanāraka 336–39
Act Two: Celebratory Speech by the Deity of Good Conscience as the Virtuous Householder Śrījāta sets off for the Realms of Higher Rebirth 339–41

Chapter Fourteen
Liberation by Wearing: Natural Liberation of the Psycho-physical Aggregates 347–79

INTRODUCTION 347–8
PART ONE
Twenty-six Line Supreme Essential Mantra of Samantabhadra 348
Twenty-nine Line Supreme Essential Mantra of Samantabhadrī 348–9
Twenty-five Mantras which Reverse Attachment 349–54
PART TWO: SEED-SYLLABLES AND MANTRAS OF THE PEACE-

FUL AND WRATHFUL DEITIES 354–74
Forty-two Peaceful Deities 354
Five Male and Five Female Buddhas 355–7
Eight Male Bodhisattvas 357–8
Eight Female Bodhisattvas 359–60
Six Sages 360–61
Eight Male and Female Gatekeepers 361–3
Sixty Wrathful Deities 364
Twelve Principal Herukas and Krodheśvarī 365–7
Eight Mātaraḥ 368–9
Eight Piśācī 369–70
Four Female Gatekeepers 370–71
Twenty-eight Īśvarī 371–2
Four Great Wrathful Male Gatekeepers 373–4
PART THREE
Six Syllables of the Six Classes of Sentient Beings 374–5
Hundred-syllable Mantra of Vajrasattva 375
Syllables of the Sixteen Vowels and Thirty-four Consonants 375–6
Heart Mantra of Dependent Origination 376
Mantras of the Four Aspects of Enlightened Activity 376–7
CONCLUSION 377–9